Oliver & Dingemans
Employer's Liability Cases

Members of the LexisNexis Group worldwide

United Kingdom	LexisNexis UK, a Division of Reed Elsevier (UK) Ltd, Halsbury House, 35 Chancery Lane, LONDON, WC2A 1EL, and 4 Hill Street, EDINBURGH EH2 3JZ
Argentina	LexisNexis Argentina, BUENOS AIRES
Australia	LexisNexis Butterworths, CHATSWOOD, New South Wales
Austria	LexisNexis Verlag ARD Orac GmbH & Co KG, VIENNA
Canada	LexisNexis Butterworths, MARKHAM, Ontario
Chile	LexisNexis Chile Ltda, SANTIAGO DE CHILE
Czech Republic	Nakladatelství Orac sro, PRAGUE
France	Editions du Juris-Classeur SA, PARIS
Germany	LexisNexis Deutschland GmbH, FRANKFURT, MUNSTER
Hong Kong	LexisNexis Butterworths, HONG KONG
Hungary	HVG-Orac, BUDAPEST
India	LexisNexis Butterworths, NEW DELHI
Ireland	Butterworths (Ireland) Ltd, DUBLIN
Italy	Giuffrè Editore, MILAN
Malaysia	Malayan Law Journal Sdn Bhd, KUALA LUMPUR
New Zealand	LexisNexis Butterworths, WELLINGTON
Poland	Wydawnictwo Prawnicze LexisNexis, WARSAW
Singapore	LexisNexis Butterworths, SINGAPORE
South Africa	LexisNexis Butterworths, DURBAN
Switzerland	Stämpfli Verlag AG, BERNE
USA	LexisNexis, DAYTON, Ohio

© Reed Elsevier (UK) Ltd 2003

All rights reserved. No part of this publication may be reproduced in any material form (including photocopying or storing it in any medium by electronic means and whether or not transiently or incidentally to some other use of this publication) without the written permission of the copyright owner except in accordance with the provisions of the Copyright, Designs and Patents Act 1988 or under the terms of a licence issued by the Copyright Licensing Agency Ltd, 90 Tottenham Court Road, London, England W1T 4LP. Applications for the copyright owner's written permission to reproduce any part of this publication should be addressed to the publisher.

Warning: The doing of an unauthorised act in relation to a copyright work may result in both a civil claim for damages and criminal prosecution.

Crown copyright material is reproduced with the permission of the Controller of HMSO and the Queen's Printer for Scotland. Any European material in this work which has been reproduced from EUR-lex, the official European Communities legislation website, is European Communities copyright.

A CIP Catalogue record for this book is available from the British Library.

ISBN 0 406 95128 4

Typeset by Columns Design Ltd, Reading, England
Printed in Great Britain by the Cromwell Press, Trowbridge, Wiltshire

Visit LexisNexis UK at www.lexisnexis.co.uk

Foreword

Employment is more than a means of earning a living. It is one of the most important things in the lives of people. It contributes to their well-being and self-esteem. It is the economic bedrock of a civil society. The contract of employment therefore touches the lives of most families and individuals.

During the last 50 years the nature of the contract of employment has been transformed. The most striking change has been the far greater duties imposed on the employer than in the past to care for the physical, financial and even psychological welfare of the employee.

These developments have largely come about by statute law. Judicial decisions have, however, played a major role in the evolution of the more benign work place. And the role of European institutions has been of fundamental importance. The result is, however, a mosaic of changes which is not easily mastered by the uninitiated. For example, the authors of this casebook on employer's liability perceptively point out that the traditional distinction between health and safety law and employment law is increasingly difficult to maintain. Thus the Working Time Directive 93/104/EC was introduced by the European Commission as a "health and safety" matter.

There has been a clear need for a book which approaches the subject in a global fashion and provides in readily accessible form a source of relevant materials. This book admirably fills that gap. It will be of great assistance to practitioners. It is, however, also likely to be of assistance to employers, employees, trade unions and insurers.

I unreservedly commend this book, which has been written by two highly experienced practitioners, to all who grapple with such problems.

Johan Steyn*
House of Lords
July 2003

---

* A Lord of Appeal in Ordinary.

Introduction

This book attempts to provide a ready source of cases relating to the common law and statutory liability of employers. It is designed to assist the busy practitioner to find, at least in summarised form, relevant authorities on issues relating to the liability of employers. It is also designed to assist employers and their insurers, employees and their representatives by providing an outline of the duties imposed by law on employers.

As a matter of tradition, law books relating to the liability of employers have either dealt with 'Health and Safety' matters, such as common law actions for negligence and for breach of duties imposed by statute and statutory instrument, or with 'Employment' related matters, such as claims for unfair dismissal and wrongful dismissal. However the boundaries of 'Health and Safety' law have become increasingly difficult to draw. Two examples illustrate the point: the Working Time Directive 93/104/EC was introduced by the European Commission as a 'health and safety' matter; section 100 of the Employment Rights Act provides that a dismissal for activities related to reducing health and safety risks is unfair.

As a result of the increasing overlap, and because both employers and employees want to know what claims can be made in any given situation, this book is intended to cover the main aspects of the liability of employers. This is so whether or not that liability is imposed by the common law, by statute, statutory instrument, or directly by European Directive, and whether or not that liability will be adjudicated upon in the High Court, the County Court or an Employment Tribunal. As such the book contains chapters on the common law liability of employers and the liability of employers under some of the most relevant statutory instruments, but also extends to cover the liability of employers for race and sex discrimination and unfair dismissal. The increasing overlap between these areas can be easily demonstrated when considering the case of an employee, who says that he or she was bullied at work because of their sex and has suffered stress, and who needs to be advised of both common law and statutory remedies. To do this effectively the adviser will need to have an understanding of procedure in both courts and tribunals and there is a chapter which deals with the relevant procedure. Further in such a case the employer will want to ensure that there is adequate insurance to cover any liability, irrespective of legal route by which the liability arises. For this reason the book is also intended to highlight some issues relating to insurance for such liabilities. There is also a short chapter highlighting some criminal liabilities. The book is not intended to deal with situations where the liability of employers arises solely through contractual terms.

This book owes something to some fantastic and very fast catamaran sailing in Turkey where the idea of summarising some of the relevant cases on the overlapping areas set out above first occurred to us (it is accepted that this is slightly sad!). The book owes more to those experienced practitioners who have helped us transform the idea into reality, in particular fellow members of 3 Hare Court including Ian Rogers, Thomas Roe, Katherine Deal, Katherine Awadalla, Sarah Crowther, Dan Saxby and Tom Poole, others at Plexus Law including Stephen Walsh and Penny Lewis and, for the 'employment' parts, Barry Stanton, Clare Young, Emma Williams, Laurie Anstis and Michael Farrier of Boyes Turner. We are also very grateful to Butterworths for all their help, encouragement and tolerance.

Our principal hope is that you find the book useful.

James Dingemans QC and Timothy Oliver

Oliver & Dingemans
Employer's Liability Cases

Timothy G Oliver BA (Law)
Senior Partner, Plexus Law

James Dingemans QC
of Inner Temple, Barrister

Contents

Foreword	v
Introduction	vii
Table of statutes	xix
Table of statutory instruments	xxv
Table of European legislation	xxix
Table of cases	xxxi

Chapter 1 Definition and scope of employment
(James Dingemans QC and Timothy Oliver)

Introduction	[1.1]
Employee	[1.2]
Who is the employer?	[1.17]
Agency workers	[1.20]
Vicarious liability	[1.25]
Authorised work in a wrongful manner	[1.26]
Express prohibition	[1.30]
Intentional acts of an employee	[1.34]
Travel	[1.38]
Practical jokes	[1.43]

Chapter 2 Common law liability
(Sarah Crowther, James Dingemans QC and Timothy Oliver)

Employer's duty of care	[2.1]
Limits to the duty	[2.18]
Causation, remoteness and contributory negligence	[2.38]

Chapter 3 Liability for non-employees
(Sarah Crowther, James Dingemans QC and Timothy Oliver)

Acts of independent contractor/sub-contractor	[3.1]
'Casual' or 'collateral' negligence	[3.7]
Ultra-hazardous activities	[3.12]
Workers subject to another's control	[3.14]
The Australian approach	[3.35]

x   Contents

Chapter 4 Breach of statutory duty
(Katherine Awadalla, Thomas Roe, James Dingemans QC and Timothy Oliver)

The nature of the action	[4.2]
Construction of penal provisions	[4.26]
The person to whom the duty is owed	[4.41]
Civil liability under health and safety legislation: Introduction: Sources of law	[4.52]
By whom and to whom are duties owed?	[4.53]
The objectives of the European legislation: Framework Directive 89/391/EEC	[4.54]
UK regulations: Workplace (Health, Safety and Welfare Regulations) 1992 (as amended)	[4.57]
Provision and Use of Work Equipment Regulations 1998 (as amended)	[4.69]
Manual Handling Operations Regulations 1992 (as amended)	[4.79]
Control of Substances Hazardous to Health Regulations 2002	[4.86]
Employer's Liability (Defective Equipment) Act 1969	[4.98]

Chapter 5 Human rights issues and Crown liability
(Ian Rogers, James Dingemans QC and Timothy Oliver)

The Human Rights Act 1998	[5.1]
The Convention rights and employer's liability	[5.13]
Analysis of The Human Rights Act	[5.22]
Principles	[5.23]
General comments on when to raise a human rights point	[5.26]
Definition of a public authority	[5.28]
Horizontal effect of the Human Rights Act	[5.30]
Proportionality and the discretionary area of judgment	[5.32]
Statutory interpretation under section 3 and declarations of incompatibility under section 4	[5.36]
Effect of HRA, s 3 on employer's liability cases	[5.41]
Human rights cases affecting employer's liability	[5.44]
Article 4	[5.45]
Article 6	[5.46]
Article 8	[5.47]
Article 9	[5.52]
Article 10	[5.56]
Article 14	[5.57]
Crown employees: statutory liability of the Crown	[5.58]
Crown Proceedings Act 1947, ss 1, 2	[5.58]
Occupiers Liability Act 1957, s 6	[5.59]
Defective Premises Act 1972, s 5	[5.60]
Occupiers Liability Act 1984, s 3	[5.61]
Contracts of employment and the Crown	[5.62]
Armed Forces: Crown Proceedings Act 1947, s 10	[5.64]
Crown Proceedings (Armed Forces) Act 1987	[5.65]
Police	[5.73]

Contents xi

Chapter 6 Industrial disease claims
(Stephen Walsh, James Dingemans QC and Timothy Oliver)

Causation and apportionment	[6.1]
Causation in disease claims	[6.1]
Medical evidence	[6.5]
Limits on decision	[6.6]
Apportionment in 'divisible' conditions	[6.7]
Date of knowledge	[6.8]
Apportionment	[6.9]
No duty to dismiss	[6.12]
Pneumoconiosis/ Chronic Obstructive Airways Disease	[6.15]
Liability and date of knowledge	[6.16]
Medical evidence, epidemiological evidence and causation	[6.17]
Apportionment	[6.18]
Asbestos: insurance policy	[6.19]
Procedural issues: jurisdiction	[6.20]
Crown immunity	[6.21]
Limitation/ accrual of cause of action	[6.25]
Legislation: The Asbestos Industry Regulations 1931	[6.28]
Factories Act 1937, s 47(1)	[6.29]
Factories Act 1961, s 4(1)	[6.30]
Regulations under the Factories Act 1961	
Shipbuilding and Ship-repairing Regulations 1961	[6.31]
Control of Asbestos Regulations 1969	[6.32]
Standards	[6.33]
Application of legislation	[6.34]
Duty of care/date of knowledge	[6.38]
Offset of benefits	[6.45]
Occupational noise-induced hearing loss/deafness claims	[6.46]
Legislation	[6.47]
Vibration White Finger	[6.48]
Date of knowledge	[6.49]
Medical evidence	[6.50]
Vascular	[6.51]
Neurological	[6.52]
Musculo-skeletal	[6.53]
Extent of disability	[6.54]
Effect of cessation of exposure	[6.55]
Diagnosis	[6.56]
Classification	[6.57]
apportionment	[6.58]
Sensitisation claims: legislation: Control of Substances Hazardous to Health Regulations	[6.63]
Asthma	[6.64]
Date of knowledge	[6.66]
COSHH Regulations	[6.67]
Dermatitis	[6.68]

Work-related upper limb disorder claims: keyboard claims: Legislation:
    Health & Safety (Display Screen Equipment) Regulations 1992 [6.69]
Cases [6.70]
Manual processes: legislation [6.76]
Cases [6.77]
Occupational stress: pre-Hatton [6.83]
Post-Hatton [6.84]
Facts [6.85]
Summary of reasons [6.89]
Cases decided post-Hatton [6.90]
Bullying and harassment [6.92]

Chapter 7 Race discrimination
(Barry Stanton, James Dingemans QC and Timothy Oliver)
Direct race and sex discrimination [7.1]
  'Less favourable' treatment [7.2]
  Racial grounds/racial group [7.6]
  Ethnic groups [7.7]
  Identifying an ethnic group in practice [7.8]
  National origins [7.9]
  Racial grounds [7.10]
  Discrimination on the grounds of another person's race [7.14]
  Religions as ethnic groups [7.16]
  Rastafarians [7.17]
  The importance of the discriminatory factor in the decision taken
  An appropriate comparator [7.21]
  Direct sex discrimination [7.22]
  Pregnancy and reasons connected with pregnancy [7.24]
  Failure to carry out a risk assessment [7.30]
  Sexual orientation discrimination [7.31]
  Indirect discrimination [7.35]
  Is full-time work the imposition of a requirement or condition? [7.40]
  'Considerably smaller proportion' [7.42]
  The meaning of 'can comply' [7.46]
  Detriment [7.47]
  Knowledge is not necessary for there to be a detriment [7.48]
  The pool for comparison [7.49]
Justification [7.50]
Discrimination on the grounds of gender reassignment [7.55]
Establishing discriminatory treatment [7.60]
  Discrimination by others [7.63]
  Discrimination by 'qualifying bodies' [7.66]
  Continuing act versus one-off act of discrimination [7.70]
Work ordinarily outside great britain [7.74]
  Freedom of Movement (EC Treaty, Art 48) [7.75]
Genuine occupational qualification defence [7.76]

Victimisation	[7.80]
Is there a need for conscious motivation?	[7.81]
Section 2(1)(b) of the RRA	[7.84]
Victimisation on the grounds of sex	[7.86]
Instructions to discriminate and pressure to discriminate: Instructions to discriminate	[7.87]
Pressure to discriminate	[7.88]
Vicarious liability or direct liability for acts of employees	[7.90]
Post-employment victimisation	[7.96]
Aiding unlawful acts	[7.100]
Damages for injury to feelings and aggravated damages	[7.103]
Exemplary damages	[7.109]
Disability discrimination	[7.110]
Definition of disability	[7.11]
Physical impairment	[7.112]
Mental impairment	[7.115]
Functional overlay	[7.118]
Substantial and long-term adverse effect	[7.120]
Normal day-to-day activities	[7.123]
Can activities at work constitute normal day-to-day activities?	[7.127]
Progressive conditions	[7.129]
Knowledge of an employee's disability	[7.131]
Scope of the Act for employment purposes	[7.134]
The date at which to assess the question of disability	[7.137]
Small employer exemption	[7.140]
Discrimination against contract workers	[7.142]
Who is an appropriate comparator?	[7.144]
Redundancy selection arrangements	[7.146]
The obligation to make reasonable adjustments	[7.147]
Personal, non-job-related adjustments	[7.150]
Is it relevant that the applicant or advisers can think of no suitable alternatives?	[7.153]
Monetary benefits	[7.154]
Employer's duty when faced with non-co-operation by the employee	[7.155]
Justification	[7.156]
Does an employer need to know of the disability, to rely upon a justification defence?	[7.161]
The role of medical evidence and treatment	[7.162]
Damages	[7.166]
Constructive dismissal and disability discrimination	[7.167]
Post-employment victimisation	[7.168]

Chapter 8 Unfair dismissal
(Barry Stanton, James Dingemans QC and Timothy Oliver)

The law of unfair dismissal – background	[8.1]
General	[8.2]

xiv Contents

Eligibility to make an unfair dismissal claim [8.5]
    Normal retiring age: Retirement age [8.7]
    Excluded classes of employees [8.12]
Was there a dismissal? [8.14]
    Termination by agreement [8.20]
    Ambiguous language [8.21]
    Frustration and fixed-term contracts [8.24]
    Date of dismissal and 'effective date of termination' [8.27]
    Dismissal with notice [8.30]
    Section 97(2) of ERA [8.35]
    Time at which the dismissal takes effect [8.36]
Reason for dismissal [8.37]
    Correctly identifying the reason for dismissal [8.40]
    Burden of proof [8.41]
    Establishing the reason [8.44]
    When is the reason to be determined? [8.46]
Capability [8.48]
    Lack of capability due to ill-health [8.50]
Conduct [8.55]
    Criminal acts [8.60]
Breach of a statutory enactment [8.62]
Redundancy: Redundancy procedure [8.65]
Some other substantial reason [8.67]
    Protection of interest of business [8.70]
    Imprisonment [8.72]
Dismissal following a transfer of an undertaking [8.74]
    Dismissal for economic, technical or organisational reasons [8.75]
    Dismissals connected with the transfer [8.76]
    Cases on dismissal for economic, technical or organisational reasons [8.77]
    Dismissals 'connected with the transfer' [8.79]
    Automatically unfair reasons: Leave for family reasons [8.80]
    Health and safety reason [8.83]
    Refusal to work on a Sunday [8.87]
    Occupational pension scheme trustee [8.88]
    Employee representative [8.89]
    Trade union reasons [8.90]
    Selection for redundancy trade union reasons [8.92]
    Public interest disclosure [8.94]
    Assertion of a statutory right [8.96]
    The national minimum wage [8.97]
    Tax credit [8.98]
    Procedure [8.99]
    A fair procedure? [8.100]
The band of reasonable responses [8.104]
Constructive dismissal [8.111]
    Duty promptly to redress grievances [8.123]

Remedies: Re-employment	[8.124]
Order for reinstatement	[8.125]
Order for re-engagement	[8.126]
Choice of order and its terms	[8.127]
Compensation: General considerations	[8.136]
The duty to mitigate	[8.141]
Deductions for contributory fault	[8.144]
Just and equitable	[8.148]
Loss of wages	[8.152]

Chapter 9 Practice and procedure
(Katherine Deal, Thomas Roe, Barry Stanton, James Dingemans QC and Timothy Oliver)

A   HIGH COURT AND COUNTY COURT

Introduction	[9.1]
Procedural steps: Default judgment	[9.2]
Summary judgment	[9.4]
Interim applications	[9.7]
Expert evidence	[9.10]
Commencing proceedings: Pre-action protocol	[9.13]
Vexatious litigants	[9.14]
Parties to the action	[9.16]
Issuing proceedings	[9.17]
Serving proceedings	[9.20]
Pleading requirements	[9.34]
Amendments	[9.35]
Resiling from admission of liability	[9.36]
Group litigation	[9.37]
Costs	[9.38]
Limitation	[9.41]
Running of time	[9.51]
Date of knowledge	[9.53]
Limitation defence	[9.65]
Extending the time-limits (section 33)	[9.69]
New claims in pending action (section 35)	[9.76]
Commencing second action out of time	[9.78]
Striking out (CPR)	[9.80]
Claim or defence itself alleged to be objectionable	[9.81]
Manner in which claim pursued	[9.84]
Trial: allocation	[9.92]
Adjournments	[9.93]
Submission of no case to answer	[9.96]
Costs (CPR)	[9.97]
Summary assessment	[9.98]
In the court's discretion	[9.100]

Effect of Part 36 [9.110]
Indemnity basis [9.113]
Conditional fee agreements [9.118]
Costs orders against non-parties [9124]
Wasted costs orders [9.125]

B EMPLOYMENT TRIBUNAL PRACTICE AND PROCEDURE
Introduction [9.128]
Chairman sitting alone or sitting with one lay member [9.129]
    Jurisdiction [9.132]
Calculating time: Unfair dismissal – 'reasonably practical' [9.132]
    Just and equitable to extend the time-limit [9.138]
    'Reasonably practicable' – effect of criminal proceedings [9.140]
    Effect of tribunal being closed on the last day to lodge IT1 [9.142]
    Lodging claim forms by post [9.144]
    Limitation period where none specified by statute [9.145]
    Amending the grounds of claim after they have been lodged with
        the tribunal [9.146]
    The jurisdiction to hear breach of contract claims [9.148]
Preliminary issues [9.149]
    The need to sit in public [9.151]
    Adjournments [9.152]
Procedure at the hearing [9.153]
    Tribunals must exercise their discretion judicially [9.154]
    The need to investigate pleaded claims [9.155]
    The power of a tribunal to limit cross examination [9.156]
    The status of a tribunal chairman's notes of evidence [9.157]
    The use of written submissions [9.158]
    Further particulars [9.160]
    Directions [9.161]
    Disclosure of documents [9.162]
    Witness orders [9.166]
Striking out (Employment Tribunal Regs) [9.168]
The tribunal's decision [9.170]
    The need to make findings of fact [9.171]
    The tribunal's power to grant a remedy for unpleaded cause of action [9.172]
    The power to review decisions [9.173]
Costs (Employment Tribunal Regs) [9.175]
    Unreasonable conduct by a trade union representative [9.176]
    The applicant's ability to pay [9.177]

Chapter 10 Health and safety prosecutions
(Dan Saxby, James Dingemans QC and Timothy Oliver)
Health and Safety at Work etc Act 1974: Introduction [10.1]
    The test of 'reasonably practicability' and 'conducting an undertaking' [10.9]
    Personal liability of corporate officers [10.16]

Limits of practicability (HSWA, s 40)	[10.19]
Sentencing and level of fines	[10.20]
Corporate manslaughter	[10.26]

Chapter 11 EU law
(Ian Rogers, James Dingemans QC and Timothy Oliver)

Introduction	[11.1]
Direct effect of Treaty provisions	[11.2]
Direct effect of Regulations and decisions	[11.3]
Direct effect of Directives	[11.5]
The concept of an emanation of the State	[11.9]
'Indirect effect' of Directives – The obligation to construe national law in conformity with Directives	[11.10]
'Incidental' horizontal effects	[11.12]
Supremacy of community law	[11.13]
Effectiveness of EC law remedies	[11.14]
State liability for breach of EC law	[11.17]
The approach to EC law taken by the UK courts: European Communities Act 1972	[11.19]
Substantive EU law	[11.24]

Chapter 12 Insurance
(James Dingemans QC and Timothy Oliver)

Compulsory insurance	[12.1]
Employers' Liability (Compulsory Insurance) Act 1969	[12.2]
Nature of liability under 1969 Act	[12.9]
Insolvency	[12.10]
Employer's liability insurance and motor insurance	[12.13]
Personal insurance	[12.14]

Table of statutes

Paragraph numbers in **bold** type indicate where the legislation is set out in part or in full.

A

Access to Justice Act 1999
  s 29 .... 9.120, 9.121

C

Children Act 1989 .... 5.43
Civil Liability (Contribution) Act
    1978
  s 1, 2 .... 3.5
Coal Industry Nationalisation Act
    1946 .... 6.16
Coal Mines Act 1911 .... 4.30
  s 2(4) 2.2
  49 .... 4.2
  55 .... 2.40, 4.3
Companies Act 1948
  s 353(6) 9.16
Companies Act 1985
  s 651 .... 9.52
  653 .... 9.16
Consumer Credit Act 1974
  s 127(3) 5.37
Control of Employment and
    Redundancy Payments Act
    (Northern Ireland) 1965
  s 4, 5 .... 2.29
County Courts Act 1984
  s 51 .... 9.34
Crown Proceedings Act 1947
  s 10 .... **5.64**, 5.72, 6.22,
                                          6.23, 6.24
    (1) 5.67
      (a) 5.66
      (b) 5.66, 5.72
    (2) 5.68
  17 .... 5.58
Crown Proceedings (Armed Forces)
    Act 1987
  s 1 .... **5.65**

D

Defective Premises Act 1972
  s 5 .... **5.60**
Disability Discrimination Act 1995 .... 5.75,
                                          7.60, 7.111, 7.126,
                                          7.164, 8.53
  s 1 .... **7.112**, 7.116
  4 .... **7.168**
    (2) 7.169
      (d) 7.167
  5 .... **7.135**, 7.161
    (1) .... .136, 7.146, 7.152
      (a) 7.137, 7.146
      (b) 7.137
    (2) .... .136, 7.146, 7.149, 7.152
    (3) **7.156**, 7.157
    (4), (5) **7.156**
  6 .... 7.137, 7.146, **7.148**,
                                  7.150, 7.153, 7.154, 7.160
    (1) 7.149
    (2) 7.149
    (3), (4) 7.149
    (6)(b) 7.134
  12 .... **7.143**, 7.144
    (6) 7.144
  68 .... 7.142
  Sch 1 .... 7.112
    para 1(1) 7.116
    2 .... 7.121
    4 .... **7.124**
      (1) 7.127
    8 .... **7.130**

E

Employer's Liability (Defective
    Equipment) Act 1969 .... 3.4
  s 1 .... **4.98**

Employers' Liability (Compulsory
   Insurance) Act 1969 .... 6.19, 12.9
  s 1 .... **12.2**
   2 .... **12.3**
   3 .... **12.4**
   4 .... **12.5**
   5 .... **12.6**
   6 .... **12.7**
   7 .... **12.8**
Employment (Prevention of
   Accidents) Act 1900 .... 4.19
Employment Protection
   (Consolidation) Act 1978 .... 11.22
  s 57A 8.84
   67(2) 9.134
   122 .... 1.23
Employment Rights Act 1996
  s 13(1) **5.75**
   Pt IVA (ss 43a–43l) 8.94
  s 95 .... **8.111**
   97 .... **8.27**
   98 .... 8.1,
                                             8.37, 8.44, 8.77
    (1) 8.68
    (2)(a) 8.39
    (4) 8.68,
                                          8.99, 8.102, 8.104
   99 .... **8.80**, 8.81
    (1)(a) 7.28, 8.82
   100 .... **8.83**, 8.84
    (1)(d) 8.85
    (e) 8.86, 9.159
   101 .... **8.87**
   102(1) **8.88**
   103(1) **8.89**
   103A **8.94**, 8.95
   104 .... **8.96**
   104A **8.97**
   104B(1) **8.98**
   108 .... 8.1
    (1) **8.5**
   109 .... 8.1, **8.7**, 8.10
   111 .... **8.12**, 8.13, **9.132**
    (3) 8.13
   112 .... 8.124
   113 .... 8.124
   114 .... 8.124,
                                                   8.125, 8.135
   115 .... 8.124, **8.126**
   116 .... 8.124, **8.127**
   117 .... 8.124
    (3) 8.135
    (a) 8.135
   123 .... **8.136**
    (1) 8.139
   124(1)(a) 8.135

Employment Rights Act 1996 – *contd*
  s 124(4) 8.135
   127(1) 8.66
   136 .... 8.20
   156 .... **8.7**, 8.10
   200(2)(a) 5.75
   203 .... 8.4
   230 .... 1.1
Employment Tribunals Act 1996 .... 9.128
  s 3(2) 9.159
   4(5) 9.131
   35(1)(a) 9.169
European Communities Act 1972
  s 2(1) **11.19**
   (2) 11.19
   (4) **11.19**
   3(1) **11.19**

F

Factories Act 1937 .... 2.51, 2.58,
                                                    2.64, 2.69, 4.17,
                                                    4.20, 4.43
  s 4 .... 2.12, 2.57, 4.34
   (1) .... .56, 2.57, 2.86
   13 .... 4.5
   (1) 2.6, 4.31, 4.37, 4.43
   14 .... 4.32, 4.33
   (1) 2.51, 2.52, 2.62,
                                                    2.68, 2.71, 4.9, 4.37,
                                                    4.38, 4.43
   16 .... 2.9, 4.33, 4.37
   17(1) 4.43
   23(1) 4.29
   25 .... 2.7, 2.19, 4.8
   26 .... 2.19
   (1) 2.70, 4.28
   (2) 2.67, 2.70
   47 .... 4.34, 6.37
   (1) 2.12, 6.29, 6.31
   49 .... 2.59,
                                                    4.7, 4.10, 4.35
   60 .... 2.52
   119 .... 4.33
Factories Act 1948 .... 4.43
Factories Act 1959 .... 4.43
Factories Act 1961 .... 2.86
  s 4(1) 6.30
   14 .... 4.13
   (1) 2.78
   29(1) 4.12, 4.13, 4.48
   31(4) 4.39
   63 .... 6.4
   126 .... 6.30
   155(2) 6.34

Factories Act 1961 – contd
s 175(1) 6.30, 6.34
  (2) 6.30
Factory and Workshop Act 1901 .... 4.17
s 79 .... 4.4, 6.36
80(1) 6.36
Fatal Accidents Act 1846 .... 2.42,
  2.54, 2.63, 2.76,
  2.80, 4.3, 4.19
Fatal Accidents Act 1864 .... 2.42,
  2.47, 2.54, 2.63, 2.76,
  2.80, 4.3, 4.19
Fatal Accidents Act 1908 .... 2.63,
  2.76, 2.80,
  4.3, 4.19
Fatal Accidents Act 1959 .... 2.42,
  2.54, 2.76, 2.80
Fatal Accident Act 1976 .... 2.42,
  2.54, 2.80, 6.45
s 2(3) **5.42**
Finance Act 1966
s 13(1) 10.16
305(3) 10.16
Fine Arts Copyright 1862 (25 & 26
  Vict c 68)
s 6, 11 .... 4.27
Fire Precautions Act 1971
s 23(1) 10.18
Foreign Enlistment Act 1870 .... 4.26

H

Health and Safety at Work etc Act
  1974 .... 4.52, 10.21,
  10.23, 10.28
s 2 .... 3.27, 10.1, **10.2**
  (1) 10.9, 10.24, 10.25
  (2)(a) 3.27
3 .... 3.27, 10.1, **10.3**
  (1) 10.9, 10.10, 10.11
  (a) 3.28
4 .... 10.1, **10.4**
5 .... 10.1
6 .... 10.1, **10.5**
7 .... 10.1, **10.6**
8 .... 10.1, **10.7**
9 .... 10.1, **10.8**
15 .... 10.1, **10.12**
33 .... **10.13**, 10.20
  (1)(a)–(b) 10.1
36 .... **10.14**
37 .... **10.15**
  (1) 10.17
40 .... **10.19**
53(1) 1.1, 4.53

Housing Act 1988
s 21(4) 5.39
Housing Act 1996
s 98 .... 5.39
Human Rights Act 1998 .... 5.27,
  5.29, 5.32, 5.38
s 1 .... **5.1**
2 .... **5.2**, 5.23, 5.25
3 .... **5.3**, 5.23, 5.25,
  5.36, 5.37, 5.39, 5.40,
  5.41, 5.42, 5.43
4 .... **5.4**, 5.23, 5.25
  (6) 5.37
5 .... **5.5**, 5.37
6 .... **5.6**, 5.23, 5.25, 5.28
  (1) 5.23, 5.31
  (3) 5.23
    (b) 5.28
7 .... **5.7**, 5.23
  (1) 5.31
8 .... **5.8**, 5.23, 5.31
9 .... **5.9**
11 .... **5.10**, 5.23
12 .... **5.11**
  (4) 5.31
13 .... **5.12**

I

Inheritance (Family Provision) Act
  1938 .... 2.76

L

Latent Damage Act 1986 .... 9.42
Law Reform (Contributory
  Negligence) Act 1945
s 1(1) 2.23
4 .... 2.46
Law Reform (Limitation of Actions)
  Act 1954 .... 9.41
Law Reform (Married Women and
  Tortfeasors) Act 1935 .... 2.30
Law Reform (Miscellaneous
  Provisions) Act 1934 .... 2.42,
  2.54, 2.63, 2.76,
  4.17, 6.45
Law Reform (Personal Injuries) Act
  1948
s 1, 4 .... 5.58
Limitation Act 1939 .... 6.26, 9.41
s 2 .... 9.41, 9.42
  (1) 2.57

Limitation Act 1939 – contd
- s 2A–2C 9.41, 9.42
- 2D 9.41, 9.42, 9.78

Limitation Act 1963
- s 4 .... 9.41, 9.42

Limitation Act 1975 .... 9.41

Limitation Act 1980 .... 9.41, 9.61, 9.67, 9.145
- s 2 .... 9.42, **9.43**
- 5 .... 9.42, **9.44**
- 10 .... 9.42
- 11 .... 9.42, **9.45**
- 12 .... **9.46**
- 13 .... 9.42, **9.47**
- 14 .... 9.42, **9.48**
  - (1)(b) 9.57
  - (2) 9.56
- 14A 9.42, **9.49**
- 14B 9.42, **9.50**
- 32A 9.69
- 33 .... 9.42, 9.52, 9.70, 9.71, 9.73, 9.78, 9.79, 9.139
  - (3)(a) 9.72, 9.75
  - (d) 9.75
- 35 .... 9.42

Sch 2
- para 9(1) 6.26

M

Mental Health Act 1983 .... 9.75
Merchant Shipping Act 1894 .... 4.16
Merchant Shipping Act 1988 ... 11.15, 11.18
Merchant Shipping (International Labour Conventions) Act 1925
- s 1(1) 4.16

Mines and Quarries Act 1954
- s 81(1) 4.22

Municipal Corporations Act 1882 .... 5.73

N

National Insurance (Industrial Injuries) Act 1965
- s 5(1) 2.27

O

Occupiers' Liability Act 1957 ..... 3.23, 4.45
- s 6 .... **5.59**

Occupiers' Liability Act 1984
- s 3 .... **5.61**

Occupiers' Liability (Scotland) Act 1960 .... 4.50

Offices, Shops and Railway Premises Act 1963 .... 2.82, 4.47
- s 16(1) 4.44

P

Pneumoconiosis etc (Workers' Compensation) Act 1979 .... 6.45
Police Act 1996 .... 1.29b, 7.96
- s 50(1), (2) 5.75

Private International Law (Miscellaneous Provisions) Act 1995
- Pt III (ss 9–15) 6.20

Public Health Act 1875
- s 150 .... 3.8

Public Interest Disclosure Act 1998 ..... 8.94

R

Race Relations Act 1976 .... 5.75, 7.7, 7.38, 7.70
- s 1 .... **7.1**
  - (1)(a) 7.14, 7.15, 7.84
    - (b)(i) 7.7, **7.35**
    - (ii) **7.35**, 7.52
    - (iii) **7.35**
- 2 .... **7.82**, 7.86
  - (1) 2.87
    - (a) 7.84
    - (b) 7.86
    - (c) 7.85
- 3(1) **7.6**, 7.9
- 4 .... 7.84
  - (2) 7.98, 7.100
- 5 .... **7.78**
- 7 .... **7.65**
- 8(1) 7.76
- 12 .... 7.69
  - (1) **7.68**
- 30 .... **7.89**, 7.91
- 31 .... **7.90**, 7.91
- 32 .... **7.92**
- 33 .... **7.102**, 7.104
- 33(1) 7.103
- 41(1)(b) 7.56
- 78 .... 1.8

Race Relations (Amendment) Act 2000 .... 7.97

Railway Employment (Prevention of Accidents) Act 1900 .... 4.19
Road Traffic Act 1998
  s 151 .... 9.7

S

Sex Discrimination Act 1975 .... 5.75, 7.33, 7.59, 7.60, 9.139, 11.7
  s 1 .... **7.1**, 11.21
    (1) (a) **7.22**, 7.23, 7.84, 11.21
      (b) 7.23
        (i) **7.35**
        (ii) **7.35**, 7.52
        (iii) **7.35**
    (2) **7.35**
      (b)(ii) 7.52
  2A **7.57**
  4 .... **7.82**
    (1)(d) 7.95
  5(3) 11.21
  6(2) 7.100
  7 .... 7.66
  7A, 7B 7.78
  9 .... **7.65**
  10 .... **7.76**
  13 .... 7.71
    (1) **7.68**
  39 .... **7.89**
  40 .... **7.90**
  41 .... **7.92**
  42 .... **7.102**
  23(1) 7.2
  82(1) **7.57**
Social Security (Recovery of Benefits) Act 1997
  s 6(1) 9.7

Supreme Court Act 1981
  s 32A 9.34
    42 .... 9.14
    51(6), (7) 9.125
Statute of Limitation 1623 .... 9.41

T

Trade Union and Labour Relations (Consolidation) Act 1992
  s 152(1) 8.90
      (b) 8.91, 8.92
    (2)(b) 8.92
    153 .... 8.92, **8.93**
      (a) 8.93

U

Unfair Contract Terms Act 1977
  s 2(1) 2.34, **2.35**

W

Widows', Orphans' and Old Age Contributory Pensions Act 1936 .... 1.3
Workmen's Compensation Act 1925 .... 1.2, 6.26
  s 29(1) 4.2

Y

Youth Justice and Criminal Evidence Act 1999
  s 41 (3) (c) 5.40

Table of statutory instruments

Paragraph numbers in **bold** type indicate where the legislation is set out in part or in full.

A

Asbestos Industry Regulations 1931, SI 1931/1140	6.36, 6.37, 6.40, 6.42
reg 1	6.28
2	6.36
(a), (b)	6.28
3–8	6.28
10	6.28
Asbestos (Licensing) Regulations 1983, SI 1983/1649	6.32
Asbestos Products (Safety) Regulations 1985, SI 1985/2042	6.32
Asbestos (Prohibitions) Regulations 1985, SI 1985/910	6.32
Asbestos (Prohibitions) Regulations 1992, SI 1992/3067	6.32
Asbestos Regulations 1969, SI 1969/690	6.28, 6.42
reg 2(a)	6.32
3(2)	6.34
5–7	6.32
8	6.32
(1)	6.34
9	6.32, 6.34
10	6.32
15(1)(a)	6.34

B

British Railways Rules 1950, SI 1950 r 234(a)	2.50
Building Regulations 1926, SI 1926	
reg 7	4.18
15	4.41
Building (Safety, Health and Welfare) Regulations 1948, SI 1948/1145	2.48, 2.55, 2.66, 4.42

Building (Safety, Health and Welfare) Regulations 1948 – *contd*	
reg 24	4.21
27(1)	2.64
97	2.67

C

Civil Legal Aid (General) Regulations 1989, SI 1989/339	9.127
Civil Procedure Rules 1998, SI 1998/3132	9.85, 9.87, 9.88, 9.91, 9.100, 9.107
Pt 1	9.1
r 1.1(2)(e)	9.89
1.3	9.104
Pt 3	
r 3.4	9.81
(2)	**9.80**
3.9	9.27
3.10	9.27
Pt 6	9.30, 9.33
r 6.4(2)	9.24
6.5(4)	9.23
6.7(1)	9.29
6.8	9.23, 9.27
6.9	9.28
Pt 7	9.30
r 7.4	9.31
7.5	9.20, 9.32
7.6	9.28, 9.32
(3)	9.25, 9.26, 9.29
(b)	9.24, 9.26
Pt 12	9.2
Pt 13	
r 13.2	9.2
13.3	9.2
Pt 16	9.17, 9.32
r 16.4(3), (4)	9.34

Civil Procedure Rules 1998 – *contd*
  Pt 16 – *contd*
    PD 16
      para 1 .... 9.42
        4.1, 4.2............................... 9.34
    Pt 19 .... 9.37
      r 19.2(1)(a), (b) 9.37
        (3) 9.37
    PD 19B
      para 29....................................... 9.37
    Pt 22 .... 9.17
    Pt 24
      r 24.2 .... 9.4, 9.5
    Pt 25 .... 9.6
      r 25.1 .... 9.6
        25.6 .... 9.7
        25.7(2) 9.7
          (4) 9.7
    Pt 27 .... 9.1
      r 27.2(5) 9.7
        27.14 .... 9.109
    Pt 28 .... 9.1
    Pt 29 .... 9.1
    Pt 31
      r 31.22 .... 9.162
    Pt 36 .... 9.33, 9.110, 9.111,
                                9.112, 9.113
      r 36.20 .... 9.110
        36.21 .... 9.110, 9.112
    Pt 43 .... 9.97
      r 43.2(1)(k)................................. 9.13
    Pt 44 .... 9.97, 9.104
      r 44.3 .... 9.101
        (2) 9.97
        (6)(f) 9.106
    PD 44
      para 13....................................... 9.97
    Pt 45 .... 9.97
    Pt 46 .... 9.97
    Pt 47 .... 9.97
    Pt 48 .... 9.97
  Sch 1
    Rules of the Supreme Court.............. 9.84
  Sch 2
    County Court Rules 9.84
Coal Mines Order 1934, SI 1934.......... 4.30
Conditional Fee Agreements Regulations 2000, SI 2000/692
  reg 4 .... 9.118
Construction (General Provisions) Regulations 1961, SI 1961/1580.. 4.46
Construction (Working Places) Regulations 1966, SI 1966/94 .... 1.6, 3.29
  reg 3(1).. 4.45

Control of Asbestos at Work Regulations 1987, SI 1987/2115.. 6.32
Control of Asbestos at Work Regulations 2002, SI 2002/2675.. 6.32
Control of Asbestos in the Air Regulations 1990, SI 1990/556... 6.32
Control of Substances Hazardous to Health Regulations 1988, SI 1988/1657 .... 2.17, 6.63
  reg 6(1).. 6.67
    7(1)... 6.67
    (7)... 6.67
    10(1), (3).................................... 6.67
    11 .... 6.67
    12 (1).. 6.67
Control of Substances Hazardous to Health Regulations 1994, SI 1994/3246 .... 6.63
  reg 7(11)... 6.67
Control of Substances Hazardous to Health Regulations 1999, SI 1999/437 .... 6.63
Control of Substances Hazardous to Health Regulations 2002, SI 2002/2677 .... 6.63
  reg 2 .... **4.87**
    (1)(e) 6.63
    3 .... **4.88**
    5 .... **4.89**
    6 .... **4.90**, 6.63
    7 .... **4.91**,
                                                 4.92, 6.63
    8 .... **4.93**, 6.63
    9 .... **4.94**, 6.63
    10 .... **4.95**, 6.63
    11 .... **4.96**, 6.63
    12 .... **4.97**, 6.63

D

Disability Discrimination (Exemption for Small Employers) Order 1998, SI 1998/2618 .... 7.141

E

Electricity (Factories Act) Special Regulations 1908, SI 1908/1312
  reg 9 .... 2.49

Employment Tribunals (Constitution and Rules of Procedure) 1993, SI 1993/2687
Sch 1
r 8(2) 9.151
12(1) 9.176, 9.177
r 13(2)(e) 9.169
Employment Tribunals (Constitution and Rules of Procedure) Regulations 2001, SI 2001/1171 .... 9.128
Sch 1
r 4(5)(a) **9.166**
11 .... **9.153**
12 .... **9.170**
13 .... **9.173**
14 .... **9.175**, 9.176
15 .... **9.168**
Employment Tribunals Extension of Jurisdiction (England and Wales) Order 1994, SI 1994/1623 .... 9.148
Explosives in Coal Mines Order 1934, SI 1934/6 .... 4.30

G

Grinding of Metals (Miscellaneous Industries) Regulations 1925, SI 1925/904 .... 2.56
reg 1 .... 2.53, 2.57, 2.58

H

Health and Safety (Display Screen Equipment) Regulations 1992, SI 1992/2792
reg 1 .... 6.69
2 .... 6.69, 6.74
3 .... 6.69, 6.74
4 .... 6.69, 6.75
6 .... 6.69, 6.75
7 .... 6.69

M

Management of Health and Safety at Work Regulations 1992, SI 1992
reg 3 .... 10.24

Management of Health and Safety at Work Regulations 1999, SI 1999/3242 .... 3.24, 10.1
Manual Handling Operations Regulations 1992, SI 1992/2793 .... 4.85, 6.81, 6.82
reg 2 .... **4.79**
4 .... **4.80**
(1)(a) 6.76
(b)(i) 4.40, 4.84, 6.76
(ii), (iii) 4.40, 6.76
(2) 6.76
5 .... **4.81**, 6.76
Sch 1 .... **4.81**
Metalliferous Mines General Regulations 1938, SI 1938/630 .... 2.47

N

Noise at Work Regulations 1989, SI 1989/1790 .... 6.47
Non-ferrous Metals (Melting and Founding) Regulations 1962, SI 1962/1667
reg 13(1) 4.11

O

Offshore Installations (Operational Safety, Health and Welfare) Regulations 1976, SI 1976/1019 .... 4.49

P

Pedestrian Crossing Places (Traffic) Regulations 1941, SI 1941/397
reg 3, 13 .... 4.6
Prevention of Accident Rules 1902, SI 1902/616 .... 4.19
r 9 .... 2.50
Protection of Eyes Regulations 1938, SI 1938/654 .... 2.59, 4.35, 4.36
Provision and Use of Work Equipment Regulations 1992, SI 1992/2932 .... 4.55, 4.75
reg 2 .... **4.69**
3 .... **4.70**
4 .... **4.71**
5 .... **4.73**

Provision and Use of Work Equipment Regulations 1992 – *contd*
reg 6(1) 4.15, **11.23**
8 .... **4.76**
9 .... **4.77**
Provision and Use of Work Equipment Regulations 1998, SI 1998/2306 .... 4.55
reg 11 .... 10.25

Q

Queen's Regulations for the Royal Navy 1967 .... 2.16

R

Reporting of Injuries, Diseases and Dangerous Occurrences Regulations 1995, SI 1995/3163 .... 10.1

S

Schools Regulations 1959, SI 1959/364 .... 8.64
Shipbuilding Regulations 1931, SI 1931/133 .... 4.4, 4.17
Shipbuilding and Ship-repairing Regulations 1960, SI 1960/1932 ...... 6.42
reg 53(2) 6.31
76 .... 6.31

T

Transfer of Undertakings (Protection of Employment) Regulations 1981, SI 1981/1794 .... 9.130, 9.176, 11.20
reg 5(1) **8.76**, 8.79
(3) **8.76**
(4a) 8.79
(5) 8.79
8 .... **8.74**
(1) 8.76, 8.78
(2) 8.76, 8.77, 8.78

W

Woodworking Machinery Regulations 1922, SI 1922/1196 .... 2.43
Workplace (Health, Safety and Welfare) Regulations 1992, SI 1992/3004 .... 4.83
reg 2 .... **4.57**, 4.68
4 .... **4.58**
(2) 4.59
(a)–(c) 4.59
4A **4.60**
5 .... **4.61**
11 .... **4.62**
12 .... 4.59, **4.64**
(1) 4.65, 4.66
(2) 4.66
(a) 4.65
(3) 4.50, 4.65
13 .... **4.67**
(4) 4.68

Table of European legislation

CONVENTIONS

EC Treaty
  art 10(ex art 5)................................ 11.10
    25(ex art 12).............................. 11.2
    28(ex art 30)............................. 11.18
    43(ex art 52)............................. 11.18
    48 .... 7.77
    52 .... 11.16
    141(ex art 119)......................... 11.22
    249(ex art 189).......................... 11.3,
                                           11.5, 11.10
European Convention of Human
    Rights 5.26
  art 2 .... **5.13**
    3 .... **5.14**
    4 .... **5.15**
    6 .... **5.16**, 5.37, 5.40,
                                       5.43, 5.46, 6.24
    8 .... **5.17**, 5.28, 5.29,
                                             5.43, 5.48
      (1)........................... 5.31, 5.35, 5.50a
    9 ....**5.18**, 5.52, 5.53
    10 ....**5.19**
      (2).. 5.25
    11 .... **5.20**
    14 .... **5.21**, 5.57
  First Protocol
    art 1 .... 5.37
European Union Charter of
    Fundamental Rights 5.23, 11.24
  Ch IV
    art 27–34 .... **11.25**
International Labour Conventions 4.16
Warsaw Convention............................... 4.23
  Hague Protocol.................................. 4.23

DIRECTIVES

EEC Council Directive 64/221 .... 11.6
EEC Council Directive 68/151
  art 11 .... 11.11
EEC Council Directive 75/117 .... 11.22
EEC Council Directive 76/207(Equal
    Treatment Directive) 7.24,
                                       7.25, 7.59, 7.98,
                                           11.10, 11.22
  art 2 (1).. 11.21
    5 (1)........................ 11.7, 11.9, 11.21
    6 .... 7.99, 11.16
EEC Council Directive 77/187 .... 11.20
EEC Council Directive 80/987 .... 11.17
EEC Council Directive 83/189
  art 8, 9 .... 11.12
EEC Council Directive 86/188 .... 6.47
EEC Council Directive 85/577 .... 11.8
EEC Council Directive 89/391
    (Framework Directive)............. 4.52,
                                       4.55, 4.86, 11.23
  preamble... **4.54**
  art 1, 5, 6 .... **4.54**
EEC Council Directive 89/665 (Work
    Equipment Directive)....... 4.55, 11.23
EEC Council Directive 90/269
    (Manual Handling Directive) 4.85
EEC Council Directive (Acquired
    Rights Directive) 8.76
EEC Council Directive 91/383
    (Temporary Workers
    Directive).................................... 1.24
EC Council Directive 2003/10
    (Physical Agents (Noise)
    Directive).................................... 6.47

Table of cases

All references in the right-hand column are to chapter and paragraph numbers. Chapter and paragraph numbers in **bold** type indicate where a case is set out.

A

A v Chief Constable of West Yorkshire Police [2002] EWCA Civ 1584, [2003] 1 All ER 255, [2003] IRLR 32, [2002] 3 FCR 751, [2003] 1 FLR 223, [2003] 01 LS Gaz R 24, 146 Sol Jo LB 254, sub nom Chief Constable of West Yorkshire Police v A (No 2) [2003] ICR 161 .... **7.59**, **7.79**
AB v South West Water Services Ltd. See Gibbons v South West Water Services Ltd
AEI Rediffusion Music Ltd v Phonographic Performance Ltd (No 2). See Phonographic Performance Ltd v AEI Rediffusion Music Ltd
Abadeh v British Telecommunications plc [2001] ICR 156, [2001] IRLR 23, EAT **7.125**, **7.164**
Abbey Life Assurance Co Ltd v Tansell [2000] IRLR 387, [2000] NLJR 651, CA **7.143**
Aberdeen Steak Houses Group plc v Ibrahim [1988] ICR 550, [1988] IRLR 420, [1988] NLJR 151, EAT **9.154**
Abernethy v Mott, Hay and Anderson [1974] ICR 323, [1974] IRLR 213, 118 Sol Jo 294, CA **8.40**, **8.47**
Adams v GKN Sankey Ltd [1980] IRLR 416, EAT **8.30**
Adamson v B & L Cleaning Services Ltd [1995] IRLR 193, EAT **8.58**
Addison v Babcock FATA Ltd [1988] QB 280, [1987] 2 All ER 784, [1987] 3 WLR 122, [1987] ICR 805, 131 Sol Jo 538, [1987] LS Gaz R 1409, sub nom Babcock FATA Ltd v Addison [1987] IRLR 173, [1987] 1 FTLR 505, CA **8.2**
Adekeye v Post Office (No 2). See Post Office v Adekeye
Ahmad v United Kingdom (1981) 4 EHRR 126, E Ct HR **5.57**
Alcan Extrusions v Yates [1996] IRLR 327, EAT **8.14**
Aldred v Nacanco [1987] IRLR 292, CA **1.45**
Alexander v Midland Bank plc [2000] ICR 464, [1999] IRLR 723, CA **6.73**
Alford v National Coal Board [1952] 1 All ER 754, [1952] WN 144, [1952] 1 TLR 687, 1952 SC 17, 1952 SLT 204, HL **1.30**
Algemene Transport-en Expeditie Onderneming van Gend en Loos NV v Nederlandse Belastingadministratie: 26/62 [1963] ECR 1, [1963] CMLR 105, ECJ **11.2**
Allen v Aeroplane and Motor Aluminium Castings Ltd [1965] 3 All ER 377, [1965] 1 WLR 1244, 109 Sol Jo 629, CA **2.71**, 2.78
Allen v British Rail Engineering [2000] CLY 454; on appeal [2001] EWCA Civ 242, [2001] ICR 942 .... **6.11**, 6.59, **9.39**
Allonby v Accrington and Rossendale College [2001] EWCA Civ 529, [2001] 2 CMLR 559, [2001] ICR 1189, [2001] IRLR 364 .... **7.39**, **7.65**
Alpine Bulk Transport Co Inc v Saudi Eagle Shipping Co Inc, The Saudi Eagle [1986] 2 Lloyd's Rep 221, CA **9.3**

Amministrazione delle Finanze dello Stato v Simmenthal SpA: 106/77 [1978]
 ECR 629, [1978] 3 CMLR 263, ECJ **11.13**
Amor v Galliard Homes Ltd (2001) EAT/47/01, EAT **8.44**
Amosu v Financial Times Ltd (1998) LTL, 31 July **6.71**
Amsterdam Bulb BV v Produktschap voor Siergewassen: 50/76 [1977] ECR 137,
 [1977] 2 CMLR 218 .... **11.4**
Anderton v Clwyd County Council [2002] EWCA Civ 933, [2002] 3 All ER 813,
 [2002] 1 WLR 3174, [2002] 35 LS Gaz R 38, [2002] NLJR 1125 .... **9.30**
Angel v New Possibilities NHS Trust [2002] EWCA Civ 304, (2002) 70 BMLR 1 .... **7.169**
Antonelli v Allen [2000] NLJR 1825, [2000] All ER (D) 2040 .... **9.103**
Anya v University of Oxford [2001] EWCA Civ 405, [2001] ICR 847, [2001]
 IRLR 377, [2001] ELR 711 .... 7.62
Anyanwu v South Bank Student Union (Commission for Racial Equality intervening) [2001] UKHL 14, [2001] 2 All ER 353, [2001] 1 WLR 638, [2001] ICR
 391, [2001] IRLR 305, [2001] 21 LS Gaz R 39, [2001] NLJR 501 .... **7.101**
Aparau v Iceland Frozen Foods plc [2000] 1 All ER 228, [2000] ICR 341, [2000]
 IRLR 196, [1999] 45 LS Gaz R 31, CA **9.174**
Appleyard v F M Smith (Hull) Ltd [1972] IRLR 19, IT **8.62**
Arbuthnot Latham Bank Ltd v Trafalgar Holdings Ltd [1998] 2 All ER 181, [1998]
 1 WLR 1426, CA **9.85**
Arkin v Borchard Lines Ltd (No 2) [2001] NLJR 970, [2001] Eu LR 232, [2001]
 CP Rep 108 .... **9.123**
Armitage v Johnson [1997] IRLR 162, EAT **7.106**
Armour v Skeen [1977] IRLR 310, 1977 JC 15, 1977 SLT 71 .... **10.17**
Armstrong v British Coal Corpn [1997] 8 Med LR 259, (1996) Times,
 6 December, CA **6.59**
Arnold v Central Electricity Generating Board [1988] AC 228, [1987] 3 All ER
 694, [1987] 3 WLR 1009, 131 Sol Jo 1487, [1987] LS Gaz R 3416, [1987]
 NLJ Rep 1014, HL 6.18, **6.26**
Artisan Press Ltd v Srawley [1986] ICR 328, [1986] IRLR 126, EAT **8.131**
Asda Stores Ltd v Thompson [2002] IRLR 245, EAT **9.164**
Ashton v Chief Constable of West Mercia Constabulary [2001] ICR 67, EAT **7.58**
Ashworth v Peterborough United Football Club (10 June 2002, unreported) **9.123**
Atkinson (Octavius) & Sons Ltd v Morris [1989] ICR 431, [1989] IRLR 158, CA **8.36**
A-G for New South Wales v Perpetual Trustee Co Ltd [1955] AC 457, [1955]
 1 All ER 846, [1955] 2 WLR 707, 119 JP 312, 99 Sol Jo 233, PC **5.74**
A-G's Reference (No 2 of 1999) [2000] QB 796, [2000] 3 All ER 182, [2000]
 3 WLR 195, [2000] IRLR 417, [2000] 2 BCLC 257, [2000] 2 Cr App Rep
 207, [2000] Crim LR 475, [2000] 09 LS Gaz R 39, CA **10.29**
Aziz v Trinity Street Taxis Ltd [1989] QB 463, [1988] 2 All ER 860, [1988]
 3 WLR 79, [1988] ICR 534, [1988] IRLR 204, 132 Sol Jo 898, [1988] 26 LS
 Gaz R 42, CA **7.83**

B

BL Cars Ltd (formerly Leyland Cars) v Vyas. See Leyland Cars v Vyas
Babcock FATA Ltd v Addison. See Addison v Babcock FATA Ltd
Babcock International Ltd v National Grid plc [2000] All ER (D) 810 .... **6.43**
Baker v T E Hopkins & Son Ltd. See Ward v T E Hopkins & Son Ltd
 Baker v Willoughby [1970] AC 467, [1969] 2 All ER 549, [1969] 2 WLR 489,
 113 Sol Jo 37, CA; revsd [1970] AC 467, [1969] 3 All ER 1528, [1970]
 2 WLR 50, 114 Sol Jo 15, HL 2.82
Baker Refractories Ltd v Bishop. See Bishop v Baker Refractories Ltd [2002]
 EWCA Civ 76

Ball v Post Office [1995] PIQR P5 .... 6.12
Ballantine v Newalls Insulation Co Ltd [2001] ICR 25, [2000] PIQR Q327, [2000] 26 LS Gaz R 36, 144 Sol Jo LB 230, CA 6.45
Banna v Delicato 1999 SLT 84, Sh Ct 4.50
Barber v Somerset County Council [2002] EWCA Civ 76, [2002] 2 All ER 1, [2002] ICR 613, 68 BMLR 115, [2002] 12 LS Gaz R 34, sub nom Somerset County Council v Barber [2002] IRLR 263 .... 6.86
Barclays Bank plc v Kapur [1991] 2 AC 355, [1991] 1 All ER 646, [1991] 2 WLR 401, [1991] ICR 208, [1991] IRLR 136, HL 7.70
Barclays Bank plc v Kapur (No 2) [1995] IRLR 87, CA 7.19
Barking and Dagenham London Borough v Oguoko [2000] IRLR 179, EAT 9.158
Barlow v Borough of Broxbourne [2003] EWHC 50, (2003) LTL, 24 January 6.91
Barnett v Chelsea and Kensington Hospital Management Committee [1969] 1 QB 428, [1968] 1 All ER 1068, [1968] 2 WLR 422, 111 Sol Jo 912 .... 2.75
Baron v Lovell [2000] PIQR P20, [1999] CPLR 630, CA 9.116
Barras v Aberdeen Steam Trawling and Fishing Co Ltd [1933] AC 402, [1933] All ER Rep 52, 102 LJPC 33, 18 Asp MLC 384, 38 Com Cas 279, 77 Sol Jo 215, 149 LT 169, 49 TLR 391, HL 4.16
Barrett v Ministry of Defence [1995] 3 All ER 87, [1995] 1 WLR 1217, CA 2.16, 5.70
Barry v Midland Bank plc [1999] 3 All ER 974, [1999] 1 WLR 1465, [1999] ICR 859, [1999] IRLR 581, [1999] 31 LS Gaz R 36, [1999] NLJR 1253, 143 Sol Jo LB 221, HL 7.37
Bastick v James Lane (Turf Accountants) Ltd [1979] ICR 778 .... 9.152
Baynton v Saurus General Engineers Ltd [2000] ICR 375, [1999] IRLR 604, EAT 7.159
Beadsley v United Steel Cos Ltd [1951] 1 KB 408, [1950] 2 All ER 872, 114 JP 565, 94 Sol Jo 704, 66 (pt 2) TLR 902, CA 4.29
Beck v United Closures and Plastics plc 2001 SLT 1299, Ct of Sess 4.75
Bell v Blackwood Morton & Sons Ltd 1960 SC 11, 1960 SLT 145 .... 1.27a
Bell v Secretary of State for Defence [1986] QB 322, [1985] 3 All ER 661, [1986] 2 WLR 248, 129 Sol Jo 871, [1986] LS Gaz R 206, [1985] NLJ Rep 847, CA 5.66
Bennett v Southwark London Borough Council [2002] EWCA Civ 223, [2002] ICR 881, [2002] IRLR 407, 146 Sol Jo LB 59 .... 9.163
Bentley v Secretary of State for Trade and Industry [2002] IRLR 768, EAT 7.44, 8.10
Berriman v Delabole Slate Ltd [1985] ICR 546, sub nom Delabole Slate Ltd v Berriman [1985] IRLR 305, CA 8.77
Bessenden Properties Ltd v Corness [1974] IRLR 338, [1977] ICR 821n, CA 8.142
Beynon v Scadden [1999] IRLR 700, EAT 9.176
Biggs v Somerset County Council [1996] 2 All ER 734, [1996] 2 CMLR 292, [1996] ICR 364, [1996] IRLR 203, [1996] 06 LS Gaz R 27, [1996] NLJR 174, 140 Sol Jo LB 59, CA 9.137
Biguzzi v Rank Leisure plc [1999] 4 All ER 934, [1999] 1 WLR 1926, CA 9.87
Bilka-Kaufhaus GmbH v Weber von Hartz: 170/84 [1986] ECR 1607, [1986] 2 CMLR 701, [1987] ICR 110, [1986] IRLR 317, ECJ 7.52
Billings (A C) & Sons Ltd v Riden [1958] AC 240, [1957] 3 All ER 1, [1957] 3 WLR 496, 101 Sol Jo 645, HL 2.60
Bilton v Fastnet Highlands Ltd 1998 SLT 1323, Ct of Sess 6.67
Birch v University of Liverpool [1985] ICR 470, [1985] IRLR 165, 129 Sol Jo 245, CA 8.20
Birkett v James [1978] AC 297, [1977] 2 All ER 801, [1977] 3 WLR 38, 121 Sol Jo 444, HL 9.84
Birmingham City Council v Equal Opportunities Commission [1989] AC 1155, [1989] 2 WLR 520, [1989] IRLR 173, 87 LGR 557, 133 Sol Jo 322, [1989] 15 LS Gaz R 36, [1989] NLJR 292, sub nom Equal Opportunities Commission v Birmingham City Council [1989] 1 All ER 769, HL 7.2

Bishop v Baker Refractories Ltd [2002] EWCA Civ 76, [2002] 2 All ER 1, [2002]
ICR 613, 68 BMLR 115, [2002] 12 LS Gaz R 34, sub nom Baker Refractories
Ltd v Bishop [2002] IRLR 263 .... **6.88**
Bloor v Liverpool Derricking and Carrying Co Ltd [1936] 3 All ER 399, CA **2.18**
Bohon-Mitchell v Common Professional Examination Board and Council of Legal
Education [1978] IRLR 525 .... **7.47, 7.68**
Bond v Hackney Citizens' Advice Bureau [2002] EWCA Civ 304, (2002) 70
BMLR 1 .... **7.169**
Bonnington Castings Ltd v Wardlaw [1956] AC 613, [1956] 1 All ER 615, [1956]
2 WLR 707, 54 LGR 153, 100 Sol Jo 207, 1956 SC (HL) 26, 1956 SLT
135 .... **2.53**, 2.55, 2.56, 2.57, 2.59, 2.81, **6.1**
Bork (P) International A/S v Foreningen af Arbejdsledere i Danmark: 101/87
[1988] ECR 3057, [1990] 3 CMLR 701, [1989] IRLR 41, ECJ 8.76
Bossa v Nordstress Ltd [1998] ICR 694, [1998] IRLR 284, EAT **7.75**
Bouchaala v Trusthouse Forte Hotels Ltd [1980] ICR 721, [1980] IRLR 382, EAT **8.63**
Boys and Girls Welfare Society v McDonald [1997] ICR 693, [1996] IRLR 129,
EAT **8.56**
Bradford City Metropolitan Council v Arora [1991] 2 QB 507, [1991] 3 All ER
545, [1991] 2 WLR 1377, [1991] ICR 226, [1991] IRLR 165, CA **7.108**
Bradley v Eagle Star Insurance Co [1989] AC 957, [1989] 2 WLR 568, [1989]
1 All ER 961, [1989] ICR 301, HL **12.12**
Brandon v Osborne Garrett & Co [1924] 1 KB 548, [1924] All ER Rep 703, 93
LJKB 304, 130 LT 670, 68 Sol Jo 460, 40 TLR 235 .... 2.39
Brasserie du Pêcheur SA v Germany: C-46/93 [1996] QB 404, [1996] All ER (EC)
301, [1996] 2 WLR 506, [1996] ECR I-1029, [1996] 1 CMLR 889, [1996]
IRLR 267, ECJ **11.18**
Brawley v Marczynski (No 2) [2002] EWCA Civ 1453, [2002] 4 All ER 1067,
[2003] 1 WLR 813, [2003] 01 LS Gaz R 23, 146 Sol Jo LB 239 .... **9.117**
Bridgeman v McAlpine Brown (19 January 2000, unreported), CA **9.68, 9.82**
Briggs v North Eastern Education and Library Board [1990] IRLR 181, NI CA **7.40**
British Coal Corpn v Keeble [1997] IRLR 336, EAT **9.139**
British Gas Services Ltd v McCaull [2001] IRLR 60, EAT **7.152, 8.50**
British Home Stores Ltd v Burchell [1980] ICR 303n, [1978] IRLR 379, 13 ITR
560, EAT **8.55**, 8.106
British Judo Association v Petty [1981] ICR 660, [1981] IRLR 484, EAT **7.69**
British Labour Pump Co Ltd v Byrne [1979] ICR 347, [1979] IRLR 94, EAT 8.100
British Leyland (UK) Ltd v Ashraf [1978] ICR 979, [1978] IRLR 330, 13 ITR 500,
EAT 8.3
British Sugar plc v Kirker [1998] IRLR 624, EAT **7.146**
Brooke v Bool [1928] 2 KB 578, [1928] All ER Rep 155, 97 LJKB 511, 72 Sol Jo
354, 139 LT 376, 44 TLR 531, DC **3.13**
Brooks v British Telecommunications plc [1991] ICR 286, [1991] IRLR 4, EAT;
affd [1992] ICR 414, [1992] IRLR 66, CA **8.8**
Brown v JBD Engineering Ltd [1993] IRLR 568, EAT **8.118**
Brown v Rentokil Ltd: C-394/96 [1998] All ER (EC) 791, [1998] ECR I-4185,
[1998] 2 CMLR 1049, [1998] ICR 790, [1998] IRLR 445, [1999] 1 FCR 49,
[1998] 2 FLR 649, [1998] Fam Law 597, 48 BMLR 126, [1998] 34 LS Gaz R
34, ECJ **7.27**
Brunsden v Humphrey (1884) 14 QBD 141, [1881–5] All ER Rep 357, 53 LJQB
476, 49 JP 4, 32 WR 944, 51 LT 529, CA 2.42
Bryant v Housing Corpn. See Housing Corpn v Bryant
Bryce v Swan Hunter Group plc [1988] 1 All ER 659, [1987] 2 Lloyd's Rep 426 . **2.86, 6.38**
Burgess v Thorn Consumer Electronics (Newhaven) Ltd (1983) Times, 16 May 6.77
Burns v Joseph Terry & Sons Ltd [1951] 1 KB 454, [1950] 2 All ER 987114 JP
613,, 49 LGR 161, 94 Sol Jo 837, [1951] 1 TLR 349, CA **4.31**
Burrett v West Birmingham Health Authority [1994] IRLR 7, EAT **7.3**

Burton v De Vere Hotels Ltd [1997] ICR 1, [1996] IRLR 596, EAT **7.92**
Butler v Grampian University Hospital NHS Trust 2002 SLT 985, Ct of Sess **4.63**
Bux v Slough Metals Ltd [1974] 1 All ER 262, [1973] 1 WLR 1358, [1974]
 1 Lloyd's Rep 155, 117 Sol Jo 615, CA **4.11**
Buxton v Equinox Design Ltd [1999] ICR 269, [1999] IRLR 158, EAT **7.166**
Byrne v Financial Times Ltd [1991] IRLR 417, EAT **9.160**

C

CIA Security International SA v Signalson: C-194/94 [1996] All ER (EC) 557,
 [1996] ECR I-2201, [1996] 2 CMLR 781, ECJ 11.12
Cachia v Faluyi [2001] EWCA Civ 998, [2002] 1 All ER 192, [2001] 1 WLR
 1966, [2002] PIQR P39, [2001] CP Rep 102, [2001] 29 LS Gaz R 39, 145 Sol
 Jo LB 167 .... **5.42**
Caisse Nationale d'Assurance Vieillesse des Travailleurs Salariés v Thibault:
 C-136/95 [1998] All ER (EC) 385, [1998] ECR I-2011, [1998] 2 CMLR 516,
 [1998] IRLR 399, sub nom Thibault v Caisse Nationale d'Assurance
 Viellesse des Travailleurs Salariés (CNAVTS) [1999] ICR 160, ECJ **7.24**
Caledonia Bureau Investment and Property v Caffrey [1998] ICR 603, [1998]
 IRLR 110, EAT **7.28, 8.82**
Callagan v Glasgow City Council [2001] IRLR 724, EAT **7.160**
Callery v Gray [2001] EWCA Civ 1117, [2001] 3 All ER 833, [2001] 1 WLR
 2112, [2001] NLJR 1129; affd sub nom Callery v Gray (Nos 1 and 2) [2002]
 UKHL 28, [2002] 3 All ER 417, [2002] 1 WLR 2000, [2003] RTR 71, [2003]
 Lloyds Rep IR 203, [2002] NLJR 1031 .... **9.119**
Callery v Gray (No 2) [2001] EWCA Civ 1246, [2001] 4 All ER 1, [2001] 1 WLR
 2142, [2001] 35 LS Gaz R 33, 145 Sol Jo LB 204 .... **9.120**
Callow (F E) (Engineers) Ltd v Johnson [1971] AC 335, [1970] 3 All ER 639,
 [1970] 3 WLR 982, 114 Sol Jo 846, HL **2.78**
Campbell v Mylchreest [1998] PIQR P20; affd [1999] PIQR Q17, CA **9.9**
Cape plc v Iron Trades Employers Insurance Association Ltd [1999] PIQR Q212 .... **6.19**
Capek v Lincolnshire County Council [2000] ICR 878, [2000] IRLR 590, CA **9.148**
Carmarthenshire County Council v Lewis [1955] AC 549, [1955] 1 All ER 565,
 [1955] 2 WLR 517, 119 JP 230, 53 LGR 230, 99 Sol Jo 167, HL **3.15**
Carmichael v National Power plc [1999] 4 All ER 897, [1999] 1 WLR 2042,
 [1999] ICR 1226, [2000] IRLR 43, [1999] 46 LS Gaz R 38, 143 Sol Jo LB
 281, HL **1.15**
Carroll v Andrew Barclay & Sons Ltd [1948] AC 477, [1948] 2 All ER 386,
 [1948] LJR 1490, 92 Sol Jo 555, 64 TLR 384, HL **2.6**, 2.68, **4.5**
Cartledge v E Jopling & Sons Ltd [1963] AC 758, [1963] 1 All ER 341, [1963]
 2 WLR 210, [1963] 1 Lloyd's Rep 1, 107 Sol Jo 73, HL 6.26, 6.27
Cast v Croydon College [1998] ICR 500, [1998] IRLR 318, [1998] 16 LS Gaz R
 26, 142 Sol Jo LB 119, CA 7.167
Caswell v Powell Duffryn Associated Collieries Ltd [1940] AC 152, [1939] 3 All
 ER 722, 108 LJKB 779, 83 Sol Jo 976, 161 LT 374, 55 TLR 1004, HL **2.40, 4.3**
Central Asbestos Co Ltd v Dodd [1973] AC 518, [1972] 2 All ER 1135, [1972]
 3 WLR 333, [1972] 2 Lloyd's Rep 413, 116 Sol Jo 584, HL **9.61**
Century Insurance Co Ltd v Northern Ireland Road Tranport Board [1942] AC
 509, [1942] 1 All ER 491, 111 LJPC 138, 167 LT 404, HL **1.27**
Chadwick v Pioneer Private Telephone Co Ltd [1941] 1 All ER 522 .... **1.3**
Chapman v Simon [1994] IRLR 124, CA **9.172**
Chapman (TGA) Ltd v Christopher [1998] 2 All ER 873, [1998] 1 WLR 12,
 [1998] Lloyd's Rep IR 1, CA 9.124
Charles v NTL Group Ltd (2002) LTL, 13 December **9.33**

Chessington World of Adventures Ltd v Reed, ex p News Group Newspapers Ltd
[1998] ICR 97, [1998] IRLR 556, EAT 7.57
Chief Constable of Avon and Somerset Constabularly v Chew [2001] All ER (D)
101 (Sep), EAT 7.43
Chief Constable of Cumbria v McGlennon [2002] ICR 1156, EAT 7.95
Chief Constable of Lincolnshire Police v Stubbs [1999] ICR 547, [1999] IRLR 81,
EAT 7.94
Chief Constable of West Yorkshire Police v A (No 2). See A v Chief Constable of
West Yorkshire Police
Chief Constable of West Yorkshire Police v Khan. See Khan v Chief Constable of
West Yorkshire Police
Chief Constable of West Yorkshire Police v Vento (No 2). See Vento v Chief
Constable of West Yorkshire Police
Choraria v Sethia [1998] CLC 625, [1998] 07 LS Gaz R 31, 142 Sol Jo LB 53, CA 9.88
Claims Direct Test Cases, Re (19 July 2002, unreported) **9.121**
Clancy v Cannock Chase Technical College [2001] IRLR 331, EAT **8.160**
Clapson v British Airways plc [2001] IRLR 184, EAT **9.166**
Clark v Associated Newspapers Ltd [1998] 1 All ER 959, [1998] 1 WLR 1558,
[1998] RPC 261, [1998] 07 LS Gaz R 31, [1998] NLJR 157 .... **9.115**
Clark v Novacold Ltd. See Clark v TDG Ltd (t/a Novacold)
Clark v Oxfordshire Health Authority [1998] IRLR 125, 41 BMLR 18, CA **1.13**
Clark v TDG Ltd (t/a Novacold) [1999] 2 All ER 977, sub nom Clark v Novacold
Ltd [1999] ICR 951, [1999] IRLR 318, 48 BMLR 1, CA **7.145**
Clarke v Air Foyle Ltd. See Crosby-Clarke v Air Foyle Ltd
Clarke v E R Wright & Son [1957] 3 All ER 486, [1957] 1 WLR 1191, 101 Sol Jo
902, CA 2.55
Clarke v Marlborough Fine Art (London) Ltd [2002] 1 WLR 1731, [2002] 03 LS
Gaz R 26, 145 Sol Jo LB 278, [2002] All ER (D) 105 (Jan) 9.18
Clarkson v Modern Foundries Ltd [1958] 1 All ER 33, [1957] 1 WLR 1210, 101
Sol Jo 960 .... 2.57
Clay v A J Crump & Sons Ltd [1964] 1 QB 533, [1963] 3 All ER 687, [1963]
3 WLR 866, 4 BLR 80, 107 Sol Jo 664, CA **3.24**, 3.26
Clayton v Woodman & Son (Builders) Ltd [1962] 2 QB 533, [1961] 3 All ER 249,
[1961] 3 WLR 987, 105 Sol Jo 889; revsd [1962] 2 QB 533n, [1962] 2 All ER
33, [1962] 1 WLR 585, 4 BLR 65, 106 Sol Jo 242, CA **3.23**, 3.24
Close v Steel Co of Wales Ltd [1962] AC 367, [1961] 2 All ER 953, [1961]
3 WLR 319, 59 LGR 439, 105 Sol Jo 586, HL 2.68
Coley v Securicor (1998) LTL, 3 February 6.80
College of Ripon and York St John v Hobbs [2002] IRLR 185, EAT 7.113
Collins v CPS Fuels Ltd [2001] EWCA Civ 1597, [2001] All ER (D) 124 (Oct) 9.90
Coltman v Bibby Tankers Ltd, The Derbyshire [1988] AC 276, [1987] 3 All ER
1068, [1987] 3 WLR 1181, [1988] ICR 67, [1988] 1 Lloyd's Rep 109, 1 S &
B AvR I/165, 131 Sol Jo 1658, [1988] 3 LS Gaz R 36, [1987] NLJ Rep 1157,
HL 4.99
Commission for Racial Equality v Dutton [1989] QB 783, [1989] 1 All ER 306,
[1989] 2 WLR 17, [1989] IRLR 8, 133 Sol Jo 19, [1989] 1 LS Gaz R 38, CA 7.8
Commission for Racial Equality v Imperial Society of Teachers of Dancing [1983]
ICR 473, [1983] IRLR 315, EAT 7.89
Conaty v Barclays Bank plc (6 April 2000, unreported), Central London County Court   6.74
Consignia plc v Sealy. See Sealy v Consignia plc [2002] EWCA Civ 878
Construction Industry Training Board v Labour Force Ltd [1970] 3 All ER 220,
114 Sol Jo 704 .... 1.5
Coote v Granada Hospitality Ltd: C-185/97 [1998] All ER (EC) 865, [1998] ECR
I-5199, [1998] 3 CMLR 958, [1999] ICR 100, [1998] IRLR 656, ECJ; apld
[1999] IRLR 452, EAT 7.97
Coote v Granada Hospitality Ltd (No 2) [1999] 3 CMLR 334, [1999] ICR 942,
[1999] IRLR 452, EAT 7.97

Corbin v Penfold Metalising Co Ltd [2000] Lloyd's Rep Med 247, [2000] 17 LS
   Gaz R 35, 144 Sol Jo LB 204, CA **9.58**, **9.70**
Cork v Kirby Maclean Ltd [1952] 2 All ER 402, 50 LGR 632, 96 Sol Jo 482,
   [1952] 2 TLR 217, CA **2.46**
Cormack v Excess Insurance Co Ltd (2000) Times, 30 March, CA 9.124
Corn v Weir's Glass (Hanley) Ltd [1960] 2 All ER 300, [1960] 1 WLR 577, 104
   Sol Jo 447, CA **2.64**
Cornelius v University College of Swansea [1987] IRLR 141, 131 Sol Jo 359,
   [1987] LS Gaz R 1141, CA **7.86**
Cosgrove v Caesar and Howie [2001] IRLR 653, EAT **7.153**
Cosgrove v Pattison [2001] 2 CPLR 177, [2000] All ER (D) 2007 .... **9.11**
Cotterell (Reece's Executrix) v Leeds Day (a firm) (2000) LTL, 3 January **9.65**, **9.67**
Courage Ltd v Crehan: C-453/99 [2002] QB 507, [2001] All ER (EC) 886, [2001]
   3 WLR 1646, [2001] ECR I-6297, [2002] ICR 457, ECJ 11.18
Cowley v Manson Timber Ltd [1995] ICR 367, [1995] IRLR 153, CA **8.128**
Cowley v Mersey Regional Ambulance NHS Trust (2001) LTL, 23 October, QBD 6.83
Cox Toner (W E) (International) Ltd v Crook [1981] ICR 823, [1981] IRLR 443,
   EAT **8.113**
Coxall v Goodyear Great Britain Ltd [2002] EWCA Civ 1010, [2003] 1 WLR 536,
   [2003] ICR 152, [2002] IRLR 742 .... **6.14**
Coxwold, The. See Yorkshire Dale Steamship Co Ltd v Minister of War
   Transport, The Coxwold
Crookall v Vickers-Armstrong Ltd [1955] 2 All ER 12, [1955] 1 WLR 659, 53
   LGR 407, 99 Sol Jo 401 .... **2.12**
Crosby-Clarke v Air Foyle Ltd [2002] EWCA Civ 745, [2002] ICR 1063, sub nom
   Clarke v Air Foyle Ltd [2002] 24 LS Gaz R 34 .... **8.79**
Crown Suppliers (Property Services Agency) v Dawkins [1993] ICR 517, sub nom
   Dawkins v Department of the Environment [1993] IRLR 284, CA **7.17**
Cruickshank v VAW Motorcast Ltd [2002] ICR 729, [2002] IRLR 24, EAT **7.112**, **7.139**
Cullen v North Lanarkshire Council 1998 SC 451, 1998 SLT 847 .... **4.82**
Cummings (or McWilliams) v Sir William Arrol & Co Ltd [1962] 1 All ER 623,
   [1962] 1 WLR 295, 106 Sol Jo 218, 1962 SC 70, 1962 SLT 121, HL **2.67**, 2.70
Curran v William Neill & Son (St Helens) Ltd [1961] 3 All ER 108, [1961]
   1 WLR 1069, 105 Sol Jo 526, CA **2.66**
Customs and Excise Comrs v Anchor Foods Ltd [1999] 3 All ER 268, [1999]
   1 WLR 1139, 143 Sol Jo LB 96 .... **9.101**

D

Dacas v Brook Street Bureau and Wandsworth Borough Council (11 February
   2003, unreported), EAT **1.24**
Dada v Metal Box Co Ltd [1974] ICR 559, [1974] IRLR 251, 9 ITR 390, NIRC **9.167**
Dale v British Coal Corpn [1993] 1 All ER 317, [1992] 1 WLR 964, [1992] PIQR
   P373, 136 Sol Jo LB 197, CA **9.74**
Daley v Allied Suppliers Ltd [1983] ICR 90, [1983] IRLR 14, EAT **1.8**
Daniels v Ford Motor Co Ltd [1955] 1 All ER 218, [1955] 1 WLR 76, 53 LGR
   171, 99 Sol Jo 74, CA **4.10**
Daniels v Walker [2000] 1 WLR 1382, [2000] CPLR 462, CA **9.10**, **9.102**
Davidson v Handley Page Ltd [1945] 1 All ER 235, 114 LJKB 81, 89 Sol Jo 118,
   172 LT 38, 61 TLR 178, CA **2.19**
Davie v New Merton Board Mills Ltd [1959] AC 604, [1959] 1 All ER 346,
   [1959] 2 WLR 331, 103 Sol Jo 177, HL **2.10**, **2.31**, **3.4**
Davies v Powell Duffryn Associated Collieries Ltd [1942] AC 601, [1942] 1 All
   ER 657, 111 LJKB 418, 86 Sol Jo 294, 167 LT 74, 58 TLR 240, HL 2.80

Dawkins v Department of the Environment. See Crown Suppliers (Property
  Services Agency) v Dawkins
Day v T Pickles Farms Ltd [1999] IRLR 217, EAT 7.30
Dedman v British Building and Engineering Appliances Ltd [1974] 1 All ER 520,
  [1974] 1 WLR 171, [1974] ICR 53, [1973] IRLR 379, 16 KIR 1, 9 ITR 100,
  117 Sol Jo 938, CA 9.141
De Freitas v Permanent Secretary of Ministry of Agriculture, Fisheries, Lands and
  Housing [1999] 1 AC 69, [1998] 3 WLR 675, [1998] 3 LRC 62, 142 Sol Jo
  LB 219, PC 5.35
Dekker v Stichting Vormingscentrum voor Jong Volwassenen (VJV – Centrum)
  Plus: C-177/88 [1990] ECR I-3941, [1992] ICR 325, [1991] IRLR 27, ECJ 7.25
Delabole Slate Ltd v Berriman. See Berriman v Delabole Slate Ltd
Del Monte Foods Ltd v Mundon [1980] ICR 694, [1980] IRLR 224, EAT 8.81
Dench v Flynn & Partners [1998] IRLR 653, CA 8.152
Denham v Midland Employers' Mutual Assurance Ltd [1955] 2 QB 437, [1955]
  2 All ER 561, [1955] 3 WLR 84, [1955] 1 Lloyd's Rep 467, 99 Sol Jo 417,
  CA 3.21, 3.22
Derbyshire, The. See Coltman v Bibby Tankers Ltd, The Derbyshire
D'Souza v Lambeth London Borough Council [2001] EWCA Civ 794 .... 7.99
Devine v Franklin [2002] EWCA Civ 1846 .... 9.109
Devis (W) & Sons Ltd v Atkins [1977] AC 931, [1977] 3 All ER 40, [1977]
  3 WLR 214, [1977] ICR 662, [1977] IRLR 314, 13 ITR 71, 8 BLR 57, 121
  Sol Jo 512, HL 8.46
Dexter v Tenby Electrical Accessories Ltd [1991] Crim LR 839, [1991] COD 288,
  DC 4.48
Deyong v Shenburn [1946] KB 227, [1946] 1 All ER 226, 115 LJKB 262, 90 Sol
  Jo 139, 174 LT 129, 62 TLR 193, CA 2.20
Dhak v Insurance Co of North America (UK) Ltd [1996] 2 All ER 609, [1996]
  1 WLR 936, [1996] 1 Lloyd's Rep 632, [1996] NLJR 247, CA 6.26
Dhatt v McDonald's Hamburgers Ltd [1991] 3 All ER 692, [1991] 1 WLR 527,
  [1991] ICR 238, [1991] IRLR 130, CA 7.11
Dillenkofer v Germany: C-178–190/94 [1997] QB 259, [1996] All ER (EC) 917,
  [1997] 2 WLR 253, [1996] ECR I-4845, [1996] 3 CMLR 469, [1997] IRLR
  60, ECJ 11.18
Din v Carrington Viyella Ltd (Jersey Kapwood Ltd) [1982] ICR 256, [1982] IRLR
  281, EAT 7.13
Dixon v BBC [1979] QB 546, [1979] 2 All ER 112, [1979] 2 WLR 647, [1979]
  ICR 281, [1979] IRLR 114, 122 Sol Jo 713, CA 8.25
Dobie v Burns International Security Services (UK) Ltd [1984] 3 All ER 333,
  [1985] 1 WLR 43, [1984] ICR 812, [1984] IRLR 329, 128 Sol Jo 872, CA 8.67
Donoghue v Poplar Housing and Regeneration Community Association Ltd. See
  Poplar Housing and Regeneration Community Association Ltd v Donoghue
Donoghue (or McAlister) v Stevenson. See M'Alister (or Donoghue) v Stevenson
Donovan v Gwentoys Ltd [1990] 1 All ER 1018, [1990] 1 WLR 472, 134 Sol Jo
  910, [1990] 15 LS Gaz R 40, HL 9.73
Dori v Recreb Srl: C-91/92 [1995] All ER (EC) 1, [1994] ECR I-3325, [1995]
  1 CMLR 665, ECJ 11.8
Douglas v Hello! Ltd [2001] QB 967, [2001] 2 All ER 289, [2001] 2 WLR 992,
  [2002] 1 FCR 289, [2001] 1 FLR 982, [2001] FSR 732, [2001] EMLR 199,
  CA 5.31
Driscoll-Varley v Parkside Health Authority [1991] 2 Med LR 346 .... 9.53
Dugmore v Swansea NHS Trust [2002] EWCA Civ 1689, [2003] 1 All ER 333,
  [2003] IRLR 164, [2003] 05 LS Gaz R 30, 146 Sol Jo LB 271 .... 4.92, 6.14, 6.65
Dundon v GPT Ltd [1995] IRLR 403, EAT 8.92
Dunnett v Railtrack plc (in administration) [2002] EWCA Civ 303, [2002] 2 All
  ER 850, [2002] 1 WLR 2434, [2002] 16 LS Gaz R 37 .... 9.104

Durham v T & N plc (1996) LTL. 2 May, CA **6.20**
Durnford v Western Atlas International Inc [2003] EWCA Civ 306, [2003] All ER
 (D) 94 (Mar) **2.37**
Dyke v Elliott, The Gauntlet (1872) LR 4 PC 184, 8 Moo PCCNS 428, 1 Asp
 MLC 211, 20 WR 497, 26 LT 45, sub nom R v Elliott 41 LJ Adm 65, PC **4.26**

E

EC Commission v Germany: 178/84 [1987] ECR 1227, [1988] 1 CMLR 780, ECJ 11.18
Eastwood v Magnox Electric plc [2002] EWCA Civ 463, [2003] ICR 520n, [2002]
 IRLR 447 .... **6.93**
Ebbs v James Whitson & Co Ltd [1952] 2 QB 877, [1952] 2 All ER 192, 50 LGR
 563, 96 Sol Jo 375, [1952] 1 TLR 1428, CA **4.34**, 6.30
Ebert v Venvil [2000] Ch 484, [1999] 3 WLR 670, [1999] NLJR 608, 143 Sol Jo
 LB 130, CA **9.15**
Edgson v Vickers plc [1994] ICR 510 .... **6.34**
Edwards v Hanson School Governors [2001] IRLR 733, EAT **8.52**, **8.151**
Edwards v Mid-Suffolk District Council [2001] ICR 616, [2001] IRLR 190, EAT **7.165**
Ekpe v Metropolitan Police Comr [2001] ICR 1084, [2001] IRLR 605, EAT **7.126**
Elkouil v Coney Island Ltd [2002] IRLR 174, EAT **8.66**
Ellis v Eagle Place Services [2002] EWHC 1201 .... **6.93**
Elmes v Hygrade Food Products plc [2001] EWCA Civ 121, [2001] CP Rep 71,
 [2001] All ER (D) 158 (Jan) **9.27**
Ely v YKK Fasteners (UK) Ltd [1994] ICR 164, [1993] IRLR 500, CA **8.43**
English v Emery Reimbold & Strick Ltd [2002] EWCA Civ 605, [2002] 3 All ER
 385, [2002] 1 WLR 2409, [2002] 22 LS Gaz R 34, [2002] NLJR 758, 146 Sol
 Jo LB 123 .... **9.106**
Equal Opportunities Commission v Birmingham City Council. See Birmingham
 City Council v Equal Opportunities Commission
Equal Opportunities Commission v Secretary of State for Employment. See R v
 Secretary of State for Employment, ex p Equal Opportunities Commission
Express and Echo Publications Ltd v Tanton [1999] ICR 693, [1999] IRLR 367,
 [1999] 14 LS Gaz R 31, CA **1.14**

F

Factortame Ltd v Secretary of State for Transport (No 2). See R v Secretary of
 State for Transport, ex p Factortame Ltd (No 2)
Fairchild v Glenhaven Funeral Services Ltd [2002] UKHL 22, [2003] 1 AC 32,
 [2002] 3 All ER 305, [2002] 3 WLR 89, [2002] ICR 798, [2002] IRLR 533,
 67 BMLR 90, [2002] NLJR 998 .... **6.4**
Farah v British Airways plc (2000) Times, 26 January, CA **9.83**
Farmer v National Coal Board [1985] CLY 2018, (1985) Times, 27 April, CA **9.60**
Farmer v Rash [1969] 1 All ER 705, [1969] 1 WLR 160, 113 Sol Jo 57 .... **2.76**
Fay v North Yorkshire County Council [1986] ICR 133, 85 LGR 87, sub nom
 North Yorkshire County Council v Fay [1985] IRLR 247, CA **8.71**
Fennelly v Connex South Eastern Ltd [2001] IRLR 390, CA **1.29**
Ferguson v John Dawson & Partners (Contractors) Ltd [1976] 3 All ER 817,
 [1976] 1 WLR 1213, [1976] IRLR 346, [1976] 2 Lloyd's Rep 669, 8 BLR 38,
 120 Sol Jo 603, CA **1.6**
Field v Perrys (Ealing) Ltd [1950] 2 All ER 521 .... **4.41**

Fisher v Oldham Corpn [1930] 2 KB 364, [1930] All ER Rep 96, 99 LJKB 569, 94 JP 132, 28 LGR 293, 29 Cox CC 154, 143 LT 281, 74 Sol Jo 299, 46 TLR 390 ...... **5.73**
Fitzgerald v Lane [1987] QB 781, [1987] 2 All ER 455, [1987] 3 WLR 249, 131 Sol Jo 976, [1987] LS Gaz R 1334, [1987] NLJ Rep 316, CA; affd [1989] AC 328, [1988] 2 All ER 961, [1988] 3 WLR 356, [1990] RTR 133, 132 Sol Jo 1064, [1988] NLJR 209, HL **6.6**
Fitzpatrick v British Railways Board [1992] ICR 221, [1991] IRLR 376, CA **8.91**
Fitzsimons v Ford Motor Co Ltd (Aero Engines) [1946] 1 All ER 429, 174 LT 233, 62 TLR 257, 39 BWCC 26, CA **6.26**
Foley v Post Office [2001] 1 All ER 550, [2000] ICR 1283, [2000] IRLR 827, CA **8.106**
Ford v Stakis Hotels and Inns Ltd [1987] ICR 943, [1988] IRLR 46, [1987] LS Gaz R 2192, EAT **9.143**
Foster v British Gas plc: C-188/89 [1991] 1 QB 405, [1990] 3 All ER 897, [1991] 2 WLR 258, [1990] ECR I-3313, [1990] 2 CMLR 833, [1991] ICR 84, [1990] IRLR 353, ECJ; apld [1991] 2 AC 306, [1991] 2 All ER 705, [1991] 2 WLR 1075, [1991] 2 CMLR 217, [1991] ICR 463, [1991] IRLR 268, [1991] 18 LS Gaz R 34, HL **11.9**
Foster v National Power plc (1997) LTL, 7 May **6.79**
Fougère v Phoenix Motor Co Ltd [1977] 1 All ER 237, [1976] 1 WLR 1281, [1976] ICR 495, [1976] IRLR 259, 11 ITR 181, 120 Sol Jo 603, EAT **8.155**
Fowles v Bedfordshire County Council [1996] ELR 51, [1995] PIQR P389, CA **3.16**
Fox v Graham Group Ltd (2001) Times, 3 August **9.93**
Fox v Spousal (Midland) Ltd [2002] UKHL 22, [2003] 1 AC 32, [2002] 3 All ER 305, [2002] 3 WLR 89, [2002] ICR 798, [2002] IRLR 533, 67 BMLR 90, [2002] NLJR 998 ...... **6.4**
Fox Maintenance Ltd v Jackson [1978] ICR 110, [1977] IRLR 306, 12 ITR 455, EAT **8.35**
Francovich and Bonifaci v Italy: C-6, 9/90 [1991] ECR I-5357, [1993] 2 CMLR 66, [1995] ICR 722, [1992] IRLR 84, ECJ **11.17**
Fraser v Winchester Health Authority (1999) 55 BMLR 122, CA **4.78**
Friend v Civil Aviation Authority [2001] EWCA Civ 1204, [2001] 4 All ER 385, [2002] ICR 525, [2001] IRLR 819 ...... **8.145**
Frydlender v France (26 June 2000, unreported), E Ct HR **5.46**
Fu v London Borough of Camden [2001] IRLR 186, EAT **7.149**
Fuller v Lloyds Bank plc [1991] IRLR 336, EAT **8.107**
Futty v D & D Brekkes Ltd [1974] IRLR 130 ...... **8.21**
Fyfe v Scientific Furnishings Ltd [1989] ICR 648, [1989] IRLR 331, EAT **8.143**

G

GUS Home Shopping Ltd v Green and McLaughlin [2001] IRLR 75, EAT **7.29**
Galashiels Gas Co Ltd v O'Donnell (or Millar) [1949] AC 275, [1949] 1 All ER 319, 113 JP 144, 47 LGR 213, [1949] LJR 540, 93 Sol Jo 71, 65 TLR 76, HL **4.55**, 11.23
Gale v Superdrug Stores plc [1996] 3 All ER 468, [1996] 1 WLR 1089, [1996] PIQR P330, [1996] 19 LS Gaz R 29, 140 Sol Jo LB 124, CA **9.36**
Gallagher v Bond Pearce [2001] CLY 1668 ...... **6.75**
Garcia v Harland & Wolff Ltd [1943] 1 KB 731, [1943] 2 All ER 477, 112 LJKB 605, 169 LT 300, 60 TLR 16 ...... **4.17**
Gardiner v Motherwell Machinery and Scrap Co Ltd [1961] 3 All ER 831n, [1961] 1 WLR 1424, 105 Sol Jo 966, 1961 SC (HL) 1, 1962 SLT 2 ...... **2.65**
Garrard v A E Southey & Co and Standard Telephones and Cables Ltd [1952] 2 QB 174, [1952] 1 All ER 597, 96 Sol Jo 166, [1952] 1 TLR 630 ...... **3.20**
Garret v Camden London Borough Council (2001) LTL, 3 April, CA **6.83**

Garry v London Borough of Ealing [2001] EWCA Civ 1282, [2001] IRLR 681 .... **7.48**
Gauntlet, The. See Dyke v Elliott, The Gauntlet
Geest plc v Lansiquot [2002] UKPC 48, [2003] 1 All ER 383n, [2002] 1 WLR
    3111, 69 BMLR 184 .... 2.83
General Cleaning Contractors Ltd v Christmas [1953] AC 180, [1952] 2 All ER
    1110, [1953] 2 WLR 6, 51 LGR 109, 97 Sol Jo 7, HL **2.8**
General Engineering Services Ltd v Kingston and St Andrew Corpn [1988] 3 All
    ER 867, [1989] 1 WLR 69, [1989] ICR 88, [1989] IRLR 35, 133 Sol Jo 20,
    [1989] 4 LS Gaz R 44, PC **1.35**
Gibbons v South West Water Services Ltd [1993] QB 507, sub nom AB v South
    West Water Services Ltd [1993] 1 All ER 609, [1993] 2 WLR 507, [1993]
    PIQR P167, [1993] NLJR 235, CA **7.109**
Gilham v Kent County Council (No 2) [1985] ICR 233, sub nom Kent County
    Council v Gilham [1985] IRLR 18, CA **8.68**
Gilham v Kent County Council (No 3) [1986] ICR 52, [1986] IRLR 56, EAT **8.159**
Gissing v Walkers Smith Snack Foods Ltd [1999] CLY 3983 .... **6.81**
Glasgow, HMS. See R v Swan Hunter Shipbuilders Ltd
Glasgow City Council v Zafar [1998] 2 All ER 953, [1997] 1 WLR 1659, [1998]
    ICR 120, [1997] 48 LS Gaz R 29, 1998 SC (HL) 27, 142 Sol Jo LB 30, 1998
    SLT 135, sub nom Zafar v Glasgow City Council [1998] IRLR 36 .... **7.61**
Godbout v City of Longueuil [1997] 3 SCR 844, [1998] 2 LRC 333, Can SC **5.51**
Godwin v Swindon Borough Council [2001] EWCA Civ 1478, [2001] 4 All ER
    641, [2002] 1 WLR 997 .... **9.29**
Gogay v Hertfordshire County Council [2000] IRLR 703, [2001] 1 FCR 455,
    [2001] 1 FLR 280, [2000] 37 LS Gaz R 40, CA **8.121**
Goodwin v Cabletel UK Ltd [1998] ICR 112, [1997] IRLR 665, EAT **8.84**
Goodwin v Patent Office [1999] ICR 302, [1999] IRLR 4, EAT **7.137**
Goodwin v United Kingdom (2002) 35 EHRR 447, [2002] IRLR 664, [2002]
    2 FCR 577, [2002] 2 FLR 487, [2002] Fam Law 738, 67 BMLR 199,
    13 BHRC 120, [2002] NLJR 1171, E Ct HR **7.79**
Goold (W A) (Pearmak) Ltd v McConnell [1995] IRLR 516, EAT **8.123**
Grad v Finanzamt Traunstein: 9/70 [1970] ECR 825, [1971] CMLR 1, ECJ **11.4**
Grant v South-West Trains Ltd: C-249/96 [1998] All ER (EC) 193, [1998] ECR
    I-621, [1998] 1 CMLR 993, [1998] ICR 449, [1998] IRLR 206, [1998] 1 FCR
    377, [1998] 1 FLR 839, [1998] Fam Law 392, 3 BHRC 578, ECJ **7.32**
Green v Yorkshire Traction Co Ltd [2001] EWCA Civ 1925, [2001] All ER (D) 42
    (Dec) **4.74**
Greenaway Harrison Ltd v Wiles [1994] IRLR 380, EAT **8.116**
Greenwich Health Authority v Skinner [1989] ICR 220, [1989] IRLR 238, [1989]
    13 LS Gaz R 43, EAT **9.145**
Greenwich Health Authority v Ward [1989] ICR 220, [1989] IRLR 238, [1989]
    13 LS Gaz R 43, EAT **9.145**
Greenwood v British Airways plc [1999] ICR 969, [1999] IRLR 600, EAT **7.138**
Grepe v Loam (1887) 37 Ch D 168, 57 LJ Ch 435, 58 LT 100, CA **9.14**
Griffiths v British Coal Corpn (1998) LTL, 23 January, QBD **6.15**
Grootcon (UK) Ltd v Keld [1984] IRLR 302, EAT **8.73**
Grovit v Doctor [1997] 2 All ER 417, [1997] 1 WLR 640, [1997] NLJR 633, 141
    Sol Jo LB 107, HL **9.86**
Gunn v Wallsend Slipway and Engineering Co Ltd (1989) Times, 23 January **6.39**

H

HSBC Bank plc (formerly Midland Bank plc) v Madden [2001] 1 All ER 550,
    [2000] ICR 1283, [2000] IRLR 827, CA **8.106**

Habib Bank Ltd v Jaffer [2000] CPLR 438, [2000] 17 LS Gaz R 34, 144 Sol Jo LB
187, CA **9.88**
Hadley v Baxendale (1854) 23 LJ Ex 179, [1843–60] All ER Rep 461, 9 Exch 341,
18 Jur 358, 2 WR 302, 2 CLR 517, 23 LTOS 69 .... **2.44**
Hadoulis v Trinatours Ltd (2002) LTL, 1 October **6.75**
Haigh v Charles W Ireland Ltd [1973] 3 All ER 1137, [1974] 1 WLR 43, [1973]
RA 449, 117 Sol Jo 939, HL **4.39**
Halford v Brookes [1991] 3 All ER 559, [1991] 1 WLR 428, CA **9.55**
Halford v United Kingdom (1997) 24 EHRR 523, [1997] IRLR 471, [1998] Crim
LR 753, 94 LS Gaz R 24, E Ct HR **5.47**
Hall v British Gas plc (1998) LTL, 1 May **6.48**
Hall v Rover Financial Services Ltd (GB) (t/a Landrover Financial Services)
[2002] EWCA Civ 1514, [2002] 45 LS Gaz R 34, 146 Sol Jo LB 257 .... **9.108**
Hallam v Avery [2001] UKHL 15, [2001] 1 WLR 655, [2001] ICR 408, [2001]
21 LS Gaz R 39, 145 Sol Jo LB 116, sub nom Hallam v Cheltenham Borough
Council [2001] IRLR 312 .... **7.102**
Hallam v Cheltenham Borough Council. See Hallam v Avery
Hamblin v Field [2000] BPIR 621, (2000) Times, 26 April, CA **9.91**
Hamilton v National Coal Board [1960] AC 633, [1960] 1 All ER 76, [1960]
3 WLR 313, 124 JP 141, 104 Sol Jo 106, 1960 SLT 24, HL **4.22**, **11.23**
Hammersmith and Fulham London Borough v Farnsworth [2000] IRLR 691, EAT **7.136**
Hammond v Haigh Castle & Co Ltd [1973] 2 All ER 289, [1973] ICR 148, [1973]
IRLR 91, 14 KIR 407, 8 ITR 199, NIRC **9.136**
Hampson v Department of Education and Science [1990] 2 All ER 25, [1989] ICR
179, [1989] IRLR 69, 133 Sol Jo 151, [1989] 13 LS Gaz R 43, CA; revsd
[1991] 1 AC 171, [1990] 2 All ER 513, [1990] 3 WLR 42, [1990] ICR 511,
[1990] IRLR 302, 134 Sol Jo 1123, [1990] 26 LS Gaz R 39, [1990] NLJR
853, HL **7.54**
Hardie v CD Northern Ltd [2000] ICR 207, [2000] IRLR 87, EAT **7.141**
Harding v People's Dispensary for Sick Animals [1994] PIQR P270, CA **9.56**
Harper v National Coal Board [1974] QB 614, [1974] 2 All ER 441, [1974]
2 WLR 775, 118 Sol Jo 67, CA **9.61**
Harris v Courage (Eastern) Ltd [1982] ICR 530, [1982] IRLR 509, CA **8.60**
Harrison v Michelin Tyre Co Ltd [1985] 1 All ER 918, [1985] ICR 696 .... **1.44**
Harrison v National Coal Board [1951] AC 639, [1951] 1 All ER 1102, 115 JP
413, 50 LGR 1, [1951] 1 TLR 1079, HL **4.30**
Harrods Ltd v Remick [1998] 1 All ER 52, [1998] ICR 156, [1997] IRLR 583, CA **7.64**
Hartley v Mayoh & Co [1954] 1 QB 383, [1954] 1 All ER 375, [1954] 1 WLR
355, 118 JP 178, 52 LGR 165, 98 Sol Jo 107, CA **2.49**
Harvest Lane Motor Bodies Ltd, Re [1969] 1 Ch 457, [1968] 2 All ER 1012,
[1968] 3 WLR 220, 112 Sol Jo 518 .... **9.16**
Harvest Press Ltd v McCaffrey [1999] IRLR 778, EAT **8.85**
Harz v Deutsche Tradax GmbH: 79/83 [1984] ECR 1921, [1986] 2 CMLR 430,
ECJ **11.10**
Hatton v Sutherland [2002] EWCA Civ 76, [2002] 2 All ER 1, [2002] ICR 613, 68
BMLR 115, [2002] 12 LS Gaz R 34, sub nom Sutherland v Hatton [2002]
IRLR 263 .... **6.84**
Hawkes v Southwark London Borough Council (20 February 1998, unreported),
CA **4.84**
Hay v London Brick Co Ltd [1989] 2 Lloyd's Rep 7, CA **9.35**
Haynes v Harwood [1935] 1 KB 146, [1934] All ER Rep 103, 104 LJKB 63, 78
Sol Jo 801, 152 LT 121, 51 TLR 100, CA **2.39**, 2.44, 2.63
Haynes v Qualcast (Wolverhampton) Ltd [1958] 1 All ER 441, [1958] 1 WLR
225, 102 Sol Jo 138; revsd sub nom Qualcast (Wolverhampton) Ltd v Haynes
[1959] AC 743, [1959] 2 All ER 38, [1959] 2 WLR 510, 103 Sol Jo 310,
HL **2.11**, 2.59, **2.61**, **2.62**, 2.67

Heasmans v Clarity Cleaning Co Ltd [1987] ICR 949, [1987] IRLR 286, [1987]
 BTLC 174, [1987] NLJ Rep 101, CA **1.34**
Hedley Byrne & Co Ltd v Heller & Partners Ltd [1964] AC 465, [1963] 2 All ER
 575, [1963] 3 WLR 101, [1963] 1 Lloyd's Rep 485, 107 Sol Jo 454, HL 2.88
Heinz (H J) Co Ltd v Kenrick [2000] ICR 491, [2000] IRLR 144, EAT **7.131**, **8.53**
Hellyer Bros Ltd v McLeod [1987] 1 WLR 728, [1987] ICR 526, 131 Sol Jo 805,
 [1987] LS Gaz R 1056, sub nom McLeod v Hellyer Bros Ltd [1987] IRLR
 232, CA **1.10**
Henderson v Temple Pier Co Ltd [1998] 3 All ER 324, [1998] 1 WLR 1540,
 [1998] 20 LS Gaz R 35, 142 Sol Jo LB 156, CA **9.62**
Henderson v Wakefield Shirt Co Ltd [1997] PIQR P413, CA **6.13**, 6.79
Hendricks v Metropolitan Police Comr [2002] EWCA Civ 1686, [2003] 1 All ER
 654, [2003] IRLR 96, sub nom Metropolitan Police Comr v Hendricks [2003]
 05 LS Gaz R 30, 146 Sol Jo LB 274 .... **7.73**
HM Prison Service v Johnson [1997] ICR 275, [1997] IRLR 162, EAT **7.106**
Herbert v Harold Shaw Ltd [1959] 2 QB 138, [1959] 2 All ER 189, [1959] 2 WLR
 681, 57 LGR 185, 103 Sol Jo 372, CA **4.42**
Hereford and Worcester County Council v Neale. See Neale v Hereford and
 Worcester County Council
Hetton Victory Club Ltd v Swainston. See Swainston v Hetton Victory Club Ltd
Heyes v Pilkington Glass Ltd [1998] PIQR P303, CA **6.60**
Hilton v Shiner Ltd – Builders Merchants [2001] IRLR 727, EAT **8.122**
Hilton v Thomas Burton (Rhodes) Ltd [1961] 1 All ER 74, [1961] 1 WLR 705,
 105 Sol Jo 322 .... **1.40**
Hilton International Hotels (UK) Ltd v Protopapa [1990] IRLR 316, EAT **8.115**
Hinks v Channel 4 Television Corpn (3 March 2000, unreported) **9.69**
Hodkinson v Henry Wallwork & Co Ltd [1955] 3 All ER 236, [1955] 1 WLR
 1195, 53 LGR 656, 99 Sol Jo 778, CA 2.51
Hoechst AG v IRC and A-G: C-397, 410/98 [2001] Ch 620, [2001] All ER (EC)
 496, [2001] 2 WLR 1497, [2001] ECR I-1727, [2001] STC 452, sub nom
 Metallgesellschaft, Hoechst AG and Hoechst Ltd v IRC and A-G [2001]
 2 CMLR 700, ECJ 11.16
Holliday v National Telephone Co [1899] 2 QB 392, [1895–99] All ER Rep 359,
 68 LJQB 1016, 47 WR 658, 81 LT 252, 15 TLR 483, CA 3.12
Hollier v Plysu Ltd [1983] IRLR 260, CA **8.147**
Hollister v National Farmers' Union [1979] ICR 542, [1979] IRLR 238, CA **8.69**
Holmes v Ashford [1950] 2 All ER 76, 94 Sol Jo 337, CA 6.68
Holtby v Brigham & Cowan (Hull) Ltd [2000] 3 All ER 421, [2000] ICR 1086,
 [2000] PIQR Q293, [2000] Lloyd's Rep Med 254, [2000] NLJR 544, 144 Sol
 Jo LB 212, CA **6.10**
Home Office v Dorset Yacht Co Ltd [1970] AC 1004, [1970] 2 All ER 294, [1970]
 2 WLR 1140, [1970] 1 Lloyd's Rep 453, 114 Sol Jo 375, HL **2.79**, 2.85
Home Office v Wainwright. See Wainwright v Home Office
Honeywill & Stein Ltd v Larkin Bros (London's Commercial Photographers) Ltd
 [1934] 1 KB 191, [1933] All ER Rep 77, 103 LJKB 74, 150 LT 71, 50 TLR
 56, CA **3.12**, 3.37
Horton v Taplin Contracts Ltd [2002] EWCA Civ 1604, [2003] ICR 179, [2003]
 BLR 74, [2003] 01 LS Gaz R 24, 146 Sol Jo LB 256 .... **4.72**
Housing Corpn v Bryant [1999] ICR 123, sub nom Bryant v Housing Corpn
 [1998] 26 LS Gaz R 31, 142 Sol Jo LB 181, CA **9.147**
Houston v Lightwater Farms Ltd [1990] ICR 502, [1990] IRLR 469, EAT **9.157**
Howden v Capital Copiers (ET No S/400005/97), (1997) IRLIB 586 .... **7.114**
Huck v Robson [2002] EWCA Civ 398, [2002] 3 All ER 263 .... **9.111**
Huckerby v Elliott [1970] 1 All ER 189, 134 JP 175, 113 Sol Jo 1001 .... **10.16**
Hudson v Ridge Manufacturing Co Ltd [1957] 2 QB 348, [1957] 2 All ER 229,
 [1957] 2 WLR 948, 101 Sol Jo 409 .... **3.3**

Hunter v Singer Manufacturing Co Ltd 1953 SLT (Notes) 84, 104 Sol Jo 58 .... **4.36**
Hurst v Leeming [2001] EWHC 1051 (Ch), [2003] 1 Lloyd's Rep 379, [2002] CP
  Rep 59, [2002] All ER (D) 135 (May) **9.105**
Hutchison v Westward Television Ltd [1977] ICR 279, [1977] IRLR 69, 12 ITR
  125, EAT **9.138**
Hyett v Great Western Rly Co [1948] 1 KB 345, [1947] 2 All ER 264, [1947] LJR
  1243, 91 Sol Jo 434, 177 LT 178, 63 TLR 411, CA **2.44**

I

ICTS (UK) Ltd v Tchoula. See Tchoula v ICTS (UK) Ltd
Iceland Frozen Foods Ltd v Jones [1983] ICR 17, [1982] IRLR 439, EAT **8.104**,
  8.106, **8.110**
Igbo v Johnson Matthey Chemicals Ltd [1986] ICR 505, [1986] IRLR 215, 130
  Sol Jo 524, [1986] LS Gaz R 2089, CA **8.3**
Infantino v MacLean [2001] 3 All ER 802, [2001] All ER (D) 137 .... **9.28**
Insurance Co of North America v Forty-Eight Insulations 633 F 2d 1212 (6th Cir
  1980); cert den 454 US 1109 (1981) **6.27**
Interlink Express Parcels Ltd v Night Trunkers Ltd [2001] EWCA Civ 360, [2001]
  RTR 338, [2001] 20 LS Gaz R 43 .... **1.19**
International Sports Co Ltd v Thomson [1980] IRLR 340, EAT **8.54**
International Transport Roth GmbH v Secretary of State for the Home Department
  [2002] EWCA Civ 158, [2002] 3 WLR 344, [2002] All ER (D) 325 (Feb) **5.35**
Ironmonger v Movefield Ltd (t/a Deering Appointments) [1988] IRLR 461, EAT **8.6**

J

James v Eastleigh Borough Council [1990] 2 AC 751, [1990] 2 All ER 607, [1990]
  3 WLR 55, [1990] ICR 554, [1990] IRLR 288, 88 LGR 756, [1990] 27 LS
  Gaz R 41, [1990] NLJR 926, HL **7.23**
James v Hepworth and Grandage Ltd [1968] 1 QB 94, [1967] 2 All ER 829,
  [1967] 3 WLR 178, 111 Sol Jo 232, CA **2.74**
Jameson v Central Electricity Generating Board (Babcock Energy, third party)
  (31 March 1995, unreported), QBD; on appeal [1998] QB 323, [1997] 4 All
  ER 38, [1997] 3 WLR 151, [1997] PIQR Q89, 141 Sol Jo LB 55, CA; revsd
  [2000] 1 AC 455, [1999] 1 All ER 193, [1999] 2 WLR 141, [1999] 1 Lloyd's
  Rep 573, 143 Sol Jo LB 29, HL **6.27**
Jebson v Ministry of Defence [2000] 1 WLR 2055, [2000] ICR 1220, [2001] RTR
  22, [2000] PIQR P 201, 144 Sol Jo LB 226, CA **5.71**
Jégo-Quéré et Cie SA v European Commission: T-177/01 [2003] 2 WLR 783,
  [2002] All ER (EC) 932, CFI **11.24**
Jeromson v Shell Tankers (UK) Ltd [2001] EWCA Civ 100, [2001] ICR 1223 .... **6.35**
Jobling v Associated Dairies Ltd [1982] AC 794, [1981] 2 All ER 752, [1981]
  3 WLR 155, 125 Sol Jo 481, HL **2.82**
Johnson v Coventry Churchill International Ltd [1992] 3 All ER 14 .... **3.33**
Johnson v Unisys Ltd [2001] UKHL 13, [2003] 1 AC 518, [2001] 2 All ER 801,
  [2001] 2 WLR 1076, [2001] ICR 480, [2001] IRLR 279 .... **8.138**
Johnstone v Bloomsbury Health Authority [1992] QB 333, [1991] 2 All ER 293,
  [1991] 2 WLR 1362, [1991] ICR 269, [1991] IRLR 118, [1991] 2 Med LR
  38, CA **2.34**
Jones v Minton Construction Ltd (1973) 15 KIR 309 .... **4.46**
Jones v Post Office [2001] EWCA Civ 558, [2001] ICR 805, [2001] IRLR 384 .... **7.157**

Jones v Sandwell Metropolitan Borough Council [2002] EWCA Civ 76, [2002]
2 All ER 1, [2002] ICR 613, 68 BMLR 115, [2002] 12 LS Gaz R 34, sub nom
Sandwell Metropolitan Borough Council v Jones [2002] IRLR 263 .... **6.87**
Jones v 3M Healthcare Ltd [2002] EWCA Civ 304, (2002) 70 BMLR 1 .... **7.169**
Jones v Tower Boot Co Ltd [1997] 2 All ER 406, [1997] ICR 254, [1997] IRLR
168, [1997] NLJR 60, CA **7.91**
Jones v University of Manchester [1993] ICR 474, [1993] IRLR 218, [1993] 10 LS
Gaz R 33, 137 Sol Jo LB 14, CA **7.49**
Jones v University of Warwick [2003] EWCA Civ 151, [2003] 1 WLR 954, [2003]
11 LS Gaz R 32, [2003] NLJR 230, 147 Sol Jo LB 179, [2003] All ER (D) 34
(Feb) **5.50**
Judson v British Transport Commission [1954] 1 All ER 624, [1954] 1 WLR 585,
98 Sol Jo 211, CA **2.50**

K

Kalac v Turkey (1997) 27 EHRR 552, E Ct HR **5.53**
Kapadia v London Borough of Lambeth [2000] IRLR 699, 57 BMLR 170, CA **7.163**
Kasapis v Laimos Bros [1959] 2 Lloyd's Rep 378 .... **2.14**
Kaur v CTP Coil Ltd (2000) LTL, 10 July **9.26**
Kay v Ayrshire and Arran Health Board [1987] 2 All ER 417, sub nom Kay's
Tutor v Ayrshire and Arran Health Board 1987 SC 145, 1987 SLT 577, HL **2.84**
Kay's Tutor v Ayrshire and Arran Health Board. See Kay v Ayrshire and Arran
Health Board
Kealey v Heard [1983] 1 All ER 973, [1983] 1 WLR 573, [1983] ICR 484, 127 Sol
Jo 288 .... **3.29**
Keene Corpn v Insurance Co of North America 667 F 2d 1034 (DC Cir 1981); cert
den 455 US 1007 (1982) **6.27**
Kenny v Hampshire Constabulary [1999] ICR 27, [1999] IRLR 76, EAT **7.151**
Kent County Council v Gilham. See Gilham v Kent County Council (No 2)
Kent County Council v Mingo [2000] IRLR 90, EAT **7.135**
Kerry Foods Ltd v Creber [2000] ICR 556, [2000] IRLR 10, EAT **8.75**
Khan v Chief Constable of West Yorkshire Police [2001] UKHL 48, [2001] 4 All
ER 834, sub nom Chief Constable of West Yorkshire Police v Khan [2001]
1 WLR 1947, [2001] ICR 1065, [2001] IRLR 830, [2001] 42 LS Gaz R 37,
145 Sol Jo LB 230 .... **2.90, 7.85**
Kiam v MGN Ltd (No 2) [2002] EWCA Civ 66, [2002] 2 All ER 242, [2002]
1 WLR 2810, [2002] EMLR 504 .... **9.114**
Kidd v Axa Equity and Law Life Assurance Society plc [2000] IRLR 301 .... **2.90**
Kilroy v Kilroy [1997] PNLR 66, CA **9.126**
King v Eaton Ltd (No 2) [1998] IRLR 686, 1999 SLT 656, Ct of Sess **8.149**
King v Great Britain-China Centre [1992] ICR 516, [1991] IRLR 513, CA **7.60**
King v RCO Support Services Ltd [2001] ICR 608, CA **4.59, 4.70**
King v Samsung Heavy Industries (2002) LTL, 10 April, CA **6.62**
King v Sussex Ambulance NHS Trust [2002] EWCA Civ 953, [2002] ICR 1413,
68 BMLR 177 .... **4.85**
Kingston v British Railways Board [1984] ICR 781, [1984] IRLR 146, CA **8.72**
Kirby v Manpower Services Commission [1980] 3 All ER 334, [1980] 1 WLR
725, [1980] ICR 420, [1980] IRLR 229, 124 Sol Jo 326, EAT **7.84**
Kirker v British Sugar plc [2002] EWCA Civ 304, (2002) 70 BMLR 1 .... **7.169**
Kirkham v Chief Constable of the Greater Manchester Police [1990] 2 QB 283,
[1990] 3 All ER 246, [1990] 2 WLR 987, 134 Sol Jo 758, [1990] 13 LS Gaz
R 47, [1990] NLJR 209, CA **3.17**
Kirton v Tetrosyl Ltd [2003] ICR 37, [2002] IRLR 840, EAT; revsd (2003) 147
Sol Jo LB 474, CA **7.122**

Table of Cases

Knight v Department of Social Security [2002] IRLR 249, EAT **9.162**
Knox v Cammell Laird Shipbuilders (30 July 1990, unreported) 6.18
Kondis v State Transport Authority (1984) 154 CLR 672, 55 ALR 225, 58 ALJR
    531, HC of A **3.36**
Konttinen v Finland (Application 24949/94) 87 DR 68, (1996) E Com HR **5.52**
Koonjul v Thameslink Healthcare Services [2000] PIQR P123, CA **4.83**, 6.76
Kooragang Investments Pty Ltd v Richardson & Wrench Ltd [1982] AC 462,
    [1981] 3 All ER 65, [1981] 3 WLR 493, 125 Sol Jo 641, PC **1.28**
Kosiek v Germany (1986) 9 EHRR 328 .... **5.56**
Kossinski v Chrysler United Kingdom Ltd (1973) 15 KIR 225 .... 6.12
Kovacs v Queen Mary and Westfield College [2002] EWCA Civ 352, [2002] ICR
    919, [2002] IRLR 414, [2002] 19 LS Gaz R 29, 146 Sol Jo LB 91 .... **9.177**
Kraft Foods Ltd v Fox [1978] ICR 311, [1977] IRLR 431, EAT 8.49

L

Lambert v Croydon College [1999] ICR 409, [1999] IRLR 346, EAT 8.29
Lambeth London Borough Council v Commission for Racial Equality [1990] ICR
    768, [1990] IRLR 231, CA 7.78
Lane v Shire Roofing Co (Oxford) Ltd [1995] IRLR 493, [1995] PIQR P417, CA 1.12
Larner v British Steel plc [1993] 4 All ER 102, [1993] ICR 551, [1993] IRLR 278,
    CA 4.12
Laszczyk v National Coal Board [1954] 3 All ER 205, [1954] 1 WLR 1426, 98 Sol
    Jo 805 .... 2.22
Latimer v AEC Ltd [1953] AC 643, [1953] 2 All ER 449, 117 JP 387, 51 LGR
    457, 97 Sol Jo 486, HL 2.7, 4.8
Lavender v Diamints Ltd [1949] 1 KB 585, [1949] 1 All ER 532, 47 LGR 231,
    [1949] LJR 970, 93 Sol Jo 147, 65 TLR 163, CA 2.70
Law Hospital NHS Trust v Rush [2001] IRLR 611, 2002 SC 24, 2002 SLT 7, Ct of
    Sess 7.127
Lawrie (Alex) Factors Ltd v Morgan (1999) Times, 18 August, CA 9.19
Lee v Nursery Furnishings Ltd [1945] 1 All ER 387, 172 LT 285, 61 TLR 263, CA 2.43
Lee Ting Sang v Chung Chi-Keung [1990] 2 AC 374, [1990] 2 WLR 1173, [1990]
    ICR 409, 134 Sol Jo 909, [1990] 13 LS Gaz R 43, PC 1.11
Leicester Wholesale Fruit Market Ltd v Grundy [1990] 1 All ER 442, [1990]
    1 WLR 107, 134 Sol Jo 374, CA 9.76
Leonard v Southern Derbyshire Chamber of Commerce [2001] IRLR 19, EAT 7.124
Lewis (John) plc v Coyne [2001] IRLR 139, EAT 8.59
Lewis v Motorworld Garages Ltd [1986] ICR 157, [1985] IRLR 465, CA 8.117
Leyland Cars v Vyas [1980] AC 1028, [1979] 3 WLR 762, [1979] ICR 921,
    [1979] IRLR 465, 123 Sol Jo 768, sub nom BL Cars Ltd (formerly Leyland
    Cars) v Vyas [1979] 3 All ER 673, HL 9.163
Lister v Hesley Hall Ltd [2001] UKHL 22, [2002] 1 AC 215, [2001] 2 All ER 769,
    [2001] 2 WLR 1311, [2001] ICR 665, [2001] IRLR 472, [2001] 2 FCR 97,
    [2001] 2 FLR 307, [2001] Fam Law 595, [2001] NPC 89, [2001] 24 LS Gaz
    R 45, [2001] NLJR 728, 145 Sol Jo LB 126 .... 1.37
Lister v Romford Ice and Cold Storage Co Ltd [1957] AC 555, [1957] 1 All ER
    125, [1957] 2 WLR 158, 121 JP 98, [1956] 2 Lloyd's Rep 505, 101 Sol Jo
    106, HL 2.30
Litster v Forth Dry Dock and Engineering Co Ltd [1990] 1 AC 546, [1989] 1 All
    ER 1134, [1989] 2 WLR 634, [1989] ICR 341, [1989] IRLR 161, 133 Sol Jo
    455, [1989] NLJR 400, HL 8.76, 11.20
Littlewoods Organisation plc v Traynor [1993] IRLR 154, EAT 7.72
Liversidge v Chief Constable of Bedfordshire Police [2002] EWCA Civ 894,
    [2002] IRLR 651 .... 7.95

Lloyd v F Evans & Sons Ltd [1951] WN 306, 95 Sol Jo 483, CA **4.7**
Lloyd v Grace, Smith & Co [1912] AC 716, [1911–13] All ER Rep 51, 81 LJKB
    1140, 56 Sol Jo 723, 107 LT 531, 28 TLR 547, HL **1.26**
Lochgelly Iron and Coal Co v M'Mullan [1934] AC 1, [1933] All ER Rep Ext
    1018, 102 LJPC 123, 26 BWCC 463, 77 Sol Jo 539, 149 LT 526, 49 TLR
    566, 1934 SC 64, 1934 SLT 114, HL **4.2**
Lock v Connell Estate Agents [1994] ICR 983, [1994] IRLR 444, EAT **8.157**
Logan Salton v Durham County Council [1989] IRLR 99, EAT **8.4**
London and North Eastern Rly Co v Berriman [1946] AC 278, [1946] 1 All ER
    255, 115 LJKB 124, 38 BWCC 109, 174 LT 151, 62 TLR 170, HL **4.19**
London Clubs Management Ltd v Hood [2001] IRLR 719, EAT **7.154**
LCC v Cattermoles (Garages) Ltd [1953] 2 All ER 582, [1953] 1 WLR 997, 97 Sol
    Jo 505, CA **1.31**
London Fire and Civil Defence Authority v Betty [1994] IRLR 384, EAT **8.51**
London International College v Sen [1993] IRLR 333, CA **9.134**
London Passenger Transport Board v Upson [1949] AC 155, [1949] 1 All ER 60,
    [1949] LJR 238, 47 LGR 333, 93 Sol Jo 40, 65 TLR 9, HL **4.6**
London Transport Executive v Clarke [1981] ICR 355, [1981] IRLR 166, 125 Sol
    Jo 306, CA **8.114**
London Underground Ltd v Edwards (No 2) [1999] ICR 494, [1998] IRLR 364,
    [1998] 25 LS Gaz R 32, [1998] NLJR 905, 142 Sol Jo LB 182, CA **7.42**
Lord v Pacific Steam Navigation Co Ltd, The Oropesa [1943] P 32, [1943] 1 All
    ER 211, 112 LJP 91, 168 LT 364, 59 TLR 103, CA **2.42**, 2.77
Lord Chancellor v Coker [2001] EWCA Civ 1756, [2002] ICR 321, [2002] IRLR
    80, 145 Sol Jo LB 268 .... **7.41**
Lownds v Home Office [2002] EWCA Civ 365, [2002] 4 All ER 775, [2002]
    1 WLR 2450, [2002] 19 LS Gaz R 28 .... **9.107**
Lubbe v Cape plc [2000] 4 All ER 268, [2000] 1 WLR 1545, [2000] 2 Lloyd's Rep
    383, 144 Sol Jo LB 250, HL **6.20**
Lubovsky v Snelling [1944] KB 44, [1943] 2 All ER 577, 113 LJKB 14, 170 LT 2,
    60 TLR 52, CA **9.66**

M

MP (by his father and litigation friend, RJP) v Mid Kent Healthcare NHS Trust.
    See Peet v Mid-Kent Healthcare Trust
Mabirizi v National Hospital for Nervous Diseases [1990] ICR 281, [1990] IRLR
    133, EAT **8.134**
M'Alister (or Donoghue) v Stevenson [1932] AC 562, 101 LJPC 119, 37 Com Cas
    350, 48 TLR 494, 1932 SC (HL) 31, sub nom Donoghue (or McAlister) v
    Stevenson [1932] All ER Rep 1, 1932 SLT 317, sub nom McAlister (or
    Donoghue) v Stevenson 76 Sol Jo 396, 147 LT 281 .... 2.63, 2.79
McArdle v Andmac Roofing Co [1967] 1 All ER 583, [1967] 1 WLR 356, 111 Sol
    Jo 37, CA **3.26**
McCabe v Cornwall County Council [2002] EWCA Civ 1887, [2003] ICR 501,
    [2003] IRLR 87, [2003] 09 LS Gaz R 27 .... 6.93
McCafferty v Metropolitan Police District Receiver [1977] 2 All ER 756, [1977]
    1 WLR 1073, [1977] ICR 799, 121 Sol Jo 678, CA **2.15**
McCarthy v British Insulated Callenders Cables plc [1985] IRLR 94, EAT **8.158**
McCarthy v Coldair Ltd (1951) 50 LGR 85, 95 Sol Jo 711, [1951] 2 TLR 1226, CA **4.28**
McConnell v Police Authority for Northern Ireland [1997] IRLR 625, NI CA **7.105**
McDermid v Nash Dredging and Reclamation Co Ltd [1987] AC 906, [1987] 2 All
    ER 878, [1987] 3 WLR 212, [1987] ICR 917, [1987] IRLR 334, [1987]
    2 Lloyd's Rep 201, 131 Sol Jo 973, [1987] LS Gaz R 2458, HL 3.5, **3.6**,
                                                                                                                                  3.11, 3.34

Macdonald v Taree Holdings Ltd [2001] CPLR 439, [2001] 06 LS Gaz R 45, [2000] All ER (D) 2204, (2000) Times, 28 December 9.98
McGarvey v Eve NCI Ltd and N G Bailey & Co Ltd (2002) LTL, 26 February, CA 3.32
McGhee v National Coal Board [1972] 3 All ER 1008, [1973] 1 WLR 1, 13 KIR 471, 116 Sol Jo 967, HL 2.81, 2.84, 6.2
McGhee v Strathclyde Fire Brigade 2002 SLT 680 .... 4.65
Machine Tool Industry Research Association v Simpson [1988] ICR 558, [1988] IRLR 212, CA 9.135
McKew v Holland & Hannen & Cubitts (Scotland) Ltd [1969] 3 All ER 1621, 1970 SC (HL) 20, 1970 SLT 68 .... 2.77
McLeod v Hellyer Bros Ltd. See Hellyer Bros Ltd v McLeod
McMaster v Manchester Airport plc [1998] IRLR 112, EAT 8.28
McMeechan v Secretary of State for Employment [1997] ICR 549, [1997] IRLR 353, CA 1.23
MacMillan v Wimpey Offshore Engineers and Constructors Ltd 1991 SLT 515 .... 4.49
McNicol v Balfour Beatty Rail Maintenance Ltd [2002] ICR 381, [2001] IRLR 644, EAT; affd [2002] EWCA Civ 1074, [2002] ICR 1498, [2002] IRLR 711 ..... 7.118
McPherson v Camden London Borough (1999) LTL, 24 May. QBD 6.74
McPhilemy v Times Newspapers Ltd (No 2) [2001] EWCA Civ 933, [2001] 4 All ER 861, [2002] 1 WLR 934, [2001] EMLR 858 .... 9.112
Maddox v Rocky Horror London Ltd (1975) LTL, 6 June 6.68
Maguire v Molin [2002] EWCA Civ 1083, [2002] 4 All ER 325, [2003] 1 WLR 644, [2002] 39 LS Gaz R 40 .... 9.92
Mahmud v Bank of Credit and Commerce International SA (in compulsory liquidation) [1998] AC 20, [1997] 3 All ER 1, [1997] 3 WLR 95, [1997] ICR 606, [1997] IRLR 462, [1997] 94 LS Gaz R 33, HL 8.120
Mains v Uniroyal Englebert Tyres Ltd [1995] IRLR 544, 1995 SLT 1115, Ct of Sess 4.13
Maintenance Co Ltd v Dormer [1982] IRLR 491, EAT 8.45
Makepeace v Evans Bros (Reading) (a firm) [2001] ICR 241, [2000] BLR 737, CA 3.31, 3.32
Malik v Bank of Credit and Commerce International SA (in liquidation) [1998] AC 20, [1997] 3 All ER 1, [1997] 3 WLR 95, [1997] ICR 606, [1997] IRLR 462, [1997] 94 LS Gaz R 33, [1997] NLJR 917, HL 8.120
Mallett v McMonagle [1970] AC 166, [1969] 2 All ER 178, [1969] 2 WLR 767, [1969] 1 Lloyd's Rep 127, [1969] NI 91, 113 Sol Jo 207. HL 2.80
Maloco v Littlewoods Organisation Ltd [1987] AC 241, [1987] 2 WLR 480, 131 Sol Jo 226, [1987] LS Gaz R 905, 1987 SC 37, 1987 SLT 425, sub nom Smith v Littlewoods Organisation Ltd [1987] 1 All ER 710, [1987] NLJ Rep 149, HL 2.85
Mandla v Dowell Lee [1983] 2 AC 548, [1983] 1 All ER 1062, [1983] 2 WLR 620, [1983] ICR 385, [1983] IRLR 209, 127 Sol Jo 242, HL 7.7
Margereson and Hancock v J W Roberts Ltd [1996] PIQR P358, [1996] Env LR 304, [1996] 22 LS Gaz R 27, CA 6.40
Marks & Spencer plc v Martins [1998] ICR 1005, sub nom Martins v Marks & Spencer plc [1998] IRLR 326, CA 7.18, 9.161
Marleasing SA v La Comercial Internacional de Alimentación SA: C-106/89 [1990] ECR I-4135, [1992] 1 CMLR 305, [1993] BCC 421, 135 Sol Jo 15, ECJ 11.11
Marren v Dawson Bentley & Co Ltd [1961] 2 QB 135, [1961] 2 All ER 270, [1961] 2 WLR 679, 105 Sol Jo 383 .... 9.51
Marsden v Johnson [1997] IRLR 162, EAT 7.106
Marshall v Southampton and South West Hampshire Area Health Authority (Teaching): 152/84 [1986] QB 401, [1986] 2 All ER 584, [1986] 2 WLR 780, [1986] ECR 723, [1986] 1 CMLR 688, [1986] ICR 335, [1986] IRLR 140, 130 Sol Jo 340, [1986] LS Gaz R 1720, ECJ 11.7, 11.9

Marshall v Southampton and South West Hampshire Area Health Authority (No
  2): C-271/91 [1994] QB 126, [1993] 4 All ER 586, [1993] 3 WLR 1054,
  [1993] ECR I-4367, [1993] 3 CMLR 293, [1993] ICR 893, [1993] IRLR 445,
  ECJ; apld sub nom Marshall v Southampton and South-West Hampshire Area
  Health Authority (Teaching) (No 2) [1994] 1 AC 530n, [1994] 1 All ER
  736n, [1994] 2 WLR 392, [1994] ICR 242n, HL **11.16**
Marshall (Cambridge) Ltd v Hamblin [1994] ICR 362, [1994] IRLR 260, EAT **8.31**
Martin v Glynwed Distribution Ltd [1983] ICR 511, sub nom Martin v MBS
  Fastenings (Glynwed) Distribution Ltd [1983] IRLR 198, CA **8.16**
Martin v MBS Fastenings (Glynwed) Distribution Ltd. See Martin v Glynwed
  Distribution Ltd
Martin v McGuiness (2003) Times, 21 April, Ct of Sess **5.50a**
Martin v Yeoman Aggregates Ltd [1983] ICR 314, [1983] IRLR 49, EAT **8.19**
Martins v Marks & Spencer plc. See Marks & Spencer plc v Martins
Maryniak v Thomas Cook Group Ltd (1999) LTL, 1 July 6.83
Masiak v City Restaurants (UK) Ltd [1999] IRLR 780, EAT **8.86**, **9.159**
Matania v National Provincial Bank Ltd and Elevenist Syndicate Ltd [1936] 2 All
  ER 633, 106 LJKB 113, 155 LT 74, 80 Sol Jo 532, CA 3.37
Matthews v Associated Portland Cement Manufacturers (1978) Ltd [2002] UKHL
  22, [2003] 1 AC 32, [2002] 3 All ER 305, [2002] 3 WLR 89, [2002] ICR 798,
  [2002] IRLR 533, 67 BMLR 90, [2002] NLJR 998 .... 6.4
Matthews v Kuwait Bechtel Corpn [1959] 2 QB 57, [1959] 2 All ER 345, [1959]
  2 WLR 702, 103 Sol Jo 393, CA 2.32
Matthews v Ministry of Defence [2003] UKHL 4, [2003] 1 All ER 689, [2003]
  2 WLR 435, [2003] ICR 247, [2003] 13 LS Gaz R 26, [2003] NLJR 261, 147
  Sol Jo LB 235 .... **5.72**, **6.24**
Matthews v Tarmac Bricks and Tiles Ltd (1999) 54 BMLR 139, [1999] CPLR
  463, [1999] 28 LS Gaz R 26, 143 Sol Jo LB 196, CA 9.95
Mattis v Pollock [2002] EWHC 2177, QBD **1.29a**
Maund v Penwith District Council [1984] ICR 143, [1984] IRLR 24, CA **8.42**
Max.mobil Telekommunikation Service GmbH v EC Commission: T-54/99 [2002]
  4 CMLR 1356, CFI 11.24
Meer v London Borough of Tower Hamlets [1988] IRLR 399, CA **7.38**
Mensah v East Hertfordshire NHS Trust [1998] IRLR 531, CA **9.155**
Mersey Docks and Harbour Board v Coggins and Griffith (Liverpool) Ltd [1947]
  AC 1, [1946] 2 All ER 345, 115 LJKB 465, 90 Sol Jo 466, 175 LT 270, 62
  TLR 533, HL **1.17**, **3.19**, 3.20, 3.21
Metallgesellschaft, Hoechst AG and Hoechst Ltd v IRC and A-G. See Hoechst AG
  v IRC and A-G
Metropolitan Police Comr v Harley [2001] ICR 927, [2001] IRLR 263, EAT **7.167**
Metropolitan Police Comr v Hendricks. See Hendricks v Metropolitan Police
  Comr
Metropolitan Police Comr v Lowrey-Nesbitt [1999] ICR 401, EAT **5.75**
Miklaszewicz v Stolt Offshore Ltd [2002] IRLR 344, sub nom Stolt Offshore Ltd v
  Miklasewicz 2002 SLT 103 .... **8.95**
Milner v Humphreys & Glasgow Ltd (2002) LTL, 25 July 6.44
Ministry of Defence v Meredith [1995] IRLR 539, EAT 7.107
Mobbs v Nuclear Electric plc [1996] IRLR 536, EAT 9.130
Mold v Hayton (17 April 2000, unreported), CA 9.71
Molins plc v GD SpA [2000] 1 WLR 1741, [2000] 2 Lloyd's Rep 234, CA 9.21
Montgomery v Johnson Underwood Ltd [2001] EWCA Civ 318, [2001] ICR 819,
  [2001] IRLR 269, [2001] 20 LS Gaz R 40 .... **1.16**
Morgan v Brith Gof Cyf [2001] ICR 978, EAT **9.129**
Morganite Electrical Carbon Ltd v Donne [1988] ICR 18, [1987] IRLR 363, EAT **8.154**
Morris v Breaveglen Ltd (t/a Anzac Construction Co) [1993] ICR 766, [1993]
  IRLR 350, [1993] PIQR P294, 137 Sol Jo LB 13, CA 3.5, **3.34**

Table of Cases

Morris v London Iron and Steel Co Ltd [1988] QB 493, [1987] 2 All ER 496, [1987] 3 WLR 836, [1987] ICR 855, [1987] IRLR 182, 131 Sol Jo 1040, [1987] LS Gaz R 2274, CA **8.17, 9.171**
Morse v Wiltshire County Council [1998] ICR 1023, [1998] IRLR 352, 44 BMLR 58, EAT **7.148**
Morton v William Dixon Ltd 1909 SC 807 .... 2.5
Motorola Ltd v Davidson [2001] IRLR 4, EAT **1.18**
Mountenay v Bernard Matthews plc [1994] 5 Med LR 293 .... **6.78**
Mowat-Brown v University of Surrey [2002] IRLR 235, EAT **7.130**
Mughal v Reuters Ltd [1993] IRLR 571, 16 BMLR 127, 137 Sol Jo LB 275 .... **6.70**
Muir (William) (Bond 9) Ltd v Lamb [1985] IRLR 95, EAT **8.156**, 8.157
Mulcahy v Ministry of Defence [1996] QB 732, [1996] 2 All ER 758, [1996] 2 WLR 474, [1996] NLJR 334, CA **5.69**
Mullan v Birmingham City Council (1999) Times, 29 July **9.96**
Murphy v Epsom College [1983] ICR 715, [1983] IRLR 395, [1983] LS Gaz R 2134, EAT; affd [1985] ICR 80, [1984] IRLR 271, [1985] LS Gaz R 199, CA **8.38, 8.69**
Murphy v Young & Co's Brewery plc and Sun Alliance and London Insurance plc [1997] 1 All ER 518, [1997] 1 WLR 1591, [1997] 1 Lloyd's Rep 236, CA 9.124
Murray v Legal & General Assurance Society [1970] 2 QB 495, [1970] 2 WLR 465, 113 SJ 720, [1969] 3 All ER 794, [1969] 2 Lloyd's Rep 405 .... **12.11**

N

Nagarajan v London Regional Transport [2000] 1 AC 501, [1999] 4 All ER 65, [1999] 3 WLR 425, [1999] ICR 877, [1999] IRLR 572, [1999] 31 LS Gaz R 36, 143 Sol Jo LB 219, HL **7.82**
Nance v British Columbia Electric Rly Co Ltd [1951] AC 601, [1951] 2 All ER 448, 95 Sol Jo 543, [1951] 2 TLR 137, [1951] 3 DLR 705, 2 WWR (NS) 665, PC 2.80
Nanglegan v Royal Free Hampstead NHS Trust [2001] EWCA Civ 127, [2001] 3 All ER 793, [2002] 1 WLR 1043, [2001] CP Rep 65, [2001] 3 CPLR 225 .... **9.23**
National Coal Board v England [1954] AC 403, [1954] 1 All ER 546, [1954] 2 WLR 400, 98 Sol Jo 176, HL **2.23**
Naylor v Volex Group plc (2003) LTL, 14 February **6.67**
Neale v Hereford and Worcester County Council [1986] ICR 471, sub nom Hereford and Worcester County Council v Neale [1986] IRLR 168, CA **8.105**
Neary v Dean of Westminster [1999] IRLR 288 .... **8.57**
Nelhams v Sandells Maintenance Ltd and Gillespie (UK) Ltd (1995) 46 Con LR 40, [1996] PIQR P52, CA **3.5**
Nelson v BBC (No 2) [1980] ICR 110, [1979] IRLR 346, 123 Sol Jo 552, CA **8.144**
Nethermere (St Neots) Ltd v Gardiner [1984] ICR 612, sub nom Nethermere (St Neots) Ltd v Taverna and Gardiner [1984] IRLR 240, CA **1.9**
Newham London Borough v Ward [1985] IRLR 509, CA **8.32**
Nicholls v F Austin (Leyton) Ltd [1946] AC 493, [1946] 2 All ER 92, 115 LJKB 329, 44 LGR 287, 175 LT 5, 90 Sol Jo 628, 62 TLR 320, HL 2.68
Nicholson v Atlas Steel Foundry and Engineering Co Ltd [1957] 1 All ER 776, [1957] 1 WLR 613, 55 LGR 297, 101 Sol Jo 355, HL **2.56**, 6.1
Niemietz v Germany (1992) 16 EHRR 97, E Ct HR **5.48**
Nkengfack v Southwark London Borough (A1/2001/1616), unreported, CA **8.110**
Nolan v Dental Manufacturing Co Ltd [1958] 2 All ER 449, [1958] 1 WLR 936, 102 Sol Jo 619 .... **2.59**
Norris v Syndic Manufacturing Co Ltd [1952] 2 QB 135, [1952] 1 All ER 935, [1952] 1 TLR 858, CA **4.33**

Norris v William Moss & Sons Ltd [1954] 1 All ER 324, [1954] 1 WLR 346, 52
  LGR 140, 98 Sol Jo 110, CA **2.48**
North West Lancashire Health Authority v A, D and G. See R v North West
  Lancashire Health Authority, ex p A
North Yorkshire County Council v Fay. See Fay v North Yorkshire County
  Council
Northern Joint Police Board v Power [1997] IRLR 610, EAT **7.9**
Norton Tool Co Ltd v Tewson [1973] 1 All ER 183, [1973] 1 WLR 45, [1972]
  ICR 501, [1972] IRLR 86, 117 Sol Jo 33, NIRC **8.137**
Notcutt v Universal Equipment Co (London) Ltd [1986] 3 All ER 582, [1986]
  1 WLR 641, [1986] ICR 414, [1986] IRLR 218, 130 Sol Jo 392, [1986] LS
  Gaz R 1314, [1986] NLJ Rep 393, CA **8.24**
Nurse v Morganite Crucible Ltd [1989] AC 692, [1989] 1 All ER 113, [1989]
  2 WLR 82, [1989] ICR 15, [1989] IRLR 88, 153 JP 398, 133 Sol Jo 81,
  [1989] 5 LS Gaz R 41, HL **6.34**

O

Oceanic Crest Shipping Co v Pilbara Harbour Services Pty Ltd (1986) 160 CLR
  626 .... 3.35
Ochwat v Watson Burton (a firm) (10 December 1999, unreported), CA **9.38**
O'Dea v ISC Chemicals Ltd (t/a as Rhône-Poulenc Chemicals) [1996] ICR 222,
  [1995] IRLR 599, CA **8.93**
O'Donoghue v Redcar and Cleveland Borough Council [2001] EWCA Civ 701,
  [2001] IRLR 615 .... **8.147**
O'Driscoll v Dudley Health Authority [1998] Lloyd's Rep Med 210, CA **9.54**
O'Flynn v Airlinks the Airport Coach Co Ltd (EAT/0269/01) **8.109**
Ogden v Airedale Health Authority [1996] 7 Med LR 153 .... **2.17**, **6.64**
Ojutiku v Manpower Services Commission [1982] ICR 661, [1982] IRLR 418, CA **7.51**
O'Kelly v Trusthouse Forte plc [1984] QB 90, [1983] 3 All ER 456, [1983]
  3 WLR 605, [1983] ICR 728, [1983] IRLR 369, 127 Sol Jo 632, [1983] LS
  Gaz R 2367, CA **1.21**
O'Laoire v Jackel International Ltd (No 2) [1991] ICR 718, [1991] IRLR 170, CA **8.132**
1–800 Flowers Inc v Phonenames Ltd [2001] EWCA Civ 721, [2001] IP & T 839,
  [2001] 2 Costs LR 286, [2001] 28 LS Gaz R 42, [2001] All ER (D) 218 (May) **9.99**
O'Neill v Symm & Co Ltd [1998] ICR 481, [1998] IRLR 233, [1999] Disc LR 59,
  EAT **7.132**
O'Reilly v ICI Ltd [1955] 3 All ER 382, [1955] 1 WLR 1155, 99 Sol Jo 778,
  CA **3.21**, 3.25
O'Reilly v National Rail and Tramway Appliances Ltd [1966] 1 All ER 499 .... **1.43**
Oropesa, The. See Lord v Pacific Steam Navigation Co Ltd, The Oropesa
O'Toole v Iarnod Eireann Irish Rail [1999] CLY 1535 .... **6.41**
Owen and Briggs v James [1982] ICR 618, [1982] IRLR 502, CA **7.20**

P

P v S: C-13/94 [1996] All ER (EC) 397, [1996] ECR I-2143, [1996] 2 CMLR 247,
  [1996] ICR 795, [1996] IRLR 347, [1997] 2 FCR 180, [1996] 2 FLR 347,
  [1996] Fam Law 609, ECJ **7.56**
Padbury v Holliday and Greenwood Ltd (1912) 28 TLR 494, CA **3.9**
Paggetti v Cobb [2002] IRLR 861, [2002] All ER (D) 394 (Mar), EAT **8.140**
Palmer v Marks & Spencer plc [2001] EWCA Civ 1528, [2001] All ER (D) 123
  (Oct) 4.66

Palmer v Southend-on-Sea Borough Council [1984] 1 All ER 945, [1984] 1 WLR 1129, [1984] ICR 372, [1984] IRLR 119, 128 Sol Jo 262, CA **9.140**
Pape v Cumbria County Council [1992] 3 All ER 211, [1992] ICR 132, [1991] IRLR 463 .... **6.68**
Paris v Stepney Borough Council [1951] AC 367, [1951] 1 All ER 42, 115 JP 22, 49 LGR 293, [1951] 1 TLR 25, 84 Ll L Rep 525, 94 Sol Jo 837, HL **2.3**
Parker v PFC Flooring Supplies Ltd [2001] PIQR P115; affd [2001] EWCA Civ 1533 .... **4.68**
Parkinson v March Consulting Ltd [1998] ICR 276, [1997] IRLR 308, CA **8.47**
Parvin v Morton Machine Co Ltd [1952] AC 515, [1952] 1 All ER 670, 116 JP 211, 96 Sol Jo 212, [1952] 1 TLR 682, HL **4.20**
Patel v Nagesan [1995] ICR 989, [1995] IRLR 370, CA **8.13**
Pearce v Governing Body of Mayfield Secondary School [2001] EWCA Civ 1347, [2002] ICR 198, [2001] IRLR 669, [2001] 37 LS Gaz R 38, 145 Sol Jo LB 218 .... **7.33**
Pearce v Secretary of State for Defence [1988] AC 755, [1988] 2 All ER 348, [1988] 2 WLR 1027, 132 Sol Jo 699, HL **5.67, 6.22**
Pearson v Cox (1877) 2 CPD 369, [1874–80] All ER Rep 1160, 42 JP 117, 36 LT 495, CA **3.7**
Peet v Mid-Kent Healthcare Trust [2001] EWCA Civ 1703, [2002] 3 All ER 688, [2002] 1 WLR 210, 145 Sol Jo LB 261, [2001] All ER (D) 58 (Nov), sub nom MP (by his father and litigation friend, RJP) v Mid Kent Healthcare NHS Trust 65 BMLR 43 .... **9.12**
Pellegrin v France (Application 28541/95) (1999) 31 EHRR 651, E Ct HR **5.46**
Pendennis Shipyard Ltd v Magrathea (Pendennis) Ltd (in liquidation) [1998] 1 Lloyd's Rep 315, [1997] 35 LS Gaz R 35 .... **9.124**
Penny v Wimbledon UDC and Iles [1899] 2 QB 72, 68 LJQB 704, 63 JP 406, 47 WR 565, 43 Sol Jo 476, 80 LT 615, 15 TLR 348, CA **3.8**
Perera v Civil Service Commission (No 2) [1983] ICR 428, [1983] IRLR 166, CA **7.36**
Petrotrade Inc v Texaco Ltd [2001] 4 All ER 853, [2002] 1 WLR 947, [2000] CLC 1341, CA **9.110**
Philco Radio and Television Corpn of Great Britain Ltd v J Spurling Ltd [1949] 2 KB 33, [1949] 2 All ER 882, 65 TLR 757, 93 Sol Jo 755, CA **2.45**
Phonographic Performance Ltd v AEI Rediffusion Music Ltd [1999] 2 All ER 299, [1999] RPC 599, sub nom AEI Rediffusion Music Ltd v Phonographic Performance Ltd (No 2) [1999] 1 WLR 1507, [1999] EMLR 335, 143 Sol Jo LB 97, CA **9.100**
Pickford v Imperial Chemical Industries plc [1998] 3 All ER 462, [1998] 1 WLR 1189, [1998] ICR 673, [1998] IRLR 435, [1998] 31 LS Gaz R 36, [1998] NLJR 978, 142 Sol Jo LB 198, HL **2.87, 6.72**
Pigney v Pointers Transport Services Ltd [1957] 2 All ER 807, [1957] 1 WLR 1121, 101 Sol Jo 851 .... **2.54**
Pinn v Rew (1916) 32 TLR 451 .... **3.18**
Polentarutti v Autokraft Ltd [1991] ICR 757, [1991] IRLR 457, EAT **8.146**
Polkey v A E Dauton (or Dayton) Services Ltd [1988] AC 344, [1987] 3 All ER 974, [1987] 3 WLR 1153, [1988] ICR 142, [1987] IRLR 503, 131 Sol Jo 1624, [1988] 1 LS Gaz R 36, [1987] NLJ Rep 1109, HL **8.100**
Poplar Housing and Regeneration Community Association Ltd v Donoghue [2001] EWCA Civ 595, [2002] QB 48, [2001] 4 All ER 604, [2001] 3 WLR 183, 33 HLR 823, [2001] 19 LS Gaz R 38, 145 Sol Jo LB 122, sub nom Donoghue v Poplar Housing and Regeneration Community Association Ltd [2001] 3 FCR 74, [2001] 2 FLR 284, [2001] Fam Law 588 .... **5.28, 5.39**
Port of London Authority v Payne [1994] ICR 555, [1994] IRLR 9, CA **8.129**
Porter v Bandridge Ltd [1978] 1 WLR 1145, [1978] ICR 943, [1978] IRLR 271, 13 ITR 340, 122 Sol Jo 592, CA **9.133**

Post Office v Adekeye [1997] ICR 110, 140 Sol Jo LB 262, sub nom Adekeye v
 Post Office (No 2) [1997] IRLR 105, CA **7.96**
Post Office v Foley. See Foley v Post Office
Post Office (Counters) Ltd v Heavey [1990] ICR 1, [1989] IRLR 513, EAT **8.41**
Potts (or Riddell) v Reid [1943] AC 1, [1942] 2 All ER 161, 111 LJPC 65, 167 LT
 301, 58 TLR 335, HL **4.18**
Power v Panasonic UK Ltd [2003] IRLR 151, EAT **7.119**
Pratley v Surrey County Council [2002] EWHC 1608, (2002) LTL, 13 August **6.90**
Pyrah v Doncaster Corpn [1949] 1 All ER 883, 113 JP 248, 47 LGR 577, 65 TLR
 347, 41 BWCC 255, 93 Sol Jo 356, CA **6.26**

Q

Qualcast (Wolverhampton) Ltd v Haynes. See Haynes v Qualcast
 (Wolverhampton) Ltd
Quinlan v B & Q plc [1999] Disc LR 76, EAT **7.128**
Quinn (or Quin) v Burch Bros (Builders) Ltd [1966] 2 QB 370, [1966] 2 All ER
 283, [1966] 2 WLR 1017, 110 Sol Jo 214, CA **2.73**
Quinn v Cameron & Roberton Ltd [1958] AC 9, [1957] 1 All ER 760, [1957]
 2 WLR 692, 55 LGR 177, 101 Sol Jo 317, HL... **2.58**
Quinn v Ministry of Defence [1998] PIQR P387, CA **5.68**, **6.23**
Quinn v Schwarzkopf [2002] IRLR 602, Ct of Sess **7.161**

R

R v A (No 2) [2001] UKHL 25, [2002] 1 AC 45, [2001] 3 All ER 1, [2001] 2
 WLR 1546, 165 JP 609, [2001] 2 Cr App Rep 351, [2001] Crim LR 908, 11
 BHRC 225, [2001] UKHRR 825 .... **5.40**, 5.43
R v Adomako [1995] 1 AC 171, [1994] 3 All ER 79, [1994] 3 WLR 288, 158 JP
 653, [1994] Crim LR 757, [1994] 5 Med LR 277, 19 BMLR 56, [1994] NLJR
 936, HL 10.26, **10.27**, 10.28
R v Associated Octel Co Ltd [1996] 4 All ER 846, [1996] 1 WLR 1543, [1996]
 ICR 972, [1997] IRLR 123, [1997] Crim LR 355, [1996] NLJR 1685,
 HL **3.28**, 10.9, **10.10**
R v Balfour Beatty Civil Engineering Ltd and Geoconsult GES (1999) LTL,
 22 March **10.22**
R v Boal [1992] QB 591, [1992] 3 All ER 177, [1992] 2 WLR 890, [1992] ICR
 495, [1992] IRLR 420, 156 JP 617, [1992] BCLC 872, 95 Cr App Rep 272,
 [1992] 21 LS Gaz R 26, 136 Sol Jo LB 100, CA **10.18**
R (on the application of ProLife Alliance) v BBC [2002] EWCA Civ 297, [2002]
 2 All ER 756, [2002] 3 WLR 1080, [2002] EMLR 902 .... **5.25**
R v Colthrop Board Mills Ltd (2002) LTL, 18 March, CA **10.25**
R v Commission for Racial Equality, ex p Westminster City Council [1985] ICR
 827, [1985] IRLR 426, CA **7.12**
R v DPP, ex p Kebilene [2000] 2 AC 326, [1999] 4 All ER 801, [1999] 3 WLR
 972, [2000] 1 Cr App Rep 275, [2000] Crim LR 486, [1999] 43 LS Gaz R 32,
 HL **5.26**, **5.33**
R v Elliott. See Dyke v Elliott, The Gauntlet
R v F Howe & Son (Engineers) Ltd [1999] 2 All ER 249, [1999] IRLR 434,
 163 JP 359, [1999] 2 Cr App Rep (S) 37, [1999] Crim LR 238, [1998] 46 LS
 Gaz R 34, CA 10.20, **10.21**,
  10.22, 10.24, 10.25

R v Friskies Petcare (UK) Ltd [2000] 2 Cr App Rep (S) 401, CA 10.20, **10.24**, 10.25
R v Gateway Foodmarkets Ltd [1997] 3 All ER 78, [1997] ICR 382, [1997] IRLR 189, [1997] 2 Cr App Rep 40, [1997] Crim LR 512, [1997] 03 LS Gaz R 28, 141 Sol Jo LB 28, CA **10.9**, 10.11
R v Great Western Trains Co Ltd (1999) LTL, 13 August **10.23**
R v Great Western Trains Co Ltd (1999) LTL, 8 November **10.28**
R (on the application of Heather) v Leonard Cheshire Foundation [2002] EWCA Civ 366, [2002] 2 All ER 936, [2002] HLR 893, 69 BMLR 22 .... **5.29**
R v Lord Chancellor's Department, ex p Nangle [1992] 1 All ER 897, [1991] ICR 743, [1991] IRLR 343, DC **5.63**
R (on the application of Rottman) v Metropolitan Police Comr [2002] UKHL 20, [2002] 2 AC 692, [2002] 2 All ER 865, [2002] 2 WLR 1315 .... 5.35
R v National Insurance Comr, ex p Michael [1977] 2 All ER 420, [1977] 1 WLR 109, [1977] ICR 121, 120 Sol Jo 856, CA **2.27**
R v Nelson Group Services (Maintenance) Ltd [1998] 4 All ER 331, [1999] 1 WLR 1526, [1999] ICR 1004, [1999] IRLR 646, CA **10.11**
R v North West Lancashire Health Authority, ex p A [2000] 1 WLR 977, [2000] 2 FCR 525, sub nom North West Lancashire Health Authority v A, D and G 53 BMLR 148, [1999] Lloyd's Rep Med 339, [1999] 2 CCL Rep 419, CA **5.27**
R v P & O European Ferries (Dover) Ltd (1990) 93 Cr App Rep 72, [1991] Crim LR 695 .... 10.28
R v Secretary of State for Employment, ex p Equal Opportunities Commission [1995] 1 AC 1, [1994] 2 WLR 409, [1995] 1 CMLR 391, [1994] IRLR 176, 92 LGR 360, [1994] 18 LS Gaz R 43, [1994] NLJR 358, sub nom Equal Opportunities Commission v Secretary of State for Employment [1994] 1 All ER 910, [1994] ICR 317, HL **11.22**
R v Secretary of State for Social Security, ex p Sutton: C-66/95 [1997] All ER (EC) 497, [1997] ECR I-2163, [1997] 2 CMLR 382, [1997] ICR 961, [1997] IRLR 524, ECJ 11.16
R (on the application of Alconbury Developments Ltd) v Secretary of State for the Environment, Transport and the Regions [2001] UKHL 23, [2001] 2 All ER 929, [2001] 2 WLR 1389, 82 P & CR 513, [2001] 2 PLR 76, 145 Sol Jo LB 140 .... **5.34**
R (on the application of Daly) v Secretary of State for the Home Department [2001] UKHL 26, [2001] 2 AC 532, [2001] 3 All ER 433, [2001] 2 WLR 1622, [2001] 26 LS Gaz R 43, 145 Sol Jo LB 156 .... **5.35**
R v Secretary of State for the Home Department, ex p Simms [2000] 2 AC 115, [1999] 3 All ER 400, [1999] 3 WLR 328, [1999] EMLR 689, [1999] 30 LS Gaz R 28, [1999] NLJR 1073, 143 Sol Jo LB 212, HL **5.38**
R (on the application of BECTU) v Secretary of State for Trade and Industry: C-173/99 [2001] All ER (EC) 647, [2001] 1 WLR 2313, [2001] ECR I-4881, [2001] 3 CMLR 109, [2001] ICR 1152, [2001] IRLR 559, ECJ 11.24
R v Secretary of State for Transport, ex p Factortame Ltd (No 2): C-213/89 [1991] 1 AC 603, [1990] 3 WLR 818, [1990] ECR I-2433, [1990] 3 CMLR 1, [1990] 2 Lloyd's Rep 351, [1990] 41 LS Gaz R 33, sub nom Factortame Ltd v Secretary of State for Transport (No 2) [1991] 1 All ER 70, [1990] NLJR 927, ECJ; apld sub nom R v Secretary of State for Transport, ex p Factortame Ltd (No 2) [1991] 1 AC 603, [1990] 3 WLR 818, [1990] 3 CMLR 375, [1990] 2 Lloyd's Rep 365n, [1991] 1 Lloyd's Rep 10, 134 Sol Jo 1189, [1990] 41 LS Gaz R 36, [1990] NLJR 1457, sub nom Factortame Ltd v Secretary of State for Transport (No 2) [1991] 1 All ER 70, HL **11.15**
R v Secretary of State for Transport, ex p Factortame Ltd (No 3): C-221/89 [1992] QB 680, [1991] 3 All ER 769, [1992] 3 WLR 288, [1991] ECR I-3905, [1991] 3 CMLR 589, [1991] 2 Lloyd's Rep 648, [1991] NLJR 1107, ECJ 11.18

R v Secretary of State for Transport, ex p Factortame Ltd: C-48/93 [1996] QB 404,
[1996] All ER (EC) 301, [1996] 2 WLR 506, [1996] ECR I-1029, [1996]
1 CMLR 889, [1996] IRLR 267, ECJ; apld [1998] 1 All ER 736n, [1998] 1
CMLR 1353, [1997] Eu LR 475; affd [1999] 2 All ER 640n, [1998] 3 CMLR
192, [1998] NPC 68, [1998] Eu LR 456, CA; affd sub nom R v Secretary of
State for Transport, ex p Factortame Ltd (No 5) [2000] 1 AC 524, [1999] 4
All ER 906, [1999] 3 WLR 1062, [1999] 3 CMLR 597, [1999] 43 LS Gaz R
32, HL **11.18**
R v Shayler [2002] UKHL 11, [2003] 1 AC 247, [2002] 2 All ER 477, [2002]
2 WLR 754, [2002] 17 LS Gaz R 34 .... 5.35
R v Stone [1977] QB 354, [1977] 2 All ER 341, [1977] 2 WLR 169, 141 JP 354,
64 Cr App Rep 186, 121 Sol Jo 83, CA 10.29
R v Swan Hunter Shipbuilders Ltd [1982] 1 All ER 264, [1981] ICR 831, [1981]
IRLR 403, [1981] Crim LR 833, sub nom R v Swan Hunter Shipbuilders Ltd
and Telemeter Installations Ltd, HMS Glasgow [1981] 2 Lloyd's Rep 605,
CA **3.27**
RS Components Ltd v Irwin [1974] 1 All ER 41, [1973] ICR 535, [1973] IRLR
239, NIRC **8.70**
Racz v Home Office [1994] 2 AC 45, [1994] 1 All ER 97, [1994] 2 WLR 23,
[1994] NLJR 89, 138 Sol Jo LB 12, HL **1.36**
Rainey v Greater Glasgow Health Board [1987] AC 224, [1987] 1 All ER 65,
[1986] 3 WLR 1017, [1987] 2 CMLR 11, [1987] ICR 129, [1987] IRLR 26,
130 Sol Jo 954, [1987] LS Gaz R 188, [1986] NLJ Rep 1161, 1987 SC 1,
1987 SLT 146, HL **7.53**
Ramsay v Wimpey & Co Ltd 1951 SC 692, 1952 SLT 46 .... **2.24**
Rands v McNeil [1955] 1 QB 253, [1954] 3 All ER 593, [1954] 3 WLR 905, 164
Estates Gazette 522, 98 Sol Jo 851, CA **2.24**, **2.25**
Rank Xerox (UK) Ltd v Stryczek [1995] IRLR 568, EAT **8.133**
Rao v Civil Aviation Authority [1994] ICR 495, [1994] IRLR 240, CA **8.150**
Raval v Department of Health and Social Security [1985] ICR 685, [1985] IRLR
370, [1985] LS Gaz R 1333, EAT **7.46**
Read v Phoenix Preservation Ltd [1985] ICR 164, [1985] IRLR 93, [1985] LS Gaz
R 43, EAT **8.61**
Ready Case Ltd v Jackson [1981] IRLR 312, EAT **8.18**
Ready Mixed Concrete (South East) Ltd v Minister of Pensions and National
Insurance [1968] 2 QB 497, [1968] 1 All ER 433, [1968] 2 WLR 775, 112
Sol Jo 14 .... 1.1, **1.4**
Reed v Stedman [1999] IRLR 299, EAT 7.167
Rees v Bernard Hastie & Co Ltd [1953] 1 QB 328, [1953] 1 All ER 375, [1953]
2 WLR 288, 97 Sol Jo 94, CA **4.35**
Reid v Galbraith's Stores 1970 SLT (Notes) 83 .... **4.44**
Reid v Rush & Tompkins Group plc [1989] 3 All ER 228, [1990] 1 WLR 212,
[1990] ICR 61, [1989] IRLR 265, [1990] RTR 144, [1989] 2 Lloyd's Rep
167, CA **2.28**, **12.15**
Reid Minty (a firm) v Taylor [2001] EWCA Civ 1723, [2002] 2 All ER 150,
[2002] 1 WLR 2800, [2002] 1 CPLR 1, [2002] EMLR 347 .... **9.113**
Rendall v Hill's Dry Docks and Engineering Co [1900] 2 QB 245 .... **9.65**
Rewe-Zentralfinanz GmbH v Landwirtschaftskammer für Saarland: 33/76 [1976]
ECR 1989, [1977] 1 CMLR 533, ECJ **11.14**
Rhys-Harper v Relaxion Group plc [2001] EWCA Civ 634, [2001] 2 CMLR 1115,
[2001] ICR 1176, [2001] IRLR 460 .... **7.98**
Richardson v Pitt-Stanley [1995] QB 123, [1995] 1 All ER 460, [1995] 2 WLR 26,
[1995] ICR 303, [1994] PIQR P496, [1994] JPIL 315, CA **12.9**
Ridehalgh v Horsefield [1994] Ch 205, [1994] 3 All ER 848, [1994] 3 WLR 462,
[1994] 2 FLR 194, [1994] Fam Law 560, [1994] BCC 390, CA **9.125**

Table of Cases

Ridgway and Fairbrother v National Coal Board. See National Coal Board v Ridgway
Ridout v T C Group [1998] IRLR 628, [1999] Disc LR 8, EAT **7.133**
Roberts v Dorman Long & Co Ltd [1953] 2 All ER 428, [1953] 1 WLR 942, 51 LGR 476, 97 Sol Jo 487, CA 2.67
Rollinson v Kimberley Clark Ltd [2000] CP Rep 85, [1999] CPLR 581, (1999) Times, 22 June, CA 9.94
Rookes v Barnard [1964] AC 1129, [1964] 1 All ER 367, [1964] 2 WLR 269, [1964] 1 Lloyd's Rep 28, 108 Sol Jo 93, HL 7.109
Rose v Plenty [1976] 1 All ER 97, [1976] 1 WLR 141, [1975] ICR 430, [1976] IRLR 60, [1976] 1 Lloyd's Rep 263, 119 Sol Jo 592, CA 1.33
Rossiter v Pendragon plc [2002] EWCA Civ 745, [2002] 2 CMLR 1119, [2002] ICR 1063, [2002] IRLR 483, [2002] 24 LS Gaz R 34 .... 8.79
Rushton v Turner Bros Asbestos Co Ltd [1959] 3 All ER 517, [1960] 1 WLR 96, 104 Sol Jo 128 .... 2.62
Rutherford v Towncircle Ltd (t/a Harvest) (in liquidation) and Secretary of Sate for Trade and Industry (No 2) [2002] IRLR 768, EAT **7.44**, **8.10**
Rylands v Fletcher (1868) LR 3 HL 330, [1861–73] All ER Rep 1, 37 LJ Ex 161, 33 JP 70, 14 WR 799, 19 LT 220 .... 2.25

S

S (minors) (care order: implementation of care plan), Re [2002] UKHL 10, [2002] 2 AC 291, [2002] 2 All ER 192, [2002] 2 WLR 720, [2002] 1 FCR 577, [2002] 1 FLR 815, [2002] LGR 251, [2002] 17 LS Gaz R 34 .... 5.43
Sainsbury (J) Ltd v Savage [1981] ICR 1, [1980] IRLR 109, CA 8.34
Sainsbury (J) plc v Hitt [2002] EWCA Civ 1588, [2003] ICR 111, sub nom Sainsbury's Supermarkets Ltd v Hitt [2003] IRLR 23, 146 Sol Jo LB 238 .... **8.108**
Salsbury v Woodland [1970] 1 QB 324, [1969] 3 All ER 863, [1969] 3 WLR 29, 113 Sol Jo 327, CA **3.10**, 3.37
Sandhu v Department of Education and Science and London Borough of Hillingdon [1978] IRLR 208, 13 ITR 314, EAT 8.64
Sandwell Metropolitan Borough Council v Jones. See Jones v Sandwell Metropolitan Borough Council
Sarwar v Alam [2001] EWCA Civ 1401, [2001] 4 All ER 541, [2002] 1 WLR 125, [2002] Lloyd's Rep IR 126, [2001] NLJR 1492 .... 9.122
Saudi Eagle, The. See Alpine Bulk Transport Co Inc v Saudi Eagle Shipping Co Inc, The Saudi Eagle
Savoia v Chiltern Herb Farms Ltd [1981] IRLR 65, EAT; affd [1982] IRLR 166, CA 8.119
Savory v Holland Hannen and Cubitts (Southern) Ltd [1964] 3 All ER 18, [1964] 1 WLR 1158, 108 Sol Jo 479, CA 3.21, **3.25**
Sayers v Merck SmithKline Beecham plc [2001] EWCA Civ 2017, [2002] 1 WLR 2274, 146 Sol Jo LB 31, [2001] All ER (D) 365 .... 9.40
Scally v Southern Health and Social Services Board [1992] 1 AC 294, [1991] 4 All ER 563, [1991] 3 WLR 778, [1991] ICR 771, [1991] IRLR 522, 135 Sol Jo LB 172, HL 2.29
Science Research Council v Nassé [1980] AC 1028, [1979] 3 All ER 673, [1979] 3 WLR 762, [1979] ICR 921, [1979] IRLR 465, 123 Sol Jo 768, HL **9.163**
Sealy v Consignia plc [2002] EWCA Civ 878, [2002] 3 All ER 801, sub nom Consignia plc v Sealy [2002] ICR 1193, [2002] IRLR 624, [2002] 30 LS Gaz R 39, 146 Sol Jo LB 162 .... **9.144**
Secretary of State for Trade and Industry v Backhouse [2001] 09 LS Gaz R 38, 145 Sol Jo LB 53, CA 9.124

Securum Finance Ltd v Ashton [2001] Ch 291, [2000] 3 WLR 1400, CA **9.89**
Seide v Gillette Industries [1980] IRLR 427, EAT **7.16**
Selfridges Ltd v Malik [1998] ICR 268, [1997] IRLR 577, EAT **8.135**
Selkent Bus Co Ltd v Moore [1996] ICR 836, [1996] IRLR 661, EAT **9.146**
Selvanayagam v University of the West Indies [1983] 1 All ER 824, [1983]
  1 WLR 585, 127 Sol Jo 288, PC **2.83**
Sexton v Scaffolding (Great Britain) Ltd [1953] 1 QB 153, [1952] 2 All ER 1085,
  51 LGR 41, 96 Sol Jo 850, [1952] 2 TLR 986, CA **4.21**
Shapland v Palmer [1999] 3 All ER 50, [1999] 1 WLR 2068, [1999] PIQR P249,
  CA **9.79**
Sheffield v Oxford Controls Co Ltd [1979] ICR 396, [1979] IRLR 133, EAT **8.15**
Sheikh v Chief Constable of Greater Manchester Police [1990] 1 QB 637, [1989]
  2 All ER 684, [1989] 2 WLR 1102, [1989] ICR 373, 133 Sol Jo 784, CA **5.75**
Shell Tankers UK Ltd v Dawson [2001] EWCA Civ 101, [2001] ICR 1223, [2001]
  PIQR P265 .... **6.35**
Showboat Entertainment Centre Ltd v Owens [1984] 1 All ER 836, [1984] 1 WLR
  384, [1984] ICR 65, [1984] IRLR 7, 128 Sol Jo 152, [1983] LS Gaz R 3002,
  EAT **7.14**
Sidhu v Aerospace Composite Technology Ltd [2001] ICR 167, [2000] IRLR 602,
  [2000] 25 LS Gaz R 38, CA **7.5**
Simmons v Heath Laundry Co [1910] 1 KB 543, 79 LJKB 395, 3 BWCC 200, 54
  Sol Jo 392, 102 LT 210, 26 TLR 326, CA **1.2**
Simpson v Norwest Holst Southern Ltd [1980] 2 All ER 471, [1980] 1 WLR 968,
  124 Sol Jo 313, CA **9.59**
Simrad Ltd v Scott [1997] IRLR 147, EAT **8.139**
Slater v Leicestershire Health Authority [1989] IRLR 16, CA **8.101**
Smith v Cammell Laird & Co Ltd [1940] AC 242, [1939] 4 All ER 381, 109 LJKB
  134, 104 JP 51, 38 LGR 1, 84 Sol Jo 149, 163 LT 9, 56 TLR 164, HL **4.4**
Smith v Gardner Merchant Ltd [1998] 3 All ER 852, [1999] ICR 134, [1998]
  IRLR 510, [1998] 32 LS Gaz R 29, 142 Sol Jo LB 244, CA **7.31**, **9.150**
Smith v George Wimpey & Co Ltd [1972] 2 QB 329, [1972] 2 All ER 723, [1972]
  2 WLR 1166, 116 Sol Jo 314, CA **4.45**
Smith v Howdens Ltd [1953] NI 131, CA **2.13**
Smith v Leech Brain & Co Ltd [1962] 2 QB 405, [1961] 3 All ER 1159, [1962]
  2 WLR 148, 106 Sol Jo 77 .... **2.69**
Smith v Littlewoods Organisation Ltd [1987] AC 241, [1987] 1 All ER 710,
  [1987] 2 WLR 480, 131 Sol Jo 226, HL **2.85**
Smith v Littlewoods Organisation Ltd. See Maloco v Littlewoods Organisation Ltd
Smith v P & O Bulk Shipping Ltd [1998] 2 Lloyd's Rep 81 .... **6.42**
Smith v Probyn [2000] 12 LS Gaz R 44, 144 Sol Jo LB 134, (2000) Times,
  29 March, [2000] All ER (D) 250 .... **9.24**
Smith v Stages [1989] AC 928, [1989] 1 All ER 833, [1989] 2 WLR 529, [1989]
  ICR 272, [1989] IRLR 177, 133 Sol Jo 324, [1989] 15 LS Gaz R 42, [1989]
  NLJR 291, HL **1.42**
Smith v White Knight Laundry Ltd [2001] EWCA Civ 660, [2001] 3 All ER 862,
  [2002] 1 WLR 616, [2001] 2 BCLC 206 .... **9.52**
Smith and Grady v United Kingdom (1999) 29 EHRR 493, [1999] IRLR 734, E Ct
  HR **5.35**, **5.49**
Sniezek v Bundy (Letchworth) Ltd [2000] PIQR P213, CA **9.63**
Sogbetun v London Borough of Hackney [1998] ICR 1264, [1998] IRLR 676, EAT ... **9.131**
Somerset County Council v Barber. See Barber v Somerset County Council [2002]
  EWCA Civ 76
Sothern v Franks Charlesly & Co [1981] IRLR 278, CA **8.23**
Sougrin v Haringey Health Authority [1992] ICR 650, [1992] IRLR 416, CA **7.71**
Sovereign House Security Services Ltd v Savage [1989] IRLR 115, CA **8.22**

Spargo v North Essex District Health Authority [1997] PIQR P235, [1997] 8 Med
LR 125, 37 BMLR 99, [1997] 15 LS Gaz R 26, 141 Sol Jo LB 90, CA **9.57**
Sparks v HSBC (2002) LTL, 9 December, CA **6.91**
Speciality Care plc v Pachela [1996] ICR 633, [1996] IRLR 248, EAT **8.90**
Spencer v Boots the Chemist Ltd (2002) 146 Sol Jo LB 251, CA **6.82**
Spring v Guardian Assurance plc [1995] 2 AC 296, [1994] 3 All ER 129, [1994]
3 WLR 354, [1994] ICR 596, [1994] IRLR 460, [1994] NLJR 971, 40 LS Gaz
R 36, 138 Sol Jo LB 183, HL **2.89**
Stapley v Gypsum Mines Ltd [1953] AC 663, [1953] 2 All ER 478, [1953] 3 WLR
279, 97 Sol Jo 486, HL **2.21**, **2.47**
Stapp v Shaftesbury Society [1982] IRLR 326, CA **8.33**
Stark v Post Office [2000] ICR 1013, [2000] PIQR P105, 144 Sol Jo LB 150,
CA **2.10**, **4.15**, **4.55**, **11.23**
Stathams (Wasted Costs Order), Re, Banks v Woodall Duckham Ltd [1997] PIQR
P464, CA **9.127**
Staton v National Coal Board [1957] 2 All ER 667, [1957] 1 WLR 893, 101 Sol Jo
592 .... **1.39**
Steenhorst-Neerings v Bestuur van de Bedrijfsvereniging voor Detailhandel,
Ambachten en Huisvrouwen: C-338/91 [1993] ECR I-5475, [1995] 3 CMLR
323, [1994] IRLR 244, ECJ 11.16
Stevens v Brodribb Sawmilling Co (1986) 160 CLR 16 .... **3.37**
Stewart v Cleveland Guest (Engineering) Ltd [1996] ICR 535, [1994] IRLR 440,
EAT **7.4**
Stokes v Guest, Keen and Nettlefold (Bolts and Nuts) Ltd [1968] 1 WLR 1776, 5
KIR 401, 112 Sol Jo 821 .... **2.86**, **6.8**
Stolt Offshore Ltd v Miklasewicz. See Miklaszewicz v Stolt Offshore Ltd
Storer v British Gas plc [2000] 2 All ER 440, [2000] 1 WLR 1237, [2000] ICR
603, [2000] IRLR 495, CA **9.151**
Storey v Ashton (1869) LR 4 QB 476, 38 LJQB 223, 33 JP 676, 10 B & S 337,
17 WR 727 .... **1.38**
Street v British Electricity Authority [1952] 2 QB 399, [1952] 1 All ER 679, 51
LGR 199, 96 Sol Jo 260, [1952] 1 TLR 799, CA **2.4**
Stringman v McArdle [1994] 1 WLR 1653, [1994] PIQR P230, CA **9.8**
Summers (John) & Sons Ltd v Frost [1955] AC 740, [1955] 1 All ER 870, [1955]
2 WLR 825, 53 LGR 329, 99 Sol Jo 257, HL **2.52**, **4.9**, **4.38**
Surrey Police v Marshall [2002] IRLR 843, EAT **7.158**
Sutherland v Hatton. See Hatton v Sutherland [2002] EWCA Civ 76
Sutton and Gates (Luton) Ltd v Boxall [1979] ICR 67, [1978] IRLR 486, EAT **8.49**
Swain v Denso Marston Ltd [2000] ICR 1079, [2000] PIQR P129, CA **4.40**
Swain v Hillman [2001] 1 All ER 91, [2000] PIQR P51, [1999] CPLR 779, CA **9.5**
Swainston v Hetton Victory Club Ltd [1983] 1 All ER 1179, [1983] IRLR 164,
127 Sol Jo 171, sub nom Hetton Victory Club Ltd v Swainston [1983] ICR
341, CA **9.142**
Symphony Group plc v Hodgson [1994] QB 179, [1993] 4 All ER 143, [1993]
3 WLR 830, [1993] 23 LS Gaz R 39, [1993] NLJR 725, 137 Sol Jo LB 134,
CA 9.124

T

Tattari v Private Patients Plan Ltd [1998] ICR 106, [1997] IRLR 586, 38 BMLR
24, CA **7.67**
Taylor v Rover Co Ltd [1966] 2 All ER 181, [1966] 1 WLR 1491 .... **2.72**
Tchoula v ICTS (UK) Ltd [2000] ICR 1191, sub nom ICTS (UK) Ltd v Tchoula
[2000] IRLR 643, EAT **7.104**

Tejani v Superintendent Registrar for the District of Peterborough [1986] IRLR
502, CA **7.10**
Tele-Trading Ltd v Jenkins [1990] IRLR 430, CA.. **8.161**
Thibault v Caisse Nationale d'Assurance Viellesse des Travailleurs Salariés
(CNAVTS). See Caisse Nationale d'Assurance Vieillesse des Travailleurs
Salariés v Thibault
Thomas v Plaistow [1997] 17 LS Gaz R 25, [1997] PIQR P540, CA **9.75**
Thomas v St Johnstone Football Club Ltd (EAT/48/02) **8.103**
Thomas (Richard) & Baldwins Ltd v Cummings [1955] AC 321, [1955] 1 All ER
285, 53 LGR 121, 99 Sol Jo 94, HL **2.9**, **4.37**
Thompson v Brown Construction (Ebbw Vale) Ltd [1981] 2 All ER 296, [1981]
1 WLR 744, 125 Sol Jo 377, HL **9.72**
Thompson v News Group Newspapers Ltd [2001] Fam 430, [2001] 2 WLR 1038,
[2001] 1 FLR 791, [2001] Fam Law 258 .... 5.31
Thompson v Smiths Shiprepairers (North Shields) Ltd [1984] QB 405, [1984] 1
All ER 881, [1984] 2 WLR 522, [1984] ICR 236, [1984] IRLR 93, 128 Sol Jo
225, [1984] LS Gaz R 741 .... **6.7**, 6.8, 6.10, **6.18**
Thurogood v Van Den Berghs and Jurgens Ltd [1951] 2 KB 537, 49 LGR 504, 95
Sol Jo 317, [1951] 1 TLR 557, sub nom Thorogood v Van Den Berghs and
Jurgens Ltd [1951] 1 All ER 682, 115 JP 237, CA **4.32**
Tottenham Green Under Fives' Centre v Marshall [1989] ICR 214, [1989] IRLR
147, [1989] 15 LS Gaz R 39, EAT **7.77**
Totty v Snowden [2001] EWCA Civ 1415, [2001] 4 All ER 577, [2002] 1 WLR
1384, [2001] 38 LS Gaz R 37, [2001] NLJR 1492 .... **9.32**
Tsangacos v Amalgamated Chemicals Ltd [1997] ICR 154, [1997] IRLR 4,
EAT **9.130**
Tuck & Sons v Priester (1887) 19 QBD 629, 56 LJQB 553, 52 JP 213, 36 WR 93,
3 TLR 826, CA **4.27**

U

Uddin v Associated Portland Cement Manufacturers Ltd [1965] 2 QB 15, [1965]
1 All ER 347, [1965] 2 WLR 827, 109 Sol Jo 151; affd [1965] 2 QB 582,
[1965] 2 All ER 213, [1965] 2 WLR 1183, 63 LGR 241, 109 Sol Jo 313,
CA 2.71, **4.43**
Unilever Italia SpA v Central Food SpA: C-443/98 [2000] ECR I-7535, [2001]
1 CMLR 566, ECJ **11.12**

V

Van der Mussele v Belgium (1983) 6 EHRR 163 .... **5.45**
Van Duyn v Home Office: 41/74 [1975] Ch 358, [1975] 3 All ER 190, [1975]
2 WLR 760, [1974] ECR 1337, [1975] 1 CMLR 1, 119 Sol Jo 302, ECJ 7.75, **11.6**
Vandyke v Fender (Sun Insurance Office Ltd, third party) [1970] 2 QB 292, [1970]
2 All ER 335, [1970] 3 WLR 929, 134 JP 487, [1970] RTR 236, [1970]
1 Lloyd's Rep 320, 114 Sol Jo 205, CA **1.41**
Venables v News Group Newspapers Ltd [2001] Fam 430, [2001] 1 All ER 908,
[2001] 2 WLR 1038, [2002] 1 FCR 333, [2001] 1 FLR 791, [2001] Fam Law
258, [2001] EMLR 255, [2001] HRLR 19, [2001] 12 LS Gaz R 41, [2001]
NLJR 57, 145 Sol Jo LB 43 .... 5.31
Vento v Chief Constable of West Yorkshire Police (No 2) [2002[EWCA Civ
1871, [2003] ICR 318, [2003] IRLR 102, 147 Sol Jo LB 181, sub nom Chief
Constable of West Yorkshire Police v Vento (No 2) [2003] 10 LS Gaz
R 28 .... **7.103**
Vicary v British Telecommunications plc [1999] IRLR 680, EAT **7.121**
Vinos v Marks & Spencer plc [2001] 3 All ER 784, [2000] CPLR 570, CA **9.25**

Von Colson and Kamann v Land Nordrhein-Westfalen: 14/83 [1984] ECR 1891, [1986] 2 CMLR 430, ECJ **11.10**

W

W (minors) (care order: adequacy of care plan), Re, [2002] UKHL 10, [2002] 2 AC 291, [2002] 2 All ER 192, [2002] 2 WLR 720, [2002] 1 FCR 577, [2002] 1 FLR 815, [2002] LGR 251, [2002] 17 LS Gaz R 34 .... **5.43**
Wainwright v Home Office [2001] EWCA Civ 2081, [2002] QB 1334, [2002] 3 WLR 405, sub nom Home Office v Wainwright [2002] 09 LS Gaz R 31, 146 Sol Jo LB 19 .... **5.31**
Waite v Government Communications Headquarters [1983] 2 AC 714, [1983] 2 All ER 1013, [1983] 3 WLR 389, [1983] ICR 653, [1983] IRLR 341, 81 LGR 769, 127 Sol Jo 536, [1983] LS Gaz R 2516, HL **8.9**
Wakeman v Quick Corpn [1999] IRLR 424, CA **7.21**
Walker v Lakhdari [1990] ICR 502, [1990] IRLR 469, EAT **9.157**
Walker v Northumberland County Council [1995] 1 All ER 737, [1995] ICR 702, [1995] IRLR 35, [1995] ELR 231, [1994] NLJR 1659 .... **6.83**
Walker v Wabco Automotive UK Ltd (1999) LTL, 11 May, CA **6.61**
Walkin v South Manchester Health Authority [1995] 4 All ER 132, [1995] 1 WLR 1543, 25 BMLR 108, CA **9.64**
Walkley v Precision Forgings Ltd [1979] 2 All ER 548, [1979] 1 WLR 606, 123 Sol Jo 354, HL **9.78**
Wallwork v Fielding [1922] 2 KB 66, [1922] All ER Rep 298, 91 LJKB 568, 86 JP 133, 20 LGR 618, 66 Sol Jo 366, 127 LT 131, 38 TLR 441, CA **5.73**
Ward v T E Hopkins & Son Ltd [1959] 3 All ER 225, 103 Sol Jo 812, sub nom Baker v T E Hopkins & Son Ltd [1959] 1 WLR 966, CA **2.63**
Waters v Metropolitan Police Comr [1997] ICR 1073, [1997] IRLR 589, CA; revsd [2000] 4 All ER 934, [2000] 1 WLR 1607, [2000] ICR 1064, [2000] IRLR 720, 144 Sol Jo 248, [2000] 39 LS Gaz R 42, HL **6.92**, **7.93**
Weathersfield Ltd (t/a Van & Truck Rentals) v Sargent [1999] ICR 425, [1999] IRLR 94, 143 Sol Jo LB 39, CA **7.15**
Webb v EMO Air Cargo (UK) Ltd [1992] 2 All ER 43, [1992] 1 CMLR 793, [1992] ICR 445, [1992] IRLR 116, [1992] 10 LS Gaz R 33, [1992] NLJR 16, 136 Sol Jo LB 32, CA; on appeal [1992] 4 All ER 929, [1993] 1 WLR 49, [1993] 1 CMLR 259, [1993] ICR 175, [1993] IRLR 27, [1993] 9 LS Gaz R 44, 137 Sol Jo LB 48, HL; refd C-32/93: [1994] QB 718, [1994] 4 All ER 115, [1994] 3 WLR 941, [1994] ECR I-3567, [1994] 2 CMLR 729, [1994] ICR 770, [1994] IRLR 482, [1994] NLJR 1278, ECJ; apld sub nom Webb v EMO Air Cargo (UK) Ltd (No 2) [1995] 4 All ER 577, [1995] 1 WLR 1454, [1996] 2 CMLR 990, [1995] ICR 1021, [1995] IRLR 645, [1995] 42 LS Gaz R 24, 140 Sol Jo LB 9, HL **7.26**, **11.21**
Weems v Mathieson (1861) 149 RR 322, 4 Macq 215, HL **2.36**
Weir v Bettison [2003] All ER (D) 273 (Jan), sub nom Weir v Chief Constable of Merseyside Police (2003) Times, 4 February, CA **1.29b**
Wellcome Foundation v Darby [1996] IRLR 538, EAT **9.149**
Welsh Development Agency v Redpath Dorman Long Ltd [1994] 4 All ER 10, [1994] 1 WLR 1409, 38 Con LR 106, [1994] 21 LS Gaz R 42, 67 BLR 1, CA........ **9.77**
West Midlands Passenger Executive v Singh [1988] 2 All ER 873, sub nom West Midlands Passenger Transport Executive v Singh [1988] 1 WLR 730, [1988] ICR 614, [1988] IRLR 186, 132 Sol Jo 933, CA **9.165**
Western Excavating (ECC) Ltd v Sharp [1978] QB 761, [1978] 1 All ER 713, [1978] 2 WLR 344, [1978] ICR 221, [1978] IRLR 27, 121 Sol Jo 814, CA **8.112**
Westwood v Post Office [1974] AC 1, [1973] 3 All ER 184, [1973] 3 WLR 287, 117 Sol Jo 600, HL **4.47**
Wheeler v Copas [1981] 3 All ER 405 .... **3.30**
Whelan (t/a Cheers Off Licence) v Richardson [1998] ICR 318, [1998] IRLR 114, EAT **8.152**, **8.153**

Whiffen v Milham Ford Girls' School [2001] EWCA Civ 385, [2001] ICR 1023,
  [2001] IRLR 468 .... **7.45**
Whitbread plc (t/a Whitbread Medway Inns) v Hall [2001] EWCA Civ 268, [2001]
  ICR 699, [2001] IRLR 275, [2001] 16 LS Gaz R 32, 145 Sol Jo LB 77 .... **8.102**
Whitehouse v Charles A Blatchford & Sons Ltd [2000] ICR 542, [1999] IRLR
  492, CA **8.78**
Wickens v Champion Employment [1984] ICR 365, 134 NLJ 544, EAT **1.22**
Wigley v British Vinegars Ltd [1964] AC 307, [1962] 3 All ER 161, [1962]
  3 WLR 731, 61 LGR 1, 106 Sol Jo 609, HL **2.70**
Wilding v British Telecommunications plc [2002] EWCA Civ 349, [2002] IRLR
  524 .... **8.141**
Wilkey v BBC [2002] EWCA Civ 1561, [2002] 4 All ER 1177, [2003] 1 WLR 1,
  [2002] 47 LS Gaz R 29, 146 Sol Jo LB 242 .... **9.31**
Williams v A & W Hemphill Ltd. See Hemphill (A & W) Ltd v Williams
Williams v Compair Maxam Ltd [1982] ICR 156, [1982] IRLR 83, EAT **8.65**
Williams v Farne Salmon and Trout Ltd 1998 SLT 1329, Ct of Sess **6.67**
Williams v Port of Liverpool Stevedoring Co Ltd [1956] 2 All ER 69, [1956]
  1 WLR 551, [1956] 1 Lloyd's Rep 541, 100 Sol Jo 381 .... **1.32**
Wilsher v Essex Area Health Authority [1988] AC 1074, [1988] 1 All ER 871,
  [1988] 2 WLR 557, 132 Sol Jo 418, [1988] 15 LS Gaz R 37, [1988] NLJR 78,
  HL **6.3**
Wilson v First County Trust Ltd [2001] QB 407, [2001] 2 WLR 302, [2001] 03 LS
  Gaz R 42, CA **5.37**
Wilson v First County Trust Ltd (No 2) [2001] EWCA Civ 633, [2002] QB 74,
  [2001] 3 All ER 229, [2001] 2 All ER (Comm) 134, [2001] 3 WLR 42, 145
  Sol Jo LB 125 .... **5.37**
Wilson v Post Office [2000] IRLR 834, CA **8.39**
Wilsons & Clyde Coal Co Ltd v English [1938] AC 57, [1937] 3 All ER 628, 106
  LJPC 117, 81 Sol Jo 700, 157 LT 406, 53 TLR 944, HL **2.2**, **3.2**, 3.5,
  3.34, 10.29
Wiltshire County Council v National Association of Teachers in Further and
  Higher Education [1980] ICR 455, [1980] IRLR 198, 78 LGR 445, CA **8.26**
Withers v Perry Chain Co Ltd [1961] 3 All ER 676, [1961] 1 WLR 1314, 59 LGR
  496, 105 Sol Jo 648, CA **6.12**, 6.14, 6.67
Wood Group Heavy Industrial Turbines Ltd v Crossan [1998] IRLR 680, EAT **8.130**
Woodrup v London Borough of Southwark [2002] EWCA Civ 1716, [2003] IRLR
  111, 146 Sol Jo LB 263 .... **7.162**
Worsley v Tambrands Ltd (3 December 1999, unreported); on appeal [2000] PIQR
  P95, [2000] Lloyd's Rep Med 280, [1999] 48 LS Gaz R 40, CA **9.96**
Wright v John Bagnall & Sons Ltd [1900] 2 QB 240, 69 LJQB 551, 64 JP 420,
  48 WR 533, 2 WCC 36, 44 Sol Jo 376, 82 LT 346, 16 TLR 327, CA **9.65**

X

X v Bedfordshire County Council [1995] 2 AC 633, [1995] 3 All ER 353, [1995]
  3 WLR 152, [1995] 3 FCR 337, [1995] 2 FLR 276, [1995] Fam Law 537,
  [1995] ELR 404, 26 BMLR 15, 160 LG Rev 103, [1995] NLJR 993, HL **4.14**
X v Germany (1985) 7 EHRR 461 .... **5.54**
X v United Kingdom (Application 8160/78) 22 DR 27 (1981) **5.55**

Y

Yorkshire Dale Steamship Co Ltd v Minister of War Transport, The Coxwold
  [1942] AC 691, [1942] 2 All ER 6, 111 LJKB 512, 86 Sol Jo 359, 167 LT
  349, 58 TLR 263, 73 Ll L Rep 1, HL **2.41**, 2.51

Young v Post Office [2002] EWCA Civ 661, [2002] IRLR 660, [2002] All ER (D) 311 (Apr) 6.83
Young & Woods Ltd v West [1980] IRLR 201, CA **1.7**

Z

Zafar v Glasgow City Council. See Glasgow City Council v Zafar
Zoan v Rouamba [2000] 2 All ER 620, [2000] 1 WLR 1509, [2000] NLJR 99, CA **9.22**
Zurich Insurance Co v Gulson [1998] IRLR 118, EAT **9.156**

Decisions of the European Court of Justice are listed below numerically. These decisions are also included in the preceding alphabetical table.

26/62: Algemene Transport-en Expeditie Onderneming van Gend en Loos NV v Nederlandse Belastingadministratie [1963] ECR 1, [1963] CMLR 105, ECJ **11.2**
9/70: Grad v Finanzamt Traunstein [1970] ECR 825, [1971] CMLR 1, ECJ 11.4
41/74: Van Duyn v Home Office [1975] Ch 358, [1975] 3 All ER 190, [1975] 2 WLR 760, [1974] ECR 1337, [1975] 1 CMLR 1, 119 Sol Jo 302, ECJ 7.75, **11.6**
33/76: Rewe-Zentralfinanz GmbH v Landwirtschaftskammer für Saarland [1976] ECR 1989, [1977] 1 CMLR 533, ECJ **11.14**
50/76: Amsterdam Bulb BV v Produktschap voor Siergewassen [1977] ECR 137, [1977] 2 CMLR 218 ...... **11.4**
106/77: Amministrazione delle Finanze dello Stato v Simmenthal SpA [1978] ECR 629, [1978] 3 CMLR 263, ECJ **11.13**
14/83: Von Colson and Kamann v Land Nordrhein-Westfalen [1984] ECR 1891, [1986] 2 CMLR 430, ECJ **11.10**
79/83: Harz v Deutsche Tradax GmbH [1984] ECR 1921, [1986] 2 CMLR 430, ECJ .. **11.10**
152/84: Marshall v Southampton and South West Hampshire Area Health Authority (Teaching) [1986] QB 401, [1986] 2 All ER 584, [1986] 2 WLR 780, [1986] ECR 723, [1986] 1 CMLR 688, [1986] ICR 335, [1986] IRLR 140, 130 Sol Jo 340, [1986] LS Gaz R 1720, ECJ **11.7**, 11.9
170/84: Bilka-Kaufhaus GmbH v Weber von Hartz [1986] ECR 1607, [1986] 2 CMLR 701, [1987] ICR 110, [1986] IRLR 317, ECJ **7.52**
178/84: EC Commission v Germany [1987] ECR 1227, [1988] 1 CMLR 780, ECJ 11.18
101/87: P Bork International A/S v Foreningen af Arbejdsledere i Danmark [1988] ECR 3057, [1990] 3 CMLR 701, [1989] IRLR 41, ECJ 8.76
C-177/88: Dekker v Stichting Vormingscentrum voor Jong Volwassenen (VJV – Centrum) Plus [1990] ECR I-3941, [1992] ICR 325, [1991] IRLR 27, ECJ **7.25**
C-106/89: Marleasing SA v La Comercial Internacional de Alimentación SA [1990] ECR I-4135, [1992] 1 CMLR 305, [1993] BCC 421, 135 Sol Jo 15, ECJ . **11.11**
C-188/89: Foster v British Gas plc [1991] 1 QB 405, [1990] 3 All ER 897, [1991] 2 WLR 258, [1990] ECR I-3313, [1990] 2 CMLR 833, [1991] ICR 84, [1990] IRLR 353, ECJ; apld [1991] 2 AC 306, [1991] 2 All ER 705, [1991] 2 WLR 1075, [1991] 2 CMLR 217, [1991] ICR 463, [1991] IRLR 268, [1991] 18 LS Gaz R 34, HL **11.9**
C-213/89 R v Secretary of State for Transport, ex p Factortame Ltd (No 2): [1991] 1 AC 603, [1990] 3 WLR 818, [1990] ECR I-2433, [1990] 3 CMLR 1, [1990] 2 Lloyd's Rep 351, [1990] 41 LS Gaz R 33, sub nom Factortame Ltd v Secretary of State for Transport (No 2) [1991] 1 All ER 70, [1990] NLJR 927, ECJ; apld sub nom R v Secretary of State for Transport, ex p Factortame Ltd (No 2) [1991] 1 AC 603, [1990] 3 WLR 818, [1990] 3 CMLR 375, [1990] 2 Lloyd's Rep 365n, [1991] 1 Lloyd's Rep 10, 134 Sol Jo 1189, [1990] 41 LS Gaz R 36, [1990] NLJR 1457, sub nom Factortame Ltd v Secretary of State for Transport (No 2) [1991] 1 All ER 70, HL **11.15**

C-221/89: R v Secretary of State for Transport, ex p Factortame Ltd (No 3) [1992]
QB 680, [1991] 3 All ER 769, [1992] 3 WLR 288, [1991] ECR I-3905,
[1991] 3 CMLR 589, [1991] 2 Lloyd's Rep 648, [1991] NLJR 1107, ECJ 11.18
C-6, 9/90: Francovich and Bonifaci v Italy [1991] ECR I-5357, [1993] 2 CMLR
66, [1995] ICR 722, [1992] IRLR 84, ECJ **11.17**
C-271/91: Marshall v Southampton and South West Hampshire Area Health
Authority (No 2) [1994] QB 126, [1993] 4 All ER 586, [1993] 3 WLR 1054,
[1993] ECR I-4367, [1993] 3 CMLR 293, [1993] ICR 893, [1993] IRLR 445,
ECJ; apld sub nom Marshall v Southampton and South-West Hampshire Area
Health Authority (Teaching) (No 2) [1994] 1 AC 530n, [1994] 1 All ER
736n, [1994] 2 WLR 392, [1994] ICR 242n, HL **11.16**
C-338/91: Steenhorst-Neerings v Bestuur van de Bedrijfsvereniging voor
Detailhandel, Ambachten en Huisvrouwen [1993] ECR I-5475, [1995]
3 CMLR 323, [1994] IRLR 244, ECJ 11.16
C-91/92: Dori v Recreb Srl [1995] All ER (EC) 1, [1994] ECR I-3325, [1995]
1 CMLR 665, ECJ **11.8**
C-32/93: Webb v EMO Air Cargo (UK) Ltd [1994] QB 718, [1994] 4 All ER 115,
[1994] 3 WLR 941, [1994] ECR I-3567, [1994] 2 CMLR 729, [1994] ICR
770, [1994] IRLR 482, [1994] NLJR 1278, ECJ; apld sub nom Webb v EMO
Air Cargo (UK) Ltd (No 2) [1995] 4 All ER 577, [1995] 1 WLR 1454, [1996]
2 CMLR 990, [1995] ICR 1021, [1995] IRLR 645, [1995] 42 LS Gaz R 24,
140 Sol Jo LB 9, HL **7.26**, **11.21**
C-46/93: Brasserie du Pêcheur SA v Germany [1996] QB 404, [1996] All ER (EC)
301, [1996] 2 WLR 506, [1996] ECR I-1029, [1996] 1 CMLR 889, [1996]
IRLR 267, ECJ **11.18**
C-48/93: R v Secretary of State for Transport, ex p Factortame Ltd [1996] QB 404,
[1996] All ER (EC) 301, [1996] 2 WLR 506, [1996] ECR I-1029, [1996] 1
CMLR 889, [1996] IRLR 267, ECJ; apld [1998] 1 All ER 736n, [1998] 1
CMLR 1353, [1997] Eu LR 475; affd [1999] 2 All ER 640n, [1998] 3 CMLR
192, [1998] NPC 68, [1998] Eu LR 456, CA; affd sub nom R v Secretary of
State for Transport, ex p Factortame Ltd (No 5) [2000] 1 AC 524, [1999] 4
All ER 906, [1999] 3 WLR 1062, [1999] 3 CMLR 597, [1999] 43 LS Gaz R
32, HL **11.18**
C-13/94: P v S [1996] All ER (EC) 397, [1996] ECR I-2143, [1996] 2 CMLR 247,
[1996] ICR 795, [1996] IRLR 347, [1997] 2 FCR 180, [1996] 2 FLR 347,
[1996] Fam Law 609, ECJ **7.56**
C-178–190/94: Dillenkofer v Germany [1997] QB 259, [1996] All ER (EC) 917,
[1997] 2 WLR 253, [1996] ECR I-4845, [1996] 3 CMLR 469, [1997] IRLR
60, ECJ 11.18
C-194/94: CIA Security International SA v Signalson SA [1996] All ER (EC) 557,
[1996] ECR I-2201, [1996] 2 CMLR 781, ECJ 11.12
C-66/95: R v Secretary of State for Social Security, ex p Sutton [1997] All ER
(EC) 497, [1997] ECR I-2163, [1997] 2 CMLR 382, [1997] ICR 961, [1997]
IRLR 524, ECJ 11.16
C-136/95: Caisse Nationale d'Assurance Vieillesse des Travailleurs Salariés v
Thibault [1998] ECR I-2011, [1998] All ER (EC) 385, [1998] 2 CMLR 516,
[1998] IRLR 399, sub nom Thibault v Caisse Nationale d'Assurance
Viellesse des Travailleurs Salariés (CNAVTS) [1999] ICR 160, ECJ **7.24**
C-249/96: Grant v South-West Trains Ltd [1998] All ER (EC) 193, [1998] ECR I-
621, [1998] 1 CMLR 993, [1998] ICR 449, [1998] IRLR 206, [1998] 1 FCR
377, [1998] 1 FLR 839, [1998] Fam Law 392, 3 BHRC 578, ECJ **7.32**
C-394/96: Brown v Rentokil Ltd [1998] All ER (EC) 791, [1998] ECR I-4185,
[1998] 2 CMLR 1049, [1998] ICR 790, [1998] IRLR 445, [1999] 1 FCR 49,
[1998] 2 FLR 649, [1998] Fam Law 597, 48 BMLR 126, [1998] 34 LS Gaz R
34, ECJ **7.27**

C-185/97: Coote v Granada Hospitality Ltd [1998] All ER (EC) 865, [1998] ECR
I-5199, [1998] 3 CMLR 958, [1999] ICR 100, [1998] IRLR 656, ECJ; apld
[1999] IRLR 452, EAT **7.97**
C-397, 410/98: Hoechst AG v IRC and A-G [2001] Ch 620, [2001] All ER (EC)
496, [2001] 2 WLR 1497, [2001] ECR I-1727, [2001] STC 452, sub nom
Metallgesellschaft, Hoechst AG and Hoechst Ltd v IRC and AG [2001]
2 CMLR 700, ECJ 11.16
C-443/98: Unilever Italia SpA v Central Food SpA [2000] ECR I-7535, [2001]
1 CMLR 566, ECJ **11.12**
C-173/99: R (on the application of BECTU) v Secretary of State for Trade and
Industry [2001] All ER (EC) 647, [2001] 1 WLR 2313, [2001] ECR I-4881,
[2001] 3 CMLR 109, [2001] ICR 1152, [2001] IRLR 559, ECJ 11.24
C-453/99: Courage Ltd v Crehan [2002] QB 507, [2001] All ER (EC) 886, [2001]
3 WLR 1646, [2001] ECR I-6297, [2002] ICR 457, ECJ 11.18
T-54/99: Max.mobil Telekommunikation Service GmbH v EC Commission [2002]
4 CMLR 1356, CFI 11.24
T-177/01: Jégo-Quéré et Cie SA v European Commision [2002] All ER (EC) 932,
[2003] 2 WLR 783, CFI 11.24

CHAPTER 1

Definition and Scope of Employment

Introduction	[1.1]
Employee	[1.2]
Who is the employer?	[1.17]
Agency workers	[1.20]
Vicarious liability	[1.25]
Authorised work in a wrongful manner	[1.26]
Express prohibition	[1.30]
Intentional acts of an employee	[1.34]
Travel	[1.38]
Practical jokes	[1.43]

INTRODUCTION

[1.1] Employers owe both statutory and common law duties to their employees. They can also be held liable for the actions of their employees. It is therefore necessary to define who is an 'employee'.

An employee is someone who works under a contract of service, as opposed to someone who works under a contract for services (who is an independent contractor). Statutory definitions do not assist in determining who is an employee. Health and Safety at Work etc Act 1974, s 53(1) defines an employee as 'an individual who works under a contract of employment'. Employment Rights Act 1996, s 230 defines an employee as 'individual who has entered into or works under (or where employment has ceased worked under) a contract of employment'.

It is therefore necessary to look at some of the cases summarised below to define who is, and who is not, working under a contract of service and therefore an employee. The courts have adopted a number of tests in order to determine whether a person is working under a 'contract of service'. These tests have included the 'control test', the 'economic reality test', the 'multiple test', and what has been described as the 'fundamental test' (whether or not someone was in business on his own account). The courts have found that there are two irreducible minimum obligations without which there cannot be a contract of employment. These are 'mutuality of obligation' and 'sufficient control'. However the presence of these two obligations does not necessarily mean that there will be a contract of employment. The formulation which seems to have attracted most judicial approval, and to have best withstood the test of time, is that of MacKenna J in *Ready Mixed Concrete (South East) Ltd v Minister of Pensions and National Insurance* [1968] 2 QB 497 (see 1.4 below).

In these circumstances the courts have had to consider: whether or not a person is as an independent contractor; which one out of two persons is the employer; and whether or not a person who is employed from time to time is still under a contract of employment when he is not working.

EMPLOYEE

Simmons v Heath Laundry Co

[1910] 1 KB 543, CA

[1.2] A 19 year old laundry girl had an accident at work and her left hand was crushed. She earned seven shillings a week in the laundry, but also earned three shillings a week from teaching children the piano. An issue arose under the Workmen's Compensation Act as to whether or not the three shillings a week were earned under a 'contract of service'.

HELD: The piano lessons were given not under a 'contract of service' but as a 'contract for services'. It was difficult to lay down any complete or satisfactory definition of the term 'contract of service'. The greater the amount of direct control exercised over the person rendering the services by the person contracting for them the stronger the grounds for holding it to be a contract of service. Similarly the greater the degree of independence from such control the greater the probability that the services rendered are of the nature of professional services and that the contract is not one of service. Whether there is a contract of service is a question of law but the answer to it includes questions of degree and fact.

Chadwick v Pioneer Private Telephone Co Ltd

[1941] 1 All ER 522 (Stable J)

[1.3] An issue arose, for the purposes of the Widows', Orphans' and Old Age Contributory Pensions Act 1936, as to whether or not Mr Chadwick was in 'employment'. He was paid by the defendant travelling expenses and commission on the orders he obtained.

HELD: There was no contract of service. A contract of service implies an obligation to serve and it comprises some degree of control. There was no degree of control in this case.

Ready Mixed Concrete (South East) Ltd v Minister of Pensions and National Insurance

[1968] 2 QB 497, QBD (MacKenna J)

[1.4] HELD: A contract of service exists if three conditions are fulfilled: (i) the servant agrees that, in consideration of a wage or other remuneration, he will provide his own work and skill in the performance of a service for his master; (ii) he agrees, expressly or impliedly, that in the performance of that service he will be subject to the other's control in a sufficient degree to make that other master; (iii) the other provisions of the contract are consistent with its being a contract of service.

Construction Industry Training Board v Labour Force Ltd

[1970] 3 All ER 220, QBD (Lord Parker CJ, Cooke and Fisher JJ)

[1.5] Labour Force supplied labour to building contractors. When a contractor required labour Labour Force supplied workmen at rates payable by the contractor to Labour Force. The workmen were paid by Labour Force on the basis of the information as to working times provided by the contractor. Labour Force had no control over the work carried out by the workmen and the contractor had the right to terminate the workmen's engagement. On each separate assignment the workman was provided with a card which contained a declaration that the workman was engaged on a sub-contract basis and would be responsible for PAYE, income tax returns and national insurance contributions. The Construction Industry Training Board was entitled to impose levies on employers in the Construction Industry to fund training. A levy was imposed by the CITB on Labour Force as an employer. Labour Force appealed to an industrial tribunal which allowed the appeal. On appeal to the Queen's Bench Division:

HELD: Appeal dismissed. Having referred to *Ready Mixed Concrete* (above), it was held that 'no list of tests which had been formulated was exhaustive and the weight to be attached to particular criteria varied from case to case'. The industrial tribunal had applied the right test to the facts.

Ferguson v John Dawson & Partners (Contractors) Ltd

[1976] 3 All ER 817, CA

[1.6] Mr Ferguson was engaged by John Dawson's site agent to work as a general labourer. He was told that there were no cards and he was 'purely working as a lump labour force'. He was paid an hourly rate and no deductions were made for tax. The site agent was responsible for hiring and dismissing workmen. The site agent told the workmen what work to do and John Dawson provided any necessary tools. Mr Ferguson was working on a flat roof removing scaffold boards when he slipped and fell. There was no guardrail and Mr Ferguson brought an action claiming damages for breach of the Construction (Working Places) Regulations 1966. John Dawson claimed that the regulations did not apply because Mr Ferguson was not an employee. Boreham J held that Mr Ferguson was an employee and awarded damages. On appeal by John Dawson:

HELD: Appeal dismissed. Although the label given to any relationship by the parties was a factor it was not necessarily decisive. The court would look to ascertain in reality what terms governed the parties' relationship even though they had not been formally discussed or recorded in writing. The fact that the site agent was responsible for hiring and firing, moving men from site to site, providing tools and controlling the work indicated beyond doubt that the reality of the relationship was employer and employee.

Young & Woods Ltd v West

[1980] IRLR 201, CA

[1.7] Mr West joined the appellants as a skilled sheet metal worker. When he joined he was offered alternative methods of payment. He could become an employee in the ordinary way, or he could be entered as a self-employed person, with no deductions for tax, no holiday pay and no sickness pay. The agreement was entered into with the knowledge of the Inland Revenue. Mr West chose to be self-employed. When his employment was terminated he brought an action for unfair dismissal. The issue arose as to whether or not he was an employee. The industrial tribunal found that he was an employee. The EAT, by a majority, dismissed the appeal. On appeal to the Court of Appeal:

HELD: Appeal dismissed. Mr West was an employee under a contract of service. The label which parties apply to their relationship cannot alter or decide their true relationship, although it is relevant evidence. The legal relationship must be characterised not by appearance but by reality. It was impossible to regard Mr West as a person employed on his own account which was the fundamental test.

Daley v Allied Suppliers Ltd

[1983] IRLR 14, EAT

[1.8] Miss Daley was on a Youth Opportunities Programme (YOP). The YOP was administered by the Manpower Services Commission, and her training was with Allied Suppliers. The issue of whether or not Miss Daley was employed arose in the context of a complaint to an industrial tribunal against Allied Suppliers of racial discrimination. The industrial tribunal found that Miss Daley was not employed by Allied Suppliers. On appeal by Miss Daley:

HELD: Appeal dismissed. The majority found that in the present case there was no legal contract binding Miss Daley and Allied Suppliers, notwithstanding the fact that the parties accepted certain obligations towards each other. The EAT were agreed that even if a contract had existed it was a contract for the training of Miss Daley and not a 'contract of service' or 'a contract personally to execute any work or labour' within the meaning of the Race Relations Act 1976, s 78.

Nethermere (St Neots) Ltd v Taverna and Gardiner

[1984] IRLR 240, CA

[1.9] Mrs Taverna and Mrs Gardiner had been employed to work at Nethermere's knitwear factory. Later they began to work from home. Mrs Taverna used a sewing machine supplied by Nethermere. Mrs Gardiner initially used her own sewing machine but later used one supplied by Nethermere. There were no fixed hours of working. On some weeks Mrs Taverna did no work. Mrs Gardiner normally stitched

200 trouser pockets a day but could do less work if she chose. She would tell the driver when he called to ask for a collection. The only requirement was that there had to be sufficient to make it worthwhile for the driver to call. After the termination of their employment an issue arose as to whether or not Mrs Taverna and Mrs Gardiner were employees. The industrial tribunal held that they were employees and the EAT, by a majority, dismissed an appeal. On appeal to the Court of Appeal:

HELD: Appeal dismissed. There must be an irreducible minimum obligation on each side to create a contract of services. There was evidence to justify the findings of such obligations in this case.

McLeod v Hellyer Bros Ltd
[1987] IRLR 232, CA

[1.10] Five persons worked as trawlermen based in Hull. They had worked exclusively for the respondent over a long period of time. On each engagement on board a fishing vessel they signed a 'crew agreement'. At the conclusion of each engagement, and before the next engagement, they registered as unemployed. At the conclusion of the final sailing there had been signed a 'mutual consent discharge'. In January 1994 the respondent announced that it was taking its vessels out of commission. The trawlermen argued that they had been dismissed on the grounds of redundancy. The issue arose as to whether or not the trawlermen had been employed under a continuing contract of employment under which the respondent had the right not to provide work. The industrial tribunal found that the trawlermen were so employed. The EAT allowed the appeal. The trawlermen appealed.

HELD: Appeal dismissed. There was not present the necessary element of continuing mutual contractual obligations in that the trawlermen were not under a legal obligation to serve when the next crew engagement was offered.

Lee Ting Sang v Chung Chi-Keung
[1990] 2 AC 374, PC

[1.11] Mr Sang was a mason and he worked for a subcontractor at a construction site chiselling concrete as directed by the subcontractor. He used tools supplied by the subcontractor. His work was inspected by the foreman employed by the main contractor. He was paid either a piece rate or a daily rate (depending on the work to be undertaken). He sometimes worked for other contractors but always gave priority to the work of the subcontractor. He was injured at work. He was found by the trial Judge and the local Court of Appeal to be an independent contractor. He appealed to the Privy Council:

HELD: English common law standards were to be applied. On those standards the fundamental test was whether he was in business on his own account. Mr Sang was not in business on his own account and he was an employee of the subcontractor.

Lane v Shire Roofing Co (Oxford) Ltd
[1995] IRLR 493, CA

[1.12] Mr Lane was a builder/roofer/carpenter. He had traded since 1982 as a one-man firm. He was treated by the tax authorities as self-employed. The defendant firm did not want to take on employees. They advertised for men to work on a large roofing job in Marlow and paid Mr Lane £45 per day. Towards the conclusion of that job he was asked by the defendant to look at reroofing a porch in Sonning. He went with the defendant and agreed what was needed by way of ladders and scaffold. The defendants agreed to pay an all-in fee. When carrying out the work at Sonning Mr Lane fell and suffered injury. The trial Judge held that Mr Lane was self-employed. Mr Lane appealed to the Court of Appeal.

HELD: The essential question 'whose business is it?' could only be answered in relation to the Sonning job as the defendant's. As, under modern legislation, there were reasons for both sides to avoid the employee label courts had to be careful in the safety at work field to ensure that the law properly discriminated between employees and independent contractors.

Clark v Oxfordshire Health Authority

[1998] IRLR 125, CA

[1.13] Mrs Clark worked for the Oxfordshire Health Authority's 'nurse bank'. She was offered work in appropriate temporary vacancies. Her conditions of service stated that 'bank nurses' were not regular employees and had no entitlement to guaranteed or continuous work. Mrs Clark's statement of employment included provisions relating to discipline and dismissal, duties of confidentiality and encouraged union membership. National insurance and PAYE was deducted from the sums paid to Mrs Clark. Mrs Clark claimed that she was dismissed in January 1994 and alleged race discrimination. An issue arose as to whether or not Mrs Clark was an employee throughout the whole period from January 1991. The industrial tribunal held that Mrs Clark was not an employee having found as a fact that although she had never refused work there was no obligation on the authority to offer her work. The EAT (by a majority) allowed Mrs Clark's appeal. On appeal by the health authority:

HELD: Appeal allowed. Case remitted to industrial tribunal. There was no global contract of employment because there was a lack of mutuality of obligation during the periods between engagements. There was no obligation on the health authority to provide work and no obligation on the part of Mrs Clark to accept any work offered.

Express and Echo Publications Ltd v Tanton

[1999] IRLR 367, CA

[1.14] Mr Tanton was originally employed as a driver by the company. He was made redundant in 1995 but in August 1995 he was re-engaged as a self-employed driver. He was sent in January 1996 a contract headed 'agreement for services'. Mr Tanton did not sign the agreement. One provision in the contract, of which use had been made by Mr Tanton, permitted Mr Tanton to arrange for another person to provide driving services. Mr Tanton later applied to an employment tribunal for a statement of written particulars. The employment tribunal held that Mr Tanton was an employee. The EAT dismissed an appeal. The company appealed to the Court of Appeal.

HELD: Appeal allowed. The employment tribunal had approached the matter on an incorrect basis by considering what had actually occurred as opposed to finding what mutual obligations governed the parties. A right to substitute another person is inherently inconsistent with a contract of employment. A contract of employment must necessarily contain an obligation on the part of the employee to provide services personally. The provision in the contract entitling Mr Tanton to arrange for another person to provide driving services was not a sham.

Carmichael v National Power plc

[2000] IRLR 43, HL

[1.15] Mrs Carmichael and Mrs Leese accepted work as guides at power stations on 'casual as required basis'. After training, both worked as guides on invitation when they were available and when they chose to work. By 1995 they were working for as many as 25 hours per week. National Insurance and PAYE were deducted from their earnings. Mrs Carmichael and Mrs Leese complained to an employment tribunal that they had not been given a written statement of the particulars of their employment. The issue arose as to whether or not they were employees. The tribunal held that they were not employees. The EAT dismissed the appeal. The Court of Appeal allowed an appeal by Mrs Carmichael and Mrs Leese. On appeal by the company:

HELD: Appeal allowed. Evidence as to what the parties understood their respective obligations to be was admissible on the basis that it was some evidence, in an objective sense, as to what was agreed. The employment tribunal had been entitled to find as a matter of fact that there were some factors which pointed to employment and others which did not and that the case foundered on the absence of mutuality of obligation to provide and perform work. The guidance given in *Ready Mixed Concrete* (see 1.4 above) represented the best test to be applied.

Montgomery v Johnson Underwood Ltd

[2001] EWCA Civ 318, [2001] IRLR 269

[1.16] Mrs Montgomery was seeking work through Johnson Underwood, an employment agency. On 30 May she was contacted by Johnson Underwood and offered a position with a local company. Hours of work were discussed and agreed with Johnson Underwood and a letter confirming the appointment was sent by Johnson Underwood. Mrs Montgomery worked at the local company for two years but was paid by Johnson Underwood on the basis of time sheets approved by the local company. The local company asked Johnson Underwood to terminate Mrs Montgomery's assignment (after a dispute about telephone use). Mrs Montgomery brought proceedings for unfair dismissal against Johnson Underwood and the local company. The employment tribunal found that Mrs Montgomery was an employee of Johnson Underwood. The EAT dismissed an appeal by Johnson Underwood. On appeal by Johnson Underwood to the Court of Appeal:

HELD: Appeal allowed. Although 'mutuality of obligation' and 'control' were irreducible legal requirements for a contract of employment, a contractual obligation concerning work to be carried out in which there was no control could not sensibly be called a contract of employment. In this case the tribunal had found that there was no control. In certain cases (but this was not one of them) an offer of work by an employment agency, even at another's workplace, accepted by an individual for remuneration to be paid by the agency could satisfy the requirement of mutual obligation.

WHO IS THE EMPLOYER?

Mersey Docks and Harbour Board v Coggins & Griffith (Liverpool) Ltd

[1947] AC 1, HL

[1.17] A harbour authority hired a crane to a firm of stevedores to assist in the unloading of a ship, together with a crane operator. The crane operator was paid by the harbour authority and could be dismissed by the harbour authority. The hiring terms and conditions provided that the crane operator should be the servants of the hirers (the stevedores). The crane operator negligently operated the crane, ran over and seriously injured John McFarlane, who was employed by forwarding agents. John McFarlane sued both the stevedores and the harbour authority.

HELD: The existence of the contract between the harbour authority and the stevedores did not affect the question as to whether or not the harbour authority was liable for the losses suffered by John McFarlane. The 'general or permanent employer', in this case the harbour authority, had a heavy burden to show that the responsibility for the negligence of servants engaged and paid by them had been shifted on to a third party. Many factors had a bearing on the question as to who was the employer. This included who was the paymaster, who could dismiss, how long the alternative service lasted, what machinery was to employed and who was entitled to tell the employee the way in which his work was to be done. If the harbour authority's contentions had been upheld it would have led to the result of the crane operator changing employer each time he embarked on the discharge of a fresh ship with all the concomitant disadvantages of uncertainty as to whom should be responsible for his insurance in respect of health, unemployment and accident.

Motorola Ltd v Davidson

[2001] IRLR 4, EAT

[1.18] Mr Davidson responded to an advertisement for a job repairing mobile telephones with Motorola at Bathgate. The interview and recruitment process was handled by Melville Craig Group Limited which had an operating agreement with Motorola for the supply of temporary workers. Mr Davidson was recruited by Melville Craig which then assigned Mr Davidson to work at Bathgate for Motorola. His contract of employment provided that Mr Davidson was bound to comply with all reasonable requests made by Motorola. In December 1998, following a disciplinary hearing, Mr Davidson's assignment to Motorola was terminated by Motorola's regional service manager. Mr Davidson brought proceedings for unfair dismissal against both Motorola and Melville Craig. The employment tribunal held that Mr Davidson was an employee of Motorola only.

HELD: Appeal dismissed. Motorola determined 'the thing to be done, the way in which it shall be done, the means to be employed in doing it, the time when and the place where it shall be done'. The tribunal had not erred in holding that Motorola had a sufficient degree of control over the first respondent so that he could properly be regarded as their employee.

Interlink Express Parcels Ltd v Night Trunkers Ltd

[2001] EWCA Civ 360, [2001] RTR

[1.19] Express Parcels Ltd traded as Interlink. Interlink delivered parcels and packages using vehicles owned or leased by Interlink. Drivers were either employed directly by Interlink or supplied by Night Trunkers. There was an agreement between Interlink and Night Trunkers. An issue arose as to whether or not the agreement was void for illegality on the basis that Night Trunkers did not have a HGV operator's licence. Night Trunkers contended that the drivers supplied by them were to be deemed temporary employees of Interlink and that there was therefore no need for them to have an operator's licence. Ferris J found that the drivers supplied by Night Trunkers remained their employees and that the agreement was void. Night Trunkers appealed.

HELD: Appeal allowed. Interlink had the right to control the way in which the Night Trunkers drivers operated, and that those drivers were to be deemed servants of Interlink.

AGENCY WORKERS

[1.20] Whether or not an agency worker is held to be an employee is a question of fact and degree.

O'Kelly v Trusthouse Forte plc

[1983] ICR 728, CA

[1.21] The banqueting department of a hotel kept a list of casual catering staff who became known as 'regulars'. Some of the 'regulars' did not have other regular employment. Three of them complained of unfair dismissal. The tribunal decided on a preliminary point that they were not employees but independent contractors.

HELD, on appeal: The answer to the question as to whether they were employees involved questions of fact and degree and the appeal tribunal ought not to interfere with the tribunal's decision except in 'unusual' circumstances.

Wickens v Champion Employment

[1984] ICR 365, EAT

[1.22] The claimant was employed as a controller of temporary staff in an employment agency. During the claimant's case for unfair dismissal a preliminary point was taken as to whether the temporary workers were employed by the employers. The employment tribunal found that they were not and declined jurisdiction.

HELD, on appeal: Dismissing the appeal, it was held that the temporary workers' contracts did not create a relationship that had the elements of continuity and care associated with a contract of employment.

McMeechan v Secretary of State for Employment

[1997] ICR 549, EAT

[1.23] The claimant worked on a series of temporary contracts for an employment agency. When the company went into liquidation the claimant claimed payments owing to him against the Secretary of State, under the Employment Protection (Consolidation) Act 1978, s 122. A tribunal dismissed the claim holding that he was not an employee of the agency.

HELD, on appeal: There is no general proposition of law that a worker whose services are supplied by an employment business to a third party client on a temporary basis does not have a contract of employment with either the employment business or with the business's client.

Dacas v Brook Street Bureau and Wandsworth Borough Council

(11 February 2003, unreported), EAT

[1.24] An agency worker brought a claim for unfair dismissal. She had been engaged by Brook Street as an agency worker and placed with Wandsworth Borough Council as a cleaner. It was said that she had been abusive to a visitor at Wandsworth's premises and she was dismissed by Brook Street. She brought proceedings against both Brook Street and Wandsworth on the basis that she was employed by one of them. The tribunal found that, although Brook Street exercised control, and there was mutuality of obligations, the agency worker was not employed by either Brook Street or Wandsworth.

HELD, on appeal: The agency worker was Brook Street's employee. It was obvious that the agency worker was not carrying on a business of her own. There was also control and mutuality of obligations.

> Note—that the Temporary Workers Directive 91/383/EC provides that agency workers should benefit from the same level of health and safety protection as other workers. This means that there may be issues of European law and remedies to be considered if an agency worker, who is not an employee, is said to be in a worse position than an employee (see Chapter 11).

VICARIOUS LIABILITY

[1.25] An employer is liable for the torts of its employees acting in the course of their employment. Having established above who is an employee, it is therefore necessary to examine what will be considered to be in the 'course of employment'. It is in these circumstances that the courts have had to decide: whether or not an employer is liable for an employee carrying out authorised work in a wrongful manner; whether or not an express prohibition will protect the employer; whether or not an employer is liable for the intentional acts of an employee; whether or not an employer is liable for injuries occurring when travelling to and from work; and whether or not an employer is liable for practical jokes that go wrong. Please also see 7.92–7.97.

Authorised work in a wrongful manner

Lloyd v Grace, Smith & Co

[1912] AC 716, HL

[1.26] A managing clerk employed by solicitors acting for a widow tricked her into signing property over to him. He then sold the property and disappeared. An issue arose as to whether or not the solicitors were liable for the fraud of the managing clerk.

HELD, on appeal: The solicitors were liable. The fraud was committed by their representative acting in the course of his employment.

Century Insurance Co v Northern Ireland Road Transport Board

[1942] AC 509, HL

[1.27] A petrol delivery driver, waiting while the delivery was being carried out, lit a match to light his cigarette. He threw the match to the floor and caused an explosion. An issue arose as to whether or not the driver was employed at that time by the petroleum company or the garage. It was held that he was employed, notwithstanding the terms and conditions, by the petroleum company. The other issue concerned whether or not the delivery driver was acting in the course of his employment. It was held that his smoking was in the course of employment.

HELD, on appeal: The delivery driver was acting in the course of his employment. The delivery driver was employed to watch over the delivery. His decision to smoke when doing so was 'plainly negligence in the discharge of his duties'.

Bell v Blackwood Morton & Sons Ltd

1960 SC 11, Ct of Sess

[1.27a] The claimant suffered injury falling downstairs when jostled by a fellow employee. At the end of the day's work, the employer laid on special buses for the transportation of employees back home. There were a limited number of seats on the buses and therefore the practice had developed for employees to rush to get a seat. The employer had placed signs on the stairs stating: 'Safety first; don't rush downstairs' and had issued regulations which provided for employees who rushed to be disciplined. The defendant resisted the claimant's claim on the basis that the claimant and others on the stairs were not acting within the scope of their employment at the time of the accident either because the time for work had ended or because in rushing and jostling the other employees were doing something which they had been expressly instructed not to do.

HELD: The defendant was vicariously liable for the negligence of its employee in jostling the claimant. Coming down the staircase was a necessary requirement of their employment and the defendant purported to regulate the manner in which it was done. The other employees were not doing something which was prohibited but rather were doing a permitted action in a prohibited way.

Kooragang Investments Pty Ltd v Richardson & Wrench Ltd

[1982] AC 462, PC

[1.28] A valuer, employed by the defendant, was instructed not to carry out valuations for a client who had not paid fees. The valuer became a director of the client and carried out valuations without the defendant's knowledge or authority but using the defendant's notepaper. The defendant was not paid for the valuations. The claimants were provided with the valuations and advanced monies. The valuations were negligently carried out and the claimants sued the defendant.

HELD, on appeal: The employers were not liable. The authority to do an act could not be inferred merely from the fact that the act itself was of a class which the employer had authorised his servant to do. The valuer was acting outside the scope of his employment.

Fennelly v Connex South Eastern Ltd

[2001] IRLR 390, CA

[1.29] A passenger was stopped at a ticket barrier. He was then offensive to a ticket inspector. He finally showed his ticket. There was an altercation and the inspector put the passenger in a headlock saying 'I've had enough of this'. Proceedings were brought against the inspector's employer. The trial judge dismissed the action on the basis that the inspector's duties had finished at the time of the assault. The passenger appealed.

HELD: Appeal allowed. It was necessary to look at what the employee was being asked to do in general terms, not concentrating on each separate step. It was artificial to say that the inspector's actions were divorced from his duties.

Mattis v Pollock

[2003] EWCA Civ 887

[1.29a] A doorman working for a nightclub went home to collect a knife and returned and stabbed Mr Mattis, a nightclub customer. Mr Mattis issued proceedings against Mr Pollock, the owner of the nightclub. There were issues as to whether or not the doorman was an employee and if so, whether or not the assault took place in the course of employment.

The trial judge held that the doorman was an employee. However, although the doorman had become aggrieved with Mr Mattis when acting in the course of his employment, his decision to return home and arm himself was not a decision made in the course of his employment. There was not a sufficiently close connection between the employment and the attack to make it fair and just for the owner to be held liable. Mr Mattis appealed.

HELD: Appeal allowed. Where an employee was expected to use violence the likelihood of establishing that an act of violence fell within the broad scope of his employment was greater than would otherwise be the case.

Weir v Bettison

[2003] All ER (D) 273, CA

[1.29b] A police constable had borrowed a police van in order to help his girlfriend move flat. He had not sought nor obtained permission to use it. Mr Weir started pestering the couple and rummaging through the girlfriend's belongings outside the flat. He refused to leave and the police constable manhandled him down the stairs and put him in the police van. Mr Weir was assaulted in the van. He brought proceedings against the Chief Constable (whose liability, by virtue of the Police Act 1996, mirrors that of an employer).

Held, on appeal: the police constable had been acting in the course of his duties as a police constable at the material time. Indeed he had told Mr Weir that he was a police officer and had locked him in the van.

Express prohibition

Alfred v National Coal Board

[1952] 1 All ER 754, HL

[1.30] A miner was injured when another miner, who was acting in breach of the Explosives In Coal Mines Order, wired up explosives when unauthorised and connected the wrong wires, causing an explosion when the claimant was still in the open.

HELD, on appeal: The miner was not acting within the scope of his employment in operating the firing apparatus and the employer was not responsible for his breach of the relevant orders.

LCC v Cattermoles (Garages) Ltd

[1953] 2 All ER 582, CA

[1.31] A garage hand, who had no driving licence, was expressly forbidden to drive vehicles. An attendant asked the garage hand to move a motor van. The garage hand moved the motor van by driving it, and because there was insufficient space drove on to the highway and collided with another motor car. In an action for damages brought by the owners of the motor car against the employer the trial judge held that the driving was unauthorised and that there was no liability on the employer.

HELD, on appeal: As the garage hand's duty was to move cars by hand, it was impossible to define the scope of his employment to exclude the driving of cars. Driving was a wrongful and unauthorised way of performing an act that he was employed to perform.

Williams v Port of Liverpool Stevedoring Co Ltd

[1956] 2 All ER 69

[1.32] The claimant and fellow employees were working as a gang stacking bags. They were told how to do it safely but ignored the order. They were given a subsequent direction to do it safely but again ignored the order. The bags collapsed and the claimant was injured. He sued his employers.

HELD: The employers were liable for each of the wrongful actions of the members of the gang, even though they had been using a method which was contrary to the orders given. There was a finding of contributory negligence of 50% to reflect the claimant's own fault and participation in the unsafe method.

Rose v Plenty
[1976] 1 All ER 97, CA

[1.33] A milkman was employed on a milk round. The employers exhibited notices prohibiting the milkmen from using children to help. The milkman invited a 13 year old boy to help. The boy suffered injury when riding on the milk float and sued the employers of the milkman. The boy's claim was dismissed.

HELD, on appeal: Appeal allowed. Although the milkman's actions had been expressly prohibited, the milkman had been carrying out actions for the purpose of the employer's business. The employers were therefore liable.

Intentional acts of an employee

Heasmans v Clarity Cleaning Co Ltd
[1987] IRLR 286, CA

[1.34] A company was employed to clean phones. An employee made unauthorised overseas phone calls. The employer was sued for the costs of the phone calls. The trial judge held that the employer was liable for wrongful acts of their employee. The employer appealed.

HELD: Appeal allowed. A master cannot be held liable for a tortious or criminal act committed by a servant which is wholly outside the scope of his employment merely because the opportunity to commit the act was created by his employment.

General Engineering Services Ltd v Kingston and St Andrew Corpn
[1988] 3 All ER 867, PC

[1.35] The local fire brigade was involved in an industrial dispute and operating a 'go slow'. They took 17 minutes (instead of the usual $3\frac{1}{2}$ minutes) to cover $1\frac{1}{2}$ miles to the fire. The property was destroyed by reason of the delay. An action was brought against the corporation, the employers of the firemen.

HELD, on appeal: The actions of the firemen could not be categorised as a wrongful and unauthorised mode of doing an act authorised by their employers. It was so unconnected with what they were supposed to do that it was outside the course of their employment. There was no vicarious liability.

Racz v Home Office
[1994] 2 AC 45, HL

[1.36] The claimant was a prisoner. He claimed to have suffered ill-treatment at the hands of prison officers. The claim, which alleged that the Home Office was vicariously liable for the acts of the prison officers, was struck out. The Court of Appeal dismissed an appeal. The claimant appealed to the House of Lords.

HELD: Appeal allowed. The question whether or not the actions of the prison officers were so unconnected with their authorised duties as to be independent of and outside them was a question of fact and degree and therefore the claim should not have been struck out.

Lister v Hesley Hall Ltd

[2001] UKHL 22, [2001] 2 All ER 769

[1.37] A warden of a boarding house sexually abused boys in his care. An action was brought against his employers.

HELD, on appeal: The employers entrusted the care of the children to the warden. The warden's actions were so closely connected with his employment that it was fair and just to hold the employers vicariously liable. Matters of degree would arise but the present case fell clearly on the side of vicarious liability.

Travel

Storey v Ashton

(1869) 4 QB 476

[1.38] A wine merchant sent his carman and clerk to deliver some wine. On the return journey the clerk persuaded the carman to drive in a different direction on his own business. The claimant was run over. The claimant sued the wine merchant.

HELD: The wine merchant was not liable. The carman was not acting in the course of his employment.

Staton v National Coal Board

[1957] 2 All ER 667, QBD

[1.39] An employee had finished work and was cycling along a road to go to his employer's offices to collect his wages. The employee took a short cut through a bus park which was on the employer's premises. He hit a passenger and killed him. An action was brought against the employer:

HELD: The employer was liable. The employee was on the employer's premises and was acting in the course of his employment in picking up his wages. It might have been different if he had been on a public road.

Hilton v Thomas Burton (Rhodes) Ltd

[1961] 1 All ER 74

[1.40] The deceased and other employees were driving in a van to go to a café, some seven miles off site, to get some tea. The employer permitted the use of the van for any reasonable purpose of the employees. The employees turned back, realising that there would not be time to have tea. On the way back to the site they had an accident caused by the negligence of the employee who was driving. In an action against the employer:

HELD: The test was whether the driver was doing something at the time that he was employed to do. He was not and accordingly the employer was not liable.

Vandyke v Fender

[1970] 2 QB 292, CA

[1.41] Two employees agreed to work for an employer some 30 miles away. The employer provided a car and paid for petrol. One employee drove one way and the other employee the other. Other employees were picked up. The car was not in fact owned by the employers. There was an accident and the injured employees sued the driver. An issue arose (for insurance purposes) about whether or not the employee had been driving 'in the course of his employment'.

HELD: The employers were liable for the negligence of their employee, whether or not he was 'in the course of his employment' because he was driving for their purposes. However, as a matter of analysis, the employee was not driving 'in the course of his employment' as it had been interpreted for the purposes of the Workmen's Compensation Acts.

Smith v Stages

[1989] AC 928, HL

[1.42] Two employees were instructed to work in Pembroke. They were paid for travelling time and a sum equivalent to the return rail fare. They drove to Pembroke. Having completed their work they drove home. There was a car accident and both employees suffered injuries. An action was brought against the employer.

HELD, on appeal: An employee who was paid wages by his employer to travel from his ordinary residence to a place other than his usual workplace to carry out a job and who was also paid wages for the return home was acting in the course of his employment when travelling. The fact that the employees had discretion as to the mode and time of travel did not take the journey out of the course of employment.

Practical jokes

O'Reilly v National Rail and Tramway Appliances Ltd

[1966] 1 All ER 499

[1.43] Employees of a foundry, who were melting scrap metal, discovered a live shell which had been delivered in a load of scrap. They played around with it and left it. The claimant, another employee, returned from lunch and was persuaded by another employee, Thompson, to hit the shell with a hammer. He did and it exploded. He brought an action against the employers.

HELD: Thompson had been negligent. However it was an isolated act of wilful misbehaviour for which the employers could not be held liable.

Harrison v Michelin Tyres Co Ltd

[1985] 1 All ER 918

[1.44] The claimant was standing on a duckboard. A fellow employee was pushing along a truck when, for a joke, he pushed his truck against the duckboard. The duckboard tipped up and the claimant fell. He brought an action against the employers.

HELD: The test was whether a reasonable man would say either that the employee's act was part and parcel of his employment (in the sense of being incidental to it) even though unauthorised and prohibited, or that it was so divergent from his employment as to be plainly alien to it. In this case a reasonable man would say that, even though the act would never have been countenanced by the employer, it was none the less part and parcel of his employment. The employer was liable.

Aldred v Nacanco

[1987] IRLR 292

[1.45] The claimant was in the washroom. Another employee came into the washroom, and pushed a loose washbasin to startle her. The claimant turned round quickly and strained her back. The claimant claimed that the washbasin was unsafe and that the employers were liable for the actions of the fellow employee. The claim was dismissed. The claimant appealed.

HELD; Appeal dismissed. The loose washbasin had not caused the injuries. It was the actions of the fellow employee. The employers were not liable for the actions of the fellow employee. The correct principle of law was that 'if a servant does negligently that which he was authorised to do carefully, or if he does fraudulently that which he was authorised to do honestly, or if he does mistakenly that which he was authorised to do carefully, his master will answer for that negligence, fraud or mistake. On the other hand, if the unauthorised and wrongful act of the servant is not so connected with the authorised act as to be a mode of doing it, but is an independent act, the master is not responsible.'

Compare paragraph 3.3 below, *Hudson v Ridge Manufacturing* and see paragraph 10.10 below, *R v Associated Octel.*

CHAPTER 2

Common Law Liability

Employer's duty of care	[2.1]
Limits to the duty	[2.18]
Causation, remoteness and contributory negligence	[2.38]
Other common law liabilities	[2.88]
Provision of references	[2.88]

EMPLOYER'S DUTY OF CARE

[2.1] An employer owes a duty to his employees to provide a safe system of work; a safe place of work; and safe fellow employees.

The cases set out below provide practical illustrations of the scope and extent of the common law duties owed. Cases on psychiatric injury (stress and bullying claims) are set out in Chapter 6:

Wilsons & Clyde Coal Co Ltd v English

[1938] AC 57, HL

[2.2] The respondent, an employee of the appellant suffered injury in an accident in the course of his employment at the appellant's mine. The Coal Mines Act 1911, s 2(4) provided that, 'The owner or agent of [a] mine required to be under the control of a manager shall not take any part in the technical management of the mine unless he is qualified to be a manager.' The appellant had duly delegated technical management of the mine to an agent who was a qualified manager. The appellant contended that it could not be liable for any failure to provide a safe system of work in circumstances where statute required it to delegate that responsibility.

HELD, affirming the decision of the Court of Session: A master cannot absolve himself of his duty to take due care in the provision of a reasonably safe system of working by appointment of a competent person to perform the duty. There is no reason in principle why a compulsory delegation should displace the vicarious responsibility of the employer if a de facto delegation would not have had that effect. An agent charged with the task of providing a safe system of work is

Paris v Stepney Borough Council

[1951] AC 367, HL

[2.3] The appellant was employed by the respondent as a garage hand. He was practically blind in one eye due to a previous injury sustained during the war. The respondent became aware of this condition and the appellant was working out two weeks' notice when the accident occurred. Whilst using a steel hammer to knock out a rusty bolt, and, in accordance with the normal practice, not wearing goggles, a fragment of metal became detached and flew into the appellant's good eye. There was nothing to suggest that the pre-accident injuries had in any way increased the risk of an accident. The Court of Appeal overturned the trial judge's decision, finding that negligence was not established on the facts.

HELD, allowing the appeal (Lord Simonds and Lord Morton of Henryton dissenting): Although there was no duty in the circumstances on the employer to provide all employees with goggles, due to their knowledge of the appellant's pre-existing injuries, the respondent ought to have provided him with goggles. The appellant was exposed to a risk of much greater injury in an accident of the nature which did in fact occur than most employees. The increased risk of serious injury was a factor relevant to the employer's consideration of the appropriate steps to be taken. There are two factors in determining the magnitude of a risk – the seriousness of the injury risked and the likelihood of the injury being in fact caused.

Street v British Electricity Authority

[1952] 2 QB 399, CA

[2.4] The claimant was a construction worker. He was working on the construction of a power station. Part of the power station was in operation and part was being constructed. As he was walking into the area where the power station was being constructed he had to pass obstructions on the gallery. He walked close to the edge and fell. His claim against his employers for common law negligence was dismissed and his claim under the Factories Act failed because the place where the accident occurred was not a factory.

HELD, on appeal: Appeal dismissed. On the facts negligence had not been proved because it was not possible to determine how the accident had happened. Further the area in which the appellant fell was not yet completed and was not therefore a factory within the meaning of the Act.

Cavanagh v Ulster Weaving Co Ltd

[1960] AC 145, HL

[2.5] The claimant was working as a labourer employed by the defendants when he suffered an accident. He was descending a roof ladder laid flat along the slated aspect of a sloping roof. As he turned to pick up a heavy bucket of cement which he was to carry to the site of works, he slipped and fell, so that his arm went through a glass section of the roof. At trial the defendant relied upon expert evidence to the effect that the system which the defendant had in place was perfectly in accord with good practice, an assertion which was never effectively challenged by the claimant. The jury found that the accident had been caused partly by the defendant's negligence. The Court of Appeal overturned that decision on the basis of the expert evidence of the defendant as to the system of work.

HELD, reinstating the decision of the jury: The concepts of system and good practice had never been properly identified at trial. It was unclear whether the jury had relied on an unsafe system in reaching their decision as there were also issues as to the provision of handrails and the rubber boots which the defendant had provided for the claimant at the time of his accident. The mere fact that the defendant's system was in accordance with good practice, although evidence of heavy weight, was not conclusive on the question of negligence. Each case must turn on its own facts as to the precise circumstances. There are many cases in which although the circumstances are not precisely similar, evidence of practice should be given some, though less, weight. Observations of Lord Normand in *Paris v Stepney Borough Council* as to the scope of Lord Dunedin's dictum in *Morton v William Dixon Ltd* 1909 SC 807, 809 applied: 'Folly' should not be read as meaning 'ridiculous' but was a formulation equivalent to a duty to take reasonable care in all the circumstances.

Carroll v Andrew Barclay & Sons, Ltd

[1948] AC 477, HL

[2.6] The claimant claimed damages following an accident in the course of his employment with the defendant, pursuant to Factories Act 1937 (FA 1937), s 13(1) which provided that, 'every part of the transmission machinery shall be securely fenced unless it is in such a position or of such construction as to be as safe to every person employed or working on the premises as it would be if securely fenced'. The claimant's accident occurred when he was struck by a part of the transmission machinery which had suddenly broken and lashed out. The claimant maintained that on a proper construction the section was absolute and that 'securely fenced' meant that the relevant persons should be protected not only from danger of contact with the transmission machinery while it was working in situ, but also against all parts of it which might fly off if it broke or came to pieces. The defendant contended that the section intended to protect employees from the working of a moving machine and not from its malfunctioning.

HELD: The section only required the machine to be securely fenced against danger of contact with the moving parts whilst the machine was properly working in situ. Obiter, their Lordships did not however exclude the possibility that in other circumstances where a machine was prone to break or to throw out moving parts, the fencing should take that into account.

Latimer v AEC Ltd

[1953] AC 643, HL

[2.7] Action in negligence and for breach of FA 1937, s 25, to ensure that floors were 'of sound construction and properly maintained'. The appellant had fallen and injured himself on a slippery floor at his employer's premises. The slipperiness was caused by flooding after an unusually heavy rainstorm. The flood waters had mixed with a cooling agent liquid which was usually carried in an open channel on the factory floor. Once the flood waters had subsided, the oily cooling agent coated the factory floor in a film which was slippery. The employers had put down sawdust, but did not have enough to protect the entire floor. The accident occurred on an untreated section of floor.

HELD, dismissing the appellant's appeal: The duty imposed by section 25 to 'maintain' the floor in 'an efficient state' is aimed primarily at the general condition of the floor and is not applicable to transient or exceptional conditions. Whilst the question of maintenance is not confined to the issue of construction, there is a question of degree as to what is efficient in all the circumstances. The mere presence of a piece of orange peel or a small pool of some slippery material will not prevent a floor being in an efficient state. In terms of the claim in negligence the employers had done all that could reasonably have been expected in the circumstances to avert the danger.

General Cleaning Contractors Ltd v Christmas

[1953] AC 180, HL

[2.8] Action in negligence brought by an employee of some 20 years' experience who fell from a first floor window which he was cleaning when due to a defect in the sash, it dropped suddenly causing him to lose his grip. The employee had not utilised a safety belt provided to him for the task as there were no hooks or supports around the window frame to which the safety belt could be attached. The appellant company had no means of knowing about the defective window sash as it was part of a client's premises. In the circumstances they were not negligent for failing to ensure the insertion of hooks. The appellants argued that their employees were all skilled window cleaners who individually made a decision in the case of each window whether it was dangerous or not. The system of work was a well-established one which had not been subject of previous complaint.

HELD, dismissing the appeal: Although there was no negligence in failing to provide hooks or a ladder, the system employed by the appellants relied entirely on the window sashes remaining entirely still, even though it was clear that from time to time a sash would move at the slightest touch. There was no instruction to employees to test windows before cleaning or to use wedges or blocks to prevent a sash from closing. It is the duty of an employer to give such general safety instructions as a reasonably careful employer who has considered the problem presented by the work would give to his workmen. Employers are not exempted from this duty by the fact that their men are experienced or that they carry out similar tasks repeatedly or frequently. Where a practice of ignoring an obvious danger has grown up it is not reasonable to expect the individual workman to devise suitable precautions.

Richard Thomas & Baldwins Ltd v Cummings

[1955] AC 321, HL

[2.9] The respondent's accident occurred in repairing an electrically powered grinding machine. The electric power was switched off at the mains. The respondent needed to move the mechanised parts manually in order to carry out his work and in doing so his finger became trapped. The respondent succeeded at trial in his claim pursuant to FA 1937, s 16 which required 'all fencing or other safeguards...shall be...maintained and kept in position while the parts required to be fenced or safeguarded are in motion or in used, except when any such parts are necessarily exposed for examination and for any lubrications or adjustment shown by such examination to be immediately necessary...'

HELD, allowing the appeal: Section 16 only requires machinery to be fenced when in 'motion or in use'. The moving parts of the machine were not 'in motion or in use' for the purpose which they were intended but for repair at the time of the accident which is not prohibited by section 16. Although there was movement as the machinery was turned over by hand, the machine could not be said to be 'in motion or use'. No negligence was proved on the facts of the case.

Davie v New Merton Board Mills Ltd

[1959] AC 604, HL

[2.10] This was an action in negligence where an employee was injured by a defective drift which had been negligently manufactured. The defect was latent and not amenable to discovery on reasonable inspection. The employee claimed damages for negligence on the basis that his employers had supplied him with a defective tool.

HELD: The duty to take reasonable care to supply a reasonably safe tool had been discharged by buying a tool from a reputable source. As the defect was latent there was no negligence on the part of the employer for failing to recognise the defect before the appellant's accident.

Note of caution—in relation to work equipment in light of the Employer's Liability (Defective Equipment Act 1969) and the Provision and Use of Work Equipment Regulations the case on the same facts would not be decided the same way today.

Qualcast (Wolverhampton) Ltd v Haynes

[1959] AC 743, HL

[2.11] The accident occurred when the respondent was casting moulding boxes when a ladle of molten metal which he was holding slipped and some of the metal splashed onto his left foot. The respondent alleged that his injury was caused by the appellant's negligent failure to provide spats. The appellants had spats available in the stores which the respondent could have had on request but the appellant was not ordered or advised by the respondent to wear spats. The trial judge held that he was bound by previous authority and found in favour of the respondent.

HELD: The trial judge misdirected himself as to the effect of authority. There was no authority which bound the trial judge as the facts of all cases differed. The issue of whether the appellants should have advised or required the wearing of spats was one of fact and not of principle. The respondent was aware that spats were available and decided not to use them. He was an experienced worker well able to decide for himself and the employer could not be criticised for failing to enforce the use of spats. Per Lord Denning, obiter, there was no evidence that an instruction to wear spats would have been followed, given the respondent's failure to wear spats since the accident.

Crookall v Vickers-Armstrong Ltd

[1955] 2 All ER 12, Liverpool Assizes

[2.12] This was an action in negligence and for breaches of FA 1937, ss 4 and 47(1). The claimant contracted silicosis after inhaling microscopic particles of silica working on the defendant's foundry floor for 20 years. The trial judge held as a fact that the defendants should have been aware of the risk of contracting silicosis and the possible benefits of wearing masks for approximately the last ten years of the claimant's employment. The defendant argued that there was great reluctance to wear masks on the part of employees carrying out heavy manual work and that masks had been available and mentioned to the employees from time to time.

HELD: The defendant was in breach of section 47(1) for the last ten years of the claimant's employment and was liable to the extent that its breach had contributed to or exacerbated the claimant's pre-existing silicosis. There was a failure to press on the employees with earnestness and ardour the need for the masks and to wear them for as long as possible.

Smith v Howdens Ltd

[1953] NI 131, CA

[2.13] The claimant was employed on board the defendant's ship and suffered an injury to his finger on a frayed section of steel rope. There was no provision for antibiotics or bandages on board ship and by the time the claimant reached medical attention at port his injury had become infected. The trial judge found for the defendant when he held that there was no failure on its part to provide or maintain proper appliances. On appeal the claimant argued that the defendant was in breach of duty to the claimant by its failure to have proper medical supplies on board.

HELD, dismissing the appeal: Contrary to the ruling of the trial judge, the defendant's duty to the claimant to take reasonable care for his safety did extend to the provision of suitable medical care. However there was no evidence upon which the jury could have found that the failure to provide medical care before the claimant reached port caused or contributed to or exacerbated his injury in any way and therefore the trial judge's decision would not be disturbed.

Kasapis v Laimos Bros

[1959] 2 Lloyd's Rep 378, QBD

[2.14] The claimant's accident occurred on board a ship at sea. He was employed by the defendants as the ship's cook and was injured when attempting to cut a heavy side of frozen beef in a narrow passageway outside the ship's refrigeration rooms. The meat was on a table and he had just stuck the point of the butcher's knife into the meat when it began to slide along the table towards him owing to the movement of the ship. In an attempt to prevent himself being crushed by the meat the claimant put his hand up and severely lacerated two fingers on the exposed blade of the knife. The allegations of negligence and breach of contract were that the table ought to have had a guard rail and that the table was unsafe because it was too smooth. Additionally the claimant alleged that there was a failure to provide reasonable medical attention after the incident.

HELD: There was no negligence proved against the defendant. There was no evidence that it was good practice to have a guard rail around the table or that such a rail would have prevented the claimant's accident. The claimant had made no complaint about the equipment provided during his six months on the ship. There was no evidence that the approach of the ship's master to medical treatment had been anything other than appropriate. Nobody had appreciated the seriousness of the claimant's injury. The duty to provide medical treatment was proportionate to the urgency of such treatment.

> Quaere whether this case really adds anything in terms of principle. It seems to be merely a first instance decision which turns on its own facts and following the comments in *Qualcast v Haynes*, 2.61 below, it may not now be relevant.

McCafferty v Metropolitan Police District Receiver

[1977] 2 All ER 756, CA

[2.15] The claimant had suffered hearing loss as a result of acoustic trauma in the course of his employment as a ballistics expert for the defendant. The claimant was a self-taught expert, whose experience had led to his becoming a leader in his field and who regularly gave expert evidence. The claimant carried out his testing work in what was originally designated temporary accommodation, but in the event remained the site of the laboratory for nearly ten years from 1965 to 1973 when he was compulsorily retired on medical grounds. The claimant claimed that his deafness was caused by the defendant's negligence in failing to provide structural acoustic protection in the building where live firing was carried out and in failing to provide personal protective equipment (ear muffs). The defendant argued that the claimant was best placed to appreciate any risk of injury and to propose precautions which should be taken and had either failed to appreciate the obvious risk or, appreciating it had failed to inform his superiors.

HELD: The duty of the employer was to take the advice of a competent adviser as to the precautions which ought to be taken. The defendant's assertion effectively was that the claimant had caused his own loss which had no basis in the facts of the case. The claimant was a ballistics expert not an acoustics expert. The defendant had failed to consider the question of health and safety in relation to the repeated firing of guns in an enclosed unprotected space and could not rely on an expectation that the claimant himself would assess health and safety information casually picked up in the course of his work.

Barrett v Ministry of Defence

[1995] 3 All ER 87, CA

[2.16] The claimant was the widow of a naval officer who died after becoming so drunk one night that he asphyxiated on his own vomit whilst on tour of duty outside the UK. The officer in command later pleaded guilty to a charge of failing to enforce the Queen's Regulations for the Royal Navy 1967, in relation to excessive drinking and drunkenness. It was widely known that the deceased was a heavy drinker and a culture of very heavy drinking had developed at the base where the deceased was stationed. The trial judge found that in exceptional circumstances it was just and reasonable to impose a duty of care on a defendant to protect a person of full age and capacity from their own weakness and that in lax application of the Queen's Regulations and other standing orders as to drunkenness and alcohol the defendant was in breach of that duty.

HELD, allowing the appeal by the defendant in part:
(i) It is fair, just and reasonable to allow a responsible adult to assume responsibility for his own actions in consuming alcoholic drink. No one is better placed to judge the amount that he can safely consume or to exercise control in his own interest as well as the interest of others. It would dilute self-responsibility to impose on one adult blame for another's lack of self-control.
(ii) Once the deceased collapsed unconscious the defendant assumed responsibility for him and the measures taken fell short of the standard reasonably to be expected. No medical assistance was summoned and no supervision was provided. However the immediate cause of death was suffocation due to inhalation of vomit and the deceased's lack of self-control was a continuing factor which caused the defendant to assume responsibility for him. The appropriate reduction for contributory negligence was therefore two-thirds.

Ogden v Airedale Health Authority

[1996] 7 Med LR 153, QBD

[2.17] The claimant claimed damages for personal injury from his employers the health authority. The injury was sustained in the course of employment as a radiographer. He had become sensitised to X-ray chemicals resulting in occupational asthma which meant that he could no longer work. He sued in negligence and for breach of the Control of Substances Hazardous to Health Regulations 1988.

HELD: Some of the chemicals used in the radiography department were capable of having a deleterious effect on health. The defendants were aware of complaints from their radiography staff of health problems. Even if the defendants were not aware of the irritant effects of the chemicals, they ought to have been, as it is incumbent upon an employer who requires an employee to use chemicals in the course of their work to make enquiry as to the safety hazards which they present. By failing to provide proper ventilation, protective equipment, a proper system for dealing with spillages or to issue warnings as to the dangers of the chemicals the defendants were negligent.

26   *Common Law Liability*

LIMITS TO THE DUTY

Bloor v Liverpool Derricking and Carrying Co Ltd

[1936] 3 All ER 399

[2.18] The respondent was the widow of a man who was employed as a derricker by the defendants. At the time of the accident the deceased had offered to act temporarily as a tipper on a different barge, in order to relieve the man employed as tipper for a short while. The deceased fell into the barge and injured his ankle. At hospital an operation was deemed appropriate and chloroform administered, which proved lethal due to an undiscovered heart problem. The appellant claimed that the deceased was a volunteer, not employed by it to act as a tipper and that it was not liable for any negligence on the part of the man employed as tipper due to the doctrine of common employment. Further the appellant claimed that the administration of chloroform was a new intervening cause of death.

HELD, allowing the appeal: The derricker was not employed by the appellant to act as a tipper and was not acting in the course of his employment at the time of his accident. The doctrine of common employment protected the appellant from liability for any negligence on the part of the fellow-employee. The administration of chloroform was not a wrongful act as there was no way of knowing that the deceased would suffer an adverse reaction.

> *Note*—this case would now be decided differently. The doctrine of common employment was that an employee agreed to run risks incidental to his employment, including the risk of injury from the defaults of fellow employees. The defence was abolished by the Law Reform (Personal Injuries) Act 1948.

Davidson v Handley Page Ltd

[1945] 1 All ER 235, CA

[2.19] This was an action in negligence and pursuant to FA 1937, ss 25, 26. The appellant slipped on suds on a walkway which she was using to access a tap in order to wash out a teacup for her own personal use. The defendant acknowledged the danger of the suds on the floor and employed labourers intermittently to clean the floor or to place sawdust on the floor to prevent slipperiness.

HELD: It could not be disputed that if the appellant had been accessing the tap for purposes directly connected with her employment by the defendant, there would have been a breach of duty. It would be an extravagant result if the common law obligation of the employer suddenly came to an end the moment the workman ceased to perform the precise acts he was employed to perform and did something which was ordinarily and reasonably incidental to his day's work. The obligation of the employer extends to cover all such acts as are normally and reasonably incidental to a man's day's work.

Deyong v Shenburn

[1946] KB 227, CA

[2.20] An action for breach of contract, breach of bailment and negligence. The appellant was employed by the respondent to play the part of the dame in a pantomime at the Palace Theatre, Camberwell. Rehearsals took place over the course of a week and on the second day someone had stolen an overcoat, two shawls and a pair of shoes which were part of his theatrical equipment from a dressing room. The trial judge found that the respondent had taken no reasonable care to safeguard its employee's property as there was no lock on the door and the security representative was absent and not replaced.

HELD: There was no implied term in the contract of service that an employer should take steps to safeguard the employee's property against loss through the wrongful act of a third person. No such duty exists in bailment, it is not a term implied through necessity or business efficacy into the contract and the duty of care to provide a safe system of working does not extend to cover for liability for failure to protect an employee's goods against theft.

Stapley v Gypsum Mines Ltd

[1953] AC 663, HL

[2.21] Action for breach of statutory duty and negligence. The appellant's husband was killed when a roof collapsed on him in the course of his employment at the respondent's mine. The deceased and a fellow employee of equal status had noticed the instability in the roof and told their foreman, whose instruction was to bring the roof down. The two employees attempted unsuccessfully to bring the roof down and re-commenced their normal work. The roof fell killing the deceased. The trial judge held that there was no breach of duty through lack of supervision and therefore gave judgment for the appellant for one half of the amount of his damages, that being the amount which he would have awarded had the deceased not also been responsible for his own death. The Court of Appeal reversed the decision, holding that any breach of the regulations or negligence on the part of the fellow employee had not caused or contributed to the deceased's death.

HELD: The fault of the fellow employee, for the which the respondent was liable, was a contributory cause of the accident which resulted in the deceased's death. Fault would be apportioned 80% in respect of the deceased and 20% in respect of the fellow employee as the deceased took the decision to enter under the dangerous section of the roof in full knowledge as to its condition. The cause of the deceased's death was the decision of both employees that the roof was safe and that they should continue with their normal work, not the fact that the deceased was present under the roof at the time when it fell.

Laszczyk v National Coal Board

[1954] 3 All ER 205, Manchester Assizes

[2.22] The claimant was injured in an accident due to the negligence of an employee of the defendant. The issue in the case was contributory negligence. The claimant was not trained as a coalface worker although he had acted as such from time to time throughout his three years' employment with the defendant. The training officer noticed him working on the coal face on one occasion, pointed out to the claimant that he should not proceed beyond a certain point in the mine towards the coal face and informed one of the claimant's two immediate managers that he was not trained and should not be employed on the coal face. The other manager however later instructed the claimant to carry on work at the coalface and to avoid the training officer. The claimant's accident took place on the coalface where a shot-firer's sentry failed to keep a proper look-out and allowed a shot to be fired whilst the claimant was in the danger zone. The issue was whether the claimant's breaches of statute and regulation were causative of his accident.

HELD: The claimant's contravention of the direct instruction given to him by the training officer was a breach of statute and regulation and therefore meant that the claimant was contributorily negligent. However, in light of the direct contrary instruction given by the claimant's immediate superior and the direction to stay away from the training officer, the proper share of the claimant's responsibility was 5%.

National Coal Board v England

[1954] AC 403, HL

[2.23] The respondent was injured in an accident at the appellant's mine where the former was employed as a miner. The accident was a premature explosion of a detonator. The respondent and a shot-firer employed by the appellant were both in breach of regulations, namely that only authorised persons should couple up the cable to the detonator, which the two employees had agreed should be done by the respondent. The shot-firer was further in breach of a regulation requiring him to ascertain that all persons in the vicinity had taken proper shelter before firing a shot. The appellant argued that the maxim ex turpi causa non oritur actio applied and that the respondent's claim could not succeed as it depended on his own criminal activity, alternatively that the appellant could not be made liable for the criminal activity of its other employee, the shot-firer, as the duties were imposed on the shot-firer himself, not the employer.

HELD: Although the duties were imposed directly on the shot-firer by statute the purpose of the regulations was to ensure safety in coal mines and the shot-firer was acting in the scope of his employment when he was carrying out the task of shot-firing. The shot-firer was clearly negligent and his negligence contributed to the accident. The maxim ex turpi causa is based on public policy which in the circumstances of health and safety legislation dictates that cases should be entertained and decided on the merits. There is no distinction in Law Reform (Contributory Negligence) Act 1945, s 1(1) between those breaches which are criminal acts and those which give rise to a liability in tort for the purposes of ex turpi causa This meant that the respondent's claim would not be defeated by his own fault. Although the Court of Appeal was incorrect to assess the respondent's contributory fault as nil, their Lordships felt that the apportionment of liability suggested by the trial judge could not be supported as the shot-firer was more at fault than the respondent and damages would be reduced by 25% instead of 50%.

Ramsay v Wimpey & Co Ltd

1951 SC 692, Ct of Sess

[2.24] The defendants were contractors working on a site. A large number of men were employed by the defendants as labourers. In order to transport the men to the site from Edinburgh (and back again after each shift) the defendants hired buses. The accident occurred as the claimant's husband was attempting to board one of these buses. A large crowd of men had been awaiting the arrival of the bus and rushed towards it when it arrived. Unfortunately the bus was already full of workers for the next shift and the men were unable to board. The claimant's husband was crushed by his fellow workers against the side of the bus. It was alleged that the accident was due to the defendants' negligence in that the pick up area was dark and the ground slippery as it had rained heavily. Further there were no foremen or conductors employed to control the boarding of buses.

HELD: The points pleaded by the claimant alleged no more than a duty to take reasonable care for her husband's safety. The pick up area formed part of the defendants' site and the hours and terms of the employees' employment included transport. In the circumstances the defendants' duty to take reasonable care for the safety of the deceased would continue to apply while he was waiting on premises controlled by the defendants for transport provided by them under their contract with him. The fact that the deceased was not required to make use of the transport made no difference. The question of causation, in particular novus actus interveniens on the part of the crowd in rushing forward, were also all matters for consideration by a jury. The defendants' applications to strike out were dismissed.

Rands v McNeil

[1955] 1 QB 253, CA

[2.25–2.26] The claimant was a senior labourer on a farm owned by the defendant. The defendant kept a dangerous bull on the farm which had been de-horned and was kept in a loose box untethered. Some workmen, not including the claimant, had been cautioned not to enter the box until the bull had been secured. One day another employee of the defendant with responsibility for the animal intended to muck it out. Without having followed the usual method of securing the bull he set about this work, asking the claimant to hold the door to the loose box open as an escape route if necessary. When the other employee still could not secure the bull the claimant volunteered to assist, when the bull charged and severely injured him. The claimant claimed that the defendant was negligent in failing to institute a safe system of work alternatively that strict liability applied in view of the fact that the animal was known to be dangerous.

HELD, by a majority, with Denning LJ dissenting: The trial judge had held that the measures taken were adequate to prevent the bull from harming anyone unless that person brought the harm upon himself. The rule in *Rylands v Fletcher* (1868) LR 3 HL 330, was not applicable as it required a dangerous animal to escape. The claimant at the time of the accident was doing something which he knew he should not have been doing in light of his considerable experience working on the farm. As a result he was working outside the scope of his employment.

Per Denning LJ: There were obvious defects in a system of working which required men never to enter the loose box whilst the bull was untethered when several employees had not been given that instruction. The tethering system, which involved poking a hooked staff at the bull's nose was inadequate as it was obvious that this was a step to which the bull would object. A chain on the ring would have made the task much easier. The fact that the claimant was also at fault for entering the box goes only to reduce damages not to expunge the defendant's fault. He would have awarded 50% of the damages.

R v National Insurance Comr, ex p Michael

[1977] 2 All ER 420, CA

[2.27] The claimant was a police officer selected to represent his police force in a football match against another force. By chance the match took place on a day when the officer was not on duty. The claimant was injured during the match and required time off work to recover. He sought to claim injury benefit pursuant to National Insurance (Industrial Injuries) Act 1965, s 5(1) which provided that benefit would be payable in respect of all injuries, 'arising out of and in the course of employment'. The commissioner rejected the claim, stating that playing football could not form part of the activities of a police officer. The Divisional Court upheld this ruling on the basis that such decisions were one of fact which could not be interfered with.

HELD, dismissing the appeal: Although the primary facts were, as so often in such cases, not in dispute, the correct inference to be drawn from them was a matter of law which could be properly reviewed by the courts where there was a matter of general principle involved or a disagreement between the commissioners. The commissioner in this case was incorrect to suggest that the statute should be interpreted as meaning injured whilst doing something which is 'reasonably incidental to his employment'. Those words are not part of the statute and should be read in the context of the cases in which they are mentioned. The sole question is whether the accident arose in the course of employment. There was no basis for saying on the facts of this particular case that such football matches were in the course of the claimant's employment.

Reid v Rush & Tompkins Group plc

[1989] 3 All ER 228, CA

[2.28] The claimant was injured in a road traffic accident in Ethiopia. He was at the time of the accident in the course of his employment with the defendant as a quarry foreman on a project in Ethiopia. The accident was the fault of the driver of a vehicle which collided with the vehicle in which the claimant was travelling. However this individual was never identified and there was no scheme to cover uninsured third parties in Ethiopia. The claimant therefore claimed against the defendant, alleging that its failure either to insure the claimant or to advise him to obtain such cover for himself amounted to a breach of its duty of care owed to him in negligence. On an application to strike out for failure to disclose a cause of action the claimant appealed to the Court of Appeal.

HELD, dismissing the appeal: It was conceded on the part of the claimant that his claim amounted to a claim for pure economic loss and that hitherto the duty of a master to his servant had not been extended to the taking of reasonable care to protect the servant from economic loss. There are several scenarios at English law where an individual might suffer injury as a result of the fault of another yet be unable to recover the money compensation to which the law entitles him. There was no basis for implying a term into the contract of employment which imposed a duty on the defendant to provide advice. Such a term would have to be express. On the basis of the facts alleged in the pleadings there could be no finding of a voluntary assumption of responsibility on the part of the defendant to advise the claimant to take out personal insurance, nor did such a duty fall within the scope of the defendant's general duty as employer which is limited to protection of the employee from physical harm.

Scally v Southern Health and Social Services Board
[1992] 1 AC 294, HL

[2.29] The claimants were all employed by various health boards and under the terms of their contracts of employment were required to contribute to the statutory superannuation scheme. To qualify for a full pension an employee had to have 40 years' contributory service. Pursuant to the regulations governing the scheme employees had a right to purchase 'added years' of pension entitlement in order to make up the 40 years' contributions to qualify for maximum pension. Added years had to be purchased within 12 months of either 10 February 1975 or from the date that the individual's employment commenced, whichever was the latter. The Department of Health possessed a discretion to extend the time limit, subject to the right to vary the terms of purchase. The claimants all claimed damages alleged to flow from the employer's failure in each case to bring to the claimants' attention the right to enhance his pension entitlement by purchase of added years on the terms available within the first 12 months. This duty was alleged to arise either by way of an implied term of the contract or a duty of care. There was also a claim for breach of statutory duty, namely the Contracts of Employment and Redundancy Payments Act (Northern Ireland) 1965, s 4.

HELD:
(i) That any breach of the above mentioned statutory provision was remediable only as provided in section 5 by an employment tribunal;
(ii) As the terms of the superannuation scheme were incorporated by reference into the claimants' contracts of employment and, without notice of their rights to buy added years that entitlement was of no effect, it was necessary to imply into the contracts an obligation on the employer to bring to that entitlement to the employee's attention.

Lister v Romford Ice and Cold Storage Co Ltd
[1957] AC 555, HL

[2.30] A lorry driver was employed by a company. He took his father with him as mate. In reversing the lorry the driver, through his negligence, injured his father who recovered damages in an action against the company. The current action was brought by the company against the lorry driver claiming that as a joint tortfeasor it was entitled to a contribution from him in respect of his father's damages or for damages for breach of an implied term in his contract of employment that he would use reasonable skill and care in driving. The lorry driver defended the action stating that it was an implied term of the contract of service that the company would indemnify him against all claims brought against him for any act done by him in the course of his employment or that he would receive the benefit of any contract of insurance which the company had in place covering its liability for the first action. He denied the existence of an implied term that he would carry out his duties with reasonable care and skill.

HELD, by a majority, Lords Radcliffe and Somervell dissenting: It is an implied term of a contract of service that an employee will perform his duties with proper care. There was no ground for making a distinction in respect of duties which involved driving vehicles. There could be no implied term for the benefit of an employee which allowed him to escape all liability. The fact that a party to an action might be insured was to be disregarded when determining the rights of that party as against another.

Per Lord Morton and Viscount Simonds: the company was also entitled to recover 100% pursuant to the Law Reform (Married Women and Tortfeasors) Act 1935.

Dissent: although the employee owes a contractual duty to exercise reasonable skill and care in the course of his employment, the company could not claim against its employee due to an implied term that the employer could not recover from his employee any damages which the reasonable person would cover with insurance.

Davie v New Merton Board Mills Ltd

[1959] AC 604, HL

[2.31] (See 2.10 above) At common law duties of an employer in respect of work tools are limited.

Matthews v Kuwait Bechtel Corpn

[1959] 2 QB 57, CA

[2.32–2.33] The claimant was injured in the course of his employment for the defendant company in Kuwait when he fell into a trench. By the terms of his contract of employment the law of England applied. There was no express term requiring the defendant to take reasonable care for the claimant's safety in the course of his employment. The company had no residence in England or Wales but only in Panama. The claimant sought leave to serve proceedings outside the jurisdiction which the defendant resisted on the basis that the only cause of action was in tort and there was no sufficient link to the jurisdiction.

HELD: The employer's duty of care to his employee existed either in tort or as a matter of implication in the contract of employment. As the claim was pleaded in contract, the court had jurisdiction to hear the claim.

Johnstone v Bloomsbury Health Authority

[1992] QB 333, [1991] 2 All ER 293, CA

[2.34] The claimant was employed by the defendant as a senior house officer in a hospital department. The terms of his employment contained an express term as to the number of hours which he was expected to work, namely a basic rate of 40 hours per week plus an additional 48 hours on average call duty. The claimant alleged that the defendants were, as an implied term of the contract, obliged to take reasonable care for his safety and well-being. The claimant alleged that in breach of this term the defendant consistently required him to work such intolerably long hours with deprivation of sleep as to damage his health. The claimant sought a declaration that he could not be required to work more than 72 hours per week or a continuous period of more than 24 hours and damages. The claimant also sought to rely on Unfair Contract Terms Act 1977, s 2(1). The defendant applied to have the particulars of claim struck out as disclosing no cause of action.

HELD, refusing the application: The contractual right of the employer to require the employee to work 88 hours a week had to be exercised subject to the duty to provide a safe system of working and the duty to take care for safety of the employee. If employers know or ought to know that a particular employee is vulnerable, they should take account of that when requiring them to do extra work. If contrary to this opinion, the defendants are allowed to rely on the contractual term to limit the scope of their duty to the claimant, UCTA clearly applies as the clause has the effect of restricting or limiting their duty to the claimant. There is however no ground of public policy for declaring the contract term void. Case of *Ottoman Bank v Chakarian* [1930] AC 277 followed, there being no distinction in cases where the inherent danger of requiring the employee to follow the strict terms of the contract arises after the instruction from the employer, from situations such as the present one where the risk to the health or safety of the employee subsisted at the time of the instruction.

[2.35] Unfair Contract Terms Act 1977 (1977 c50) provides at section 2:

(1) A person cannot be reference to any contract term or to a notice given to persons generally or to particular persons exclude or restrict his liability for death or personal injury resulting from negligence.

Weems v Mathieson

(1861) 4 Macq 215, HL

[2.36] Mrs Mathieson's son was a journeyman tinsmith killed in the course of his employment when a two-ton air-heater fell on him due to it being insufficiently secured. The defendant employer appealed the decision against it, stating that there were no allegations which amounted to negligence on his part to justify a finding against him.

HELD, dismissing the appeal: It was averred in the claim that by reason of want of reasonable care on the part of the defendant, or some person or persons in his employ, the chains were negligently or unskilfully attached which led to the accident and the deceased's death, upon which there had been a finding in favour of the claimant. The master is bound to do is to provide machinery fit and proper for the work, and to take care to have it superintended by himself or his workmen in a fit and proper manner.

Durnford v Western Atlas International Inc

[2003] EWCA Civ 306, [2003] All ER (D) 94 (Mar)

[2.37] An employee had to travel to Nigeria to work on a vessel. He flew from London to Paris, from Paris to Nigeria, had a coach journey, a minibus journey, and finally a 3 hour trip on a speed boat. He suffered back injuries which were held to have been caused on the minibus journey. The trial judge found that the defendant had failed to provide suitable transport. The defendant appealed.

HELD: dismissing the appeal. The trial judge was entitled to find that the back injury had been caused by the journey and that the defendant had not discharged its duties to the claimant.

CAUSATION, REMOTENESS AND CONTRIBUTORY NEGLIGENCE

[2.38] Even though a duty on the part of an employer can be shown to have been breached there may be issues as to remoteness, causation and contributory negligence to be addressed.

The cases summarised below are intended to show these principles in practice.

Haynes v Harwood

[1935] 1 KB 146, CA

[2.39] A rescue case in which the plaintiff police constable, whilst on duty inside a police station, saw the defendants' runaway horses, attached to a van, bolting down a crowded highway endangering passers-by. He sustained personal injuries whilst bringing the animals under control.

HELD, on appeal: Approving *Brandon v Osborne Garrett & Co* [1924] 1 KB 548, the plaintiff had acted to avoid loss or damage to others. Accordingly, because his injuries were precipitated by the defendants' wrongful act, the defence of volenti non fit injuria did not apply. On the facts the defendants' servant was negligent in leaving the horses unattended in a busy street; he should have appreciated that someone, especially the police, who are under a moral and legal duty to act to protect property and lives, would intervene in order to prevent loss of life or limb. Accordingly, the injuries sustained were foreseeable and the maxim volenti non fit injuria did not apply.

The fact that the horses bolted as a result of a novus actus interveniens, apparently having been startled by a stone thrown by a small boy, did not save the defendants. Having found that the animals should not have been left unattended, Greer LJ said that damage was 'one of the natural and probable consequences of the wrongful act'. The likelihood that the animals might cause injury unless brought under control was relevant to the reasonableness of the actions of the police officer.

Caswell v Powell Duffryn Associated Collieries Ltd

[1940] AC 152, HL

[2.40] A fatal accident claim brought by the mother of the deceased under Coal Mines Act 1911, s 55, which required dangerous and exposed parts of mining equipment to be securely fenced. The deceased was employed by the respondents at their colliery to clean the top of a roller on a machine used to transport coal. Mr Caswell's job was to clean the machine when not in motion and then to replace a plate which operated the belt. He died having been trapped by the arm between belt and roller. There was no system of signalling to him when the machine was about to be restarted.

HELD, overturning a decision at first instance and in the Court of Appeal: That the machinery was dangerous when unfenced and in motion and this omission materially contributed to the deceased's death notwithstanding that the precise circumstances of the accident were not known. The respondents failed in their duty to ensure that the plate was replaced before the machine was restarted, the system of working necessitated a means of alerting the deceased to the machine being switched on and in the absence of establishing that it was not reasonably practicable to avoid a breach of duty, the respondents were liable in damages.

The case confirms that actions for breach of statutory duty leading to injury are similar to claims based on other causes of action although they often impose absolute or strict liability. To establish liability the claimant must prove (a) breach of statutory duty and (b) that such breach caused the injury.

The House of Lords also considered when contributory negligence affords a defence in these cases. Where there is breach of statutory duty the onus is on the defendant to prove that contributory negligence was a substantial or material co-operating cause of injury. The key issue is causation. For example, where injury is entirely due to the claimant's wilful act or the claimant establishes that injury was caused wholly or in part by a workman's failure to take the ordinary care which the circumstances of the accident demanded, his claim will fail. Conditions, hours of work and repetition of tasks are relevant factors. The degree of care expected of an individual varies according to the facts and is not limited to wilful or serious misconduct. The standard adopted is that of the reasonable man. However, as a general rule, if the claimant's negligence did not result in the injury a contributory negligence defence will not operate.

Yorkshire Dale Steamship Co v Minister of War Transport, The Coxwold

[1942] AC 691, HL

[2.41] A merchant ship, the *Coxwold*, requisitioned for naval use by the Minister of War Transport, became grounded on the Damsel Rocks off the Isle of Skye during a substantial deviation to avoid suspected hostile submarine activity in 1940. The operation of the tide contributed to the loss. At the material time the ship was carrying petrol for military use. It had been insured by the owners against marine risks and the government assumed responsibility for damage occasioned by war risks. Ordinary Lloyd's cover excepted 'the consequences of hostilities and warlike operations.' The court considered whether stranding, an obvious marine risk, precluded the operation of the war risks exception.

HELD, overturning the decision reached in the Court of Appeal: That common sense must be used to decide which of several factors amounts to the proximate cause of loss of a ship. The test is, was loss caused *'effectively and proximately'* by the warlike operation? This means identifying the dominant cause of loss, not necessarily the one which operates last.

Here, the vessel was sailing in convoy, ferrying war stores between military bases and had set an altered course because of threat of submarine attack; the proximate cause of damage was a warlike operation. Negligent navigation was not established. Once a warlike operation is found to exist the onus is on the party seeking to displace the presumption that, as matter of fact, this was not the cause of loss. Lord Wright described the warlike operation as 'an umbrella which covers every active step taken to carry it out, including the navigation, the course and helm action intended to bring the vessel to the position required by the warlike operation.' A wilful act such as scuttling 'would raise different questions'.

The Oropesa

[1943] P 32, CA

[2.42] In December 1939 a collision occurred between two steam vessels, the *Oropesa* and the *Manchester Regiment*, off the coast of Nova Scotia. The master of the latter erroneously believed that, despite severe damage, his ship could be salvaged. Whilst transferring crew to the *Oropesa* by lifeboat in deteriorating weather conditions, the craft capsized with a loss of nine lives. The parents of one of the lost crewmembers, Arthur Lord, the sixth engineer, qua personal representatives, were joined as plaintiffs, together with the *Manchester Regiment's* owners in an action against the *Oropesa's* owners, the Pacific Steam Navigation Co, claiming for the deceased's personal effects. Liability was apportioned.

The parents brought a second action against the same defendants under the Law Reform (Miscellaneous Provisions) Act 1934 qua administrators for: (a) loss of expectation of life and (b) damages as dependants under the Fatal Accidents Acts.

HELD, affirming the decision of Langton J below: The Court of Appeal found firstly, that reasonable conduct in an emergency situation does not break the chain of causation even if further loss is sustained. The *Manchester Regiment's* master acted reasonably in a crisis. Accordingly, the engineer's death was not the result of a novus actus interveniens but of the collision.

Secondly, the cause of action in the second claim differing from that contained within the first set of proceedings, the plaintiffs were entitled to further damages. Estoppel did not operate to defeat the second action because although both claims arose out of identical acts of negligence, the rights infringed differed. Applying *Brunsden v Humphrey* (1884) 14 QBD 141, Lord Wright found that damages in respect of personal injury including loss of life present a distinct cause of action to a claim in respect of lost chattels.

On the facts, the holed *Manchester Regiment* was 'a dead lump in the water'. The captain of a ship had a duty to take reasonable steps to prevent further loss and his crew to obey his instructions. What is reasonable must be judged in the context of the case; here an emergency. In the factual matrix of the case it was reasonable for the master to seek advice and assistance from the second vessel even if his assessment of the prospects of saving the ship was mistaken, an error which 'might be regarded as a natural consequence of the emergency'. It was equally reasonable for the crew to obey orders to man the lifeboat. The rescue party was 'dictated by the exigencies of the position' and could not be severed from the context in which it was launched.

To break the chain of causation requires 'something ultroneous, something unwarrantable, a new cause which disturbs the sequence of events'.

Lee v Nursery Furnishings Ltd

[1945] 1 All ER 387, CA

[2.43] The appellant operated a circular saw for cutting wood in the respondents' factory. Whilst cutting up chair legs she injured the fourth finger of her right hand on the saw. Precisely how the accident happened was not plain. The question which arose was whether a guard over the saw was low enough.

HELD: On the facts there was a gap of $\frac{1}{2}$ inch between the top of the wood being cut and the lower edge of the guard. As a matter of construction this was insufficiently 'low as practicable' within the meaning of the Use of Woodworking Machinery Regulations 1922. It was higher than it should have been to accommodate a crossbar which was higher than the pieces of wood being cut. The guard should have been capable of adjustment to avoid injury.

On a point of more general interest, the court indicated that where there is a breach of safety regulations, and the accident which has occurred is of a class which those regulations are designed to prevent, the court should not strive to find that the cause of injury was unconnected to the breach.

Hyett v Great Western Rly Co

[1948] 1 KB 345, CA

[2.44] The plaintiff sustained leg injuries whilst attempting to extinguish a fire which had broken out in a wagon on railway sidings due to the defendant's negligence. At the time of the accident he was on the defendant's property in order to repair rolling stock belonging to the railway company when he saw smoke coming from the wagon. Paraffin drums within it had leaked and fire had taken hold.

The question was whether the accident was a natural and probable result of breach of duty in leaving leaking paraffin drums on site within the meaning of *Hadley v Baxendale* (1854) or whether there was a novus actus interveniens.

HELD: That the rule in *Haynes v Harwood & Son* (1935) (see 2.39 above) that someone can recover damages if it is a natural and probable consequence of a defendant's negligence that someone will intervene to prevent loss, applies where the risk is of property damage only.

The test is ultimately one of foreseeability, namely, whether, looking at the broad facts of the case, the plaintiff's conduct was reasonable and justifiable and a natural and probable consequence of the defendant's negligence.

Philco Radio and Television Corpn of Great Britain Ltd v J Spurling Ltd

[1949] 2 All ER 882, CA

[2.45] Packing cases containing combustible celluloid film scrap were delivered in error by the defendants to the plaintiffs' premises. The plaintiffs' foreman realising the potential danger, warned the workmen in charge of the cases not to smoke and instructed them to remove them. Before this happened, a typist employed by the plaintiffs, Mrs Brady, caused an explosion when she lit a cigarette and put it against the scrap material. There was some suggestion that Mrs Brady realised that her actions would lead to a small fire, but not an explosion.

HELD: That the defendants had a duty to warn those to whom they had delivered the materials of the risk of damage from some foolish act and the onus was on them to establish that the damage which occurred was the result, not of their negligence, but of some novus actus interveniens. Short of a 'conscious act of volition' that is, some deliberate or reckless act to set fire to the material, so as to cause damage, this burden would not be discharged.

There was some discussion as to whether, if Mrs Brady had deliberately set fire to the packing material, this would have broken the chain of causation or whether this would only happen if she had realised precisely what would happen. On the facts and since she was not called to give evidence, her knowledge on the point could not be established.

Cork v Kirby Maclean Ltd

[1952] 2 All ER 402, CA

[2.46] A painter accepted employment with the defendants deliberately concealing from them that he suffered from epilepsy and that he ought not on medical grounds work above ground level because of the danger of having an epileptic fit. Two days into his new job, in order to paint a roof at a factory in Colchester, he worked on a platform 20 feet above the ground. Contrary to Building Regulations the platform was insufficiently wide and lacked guard-rails and toe-boards. He had an epileptic fit and fell to his death. His widow brought a claim based on breach of statutory duty.

The relevance of the deceased's failure to disclose his illness to the claim was explored in the context of the Law Reform (Contributory Negligence) Act, 1945. It was likely that had the deceased revealed his illness, he either would not have been employed at all or at least not engaged in the task which provided the opportunity for the accident.

HELD: That it was not necessary for the defendants to prove that the deceased would have fallen even if the regulations had been complied with. On the evidence there were two causes of the accident, namely, the deceased's failure to inform his employers of his medical condition and the breach of safety regulations. Accordingly, liability was apportioned equally and recoverable damages would be reduced by 50%.

Despite being unable to say affirmatively whether the breach of safety regulation contributed to the accident the court found that as a matter of law, there were two causes of the fall. One of these was the deceased's negligence in failing to inform his employers of his illness. Such omission fell within the meaning of 'fault' under the Law Reform (Contributory Negligence) Act, 1945, s 4 and would thus be relevant to the amount of damages awarded in the claim.

Stapley v Gypsum Mines Ltd

[1953] AC 663, HL

[2.47] See 2.21 above.

Norris v William Moss & Sons Ltd

[1954] 1 All ER 324, CA

[2.48] The plaintiff's job was to erect scaffolding for the defendant builders and contractors in a brick ventilating shaft. The foreman had, several days earlier, noticed that one of the standards of the scaffolding was not vertical but failed to notify the plaintiff when he was asked to put up an extra platform.

The plaintiff noticed the fault and attempted to straighten the standard but by a method described by the trial judge as 'fantastically wrong' in that he did not seek to fasten couplings at the base and centre of the platform. The platform collapsed and the plaintiff fell. In a claim for personal injuries against his employers he claimed negligence and breach of the Building (Safety, Health and Welfare) Regulations 1948. The latter required, where practical, that standards or uprights of scaffolds to be in a vertical position or slightly inclined towards the building.

HELD: Rejecting the plaintiff's claim, that despite a breach by the defendants of building regulations, in that the standard was out of alignment, the accident was due solely to the plaintiff's negligence in that he had resorted to an inappropriate method of rectifying the fault and the subsequent accident could not be attributed to either the foreman's failure to warn him of the defect or the breach of regulation. Had the plaintiff sustained injury whilst working on the platform but in ignorance of the faulty positioning of the scaffolding he would have been able to recover damages. As it was Vaisey J found no favour in 'the argument in the old fable in which the loss of a kingdom is traced back to an originating and ultimate cause in the loss of a single nail from a horse's shoe'.

Hartley v Mayoh & Co

[1954] 1 QB 383, CA

[2.49] Having been summoned to a fire at a pickle factory, fire brigade officers asked the factory manager to direct them to the main electric switch so that they could turn off the current in accordance with standard practice. Unbeknown to the manager, Mr Holland, the main switch comprised two tumbler switches which needed to be turned off and instead the firemen were told to turn off other master switches. Unfortunately, because of the manner in which the latter had been transposed by the area electricity authority, the current remained live in the neutral wire and a fire officer was fatally electrocuted. His widow brought a claim against the factory and the electricity board.

At first instance Barry J found against both defendants apportioning liability as to 90% against the board and 10% against the factory. The latter appealed against his ruling.

HELD, dismissing the appeal: That regulation 9 of the Electricity Regulations 1908 imposed a duty on occupiers of a factory to familiarise themselves with their own main switch. Accordingly, the manager should have known about the tumbler switches. His lack of knowledge and resultant failure to turn them off presented a danger to the firemen to whom the factory, as invitors and occupiers, owed a duty as invitees. This omission and his failure to warn and protect the firemen against the unusual danger persisted regardless of his lack of knowledge of the intricacies in the wiring relating to the master switches which had been transposed by the electricity board. Accordingly there was liability at common law.

Singleton LJ specifically referred to the manager's evidence in relation to the tumbler switches. The fact that he knew that they did not control any local lighting points should have been put him 'on enquiry as to their true function'.

No claim could be brought in respect of a breach of the statutory regulations the purpose of which was to protect a limited class of person, namely factory employees. The firemen did not fall within this class and were thus not entitled to claim for breach of statutory duty.

Judson v British Transport Commission

[1954] 1 All ER 624, CA

[2.50] An accident took place whilst the plaintiff was working on a railway line. At the time he and a ganger, who was senior to him, were inspecting a section of the line in order to determine how much material would be needed to relay it the next day. In order to avoid an oncoming train he stepped onto an adjoining track where he was injured by a train approaching from behind. As a result of the incident his leg was amputated above the knee. In effecting this manoeuvre the plaintiff breached instructions that he 'move clear of all lines unless' he could 'distinctly see that (he was) in a position of safety' within the British Railway Rules 1950, r 234(a).

The plaintiff argued that the defendants had failed in its statutory duty to provide a look-out in accordance with the Prevention of Accident Rules 1902, r 9 and further, that they were negligent in that the ganger had failed to ensure that he stepped clear of the lines. Donovan J found breach of statutory duty but dismissed the claim for damages on the grounds that the plaintiff was the author of his own misfortune.

HELD, dismissing the plaintiff's appeal and distinguishing this case from *Stapley v Gypsum Mines* (1953): That the plaintiff alone was responsible for his injuries. Had both men moved clear of both tracks when the first train was approaching, as they both knew that they ought, the accident would have been avoided.

Disagreeing with Donnovan J it was held first, that the defendants were not in breach of statutory duty in failing to provide a look-out. The requirement to do so arose when someone was relaying or repairing the line. Here, inspection was preparatory to repair/relaying which was to be carried out the next day. Also the plaintiff was moving along the track. Accordingly, any look-out would have been in no better position to notice approaching trains than the plaintiff. The duty to provide a stationary look-out to protect workmen did not apply to peripatetic workmen inspecting what might be a lengthy section of track.

Secondly, the plaintiff's colleague, a ganger, was not to blame since he did not influence the direction in which the plaintiff moved across the track and the plaintiff moved first.

Hodkinson v Henry Wallwork & Co Ltd

[1955] 3 All ER 236, CA

[2.51] The plaintiff operated an electric machine in a Manchester factory known as a wheelabrator. When the power was turned on a bucket filled with metal castings would be lifted up and travel along wire ropes over pulleys nine feet above the ground. Neither pulleys nor ropes were fenced. Sometimes the ropes would come off the pulleys causing the machine to stop. When this happened the matter would be reported to the factory foreman or the charge hand who would summon fitter-mechanics to fix the fault. They would usually arrive within minutes. No one else had authority to rectify the problem.

One day, when the rope became detached, the plaintiff reported this to the foreman but nevertheless he unaccountably sought to rectify the problem himself. The electricity power was still on and, before he had slipped the second rope back onto the pulley, the machine began to move and he injured his left hand badly, losing two middle fingers. The plaintiff sought to recover damages from his employers for breach of statutory duty under the FA 1937 on the grounds that they had failed to fence in transmission machinery.

HELD, in an appeal by the defendants against a fifty:fifty apportionment of liability: That firstly, there was a breach of statutory duty in that the equipment, although suspended nine feet above ground level, was not as safe as it would have been had it been fenced in. Singleton LJ referred to the evidence of one witness that a ladder close by which the fitter-mechanics used served as 'a temptation'.

Secondly, approving the test of causation in *Yorkshire Dale Steamship Co Ltd v Minister of War Transport* (1942) (see 2.41 above) that: 'Causation is to be understood as the man in the street, and not as either the scientist or the metaphysician, would understand it.' Despite the breach of statutory duty the plaintiff was negligent in that he had consciously acted contrary to established practice thereby taking what was described as an 'amazing risk' and accordingly damages should be reduced by 90%. It was perhaps significant that the plaintiff's evidence was considered unreliable by the trial judge in that he falsely represented that the defendants had approved his course of action in order to shift blame to them.

Some liability had to be borne by the defendants in circumstances in which the type of injury which occurred was that which the statute was designed to prevent. A guard over the equipment might have deterred the plaintiff from attempting to remedy the problem. Moreover, by the time he had reached over the guard, the fitters would have arrived on the scene.

John Summers & Sons Ltd v Frost

[1955] AC 740, HL

[2.52] An experienced maintenance fitter in a steel works injured his thumb when grinding metal using a power driven grindstone which revolved at the rate of approximately 1,450 revolutions a minute and part of which was unfenced. The machine was in common use at the time.

The material issue was the ambit of the statutory duty under FA 1937, s 14(1) to securely fence off dangerous parts of machinery unless the position or construction of the machinery made it as safe as it would be were it fenced.

HELD, dismissing an appeal by the appellant company from a finding of liability made by the Court of Appeal: That there was a breach of statutory duty there was insufficient evidence of contributory negligence on the part of the respondent.

The language with which s 14 was framed imposed an absolute duty to fence the grinding wheel notwithstanding that compliance with s 14 might render such a machine unusable and in effect a 'museum piece'. Significantly, there were no qualifying words in the section to limit the duty. Modifying regulations could be made by the Minister under s 60 of the Act but these had not been devised.

Per Lord Reid: 'the object of fencing is to remove the danger which would exist in its absence'. Whether something is dangerous is a question of whether it is a reasonably foreseeable cause of injury. Here, the hazard posed by the equipment justified making the standard of care in fencing one which not only would protect the vigilant, experienced worker but also the lazy and careless worker.

Considering the meaning of the word 'securely' in the context of fencing in a dangerous part of machinery, Lord Morton said that this meant doing so in a manner so as prevent a person working at or near the machinery or his clothing from coming into contact with it.

Bonnington Castings Ltd v Wardlaw

[1956] AC 613, HL

[2.53] The respondent steel dresser contracted pneumoconiosis whilst working for the appellants at their foundry in Leith and he brought a claim against them for personal injury. He was so employed for a period of eight years. The job exposed him to silica dust from the pneumatic hammer and also from swing grinders.

The swing grinders were fitted with a dust extraction plant which was not maintained properly throughout a substantial period, if not the whole, of the respondent's employment. This negligence constituted a breach of regulation 1 of the Grinding of Metals (Miscellaneous Industries) Regulations 1925 which imposed a duty to provide adequate appliances to intercept and remove dust created by certain operations.

There was apparently no equivalent protective equipment for use with a pneumatic hammer at the time and the respondent's complaint related solely to the failure to maintain the dust extraction plant for the swing grinders.

Despite an admitted breach of statutory duty the appellants argued that this had not been a cause of or materially contributed to the respondent's condition.

HELD, in a leading judgment delivered by Lord Reid: That the correct test was one which meant that:

> the employee must, in all cases, prove his case by the ordinary standard of proof in civil actions; he must make it appear at least that, on a balance of probabilities, the breach of duty caused, or materially contributed to, his injury.

The possibility that the breach might have caused the injury would not be enough to found liability. On the facts he had adduced sufficient evidence from which an inference could be drawn that the dust from the swing grinders had materially contributed to the disease.

It is in the nature of pneumoconiosis that it is caused by a gradual accumulation in the lungs of minute particles of silica. This may have come from more than one source but only if it could be established that a de minimus or negligible amount of dust emanated from the swing grinders would the appellants have escaped a finding of liability.

Pigney v Pointers Transport Services Ltd

[1957] 2 All ER 807

[2.54] A first instance decision in which the widow of a lorry driver who had committed suicide 18 months after an accident at work, brought a claim against his employers under the LR(MP)A 1934 and the Fatal Accidents Acts. Her husband had suffered from severe depression and neurosis following the incident in which he had sustained a serious cut to his head. Despite receiving psychiatric treatment, Mr Pigney took his own life. The court found against his employers in negligence in a case which concluded after he had died.

The court also considered a separate issue in fresh proceedings brought by Mrs Pigney namely, whether she was entitled to damages in her own right. Had the fact that Mr Pigney committed suicide broken the chain of causation and further, could she derive a benefit in circumstances in which the deceased had committed a felony, suicide amounting to a felonious act?

HELD: That the plaintiff was entitled to damages due to her husband's death because the Fatal Damages Act 1846 created a new cause of action arising out of a person's death even where this occurred as a result of what amounted to a felony. The Act provided statutory compensation to dependants which does not form part of the deceased's estate. This scenario can be distinguished from a situation in which someone deliberately takes their own life so as to enable their estate to benefit from say, the fruits of a life insurance policy. Accordingly, whilst it was against public policy to allow someone to benefit from a felony, that rule did not apply since the damages awarded belonged to the deceased's widow and did not form part of his estate.

On the facts, the medical evidence was that Mr Pigney's death was directly attributable to the injury which he had sustained at work. He hanged himself during a bout of depression induced by the accident. Whilst his condition did not amount to insanity within the meaning of the M'Naghten rules, he was sufficiently mentally disturbed that he could no longer cope with relatively minor tribulations of life.

Although the deceased was a worrier before the accident this did not absolve the defendants because of the maxim that you must take your victim as you find him.

Clarke v ER Wright & Son

[1957] 3 All ER 486, CA

[2.55] The plaintiff glazier was employed by the first defendants who in turn were sub-contracted by the second defendant building contractors to glaze a house which they were building. The latter had erected scaffolding around the house and the mechanics by which this was secured in position was altered by them at the last minute in anticipation of the plaintiff commencing work. The plaintiff fell, injuring himself in the process, whilst standing on a ladder which he had balanced on planks across the scaffolding. The planks had slipped because they were not as well supported as they were originally before the method of securing them had been changed. His employers had not inspected the scaffolding for safety nor made enquiries about its suitability for their employee to work upon. The court found in favour of the plaintiff against the second defendants.

HELD: Allowing an appeal by the plaintiff against a dismissal of his claim against the first defendants and increasing the award of general damages from £100 to £250, that the plaintiff's employers failure to take *'express'* steps to satisfy themselves as to the stability of the scaffolding placed them in breach of the Building (Safety, Health and Welfare) Regulations 1948.

Further, following the test laid down by Lord Reid in *Bonnington Castings Ltd v Wardlow* [1956] 1 All ER 615 (see 2.53 above), that this breach materially contributed to the injury sustained by the plaintiff. Liability was apportioned as between the defendants in the ratio one-fifth:four-fifths, reflecting the greater duty on the second defendants who were in charge of the site and who had erected the scaffolding, to ensure its safety.

Nicholson v Atlas Steel Foundry and Engineering Co Ltd

[1957] 1 All ER 776, HL

[2.56] Mr Nicholson, the appellants' husband and father, worked for an aggregate of nine years over a 15-year period for the respondents at their steel foundry. It was his job to dress metal castings using a pneumatic hammer. This process caused silica dust to be emitted. The section of the factory where Mr Nicholson worked lacked ventilation apart from doors through which vehicles passed. In close proximity were two swing frame grinders which did not have dust extraction equipment.

Two years after leaving the respondent's employment, Mr Nicholson died of pneumoconiosis, a progressive disease contracted from silica dust. The appellants' claim cited, first, a failure to provide adequate means of circulating fresh air and rendering harmless impurities in the air in breach of section 4(1); second, a breach of statutory duty under regulation 1 of the Grinding of Metals (Miscellaneous Industries)

Regulations 1925 in respect of the absence of a dust extraction system for the swing grinders; and third, negligence at common law.

HELD: Following the test laid down in *Bonnington Castings Ltd v Wardlaw* [1956] 1 All ER 615 (see 2.53 above), namely 'that a contribution is material unless the maxim "de minimis" can be applied to it,' that the respondents were in breach of FA 1937, s 4(1).

The most dangerous particles of silica are light ones which rise. Improved ventilation in the dressing shop would have more rapidly dispersed the dust cloud and reduced its concentration. Thus, although no fault attached to the respondents in respect of the generation of silica dust from the operation of the hammer, their failure to provide adequate ventilation, particularly in the roof area above Mr Nicholson's working area, exposed him to a greater risk of contracting the fatal illness than otherwise would have been the case. Prolonged exposure to silica particles contributed to his illness to a material degree.

It having been established that dust from the hammer was a material cause of Mr Nicholson's illness, it was unnecessary to consider what proportion of dust emanated from the swing frame grinders.

Clarkson v Modern Foundries Ltd

[1958] 1 All ER 33 (Donovan J)

[2.57] The plaintiff worked for the defendants over an eleven-year period from 1940–1951 as a metal dresser in their iron foundry. The operations carried out in the factory produced a quantity of dust and although he was supplied with a mask he was still exposed to dust when he worked without the mask on.

In 1951 the plaintiff discovered that he was suffering from pneumoconiosis which had developed as a result of breathing in silica particles in the factory. In an action against the defendants for negligence and breach of statutory duty which was issued in August 1955 the court considered whether liability in damages would be limited to the exposure post August 1949 by virtue of Limitation Act 1939, s 2(1).

HELD, at first instance: That the defendants were in breach of their statutory duty inter alia in failing to provide adequate ventilation and a means of removing impurities in the air contrary to FA 1937, s 4, and further that there had been a breach of regulation 1 of the Grinding of Metals (Miscellaneous Industries) Regulations 1925. On the question of whether the breaches had caused or materially contributed to the disease it was a reasonable inference that the breach of section 4(1) alone had made a material contribution to the disease.

Applying *Bonnington Castings Ltd v Wardlaw* [1956] 1 All ER 615 (see 2.53 above), Donovan J also held that the plaintiff was entitled to recover damages for the whole injury since exposure to dust after 1949 had materially contributed to his illness. The onus would have been on the defendants to prove that Mr Clarkson's illness was contracted before the cut-off date when in fact they could only prove that an unidentifiable part of his injuries related to the earlier period.

Quinn v Cameron & Roberton Ltd

[1958] AC 9, HL

[2.58] The appellant was a grinder at the respondents' Kirkintilloch iron foundry from 1942–1951 and contracted pneumoconiosis which he attributed to his working environment. The work at the factory involved iron castings being cast in sand in moulding boxes. They were then knocked out and most of the sand was removed in the moulding shop before being taken to the dressing shop where the appellant worked.

In the dressing area superfluous metal and remaining sand was removed by a grinding machine, known as a plough buff, operated by the appellant. This comprised a frame hinged at one end to a vertical grinder. The frame contained carborundum, a silica carbide. There was no means of drawing off the dust, including silica dust, which operation of the plough buff generated. Inhalation of this dust causes pneumoconiosis. Accordingly, those working in the shop were exposed to an inherently dangerous substance.

The material issue concerned the extent of the obligations of ironfounders to employees at common law and under regulations made under the FA 1937.

HELD: That the respondents were guilty of breach of statutory regulation. The duty to provide proper ventilation equipment under regulation 1 of the Grinding of Metals (Miscellaneous Industries) Regulations 1925 was absolute. The regulation gave examples of some types of appliances (such as a fan or duct) which should be used to intercept and remove dust in discharge of this duty. No such safeguards had been deployed and accordingly the respondents were in breach of statutory regulation.

It was further held that operation of the plough buff fell within the definition of 'grinding' within the regulations. Approving *Bonnington Castings Ltd*, there was a sufficient causal nexus between the respondents' regulatory breach and the appellant's disease. In order to ground a claim the breach must have caused or made a material contribution to the injury. Viscount Simonds confirmed that 'a contribution is material unless the maxim "de minimis non curat lex" can be applied to it'.

The appellant was entitled to rely on the breach of regulation because his job involved grinding and the purpose of the regulations was to protect workmen against the danger caused by the dust emitted during such an operation.

Nolan v Dental Manufacturing Co Ltd

[1958] 2 All ER 449, Manchester Assizes

[2.59] The plaintiff was an experienced toolsetter in the defendants' factory. Part of his daily job entailed sharpening tools using a carborundum wheel several times during the day. This task occupied no more than a half hour in total. Whilst the risk of accident was minute, the injuries which might result from this activity could be severe. Like many of his colleagues, the evidence given by the plaintiff was that he did not see any need to wear goggles and he had never in fact done so. He lost his left eye when a chip flew off the wheel whilst he was sharpening tools.

The defendants kept some protective eyewear in the factory but had not provided the plaintiff with any when he was operating the wheel, in breach of FA 1937, s 49 and the Protection of Eyes Regulations 1938. These imposed a duty to provide protective eyewear to those engaged in dry grinding of metals where there was a special risk of eye injury.

There were neither proper notices reminding employees of the availability of protective spectacles nor was an adequate supply of goggles kept for use by a number of machines simultaneously. Mr Nolan brought a claim based on negligence and breach of statutory duty.

HELD, applying *Bonnington Castings Ltd v Wardlaw* [1956] 1 All ER 615 (see 2.53 above): That the claim based on breach of statutory duty failed because the plaintiff had not demonstrated that his injury was caused by the defendants' breach of statutory duty. This was because the plaintiff was unable to satisfy the court that he would have worn goggles.

Approving *Haynes v Qualcast (Wolverhampton) Ltd* [1958] 1 All ER 441 (see 2.11 above), that the defendants had a duty to provide a safe system of work by taking reasonable steps to ensure that someone was not exposed to unnecessary risk. This meant: (a) providing safety equipment, and (b) ensuring that it was used. In the context of the accident there was therefore a breach of their common law duty not to expose the plaintiff to unreasonable risk of harm. In the factual matrix here there was an appreciable likelihood of serious injury occurring in the event of an accident, albeit that the risks of accident were not considered to be great. As a corollary, the defendants should have taken steps to ensure that goggles were worn by means of express orders and strict supervision.

AC Billings & Sons Ltd v Riden

[1958] AC 240, HL

[2.60] The respondent was injured during a fall into an unfenced sunken area of land. The accident happened when she was leaving a house in Cheltenham occupied by her friends, a caretaker and his wife, late one November evening.

Normal access to the property via a ramp had been blocked by the appellant contractors who were instructed by the Ministry of Works to remove the ramp. As a temporary measure the contractors recommended to the caretaker's wife that anyone entering or leaving the property should do so by the forecourt of the neighbouring property, around the muddy front of the two properties, then to step up some 2–3 feet onto the ramp near the front door of her house. In order to facilitate this route the contractors removed a side fence. The pathway so exposed was dangerous because it meant traversing an area close to an unfenced sunken part of the next door property.

This information was relayed to the respondent by the caretaker's wife who successfully negotiated the journey when she entered the property but lost her footing as she left, falling into the sunken area next door in the process. The question posed in the appeal concerned the extent of the duty owed by contractors to third parties in relation to a risk of danger created by them.

HELD, dismissing an appeal against a ruling by the Court of Appeal: That the appellants be held liable to the respondent in damages, such damages to be reduced by 50% on grounds of contributory negligence; that the contractors were negligent and that the respondent was entitled to damages albeit reduced on account of her contributory negligence in that she had declined to be escorted.

Per Lord Reid, the appellant contractors:

> owed a duty to all persons who might be expected lawfully to visit the house, and that duty was the ordinary duty to take such care, as in all the circumstances of the case, was reasonable to ensure that visitors were not exposed to danger by their actions.

This included everyone who might reasonably be expected to visit the property and to protect them from danger on an adjacent property when the need to enter such land was the direct result of their conduct in blocking off the normal route of entry to the house.

The fact that the respondent had voluntarily used the alternative route of access cognisant of the hazard did not defeat her claim because it could not be said that the risk was not one which no ordinary and sensible person would have taken.

Qualcast (Wolverhampton) Ltd v Haynes

[1959] AC 743, HL

[2.61] The respondent was an experienced moulder working with molten metal at the appellants Wolverhampton factory. He sustained an injury to his left foot when he slipped whilst carrying a ladle of hot metal. His employers kept a supply of protective 'spats' but they had not insisted on his donning them apparently because of his experience in the job. The respondent had chosen not to wear spats either before or after the incident when he returned to work.

In a claim against his employers the county court judge found no negligence on the part of the foundry but considered that he ought make a finding of liability against them because of existing legal authority. Both at first instance and on appeal the court held that the respondent was three-quarters liable for the accident and his employers one quarter liable.

The material issue on appeal was whether the appellants had provided the respondent with protective clothing as a matter of common law, there being no specific statutory duty to provide workmen with protective footwear.

HELD, allowing an appeal by the employers: That the issue of whether reasonable care had been taken by an employer was one of fact and that in this instance there was no negligence on the employers' part.

Lord Radcliffe commented that whilst there may be cases where an employer's duty is not discharged simply by making available protective equipment, courts should be slow to find against them solely because no order was given insisting on such equipment being regularly used. The duty owed towards an employee will vary and is not identical in every case, for example, it depends on the degree of experience and knowledge of a given employee.

It is perhaps noteworthy that the respondent's evidence was disbelieved in that he alleged first, that he had tripped on some obstacle and second, that he was not provided with spats. These facts were not proven. There was a suggestion that perhaps if he instead had pleaded a failure to advise him to use the spats the outcome might have been different.

(See also at 2.11 above.)

Rushton v Turner Bros Asbestos Co Ltd

[1959] 3 All ER 517 (Ashworth J)

[2.62] The plaintiff was a fibre packer. His duties included operating equipment known as a fibre crushing machine. Although he understood from the training which he had received at work that he was not to clean grooves in the machine without first stopping it and he was given a knife with which to perform this task, the plaintiff nevertheless attempted to clean an obstruction both whilst the machine was moving and with his bare hand. Compounding his folly he knew that this manoeuvre was particularly dangerous on the day because of an earlier breakage of part of machine. Because of his actions the plaintiff's fingers were crushed and he underwent partial amputation of four of them.

HELD: That despite a breach of statutory duty by the defendants under FA 1937, s 14(1), namely a failure to fence a dangerous part of machinery, they were not liable in damages to the plaintiff because the operative cause of injury was the plaintiff's negligence in putting his hand into the rotating machine. Ashworth J described the plaintiff's act as 'about as foolish a piece of negligence as anyone could conceive.'

The decision reached in this case is an illustration of the principle that if a claimant is the sole author of his misfortune then he will be barred from recovering damages notwithstanding breach of statutory duty.

Ward v TE Hopkins & Son Ltd

[1959] 3 All ER 225, CA

[2.63] A tragic accident took place in a well at Tadser Farm in Derby county in which three people died, two workmen employed by the defendants, the other, Dr Baker, a doctor who died in a failed rescue bid. The first plaintiff, Mrs Ward, was the widow of one of the workmen, the second plaintiffs being the executors of Dr Baker.

The defendant building contractors were engaged to clean the well which meant first emptying it of water. The managing director, Mr Hopkins, together with two employees, including Mr Ward, erected a platform 29 feet down the well on which they set a petrol-driven pump. The engine generated lethal odourless carbon monoxide gas. Mr Hopkins noticed a haze of gas and next morning instructed the workmen not to enter the well until he arrived although he failed to spell out the risks if they ignored him. Contrary to his orders the two men descended the well without him and were overcome by fumes. Dr Baker who attempted their rescue also died when the rope he was secured by became snagged on an obstruction.

An action was brought against the defendant employers under the Fatal Accidents Acts 1846 to 1908 and the LR(MP)A 1934 for negligently causing the deaths. At first instance the court found in favour of both plaintiffs but held that Mr Ward's damages should be reduced by 10% on grounds of contributory negligence. The defendant company appealed against this finding and against the amount of damages sought by the doctor's estate.

HELD: That the defendants were liable because the system used to empty the well was extremely unsafe, creating lethal conditions for anyone entering it and, that further, no explicit warning of the danger was given. The instruction not to go down was insufficiently precise to discharge the defendants' duty of care although the apportionment of liability in the case of Mr Ward would stand. Expert advice was not sought by Mr Hopkins who had not appreciated the degree of danger presented by the noxious fumes.

Applying *Haynes v Harwood* [1935] 1 KB 146, CA (see 2.39 above), the defendants were liable in negligence for the doctor's death. It was a natural and foreseeable consequence of their negligence that a rescue attempt would be launched. A doctor in particular was likely to be summoned. Dr Baker, said Morris LJ, placed his own life in danger 'prompted by the finest instincts of humanity'. He acted courageously without being foolhardy. Unreasonable disregard for his own safety can defeat a rescuer's claim but conduct will be judged from the rescuer's perspective, ie as events appeared to him. Danger invites rescue and the courts are reluctant in these circumstances to criticise a rescuer's conduct.

The classic definition of neighbours in *Donoghue v Stevenson* [1931] AC 562, [1932] All ER Rep 1 was followed. These are persons 'who are so closely and directly affected by my act that I ought reasonably to have them in contemplation as being so affected when I am directing my mind to the acts or omissions which are called in question'. Rescuers fall within the class of persons whose actions are likely to follow from a grave situation in which life and limb is put in peril and only immediate action might assist.

Corn v Weir's Glass (Hanley) Ltd (L Bates Ltd Third Party)

[1960] 2 All ER 300, CA

[2.64] The plaintiff glazier employed by the defendants fell whilst descending a short flight of stairs in a building under construction. He was carrying a sheet of glass measuring five feet by two and a half feet using both hands when he lost his balance falling a couple of feet.

The plaintiff brought an action for negligence and breach of statutory duty focusing upon regulation 27(1) of the Building (Safety, Health and Welfare) Regulations 1948 made under the FA 1937. This imposed a duty to provide stairs 'with hand-rails or other efficient means to prevent the fall of persons except for the time and to the extent necessary for the access of persons or the movement of materials'.

HELD, dismissing an appeal by the plaintiff: That there was a breach of statutory duty on the part of the defendants but the claim nevertheless failed.

As a matter of interpretation the regulation applied to partially completed stairs. Further, the defendants could not assert that there was no hand-rail in order to facilitate equipment being carried.

However, following *Bonnington Castings Ltd v Wardlaw* (see 2.53 above), the claim failed because Mr Corn had failed to establish that a hand-rail would have averted the injury as he had no free hand to hold onto any such rail. The plaintiff must show that on balance of probabilities the breach of duty caused or materially contributed to his injury. Devlin LJ commented that the court should consider how the regulation would have been complied with. If there is more than one means of doing so, one of which might have protected the plaintiff, but it is unknown which method would have been adopted, the claim fails.

Gardiner v Motherwell Machinery and Scrap Co Ltd

[1961] 3 All ER 831n, HL

[2.65] The appellant worked for the respondents from May to August 1955 demolishing buildings and boilers. This work was likely to cause dermatitis which he contracted, the disease spreading from his hands to the whole of his body. He brought a claim against his employers at common law in respect of their failure to provide proper washing amenities. The material issue was whether the appellant's injury could be attributed to his work on which the medical evidence had been divided.

HELD, in a leading judgment delivered by Lord Reid, allowing the appeal: That the appellant had not suffered from dermatitis prior to being exposed by his employers to the conditions likely to cause the disease. When someone contracts a disease after being subjected to conditions likely to cause it and shows that it starts in a way typical of disease caused by such conditions, there is a prima facie presumption that the disease was caused by those conditions. Whilst this presumption can be displaced, it had not been done so here.

Curran v William Neill & Son (St Helens) Ltd

[1961] 3 All ER 108, CA

[2.66] The plaintiff was employed by the defendant steel erectors in erecting a gutter between bays in a factory roof. The gutter was supposed to have an overlay consisting of ten foot pieces bolted to each other. Because of industrial action the intended method of securing the overlay was not used. Whilst walking along the guttering the plaintiff fell 23 feet onto a concrete floor. The accident was due to a defective hook bolt which meant that the gutter was unstable, the section Mr Curran was walking on pivoted on its central strap and the supporting strap gave way. At first instance the court found for the defendants since the breakage was not foreseeable.

HELD, dismissing the plaintiff's appeal in his action for negligence and breach of statutory duty under the Building (Safety, Health and Welfare) Regulations 1948:

52 Common Law Liability

Whilst there was a breach of statutory duty by the defendants in failing to provide a guard rail of adequate strength in a working place from which a person might fall more than six feet six inches, non-compliance with the regulation had not caused the accident. Although a court should not be astute to find that the breach did not cause the accident 'that only means that one approaches with benevolence and sympathy the argument put forward by the plaintiff ' – Holroyd Pearce LJ.

On the facts there was no separate duty to provide scaffolding nor did the gutter constitute a working platform, gangway or scaffold to which further regulations would have applied. Accordingly, no amendment of the claim to encompass these additional regulations was allowed.

Cummings (or Mcwilliams) v Sir William Arrol & Co Ltd

[1962] 1 All ER 623, HL

[2.67] An experienced steel erector fell 70 feet to his death from a steel tower under construction at the Kingston shipyard at Port Glasgow. His estate sought damages for negligence against his employers and from the occupiers of the shipyard for breach of statutory duty under FA 1937, s 26(2) in respect of a failure to provide him with a safety belt. Had he worn a belt it would have saved his life.

Safety belts had been removed from the site shortly before the accident but there was compelling evidence that the deceased would not have used one. It was not mandatory for them to be worn.

HELD, dismissing an appeal by the estate for damages: That, notwithstanding any obligation to provide safety equipment, any breach of duty was not causative of the injury because first, there was overwhelming evidence that the deceased would not have agreed to wear a safety belt and second, his employers were not under a duty to insist that he did so.

An interesting consideration was whether employees should have been ordered to wear safety belts. Citing Lord Radcliffe in *Qualcast (Wolverhampton) Ltd v Haynes* [1959] 2 All ER 38 (see 2.61 above), Viscount Kilmuir LC agreed that courts should be circumspect about saying that the duty on an employer extends beyond providing safety equipment to requiring employees to use it. He was disinclined to find that the defendants should have insisted on belts being worn in this case for two reasons. There was an established practice amongst steel erectors not to wear safety belts, which were considered to be cumbersome and dangerous except in special circumstances. Furthermore, the language of reg 97 Building (Safety, Health and Welfare) Regulations 1948 (relied upon in *Roberts v Dorman Long & Co Ltd* [1953] 2 All ER 428) makes use of this type of safety equipment voluntary.

Close v Steel Co of Wales Ltd

[1962] AC 367, HL

[2.68] The appellant instrument machinist suffered an eye injury whilst operating an electric drill at the respondents' Glamorganshire factory when the high speed steel bit shattered causing fragments to strike him. Mr Close sought damages from his employers at common law and for breach of statutory duty under FA 1937, s 14(1) in respect of an alleged failure to securely fence off every dangerous part of any machinery. The material question was whether this duty extended to fencing parts of a machine which might fly off or break causing injury to the operator and if so whether the degree of danger must be foreseeable.

HELD: In an appeal by Mr Close against the Court of Appeal's dismissal of his claim for breach of statutory duty, dismissing the appeal and finding in the respondents favour, that the risk of serious injury was not reasonably foreseeable. The bit was not a 'dangerous part of any machinery' within s 14(1).

As a matter of general principle the House reaffirmed the decisions of *Nicholls v F Austin (Leyton) Ltd* [1946] AC 493 and *Carroll v Andrew Barclay & Sons Ltd* [1948] AC 477. The duty to fence under s 14(1) is confined to keeping someone away from moving parts of a machine, rather than preventing injury from broken off pieces from the machine or material on which a machine might be working. The latter can be separately regulated.

However, if in a factory there is a machine which has a tendency to throw out parts of the machine or material on which it is working so as to be a danger to the operator the absence of a protective shield may well ground an action at common law (Lord Goddard).

Lord Denning cited the established test of foreseeability laid down by Wills J in *Hindle v Birtwistle* [1897] 1 QB 192, namely that 'machinery or parts of machinery is and are dangerous if in the ordinary course of human affairs danger may be reasonably anticipated from the use of them without protection'. Something that happens regularly can be a reasonably foreseeable cause of injury. If the item in question is then not fenced a claim might lie.

The equipment in this case was one which people often used at home as well as at work and whilst the bit might be prone to breaking there was no evidence of earlier accidents. This was because the broken fragments tend to be small and light and the possibility of serious injury was therefore extremely remote. For this reason the wearing of goggles had not been mooted previously.

Smith v Leech Brain & Co Ltd

[1962] 2 QB 405, CA

[2.69] A fatal accidents claim was brought by the widow of the deceased against her late husband's employers alleging negligence and breach of statutory duty under the FA 1937 in respect of their failure to provide a safe system of work. Mr Smith had been a labourer and galvaniser at the defendants' Poplar iron works. His job included lowering items by crane into a tank filled with molten metal which was maintained at a temperature of 400 degrees centigrade and then removing galvanised articles. His back was usually facing a firebrick wall and he was supplied with a protective corrugated iron sheet.

In 1950, whilst performing this task, he poked his head round the shield and sustained a burn to his lower lip when spattered by some hot metal. The wound ulcerated, triggering cancer in pre-malignant lip tissue, from which he died three years later. Although the deceased was prone to cancer, there was no certainty that it would have developed but for the accident, although it might equally have developed in any event.

HELD, by Lord Parker CJ: That on the issue of liability, the defendants were negligent at common law in failing to protect the deceased from a foreseeable risk of harm, namely the clear and known danger of being injured by molten metal when undertaking the operation in question. In these circumstances it would have been foreseeable to a reasonable employer that a workman, unless protected, would be liable to be struck by molten metal and badly injured. Sooner or later it was natural that someone would look around the temporary corrugated screen. The actual protection afforded was described by counsel for the plaintiff as 'Heath Robinson'.

In so far as the deceased had a pre-disposition to illness, the maxim that a tortfeasor must take his victim as he finds him applied. This is colloquially known as the 'thin skull' rule. The correct test was whether the employer could reasonably have foreseen the type of injury which occurred, that is, a burn, and the fact that the consequences were in fact more severe did not absolve the defendants from liability. Here 'the burn did contribute to, or cause in part, at any rate, the cancer and the death'.

Wigley v British Vinegars Ltd

[1964] AC 307, HL

[2.70] The deceased, an experienced window cleaner who operated in business as 'Ever Ready Cleaning Services', fell 30 feet to his death whilst cleaning a swinging window in the respondents' factory premises. Mr Wigley's services had been engaged as an independent contractor and he had previously cleaned the window approximately a dozen times.

Immediately before the accident Mr Wigley was standing on a ladder balanced inside the building. The ladder had been provided by the respondents and was perfectly good although it lacked hooks or bars to which a safety belt could have been attached. One part of the window did not have a catch to fasten it closed. This meant that the deceased needed to hold it closed using one hand whilst using the other hand to clean it.

The deceased's widow brought a claim based on an alleged breach of FA 1937, s 26(2) in respect of the respondents alleged failure to ensure her late husband's safety whilst working at a height of more than ten feet at a place without a secure foothold or handhold. The claim was dismissed.

HELD, dismissing an appeal: That, following *Lavender v Diamints Ltd* [1949] 1 KB 585, CA, FA 1937, s 26 applied both to an independent contractor and one of its employees. Viscount Kilmuir clarified that the words 'any person' in subsections (1) and (2) meant a distinction between 'those who are to work for the purposes of the factory and those who are not'. Maintenance embraced cleaning windows and constituted work for the factory but the provision would not protect firemen, policemen or film actors on a film shoot.

There was no breach of duty under section 26(2) because the 'place from which' the deceased 'was liable to fall' was the ladder which had both a secure foothold and handhold. The fact of an accident does not convert a secure foothold or handhold into one which is inadequate.

On the evidence the appellant had also failed to prove that her husband would have worn a safety belt. Accordingly, following *Cummings v Sir William Arrol & Co Ltd* [1962] 1 WLR 295, any claim based on breach of statutory duty would have failed on causation. A plaintiff needed to prove on balance of probabilities both that the safety measures would have been effective and that the injured person would have made use of them.

Allen v Aeroplane and Motor Aluminium Castings Ltd

[1965] 3 All ER 377, CA

[2.71] A recently recruited school leaver aged 15, working in the defendants' factory, caught his finger between a conveyor belt and some bars in a machine. The circumstances of the accident were unclear and at the trial of a claim brought on his behalf by his father and next friend, based on a breach of statutory duty in failing to securely fence every dangerous part of any machinery under the Factories Act 1961, s 14(1), the trial judge rejected the youth's account and dismissed his case concluding that he had been 'on a frolic of his own' at the time.

HELD, by Sellers LJ allowing an appeal: That the boy was employed at the defendants' premises and but for the breach of statutory duty the accident would not have happened.

Despite the absence of credible evidence of what took place and even were the youth on a frolic of his own, he was nevertheless entitled to damages – *Uddin v Associated Portland Cement Manufacturers Ltd* [1965] 1 All ER 347 followed. The issue was not whether the employee, when injured, was injured in the course of his employment, but that he was employed at the premises.

> *Note*: Sellers LJ made it clear that this was 'an exceptional case' - the facts demonstrated that the accident would not have happened but for the 'dangerous nip'.

Taylor v Rover Co Ltd (Richard W Carr & Co Ltd, third party)

[1966] 2 All ER 181, Birmingham Assizes

[2.72] The plaintiff lost an eye after being struck by a steel splinter from a chisel made from alloyed steel. He and a superior, Mr Jones, were the only ones to use this defective chisel on the factory assembly line. Some weeks before the accident Mr Jones hurt his cheek when a piece flew off the same chisel, yet he failed to withdraw the instrument from use.

The first defendants were the plaintiff's employers, the second, the company which fashioned the chisel according to specifications and a blue print provided by the first defendants. The third party supplied and then heat treated the steel alloy (a hardening process) for the second defendants after it had been fashioned. The incident was caused by negligent heat treatment of the chisel by the third party. The first defendants sought to pass the blame onto the second defendants on the grounds that they would have known that the former would not test the chisel for safety.

HELD: In relation to the question as to whether there was a reasonable probability of independent testing of the tool by the first defendants once it had left the second defendants' hands, that this was unlikely.

The first defendants however had actual knowledge of a defect. Their failure to withdraw the chisel from circulation knowing that it was dangerous meant that they were liable. The second defendants escaped liability (a) because the chain of causation was broken by the first defendants' continued use of the tool after the first accident, and (b) because they had engaged a competent third party to harden the chisel and were entitled to assume that the tool had been hardened properly.

> Note—as a general rule, Baker J commented on whether someone can ever be responsible for negligence or breach of duty by a third party. A manufacturer's duty extends beyond parts of a product which he manufactures to components supplied by others. The manufacturer must take reasonable care, by inspection or otherwise, to see that components can properly be used.

Quinn v Burch Bros (Builders) Ltd

[1966] 2 QB 370, CA

[2.73] The plaintiff plasterer and builder was engaged as an independent sub-contractor by the defendants to carry out plastering work on a building site in Lewisham. The defendants agreed to supply the plaintiff's firm with all equipment as was reasonably necessary to perform its job within a reasonable time of a request being made.

In order to work upon the ceilings, the plaintiff asked for a step-ladder. However, when this did not materialise, he chose to make use of a folded trestle table as a substitute. Because of its width someone was needed to hold onto the bottom rung to prevent it slipping. Mr Quinn's colleague had already left the premises and he decided to proceed alone, falling when the table slipped. The plaintiff sought damages for breach of contract on the grounds that the defendants had failed to supply him with the appropriate equipment. At first instance the judge found the defendants in breach of contract in failing to supply the ladder but that the claim failed on causation.

HELD, dismissing the plaintiff's appeal: That the claim failed on grounds of causation. Sellers LJ cast doubt on whether on the facts the defendants were in breach of contract in failing to provide a step-ladder. However, even were there to have been a breach, this had not give risen to the damage suffered by the plaintiff. The plaintiff could have purchased his own ladder and charged the defendants for it.

Further, although the lack of a ladder might have led the defendants to foresee the resulting accident, this was not the immediate cause of the injury, merely the setting in which it took place. The plaintiff was not obliged to proceed with the work in the absence of a ladder but voluntarily chose to do so. His injury was not a natural and probable consequence of the breach of contract but the result of the plaintiff's failure to take reasonable precautions for his own safety before he used the trestle table.

Note—this claim was not one between a master and servant, nor a claim based on tort or the provision of faulty equipment, but one of pure breach of contract. Foreseeability of injury is the true criterion when negligence is in issue. In contract claims foreseeability determines whether damages are too remote – damages that is, which are caused by the breach of contract. The issue of recoverability is whether the damage sustained was reasonably foreseeable when the contract was entered into as likely to result from its breach.

James v Hepworth & Grandage Ltd

[1968] 1 QB 94, CA

[2.74] The plaintiff was, unbeknown to his employers, illiterate. After working for them for over three years he applied for work in their foundry as a metal spinner. Following a four-week induction period he worked for six months as a spinner when he sustained an injury to his foot and leg whilst pouring molten metal which splashed on him.

The safety equipment he was given comprised goggles, gloves and boots but he was not informed verbally about safety spats. Two prominent notices in the workshop said that the safety equipment, including spats, was available and should be worn. The plaintiff, despite his learning deficiency, did not ask his colleagues what the notices said. Only two out of 24 of the workmen opted to wear spats, the prevailing view being that they were no safer than trousers.

The plaintiff's claim against the defendants was upheld at first instance on grounds that the latter had negligently failed to make available spats to him by virtue of his inability to read the notices.

HELD, allowing an appeal by the defendants: That employers have a duty to take reasonable care for the safety of their workmen. In the present instance this entailed making provision for spats, informing employees of their availability and letting them make their choice. The defendants had given adequate notice of the availability of spats by the notice board and also the plaintiff had seen people wearing them. The defendants were not obliged to investigate whether employees could read and write when they had no reason to suspect to the contrary, and since the availability of the spats was averted to in the notices, they had not been negligent.

Further, even had they negligently failed to make available spats, the claim failed on causation, it being unlikely that the plaintiff would have chosen to wear spats.

Barnett v Chelsea and Kensington Hospital Management Committee

[1969] 1 QB 428, QBD

[2.75] Three night watchmen attended the casualty department of St Stephen's Hospital, Chelsea, complaining of prolonged vomiting after drinking tea on their shift on New Year's Day 1966. The nurse relayed their symptoms to a duty medical casualty officer by telephone and she was told to advise the men to go home to bed and call their own doctors. Five hours later one of the men died from arsenic poisoning. The medical evidence strongly suggested that the deceased would probably have died even had he been admitted to hospital.

Mr Barnett's widow brought a claim on behalf of his estate against the defendants who were responsible for managing St Stephens, alleging negligence in failing either to diagnose or treat her late husband.

HELD, by Nield J dismissing the claim: that the health authority were responsible for the actions of their casualty department. That department owes a duty to a patient to exercise the average amount of competence associated with a nurse and medical casualty officer even if someone is not admitted into a ward.

The defendants were in breach of duty to the deceased in that the casualty officer was negligent in not having seen and examined him, admitting him to a ward and treating him. However, since his death was inevitable, the plaintiff had failed to establish on balance of probabilities that the defendants' negligence was the cause of death.

Farmer v Rash

[1969] 1 All ER 705, QBD (Willis J)

[2.76] A year after being seriously injured by the defendant motor cyclist who ran him down whilst he was on a pedestrian crossing, Sidney Ward committed suicide. Although Mr Ward appeared to be making a good recovery from his injuries, he began to suffer from depression. He received psychiatric treatment in hospital for a month before he took his own life. The coroner recorded an open verdict.

Mr Ward was living with a woman and their child before his death and was also supporting his estranged wife and their son. Having bequeathed his entire estate to his partner, his wife issued proceedings under the Inheritance (Family Provision) Act 1938. Separate proceedings were brought by the deceased's executor against the defendant in respect of his death, under the LR(MP)A 1934 and under the Fatal Accidents Acts 1846 to 1959.

HELD, in an application to endorse a settlement of the case: That monies paid into court by the defendant should be attributed to a claim under the Law Reform Act because a contested Fatal Accidents Act claim was unlikely to have succeeded. On the evidence it was felt that the estate may have been in difficulty in establishing on balance of probabilities that there was a causal link between the accident and the deceased's depression and that the latter had caused the death. Lapse of time between an accident and death would not necessarily preclude a claim but, the longer the time lag, the weaker is the probability of a causative link being established.

McKew v Holland & Hannen & Cubitts (Scotland) Ltd

[1969] 3 All ER 1621, HL

[2.77] After a minor accident at work which was the respondent employers' fault, the appellant would occasionally, and without warning, lose control of his left leg. He would have recovered from his injuries fairly speedily but for a further injury when he fell down a steep flight of stairs suffering a severe ankle fracture. The staircase had no hand rail and, sensing that he was about to fall, the appellant leapt, landing badly. He had started to descend the stairs on his own although he could have sought assistance from either his wife or brother-in-law both of whom were close by. The appellant sought to hold the respondents liable for the second accident.

HELD, dismissing the appeal: That the chain of causation had been broken by the appellant in that he had acted unreasonably in attempting the descent on his own or without a stick or other support notwithstanding that his leg had '*gone away*' from him previously. Accordingly, the second accident was not the natural and probable result of the first one.

Per Lord Reid: if someone 'is injured in such a way that his leg may give way at any moment he must act reasonably and carefully'. Only if that person takes proper care can he or she recover for a second injury. Unreasonable conduct '*is* novus actus interveniens'. Here it was the fact that the appellant had started to descend the stairs unaided thus putting himself in peril that went against him rather than the act of jumping once an emergency had arisen.

Dicta of Lord Wright in *Lord v Pacific Steam Navigation Co Ltd, The Oropesa* [1943] 1 All ER 211 (see 2.42 above) followed.

FE Callow (Engineers) Ltd v Johnson
[1970] 3 All ER 639, HL

[2.78] The respondent operated a piece of boring machinery, known as a Ward 10 lathe, at the appellants' Skelmersdale factory. There was an unfenced gap between a boring bar and the bore to which a cutting implement was attached. The respondent as a matter of routine used a 'squeezie' bottle belonging to him to inject coolant onto the inside of the cutting tool instead of relying on an automated system. The appellants knew of but did not condone use of a squeezie. The respondent lost three fingers when he reached out for the squeezie and somehow slipped. In attempting to steady himself his hand became trapped in the machine between the rotating inside of the workpiece and the boring bar. He asserted breach of statutory duty by his employers in failing to fence a dangerous part of machinery contrary to the Factories Act 1961, s 14(1).

HELD: That, although the movement of the boring bar was imperceptible to the naked eye and could be regarded as stationary, when the machine was working there was a dangerous nip between the boring bar and the workpiece and accordingly the boring bar became a dangerous part of the machinery. It was immaterial once a dangerous nip appears if this is the result of two moving parts or the interaction of one moving and one stationary part of a machine.

The appellants had breached section 14(1) because they knew that the respondent and other employees made manual use of squeezies to insert coolant into the equipment. It was foreseeable that one of them might inadvertently place his hand too far inside trapping it in a nip between the boring bar and the workpiece and causing an accident of the type which occurred.

Damages were reduced by one third on grounds of contributory negligence because the plaintiff had deliberately incurred a risk to himself in placing his hand between the boring bar and the back of the workpiece.

Note—Fenton Atkinson LJ in the Court of Appeal appears to have taken a critical view of the manner in which the case had been pleaded by the respondent and, in particular, the fact that use of the squeezie was not mentioned in the original statement of claim but was first referred to in the defence. He attributed this to the fact that the respondent must have realised that use of the hand held bottle was dangerous.

Lord Hailsham LC, on further appeal, affirmed the principle in *Allen v Aeroplane and Motor Aluminium Castings Ltd* [1965] 3 All ER 377, CA, namely, that once it is established by the plaintiff on the balance of probabilities that there was a breach of section 14 and that the accident occurred as a result of that breach, it does not matter that he is unable to establish exactly how the accident came about.

Whether a part of machinery is dangerous and thus creates a foreseeable risk of injury includes where the danger is present for skilled prudent workers as well as careless inattentive workers. Danger is dependent on the machine being in operation at the time.

Home Office v Dorset Yacht Co Ltd

[1970] AC 1004, HL

[2.79] The respondent's yacht, *Silver Mist*, was damaged at night by a group of seven Borstal boys who had been working on Brownsea Island near Poole Harbour in the custody of the Portland Borstal institution and whilst under the supervision of three officers. The boys absconded, appropriating a vessel which collided with the *Silver Mist*, which they then damaged.

The respondent brought a claim based on the officers' negligence in failing properly to control the youths in circumstances in which they maintained that an escape bid was foreseeable. All seven had criminal records and the officers ignored instructions in leaving the boys to their own devices when they went to bed.

A preliminary issue was heard on the question of whether the Home Office owed a duty of care to third parties giving rise to a liability in damages.

HELD, applying dicta of Lord Atkin in *Donoghue v Stevenson* [1932] AC 562, dismissing an appeal by the Home Office: That public policy would not, in the circumstances, prevent the officers owing the respondent a duty to take such care in the exercise of their powers of control as was reasonable in all the circumstances in order to prevent the boys under their care from causing damage to the respondent's property if that was a happening of which there was a manifest and obvious risk.

Whether a duty was owed to someone who suffers loss depends on whether they can reasonably be foreseen to have been at risk. In the case of escaping inmates, those with property in the vicinity of the place of detention, or likely to suffer damage from the detainees in the course of eluding immediate pursuit and recapture would be likely to be owed such a duty.

Per Lord Reid, commenting on Lord Atkin's 'neighbour' speech: 'the time has come when we can and should say that it ought to apply unless there is some justification or valid explanation for its exclusion'.

The argument against liability was that the boys were not employees or acting with Home Office authority. However liability was based on the officers' negligence. *Novus actus interveniens* did not apply. Accordingly, recoverability became a matter of remoteness of damage.

There was an obvious risk of damage to a boat, given the criminal records of the seven boys, the fact that five of them had attempted to escape before and their being physically located on an island. Accordingly, 'the taking of a boat by the escaping trainees and their unskilled navigation leading to damage to another vessel were the very kind of thing that these Borstal officers ought to have seen to be likely.'

Mallett v McMonagle (a Minor by Hugh Joseph McMonagle, His Father and Guardian Ad Litem)

[1970] AC 166, HL

[2.80] The appellant was a widow with three infants whose husband died at the age of 25 in a minibus accident caused by the respondent's negligence. The deceased had been a machine operator who supplemented his earnings by working part time in a band. There was evidence to suggest that he might have become an asphalter, which was a more lucrative form of employment, in due course.

The appellant brought a Fatal Accident Acts claim as his administratrix and was awarded a total of £22,000 by the jury of which £21,500 comprised the Fatal Accidents Acts claim. Quantum was disputed. The Court of Appeal found that the original award was excessive, exceeding that which any reasonable jury could properly award. It directed there to be a new trial on damages under the Fatal Accidents Acts.

HELD, by Lord Morris delivering the leading judgment, dismissing an appeal from the Court of Appeal in Northern Ireland: That the approach of an appellate court must differ according to whether an assessment of damages has been made by a judge or jury. A jury's assessment of damages should not be disturbed unless the appellate court was satisfied that no reasonable jury could have made it, namely, that it was out of all proportion to the facts of the case. In the present instance the Court of Appeal had been so satisfied. Had the award been made by a single judge, the Court of Appeal would have regarded it as a 'wholly erroneous estimate'.

Per Lord Morris and following guidance in *Davies v Powell Duffryn Associated Collieries Ltd* [1942] AC 601, 616 and in *Nance v British Columbia Electric Rly Co Ltd* [1951] AC 601, 614:

> In cases such as that now being considered it is inevitable that in assessing damages there must be elements of estimate and to some extent of conjecture. All the chances and the changes of the future must be assessed. They must be weighed not only with sympathy but with fairness for the interests of all concerned and at all times with a sense of proportion.

Lord Diplock: in assessing damages in a Fatal Accidents Acts claim further inflation should be disregarded as should high interest rates and capital appreciation.

McGhee v National Coal Board

[1972] 3 All ER 1008, HL

[2.81] The appellant was instructed by his employers, the respondents, to clean out brick kilns at their Prestongrange brickworks. Normally he worked in the cooler pipe kilns. The new task was hot and dirty work because the air was contaminated by abrasive brick dust. The lack of washing facilities on site meant that the appellant travelled home by bicycle still covered in dirt. Some days later he contracted dermatitis.

The appellant subsequently brought a claim against the respondents alleging that, as a result of their negligence in failing to provide adequate washing facilities, he had developed this condition. Medical evidence adduced at trial supported a link between the conditions in the kiln and dermatitis although the relevance of the washing facilities was unclear. The appellant's medical experts could only say that the lack of them increased the risk of developing the condition. Nevertheless, the respondents argued that despite an admitted breach of duty, this had not caused the onset of the disease. They claimed too that the additional exertion involved in the appellant cycling home was pertinent.

HELD, on appeal, in favour of the appellant: That there would be liability in negligence where a breach of duty had caused or materially contributed to an injury despite the presence of other contributory factors for which the negligent party was not responsible. Here the practical and reasonable measure of installing showers or other proper washing facilities would have reduced the risk of exposure to dermatitis, prudent employers would have installed them, and the failure to do so amounted to breach of duty.

Per Lord Simon of Glaisdale: where an injury is caused by two or more factors operating cumulatively, one of which is a breach of duty and one not, and it is impossible to ascertain the proportion in which the factors were effective, the plaintiff is not required to prove the impossible but 'holds that he is entitled to damages for the injury if he proves on a balance of probabilities that the breach or breaches of duty contributed substantially to causing the injury'.

The precise means by which dermatitis develops was found to be scientifically unknown. However, per Lord Reid:

> in cases like this we must take a broader view of causation....From a broad and practical viewpoint I can see no substantial difference between saying that what the respondents did materially increased the risk of injury to the appellant and saying that what the respondents did made a material contribution to his injury.

Bonnington Castings v Wardlaw [1956] 1 All ER 615 (see 2.53 above) followed.

See now Fairchild (6.4 below).

Jobling v Associated Dairies Ltd

[1982] AC 794, HL

[2.82] The plaintiff brought proceedings against his employers in respect of a work related 'slip and trip' accident under the Offices, Shops and Railway Premises

Act 1963. The accident, which happened in January 1973, caused the plaintiff continuing back pain and he sought compensation which included future loss of earnings. Three years before the trial (1979) in 1976 the plaintiff was diagnosed with a condition known as spondylotic myelopathy. This neck condition was dormant at the date of the accident but would have disabled him completely from 1976 onwards irrespective of the accident.

The question which arose was whether the disability caused by myelopathy should reduce the quantum of damages awarded to the plaintiff at first instance. The Court of Appeal so found.

HELD, dismissing an appeal by the appellant: That in assessing damages, the appellant's medical condition had to be taken into account to enable the court to 'provide just and sufficient but not excessive compensation, taking all factors into account' – Lord Wilberforce.

> *Note*—A court is obliged to take account of vicissitudes of life, ie the actual circumstances, as well as anticipating those in which a plaintiff would have been in but for the accident. This includes supervening non-tortious events. On the facts the appellant's illness would have developed in any event reducing his earning capacity.
>
> *Baker v Willoughby* [1970] AC 467 involved successive tortious events and thus was distinguished.

Selvanayagam v University of the West Indies

[1983] 1 All ER 824, PC (Lord Scarman)

[2.83] The appellant was plaintiff in a personal injury action against his employers brought in the High Court of Trinidad and Tobago. In 1975 he was professor of civil engineering when he fell on campus into a trench because the passageway he was walking along was poorly lit due to building works.

Following the accident he declined to undergo a neck operation which, if successful, could have restored some 80% of his mobility so enabling him within six months to resume his career as a highly qualified professional engineer. The appellant was diabetic and was concerned about the risks of infection from surgery. The respondent asserted that there had been contributory negligence and further, that the refusal to undergo the operation had been unreasonable.

HELD, allowing the appellant's appeal: That in a personal injuries claim the plaintiff has a duty to mitigate his damage. Where medical advice to undergo surgery is not taken, the burden is on the plaintiff to prove that the decision was reasonable and that he acted reasonably to mitigate his damage. Per Lord Scarman: 'the true question is whether in all the circumstances, including particularly the medical advice received, the plaintiff acted reasonably in refusing surgery'.

On the issue of damages in appeals to the Judicial Committee of the Privy Council, whilst there was the power to substitute their own assessment of damages for that of the trial judge, the Board was reluctant to do so, lacking local knowledge and instead referred the case back to the local court on the basis of rulings given on the appeal.

This case has just been distinguished in *Geest v Lasinqoot* [2002] ULPC 48, [2002] I WLR 3111. In *Geest* Lord Bingham held that the obligation of proving a failure to mitigate is on the defendant employer. It was also noted that there would be difficulties in showing an unreasonable failure to undergo an operation without clear medical evidence in which any risks were brought fairly to the attention of the employee

Kay v Ayrshire and Arran Health Board

[1987] 2 All ER 417, HL

[2.84] The appellant's young son was hospitalised with pneumococcal meningititis, a virulent form of meningitis. Due to an error on the part of the senior house officer, the child negligently received a massive overdose of penicillin. Despite immediate corrective treatment the little boy was found to be profoundly deaf.

In an action for personal injury against the respondent in which liability was admitted, the respondent denied that the boy's residual disability was due to the overdose. The medical evidence adduced by the respondent supported the view that deafness was a common side effect of meningitis, but not of a penicillin overdose. The appellant argued that the administration of the drug had increased the risk of neurological damage and thus created or increased the risk of injury of the kind which his son sustained.

HELD, dismissing an appeal by the appellant: That he had failed to establish that the overdose had any causal connection with his son's deafness.

Where there are two competing causes of damage the law does not presume in favour of a plaintiff that the tortious cause was responsible for the damage *unless* the plaintiff has first established that the tortious act was capable of causing or aggravating the damage. Here, no acceptable medical evidence had been adduced by the appellant to support the proposition that an overdose of penicillin could cause or contribute to deafness. The principle in *McGhee v National Coal Board* [1972] 3 All ER 1008 did not therefore apply.

Note—their Lordships relied heavily on the fact that there was no evidence of any recorded case in which a penicillin overdose had caused deafness.

Smith v Littlewoods Organisation Ltd, Maloco v Same (Consolidated Appeals)

[1987] AC 241, HL

[2.85] In 1976 the defenders purchased the Regal Cinema in Dunfermline for development purposes. After the work had started, the disused cinema was left empty and occasionally children and youngsters broke in and committed acts of vandalism including two attempts to start fires. Shortly afterwards the premises were burnt to the ground by arson, the culprits believed to have been children or teenagers. The fire spread to adjacent buildings which were seriously damaged. The occupiers of these buildings brought a claim against the defenders alleging that the fire had been caused as a result of their negligence. The defenders had no knowledge of the earlier fires although the neighbours were aware of vandalism which they did not draw to the defenders' attention or to the notice of the police.

HELD: That liability of an occupier to his neighbour for acts of trespass committed by third parties depended on the circumstances, that the existence of such a duty of care was likely to be rare.

Per Lord Brandon: The defenders owed a general duty to the appellants to exercise reasonable care to ensure that the cinema was not, and did not become, a source of danger to neighbouring properties. Whether such encompassed a specific duty to prevent youngsters from unlawfully entering and causing damage depended on whether such behaviour was reasonably foreseeable.

On the facts, the defenders were unaware of the previous attempts to light fires and because the cinema premises did not amount to an obvious fire risk, they were not to be held responsible for failing to foresee the risk of it being set alight by putting in place greater security measures.

As to the correct test, Lord Mackay of Clashfern stated:

> what the reasonable man is bound to foresee in a case involving injury or damage by independent human agency ... is the probable consequences of his own act or omission, but, in such a case, a clear basis will be required on which to assert that the injury or damage is more than a mere possibility. When 'the word 'probable' is used in this context in the authorities, it is used as indicating a real risk as distinct from a mere possibility of danger.

Home Office v Dorset Yacht Co Ltd [1970] AC 1004, HL followed.

Bryce v Swan Hunter Group plc and others

[1988] 1 All ER 659, QBD (Phillips J)

[2.86] The deceased, John Bryce, was a painter who was employed in shipyards owned by the three defendants for the greater part of 1937 to 1975. As a result of exposure to asbestos he contracted malignant mesothelioma, a rare form of cancer, from which he died in 1981. His widow, qua administratrix, issued proceedings against the defendants on the basis that the work practices and processes with each employer's business had caused asbestos dust to be released into the deceased's places of work.

HELD: In relation to the allegation that the defendants had breached a duty at common law in the form of negligent failure to take precautions which would materially have reduced her husband's exposure to the dust, that based on the standards of knowledge at the material times, the defendants were under a duty to take all reasonable steps to reduce the deceased's exposure to asbestos dust. On the facts this duty had been breached.

Phillips J approved the test of an employer's duty of care to his employee as formulated by Swanwick J in *Stokes v Guest Keen & Nettlefold (Bolts and Nuts) Ltd* [1968] 1 WLR 1776 namely, the conduct of the reasonable and prudent employer, taking positive thought for the safety of his workers in the light of what he knows or ought to know.

In relation to statutory duties, the defendants were subject to inter alia, FA 1937, s 4(1) as re-enacted in the 1961 Act, to provide effective ventilation of all harmful dust. Accordingly, they were under a duty to take all practical measures to protect their employees against inhalation of the dust. On the facts there were breaches of duty by all defendants.

Despite the breaches of duty the plaintiff had failed to establish on balance of probabilities a causal link between the breach and the deceased's contraction of the disease.

However, the judge found that it was immaterial whether the breaches of duty either added to the number of possible initiators of mesothelioma or whether they also produced a cumulative effect on the reduction of the deceased's defence mechanism. The fact remained that they increased the risk of his developing the disease and each defendant was thus liable.

Pickford v Imperial Chemical Industries plc

[1998] 3 All ER 462, HL

[2.87] The plaintiff was a secretary employed by the defendants. Part, but not all of her duties involved typing. In May 1989 she consulted her GP about pain in her hands from which she had been suffering for a few months. Neither the GP nor several other doctors could identify any physical explanation for her symptoms. ICI terminated her employment with them in late 1990 on the grounds that there was no work which she was able to perform. The plaintiff issued proceedings against ICI alleging that as a result of their negligence, she had contracted a condition known as PDA4, a prescribed disease for the purpose of industrial injury benefit.

HELD: That the crucial issue was causation. The onus was on the plaintiff to establish that her condition was caused by repetitive movements during typing and it was not for the defendants to have to prove an alternative cause of injury.

Note—on the facts the court was influenced by the fact that the judge at first instance had found that the condition was not reasonably foreseeable and that ICI had not been negligent.

OTHER COMMON LAW LIABILITIES

Provision of References

[2.88] The provision of a reference on a former employee to a prospective employer can create legal liabilities. Firstly duties may be owed to the prospective employer, see *Hedley Byrne v Heller* [1964] AC 465. Secondly the employee may have remedies for libel (although providing a reference is likely to be an occasion of qualified privilege and the employee will have to demonstrate malice to defeat the claim of qualified privilege) and malicious falsehood. Thirdly it has now been established that the employer owes a duty of care to an ex-employee and could be liable for economic loss suffered as a result of failing to obtain new employment because of a carelessly supplied reference.

Spring v Guardian Assurance

[1995] 2 AC 296, HL

[2.89] The claimant, a life assurance salesman, had been dismissed from his position as sales director and office manager. He sought employment with another company. That company sought and the defence provided a reference. As a result of the unfavourable reference the claimant was not employed by the prospective employers. The trial judge found that the defendant had acted in breach of a duty of care by carelessly giving a reference which was false. The court of appeal allowed an appeal by the defendant. On appeal to the house of lords.

HELD: Appeal allowed. An employer who gave a reference owed the employee a duty of care. The availability of a claim in libel did not bar such an action.

Kidd v Axa Equity & Law Life

[2000] IRLR 301 Burton J

[2.90] The claimant had been employed the defendant and was the subject of seven complaints by customers and was the subject of a customer care exercise. The claimant sought employment with Allied Dunbar, who sought references from the defendant. The defendant provided a reference which referred to the customer care exercise. Allied Dunbar did not engage the claimant who issued proceedings against the defendant.

Held: Claim dismissed. The claimant had to prove: that misleading information had been provided; that the misleading information had been carelessly provided; and that the misleading information was likely to have a material effect on the mind of a reasonable recipient. The information provided was not misleading.

Note: Employers in ongoing litigation for race discrimination could protect themselves by preserving the position as to the giving of references, see *Chief Constable of West Yorkshire v Khan* [2001] 4 All ER 834.

CHAPTER 3

Liability for Non-Employees

Acts of independent contractor/sub-contractor	[3.1]
'Casual' or 'collateral' negligence	[3.7]
Ultra-hazardous activities	[3.12]
Workers subject to another's control	[3.14]
The Australian approach	[3.35]

[3.1] Employers have been held liable for the actions of independent contractors and sub-contractors.

ACTS OF INDEPENDENT CONTRACTOR/SUB-CONTRACTOR

Wilsons & Clyde Coal Co Ltd v English

[1938] AC 57, HL

[3.2] The claimant claimed damages for injuries he sustained when working in the defendant's coal mine. On the day in question the claimant was leaving the mine, at the end of the day shift, when the haulage plant was put in motion, and before he could reach one of the manholes provided he was caught by a rake of hutches and crushed between it and the side of the road.

The claimant alleged that his accident was caused by the defendant's failure to provide a reasonably safe system of working. This failure was not known to the defendant's board of directors but was known to its servants to whom it had delegated the management of the mine.

HELD, on appeal: The provision of a safe system of working in a mine is an obligation of the owner who, if he appoints an agent to perform it, remains vicariously responsible for the agent's negligence. This liability cannot be escaped by delegating performance of the duty to someone else (even where, as in the case of coal mines, delegation of the management to a qualified official is required by law). It is not sufficient for the employer merely to select a competent person to perform the duty: See Lord Thankerton at page 64 and Lord Wright at page 78.

See paragraph 2.2 above.

Hudson v Ridge Manufacturing Co Ltd

[1957] 2 QB 348 (Steatfeild J)

[3.3] The claimant claimed damages from the defendant for injuries received when he was tripped up by a fellow employee as a practical joke. For nearly four years one of the defendant's employees had made a nuisance of himself to his fellow employees, including the claimant, by persistently engaging in horseplay such as tripping them up. Many times he had been reprimanded by the defendant's foreman and warned that he would hurt someone, but without effect. No further steps were taken to check this conduct by dismissal or otherwise. The claimant claimed against the defendant for damages on the ground that it had failed to maintain such discipline among its employees as would protect him from dangerous horseplay.

HELD, per Steatfeild J: It is the duty of employers, for the safety of their employees, to have: reasonably safe plant and machinery; premises which are reasonably safe; a reasonably safe system of work; and to employ reasonably competent fellow workmen. In the circumstances the defendant was liable to the claimant for failing to take proper care for his safety.

Davie v New Merton Board Mills Ltd

[1959] AC 604, HL

[3.4] The claimant claimed damages against his employer on the ground that it had supplied him with a defective tool, and against the manufacturers on the ground that they were under a duty to those who they contemplated might use it. The claimant, a maintenance fitter, was working on a machine and had occasion to separate certain parts which were fitted together too tightly for separation by hand. The appropriate tool for this purpose was a drift, which may be described as a tapered bar or strip of metal approximately 12 inches long. The claimant took a drift, provided by the first defendant and manufactured by the second defendant, and began to strike it with a hammer. At the second stroke the drift broke and a piece flew off, striking, and destroying the sight of, the claimant's left eye.

The drift was defective in that the steel from which it was made was excessively hard and consequently liable to fracture when subjected to blows of the force to which a drift in ordinary use would be subjected. This was a defect which ought to have been discovered by a manufacturer using reasonable skill and care in the making of drifts.

This was an appeal from an order of the Court of Appeal, allowing an appeal by the first defendant (the employer) from a judgment of Ashworth J. whereby he gave judgment for the claimant against both defendants, and ordered that the second defendant (the manufacturers) should wholly indemnify the employer with regard to damages.

HELD, on appeal, per Lord Tucker:

> the employer may delegate the performance of his obligation in this sphere to someone who is more properly described as a contractor than a servant, but this does not affect the liability of the employer, he will be just as much liable for his negligence as for that of his servant. Such a contractor is entrusted by his employer with the performance of the employer's personal duty.
>
> *Note*—the employer's liability was held not to extend to cover the negligent manufacture of a tool. This case led to the enactment of the Employer's Liability (Defective Equipment) Act 1969.

Nelhams v Sandells Maintenance Ltd and Gillespie (UK) Ltd

[1996] PIQR P52, CA

[3.5] The claimant claimed damages against the defendants for an injury sustained while temporarily assigned to work for the second defendant, G Ltd, by the first defendant, his employer. The second defendant's supervisor had instructed the claimant to use a ladder when painting. The claimant had pointed out the floor was slippery and that the ladder ought to be footed. He was told there was no one available to foot the ladder. He then climbed it, the ladder slipped and he was injured.

HELD, on appeal: In dismissing the second defendant's appeal, it was held that the contractor is, in effect, the employer's agent. The correct approach to determining liability for injuries sustained in the course of employment under the direction of a second employer was to recognise that the first employer retained a duty of care to ensure the safety of its employees: *Morris v Breavegien Ltd* [1993] ICR 766 (see 3.34 below), *Wilsons and Clyde Coal Co v English* [1938] AC 57, HL (see 3.2 above) and *McDermid v Nash Dredging Co Ltd* [1987] AC 906, HL (see 3.6 and 3.11 below) considered. Where an employer assigns his employee to work for another employer, both employers are liable to the employee for any injury sustained in consequence of the other employer's negligence, although under the Civil Liability (Contribution) Act 1978, ss 1 and 2, the court may apportion damages between the defendants.

In terms of blameworthiness and causative potency the judge had found that the accident was attributable wholly to the second defendant's instruction to the claimant to use the ladder without footing it. Therefore although the claimant was entitled to recover against both defendants the contribution to be recovered by the first defendant from the second defendant should amount to a complete indemnity.

McDermid v Nash Dredging & Reclamation Co Ltd

[1987] AC 906, HL

[3.6] The claimant claimed against the defendant, his employer, for injuries sustained whilst working as a deckhand. In the course of his employment the claimant was working on board a tugboat owned by a Dutch company. The tugboat was under the control of a Dutch captain employed by the Dutch company. The claimant's work included untying ropes mooring the tug for and aft to a dredger. At the time in question the claimant had untied the aft rope but was still in the course of untying the forward rope when the captain, without waiting for the signal, put the engine of the tug hard astern. As a result the rope snaked around the claimant's leg causing serious injury.

The defendant employer was held liable to the claimant for the injury caused by the tugboat captain's negligence, the tug owner itself being the holding company of the defendant, the defendant being its wholly owned subsidiary.

HELD, on appeal: In dismissing an appeal by the defendant on the question of liability it was held that an employer could not delegate its duty to provide a safe system of work for its workers. It was no defence to show the delegation was to a person who was reasonably believed to be competent. Accordingly, although the defendant had delegated the performance of their duty of care to the captain, it could not thereby avoid its own liability to the claimant.

> *Note*—The House of Lords extended the employers' duty to the operation as well as the provision of a safe system of work (see Lord Hailsham at page 911 and Lord Brandon at page 919).

See also 3.11 below.

'Casual' or 'collateral' negligence

[3.7] In the past employers could escape liability for acts of 'casual' or 'collateral' negligence which did not arise in the course of the act which the contractor was employed to perform: *Pearson v Cox* (1877) 2 CPD 369. Today, however, the employer remains liable for failure to impose a safe system of work even when the system is in the hands of a third party.

Penny v Wimbledon UDC and Iles

[1899] 2 QB 72, CA

[3.8] The claimant claimed damages against the defendants for an injury sustained when walking along a road after dark and falling over a heap of soil and grass. The first defendant, a district council, acting under the Public Health Act 1875, s 150, employed the second defendant, an independent contractor, to make up a highway, which was used by the public, but had not become repairable by the inhabitants at large. In carrying out the work the second defendant negligently left on the road a heap of soil, unlighted and unprotected. The first defendant contended that the negligence complained of was casual or collateral, having regard to the nature of the employment, and that it was therefore not liable.

HELD, on appeal: As, from the nature of the work, danger was likely to arise to the public using the road unless precautions were taken, the negligence of the contractor was not casual, or collateral to his employment, and the first defendant was liable.

Per Romer LJ: The usual precaution to take in such a case is to put up lights or other warnings to prevent persons falling into holes or over heaps of soil. It is unreasonable not to take those precautions.

72 *Liability for Non-Employees*

Per Smith LJ: Such casual or collateral acts of negligence could include leaving a pickaxe, or such like, in the road but could not extend to leaving heaps of soil in the road, which would by the very nature of the contract have to be dug up and dealt with.

Padbury v Holliday and Greenwood Ltd

(1912) 28 TLR 494

[3.9] The defendants were employed to erect certain premises, and the contract involved the employment by the defendants of sub-contractors to execute the special work of putting metallic casements into the windows. While one of these casements was being fitted an iron tool was left on the windowsill by a servant of the sub-contractors which fell to the road below injuring the claimant who was passing. It was noted that the tool was not placed on the windowsill in the normal course of doing the work which the sub-contractors were employed to do.

HELD: The injuries were caused to the claimant by an act of collateral negligence on the part of the workman who was a servant of the sub-contractors and not of the defendants, and that the latter were therefore not liable for the consequences of that negligence.

Salsbury v Woodland

[1970] 1 QB 324, CA

[3.10] The first defendant, an occupier of a house, employed the second defendant, a tree-felling contractor, to remove a hawthorn tree from the front garden of his house adjoining the highway. Owing to the negligent manner in which the second defendant removed the tree it fouled and broke telephone wires, which fell into the road, causing an obstruction. The claimant, who was watching out of curiosity, went into the road to remove the wires when the third defendant approached in his car driving at a fast speed and accelerating. The claimant, realising that a collision between the third defendant's car and the wires was inevitable threw himself onto the grass verge adjoining the road to avoid injury by the wires but his fall caused a tumour in his spine to bleed and the effect of that upon his adjacent spinal chord was to cause paralysis.

The claimant was awarded damages against all three defendants.

HELD, on appeal: Allowing the first defendant's appeal it was held that the first defendant was not liable for the negligence of the second defendant, since the first defendant fell within the general rule that an employer of an independent contractor was not responsible for his contractor's acts or omissions and did not come within the exceptions to that rule; for the removal of the tree was not work of an inherently dangerous nature nor was it work carried out on the highway and there was no exception in respect of work carried out near to a highway which might caused injury to persons on the highway.

Sachs LJ 'derived no assistance at all from any distinction between 'casual and collateral' negligence and other negligence'.

McDermid v Nash Dredging and Reclamation Co Ltd

[1987] AC 906, HL

[3.11] In this case, as set out in 3.6 above, it was argued that the fact that the captain operated the engine in such dangerous circumstances was the 'casual' or 'collateral' negligence of an employee of an independent contractor, ie the Dutch company. The exemption was given short shrift by the House of Lords.

Per Lord Brandon, at 919–920:

> The negligence [of the captain] was not casual but central. It involved abandoning a safe system of work which he had devised and operating in its place a manifestly unsafe system.

Ultra-hazardous activities

Honeywill & Stein Ltd v Larkin Bros (London's Commercial Photographers) Ltd

[1934] 1 KB 191, CA

[3.12] The claimants, who were specialists in acoustic work, claimed against the defendant, an independent contractor, for breach of contract or negligence. The claimants employed the defendant to take photographs of the interior of a cinema where the claimants had installed sound reproduction apparatus. In taking a photograph with a flashlight the defendant set fire to the theatre's curtain and damage was done before the fire could be extinguished. The claimants paid the cinema company the amount claimed as the cost of repairing the damage caused by the fire, and claimed to recover the same amount from the defendant. The defendant contended that that payment was a purely voluntary payment, because the claimants would have had a defence to any claim brought against it by the cinema company based on the ground that the damage was caused by the negligence of the defendant, who were independent contractors, and not servants or agents of the claimants, so that the claimants were not responsible for the defendant's acts or defaults.

HELD, on appeal: An employer is primarily liable for damage caused by 'extra-hazardous or hazardous operations', acts which are 'inherently dangerous', whether that damage is caused by a third party or an employee.

The principle is that if a man does work on or near another's property which involves danger to that property unless proper care is taken, he is liable to the owners of the property for damage resulting to it from the failure to take proper care, and is equally liable if, instead of doing the work himself, he procures another, whether agent, servant or otherwise, to do it for him.

In attempting to define the precise scope of that which is classed as 'extra-hazardous' Slesser LJ stated at page 197: 'acts which, in their very nature, involve in the eyes of the law special danger to others; of such acts the causing of fire and explosion are obvious and established instances'.

Note—Liability is not strict but the duty is high and this duty, too, cannot be delegated. See *Holliday v National Telephone Co* [1899] 2 QB 392, CA.

Brooke v Bool

[1928] 2 KB 578, DC

[3.13] The claimant claimed for damage done to her goods when an explosion occurred in a lock-up shop let to her by the defendant, who lived next door. It was arranged that the defendant might enter the shop after the claimant had left for the day to see that it was secure. On the day in question the defendant's lodger informed the defendant that he thought he could smell gas coming from the shop, and the defendant thereupon entered the shop followed by the lodger. The defendant examined the lower part of a gas pipe in the shop with a naked light, and the lodger examined the upper part of the pipe with a naked light, when an explosion occurred which did damage to the claimant's goods.

HELD, on appeal: The defendant was liable to the claimant for the damage done to her property by the negligent act of the lodger on any one of the following grounds:
 i That the act of the lodger was done by him as agent;
 ii That that act was done in the course of proceedings of which the defendant had the control;
 iii That the act was done in pursuance of a concerted enterprise of the defendant and the lodger and was their joint tort;
 iv Per Talbot J: The defendant having undertaken the examination was under a duty to take reasonable care to avoid danger resulting from it, and that he could not escape liability for the consequences of his failure to do so by getting some one else to make the examination or part of it for him.

WORKERS SUBJECT TO ANOTHER'S CONTROL

[3.14] The courts generally impose a duty of care on a non-employer analogous to that owed by an employer where there is a relationship characterised by factual or legal control. The nature of this duty will vary with the circumstances.

Carmarthenshire County Council v Lewis

[1955] AC 549, HL

[3.15] A four-year old boy attending nursery school under the management of the county council strayed onto a public highway, and the claimant's husband, who was driving a lorry, struck a telegraph post in trying to avoid him and was killed. The claimant sued the council for damages, alleging that the death was caused by their negligence or that of the teacher who had left the child temporarily unattended.

HELD, on appeal: Educational authorities owe duties to their students. The appellant council were liable to the respondent in damages, since the unexplained fact that in the temporary absence of the teacher (who, on the evidence, was not negligent) it was possible for a young child to wander from the school premises onto the highway, through a gate which was either open or very easy for him to open, disclosed negligence on their part.

Fowles v Bedfordshire County Council

[1996] ELR 51, CA

[3.16] The claimant suffered serious and permanent spinal injury when he failed to perform a successful somersault in the activities hall at the Bedford Youth House. The defendant provided these premises. The defendant appealed against a decision that they were liable to the claimant in negligence alleging that the accident happened because the claimant had placed landing gym mats too close to a wall and had attempted a dangerous gymnastic exercise without assistance, knowing the potential risks.

HELD, on appeal: Youth centres owe duties to gymnasts. The defendant was liable in negligence because a youth worker employed by them had assumed the task of teaching the claimant to do forward somersaults and thereon assumed a duty to make him aware of the risks and dangers. The defendant provided no warnings of the dangers, whether verbal or written, and compounded that failure by allowing unsupervised access to the gym mats. The claimant did, however, have to bear a substantial part of the blame for the accident, since the risks were obvious to a reasonably intelligent person.

Kirkham v Chief Constable of the Greater Manchester Police

[1990] 2 QB 283, CA

[3.17] The claimant's husband committed suicide whilst in prison. The police knew that he was a suicide risk and that he had made recent attempts to commit suicide, but did not communicate that information to the prison authorities. Had the prison authorities known of the husband's suicidal tendencies they would probably have taken steps which would have prevented, or at least lessened the risk of, his suicide. The claimant, the administratrix of her husband's estate, brought an action in negligence against the chief constable of police.

HELD, on appeal: The police owe duties to prisoners. When the police took the husband into custody they assumed the responsibility to him of passing to the prison authorities information which might affect his well-being. On the balance of probabilities the husband would have been prevented from taking his own life had the prison authorities been informed of the risk. The claimant's claim that breach of duty had caused the husband's death had been made out.

Per Lloyd LJ: Where a man of sound mind commits suicide in hospital or prison his estate would be unable to maintain an action against the hospital or prison authorities. Volenti non fit injuria would provide them with a complete defence.

Pinn v Rew

(1916) 32 TLR 451

[3.18] The defendant through an agent bought a cow and a calf, and by the defendant's instructions the agent employed a drover to drive them to the defendant's farm. The drover got another man, who was about to drive bullocks in the same direction, to drive the cow and calf along with them. On the way the cow tossed a dog and then the claimant, who sustained injuries. Evidence was given that if a cow with a calf met a dog it might become dangerous.

HELD: The drover was negligent as it was his duty to ensure the cow was under control. The defendant was negligent in employing one man to do a dangerous thing on the highway. Therefore, even if the drover was an independent contractor this was no defence. The duty, therefore, should extend to selecting competent independent contractors to do the work.

Mersey Docks and Harbour Board v Coggins & Griffith (Liverpool) Ltd

[1947] AC 1, HL

[3.19] The claimants owned a number of mobile cranes, each driven by a skilled workman engaged and paid by them. The claimants lent one of these cranes to a firm of stevedores for loading a ship. One of the conditions on which the crane was supplied provided that the crane driver so provided shall be the servant of the hirer. In the course of his employment he injured a third person by negligently driving the crane. At the time of the accident the stevedores had the immediate direction and control of the operation of picking up and moving each piece of cargo but had no power to direct how the crane should be worked or the controls manipulated.

HELD, on appeal: An employer which lends an employee to another enterprise has a heavy burden of proof to shift to the latter its liabilities as an employer.

Per Lord Porter and Lord Simonds: The claimant harbour authority, as general permanent employer, was liable, not having discharged the heavy burden of proof so as to shift to the stevedores its prima facie responsibility for the negligence of the crane man, who in the manner of his driving was exercising the discretion it had vested in him. The question who was the employer responsible for his negligence was not determined by any agreement between the harbour authority and the stevedores. The proper test is whether or not the hirer had authority to control the manner of execution of the act in question.

Gerrard v AE Southey & Co and Standard Telephones and Cables Ltd

[1952] 2 QB 174 (Parker J)

[3.20] The claimant's general employers lent his services for hire to temporary employers to carry out electrical work. The foreman of the temporary employers not only told the claimant what work to do but also specifically controlled the way in which he did it. The claimant sustained injuries when a defective rung of a builders' trestle broke away causing him to fall backwards.

HELD, per Parker J: The temporary employer was in relation of master and servant with the workman, and so liable to him for breach of duty to take reasonable care to provide proper plant and equipment for the work.

Note—This case demonstrates that the heavy burden laid down in *Mersey Docks and Harbour Board v Coggins and Griffith* [1947] AC 1, HL (see 3.19 above) is not insurmountable.

O'Reilly v Imperial Chemical Industries Ltd

[1955] 3 All ER 382, CA

[3.21] The claimant was a lorry driver employed by British Road Services. A number of their lorries and drivers, of whom the claimant was one, were put at the defendants' disposal on a full-time basis. The lorries bore the name of the defendants but the drivers were paid by the British Road Services and could be dismissed only by them. The defendants controlled and assisted in the loading and unloading of the lorries in a general way; they made suggestions and requests and supplied unloading gear, but it was not established that British Road Services had in any sense delegated to the defendants the right to give orders how the work was to be done and the claimant was not bound to take orders in that regard from the defendants. On the day in question the claimant was unloading drums of Terylene from his lorry at the defendants' plant on to a tiering truck provided by the defendants. The method of unloading was unsafe and one of the drums fell onto the claimant causing injuries.

HELD, on appeal: The defendants did not owe to the claimant the duty of providing a safe system of work, because the contractual relationship of master and servant was between British Road Services and the claimant, and because the heavy onus of proving that a relationship of employer and employee existed between the defendants and the claimant had not been discharged, as the claimant had failed to show that the defendants had the right to direct how the unloading was to be carried out by him.

Principle stated in *Mersey Docks and Harbour Board v Coggins & Griffith (Liverpool) Ltd* [1946] 2 All ER 345 (see 3.19 above) applied.

> *Note*—This case may be compared with the decision of the Court of Appeal in *Denham v Midland Employers' Mutual Assurance Ltd* [1955] 2 All ER 561.

It must be noted, however, that today, the Occupiers Liability Act 1957 would make it clear that the defendants owed a duty to use reasonable care towards the claimant, and would be guilty of a breach of that duty: see *Savory v Holland, Hannen and Cubitts (Southern) Ltd* [1964] 3 All ER 18, CA – 3.25 below – per Lord Denning MR at 21.

Denham v Midland Employers' Mutual Assurance Ltd

[1955] 2 All ER 561, CA

[3.22] This was a claim by a widow for a fatal accident which killed her husband. An employer engaged an engineering company to do certain work on his land, and he provided one of his own unskilled labourers (the claimant's husband) to help with the work. The labourer continued to be paid by his employer, who alone had power to dismiss him, but he worked alongside the company's skilled employees and under the specific direction of that company's foreman. The labourer was killed in circumstances making the company liable to pay damages to his widow on the ground that his death was due to the company's negligence or that of its servants. The company was covered by: (1) an employers' liability policy covering liability to 'any person under a contract of service...with the insured'; (2) a public liability policy excluding the liability mentioned in (1).

HELD, on appeal: Although the engineering company would have been liable as a temporary employer for injury to a third person by the negligence of the labourer in the course of his work, and similarly the company were liable to his widow in the present case, the labourer's contract of service was with his original employer alone; that it was only the use and benefit of his services which had been transferred to the company; and that such a transfer did not render him 'a person under a contract of service' with the company within the meaning of the employers' liability policy, but it was entitled to recover under the public liability policy.

Denning LJ stated that where a worker was controlled by someone not his employer he 'becomes so much a part of the organisation to which he is seconded that the temporary employer is responsible for him and to him...The right of control carries the burden of responsibility'.

Clayton v Woodman & Son (Builders) Ltd
[1962] 2 QB 533

[3.23] The claimant was injured when working as a bricklayer. The claimant was employed by the first defendants, a firm of builders who had contracted with the second defendants, a regional hospital board, to install a lift and motor-room in one of their hospitals. An architect, employed by the third defendants, instructed the claimant to cut the chase in the gable. The chase was cut and later that day the gable toppled inwards injuring the claimant.

The claimant claimed damages for personal injuries against the builders, alleging negligence and breach of statutory duty; against the hospital board, alleging breach of duty under the Occupiers Liability Act 1957, and vicarious liability for the negligence of the architects; and against the architects alleging negligence.

HELD: The builders were liable in negligence and breach of statutory duty for not shoring or strutting the gable when they knew the chase was to be cut. The hospital board were not liable.

Having regard to the close relationship between the claimant and the architects, and on the particular facts of the case, the architects owed a duty of care to the claimant as to the instructions they gave him. Their duty was to take reasonable care for the safety of the claimant, and as they should have realised that the instructions to cut the chase would have been promptly obeyed and would have probably resulted in death or injury, they were negligent in issuing such instructions.

> *Note*—On appeal the Court of Appeal held that the evidence did not justify the judge's finding that the architect had instructed the claimant to do anything which he knew to be dangerous, or that he had acted negligently. This shows that where a person does not supervise others the courts have declined to impose liability.

Clay v AJ Crump & Sons Ltd

[1964] 1 QB 533, CA

[3.24] The owner of a site on which there were some old buildings appointed an architect to plan and supervise its redevelopment. Demolition contractors were instructed to clear the site in accordance with the architect's plan and to excavate it to the level of a datum point shown on the plan. According to the plan a wall was to be demolished. However, at the building owner's request the wall was left standing after the architect had sanctioned that course during a telephone conversation with the demolition contractor's managing director. Several weeks later building contractors came onto the site. The claimant, a labourer employed by the building contractors, was injured when the wall collapsed and fell on him and claimed damages for the personal injuries he sustained.

HELD, on appeal: Since both the architect and the demolition contractors knew that the building contractors would be working on the site, they should reasonably have foreseen that if they left a dangerous wall standing it might fall and injure the building contractors' employees and, accordingly, they were both under a duty to the claimant to make careful inspection of the wall.

Per Davies LJ: *Clayton v Woodman & Son (Builders) Ltd* [1962] 2 QB 533 (above) distinguished because that was a case of refusal by an architect to vary the contract, but the present case is one where the architect directed a variation of the contract which was dangerous.

> *Note*—When working on a site it is sensible to treat the organising body as having a legal responsibility to co-ordinate safety measures: see the Management of Health and Safety at Work Regulations 1999.

Savory v Holland, Hannen and Cubitts (Southern) Ltd

[1964] 3 All ER 18, CA

[3.25] The defendant contractors were employed by manufacturers to build a factory. In the course of excavation the defendant contractors called in H Ltd to help them blasting rock. H Ltd sent the claimant, a skilled man, to do the blasting; he brought the necessary materials with him, the defendant provided any men who were necessary. On the day in question the defendant was injured whilst acting as his own flagman due to the absence of one of the workers the defendant should have provided. He brought an action for damages against the defendant claiming that he had become for the time being their servant.

HELD, on appeal: In the circumstances of the case the claimant did not become for the time being the servant of the defendant, for they had no power to dictate to him how his skilled work of blasting should be done.

Per Lord Denning MR: *O'Reilly v Imperial Chemical Industries Ltd* [1955] 3 All ER 382, CA (see 3.21 above) is of no authority today.

Per Diplock LJ: The doctrine of master and servant pro hac vice today seems to be relevant only to a question of vicarious liability; it is a mere adjunct of the doctrine of respondeat superior for determining whether A is the superior of B.

McArdle v Andmac Roofing Co

[1967] 1 All ER 583, CA

[3.26] The claimant was employed by the first defendant sub-contractors, who were laying felt and bitumen on a roof. The third defendant sub-contractors were engaged to provide labour to place joists over a strip of the roof. Both sub-contractors were employed by the second defendants, who were responsible for carrying out the structural work to the roof. On the day of the accident the second defendants sent the first defendant's men to work on the roof while the third defendant's men were at lunch. An aperture in the roof had temporarily been left uncovered by the third defendant's men. The claimant fell through this aperture and sustained injuries for which he sued the defendants for damages.

HELD, on appeal: A principal contractor directing operations on a site who engages sub-contractors and their employees to do work is under a duty, even when not strictly the occupier, to co-ordinate the work and to ensure that reasonable safety measures are taken for the benefit of the workers on the site. *Clay v AJ Crump & Sons Ltd* [1963] 3 All ER 687,CA (see above) applied.

Per Sellers LJ: The law to be applied in the present case is the same as that applied in the *Clay* case, but the facts are stronger against the second defendants, who came closer to the practical work than did the architect in that case.

R v Swan Hunter Shipbuilders Ltd

[1982] 1 All ER 264, CA

[3.27] Sub-contractors who had no contractual relationship with the shipbuilders were working on the construction of a ship. The work involved the use of oxygen hoses. Due to the risk of fire in the confined and poorly ventilated working environment the shipbuilders issued their own employees with a rulebook on the use of fuel gases and oxygen. The rulebook was not however given to the sub-contractors. An employee of the sub-contractors failed to disconnect an oxygen hose and a fire resulted. The shipbuilders were charged, among other things, with failing to provide and maintain a system of work that was, so far as was reasonably practicable, safe and without risks to health contrary to the Health and Safety at Work etc Act 1974, s 2(2)(a).

HELD, on appeal: The duties imposed on an employer by sections 2 and 3 of the 1974 Act followed the common law duty of care of a main contractor to co-ordinate operations at a place of work so as to ensure not only the safety of his own employees but also of the sub-contractors' employees. It was for the main contractor to prove, on a balance of probabilities, that it was not reasonably practicable in all the circumstances for him to carry out those duties.

R v Associated Octel Co Ltd

[1996] 4 All ER 846, HL

[3.28] The appellant operated a large chemical plant which was designated by the Health and Safety Executive as a 'major hazard site'. The appellant used a small firm of specialist contractors for certain repairs. The contractors were employed under a 'permit to work' system which required them to fill in a form before every job stating what work was going to be done and to obtain authorisation from the appellant's engineers, who would decide what safety precautions were needed and how the work was to be carried out. While undertaking repairs an employee of the contractors was badly burned. The appellant was prosecuted for breach of the Health and Safety at Work etc Act 1974, s 3(1)(a).

HELD, on appeal: The decisive question in determining culpability under section 3 was not whether the employer was vicariously liable or in a position to exercise control over work carried out by an independent contractor but simply whether the activity in question could be described as part of the employer's undertaking, that being a question of fact in each case. If the employer engaged an independent contractor to do work which formed part of the conduct of his undertaking, he was required by section 3(1) to stipulate whatever conditions were reasonably practicable to avoid employees of the independent contractor being exposed to such risks.

Kealey v Heard

[1983] 1 All ER 973, QBD

[3.29] The claimant suffered injuries when scaffolding collapsed causing him to fall. The claimant had been employed by the defendant as a specialist plasterer. The defendant wished to convert two adjoining properties into flats. For this purpose he employed a number of specialist tradesmen rather than a building contractor. The scaffolding was erected by an unknown workman. The claimant sued the defendant for breach of the Construction (Working Places) Regulations 1966 and for negligence under the principle of res ipsa loquitur.

HELD: The defendant was not liable for breach of statutory duty as he was not a 'contractor' within the meaning of the 1966 Regulations. The defendant was however liable in negligence under the principle of res ipsa loquitur since, by not providing superintendence of the scaffolding, he had failed to discharge the duty he owed to the claimant to exercise proper care and control over the building appliances on his property; therefore he could not rebut the inference that the claimant's injuries resulted from a breach of that duty.

Wheeler v Copas

[1981] 3 All ER 405 (Chapman J)

[3.30] The claimant was a partner in a firm of bricklayers. The defendant was a farmer who wished to build a house and negotiated directly with the claimant and his partner. A labour-only contract was agreed whereby the claimant and his partner were to lay bricks and erect and dismantle scaffolding. The defendant agreed to provide the building materials and any equipment necessary for the work. The claimant needed a long ladder and was offered two farm ladders belonging to the defendant. The defendant did not ask whether the ladder was adequate for their use, nor was he told it was unsuitable. The claimant fell off the ladder and was injured. Expert evidence was given at trial that the ladder was too flimsy for building work and that that was the cause of the accident.

82 Liability for Non-Employees

HELD, per Chapman J: The defendant was liable to the claimant in negligence, either as the bailor or lender of a chattel, or as an occupier of property who intended that others should come onto it for the purposes of work or business and use appliances owned or supplied by him. In either case the duty of care is the same, namely to take reasonable care to see that the appliance or chattel was fit and safe for the purpose for which it was to be used. Since the defendant had taken on the obligation to provide equipment, he was liable in negligence for failure to ensure that the ladder was suitable.

However, since the claimant was an experienced builder and had accepted use of the ladder in spite of its apparent inadequacy, he was therefore contributorily negligent and the damages awarded would be reduced accordingly.

Makepeace v Evans Bros (Reading) (a firm)

[2001] ICR 241, CA

[3.31] The defendant was a firm of painters and decorators. It became engaged by a major site contractor, Alfred McAlpine Construction Ltd (McAlpine), to work on a large residential development. The claimant was employed by the defendant as a painter and decorator. On the day in question the claimant was working from a tower scaffold when it fell to the ground. He suffered severe head injuries and was left permanently disabled. The scaffolding had been provided by McAlpine and he had been given permission to use it by McAlpine's site agent. The claimant sued McAlpine and the defendant for his injuries.

HELD, on appeal: While there may be occasions when the main contractor or occupier would owe a duty of care to the employees of others who came upon the premises, as distinct from any duty that existed in relation to the state of the premises themselves, an occupier would not usually be liable to an employee of a contractor employed to carry out work at the occupier's premises if the employee was injured as a result of any unsafe system of work used by the employer, the contractor. It was not generally reasonable to expect an occupier of premises, having engaged a contractor whom he had reasonable grounds to regard as competent, to supervise the contractor's activities in order to ensure that he was discharging his duties to ensure a safe system of work for his employees.

McGarvey v Eve NCI Ltd and N G Bailey & Co Ltd

(2002) LTL, 26 February, CA

[3.32] The claimant was employed by the first defendant in the construction of a warehouse. The first defendant had been sub-contracted by the second defendant, the electrical contractor for the warehouse. The claimant was injured when he fell from a ladder whilst working at the construction site. The claimant was assigned the task which he was doing at the time of his accident by the first defendant. However, the second defendant's foreman pointed the claimant in the direction of the ladder he used which was dangerous and inappropriate for the task in that it was too long to have been placed at an acute angle.

HELD, on appeal: The judge distinguished *Makepeace v Evans Bros (Reading) (a firm)* [2001] ICR 241, CA (above) on the basis that in that case, the sub-contractor who was injured was an experienced painter who had fallen from a scaffold tower that was erected incorrectly. The scaffold tower was the appropriate piece of equipment to have used for the task. The ladder that the claimant was told to use was too long and not safe. Further, it must have been apparent to the second defendant's foreman that the claimant was working alone and accordingly that nobody was able to hold the ladder for him. Those reasons provide a clear distinction between the instant case and *Makepeace*.

Johnson v Coventry Churchill International Ltd

[1992] 3 All ER 14

[3.33] The claimant was sent to work in Germany by the defendants, an English employment agency. The claimant, an experience joiner/carpenter, was hired by the defendants under a contract which described him as a 'sub-contractor' and provided that he was at all times to work as and where directed by the defendants and their clients. The defendants would pay the claimant his remuneration. When in Germany the claimant sustained serious injuries whilst at work and brought an action in England claiming damages for negligence on the ground that the defendants, as his employers, had failed to comply with their duty to provide a safe system of work.

HELD: The claimant was employed by the defendants under a contract of service and not a contract for the supply of 'labour only' services, notwithstanding the references in the contract to 'sub-contractor' and 'fee', since on the facts it was clear that the defendants had dealt with the claimant as they would an ordinary employee and had not transferred any of their responsibilities as employers to their German client.

Morris v Breaveglen Ltd (t/a Anzac Construction Co)

[1993] ICR 766, CA

[3.34] The defendants were sub-contractors on a building site and their employee, the claimant, was working under the control of the main contractors. While driving the main contractors' dumper truck the claimant was injured.

HELD, on appeal : Where a third party was injured by the employee the right of control was the right test but if the employee was injured, his employer remained liable to him. Also his employer was liable for having previously allowed the employee to drive the dumper truck without proper instruction. *Wilsons & Clyde Coal Co v English* [1938] AC 57, HL (see 3.2 above) and *McDermid v Nash Dredging and Reclamation Co Ltd* [1987] AC 906, HL (see 3.6 and 3.11 above) followed.

Per Beldam LJ, at 773: 'If the work on which [the worker] is employed is so closely connected with work being done by another contractor that contractor too owes him a duty to take care for his safety'.

THE AUSTRALIAN APPROACH

[3.35] In Australia there is a general principle, based upon the fact of control or supervision, whereby circumstances may place an employer under a primary duty to supervise other workers or to co-ordinate their activities, even if they are not its employees. See also *Oceanic Crest Shipping Co v Pilbara Harbour Services Pty Ltd* (1986) 160 CLR 626.

Kondis v State Transport Authority

(1984) 154 CLR 672, High Court of Australia

[3.36] During the manual extension of a jib of the crane, operated by the defendant's independent contractor, part of the crane fell on to the claimant. The contractor had deliberately dropped the part and was found to have failed to keep a proper look out or to have warned of his intention to drop the part. The claimant's foreman had failed to instruct him not to stand under the jib during the extension operation.

HELD, on appeal: The defendant was in breach of his duty to provide a safe system of work because the foreman had failed to direct the claimant not to stand under the crane jib during the extension operation. Further, the contractor's failure to adopt a safe system of work constituted a failure by the defendant to satisfy a non-delegable duty to provide a safe system.

Stevens v Brodribb Sawmilling Co

(1986) 160 CLR 16, High Court of Australia

[3.37] A saw-miller employed 'sniggers' to move felled trees to a loading zone and truckers to carry the trees to the mill. Sniggers and truckers used their own vehicles, set their own hours of work, and were paid according to the volume of timber delivered to the mill. The saw-miller did not deduct income tax instalments from the payments. An employee of the saw-miller had general supervision over operations, but exercised no control over the manner in which sniggers and truckers carried out their tasks. While a log was being manoeuvred onto a truck, a trucker was injured by the negligence of a snigger.

HELD, on appeal: The notion that a principal is liable for the negligence of an independent contractor on the basis that the activities he was engaged to perform were extra-hazardous has no place in Australian law (*Honeywill & Stein v Larkin Bros (London's Commercial Photographers) Ltd* [1934] 1 KB 191, CA – see 3.12 above, *Matania v National Provincial Bank Ltd* [1936] 2 All ER 633, CA, and *Salsbury v Woodland* [1970] 1 QB 324, CA – see 3.10 above – not followed).

CHAPTER 4

Breach of Statutory Duty

The nature of the action	[4.2]
Construction of penal provisions	[4.26]
The person to whom the duty is owed	[4.41]
Civil liability under health and safety legislation	
Introduction	
Sources of law	[4.52]
By whom and to whom are duties owed?	[4.53]
The objectives of the European legislation: Framework Directive 89/391/EEC	[4.54]
UK regulations: Workplace (Health, Safety and Welfare Regulations) 1992 (as amended)	[4.57]
Provision and Use of Work Equipment Regulations 1998 (as amended)	[4.69]
Manual Handling Operations Regulations 1992 (as amended)	[4.79]
Control of Substances Hazardous to Health Regulations 2002	[4.86]
Employer's Liability (Defective Equipment) Act 1969	[4.98]

[4.1] Many of the cases summarised below have been decided under statutes which have since been repealed. However they have been included because they illustrate arguments, and possible arguments, on the construction of 'health and safety' statutes. This is of continuing relevance in circumstances where the governing statutes and regulations are regularly repealed and amended.

THE NATURE OF THE ACTION

Lochgelly Iron and Coal Co Ltd v M'Mullan

[1934] AC 1, HL

[4.2] The pursuer of an action for damages alleged that the defender was negligent for failing to secure the roof of the place where his son had been working, contrary to Coal Mines Act 1911, s 49. The Act imposed a duty on the defender employer to provide that the roof of every working place was made secure and the pursuer claimed that the defender had been negligent in failing to perform a duty imposed on them by statute in the interests of the safety of their workmen. The defender argued that the action was excluded by Workmen's Compensation Act 1925, s 29(1), which excluded an employer's liability in proceedings brought independently of the 1925 Act except where injury to a workman was caused by personal negligence or wilful act of the employer.

HELD, on appeal: Where a duty is imposed on an employer to take precautions for the safety of employees then if the employer fails to fulfil that duty and consequently the employee is injured, there is a clear case of negligence. It is immaterial whether the duty derives from the common law or is imposed by statute.

Caswell v Powell Duffryn Associated Collieries Ltd

[1940] AC 152, HL

[4.3] This was an action for damages under the Fatal Accidents Act following the death of the plaintiff's son while working on the conveyor belt at the defendant's colliery. The deceased was employed to clean the roller of the conveyor belt by means of a scraper. He was instructed not to clean the belt when it was in motion and to replace the plate across the belt upon finishing the cleaning process. One day the belt stopped and the deceased's body was found with the arm caught between the belt and the roller with the plate removed. The lever to start and stop the roller was located some distance away from where the deceased worked and there had been no system of signalling to him before restarting the machine. It was therefore possible that the conveyor belt had been restarted while the roller was being cleaned. The deceased's mother alleged that the defendant was under a duty to ensure that the plate had been replaced before the machine was restarted pursuant to the Coal Mines Act 1911, s 55 and that her son's death was caused by the defendant's breach of that duty.

HELD, on appeal: The action was based upon negligence and the plaintiff needed to show that the defendant owed the deceased a duty, that the duty was breached and that the cleaner's death was attributable to the defendant's breach. The statutory duty imposed by the 1911 Act assisted the plaintiff in proving the existence and the nature of the defendant's duty but the plaintiff was still required to prove the causal link with her son's death. Having causally connected the accident with the defendant's duty, the plaintiff's action succeeded.

Smith v Cammell, Laird & Co Ltd

[1940] AC 242, HL

[4.4] An action for damages was brought for breach of the Shipbuilding Regulations 1931 made under Factory and Workshop Act 1901, s 79, requiring all staging to be securely constructed of sound and substantial material and maintained in such condition as to ensure the safety of all persons employed. The respondents were shipbuilders engaged in constructing a vessel which had been launched and placed in a wet dock for finishing works. Staging had been erected in the vessel to assist those firms employed to carry out the finishing works. The appellant was employed to do certain of the finishing work from the staging. Owing to a defect in the staging, the appellant fell from it and sustained serious injuries. This action was brought against the respondents claiming damages for injuries sustained as a result of the respondents' negligence and breach of the statutory duties imposed by the 1931 Regulations. The claim had been dismissed.

HELD, on appeal: The duty imposed by the 1931 Regulations on the occupiers of the shipbuilding yard, the respondents, was an absolute one giving the wording of statutory duty its plain meaning. Appeal allowed.

Carroll v Andrew Barclay & Sons Ltd

[1948] AC 477, HL

[4.5] The appellant brought an action for damages for injuries suffered when he was employed as a machinist by the respondent engineers. The appellant was operating a lathe at the respondent's premises and was protected from the motor by a 5 feet high fence. Between the fence and the overhead driving shaft there was an area of 20 feet in which the belt was unprotected and the appellant's position was such that the lathe placed him in a direct line with the revolving belt. On the day of the accident, the belt broke and lashed over the fence, striking the appellant causing him serious injury. The appellant relied upon FA 1937, s 13 and alleged that the respondent had failed to ensure that 'every part of the transmission machinery' was securely fenced. Before the court, it was argued that the breaking of the belt was a very infrequent occurrence which had never been known to happen within the experience of the witnesses examined on both sides. It was not the practice in comparable factories to fence a motor and vertical belt above a distance of 5 or 6 feet to a maximum of 8 feet. The practice was to fence to such a height and that was sufficient to prevent any machine operator or other person coming into contact with any part of the belt. It was impracticable and commercially unviable to fence the belt to a greater height above the floor.

The appellant argued that section 13 imposed an absolute obligation upon the respondent, as occupier of the premises, to securely fence transmission machinery not only against any risk resulting from its working but against any dangers, foreseen or unforeseen, foreseeable or unforeseeable, and whether in the course of working or in the accidental breaking of the machinery involved.

HELD: While to construe section 13 as to impose an absolute duty would mean a heavy obligation on an employer, if the section so enacts, its terms must be followed. However, their Lordships held that the wording of the relevant sections indicated that the breakage of machinery was not under consideration. The duty of the respondent to fence the transmission machinery meant the erection of a barricade to prevent any employee from making contact with the machine, not an enclosure to prevent broken machinery from flying out. Appeal dismissed.

London Passenger Transport Board v Upson

[1949] AC 155, HL

[4.6] This was an action for damages brought by a pedestrian who was injured when she attempted to cross a road at a pedestrian crossing from behind a parked taxi and into the path of an oncoming bus. The respondent relied upon the Pedestrian Crossing Places (Traffic) Regulations 1941, reg 3, which provided that

88 Breach of Statutory Duty

'the driver of every vehicle approaching a crossing shall, unless he can see that there is no passenger thereon, proceed at such a speed as to be able if necessary to stop before reaching such crossing'.

HELD, ON APPEAL: Taking reg 3 in its literal sense would require vehicles to come to a dead stop at every pedestrian crossing however slowly they were going, in case someone might step in front of them at the last moment and be injured. The driver must be able to see whether the crossing is clear or not up to the time when, going at a reasonable speed, he would be able to stop before reaching the crossing. If he is unable to do so, the statutory duty is breached. The appellant's vision was hindered by the taxi and he was therefore unable to see whether there was anyone on the crossing at the moment when he would have been able to stop. Appeal dismissed.

Lloyd v F Evans & Sons Ltd

[1951] WN 306, CA

[4.7] The claimant was working at the defendant's factory welding steel using an electrical welding plant. He was working outside the factory building in windy conditions. The defendant provided goggles and a screen which the claimant was using but he felt something in his eye and later attended at the hospital where it was found that the eye was seriously injured and it was removed. An action for damages was brought alleging negligence and breach of statutory duty for failure to provide 'suitable goggles or effective screens' contrary to the FA 1937, s 49.

HELD: As the screen was a well recognised form of screen and the goggles were the normal type of goggles provided for oxy-acetylene welding, the claimant failed to prove any breach of common law duty. As far as the breach of statutory duty was concerned, this was resolved in the claimant's favour as it was found that the screen provided had not been effective to protect his eyes. Upheld on appeal.

Latimer v AEC Ltd

[1953] AC 643, HL

[4.8] An employee brought a claim for damages against his employers for negligence and breach of statutory duty to maintain one of the gangways in their works in an efficient state pursuant to the provisions of the FA 1937, s 25. The claimant was employed to collect and transport barrels along a gangway in the defendant's factory. One afternoon an exceptionally heavy rainstorm caused the whole of the defendant's factory to become flooded with surface water. That water became mixed with an oily liquid which was normally collected in channels in the floor of the factory. After the rainfall subsided the defendant spread sawdust on the floor, so far as supplies permitted. Later that day, while working in a gangway that had not been treated with sawdust, the claimant slipped and injured his ankle.

HELD: The employers were not negligent, as they had done all a reasonable employer could be expected to do for the safety of their servants, having regard to the degree of risk. The question whether there has been a breach of statutory duty turned upon the true construction of the FA 1937, s 25. In the circumstances, there was no breach of statutory duty since the floor was structurally sound and could not be said not to be properly maintained because it was in a transient and exceptional condition of being wet and oily. Whether such temporary inefficiency constituted a breach of duty was a question of degree.

John Summers & Sons Ltd v Frost

[1955] AC 740, HL

[4.9] An employee brought a claim for damages against his employer for breach of statutory duty for failing to securely fence a dangerous part of machinery pursuant to the provisions of the FA 1937, s 14(1). The claimant was employed as a maintenance fitter in the defendant's factory. While grinding a piece of metal in the defendant's factory the claimant injured his thumb by contact with the grinding wheel which was moving at about 1,450 rpm. The back and top of the wheel were fenced by a guard in the shape of a hood so that the only part of the revolving stone which was exposed was an arc about seven inches long between the hood and a rest. Section 14(1) of the FA 1937 provides that: 'Every dangerous part of any machinery…shall be securely fenced unless it is in such position or of such construction as to be as safe to every person employed or working on the premises as it would be if securely fenced…'.

HELD, ON APPEAL: In the absence of Regulations modifying these requirements of section 14(1), the duty of the defendant to fence the grinding wheel securely was an absolute one, and the fact that compliance with them might render the machine unusable did not absolve the factory owner from that duty. Since the machine was not so fenced, there was therefore a breach of the statutory duty giving rise to a right to damages.

See also 4.38 below.

Daniels v Ford Motor Co Ltd

[1955] 1 All ER 218, CA

[4.10] This was an action for damages by an employee against his employer for breach of statutory duty for failing to provide suitable goggles pursuant to the provisions of the FA 1937, s 49. The claimant was employed in the process of fettling in the defendant's factory, a process where there is a well-known risk of injury to the eye from fragments of flying metal. Fettling is one of the processes to which the FA 1937, s 49 applies and accordingly goggles of the types best adapted to the process were made available by the defendant for their employees. The goggles selected and worn by the claimant, however, had a tendency to mist over while being worn. While the claimant was at work on the day in question his goggles misted over and he pulled them away from his face to clean them with his a thumb and finger. At that time a piece of metal hit the claimant's right eye causing injury.

HELD: The obligation on the defendant under the FA 1937, s 49 was to provide goggles which were suitable and would protect the wearer's eyes. While this obligation to provide suitable goggles is quite clearly an absolute obligation, there is no absolute obligation that the goggles so provided shall ensure protection. On the facts, therefore, the defendant had provided the claimant with suitable goggles and was not in breach of their duty under the section.

Bux v Slough Metals Ltd

[1974] 1 All ER 262, CA

[4.11] An employee at the defendants' die-casting foundry brought an action for damages. The plaintiff's work involved removing molten metal from a furnace by means of a ladle and pouring it from the ladle into a die. During his training for the work, no goggles were provided or worn nor were instructions given that they should be worn. Sometime later, a new works director decided that goggles should be supplied to the employees and suitable goggles were obtained. The plaintiff tried them but found they hampered his work because they misted up every three or four minutes. He informed his superintendent that the goggles were useless and asked if there were better ones available. The matter was not taken any further. While engaged in making a left turn from the furnace to the die, the ladle struck one of the pinions throwing some of the molten metal into the plaintiff's eyes. He brought an action claiming damages for breach of the defendants' statutory duties under the Non-Ferrous Metals (Melting and Founding) Regulations 1962, reg 13(1), and negligence.

HELD, on appeal: The duty imposed upon the defendants by regulation 13(1) did not in this instance exceed the common law duties of the employer. A statutory obligation may exceed a duty at common law or it may fall short of it or equal it. However, the court has always to construe the statute or statutory instrument which imposes the obligation, consider the facts of the particular case and the allegations of negligence made by a particular employee and the decide whether, if the statutory duties have been fulfilled, any negligence is proved.

Larner v British Steel plc

[1993] 4 All ER 102, CA

[4.12] The plaintiff, a mechanical fitter, brought this action for damages for injuries he suffered when a roller he had been instructed to dismantle for repair fell and crushed his leg. It was alleged that the defendant was in breach of its statutory duty under the Factories Act 1961, s 29(1) for failing, so far as was reasonably practicable, to ensure that the plaintiff's workplace was 'made and kept safe'. The defendant sought to argue that 'safe' in section 29(1) meant 'safe from a reasonably foreseeable danger' and therefore in order to succeed, the plaintiff needed to prove that the danger to which he was exposed was reasonably foreseeable by the defendant.

HELD, on appeal: The burden upon the plaintiff was to prove that he had suffered injury from working at a place which was not made or kept safe. In order to avoid liability, a defendant had to show that it was not reasonably practicable to keep the premises safe in the manner alleged by the plaintiff. The duty under section 29(1) to make and keep the working place safe was qualified by 'so far as is reasonably practicable' and it was not necessary to imply another qualification. Implying a requirement of foreseeability would limit success in a claim for breach of statutory duty to circumstances where the employee will also succeed in a parallel claim for negligence, thereby reducing the utility of the section. Appeal allowed.

Mains v Uniroyal Englebert Tyres Ltd

[1995] IRLR 544, Court of Session

[4.13] The pursuer sustained an injury to his hand while working at a large tyre-building machine. The machine had two modes of operation, automatic and manual. When in manual, the machine depended upon activation by the operator in order for any part of it to be set in motion. On the day of the accident, the operator was adjusting a part of the machine known as the back stitcher, a task which required the machine to be in manual mode. The stitcher arm suddenly moved, trapping the pursuer's finger.

An action for damages was brought against the defender, alleging negligence at common law and breach of statutory duties under the Factories Act 1961, ss 14 and 29(1). It was found that the movement of the stitcher arm while the machine was in manual mode was something which was unforeseeable and the common law claim and claim under section 14 were therefore dismissed. The action under section 29(1) was also dismissed on the grounds that the accident was not reasonably foreseeable.

HELD, on appeal: It was not necessary for an employee, seeking a remedy under section 29(1) to show that the unsafe state of the workplace should have been reasonably foreseeable by the employers. There is nothing in the section to suggest that the obligation is only to prevent any risk arising if that risk is of a reasonably foreseeable nature. Where a statute is designed to protect the safety of employees, it is not appropriate to read into it qualifications which derogate from that purpose.

However, reasonable foreseeability is a factor to be considered when determining whether an employer has discharged the onus of showing that no reasonably practicable precautionary measures could have been taken to avoid the accident. These considerations involve weighing the degree and extent of the risk on the one hand, against the time, trouble and expense of preventing the risk on the other. In the present case, the defender had not invoked the reasonably practicable defence. Appeal allowed.

X v Bedfordshire County Council

[1995] 2 AC 633, HL

[4.14] In this group of cases, some claimants brought actions for damages for personal injury arising out of breach of statutory duty and negligence alleging that they had suffered parental abuse and neglect as a result of the council's failure adequately to investigate reports of such treatment and to protect the claimants from further harm. In other actions, the claimants were claiming damages for breach of statutory duty and negligence alleging that the council had wrongly advised parents regarding their childrens' special educational needs and failed to diagnose a special learning disorder.

HELD, on appeal: An action for breach of statutory duty might arise where, on its true construction, the statute imposed a duty for the protection of a limited class of the public and there was a clear Parliamentary intention to confer a private right of action for breach on members of that class. Whilst there was no general rule for ascertaining whether a statute conferred such a right of action, the absence of another remedy for breach and a clear intention to protect the limited class were indications that a private right of action existed. Further, the existence of some other remedy was not necessarily decisive that no private right existed and a plaintiff basing his claim on a careless exercise of a statutory duty had to show the existence of circumstances giving rise to a duty of care at common law.

Stark v Post Office

[2000] PIQR P105, CA

[4.15] The claimant was a postman and was provided with a bicycle to make his deliveries. In the course of his employment he was riding the bicycle when the front wheel locked and he was propelled over the handlebars and suffered serious injury. The front wheel locked because part of the front brake had broken in two and one part had lodged in the front wheel. In bringing an action for damages for personal injury, the claimant alleged that his employer had been negligent and in breach of its statutory duties pursuant to the Provision and Use of Work Equipment Regulations 1992, reg 6(1) which provides that an employer shall ensure that work equipment is maintained in an efficient state, in efficient working order and in good repair.

At first instance, the judge dismissed the claims as the employer had followed its established policy of replacing the bicycle after ten years. He held that although on the face of it regulation 6(1) imposed strict liability, the primary obligation on an employer was to institute and carry out a system of maintenance to the very best of its ability. The judge found that the Post Office had fulfilled this obligation.

HELD, on appeal: It was clear from the European Work Equipment Directive to which the 1992 Regulations gave effect, that it was intended that regulation 6(1) should impose an absolute obligation and as the bicycle was not in an efficient state or in efficient working order when the front brake broke, the Post Office were in breach of their statutory duty.

CONSTRUCTION OF LEGISLATION ON HEALTH AND SAFETY

Barras v Aberdeen Steam Trawling and Fishing Co Ltd

[1933] AC 402, HL

[4.16] A seaman was engaged to serve for six months as chief engineer on a steam trawler. On returning to port during the term of six months, the trawler collided with aother vessel and went into dry dock for repairs and the crew were paid off. After 14 days, the seaman was re-engaged as chief engineer. He sought to claim from the owners of the trawler wages for the time during which the vessel was under repair, alleging that his service had been terminated by reason of the 'wreck' of the trawler within the meaning of the Merchant Shipping (International Labour Conventions) Act 1925, s 1(1).

HELD, on appeal: It was a well established principle to be applied in the consideration of Acts of Parliament that where a word of doubtful meaning had received a clear judicial interpretation, a subsequent statute which incorporates the same word or the same phrase in a similar context, must be construed so that the word of phrase is interpreted according to the meaning that has previously been assigned to it. The 1925 Act, while intending to embody the International Labour Conventions, did not intend to restrict or limit the rights which seamen already possessed under the earlier Merchant Shipping Act 1894. It did not follow that because the Conventions had agreed to something less than that which seamen had previously enjoyed, their rights should be reduced. The word 'wreck' must be construed in the 1925 Act as it was in the 1894 Act.

Garcia v Harland & Wolff Ltd

[1943] 1 KB 731, KBD

[4.17] The defendants had undertaken the wiring of a 'tween deck of a ship while in wet dock. The hatchway in the 'tween deck was left uncovered and a number of articles, including two piles of hatch covers, were lying around leaving little space for persons to pass. The claimant's husband was employed by the defendants and was returning to his work after dinner when he tripped over a pile of hatch covers, fell into the hold and was killed. This action was brought under the Law Reform (Miscellaneous Provisions) Act 1934, to recover damages for breach of the Shipbuilding Regulations 1931. The issue was whether the obligations imposed by the 1931 Regulations had been extended by the FA 1937 to impose duties on persons undertaking works of repair on a ship in harbour or wet dock.

HELD: The 1931 Regulations impose liability on the occupier of a shipbuilding yard for breach of the statutory duties. If the ship is being repaired in a public dry dock, the person undertaking the work of repair of the ship is also bound by the Regulations and that would have been the case if the defendants in the present case had carried out the wiring with the ship in a public dry dock. In 1937 a new Factories Act was passed which repealed the Factory and Workshop Act 1901 and, in doing so, repealed the Regulations made under the 1901 Act. While the provisions of the new 1937 Act provide the Secretary of State with power to make Regulations which refer to a ship in wet dock and to impose on persons undertaking work on it any duties which he thinks fit, the mere fact that the statutory authority existed to make such Regulations did not alter the meaning of the Regulations imposing duties on occupiers of shipbuilding yards except persons undertaking work in a public dry dock. The claimant's case so far as it is based on the 1931 Regulations failed.

Potts (or Riddell) v Reid

[1943] AC 1, HL

[4.18] A workman was working on scaffolding and stepped onto a plank which had been placed on the working platform without authority in a manner not conforming with the Building Regulations 1926, reg 7, which required that boards or planks forming part of a working platform were to have certain support and were not to project more than a specified distance beyond the end support. As a result of standing on the plank, the workman fell and sustained fatal injuries. The question arose as to whether the 1926 Regulations applied where the Secretary of State had set out in the preamble that they shall apply 'to all premises on which machinery ... is temporarily used for the purpose of the construction of a building', but not where the only machinery consists of 'machinery which is not used for hoisting purposes and is outside the areas of the building under construction'. In the present case there had been a cement mixer situated about 23 yards from the place where the workmen were engaged.

HELD, on appeal: A narrow construction of the words in the preamble would give the Regulations limited application and would not meet the necessity of the case regarding that which the Secretary of State had certified as dangerous. The Regulations were intended to protect workmen equally, whether they were working on the outside of the four walls or inside, where they were engaged in building operations which were associated with the temporary use of machinery. Their Lordships departed from the strict literal construction of the words to hold that the Regulations applied in this case.

London and North Eastern Rly Co v Berriman

[1946] AC 278, HL

[4.19] This was an action for damages under the Fatal Accidents Act 1846 to 1908 brought following the death of the respondent's husband when he was killed by a train while engaged in his routine work of oiling signalling apparatus connecting signal boxes with signals and points in a particular area. The Railway Employment (Prevention of Accidents) Act 1900 authorises the making of rules with the object of reducing dangers incidental to railway services including 'the protection of permanent way men when relaying or repairing permanent way'. The Prevention of Accidents Rules 1902 provided for the protection of men working singly or in gangs on or near railway lines when relaying or repairing the permanent way by providing persons or apparatus for maintaining a good look-out or giving warning against a train or engine approaching. The appellant argued that the deceased was not engaged in any work of relaying or repairing and that if he was repairing, it was not the permanent way that he was repairing.

HELD: The relaying or repairing of apparatus was an operation presenting the same dangers as the relaying or repairing of the rails themselves and, having regard to the purpose of the statute and the rules, there is no adequate reason for providing protection in one case and not in the other. However, the deceased was engaged in oiling and cleaning. The critical word is 'repairing' and the ordinary usage of the English language cannot characterise the work of oiling and cleaning as a work of repair. There may well have been a good reason for limiting the requirement of protection to the case of men engaged in the work of relaying and repairing which might occupy time and require concentration, precluding them from looking after their own safety. While the statute and the rules have a beneficent purpose of providing protection for workmen, their contravention involves penal consequences so that it is not legitimate to stretch the language of the rules beyond the fair and ordinary meaning of the language.

Parvin v Morton Machine Co Ltd

[1952] AC 515, HL

[4.20] The appellant was a minor employed by the respondents as an apprentice fitter. He was instructed to clean a dough-brake which had been manufactured and assembled in the respondents' factory. While he was working, a rag he was holding was drawn into the dough-brake rollers and his hand and forearm followed causing him injury. The appellant brought an action for damages for negligence and for breach of duties imposed by the FA 1937 which required the fencing of machinery. The issue before the court was whether the provisions of the 1937 Act applied to machinery manufactured in the factory.

HELD: There was no ambiguity or difficulty in construing the sections relied upon by the appellant and it was therefore unnecessary to have recourse to presumption or maxims which may be an aid to construction when there is ambiguity or doubt.

Sexton v Scaffolding (Great Britain) Ltd

[1953] 1 QB 153, CA

[4.21] This was an action brought for damages following an accident at work where the claimant fell from a scaffold where there was no guard-rail. The building works had finished and the lowest level of scaffolding used in the works was about to be dismantled, the guard-rail having been removed upon the instruction of the defendant's charge-hand. The claimant sought damages for breach of statutory duty under the Building (Safety, Health and Welfare) Regulations 1948, reg 24, which provided that every side of a working platform or working place from which a person in liable to fall more than 6 feet 6 inches, was to be given a suitable guard-rail.

HELD, on appeal: The scaffolding having served its purpose and the work having been completed, nothing remained to be done except to dismantle it. As to the application of the 1948 Regulations in general, it is unnecessary to decide that none of those Regulations in any circumstances applies to persons employed in the erection or dismantling of scaffolding, but it does not follow that all of the Regulations necessarily do apply. As far as regulation 24 is concerned, it is difficult to see how it can be applied to the operation of dismantling as it seems inevitable that at some time in the course of dismantling a guard-rail, being itself part of the scaffolding, must be taken down and removed and there will be people on the scaffolding after the guard-rail has been removed. Otherwise, the operation of dismantling could not be carried out at all. There was no breach of the Regulations.

Hamilton v National Coal Board

[1960] AC 633, HL

[4.22–4.25] A miner had been working a hand-operated winch which tipped forward and pinned his hand against a roof girder. He brought an action for damages for injury suffered. It was alleged that the employer was in breach of statutory duties imposed by the Mines and Quarries Act 1954, s 81(1), requiring all parts and working gear, including the anchoring and fixing appliances, of all machinery and apparatus to be properly maintained. The miner claimed that it was through the absence of stells to anchor the winch that the accident had occurred.

HELD, on appeal: There was no reason for departing from the ordinary meaning of the word 'maintain' and the principles of construction which rested either on the penal consequences of failure to perform the statutory obligations or alternatively the basic purpose of the Act to protect the workmen, could not usefully be invoked. Giving the language its ordinary meaning, the duty imposed on the owners of the mine was absolute and continuing to keep the winch in a proper and efficient state and was not limited to a duty to service the winch properly.

CONSTRUCTION OF PENAL PROVISIONS

Dyke v Elliott

(1872) LR 4 PC 184, PC

[4.26] A French ship captured a Prussian ship as a prize of war in the English Channel. A French naval officer was put on board and the prize ship was anchored within British waters The French consul engaged an English steam-tug to tow the captured ship from British waters to a French port. Proceedings were brought by the Crown for violation of the Foreign Enlistment Act 1870 and the issue arose as to whether the steam-tug had been employed in the military or naval service of France, a belligerent, as defined within the Act.

HELD, on appeal: The definition section of the 1870 Act does not restrict the meaning to be given to the words appearing in the prohibition section. Within the plain meaning, the words and the spirit of the Act, the sending of an English steam-tug for the express purpose of taking the prize ship and crew speedily and safely to French waters was despatching a ship for the purpose of taking part in the naval service of the belligerent.

Tuck & Sons v Priester

(1887) 19 QBD 629, CA

[4.27] The plaintiffs were art publishers in London who purchased the copyright to a watercolour painting from the artist. The plaintiffs sent a written order to the defendant for 2000 copies of the painting to be made for them. The defendant carried out the order and made a number of copies for himself. The plaintiffs then registered the copyright before the defendant then sold some of the copies he had made for himself. The plaintiffs sought damages and penalties under 25 & 26 Vict c 68, ss 11 and 6.

HELD, on appeal: Great care must be taken when construing a section which imposes a penalty. If there is a reasonable interpretation which will avoid the penalty in any particular case, that construction is to be adopted. If there are two reasonable interpretations, effect must be given to the more lenient one, as is the settled rule for the construction of penal sections. In this case, section 6 (the penal section) might reasonably be read so as not to impose a penalty when the copy of the art work sold was made in a foreign country.

McCarthy v Coldair Ltd

[1951] 2 TLR 1226, CA

[4.28] The claimant was an electrician employed by another company at premises constituting a factory and owned and occupied by the defendant. On the day of the accident, he had begun to climb a 10 ft ladder to reach electric wiring, the ladder slipped and he fell and sustained injury to his right wrist. An action for damages was brought for failure to provide a safe means of access to his place of work 'so far as is reasonably practicable' contrary to the FA 1937, s 26(1).

HELD, on appeal: The use of the phrase 'so far as is reasonably practicable' meant that the duty to provide a safe means of access was not absolute but depended upon what was reasonably practicable having regard to the degree of risk and the steps necessary to eliminate the risk. There was a substantial risk of the ladder slipping and measures should have been taken to prevent it. Measures such as asking a charge-hand to stand at the foot of the ladder or seeing that some heavy weight was put at the bottom were reasonably practicable and the failure to adopt any one of them made the defendant guilty of a breach of the Factories Act.

Beadsley v United Steel Cos Ltd

[1951] 1 KB 408, CA

[4.29] The deceased was engaged in setting moulds on a casting car at the defendant's steel works employee was slinging moulds so that they could be lifted overhead by a crane and taken to another part of the works. The defendant provided stirrup slings but on this occasion the other employee used a three-fold sling which was intended to be used for a separate purpose and was therefore already attached to the crane. The result was that the mould slipped from the sling and fell on the deceased. The deceased's widow was claiming a breach of statutory duty under the FA 1937, s 23(1), which provided that no chain, rope or lifting tackle shall be used unless it is of good construction, sound material, adequate strength and free from patent defect.

HELD, on appeal: There was no breach of section 23(1) in the absence of any evidence that the chain or lifting tackle had any defect in its construction. Being of good construction could not mean 'good construction for the purpose for which it was used' 'and' for the particular purpose for which it was being used at the time of the accident. This would mean that on one day the chain or lifting tackle would be of good construction and on the next day not, depending on the use. The Act put a heavy burden on employers, laying down a duty which was absolute and the breach of which could entail criminal prosecution. It did not, however, make an employer responsible for everything that a workman did.

Harrison v National Coal Board

[1951] AC 639, HL

[4.30] The Explosives in Coal Mines Order 1934, made under the Coal Mines Act 1911, imposed a duty on a shot-firer to see that all persons in the vicinity had taken proper shelter before firing a shot or coupling the cable to the firing apparatus.

A coalface worker suffered injury through the failure of a shot-firer to perform his statutory duty and sought damages against his employers, the mine-owners. The issue was whether the mine-owners were liable in damages for a fellow employee's breach of statutory duty as the statutory provisions did not impose a direct or personal duty on the mine-owners, rendering the (now historic) doctrine of common employment inapplicable.

HELD, on appeal: The question of whether the duty which is laid upon the shot-firer is one for which the owner is personally liable or whether he has some lesser responsibility rests upon the true construction of the 1911 Act. The Act and the Order do not provide a general requirement that they shall be observed. A duty on the owner personally to see that requirements are complied with can be inferred in some cases and in many cases the duty is prescribed by the Act. In those cases they impose an obligation, but not an absolute one. The true meaning of the provisions must be that where no personal duty is laid upon the owner, the only obligation is to enforce the provisions to the best of his ability. In the case of a shot-firer whom the owner of the mine cannot himself appoint and with whose activities he cannot interfere, there is no reason for the owner to have any duty beyond the obligations to enforce the provisions to the best of his ability. There was no breach of that duty. The mine-owners were not therefore liable in damages to the employee for the shot-firer's breach of duty.

Burns v Joseph Terry & Sons Ltd

[1951] 1 KB 454, CA

[4.31] The claimant was employed by the defendant at a machine for cleaning chocolate beans at their factory. His everyday duties involved keeping the floor around the machine clean and collecting any beans which had spilled in the course of operating the machine. On Friday afternoons, when the machine was stopped, he assisted in the cleaning and went up a ladder and collected any beans that had been spilt over onto a shelf seven feet above the floor. At the back of the machine was a cogged rotating pulley wheel, a shaft and pinion behind a circular wire mesh which barricaded the wheel from a frontal approach but there was no circular return guard behind the wheel from the top edge of the mesh. On one occasion, the claimant placed a ladder against a rotating shaft at the top of the machine, above the shelf. The ladder started to slip sideways and the claimant put his hand out for support and got hold of the cogged pulley wheel, behind the mesh which took his hand downwards between the pulley wheel and pinion. The claimant alleged that his injuries were due to the defendant's breach of statutory duty pursuant to the FA 1937, s 13(1), which required transmission machinery to be 'securely fenced'.

HELD, on appeal: The same test should be applied in deciding whether machinery is 'securely fenced' as is applied in deciding whether it is 'dangerous'. To an allegation that machinery which has in fact caused injury is dangerous, it is enough to prove that it was not dangerous in any reasonably foreseeable circumstances. A prosecution based upon the words of the section depends upon the prosecution being able to establish that in reasonably foreseeable circumstances the machinery was not as safe as it would be if securely fenced. As this construction is a reasonably possible construction then, this being a statute imposing criminal penalties, it should be adopted.

Thurogood v Van Den Berghs & Jurgens Ltd

[1951] 2 KB 537, CA

[4.32] The claimant brought an action for damages following an accident at work when he was testing an electric wall fan. The claimant was employed at the defendants' premises which were used for the manufacture of margarine and were a factory within the meaning of the FA 1937. To test the electric wall fan, he had taken it to a separate building where repair work was done. He felt the motor to check for vibration and heat and while doing so his right hand was caught by the revolving blades. The claimant alleged that the blades should have been securely fenced as required by section 14 of the 1937 Act.

HELD, on appeal: The rules of construction which apply to provisions imposing a penalty mean that a penalty should be avoided if a common sense meaning can be given to the statutory language. However, whether penal or remedial, the statute should be interpreted according to the plain, literal and grammatical meaning of the words unless that would lead to a clear contradiction to the apparent purpose of the Act. It was unnatural and required a straining of the language of the provision to deem the repair of the electric fan as incidental to the process of manufacture of margarine being the work undertaken at the defendant's factory. It would further be inconsistent with the scope of other Factories Acts to extend the requirements for health and safety in the 1937 Act to the plant and equipment installed in the factory.

Norris v Syndic Manufacturing Co Ltd

[1952] 2 QB 135, CA

[4.33] The claimant was employed as a tool setter in the defendant's metal toy factory. He was engaged in adjusting a power press into which metal strips were fed and stamped into shape. Pressure on the foot pedal caused the press to descend by electric power. The defendant had provided the claimant with a guard but he had removed it in order to carry out his work. The claimant sought damages from the defendant for breach of its statutory duties under the FA 1937, ss 14 and 16, which required the press be securely fenced and that the fencing be maintained and kept in position, respectively. Section 119 of the 1937 Act imposed a duty on workmen to use the guard once it was provided and available for use. The question to be determined was whether the claimant was in breach of section 119 by not using the guard in circumstances where the defendant had demonstrated his work to him without the guard and had acquiesced in his not using it.

HELD, on appeal: It was no defence for the claimant to say that the defendant did not insist upon his using the guard. The award of damages was reduced to reflect the fact that the claimant had failed to use the guard once it was provided and available for use.

Ebbs v James Whitson & Co Ltd

[1952] 2 QB 877, CA

[4.34] The claimant was employed by the defendant as a coachbuilder at their factory. In the course of his employment, the claimant used a process involving the scraping and sandpapering of Monsonia wood which gave off a fine peppery powder. The powder settled on him causing intense skin irritation and a diagnosis of contact dermatitis. An action was brought against the defendant alleging breaches of the FA 1937, ss 4 and 47, which provided for ventilation and other specific measures to be taken in certain circumstances to prevent the inhalation of dust or fumes.

HELD, on appeal: The defendant was not in breach of the statutory provisions. The Act required that an employer provide ventilation or such other means as would render harmless, so far as practicable, all fumes dust etc that may be injurious to health. The trial judge found that the defendant had effective and suitable provision for ventilation and the evidence showed that the only suitable protective measures were gloves and ointment. However, these measures would not render the dust harmless but serve instead to protect the workmen. There was therefore no breach of section 4 of the Act. Section 47 dealt with the removal of dust or fumes to prevent inhalation by workers. It was aimed primarily at preventing dust being present in substantial quantities so that it was likely to be injurious. The evidence was that the dust from the Monsonia wood was not present in substantial quantities nor was it likely to be injurious except to a worker with a particular sensitivity to it.

Rees v Bernard Hastie & Co Ltd

[1953] 1 QB 328, CA

[4.35] The claimant was a cutter at the defendant's factory. He used electrical shears to cut sheets of steel. While holding the shears in his hand and bending over the steel sheet to be cut, a strip of steel sprang up and pierced his eye causing him to lose the sight of that eye. An action was brought against the defendant for failing to provide goggles or an effective screen, contrary to the FA 1937, s 49, which provided that an employer should provide suitable goggles or effective screens for processes involving special risk of eye injury from particles or fragments thrown off in the course of that process. By virtue of the Protection of Eyes Regulations 1938, the process of 'welding or cutting of metals by means of an electrical, oxy-acetylene or similar process' was specified as a process to which section 49 applied. The issue to be determined was whether the process of cutting the steel sheets by means of the electrical shears was a 'process' to which the Regulations applied.

HELD, on appeal: The Regulations applied to high temperature electrical processes involving special risk to the eyes of fragments or particles being thrown off. The use of the metal sheers was a cold process which did not therefore involve any risk falling within the Regulations. The 1937 Act created an offence and therefore a natural construction prevailed for the benefit of the party against whom the breach was alleged.

Hunter v Singer Manufacturing Co Ltd

1953 SLT (Notes) 84, Outer House

[4.36] The pursuer was an employee working at the installation of a new fire alarm system at the defender's factory. The new system required the fitting up of a bell in a certain room where the bell had to be fixed to a steel column by means of cutting three holes in the steel column at a point about 9 ft from ground level. While the pursuer was standing near the top of the ladder cutting the holes in the steel column, a piece of the electric drill broke off and damaged his left eye. An action for damages was brought for breach of the Protection of Eyes Regulations 1938 for failure to provide goggles or effective screens to protect his eyes.

HELD, on appeal: The correct construction of the Regulations was that which prevailed for the benefit of the person against whom the breach is alleged. The decision in *Rees v Bernard Hastie* (see 4.35 above) interpreted the Regulations to apply only to high-temperature processes and did not extend to cold cutting process. Decision followed. Claim for breach of the Regulations failed.

Richard Thomas & Baldwins Ltd v Cummings

[1955] AC 321, HL

[4.37] The claimant was employed as a fitter at the defendant's factory and was assisting a co-worker to make adjustments to an electric grinding machine. In order to make the adjustments, the motive power had been cut off. When he attempted to pull a belt to rotate the face plate, his finger was crushed between the belt and a pulley. An action was brought for damages for the defendant's failure to securely fence or safeguard the machinery, contrary to the FA 1937, ss 13(1) and 14(1), and the failure to maintain the fencing and keep it in position, contrary to section 16 of the 1937 Act.

HELD, on appeal: The matter turned upon the true construction of section 16 and whether the machinery was 'in motion or in use', within the meaning of that section, at the time of the accident. While the belt and pulley were in motion, it was not motion for the purpose for which they were intended, but for repair. Further, it was not motion when it was turned by hand and there is no prime motion in the prime mover. The phrase 'in motion' also imported a continuing state of motion lasting an appreciable period of time. The context of the phrase 'in motion' meant that it was not unreasonable to apply its more limited meaning. The belt and pulley had not been 'in motion' within the meaning of section 16 and there was therefore no statutory prohibition on the removal of the fence when the machinery was being repaired.

John Summers & Sons Ltd v Frost

[1955] AC 740, HL

[4.38] See 4.9 above. The claimant was a maintenance fitter at the defendant's factory. While grinding a piece of metal, he injured his thumb through contact with a grinding wheel moving at about 1,450 rpm. The upper part of the machine was guarded by a fixed hood and at the base there was an adaptable tool rest, however the rest of the stone was unguarded. This action was brought for damages for the defendant's breach of the FA 1937, s 14(1), providing that every dangerous part of machinery shall be securely fenced unless it is in such a position or of such construction as to be as safe to every person employed or working on the premises as it would be if securely fenced.

HELD, on appeal: The question was whether the grinding wheel was securely fenced within the meaning of the 1937 Act. The intention of Parliament was to be ascertained only from the words of the Act. When it was intended to add a proviso or qualification to a statutory duty, Parliament had done so. Without such a qualification, the obligation to securely fence the machinery within the meaning of the Factories Act, s 14 was an absolute one. 'Securely fenced' meant secured against all dangers whether foreseeable or not. The commercial impracticability was not a consideration.

Haigh v Charles W Ireland Ltd

[1973] 3 All ER 1137, HL

[4.39] The claimant was an employee of the defendant whose business was in the acquisition of scrap metal that was cut up and sold to steel works. Among a load of scrap was an old safe which was locked and without a key. The claimant, in the course of his employment, cut it open with an oxyacetylene cutter. The safe exploded causing the claimant serious injuries. Unbeknown to the defendant, the safe had contained gelignite. An action for damages was brought for breach of statutory duty imposed by the Factories Act 1961, s 31(4), providing that plant containing explosive substance was not to be subjected to cutting operations that involved the application of heat until all practicable steps had been taken to remove the explosive material or to render it non-explosive. The issue was whether the safe was 'plant' within the meaning of the 1961 Act.

HELD, on appeal: The purpose of the 1961 Act was to secure the safety, health and welfare of those working in factories. Primarily, the legislation sought to ensure that the precautions of the Act and the Regulations made thereunder were imposed on the employer as opposed to providing a civil remedy in damages for employees who sustained personal injuries at work. Where the employer had taken all reasonable care for an employee's safety, it was not the purpose of the 1961 Act to transfer the burden of loss sustained by an injured employee to the employer irrespective of any causative fault. When construing the 1961 Act, the court was not to give a strained meaning to words so as to provide a way of serving the social purpose of compensating an injured employee. The legislation was intended to lay down specific precautions which were to be taken by employers in factories to ensure their employees safety, together with the necessary penal sanctions. An ordinary meaning was to be given to the word 'plant', being the apparatus in a factory used in carrying out an industrial process of the factory. In contrast, the safe was an item brought into the factory for the purpose of being subjected to that industrial process and was therefore not a part of it.

Swain v Denso Marston Ltd

[2000] PIQR P129, CA

[4.40] The claimant was a production fitter employed by the defendant. In the course of his employment, he was required to strip down a conveyor system at the defendant's premises. He removed various components of the system and then removed the roller. He expected the roller to be hollow, however it was solid, weighing around 20 kg. The weight of the roller trapped his hand against the metal frame causing him a crush injury. An action for damages was brought alleging breaches of the Manual Handling Operations Regulations 1992 for failure to carry out risk assessments, contrary to regulation 4(1)(b)(i); failure to reduce the risk of injury to the lowest level reasonably practicable, contrary to regulation 4(1)(b)(ii) and failure to give precise information as to the weight of the load, contrary to regulation 4(1)(b)(iii).

HELD, on appeal: Regulation 4(1)(b) of the 1992 Regulations imposed three separate and distinct obligations upon an employer. The duties under that sub-section were not to be considered conjunctively. As the defendant had not carried out an assessment under regulation 4(1)(b)(i), the claim succeeded.

THE PERSON TO WHOM THE DUTY IS OWED

Field v Perrys (Ealing) Ltd

[1950] 2 All ER 521, KBD

[4.41] The claimant was a night watchman employed by the defendant on a site on which a block of flats was under construction. The claimant was making his round at 10:30 pm during a weekend when there was no work on site. He had been provided with a hurricane lamp but was injured when he fell over a loose plank left in the roadway. He brought an action for damages alleging breach of common law duty owed by the defendant and breach of statutory duty to efficiently light his 'working-place' under the Building Regulations 1926, reg 15. The defendant sought to avoid liability under the Regulations arguing that they did not apply to the site as at the weekend it was not 'temporarily used for the purpose of the construction of a building'.

HELD: The regulation was not designed to provide that the whole of the premises should be 'efficiently lighted'. It said 'Every working-place and approach thereto' thereby contemplating a specific working-place where people are doing a specific piece of work. It cannot extend to the case of a night watchman who has no specific working-place at all. Once work for the day has ceased and there is only a night watchman on duty, there is no longer on the site any specific working-place that the regulation requires to be efficiently lit.

Herbert v Harold Shaw Ltd

[1959] 2 QB 138, CA

[4.42] The claimant, a roofer, was fixing asbestos roofing sheets to the steel framework of a shed that had been erected by the defendant. He was injured when his foot slipped and he fell over the edge of the roof. The claimant had been a skilled roofer for many years, at first as a roofing and tiling contractor and then employed by the defendant as a foreman. He later decided that he would be his own boss and had occasionally worked for persons other than the defendant but for the five years prior to the accident he had worked exclusively for the defendant. His method of payment varied; sometimes an hourly rate, sometimes by piecework. He paid and engaged his own assistant, charging his wages to the defendant. The claimant stamped his own national insurance card as a self-employed person and for tax purposes he was treated as a man running his own business. The defendant did not supply any equipment though on the day of the accident the claimant had borrowed two ladders, but he could not borrow a plank, which he thought to be necessary to give himself a better foothold on the roof. The claimant brought an action for damages for breach of the Building (Safety, Health and Welfare) Regulations 1948, alleging that the defendant had failed to provide proper equipment.

HELD, on appeal: The contract between the claimant and the defendant was not a contract for work but a contract for the results of the work. He was paid by the hour at the standard rate at the material time and the defendant allowed him to add in his bill the wages which he paid to his assistant. It was a contract between independent contractors and no question of employer and employee or master and servant arose. The 1948 Regulations had no application to independent contractors outside the master and servant relationship.

Uddin v Associated Portland Cement Manufactures Ltd

[1965] 2 QB 15, QBD

[4.43] The claimant was employed by the defendant as a gear attendant in the packing plant of their cement factory. The packing plant and the dust collecting plant were housed in a single five-storeyed building. The claimant was a machinery attendant whose duty it was to see that the hoppers or silos were kept at an adequate level with the different types of cement. His place of work was on the second and third floors of the packing plant, he had no duties in connection with the dust collecting plant. Though he was not expressly prohibited from going up to the dust collecting plant, he knew that he was not authorised to go there except when specially instructed to do cleaning work there when the plant was shut down. On the day of the accident, he climbed the ladder of the dust collecting plant and saw a pigeon roosting behind a revolving shaft. He attempted to catch the pigeon by climbing on top of a metal cabinet and leaning over the shaft. Part of his boiler suit became caught in the coupling of the revolving shaft and he suffered a traumatic amputation of his right arm. The claimant brought an action for damages alleging negligence and breaches of statutory duties under the Factories Acts 1937–1959, ss 13(1), 14(1) and 17(1).

HELD: Section 13(1) provided that every part of transmission machinery shall be securely fenced. It was held that the revolving shaft was not a shaft by which the motion or motive power of the prime mover was transmitted and was not therefore transmission machinery within the meaning of the sub-section. Section 17(1) provided for effective guarding of components of factory machinery intended to be driven by mechanical power. It was held that this obligation was placed solely upon the person who sells or lets on hire the machinery referred to or who acts as agent for such person. Section 14(1) provided for dangerous parts of machinery to be securely fenced and the issue before the court was whether the shaft was a 'dangerous part of any machinery' and, if so, whether the defendant was in breach of its statutory duty towards the claimant at a time when he was doing an act wholly outside the scope of his employment, for his own benefit, at a place to which he was not authorised to go and at a place to which he knew he was not authorised to go. The precautions were found to be inadequate and there was a foreseeable risk that an over-zealous employee, hearing something wrong in the plant might hurriedly mount the ladder and slip or fall and grasp the revolving shaft to prevent himself falling. The defendant was in breach of section 14(1) and the claimant was not wholly debarred from recovery by reason of the fact that at the time of his injury he was doing an act wholly outside the scope of his employment, though there was a reduction of damages by 80% to reflect the claimant's folly in attempting to seize the pigeon in the manner he did.

Reid v Galbraith's Stores

1970 SLT (Notes) 83, Court of Session Outer House

[4.44] The pursuer was a customer at the greengrocery counter of the defender's department store. She stepped on a leek which was lying on the floor and fell, sustaining an injury. An action for damages was brought alleging breach of the defender's common law duty of care and failure to properly maintain the floor to keep it free from obstruction and from any substance likely to cause a person to slip, so far as is reasonably practicable, contrary to the Offices, Shops and Railway Premises Act 1963, s 16(1).

HELD, on appeal: The common law duty of care did not require the defender to 'immediately' clear up a vegetable which had spilt on the floor. The duty was to clear up the vegetable as soon as possible. As far as the statutory duty was concerned, the 1963 Act was clearly aimed at the protection of employees, and customers were not entitled to bring an action founded upon it. To this extent the claim was held irrelevant.

Smith v George Wimpey & Co Ltd

[1972] 2 QB 329, CA

[4.45] The claimant was employed by George Wimpey & Co who were sub-contractors to John Laing & Son, the main contractors for the construction of a bridge over the M1. The workmen had trodden a path down the side of a cutting and up the other side. It was a well trodden path. On the day in question, the claimant used the path, which was steep with pieces of rubble on it. He put his foot on to a loose piece of rubble and slipped. This action was brought against the defendants for damages alleging against his employer, Wimpey, breaches of the common law duty of an employer to take reasonable care for the safety of workmen and of statutory duty under the Construction (Working Places) Regulations 1966 and, against the main contractors, Laing, breach of the statutory duty owed as occupier under the Occupiers Liability Act 1957 and for breach of the duty to ensure that sub-contractors were not confronted with unnecessary risk when co-ordinating their activities. On appeal the point was raised whether the main contractors owed a statutory duty to the claimant, an employee of the sub-contractors, under the 1966 Regulations.

HELD: There were conflicting decisions on the application of the 1966 Regulations vis-à-vis main contractors and the employees of sub-contractors, two decisions having been decided against the main contractor and two in its favour. It was held that the wording of the Regulations showed an intention that the statutory duty did not extend to the employees of sub-contractors. The scope of the Regulations imposed statutory duties upon 'every contractor, and every employer of workmen undertaking any of the operations or works to which these regulations apply' and such duties required that such party must 'comply with such of the requirements of the following regulations as affect him or any workman employed by him' (reg 3(1)). The use of the words 'by him' showed that it was the intention of the legislature not to extend the liability of the main contractor so as to make him liable to the servants of the sub-contractor.

Jones v Minton Construction Ltd

(1973) 15 KIR 309

[4.46] The claimant was contracted on a labour-only basis by the defendants to carry out bricklaying work at their building site. There was a cement mixer on the site which was used by the contractors. The cement mixer was old and had not been used for at least six weeks. The claimant attempted manually to rotate the mixer but caught his right hand in the nip formed by the engagement of the bevel gear ring and the gear pinion. The guard used to cover the nip had been removed unbeknownst to the defendants. An action for damages was brought for breach of contract and negligence.

HELD: The Construction (General Provisions) Regulations 1961 required that every dangerous part of machinery was to be securely fenced unless in such a position or of such construction as to be as safe to every person employed or working on the site of the operations or works as it would be if it were securely fenced. There was a statutory duty upon the claimant to use the equipment to which the provisions of the 1961 Regulations applied, in such a manner which complied with those provisions. The claimant contracted to himself the statutory obligations and forewent the benefit of the common law duty of care owed by a master to a servant. The relationship between the parties was not one of master and servant and therefore the statutory duties could not be implied into the contract nor were there any of the ordinary duties arising from such a relationship. Claim failed.

Westwood v Post Office

[1974] AC 1, HL

[4.47] The claimant was the widow and administrator of the estate of the deceased who had been an employee of the defendant. He was employed as a technical officer at the defendant's telephone exchange. The building was a three-storey building with a flat roof. The normal means of access to the roof was through one of two doors at the tops of stairways at each side of the roof. Adjacent to one of the doors to the roof was a door into the lift motor room. It was possible to gain access to the roof through the lift motor room, via a window. Between the door of the lift motor room and the window there was a trap door used to move materials up and down. On the day in question, the deceased had gone to the roof via the window in the lift motor room, following a group of his colleagues. When leaving the roof, they used the same route. When the deceased crossed the trap door, it broke under his weight and fell through to the next floor and suffered fatal injuries. The claimant brought this action alleging breach of their statutory duties to provide a safe floor contrary to the Offices, Shops and Railway Premises Act 1963. This Act provided for the health and safety of persons employed to work in office premise and the issue was whether the lift motor room was 'office premises' within the meaning of the Act. It was conceded that the trap door had not been of sound construction.

HELD, on appeal: It was conceded that the building was office premises save that this did not extend to the lift motor room, the principal use of which was not as an office or for office purposes. It was held that the principal purpose for which the telephone exchange was occupied was for telephone and telegraph operating. As the building as a whole constituted office premises, the parts to be excluded were those not used as an office or for office purposes. Washrooms, cloakrooms, rest rooms, boiler rooms and lifts were examples which were not used as offices but were all used for office purposes. If the lift is solely or principally used for office purposes so must the lift shaft, the lift motor and the lift motor room. The trap door formed part of the floor of the office premises as defined in the Act and the defendant had failed to maintain the floor in a safe condition contrary to their statutory duties.

Dexter v Tenby Electronics Accessories Ltd

[1991] Crim LR 839, DC

[4.48] The claimant was an employee of an independent contractor. The defendant was the occupier of the premises at which the work was being carried out. He was instructed to work on the roof and in doing so fell through the roof which, it was conceded, was defective. An action was brought for damages for breach of the Factories Act 1961, s 29(1), which provides that there should be provided and maintained a safe means of access to every place at which 'any person has at any time to work'. At first instance the claim was dismissed as the claimant had been acting under the direct instructions of his employer, the contractors, and the defendants exercised no influence over the way the work was being carried out.

HELD, on appeal: The occupier of the premises was responsible for compliance with the duties arising under the 1961 Act throughout the factory and the occupier's knowledge of contravention of the Act was irrelevant to criminal liability.

MacMillan v Wimpey Offshore Engineers and Constructors Ltd

1991 SLT 515, Ct of Sess

[4.49] The pursuer was employed by the defender as a rigger on an oil rig in the North Sea. He was standing outside the defenders' office on the rig discussing a job with the foreman. The foreman suddenly grabbed the pursuer and battered his head against a metal skip. An action for damages for personal injury and consequential losses was brought for breach of the Offshore Installations (Operational Safety, Health and Welfare) Regulations 1976, reg 32(2), which imposes a duty upon an employer to ensure that an employee employed by him for work on an offshore installation complies with any provision of the Regulations imposing a duty on him or expressly prohibiting him from doing a specified act.

HELD: It was not a defence in civil proceedings for breach of regulation 32(2) that the employer had used all due diligence to enforce the execution of the Regulations. The responsibility placed on an employer by regulation 32(2) was an absolute one and effectively required an employer to guarantee compliance with the Regulations by employees. It would be contrary to the whole legislative scheme if an employer could wash his hands of his employees as soon as their day's work was finished. Claim allowed to proceed.

Banna v Delicato

1999 SLT 84, Sheriff Court

[4.50–4.51] The pursuer was shopping in the defender's store when she caught her foot in a bread basket on the floor and fell suffering personal injury. This action was brought for damages for breach of common duty of care under the Occupiers' Liability (Scotland) Act 1960 and breach of statutory duty under the Workplace (Health, Safety and Welfare) Regulations 1992, reg 12(3). Regulation 12(3) provides that: 'so far as is reasonably practicable, every floor in a workplace shall be kept free from obstructions and from any article or substance which may cause a person to slip, trip or fall'. The question was whether this statutory provision was intended to protect a particular class of persons to which the pursuer belonged. The defender argued that the provision applied to employees only and sought to have the claim struck out on that basis.

HELD: The reference to 'a person' means to any person and could not be restricted to employees or persons working there unless there was a clear indication in the Regulations as a whole that such a restriction was intended. There was no reason to import such a restriction to regulation 12(3), although such restriction had been introduced to other provisions. If Parliament had intended to restrict regulation 12(3) to persons at work it would have done so. Defender's application dismissed and the claim remitted.

CIVIL LIABILITY UNDER HEALTH AND SAFETY LEGISLATION

INTRODUCTION

Sources of law

[4.52] By far the main source of statutory duties on employers in the field of health and safety is now European law. In particular, Directives made under the Framework Directive 89/391/EEC, and transposed into English law by Regulations under the Health and Safety at Work etc Act 1974 (HSWA), lay down generally applicable rules in the fields which they cover. Further detailed provision is also to be found in other Regulations derived from European law.

For a full account of the relevant principles of construction, see above. In summary, however, the court in construing legislation enacted to give effect to European law should adopt a purposive approach, ie should construe the legislation wherever possible so as to give effect to the purpose of the relevant European provision. In the context of health and safety legislation, that is likely to involve a construction which enlarges rather than diminishes employers' obligations with regard to workers' health. The court will in particular have regard to the fundamental principles which are set out in the relevant Directive.

This work sets out some of the most commonly encountered provisions of legislation of general application to the workplace together with case law relating to them. It should be noted that the pace of change in this area is very rapid, and even an apparently up-to-date source should be checked to ensure that no relevant amendments have occurred since publication.

By whom and to whom are duties owed?

[4.53] Duties under these Regulations are principally owed by employers to employees. By HSWA, s 53(1), an employee is an individual who works under a contract of employment, and employer is construed accordingly. But, as will be seen below, certain Regulations place duties on persons other than employers, and extend duties to persons other than employees, eg others who may be affected by a breach of the duty. Care must be taken in each case to refer to the full text of the relevant Regulation.

The objectives of the European Legislation

Framework Directive 89/391/EEC

[4.54] The Directive, though not generally directly effective in English law, is important because it sets out the basic approach to the employer's obligations which is reflected in individual Directives and the UK Regulations which give them effect. Reference should be made to the Directive whenever a question of construction arises which can only be answered by looking to the purpose of the legislation.

From the Preamble

[4.55] This Directive does not justify any reduction in levels of protection already achieved in individual Member States.

Article 1

Object
1. The object of this Directive is to introduce measures to encourage improvements in the safety and health of workers at work.

Article 5

General Provision
1. The employer shall have a duty to ensure the safety and health of workers in every aspect related to the work.

2. Where an employer enlists competent external services or persons, this shall not discharge him from his responsibilities in this area.
3. The workers' obligations in the field of safety and health at work shall not affect the principle of the responsibility of the employer.
4. This Directive shall not restrict the option of Member States to provide for the exclusion or the limitation of employers' responsibility where occurrences are due to unusual and unforeseeable circumstances, beyond the employers' control, or to exceptional events, the consequences of which could not have been avoided despite the exercise of all due care. ...

Article 6

General obligations on employers

1. Within the context of his responsibilities, the employer shall take the measures necessary for the safety and health protection of workers, including prevention of occupational risks and provision of information and training, as well as provision of the necessary organization and means. The employer shall be alert to the need to adjust these measures to take account of changing circumstances and aim to improve existing situations.
2. The employer shall implement the measures referred to in the first sub-paragraph of paragraph 1 on the basis of the following general principles of prevention:
   (a) avoiding risks;
   (b) evaluating the risks which cannot be avoided:
   (c) combating the risks at source;
   (d) adapting the work to the individual, especially as regards the design of work places, the choice of work equipment and the choice of working and production methods, with a view, in particular, to alleviating monotonous work and work at a predetermined work-rate and to reducing their effect on health.
   (e) adapting to technical progress;
   (f) replacing the dangerous by the non-dangerous or the less dangerous;
   (g) developing a coherent overall prevention policy which covers technology, organization of work, working conditions, social relationships and the influence of factors related to the working environment;
   (h) giving collective protective measures priority over individual protective measures;
   (i) giving appropriate instructions to the workers.
3. Without prejudice to the other provisions of this Directive, the employer shall, taking into account the nature of the activities of the enterprise and/or establishment:
   (a) evaluate the risks to the safety and health of workers, inter alia in the choice of work equipment, the chemical substances or preparations used, and the fitting-out of work places.
   Subsequent to this evaluation and as necessary, the preventive measures and the working and production methods implemented by the employer must:

- assure an improvement in the level of protection afforded to workers with regard to safety and health,
- be integrated into all the activities of the undertaking and/or establishment and at all hierarchical levels;

(b) where he entrusts tasks to a worker, take into consideration the worker's capabilities as regards health and safety;

(c) ensure that the planning and introduction of new technologies are the subject of consultation with the workers and/or their representatives, as regards the consequences of the choice of equipment, the working conditions and the working environment for the safety and health of workers;

(d) take appropriate steps to ensure that only workers who have received adequate instructions may have access to areas where there is serious and specific danger.

4. Without prejudice to the other provisions of this Directive, where several undertakings share a work place, the employers shall cooperate in implementing the safety, health and occupational hygiene provisions and, taking into account the nature of the activities, shall coordinate their actions in matters of the protection and prevention of occupational risks, and shall inform one another and their respective workers and/or workers' representatives of these risks.

5. Measures related to safety, hygiene and health at work may in no circumstances involve the workers in financial cost.

Stark v Post Office

[2000] ICR 1013, CA

[4.56] (See also 4.15 above.) The Provision and Use of Work Equipment Regulations 1992 (see now the 1998 Regulations (below at 4.64)), required the employer to 'ensure that work equipment is maintained in an efficient state, in efficient working order and in good repair.' The claimant postman was hurt when his bicycle broke for a reason that (as the judge found) nobody could have anticipated. The judge dismissed the claim under the Regulations.

HELD: (1) The words of the Regulation had long been used in domestic legislation to import an obligation to keep an item in repair rather than an obligation merely to take reasonable care to keep it in repair: see *Galashiels Gas Co Ltd v O'Donnell* [1949] AC 275, HL. (2) Although the relevant Directive (Work Equipment Directive) did not require member states to lay down absolute obligations, it did not prevent them from doing so; on the contrary, by the Framework Directive member states were positively encouraged to impose more stringent standards and not to water down existing ones. (3) Accordingly the employer was liable since (though not at fault) it had not kept the bicycle in repair.

The court here began by looking at the historic meaning in domestic law of the words chosen by the draftsman to incorporate the Directive. However, although one should not disregard this useful aid to construction in an appropriate case, it is submitted that *Stark v Post Office* should not be seen as an general encouragement to approach all Regulations with a European origin by looking first for earlier cases on similar words in domestic law. Rather, since the Regulations are a completely new code which do not derive from domestic law, it is submitted that the starting-point should be the plain words of the relevant Regulation considered in the light of the purpose of the relevant Directive.

UK REGULATIONS

WORKPLACE (HEALTH, SAFETY AND WELFARE REGULATIONS) 1992 (AS AMENDED)

INTERPRETATION

[4.57]

2.—(1) In these Regulations, unless the context otherwise requires—

...

'traffic route' means a route for pedestrian traffic, vehicles or both and includes any stairs, staircase, fixed ladder, doorway, gateway, loading bay or ramp;

'workplace' means, subject to paragraph (2), any premises or part of premises which are not domestic premises and are made available to any person as a place of work, and includes—
(a) any place within the premises to which such person has access while at work; and
(b) any room, lobby, corridor, staircase, road or other place used as a means of access to or egress from that place of work or where facilities are provided for use in connection with the place of work other than a public road.

(2) Any reference in these Regulations, except in paragraph (1), to a modification, an extension or a conversion is a reference, as the case may be, to a modification, an extension or a conversion of a workplace started after 31st December 1992.

(3) Any requirement that anything done or provided in pursuance of these Regulations shall be suitable shall be construed to include a requirement that it is suitable for any person in respect of whom such thing is so done or provided.

Requirements under these Regulations

[4.58]

4.—(1) Every employer shall ensure that every workplace, modification, extension or conversion which is under his control and where any of his employees works complies with any requirement of these Regulations which—
(a) applies to that workplace or, as the case may be, to the workplace which contains that modification, extension or conversion; and

(b) is in force in respect of the workplace, modification, extension or conversion.

(2) Subject to paragraph (4), every person who has, to any extent, control of a workplace, modification, extension or conversion shall ensure that such workplace, modification, extension or conversion complies with any requirement of these Regulations which—
(a) applies to that workplace or, as the case may be, to the workplace which contains that modification, extension or conversion;
(b) is in force in respect of the workplace, modification, extension, or conversion; and
(c) relates to matters within that person's control.

(3) Any reference in this regulation to a person having control of any workplace, modification, extension or conversion is a reference to a person having control of the workplace, modification, extension or conversion in connection with the carrying on by him of a trade, business or other undertaking (whether for profit or not).

(4) Paragraph (2) shall not impose any requirement upon a self-employed person in respect of his own work or the work of any partner of his in the undertaking.

(5) Every person who is deemed to be the occupier of a factory by virtue of section 175(5) of the Factories Act 1961 shall ensure that the premises which are so deemed to be a factory comply with these Regulations.

King v RCO Support Services Ltd

[2001] ICR 608, CA

[4.59] The claimant was employed by the first defendant to service buses at the second defendant's premises. One morning there was ice in the yard. In accordance with established arrangements between the defendants it was for the first defendant to grit the yard, and the claimant began do so. He slipped and was hurt. The first defendant was liable for this under regulation 12 (see below) – keeping floors free from slippery substances. The question arose whether the second defendant also owed a duty by virtue of regulation 4(2). It was admitted that the second defendant retained a degree of control over the premises.

HELD: (1) The Regulations did apply to the workplace and were in force in relation to it: thus sub-paragraphs (a) and (b) of regulation 4(2) were satisfied. What was critical was whether the requirement under regulation 12 on which the claimant relied was one which related to matters within the control of the second defendant: sub-paragraph (c). (2) Since the second defendant had entrusted the task of gritting to the first defendant, an independent contractor, the second defendant retained no control over the relevant matter and owed no duty pursuant to regulation 4(2).

Note— This case is not authority that it can simply be assumed in every case that a defendant has no case to answer under the Regulations if a sub-contractor is on the site. Rather, as in this case, the court should consider carefully whether the requirement relied upon relates to a matter under the defendant's control.

[4.60]

4A. Where a workplace is in a building, the building shall have a stability and solidity appropriate to the nature of the use of a workplace.

Maintenance of workplace, and of equipment, devices and systems

[4.61]

5.—(1) The workplace and the equipment, devices and systems to which this regulation applies shall be maintained (including cleaned as appropriate) in an efficient state, in efficient working order and in good repair.

(2) Where appropriate, the equipment, devices and systems to which this regulation applies shall be subject to a suitable system of maintenance.

(3) The equipment, devices and systems to which this regulation applies are—
(a) equipment and devices a fault in which is liable to result in a failure to comply with any of these Regulations;
(b) mechanical ventilation systems provided pursuant to regulation 6 (whether or not they include equipment or devices within sub-paragraph (a) of this paragraph); and
(c) equipment and devices intended to prevent or reduce hazards.

Note—See *Stark v Post Office* (4.15 above) as to 'shall be maintained … in an efficient state, in efficient working order and in good repair'.

Workstations and seating

[4.62]

11.—(1) Every workstation shall be so arranged that it is suitable both for any person at work in the workplace who is likely to work at that workstation and for any work of the undertaking which is likely to be done there.

(2) Without prejudice to the generality of paragraph (1), every workstation outdoors shall be so arranged that—
(a) so far as is reasonably practicable, it provides protection from adverse weather;
(b) it enables any person at the workstation to leave it swiftly or, as appropriate, to be assisted in the event of an emergency; and
(c) it ensures that any person at the workstation is not likely to slip or fall.

(3) A suitable seat shall be provided for each person at work in the workplace whose work includes operations of a kind that the work (or a substantial part of it) can or must be done sitting. (4) A seat shall not be suitable for the purpose of paragraph (3) unless—
(a) it is suitable for the person for whom it is provided as well as for the operations to be performed; and
(b) a suitable footrest is also provided where necessary.

Butler v Grampian University Hospitals NHS Trust

2002 SLT 985, Ct of Sess, Outer House

[4.63] The pursuer was a nurse a clinic. She was helping a wheelchair-bound patient to use the lavatory when, owing (as she alleged) to the insufficient size of the cubicle, she hurt her back. The defender sought to strike out an allegation that the cubicle was a workstation.

HELD: (1) The word 'workstation' connotes a place at which there is gathered together or assembled or set up an item or items of equipment or apparatus for the purpose of enabling a certain category or certain categories of work to be done there. (2) The mere fact that the pursuer's work included assisting disabled persons to make use of the lavatory did not convert the lavatory into a workstation.

Condition of floors and traffic routes

[4.64]

12.—(1) Every floor in a workplace and the surface of every traffic route in a workplace shall be of a construction such that the floor or surface of the traffic route is suitable for the purpose for which it is used.

(2) Without prejudice to the generality of paragraph (1), the requirements in that paragraph shall include requirements that—
(a) the floor, or surface of the traffic route, shall have no hole or slope, or be uneven or slippery so as, in each case, to expose any person to a risk to his health or safety; and
(b) every such floor shall have effective means of drainage where necessary.

(3) So far as is reasonably practicable, every floor in a workplace and the surface of every traffic route in a workplace shall be kept free from obstructions and from any article or substance which may cause a person to slip, trip or fall.

(4) In considering whether for the purposes of paragraph (2)(a) a hole or slope exposes any person to a risk to his health or safety—
(a) no account shall be taken of a hole where adequate measures have been taken to prevent a person falling; and
(b) account shall be taken of any handrail provided in connection with any slope.

(5) Suitable and sufficient handrails and, if appropriate, guards shall be provided on all traffic routes which are staircases except in circumstances in which a handrail can not be provided without obstructing the traffic route.

McGhee v Strathclyde Fire Brigade

2002 SLT 680, Court of Session, Outer House

[4.65] A fireman slipped on a floor at the fire station which, he claimed, was worn and also covered in residue from cleaning and polishing. He complained of breaches of regulation 12(1) and 12(3).

HELD: (1) The obligation under regulation 12(1) is a continuing one, so it is necessary throughout the life of the floor to consider its suitability for the purpose for which it is at any time being used; any change to the state of the floor by, for example the effect of wear will require to be kept under review. (2) This requirement is not limited by any qualification as to reasonable practicability. (3) The notion of risk (in regulation 12(2)(a)) involves some measure of foreseeability. That measure (described by the court as 'a real risk') appears to lie somewhere between a prospect of adverse affect to health or safety which is so remote as may properly be discounted and a likelihood in the sense of something which has a more than even chance of coming to pass. The standard of care imposed on the employer may well be higher than merely reasonable foreseeability. (4) To establish a breach of regulation 12(3) the employee must prove that immediately prior to his accident there was on the floor a substance which presented a real risk that someone might slip.

Palmer v Marks & Spencer plc

[2001] EWCA Civ 1528, [2001] All ER (D) 123 (Oct)

[4.66] The claimant, a lady of 63, tripped on an 8.5–9 mm 'weather strip' across the mouth of a doorway and fell down some stairs.

HELD: (1) Regulation 12(1) read with regulation 12(2) involves considering a question of foreseeability. (2) Expressions such as 'real risk' or 'slight risk' do not necessarily encapsulate the exercise which must be performed. If the risk is slight but of a very serious injury or death, then the fact that it is slight may not outweigh the cost of taking precautions. It might be different if the risk is only of someone tripping over and suffering a not very serious injury. The court should take into account all relevant factors. (3) Here, the relevant factors were that the weather strip was in a doorway next to some steps, that the claimant was known not always to pick her feet up; but the strip was only slightly raised and there had been many exits through the doorway without incident. (4) On balance the floor was suitable.

Falls or falling objects

[4.67]

13.—(1) So far as is reasonably practicable, suitable and effective measures shall be taken to prevent any event specified in paragraph (3).

(2) So far as is reasonably practicable, the measures required by paragraph (1) shall be measures other than the provision of personal protective equipment, information, instruction, training or supervision.

(3) The events specified in this paragraph are:
(a) any person falling a distance likely to cause personal injury;
(b) any person being struck by a falling object likely to cause personal injury.

(4) Any area where there is a risk to health or safety from any event mentioned in paragraph (3) shall be clearly indicated where appropriate.

(5) So far as is practicable, every tank, pit or structure where there is a risk of a person in the workplace falling into a dangerous substance in the tank, pit or structure, shall be securely covered or fenced.

(6) Every traffic route over, across or in an uncovered tank, pit or structure such as is mentioned in paragraph (5) shall be securely fenced.

(7) In this regulation, 'dangerous substance' means—
(a) any substance likely to scald or burn;
(b) any poisonous substance;
(c) any corrosive substance;
(d) any fume, gas or vapour likely to overcome a person; or
(e) any granular or free-flowing solid substance, or any viscous substance which, in any case, is of a nature or quantity which is likely to cause dange to any person.

Parker v PFC Flooring Supplies

[2001] PIQR P115, QBD

[4.68] The claimant went onto the roof of the defendant's warehouse to investigate a cable which had been left there. Ordinarily work on the roof was carried out by specialist contractors, but the claimant was responsible for security and feared that vandals might have left the cable with a view to breaking in at the earliest opportunity. The claimant used a ladder kept at the warehouse. He slipped and fell.

HELD: (1) The roof was part of the claimant's workplace within regulation 2. (2) There had been a breach of regulation 13(4) in the failure to display any warning as to the dangers of climbing on the roof.

Note— On appeal the Court of Appeal ([2001] EWCA Civ 1533) dealt with the case entirely at common law and did not consider the Regulations.

PROVISION AND USE OF WORK EQUIPMENT REGULATIONS 1998 (AS AMENDED)

Interpretation

[4.69]

2.—(1) In these Regulations, unless the context otherwise requires –

...

'employer' except in regulation 3(2) and (3) includes a person to whom the requirements imposed by these Regulations apply by virtue of regulation 3(3)(a) and (b);

'inspection' in relation to an inspection under paragraph (1) or (2) of regulation 6—
(a) means such visual or more rigorous inspection by a competent person as is appropriate for the purpose described in the paragraph;
(b) where it is appropriate to carry out testing for the purpose, includes testing the nature and extent of which are appropriate for the purpose;

'use' in relation to work equipment means any activity involving work equipment and includes starting, stopping, programming, setting, transporting, repairing, modifying, maintaining, servicing and cleaning;

'work equipment' means any machinery, appliance, apparatus, tool or installation for use at work (whether exclusively or not);

and related expressions shall be construed accordingly …

Application

[4.70]

3.—(1) …

(2) The requirements imposed by these Regulations on an employer in respect of work equipment shall apply to such equipment provided for use or used by an employee of his at work.

(3) The requirements imposed by these Regulations on an employer shall also apply—
(a) to a self-employed person, in respect of work equipment he uses at work;
(b) subject to paragraph (5), to a person who has control to any extent of—
   (i) work equipment;
   (ii) a person at work who uses or supervises or manages the use of work equipment; or
   (iii) the way in which work equipment is used at work,
and to the extent of his control.

(4) Any reference in paragraph (3)(b) to a person having control is a reference to a person having control in connection with the carrying on by him of a trade, business or other undertaking (whether for profit or not).

(5) The requirements imposed by these Regulations shall not apply to a person in respect of work equipment supplied by him by way of sale, agreement for sale or hire-purchase agreement. …

Note—See *King v RCO Support Services Ltd* and the note thereto (above paragraph 4.54) as to the extent of control.

Suitability of work equipment

[4.71]

4.—(1) Every employer shall ensure that work equipment is so constructed or adapted as to be suitable for the purpose for which it is used or provided.

(2) In selecting work equipment, every employer shall have regard to the working conditions and to the risks to the health and safety of persons which exist in the premises or undertaking in which that work equipment is to be used and any additional risk posed by the use of that work equipment.

(3) Every employer shall ensure that work equipment is used only for operations for which, and under conditions for which, it is suitable.

(4) In this regulation 'suitable' ... means suitable in any respect which it is reasonably foreseeable will affect the health or safety of any person ....

Horton v Taplin Contracts Ltd

[2002] EWCA Civ 1604, [2003] ICR 179

[4.72] There is no breach of regulation where an otherwise stable scaffolding tower turns out to be capable of being pushed over by a disgruntled colleague of the claimant.

Maintenance

[4.73]

5.—(1) Every employer shall ensure that work equipment is maintained in an efficient state, in efficient working order and in good repair.

(2) Every employer shall ensure that where any machinery has a maintenance log, the log is kept up to date.
> *Note*—See *Stark v The Post Office* (4.15 above) as to 'is maintained in an efficient state, in efficient working order and in good repair.'

Green v Yorkshire Traction Co Ltd

[2001] EWCA Civ 1925, [2001] All ER (D) 42 (Dec)

[4.74] The claimant bus driver slipped on the step of his bus as he got off at the end of the day. The step was slippery because it had been raining all day.

HELD: The bus was work equipment. But it could not be said that the bus had not been maintained in an efficient state just because on a rainy day some water had got onto the step.

Beck v United Closures and Plastics plc

2001 SLT 1299, Ct of Sess, Outer House

[4.75] There was a pair of doors at the defendant's premises each of which had a door handle situated close to the leading edge of the door. Behind the doors was a machine which only worked when the doors were closed. The claimant shut the doors with one hand on each and in the process trapped a hand.

HELD: (1) The doors were 'work equipment'.
> *Note*—the case was decided under the 1992 Regulations which included within the definition of 'work equipment' an 'assembly of components which, in order to achieve a common end, are arranged and controlled so that they function as a whole', and this was the basis of the decision. It is submitted that the same result would follow under the 1998 Regulations, since the doors were an 'installation for use at work'.

(2) Construing 'use' broadly, the 'use' for which the doors were provided was opening and closing them.

(3) The doors were not suitable for this purpose.

Information and instructions

[4.76]

8.—(1) Every employer shall ensure that all persons who use work equipment have available to them adequate health and safety information and, where appropriate, written instructions pertaining to the use of the work equipment.

(2) Every employer shall ensure that any of his employees who supervises or manages the use of work equipment has available to him adequate health and safety information and, where appropriate, written instructions pertaining to the use of the work equipment.

(3) Without prejudice to the generality of paragraphs (1) or (2), the information and instructions required by either of those paragraphs shall include information and, where appropriate, written instructions on—
(a) the conditions in which and the methods by which the work equipment may be used;
(b) foreseeable abnormal situations and the action to be taken if such a situation were to occur; and
(c) any conclusions to be drawn from experience in using the work equipment.

(4) Information and instructions required by this regulation shall be readily comprehensible to those concerned.

Training

[4.77]

9.—(1) Every employer shall ensure that all persons who use work equipment have received adequate training for purposes of health and safety, including training in the methods which may be adopted when using the work equipment, any risks which such use may entail and precautions to be taken.

(2) Every employer shall ensure that any of his employees who supervises or manages the use of work equipment has received adequate training for purposes of health and safety, including training in the methods which may be adopted when using the work equipment, any risks which such use may entail and precautions to be taken.

Fraser v Winchester Health Authority

(1999) 55 BMLR 122, CA

[4.78] The claimant, a young and inexperienced care worker, was sent on a camping holiday with a patient. She was provided with a lamp the batteries of which were missing, a gas stove and some candles. Nobody told her how to change the gas cylinder on the stove. She lit the candles in the tent and set about changing the cylinder. Gas escaped and was ignited by the candles causing serious injuries. The defendant on appeal sought to displace the judge's finding of a breach of the obligations to provide instructions and training by contending that this was a case in which the real risk – of explosion if one changed the cylinder by a naked flame – was so obvious that neither warning nor instruction was needed.

HELD: The Court of Appeal rejected this submission, but reduced the award by a third for contributory negligence.

MANUAL HANDLING OPERATIONS REGULATIONS 1992 (AS AMENDED)

Interpretation

[4.79]

2.—(1) In these Regulations, unless the context otherwise requires—

'injury' does not include injury caused by any toxic or corrosive substance which—
(a) has leaked or spilled from a load;
(b) is present on the surface of a load but has not leaked or spilled from it; or
(c) is a constituent part of a load;

and 'injured' shall be construed accordingly;

'load' includes any person and any animal;

'manual handling operations' means any transporting or supporting of a load (including the lifting, putting down, pushing, pulling, carrying or moving thereof) by hand or by bodily force.

(2) Any duty imposed by these Regulations on an employer in respect of his employees shall also be imposed on a self-employed person in respect of himself.

Duties of employers

[4.80]

4.—(1) Each employer shall—
(a) so far as is reasonably practicable, avoid the need for his employees to undertake any manual handling operations at work which involve a risk of their being injured; or
(b) where it is not reasonably practicable to avoid the need for his employees to undertake any manual handling operations at work which involve a risk of their being injured—
   (i) make a suitable and sufficient assessment of all such manual handling operations to be undertaken by them, having regard to the factors which are specified in column 1 of Schedule 1 to these Regulations and considering the questions which are specified in the corresponding entry in column 2 of that Schedule,
   (ii) take appropriate steps to reduce the risk of injury to those employees arising out of their undertaking any such manual handling operations to the lowest level reasonably practicable, and

(iii) take appropriate steps to provide any of those employees who are undertaking any such manual handling operations with general indications and, where it is reasonably practicable to do so, precise information on—
    (aa) the weight of each load, and
    (bb) the heaviest side of any load whose centre of gravity is not positioned centrally.

(2) Any assessment such as is referred to in paragraph (1)(b)(i) of this regulation shall be reviewed by the employer who made it if—
(a) there is reason to suspect that it is no longer valid; or
(b) there has been a significant change in the manual handling operations to which it relates;

and where as a result of any such review changes to an assessment are required, the relevant employer shall make them.

(3) In determining for the purposes of this regulation whether manual handling operations at work involve a risk of injury and in determining the appropriate steps to reduce that risk regard shall be had in particular to—
(a) the physical suitability of the employee to carry out the operations;
(b) the clothing, footwear or other personal effects he is wearing;
(c) his knowledge and training;
(d) the results of any relevant risk assessment carried out pursuant to regulation 3 of the Management of Health and Safety at Work Regulations 1999;
(e) whether the employee is within a group of employees identified by that assessment as being especially at risk; and
(f) the results of any health surveillance provided pursuant to regulation 6 of the Management of Health and Safety Regulations 1999.

Duty of employees

[4.81]

5. Each employee while at work shall make full and proper use of any system of work provided for his use by his employer in compliance with regulation 4(1)(b)(ii) of these Regulations.

SCHEDULE 1

Regulation 4(1)(b)(i)

FACTORS TO WHICH THE EMPLOYER MUST HAVE REGARD AND QUESTIONS HE MUST CONSIDER WHEN MAKING AN ASSESSMENT OF MANUAL HANDLING OPERATIONS

Column 1
Column 2

Factors
Questions

1. The tasks

Do they involve:
—holding or manipulating loads at distance from trunk?
—unsatisfactory bodily movement or posture, especially:
—twisting the trunk?
—stooping?
—reaching upwards?
—excessive movement of loads, especially:
—excessive lifting or lowering distances?
—excessive carrying distances?
—excessive pushing or pulling of loads?
—risk of sudden movement of loads?
—frequent or prolonged physical effort?
—insufficient rest or recovery periods?
—a rate of work imposed by a process?

2. The loads

Are they:
—heavy?
—bulky or unwieldy?
—difficult to grasp?
—unstable, or with contents likely to shift?
—sharp, hot or otherwise potentially damaging?

3. The working environment

Are there:
—space constraints preventing good posture?
—uneven, slippery or unstable floors?
—variations in level of floors or work surfaces?
—extremes of temperature or humidity?
—conditions causing ventilation problems or gusts of wind?
—poor lighting conditions?

4. Individual capability

Does the job:
—require unusual strength, height, etc?
—create a hazard to those who might reasonably be considered to be pregnant or to have a health problem?
—require special information or training for its safe performance?

5. Other factors

Is movement or posture hindered by personal protective equipment or by clothing?

Cullen v North Lanarkshire Council

1998 SC 451, Ct of Sess, Inner House

[4.82] The test for whether an operation involves a risk of being injured is that of a foreseeable possibility of injury; it need not be a probability.

Koonjul v Thameslink Healthcare Services NHS Trust

[2000] PIQR P123, CA

[4.83] The claimant nurse in a children's home changed beds by first bending down almost to the ground and pulling them out from the wall. On one occasion she ricked her back. She contended that changing the bed was a manual handling operation which involved a risk of her being injured, so that the defendant should have carried out a risk assessment.

HELD: (1) *Cullen v North Lanarkshire Council* sets out the correct test. (2) The purpose of the Regulations is to place on employers obligations which they would not otherwise have. (3) The employer must not assume that employees will always act with full and proper concern for their own safety. (4) But there has to be a degree of realism. Here, the claimant, an experienced employee, was carrying out a common domestic task which carried a very small risk of injury. There were innumerable such tasks in the home and the notion of carrying out a precise evaluation of each task and giving precise warnings to staff about how to carry them out was beyond the realms of practicability. The defendant was not in the circumstances obliged to carry out a risk assessment.

Note— See also *McGhee v Strathclyde Fire Brigade* and *Palmer v Marks & Spencer plc* (above 4.65 and 4.66) as to risk under the Workplace (Health, Safety and Welfare) Regulations 1992.

Hawkes v Southwark London Borough Council

(20 February 1998, unreported), CA

[4.84] The claimant was required to carry a heavy door up a flight of stairs and around a landing. As he navigated the landing the door hit the wall, unbalanced him and made him fall back down the stairs. His employer had not made any assessment of the task.

HELD: This was a manual handling operation which involved a risk of injury, and it could not practicably be avoided. An assessment was required under regulation 4(1)(b)(i). No assessment had been made. The court then had to consider what the result of an assessment would have been. On the facts, the employer would have concluded that the task needed to be carried out by two men. The employer could not show (the burden being on it to show) that this was not a reasonably practicable step. The only remaining issue was whether the claimant would in practice have accepted help if it had been arranged. Since he probably would have done, the claim was made out.

King v Sussex Ambulance NHS Trust

[2002] EWCA Civ 953, (2002) 68 BMLR 177

[4.85] The claimant was a member of an ambulance crew sent to collect a patient urgently. The patient lived on the first floor, with only a steep and narrow staircase for access, and could not walk. In accordance with standard practice the crew put the patient into a carrying chair and began to lift him down the stairs, whereupon the claimant suffered a strain injury. There was expert evidence that the method adopted was clearly risky, but there was no alternative short of calling the fire brigade to lift the patient out through a window. The latter option required careful planning and could be distressing for the patient. The judge, basing his decision on the Manual Handling Directive (not reproduced here), found the Trust liable for failing to take steps to reduce the risk of injury by having a policy of giving more serious consideration to calling out the fire brigade in these circumstances.

HELD, on appeal: It was not necessary to consider the case based on the Directive, for the result was the same under the Regulations as under the Directive. There might be some cases in which calling for help was necessary: this would depend upon the magnitude of the risk, the urgency of the matter, the views of the patient and the availability of the help. Here, although the method adopted was risky, it was on the evidence the only practical method of collecting the patient in the time available. The Trust was not liable.

> Note—Compare *King v RCO Support Services Ltd* (above 4.59) in which the claimant also contended that his injury sustained while gritting a road by hand was a breach of the Manual Handling Operations Regulations 1992. The court held in the absence of any evidence from the defendant on the point that it was reasonably practicable to avoid the need for him to do this – the defendant could have used a mechanical gritter.

CONTROL OF SUBSTANCES HAZARDOUS TO HEALTH REGULATIONS 2002

[4.86] Although these Regulations have a European source, it is not the Framework Directive. Nevertheless, it is submitted that the same approach to their construction ought to apply.

The general warning above as to the importance of reference to the full and up-to-date text of the relevant regulation applies with particular force to these Regulations, which contain detailed provision – not reproduced here – as to the substances to which they apply. In all but the most straightforward cases it will be necessary to consider obtaining expert evidence as to the nature of the relevant substance, whether it falls within the terms of the Regulations, and the mechanism by which it is alleged (or denied) that exposure to it caused injury.

Interpretation

[4.87]

2.—(1) In these Regulations—

...

'control measure' means a measure taken to reduce exposure to a substance hazardous to health (including the provision of systems of work and supervision, the cleaning of workplaces, premises, plant and equipment, the provision and use of engineering controls and personal protective equipment);...

'hazard', in relation to a substance, means the intrinsic property of that substance which has the potential to cause harm to the health of a person, and 'hazardous' shall be construed accordingly;...

'substance hazardous to health' means a substance ...[here follows at sub-paragraphs (a) to (d) a detailed list of substances or classes of substance]

[or] which, not being a substance falling within sub-paragraphs (a) to (d), because of its chemical or toxicological properties and the way it is used or is present at the workplace creates a risk to health;

'workplace' means any premises or part of premises used for or in connection with work, and includes—
  (a) any place within the premises to which an employee has access while at work; and
  (b) any room, lobby, corridor, staircase, road or other place—
      (i) used as a means of access to or egress from that place of work, or
      (ii) where facilities are provided for use in connection with that place of work,
  other than a public road.

(2) In these Regulations, a reference to an employee being exposed to a substance hazardous to health is a reference to the exposure of that employee to a substance hazardous to health arising out of or in connection with work at the workplace.

Duties under these Regulations

[4.88]

3.—(1) Where a duty is placed by these Regulations on an employer in respect of his employees, he shall, so far as is reasonably practicable, be under a like duty in respect of any other person, whether at work or not, who may be affected by the work carried out by the employer except that the duties of the employer—
  (a) under regulation 11 (health surveillance) shall not extend to persons who are not his employees; and
  (b) under regulations 10, 12(1) and (2) and 13 (which relate respectively to monitoring, information and training and dealing with accidents) shall not extend to persons who are not his employees, unless those persons are on the premises where the work is being carried out.

(2) These Regulations shall apply to a self-employed person as they apply to an employer and an employee and as if that self-employed person were both an employer and an employee, except that regulations 10 and 11 shall not apply to a self-employed person

...

Application of regulations 6 to 13

[4.89]

5.—(1) Regulations 6 to 13 shall have effect with a view to protecting persons against a risk to their health, whether immediate or delayed, arising from exposure to substances hazardous to health [subject to certain exceptions not set out here, including an exception in respect of substances hazardous only by virtue of their temperature or flammability].

Assessment of the risk to health created by work involving substances hazardous to health

[4.90]

6.—(1) An employer shall not carry out work which is liable to expose any employees to any substance hazardous to health unless he has—
(a) made a suitable and sufficient assessment of the risk created by that work to the health of those employees and of the steps that need to be taken to meet the requirements of these Regulations; and
(b) implemented the steps referred to in sub-paragraph (a).

(2) The risk assessment shall include consideration of—
(a) the hazardous properties of the substance;
(b) information on health effects provided by the supplier, including information contained in any relevant safety data sheet;
(c) the level, type and duration of exposure;
(d) the circumstances of the work, including the amount of the substance involved;
(e) activities, such as maintenance, where there is the potential for a high level of exposure;
(f) any relevant occupational exposure standard, maximum exposure limit or similar occupational exposure limit;
(g) the effect of preventive and control measures which have been or will be taken in accordance with regulation 7;
(h) the results of relevant health surveillance;
(i) the results of monitoring of exposure in accordance with regulation 10;
(j) in circumstances where the work will involve exposure to more than one substance hazardous to health, the risk presented by exposure to such substances in combination;
(k) the approved classification of any biological agent; and
(l) such additional information as the employer may need in order to complete the risk assessment.

(3) The risk assessment shall be reviewed regularly and forthwith if—
(a) there is reason to suspect that the risk assessment is no longer valid;
(b) there has been a significant change in the work to which the risk assessment relates; or
(c) the results of any monitoring carried out in accordance with regulation 10 show it to be necessary,

and where, as a result of the review, changes to the risk assessment are required, those changes shall be made

...

Prevention or control of exposure to substances hazardous to health

[4.91]

7.—(1) Every employer shall ensure that the exposure of his employees to substances hazardous to health is either prevented or, where this is not reasonably practicable, adequately controlled.

(2) In complying with his duty of prevention under paragraph (1), substitution shall by preference be undertaken, whereby the employer shall avoid, so far as is reasonably practicable, the use of a substance hazardous to health at the workplace by replacing it with a substance or process which, under the conditions of its use, either eliminates or reduces the risk to the health of his employees.

(3) Where it is not reasonably practicable to prevent exposure to a substance hazardous to health, the employer shall comply with his duty of control under paragraph (1) by applying protection measures appropriate to the activity and consistent with the risk assessment, including, in order of priority—
(a) the design and use of appropriate work processes, systems and engineering controls and the provision and use of suitable work equipment and materials;
(b) the control of exposure at source, including adequate ventilation systems and appropriate organisational measures; and
(c) where adequate control of exposure cannot be achieved by other means, the provision of suitable personal protective equipment in addition to the measures required by sub-paragraphs (a) and (b).

(4) The measures referred to in paragraph (3) shall include—
(a) arrangements for the safe handling, storage and transport of substances hazardous to health, and of waste containing such substances, at the workplace;
(b) the adoption of suitable maintenance procedures;
(c) reducing, to the minimum required for the work concerned -
   (i) the number of employees subject to exposure,
   (ii) the level and duration of exposure, and
   (iii) the quantity of substances hazardous to health present at the workplace;
(d) the control of the working environment, including appropriate general ventilation; and
(e) appropriate hygiene measures including adequate washing facilities.

(5) Without prejudice to the generality of paragraph (1), where it is not reasonably practicable to prevent exposure to a carcinogen, the employer shall apply the following measures in addition to those required by paragraph (3)—
(a) totally enclosing the process and handling systems, unless this is not reasonably practicable;

(b) the prohibition of eating, drinking and smoking in areas that may be contaminated by carcinogens;
(c) cleaning floors, walls and other surfaces at regular intervals and whenever necessary;
(d) designating those areas and installations which may be contaminated by carcinogens and using suitable and sufficient warning signs; and
(e) storing, handling and disposing of carcinogens safely, including using closed and clearly labelled containers.

...

Dugmore v Swansea NHS Trust

[2002] EWCA Civ 1689, [2003] 1 All ER 333

[4.92] The claimant nurse, who was given latex gloves to wear at work, became sensitised to latex as a result. It was agreed that latex was a substance hazardous to health. The defendant had not at the relevant time (it was held) known of the risk posed to the claimant, nor should it have known.

HELD: (1) The duty in regulation 7 is an absolute one to ensure that exposure to substances hazardous to health is prevented or controlled. The Regulations involve positive obligations to seek out risks and take precautions against them. Neither knowledge nor foreseeability are relevant. (2) Here the hospital had failed to prevent the claimant's exposure. It was for the hospital to prove that it was not reasonably practicable to prevent it. On the evidence it failed: it could without undue difficulty have given the claimant vinyl gloves instead. (3) Only the primary duty to prevent exposure was qualified by reasonable practicability. Here, if it had not been reasonably practicable to prevent the claimant's exposure, the issue would have arisen whether it had been adequately controlled. Adequately was defined without reference to either foreseeability or practicality: it was a purely practical matter depending upon the nature of the substance and the nature and degree of the exposure and nothing else. Here the claimant's exposure was not adequately controlled.

Use of control measures etc.

[4.93]

8. — (1) Every employer who provides any control measure, other thing or facility in accordance with these Regulations shall take all reasonable steps to ensure that it is properly used or applied as the case may be.

(2) Every employee shall make full and proper use of any control measure, other thing or facility provided in accordance with these Regulations and, where relevant, shall—
(a) take all reasonable steps to ensure it is returned after use to any accommodation provided for it; and
(b) if he discovers a defect therein, report it forthwith to his employer. Maintenance, examination and testing of control measures

[4.94]

9.—(1) Every employer who provides any control measure to meet the requirements of regulation 7 shall ensure that, where relevant, it is maintained in an efficient state, in efficient working order, in good repair and in a clean condition.

Monitoring exposure at the workplace

[4.95]

10.—(1) Where the risk assessment indicates that—
(a) it is requisite for ensuring the maintenance of adequate control of the exposure of employees to substances hazardous to health; or
(b) it is otherwise requisite for protecting the health of employees,

the employer shall ensure that the exposure of employees to substances hazardous to health is monitored in accordance with a suitable procedure.

(2) Paragraph (1) shall not apply where the employer is able to demonstrate by another method of evaluation that the requirements of regulation 7(1) have been complied with.

(3) The monitoring referred to in paragraph (1) shall take place—
(a) at regular intervals; and
(b) when any change occurs which may affect that exposure

....

Health surveillance

[4.96]

11.—(1) Where it is appropriate for the protection of the health of his employees who are, or are liable to be, exposed to a substance hazardous to health, the employer shall ensure that such employees are under suitable health surveillance.

(2) Health surveillance shall be treated as being appropriate where—
(a) the employee is exposed to one of the substances specified in Column 1 of Schedule 6 and is engaged in a process specified in Column 2 of that Schedule, and there is a reasonable likelihood that an identifiable disease or adverse health effect will result from that exposure; or
(b) the exposure of the employee to a substance hazardous to health is such that—
  (i) an identifiable disease or adverse health effect may be related to the exposure,
  (ii) there is a reasonable likelihood that the disease or effect may occur under the particular conditions of his work, and
  (iii) there are valid techniques for detecting indications of the disease or effect,
and the technique of investigation is of low risk to the employee.

...

Information, instruction and training for persons who may be exposed to substances hazardous to health

[4.97]

12.—(1) Every employer who undertakes work which is liable to expose an employee to a substance hazardous to health shall provide that employee with suitable and sufficient information, instruction and training.

(2) Without prejudice to the generality of paragraph (1), the information, instruction and training provided under that paragraph shall include—
(a) details of the substances hazardous to health to which the employee is liable to be exposed including—
  (i) the names of those substances and the risk which they present to health,
  (ii) any relevant occupational exposure standard, maximum exposure limit or similar occupational exposure limit,
  (iii) access to any relevant safety data sheet, and
  (iv) other legislative provisions which concern the hazardous properties of those substances;
(b) the significant findings of the risk assessment;
(c) the appropriate precautions and actions to be taken by the employee in order to safeguard himself and other employees at the workplace;
(d) the results of any monitoring of exposure in accordance with regulation 10 and, in particular, in the case of a substance hazardous to health for which a maximum exposure limit has been approved, the employee or his representatives shall be informed forthwith, if the results of such monitoring show that the maximum exposure limit has been exceeded;
(e) the collective results of any health surveillance undertaken in accordance with regulation 11 in a form calculated to prevent those results from being identified as relating to a particular person;

...

EMPLOYER'S LIABILITY (DEFECTIVE EQUIPMENT) ACT 1969

Coltman v Bibby Tankers Ltd

[1988] AC 276, HL

[4.98] The claimant was killed when *The Derbyshire* sank as a result of its unseaworthy design.

HELD: The House of Lords held that the ship itself constituted equipment within the meaning of the Act.

CHAPTER 5

Human Rights Issues and Crown Liability

The Human Rights Act 1998	[5.1]
The Convention rights and employer's liability	[5.13]
Analysis of The Human Rights Act	[5.22]
Principles	[5.23]
General comments on when to raise a human rights point	[5.26]
Definition of a public authority	[5.28]
Horizontal effect of the Human Rights Act	[5.30]
Proportionality and the discretionary area of judgment	[5.32]
Statutory interpretation under section 3 and declarations of incompatibility under section 4	[5.36]
Effect of HRA, s 3 on employer's liability cases	[5.41]
Human rights cases affecting employer's liability	[5.44]
Article 4	[5.45]
Article 6	[5.46]
Article 8	[5.47]
Article 9	[5.52]
Article 10	[5.56]
Article 14	[5.57]
Crown employees: statutory liability of the Crown	[5.58]
Crown Proceedings Act 1947, ss 1, 2	[5.58]
Occupiers Liability Act 1957, s 6	[5.59]
Defective Premises Act 1972, s 5	[5.60]
Occupiers Liability Act 1984, s 3	[5.61]
Contracts of employment and the Crown	[5.62]
Armed Forces: Crown Proceedings Act 1947, s 10	[5.64]
Crown Proceedings (Armed Forces) Act 1987	[5.65]
Police	[5.73]

THE HUMAN RIGHTS ACT 1998 (HRA)

[5.1]

Introduction

1 The Convention rights

(1) In this Act 'the Convention rights' means the rights and fundamental freedoms set out in—

(a) Articles 2 to 12 and 14 of the Convention,
(b) Articles 1 to 3 of the First Protocol, and
(c) Articles 1 and 2 of the Sixth Protocol, as read with Articles 16 to 18 of the Convention. ...

[5.2]

2 Interpretation of Convention rights

(1) A court or tribunal determining a question which has arisen in connection with a Convention right must take into account any—
(a) judgment, decision, declaration or advisory opinion of the European Court of Human Rights,
(b) opinion of the Commission given in a report adopted under Article 31 of the Convention,
(c) decision of the Commission in connection with Article 26 or 27(2) of the Convention, or
(d) decision of the Committee of Ministers taken under Article 46 of the Convention, whenever made or given, so far as, in the opinion of the court or tribunal, it is relevant to the proceedings in which that question has arisen.

[5.3]

Legislation

3 Interpretation of legislation

(1) So far as it is possible to do so, primary legislation and subordinate legislation must be read and given effect in a way which is compatible with the Convention rights.

(2) This section—
(a) applies to primary legislation and subordinate legislation whenever enacted;
(b) does not affect the validity, continuing operation or enforcement of any incompatible primary legislation; and
(c) does not affect the validity, continuing operation or enforcement of any incompatible subordinate legislation if (disregarding any possibility of revocation) primary legislation prevents removal of the incompatibility.

[5.4]

4 Declaration of incompatibility

(1) Subsection (2) applies in any proceedings in which a court determines whether a provision of primary legislation is compatible with a Convention right.

(2) If the court is satisfied that the provision is incompatible with a Convention right, it may make a declaration of that incompatibility.

(3) Subsection (4) applies in any proceedings in which a court determines whether a provision of subordinate legislation, made in the exercise of a

power conferred by primary legislation, is compatible with a Convention right.

(4) If the court is satisfied—
(a) that the provision is incompatible with a Convention right, and
(b) that (disregarding any possibility of revocation) the primary legislation concerned prevents removal of the incompatibility,

it may make a declaration of that incompatibility.

(5) In this section 'court' means—
(a) the House of Lords;
(b) the Judicial Committee of the Privy Council;
(c) the Courts-Martial Appeal Court;
(d) in Scotland, the High Court of Justiciary sitting otherwise than as a trial court or the Court of Session;
(e) in England and Wales or Northern Ireland, the High Court or the Court of Appeal.

(6) A declaration under this section ('a declaration of incompatibility')—
(a) does not affect the validity, continuing operation or enforcement of the provision in respect of which it is given; and
(b) is not binding on the parties to the proceedings in which it is made.

[5.5]

5 Right of Crown to intervene

(1) Where a court is considering whether to make a declaration of incompatibility, the Crown is entitled to notice in accordance with rules of court.

(2) In any case to which subsection (1) applies—
(a) a Minister of the Crown (or a person nominated by him),
(b) a member of the Scottish Executive,
(c) a Northern Ireland Minister,
(d) a Northern Ireland department,

is entitled, on giving notice in accordance with rules of court, to be joined as a party to the proceedings

(3) Notice under subsection (2) may be given at any time during the proceedings.

(4) A person who has been made a party to criminal proceedings (other than in Scotland) as the result of a notice under subsection (2) may, with leave, appeal to the House of Lords against any declaration of incompatibility made in the proceedings.

(5) In subsection (4)—
'criminal proceedings' includes all proceedings before the Courts-Martial Appeal Court; and
'leave' means leave granted by the court making the declaration of incompatibility or by the House of Lords.

[5.6]

Public authorities

6 Acts of public authorities

(1) It is unlawful for a public authority to act in a way which is incompatible with a Convention right.

(2) Subsection (1) does not apply to an act if—
(a) as the result of one or more provisions of primary legislation, the authority could not have acted differently; or
(b) in the case of one or more provisions of, or made under, primary legislation which cannot be read or given effect in a way which is compatible with the Convention rights, the authority was acting so as to give effect to or enforce those provisions.

(3) In this section 'public authority' includes—
(a) a court or tribunal, and
(b) any person certain of whose functions are functions of a public nature,

but does not include either House of Parliament or a person exercising functions in connection with proceedings in Parliament.

(4) In subsection (3) 'Parliament' does not include the House of Lords in its judicial capacity.

(5) In relation to a particular act, a person is not a public authority by virtue only of subsection (3)(b) if the nature of the act is private.

(6) 'An act' includes a failure to act but does not include a failure to—
(a) introduce in, or lay before, Parliament a proposal for legislation; or
(b) make any primary legislation or remedial order.

[5.7]

7 Proceedings

(1) A person who claims that a public authority has acted (or proposes to act) in a way which is made unlawful by section 6(1) may—
(a) bring proceedings against the authority under this Act in the appropriate court or tribunal, or
(b) rely on the Convention right or rights concerned in any legal proceedings,

but only if he is (or would be) a victim of the unlawful act.

(2) In subsection (1)(a) 'appropriate court or tribunal' means such court or tribunal as may be determined in accordance with rules; and proceedings against an authority include a counterclaim or similar proceeding.

(3) If the proceedings are brought on an application for judicial review, the applicant is to be taken to have a sufficient interest in relation to the unlawful act only if he is, or would be, a victim of that act.(4) If the proceedings are

made by way of a petition for judicial review in Scotland, the applicant shall be taken to have title and interest to sue in relation to the unlawful act only if he is, or would be, a victim of that act.

(5) Proceedings under subsection (1)(a) must be brought before the end of—
(a) the period of one year beginning with the date on which the act complained of took place; or
(b) such longer period as the court or tribunal considers equitable having regard to all the circumstances,
but that is subject to any rule imposing a stricter time limit in relation to the procedure in question.

(6) In subsection (1)(b) 'legal proceedings' includes—
(a) proceedings brought by or at the instigation of a public authority; and
(b) an appeal against the decision of a court or tribunal.

(7) For the purposes of this section, a person is a victim of an unlawful act only if he would be a victim for the purposes of Article 34 of the Convention if proceedings were brought in the European Court of Human Rights in respect of that act.

(8) Nothing in this Act creates a criminal offence.

(9) In this section 'rules' means—
(a) in relation to proceedings before a court or tribunal outside Scotland, rules made by the Lord Chancellor or the Secretary of State for the purposes of this section or rules of court,
(b) in relation to proceedings before a court or tribunal in Scotland, rules made by the Secretary of State for those purposes,
(c) in relation to proceedings before a tribunal in Northern Ireland–
(i) which deals with transferred matters; and
(ii) for which no rules made under paragraph (a) are in force,
rules made by a Northern Ireland department for those purposes,

and includes provision made by order under section 1 of the Courts and Legal Services Act 1990.

(10) In making rules, regard must be had to section 9.

(11) The Minister who has power to make rules in relation to a particular tribunal may, to the extent he considers it necessary to ensure that the tribunal can provide an appropriate remedy in relation to an act (or proposed act) of a public authority which is (or would be) unlawful as a result of section 6(1), by order add to—
(a) the relief or remedies which the tribunal may grant; or
(b) the grounds on which it may grant any of them.

(12) An order made under subsection (11) may contain such incidental, supplemental, consequential or transitional provision as the Minister making it considers appropriate.

(13) 'The Minister' includes the Northern Ireland department concerned.

[5.8]

8 Judicial remedies

(1) In relation to any act (or proposed act) of a public authority which the court finds is (or would be) unlawful, it may grant such relief or remedy, or make such order, within its powers as it considers just and appropriate.

(2) But damages may be awarded only by a court which has power to award damages, or to order the payment of compensation, in civil proceedings.

(3) No award of damages is to be made unless, taking account of all the circumstances of the case, including—
(a) any other relief or remedy granted, or order made, in relation to the act in question (by that or any other court), and
(b) the consequences of any decision (of that or any other court) in respect of that act,

the court is satisfied that the award is necessary to afford just satisfaction to the person in whose favour it is made.

(4) In determining—
(a) whether to award damages, or
(b) the amount of an award,

the court must take into account the principles applied by the European Court of Human Rights in relation to the award of compensation under Article 41 of the Convention.

(5) A public authority against which damages are awarded is to be treated—
(a) in Scotland, for the purposes of section 3 of the Law Reform (Miscellaneous Provisions) (Scotland) Act 1940 as if the award were made in an action of damages in which the authority has been found liable in respect of loss or damage to the person to whom the award is made;
(b) for the purposes of the Civil Liability (Contribution) Act 1978 as liable in respect of damage suffered by the person to whom the award is made.

(6) In this section—
'court' includes a tribunal;
'damages' means damages for an unlawful act of a public authority; and
'unlawful' means unlawful under section 6(1).

[5.9]

9 Judicial acts

(1) Proceedings under section 7(1)(a) in respect of a judicial act may be brought only—
(a) by exercising a right of appeal;
(b) on an application (in Scotland a petition) for judicial review; or
(c) in such other forum as may be prescribed by rules.

(2) That does not affect any rule of law which prevents a court from being the subject of judicial review.

(3) In proceedings under this Act in respect of a judicial act done in good faith, damages may not be awarded otherwise than to compensate a person to the extent required by Article 5(5) of the Convention.

(4) An award of damages permitted by subsection (3) is to be made against the Crown; but no award may be made unless the appropriate person, if not a party to the proceedings, is joined.

(5) In this section—
'appropriate person' means the Minister responsible for the court concerned, or a person or government department nominated by him;
'court' includes a tribunal;
'judge' includes a member of a tribunal, a justice of the peace and a clerk or other officer entitled to exercise the jurisdiction of a court;
'judicial act' means a judicial act of a court and includes an act done on the instructions, or on behalf, of a judge; and
'rules' has the same meaning as in section 7(9).

...

[5.10]

Other rights and proceedings

11 Safeguard for existing human rights

A person's reliance on a Convention right does not restrict—
(a) any other right or freedom conferred on him by or under any law having effect in any part of the United Kingdom; or
(b) his right to make any claim or bring any proceedings which he could make or bring apart from sections 7 to 9.

[5.11]

12 Freedom of expression

(1) This section applies if a court is considering whether to grant any relief which, if granted, might affect the exercise of the Convention right to freedom of expression.

(2) If the person against whom the application for relief is made ('the respondent') is neither present nor represented, no such relief is to be granted unless the court is satisfied—
(a) that the applicant has taken all practicable steps to notify the respondent; or
(b) that there are compelling reasons why the respondent should not be notified.

(3) No such relief is to be granted so as to restrain publication before trial unless the court is satisfied that the applicant is likely to establish that publication should not be allowed.

(4) The court must have particular regard to the importance of the Convention right to freedom of expression and, where the proceedings relate to material which the respondent claims, or which appears to the court, to be journalistic, literary or artistic material (or to conduct connected with such material), to—
(a) the extent to which—
  (i) the material has, or is about to, become available to the public; or
  (ii) it is, or would be, in the public interest for the material to be published;
(b) any relevant privacy code.

(5) In this section—
'court' includes a tribunal; and
'relief' includes any remedy or order (other than in criminal proceedings).

[5.12]

13 Freedom of thought, conscience and religion

(1) If a court's determination of any question arising under this Act might affect the exercise by a religious organisation (itself or its members collectively) of the Convention right to freedom of thought, conscience and religion, it must have particular regard to the importance of that right.

(2) In this section 'court' includes a tribunal.
Note—the Interpretation clause, section 21 does not define 'public authority'.

THE CONVENTION RIGHTS AND EMPLOYER'S LIABILITY

Note—Articles 1 and 13 of the ECHR are not included within the definition of 'Convention rights' in HRA, s 1. For the purposes of considering employer's liability, the following Convention rights are most likely to be relevant.

Article 2 – Right to Life

[5.13]

1. Everyone's right to life shall be protected by law. No one shall be deprived of his life intentionally save in the execution of a sentence of a court following his conviction of a crime for which this penalty is provided by law. ...

Article 3 – Prohibition of torture

[5.14]

No one shall be subjected to torture or to inhuman or degrading treatment or punishment.

Article 4 – Prohibition of slavery and forced labour

[5.15]

1. No one shall be held in slavery or servitude.

2. No one shall be required to perform forced or compulsory labour.

3. For the purpose of this Article the term 'forced or compulsory labour' shall not include:
(a) any work required to be done in the ordinary course of detention imposed according to the provisions of Article 5 of this Convention or during conditional release from such detention;
(b) any service of a military character or, in case of conscientious objectors in countries where they are recognised, service exacted instead of compulsory military service;
(c) any service exacted in case of an emergency or calamity threatening the life or well-being of the community;
(d) any work or service which forms part of normal civic obligations.

Article 6 – Right to a fair trial

[5.16]

1. In the determination of his civil rights and obligations or of any criminal charge against him, everyone is entitled to a fair and public hearing within a reasonable time by an independent and impartial tribunal established by law. Judgment shall be pronounced publicly but the press and public may be excluded from all or part of the trial in the interest of morals, public order or national security in a democratic society, where the interests of juveniles or the protection of the private life of the parties so require, or to the extent strictly necessary in the opinion of the court in special circumstances where publicity would prejudice the interests of justice.

2. Everyone charged with a criminal offence shall be presumed innocent until proved guilty according to law.

3. Everyone charged with a criminal offence has the following minimum rights:
(a) to be informed promptly, in a language which he understands and in detail, of the nature and cause of the accusation against him;
(b) to have adequate time and facilities for the preparation of his defence;
(c) to defend himself in person or through legal assistance of his own choosing or, if he has not sufficient means to pay for legal assistance, to be given it free when the interests of justice so require;
(d) to examine or have examined witnesses against him and to obtain the attendance and examination of witnesses on his behalf under the same conditions as witnesses against him;
(e) to have the free assistance of an interpreter if he cannot understand or speak the language used in court.

Article 8 – Right to respect for private and family life

[5.17]

1. Everyone has the right to respect for his private and family life, his home and his correspondence.

2. There shall be no interference by a public authority with the exercise of this right except such as is in accordance with the law and is necessary in a

democratic society in the interests of national security, public safety or the economic well-being of the country, for the prevention of disorder or crime, for the protection of health or morals, or for the protection of the rights and freedoms of others.

Article 9 – Freedom of thought, conscience and religion

[5.18]

1. Everyone has the right to freedom of thought, conscience and religion; this right includes freedom to change his religion or belief and freedom, either alone or in community with others and in public or private, to manifest his religion or belief, in worship, teaching, practice and observance.

2. Freedom to manifest one's religion or beliefs shall be subject only to such limitations as are prescribed by law and are necessary in a democratic society in the interests of public safety, for the protection of public order, health or morals, or for the protection of the rights and freedoms of others.

Article 10 – Freedom of expression

[5.19]

1. Everyone has the right to freedom of expression. This right shall include freedom to hold opinions and to receive and impart information and ideas without interference by public authority and regardless of frontiers. This Article shall not prevent States from requiring the licensing of broadcasting, television or cinema enterprises.

2. The exercise of these freedoms, since it carries with it duties and responsibilities, may be subject to such formalities, conditions, restrictions or penalties as are prescribed by law and are necessary in a democratic society, in the interests of national security, territorial integrity or public safety, for the prevention of disorder or crime, for the protection of health or morals, for the protection of the reputation or rights of others, for preventing the disclosure of information received in confidence, or for maintaining the authority and impartiality of the judiciary.

Article 11 – Freedom of assembly and association

[5.20]

1. Everyone has the right to freedom of peaceful assembly and to freedom of association with others, including the right to form and to join trade unions for the protection of his interests.

2. No restrictions shall be placed on the exercise of these rights other than such as are prescribed by law and are necessary in a democratic society in the interests of national security or public safety, for the prevention of disorder or crime, for the protection of health or morals or for the protection of the rights and freedoms of others. This Article shall not prevent the imposition of lawful restrictions on the exercise of these rights by members of the armed forces, of the police or of the administration of the State.

Article 14 – Prohibition of discrimination

[5.21]

The enjoyment of the rights and freedoms set forth in this Convention shall be secured without discrimination on any ground such as sex, race, colour, language, religion, political or other opinion, national or social origin, association with a national minority, property, birth or other status.

ANALYSIS OF THE HUMAN RIGHTS ACT

[5.22] The progress of the courts has been somewhat patchy in developing the principles of the new national human rights jurisdiction established by the HRA. The following is a suggested analysis of the way in which the principles of the British system of human rights protection emerge from the text of the HRA.

Principles

[5.23]
(1) HRA, s 2 and HRA, s 11 may be viewed as constraints on the courts' use of sources to resolve questions raising human rights. They require the domestic courts to 'take into account' both the substantive content of the ECHR rights and the principles (such as proportionality, positive obligations and the margin of appreciation), as explained in Strasbourg case law. The courts, acting compatibly with Convention rights under section 6 ought to treat Strasbourg jurisprudence as a 'floor' level of rights not a 'ceiling'. The domestic human rights jurisdiction cannot offer less protection than the Strasbourg base. Likewise, the courts are constrained by domestic law (existing before the HRA) concerning rights, freedoms and remedies through the mechanism of s11. They cannot offer less protection than existing domestic law.
(2) HRA, s 2 may be viewed as containing an invitation element. By merely obliging the courts to 'take into account' Strasbourg jurisprudence, section 2 permits consideration of global human rights jurisprudence and instruments: the Commonwealth, Privy Council decisions, ECJ case-law and the European Union Charter of Fundamental Rights, decisions from the local level of other ECHR states, international law treaty obligations and judicial or quasi-judicial jurisprudence, US and other jurisdictions' decisions, and influential dissenting judgments. The courts are free to go their own way in developing local human rights law, subject to the requirement to give at least the same level of protection that is required by the Strasbourg Court or was required by domestic law prior to the Act.
(3) Use of HRA, s 3 (the interpretive obligation) is mandatory where the application of primary or secondary legislation would violate a Convention right. The legislation must then be subject to a stronger approach to statutory interpretation, to find an interpretation which is compatible with the Convention, 'so far as possible'. This obligation applies in purely private litigation, as well as in

cases where a standard public authority is involved; it is clear from the text of the HRA that horizontal effect exists to this extent at least.

(4) HRA, s 4 determines when there is a referral back to Parliament to take a decision. In the event that the domestic courts find it impossible to accord to a statute a meaning compatible with a Convention right, the courts may make a declaration of incompatibility. This preserves the principle of Parliamentary supremacy over the courts in areas governed by statutory law. Parliament, having been alerted to the incompatibility of its legislation, is then able to decide whether it wishes to remedy or maintain the incompatibility.

(5) HRA, s 6 makes it unlawful for a public authority to act in a way which is incompatible with a Convention right. This duty applies to standard public authorities, persons certain of whose functions are functions of a 'public nature' (hybrid, or functional, public authorities), and also courts and tribunals.

(6) HRA, s 6(1) and (3) impose an obligation of the courts to act compatibly with Convention rights. They must do so when exercising their discretion. It is strongly arguable that an effect is to ensure that the common law must also be developed consistently with the Convention, in private as well as public law. The courts have yet to provide an authoritative ruling on the nature and extent of this duty.

(7) HRA, s 7 and s 8 enable, and provide conditions for (a) an action to be brought in a court or tribunal against a standard or hybrid public authority for breach of the duty to act compatibly with Convention rights; and (b) the breach of duty to be relied upon in any legal proceedings. Section 8 of HRA directs how a challenge to a judicial act should be made.

[5.24] Practitioners and employers should be alert to the fact that the HRA does not 'incorporate' the ECHR, but creates an autonomous national level of protection of human rights. The content of the rights and principles governing them will differ from the content and principles applied at the supranational level by the European Court of Human Rights.

R (on the application of the Pro-Life Alliance) v British Broadcasting Corpn

[2002] EWCA Civ 297, [2002] 2 All ER 756

[5.25]

The English court is not a Strasbourg surrogate. The very difference between the international margin of appreciation and the municipal margin of discretion illustrates the confusion that would arise if the court so regarded itself. Our duty is to develop, by the common law's incremental method, a coherent and principled domestic law of human rights. In doing it, we are directed by the HRA (s 6) to insist on compliance by public authorities with the standards of the convention, and to comply with them ourselves. We are given new powers and duties (ss 3 and 4 of the HRA) to see that that is done. In all this we are to take account of the Strasbourg cases (s 2, to which I have already referred).

The need to make good an autonomous human rights jurisprudence is promoted by a further consideration. Treating the ECHR text as a template for our own law runs the risk of an over-rigid approach. Travelling through the words of provisions like art 10(2), with stops along the way to pronounce that this or that condition is met or not met, smacks to my mind of what Lord Wilberforce once condemned as the 'austerity of tabulated legalism' ... I accept of course that such a wintry process would be tempered by what I have called ... the strong pragmatic philosophy of the Strasbourg court.

General comments on when to raise a human rights point

R v DPP, ex p Kebilene

[1999] 3 WLR 972

[5.26] Per Lord Hope at 988E:

It is now plain that the incorporation of the European Convention on Human Rights into our domestic law will subject the entire legal system to a fundamental process of review and, where necessary, reform by the judiciary.

R v North West Lancashire Health Authority, ex p A

[2000] 1 WLR 977, 1003

[5.27] Per Buxton LJ at 1003:

I am disturbed by the appeal to Convention and Community authority that has no sensible connection with the issues in the case; and by the alternative argument that since those systems protect rights that are in some ways related to the rights asserted in this case, they can be used as some support for the applicant's primary case. That approach is misconceived. In a case where neither Convention or Community rights can be asserted, the case either succeeds or fails on domestic grounds and not other. And with the imminent coming into force of the Human Rights Act it will be even more important than it is at present to ensure that Convention rights are not asserted in inappropriate circumstances; so that they play their proper and important role, but only their proper role, in the protection of the citizen's interest.

Note—Warnings such as that of Buxton LJ have generally been adhered to. Statistical evidence shows that the Act did not expose the courts or legal aid system to the feared flood of claims. The impact is greatest in the higher courts (6.2% of cases in the Court of Appeal raised human rights issues between April and June 2001), whilst in the county court human rights points appear to be frequently overlooked (the corresponding figure being less than 0.01% of cases). [Source: 'Impact on Court Workloads' *http://www.lcd.gov.uk.*]

Definition of a public authority

(See HRA, s 6, above.)

Poplar Housing and Regeneration Community Association Ltd v Donoghue

[2001] EWCA Civ 595, [2002] QB 48

[5.28] Poplar Housing Association was a registered social landlord. Mrs Donoghue, a tenant, sought to defend a claim for possession. She did so on the ground that the Association was acting incompatibly with her right to respect for private life under ECHR, Art 8, by seeking an order for possession against her. One of the issues was whether the Association was a 'public authority' within section 6.

HELD, on appeal: Per Lord Woolf CJ: Section 6 of HRA requires a generous interpretation of who is a public authority for the purposes of the HRA. But it is clearly inspired by the courts' approach to determining the bodies and activities subject to judicial review. The Association's role was so closely assimilated to that of a local housing authority that it was carrying out a public function in relation to Mrs Donoghue, and was therefore a hybrid or 'functional public authority' within the HRA. This does not mean that all of Poplar's activities are public. The fact that a body performs an activity which otherwise a public body would be under a duty to perform cannot mean that such performance is necessarily a public function. Section 6(3)(b)'s purpose is to deal with bodies which are hybrid in that they have both public and private functions. An act may remain of a private nature even though it is performed because another body is under a public duty to ensure that the act is performed. For example, if a local authority sent a child to a private school in order to fulfil its duties, it would not mean that the private school was performing public functions. The local authority could not escape its responsibility by delegation, however: the local authority and not the school would be responsible for a breach of its Convention obligations. The fact that a body is motivated by its perception of the public interest (eg many charities and not-for-profit organisations) does not indicate that such a body is a public authority. The court looks for features which impose a public character or stamp' on the act considered, such as statutory authority for the act; the extent of a public authority's control over the function exercised by the body in question; and acts of a private nature being closely enmeshed with a public body's activities. Supervision of the acts by a public regulatory body does not necessarily indicate that the acts are of a public nature, as in judicial review cases.

R (on the application of Heather) v Leonard Cheshire Foundation

[2002] EWCA Civ 366, [2002] 2 All ER 936

[5.29] A long-term resident of a care home operated by the Foundation sought judicial review of the Foundation's decision to close the care home The Foundation provided the accommodation and support services under contracted out arrangements with various local authorities.

HELD, on appeal: The Foundation was not a public authority. This was so even though in relation to the resident, the Foundation was providing its services pursuant to contracts with local authorities, who were subject to a statutory duty to arrange for the provision of those services. However, Lord Woolf CJ noted that it was arguable that the HRA allowed a resident to require the local authority to enter into a contract with its service provider which gave full protection to the resident's Article 8 rights (paragraph 34 of the judgment). The House of Lords refused an application for leave to appeal on 18 November 2002.

HORIZONTAL EFFECT OF THE HUMAN RIGHTS ACT

[5.30] The question of the effect of the HRA in cases where neither party is a public authority has proved controversial, and has yet to be fully worked out by the courts. The authorities to date are in favour of some form of indirect horizontal effect. See further, Murray Hunt, 'The Horizontal Effect of the Human Rights Act' [1998] PL 423, which has received a certain degree of judicial support (eg Sedley LJ in *Hello!*, below).

Douglas v Hello! Ltd

[2001] QB 967, CA

[5.31] A celebrity couple agreed with Northern & Shell that its magazine, 'OK', would have exclusive rights to publish photographs of the couple's wedding. The rival magazine of the defendants, 'Hello!', obtained photographs taken surreptitiously at the wedding, although it was not known who had taken the photographs. The claimants obtained an interim injunction to restrain publication on grounds of breach of confidence.

HELD, on appeal: The injunction would be discharged, as the balance of convenience came down against prior restraint. A number of obiter remarks were made. Per Brooke LJ:

> Section 8 of the Human Rights Act 1998 is concerned only with the power of a court to award compensation against acts of public authorities for unlawful acts which are incompatible with a Convention right. The Act gives the court no such statutory power to order one private entity to pay compensation to another in respect of a breach of Convention rights ...

Referring to the consistent line of the Strasbourg Court's reasoning that state authorities may have a positive duty to take measures designed to secure effective respect for private life even in the sphere of relations between individuals themselves, it was explained that, in relation to the law of privacy, the Strasbourg institutions indicate:

> ... since the authorities in this country have been content to leave it to the judges to develop the law in this sensitive field, it is the judges who must develop the law so that it gives appropriate recognition to Article 8(1) rights. Whether they do so in future by an extension of the existing frontiers of the law of confidence, or by recognising the existence of new relationships which give rise to enforceable legal rights (as in *Donoghue v Stevenson* ...) is not for this court, on this occasion, to predict ...

Sedley LJ expressed the view that if the step from the existing common law of confidence to a law of privacy was not already accommodated by pre-HRA law, then it would be precisely the kind of incremental change for which the Act is designed, and consonant with the Strasbourg jurisprudence of the positive obligation inherent in ECHR, Art 8. Furthermore, HRA, s 12(4) puts beyond question the direct applicability of at least one ECHR article (freedom of expression, see 5.11 above). But whether its horizontal effect is an illustration of the intended mechanism of the entire Act cannot be considered in this case.

Per Keene LJ:

> ... The courts as a public authority cannot act in a way which is incompatible with a Convention right: section 6(1). That arguably includes their activity in interpreting and developing the common law, even where no public authority is a party to the litigation. Whether this extends to creating a new cause of action between private persons and bodies is more controversial, since to do so would appear to circumvent the restrictions on proceedings contained in section 7(1) of the Act and on remedies in section 8(1). But it is unnecessary to determine that issue in these proceedings ... [Due to] developments in the common law relating to confidence and the apparent obligation on English courts now to take account of the right to respect for private and family life under Article 8 when interpreting the common law, it seems unlikely that *Kaye v Robertson*, which held that there was no actionable right of privacy in English law, would be decided the same way on that aspect today.
>
> *Note*— In *Venables and Thompson v Newspapers* [2001] Fam 430, Dame Butler-Sloss P, considered *Hello!*, and expressed views against the argument that the HRA created a freestanding cause of action based directly on the ECHR Articles, and regarded the judge's duty as being 'to act compatibly with Convention rights in adjudicating upon existing common law causes of action, and that includes a positive as well as a negative obligation'. Having argued, extra-judicially, against a horizontal interpretation of the HRA ('The Human Rights Act and Private Law' [2000] 116 LQR 48), Buxton LJ sought to limit the effect of some of the comments in *Hello!* which supported the statement of a broad principle or tort of privacy in *Wainwright v Home Office* [2001] EWCA Civ 2081, [2002] QB 1334. In his view, the barrier to the recognition of a tort of privacy erected by *Kaye v Robertson* could only be removed by Parliament.

Uncertainty as to the circumstances in which resort can be had to the HRA in purely private litigation may continue for some time. The following article assists in identifying areas where horizontal effect should be considered: Ian Rogers, 'How to spot a human rights point in a private law case' (2002) NLJ Vol 152 No 7056 p 1723.

PROPORTIONALITY AND THE DISCRETIONARY AREA OF JUDGMENT

[5.32] Proportionality lies at the heart of the ECHR. It is the standard of review applied by the Strasbourg Court when assessing the lawfulness of the actions of state authorities. Under the HRA, the national courts have the task of determining whether actions of other state authorities have interfered with Convention rights in a way which can be justified having regard to the standard of proportionality. The proportionality test may be applied with a level of scrutiny which is more or less intense according to the context. The courts must apply this standard having regard to their constitutional position, relative to the body whose actions are being reviewed. They are in the process of developing a principle of 'deference' or 'discretionary area of judgment', which is to some extent informed by, but is not the same as, the Strasbourg Court's doctrine of the margin of appreciation.

R v DPP, ex p Kebilene

[2000] 2 AC 326, [1999] 4 All ER 801, HL

[5.33] Per Lord Hope:

... Difficult choices may have to be made by the executive or the legislature between the rights of the individual and the needs of society. In some circumstances it will be appropriate for the courts to recognise that there is an area of judgment within which the judiciary will defer, on democratic grounds, to the considered opinion of the elected body or person whose act or decision is said to be incompatible with the Convention. ... the area in which these choices may arise is conveniently and appropriately described as the 'discretionary area of judgment'. It will be easier for such an area of judgment to be recognised where the Convention itself requires a balance to be struck, much less so where the right is stated in terms which are unqualified. It will be easier for it to be recognised where the issues involve questions of social or economic policy, much less so where the rights are of high constitutional importance or are of a kind where the courts are especially well placed to assess the need for protection.

R (on the application of Alconbury Developments Ltd) v Secretary of State for the Environment, Transport and the Regions

[2001] UKHL 23, [2001] 2 All ER 929

[5.34] Per Lord Hoffmann:

Respect for human rights requires that certain basic rights of individuals should not be capable in any circumstances of being overridden by the majority, even if they think that the public interest so requires. Other rights should be capable of being overridden only in very restricted circumstances. These are rights which belong to individuals simply by virtue of their humanity, independently of any utilitarian calculation. The protection of these basic rights from majority decision requires that independent and impartial tribunals should have the power to decide whether legislation infringes them and either (as in the United States) to declare such legislation invalid or (as in the United Kingdom) to declare that it is incompatible with the governing human rights instrument. But outside these basic rights, there are many decisions which have to be made every day (for example, about the allocation of resources) in which the only fair method of decision is by some person or body accountable to the electorate.

R (on the application of Daly) v Secretary of State for the Home Department

[2001] UKHL 26, [2001] 2 AC 532, [2001] 3 All ER 433

[5.35] Lord Steyn referred to the three-stage test for proportionality formulated by the Privy Council in *De Freitas v Permanent Secretary of Ministry of Agriculture* [1999] 1 AC 69:

> ... In determining whether a limitation (by an act rule or decision) is arbitrary or excessive the court should ask itself:
> 'whether: (i) the legislative objective is sufficiently important to justify limiting a fundamental right;
> (ii) the measures designed to meet the legislative objective are rationally connected to it; and
> (iii) the means used to impair the right or freedom are no more than is necessary to accomplish the objective.'

Lord Steyn also noted three differences between the traditional grounds of review and proportionality:

> First, the doctrine of proportionality may require the reviewing court to assess the balance which the decision maker has struck, not merely whether it is within the range of rational or reasonable decisions.

> Secondly, the proportionality test may go further than the traditional grounds of review inasmuch as it may require attention to be directed to the relative weight accorded to interests and considerations.

> Thirdly, even the heightened scrutiny test developed in *R v Ministry of Defence, Ex p Smith* ... is not necessarily appropriate to the protection of human rights. The European Court of Human Rights came to the opposite conclusion [from the Court of Appeal's decision on the Ministry's ban on employing gay and lesbian servicemen and women]: *Smith and Grady v United Kingdom* (1999) 29 EHRR 493.

The court concluded:

> ... the threshold at which the High Court and the Court of Appeal could find the Ministry of Defence policy irrational was placed so high that it effectively excluded any consideration by the domestic courts of the question of whether the interference with the applicants' rights answered a pressing social need or was proportionate to the national security and public order aims pursued, principles which lie at the heart of the court's analysis of complaints under article 8 of the Convention.
>
> *Note*—*Daly's* apparent approval of a fairly intensive proportionality test has been applied in several subsequent cases, eg *International Transport GmbH v Secretary of State for the Home Department* [2002] EWCA Civ 158, [2002] 3 WLR 344. In other cases, where the court perceives greater deference should be shown, there is barely any consideration of proportionality at all. Whilst it is true that the application of the proportionality test will

vary according to its context, the intensity of the review will depend on a judge's appreciation of how much deference ought to be shown to the body in question. In *R v Shayler* [2002] UKHL 11, [2002] 2 All ER 477, Lord Hope applied an even more intensive test of proportionality (which he subsequently applied in his dissenting speech in *R (on the application of Rottman) v Metropolitan Police Comr* [2002] UKHL 20, [2002] 2 AC 692, a case concerned with a search of a home, constituting a prima facie interference with Article 8(1)). Lord Hope's three stages are as follows:

(i) Was the pressing social need (or objective to be achieved) sufficiently important to justify limiting the fundamental right?
(ii) Were the means chosen to limit that right rational, fair and not arbitrary?
(iii) Did the means used impair that right as minimally as reasonably possible?

It should be noted that Lord Hope's third limb resembles a test sometimes applied by the Strasbourg Court, but it is generally reserved for occasions where a very intensive level of review is deemed to be required.

STATUTORY INTERPRETATION UNDER SECTION 3 AND DECLARATIONS OF INCOMPATIBILITY UNDER SECTION 4

[5.36] It is accepted that the obligation under HRA, s 3 to interpret statutes compatibly with the Convention rights is applicable whether a public authority is a party to the litigation or all litigants are private bodies. Indeed the first declaration of incompatibility was made in a private law case, see 5.37 below.

Wilson v First County Trust Ltd

[2001] QB 407, CA, and Same v Same (No 2) *[2001] EWCA Civ 633, [2002] QB 74*

[5.37] The claimant asserted that a loan agreement made between herself and the defendant pawnbrokers breached Regulations made under the Consumer Credit Act 1974, which rendered the agreement unenforceable under the 1974 Act, s 127(3). In the first hearing, the court of its own motion recognised that it might have to make a declaration of incompatibility in respect of the legislation, and adjourned to give the Crown notice under HRA, s 5.

HELD, at the second hearing: The court made the declaration of incompatibility. Section 3 required the court to give effect to the Regulations in a way which would be compatible with the Convention rights. The loan agreement did not contain the prescribed terms set out in the Regulations. The policy aim of requiring a written credit agreement setting out the terms of the document was held to be legitimate, but section 127(3) prevented the court from enforcing the agreement. Counsel for the Secretary of State was held to have correctly identified that consumer credit legislation was an area of social policy, where the courts should be ready to defer on democratic grounds to the elected body. However, the court was critical that it had not been provided with explanations in the form of reports, preparatory material and debates in Parliament to explain why the Minister thought it just to exclude the judicial remedy in this type of situation. Nor was there any explanation from the Minister as to why he saw fit to prescribe the terms which he did in the Regulations. There was a disproportionate interference with the creditor's rights under Article 6 and Article 1 of Protocol 1, in that the 1974 Act, s 127(3) prevented the court from doing what was just in the case of a non-compliant agreement. It could not read the provisions in a compatible way, and in its discretion, the court made the declaration.

> *Note*—Thus, one of the first groups to whom the domestic courts came to aid under the HRA was that of private commercial lenders seeking to recover a debt from a private individual. The court did not discuss the issue of horizontality, but simply followed the general words of sections 3 and 4. By HRA, s 4(6), however, a declaration does not affect the validity of the provision impugned – Parliament is left to take the decision whether to remedy the incompatibility – and the declaration does not bind the parties.

R v Secretary of State for the Home Department, ex p Simms

[2000] 2 AC 115, HL

[5.38] Per Lord Hoffmann:

Parliamentary sovereignty means that Parliament can, if it chooses, legislate contrary to fundamental principles of human rights. The Human Rights Act 1998 will not detract from this power. The constraints upon its exercise by Parliament are ultimately political, not legal. But the principle of legality means that Parliament must squarely confront what it is doing and accept the political cost. Fundamental rights cannot be overridden by general or ambiguous words. This is because there is too great a risk that the full implications of their unqualified meaning may have passed unnoticed in the democratic process. In the absence of express language or necessary implication to the contrary, the courts therefore presume that even the most general words were intended to be subject to the basic rights of the individual....

The Human Rights Act 1998 will make three changes to this scheme of things. First, the principles of fundamental human rights which exist at common law will be supplemented by a specific text [the ECHR]. Secondly, the principle of legality will be expressly enacted as a rule of construction in s 3 ... Thirdly, in those unusual cases in which the legislative infringement of fundamental human rights is so clearly expressed as not to yield to the principle of legality, the courts will be able to draw this to the attention of Parliament by making a declaration of incompatibility. It will then be for the sovereign Parliament to decide whether or not to remove the incompatibility.

Poplar Housing and Regeneration Community Association Ltd v Donoghue

[2002] EWCA Civ 595, [2002] QB 48

[5.39] The facts are stated above (at 5.28); see the sub-section dealing with the definition of a public authority. Lord Woolf CJ gave the following guidance on HRA, s 3:

[Section 3] applies to legislation passed both before and after the Human Rights Act 1998 came into force. Subject to the section not requiring the court to go beyond that which is possible, it is mandatory in its terms. In the case of legislation predating the Human Rights Act 1998 where the legislation would otherwise conflict with the Convention, section 3 requires the court to now interpret legislation in a manner which it would not have done before the Human Rights Act 1998 came into force. When the court interprets legislation usually its primary task is to identify the intention of Parliament. Now, when section 3 applies, the courts have to adjust their traditional role in relation to interpretation so as to give effect to the direction contained in section 3. It is as though legislation which predates the Human Rights Act 1998 and conflicts with the Convention has to be treated as being subsequently amended to incorporate the language of section 3. ... The following points ... should be noted.

(a) Unless the legislation would otherwise be in breach of the Convention section 3 can be ignored (so courts should always first ascertain whether, absent section 3, there would be any breach of the Convention).

(b) If the court has to rely on section 3 it should limit the extent of the modified meaning to that which is necessary to achieve compatibility.

(c) Section 3 does not entitle the court to legislate (its task is still one of interpretation, but interpretation in accordance with the direction contained in section 3).

(d) The views of the parties and of the Crown as to whether a 'constructive' interpretation should be adopted cannot modify the task of the court (if section 3 applies the court is required to adopt the section 3 approach to interpretation).

(e) Where, despite the strong language of section 3, it is not possible to achieve a result which is compatible with the Convention, the court is not required to grant a declaration and presumably in exercising its discretion as to whether to grant a declaration or not it will be influenced by the usual considerations which apply to the grant of declarations.

The most difficult task which courts face is distinguishing between legislation and interpretation. Here practical experience of seeking to apply section 3 will provide the best guide. However, if it is necessary in order to obtain compliance to radically alter the effect of the legislation this will be an indication that more than interpretation is involved.

HELD, on appeal: That the effect of such an interpretation would be very wide, significantly reducing the ability of landlords to recover possession and defeating Parliament's original objective of providing certainty. The court claimed that it would involve legislating.

R v A (No 2)

[2001] UKHL 25, [2002] 1 AC 45

[5.40] The defendant was charged with rape. His defence was that the complainant had consented to the sexual intercourse in question. He sought leave under the Youth Justice and Criminal Evidence Act 1999 to adduce evidence and ask questions in relation to an alleged consensual sexual relationship with the complainant over the course of the preceding three weeks, up to one week before the alleged rape.

HELD, on appeal: Ordinary methods of purposive construction of the 1999 Act, s 41(3)(c) cannot cure the problem of the excessive breadth of section 41, read as a whole, so far as it relates to previous sexual experience between a complainant and the accused. Whilst the statute pursued desirable goals, the methods adopted amounted to legislative overkill. On the other hand, the interpretative obligation under the HRA, s 3 is a strong one. It applies even if there is no ambiguity in the language in the sense of the language being capable of two different meanings. It is an emphatic adjuration by the legislature. Section 3 places a duty on the court to strive to find a possible interpretation compatible with Convention rights. It is a general principle of the interpretation of legal instruments that the text is the primary source of interpretation: other sources are subordinate to it. Section 3 qualifies this general principle because it requires a court to find an interpretation compatible with Convention rights if it is possible to do so.

In the progress of the Bill through Parliament the Lord Chancellor observed that: 'in 99% of the cases that will arise, there will be no need for judicial declarations of incompatibility', and the Home Secretary said: 'We expect that, in almost all cases, the courts will be able to interpret the legislation compatibility with the Convention'. This is at least relevant as an aid to the interpretation of s 3 against the executive. In accordance with the will of Parliament as reflected in s 3 it will sometimes be necessary to adopt an interpretation which linguistically may appear strained. The techniques to be used will not only involve the reading down of express language in a statute but also the implication of provisions. A declaration of incompatibility is a measure of last resort. It must be avoided unless it is plainly impossible to do so. If a clear limitation on Convention rights is stated in terms, such an impossibility will arise (*R v Secretary of State for the Home Department, ex parte Simms*, above.) There is, however, no limitation of such a nature in the present case.

Section 3 requires the court to subordinate the niceties of the language of s 41(3)(c) of the 1999 Act to broader considerations of relevance judged by logical and commonsense criteria of time and circumstances. The legislature would not, if alerted to the problem, have wished to deny the right to an accused to put forward a full and complete defence by advancing truly probative material. It is therefore possible under s 3 to read s 41, and in particular s 41(3)(c), as subject to the implied provision that evidence or questioning which is required to ensure a fair trial under art 6 of the Convention should not be treated as inadmissible. Through the adoption of this approach s 41 achieves a major part of its objective but its excessive reach is attenuated in accordance with the will of Parliament as reflected in s 3 of the 1998 Act.

Effect of HRA, s 3 on employer's liability cases

[5.41] So how can all this effect employers liability cases? The following cases illustrate the practical effect of HRA, s 3 on such cases.

Cachia v Faluyi

[2001] EWCA Civ 998, [2001] 1 WLR 1966

[5.42] This private law case turned on the Fatal Accidents Act, s 2(3) which stated: 'Not more than one action shall lie for and in respect of the same subject matter of complaint'. The claimant, a widower, had issued a writ under the Act, claiming damages on behalf of the estate and loss for her dependants, but the writ had lapsed without having been served. Six years later, when a second writ was issued, the claims of the youngest children (three of the dependants named in the first writ) were still within the limitation period. The question for the court was whether section 2(3) barred the claim of the three children. There was authority in other contexts that 'action' included *unserved* writs.

HELD, on appeal: The traditional methods of statutory interpretation did not permit them to construe 'action' as 'served process', but under section 3 of the Human Rights Act it was 'possible' to do so. It was conceded that the children's right of access to the court was barred by section 2(3), and that this restriction had no legitimate aim – being a mere procedural quirk which existed 'because our traditional English methods of interpreting statutes could not right an obvious injustice'. Brooke LJ concluded: 'This is a very good example of the way in which the enactment of the Human Rights Act now enables English judges to do justice in a way which was not previously open to us.'

Re S (Minors) (Care Order: Implementation of Care Plan); Re W (Minors) (Care Order: Adequacy of Care Plan)

[2002] UKHL 10, [2002] 1 FLR 815

[5.43] The Court of Appeal (Sedley, Hale and Thorpe LJJ) had proposed new solutions to a local authority child care problem, acknowledged in the House of Lords as needing 'urgent consideration'. The Court of Appeal had deployed section 3 as an exhortation to find compatibility rather than incompatibility. Most notably the Court of Appeal proposed a new system of 'starred milestones' by which at the trial the essential milestones of a care plan would be identified and elevated to a 'starred status'. If a starred milestone was not achieved within a reasonable time after the date set at trial, the local authority was obliged to reactivate the interdisciplinary process that contributed to the creation of the care plan. At the least the local authority must inform the child's guardian of the position. Either the guardian or the local authority would then have the right to apply to the court for further directions. The starred milestones system was not canvassed in argument by counsel and appeared for the first time in the judgments of the Court of Appeal.

HELD, on appeal: By the court's introduction of a 'starring system' it exceeded the bounds of its judicial jurisdiction under section 3. Even if the Children Act 1989 is inconsistent with Articles 6 or 8 of the Convention, section 3 does not in this case have the effect suggested by the Court of Appeal. Section 3 is a powerful tool whose use is obligatory, but its reach is not unlimited. It is concerned with interpretation. The HRA reserves the amendment of primary legislation to Parliament in order to preserve parliamentary sovereignty and to maintain the constitutional boundary. Interpretation of statutes is a matter for the courts; the enactment of statutes, and the amendment of statutes, are matters for Parliament. The area of real difficulty lies in identifying the limits of interpretation in a particular case. A meaning which departs substantially from a fundamental feature of an Act of Parliament is likely to have crossed the boundary between interpretation and amendment. This is especially so where the departure has important practical repercussions which the court is not equipped to evaluate. In such a case the overall contextual setting may leave no scope for rendering the statutory provision Convention compliant by legitimate use of the process of interpretation. The boundary line may be crossed even though a limitation on Convention rights is not stated in express terms. Lord Steyn's observations in *R v A (No 2)* [2001] UKHL 25, ([2002] 1 AC 45) are not to be read as meaning that a clear limitation on Convention rights in terms is the only circumstance in which an interpretation incompatible with Convention rights may arise. Parliament entrusted to local authorities, not the courts, the responsibility for looking after children who are the subject of care orders. The new starring system would depart substantially from this principle. In short, under the starring system the court will exercise a newly created supervisory function. I consider this judicial innovation passes well beyond the boundary of interpretation. These are matters for decision by Parliament, not the courts. It is impossible for a court to attempt to evaluate the ramifications or assess what would be the views of Parliament if changes are needed.

HUMAN RIGHTS CASES AFFECTING EMPLOYER'S LIABILITY

[5.44] Plainly, it is not only public authority employers, but all employers, who need to consider the HRA, insofar as and to the extent that, the Act is being given a horizontal interpretation. Examples of cases whose facts touch upon issues relevant to employer's liability are too numerous to list here. The following examples are simply that, space does not allow for a comprehensive list. Practitioners must develop a general awareness of human rights law and its potential relevance to all litigation.

Article 4

Van der Mussele v Belgium

(1983) 6 EHRR 163, ECtHR

[5.45] Forced labour connotes physical or mental constraint, and is an evolving concept; an obligation to provide free legal services as part of a barrister's training was not compulsory labour.

Article 6

Pellegrin v France

(1999) 31 EHRR 651, ECtHR; Frydlender v France (26 June 2000, unreported), ECtHR

[5.46] A distinction was drawn by the court between civil servants' Article 6 rights and those of other employees. Typically civil service employment disputes relating to the recruitment, careers and termination or reinstatement of civil servants have been outside Article 6 protection, except that disputes relating to 'purely economic' rights, eg wage and pension claims, have attracted Article 6 protection. It is questionable whether this unattractive distinction would be applied by UK courts, who are free to offer greater protection than Strasbourg.

Article 8

Halford v United Kingdom

(1997) 24 EHRR 523, ECtHR

[5.47] Interception of communications at work constitutes an interference with respect for private life and correspondence (paras 45, 48, 51).

Niemietz v Germany

(1992) 16 EHRR 97, ECtHR

[5.48] A professional's office was to be regarded as within the meaning of 'home' for Article 8 purposes; the notion of private life extends to the development of relations with others at work and elsewhere, and generally includes activities of a business or professional nature.

Smith and Grady v United Kingdom

[1999] IRLR 734, ECtHR

[5.49] Sexual orientation is an intimate aspect of private life; investigations into, and dismissal on grounds of, sexual orientation of armed forces employees breached Article 8.

Jones v University of Warwick

[2003] EWCA Civ 151, [2003] 1 WLR 954

[5.50] Private video surveillance was used by the defendants in personal injury claims; discretion to admit such evidence was to be determined by reference to the Article 8 right to privacy, and balanced against matters such as any deception on the part of the claimant.

Martin v McGuiness

Times 21 April 2003

[5.50a] A private investigator's investigations and inquiries, involving pretences to the claimant's spouse be a former colleague of the claimant, and filming events in the claimant's garden with a telephoto lens, engaged rights to privacy and family life protected by article 8(1). Nevertheless the investigations and inquiries were reasonable and proportionate steps taken by the defendant to protect his rights and the wider rights of society.

Godbout v Longueuil

[1997] 3 SCR 844 (Canada)

[5.51] A requirement for an employee to live in a certain geographical location violates right to privacy unless a very good justification is shown.

Article 9

Konttinen v Finland

(Application 24949/94) 87 DR 68 (1996), E Com HR

[5.52] There was held to be no violation of Article 9 where a Seventh Day Adventist was dismissed for refusing to work after sunset on Fridays.

Kalac v Turkey

(1999) 27 EHRR 552, ECtHR

[5.53] This case concerned whether a dismissal was related to the way the applicant manifested his religion, and whether there was a violation of Article 9.

X v Germany

(Application 10365/83)(1985) 7 EHRR 461

[5.54] A teacher on strike was disciplined because of participation, not for holding or expressing a belief or opinion.

X v United Kingdom

(Application 8160/78) 22 DR 27 (1981), E Com HR

[5.55] The obligation of a public employer to give due consideration to employee's religious position was considered. A teacher had accepted a post without notifying the school of his religious position; a refusal to rearrange a school timetable to accommodate the teacher's wish to practise religion did not violate Article 9.

Article 10

Kosiek v Germany

(1986) 9 EHRR 328, ECtHR

[5.56] Workers have a right of freedom of expression; those in public duty may owe a duty of moderation during their employment.

Article 14

Ahmad v UK

(1981) 4 EHRR 126

[5.57] A case on refusal to allow a Muslim employee time off to attend his mosque; there was no violation of Article 14 in circumstances where all employees were refused time off.

CROWN EMPLOYEES

STATUTORY LIABILITY OF THE CROWN

CROWN PROCEEDINGS ACT 1947

[5.58] The Crown Proceedings Act 1947 governs civil proceedings against the Crown, and contains provisions affecting both substantive law relating to Crown proceedings and the procedure to be followed. Judicial review does not fall within the scope of the Act. The general effect of the Act is to put the Crown in a similar position to that of an ordinary defendant, subject to certain exceptions. Proceedings should be issued by or against the appropriate Government department, as determined by section 17 of the Act. The Crown is bound by the Law Reform (Personal Injuries) Act 1948, which abolished the doctrine of common employment (see sections 1 and 4 of that Act). Care should be taken when dealing with statutory causes of action to ascertain whether there are any particular provisions of the enactment dealing with the application of the Act to the Crown. Some examples follow.

Occupiers' Liability Act 1957, section 6

[5.59]

> This Act shall bind the Crown, but as regards the Crown's liability in tort shall not bind the Crown further than the Crown is made liable in tort by the Crown Proceedings Act 1947, and that Act and in particular section two of it shall apply in relation to duties under sections two to four of this Act as statutory duties.

Defective Premises Act 1972, section 5

[5.60]

> This Act shall bind the Crown, but as regards the Crown's liability in tort shall not bind the Crown further than the Crown is made liable in tort by the Crown Proceedings Act 1947.

Occupiers' Liability Act 1984, section 3

[5.61]

> This Act shall bind the Crown, but as regards the Crown's liability in tort shall not bind the Crown further than the Crown is made liable in tort by the Crown Proceedings Act 1947.

CONTRACTS OF EMPLOYMENT AND THE CROWN

[5.62] Former doubts as to whether civil servants were subject to a contract of employment have been largely resolved by the following decision. Practitioners should be aware of the possibility, and occasional advantages, of public law proceedings in this area (see eg De Smith, Woolf and Jowell, *Judicial Review of Administrative Action* (5th edn. 1995, Sweet & Maxwell) 3–055*ff*.).

R v Lord Chancellor's Department, ex p Nangle

[1991] ICR 743, DC

[5.63] The applicant was an executive grade civil servant in the Lord Chancellor's Department. He was accused of having assaulted and sexually harassed a woman working in the same department. It was determined after a hearing that he would be transferred to another division with loss of increment. He sought judicial review. His appointment was subject to the Civil Service Pay and Conditions of Service Code. Paragraph 14 of the Code stated: 'A civil servant does not have a contract of employment enforceable in the courts.' The Department argued that the judicial review application should be dismissed, on the basis that the application of disciplinary procedures to a Crown servant is not a matter of public law susceptible to judicial review.

HELD: The applicant was employed by the Crown under a contract of service, as the necessary intention to create legal relations existed. The application for judicial review was therefore dismissed. In determining whether the parties had entered into legal relations, the word 'appointment' was neutral and the question had to be determined not by the parties' subjective belief of the effects of the appointment, but by an objective construction of the documents. Paragraph 14 of the Code apart (which must in any event be read in context), the documents of appointment showed that the parties had entered into obligations, rights and entitlements consistent with a contract of employment (dealing with matters which are standard items covered by employment contracts, such as pay, pensions, holidays, sick pay etc). The applicant's claim was a matter of private law not susceptible to judicial review. The applicant would have a private law action in damages for breach of contract if he could establish a breach of the disciplinary code. Even if there was no legal relationship, the mere absence of a private law remedy did not give rise to a remedy in public law. The internal disciplinary proceedings, being of a domestic nature, did not have a sufficient element of public law to make them subject to judicial review.

ARMED FORCES

Crown Proceedings Act 1947, Section 10

[5.64]

(1) Nothing done or omitted to be done by a member of the armed forces of the Crown while on duty as such shall subject either him or the Crown to liability in tort for causing the death of another person, or for causing personal injury to another person, in so far as the death or personal injury is due to anything suffered by that other person while he is a member of the armed forces of the Crown if—

(a) at the time when that thing is suffered by that other person, he is either on duty as a member of the armed forces of the Crown or is, though not on duty as such, on any land, premises, ship, aircraft or vehicle for the time being used for the purposes of the armed forces of the Crown; and

(b) [the Secretary of State] certifies that his suffering that thing has been or will be treated as attributable to service for the purposes of entitlement to an award under the Royal Warrant, Order in Council or Order of His Majesty relating to the disablement or death of members of the force of which he is a member:

Provided that this subsection shall not exempt a member of the said forces from liability in tort in any case in which the court is satisfied that the act or omission was not connected with the execution of his duties as a member of those forces.

(2) No proceedings in tort shall lie against the Crown for death or personal injury due to anything suffered by a member of the armed forces of the Crown if—

(a) that thing is suffered by him in consequence of the nature or condition of any such land, premises, ship, aircraft or vehicle as aforesaid, or in consequence of the nature or condition of any equipment or supplies used for the purposes of those forces; and

(b) [the Secretary of State] certifies as mentioned in the preceding subsection; nor shall any act or omission of an officer of the Crown subject him to liability in tort for death or personal injury, in so far as the death or personal injury is due to anything suffered by a member of the armed forces of the Crown being a thing as to which the conditions aforesaid are satisfied.

(3) ... a Secretary of State, if satisfied that it is the fact:—

(a) that a person was or was not on any particular occasion on duty as a member of the armed forces of the Crown; or

(b) that at any particular time any land, premises, ship, aircraft, vehicle, equipment or supplies was or was not, or were or were not, used for the purposes of the said forces; may issue a certificate certifying that to be the fact; and any such certificate shall, for the purposes of this section, be conclusive as to the fact which it certifies.

Crown Proceedings (Armed Forces) Act 1987

[5.65]

1. Subject to section 2 below, section 10 of the Crown Proceedings Act 1947 (exclusions from liability in tort in cases involving the armed forces) shall cease to have effect except in relation to anything suffered by a person in consequence of an act or omission committed before the date on which this Act is passed.

(This Act was passed on 15 May 1987.)

Note—Section 2 of this Act enables the Secretary of State to revive the Crown Proceedings Act 1947, s 10, if the Minister considers it necessary or expedient to do so, in times of imminent national danger, great emergency or warlike operations.

Bell v Secretary of State for Defence

[1986] QB 322, CA

[5.66] A serviceman stationed in West Germany died from a head injury suffered when he fell in barracks. The plaintiff (the administrator of the estate) brought an action in negligence. It was alleged that the Ministry had sent the deceased to a German civilian hospital with a misleading case history, omitting to refer to the head injury. The defendant issued a certificate under the Crown Proceedings Act 1947, s 10(1)(b) and pleaded immunity from suit. The deceased's parents were refused a pension.

HELD (on a preliminary issue), Donaldson MR, Neill and Balcombe LJJ: The certificate was valid, even though the parents were not at this time entitled to a pension. It was not a guarantee that an award would be made.

Per Neill and Balcombe LJJ (Donaldson MR dissenting): a failure to provide all necessary information to the civilian hospital to treat the deceased was an omission. Further, within the meaning of the 1947 Act, s 10(1)(a), it was 'the thing suffered' by the deceased. The omission was continuing, but was suffered by the deceased from the time he arrived at the civilian hospital. Accordingly, from that time, he was not on Crown land, and therefore the Crown was unable to rely upon the claim to immunity in section 10.

Note— *Bell* was overruled in the following case.

Pearce v Secretary of State for Defence

[1988] AC 755, HL

[5.67] The plaintiff brought an action in negligence alleging that he had sustained injuries due to radiation exposure during his service on Christmas Island, and that employees of the UK Atomic Energy Authority (who were not members of the armed forces) had been negligent in failing to take reasonable care to advise armed forces members as to safety precautions.

HELD: The defendants were not entitled to rely on the Crown Proceedings Act 1947, s 10. This was a case in which liability was transferred to the Secretary of State from the UK Atomic Energy Authority by means of specific legislation, and the Energy Authority would not have been able to rely on section 10.

Per curiam: All references to 'anything suffered' or to a 'thing' being 'suffered' in both sub-section (1) and sub-section (2) of section 10 are references, not to the acts or omissions relied on as giving rise to liability, but to the casualty or other event caused by the acts or omissions from which personal injury or death resulted. Applying the interpretation of the expression 'anything suffered' to the facts of the present case, the thing suffered by the plaintiff was his exposure to radiation. That exposure was suffered by him in consequence of the nature or condition of the land, premises, etc, used by the armed forces of the Crown; and that the defendants therefore, if they had been entitled to rely on section 10 at all, would have been able to bring themselves within the protection from liability given by sub-section (2) of that section.

In relation to the meaning of the expressions 'anything suffered' or a 'thing' being 'suffered' in section 10(1) of the Act of 1947, *Bell* was wrongly decided.

Quinn v Ministry Of Defence

[1998] PIQR P387, CA

[5.68] HELD: (1) The *per curiam* statement in *Pearce* (above) was applied. The court rejected an argument that under the provisions of section 10(2), the Crown is not exempt from a liability in tort in respect of an unsafe system of work.

(2) When the plaintiff enlisted in the Royal Navy pursuant to the King's Regulations neither he nor the Crown had any intention to create legal relations. Further, as a matter of public policy, there is binding authority that there is no such contract. In relation to members of the armed forces, as with police officers, there is no reason to find that those long standing public policy considerations should be changed.

Mulcahy v Ministry Of Defence

[1996] QB 732, CA

[5.69] The plaintiff was a soldier serving as part of a team of gunners in the Gulf War in 1991. He brought a claim in negligence in respect of injuries suffered as a result of negligence of the gun commander during the course of live fire into Iraq.

HELD: The statement of claim was struck out. The plaintiff was in a war zone and was participating in warlike actions. A soldier does not owe a fellow soldier a duty of care in tort when engaging the enemy in battle conditions in the course of hostilities. In those circumstances, the defendant did not owe a duty to maintain a safe system of work.

Barrett v Ministry Of Defence

[1995] 3 All ER 87, CA

[5.70] The deceased was an airman who died after becoming so drunk at the base where he served that he fell into a coma, and choked to death on his own vomit. It was well known that he was a heavy drinker. There was a lax attitude to drinking at the base. The commanding officer pleaded guilty of a breach of the Queen's Regulations for the Royal Navy 1967 (which imposed a duty on all officers actively to discourage drunkenness by navy personnel, and in the event of alcohol abuse a duty to prevent injury or fatality.) The plaintiff was the widow and executrix of the deceased. She brought a claim against the defendant as employer, on the basis that it owed a duty of care to prevent the deceased becoming so drunk that he caused his own death or injury.

HELD: It was wrong to equate the Queen's Regulations for the Royal Navy with the Highway Code, as the trial judge had done. They could not be directly invoked for the purpose of determining whether a duty of care was owed or whether there was a breach of duty. As to the existence of a duty of care, it was not fair, just or reasonable to blame one adult for another's lack of self-control. Until the deceased collapsed, it was the deceased alone who was responsible in law for his drunken condition. However, once the deceased had collapsed and the defendant had assumed responsibility for his care, the defendant was in breach of a duty of care. The trial judge held that no medical officer had been informed, and the supervision of the deceased had been wholly inadequate. To that extent the defendant was liable. The deceased's own contributory negligence was increased to two thirds.

Jebson v Ministry Of Defence

[2000] 1 WLR 2055, CA

[5.71] The claimant was a soldier, part of a group of 20, returning from an off duty outing organised by the commander for the purposes of relaxation. The commander had provided the transport, a lorry. Most of the group were in the lorry with the claimant, and most, including the claimant, were drunk. He climbed through the hinged tailgate and onto the roof. He was injured when he fell onto the road from the roof.

HELD: The court rejected the argument that an adult is never entitled to pray in aid his own drunkenness as giving rise to a duty or responsibility in others to exercise special care. It is not an invariable rule, nor is it fair, just and reasonable to apply such a rule in circumstances where an obligation of care is assumed or impliedly undertaken in respect of a person who it is appreciated is likely to be drunk. It was known that the outing would involve the consumption of a lot of alcohol. This was held to be a case where a duty exists on others to make allowance for reckless actions of drunken adults, and to take precautions for the perpetrator's safety. In the absence of supervision, the transport 'package' provided had not been safe. However, the claimant was largely the author of his own misfortune, and contributory negligence was assessed as 75%.

Matthews v Ministry of Defence

[2003] UKHL 4, [2003] 1 All ER 689

[5.72] The claimant was a former Navy mechanic who alleged he had suffered injury as a result of exposure to asbestos during the course of his work on board a ship between 1955 and 1968. The Secretary of State issued a certificate under the Crown Proceedings Act 1947, s 10.

Keith J held that the bar to the claim resulting from section 10 was a procedural bar only, and, having regard to Strasbourg jurisprudence, the immunity provision was incompatible with ECHR, Art 6, in that the claimant's right of access to the courts was denied. The Court of Appeal held that section 10 was a substantive bar, not procedural. ECHR, Art 6 did not apply.

HELD: The issue of a section 10(1)(b) certificate by the Secretary of State was not incompatible with ECHR, Art 6(1). It was conceded by the plaintiff that he had to show that section 10 was a procedural bar. Section 10 was not a procedural bar. It had the effect of substituting a no-fault system of compensation for a claim in damages in very many cases before 1987, and still does for cases of latent injury since 1987. This is a matter of substantive law, notwithstanding the provision for a certificate from the Secretary of State, although the distinction between procedural and substantive bars is a difficult distinction to determine (as shown by the case-law of the Strasbourg Court). Other jurisdictions had chosen as a matter of policy not to have a system of fault-based liability. There was no human right which dictated otherwise. The claimant's appeal was dismissed.

Police

Fisher v Oldham Corpn

[1930] 2 KB 364 (McCardie J)

[5.73] This was a case of admitted wrongful arrest and detention. It was argued that the watch committee of the borough corporation was the employer of the police in their borough and that there was vicarious liability.

HELD: The police appointed by the watch committee, if they arrest and detain a person unlawfully, do not act as the servants or agents of the corporation so as to render that body liable to an action for false imprisonment.

Prima facie a police constable is not the servant of the borough. He is a servant of the state, a ministerial officer of the central power, though subject, in some respects, to local supervision and local regulation.

In *Wallwork v Fielding* [1922] 2 KB 66, a constable had successfully sued the watch committee in the county court for his wages, but the Court of Appeal allowed the committee's appeal. The point at issue turned on the proper interpretation of a provision in the Municipal Corporations Act 1882. In the course of his judgment in the Court of Appeal, Warrington LJ had said that the relations are those of employer and employed. This was only an obiter dictum. It goes too far if it is meant to imply that the relation between a corporation and a police officer is the normal relation of master and servant. Only in a special and limited sense can a police officer be said to be in the employ of a municipal corporation. With respect to the action for 'wages', the point may well be raised some day whether any such action will lie in so far as it is framed upon an alleged contract of service in the ordinary sense. Any such action may perhaps be more properly brought on a special footing – namely, on the duty of the defendants to pay such sum as is due by virtue of statutory obligation plus a certain degree of contractual relationship.

Note: the position is now governed by the Police Act 1996.

A-G for New South Wales v Perpetual Trustee Co Ltd

[1955] AC 457, PC, on appeal from the High Court of Australia

[5.74] The Crown claimed damages for the loss of services of a policeman by the alleged negligent driving of a motor-vehicle by one of the respondents. The suit out of which the appeal arose was commenced by the Attorney-General for New South

Wales. A member of the police force of New South Wales was passing along the highway in a tram car when the motor-vehicle was negligently driven against the tram car whereby the police officer received bodily injury disabling him from the performance of his duties as a member of the police force. During his period of disability and whilst he continued as a member of the police force the officer was paid the salary and allowances appropriate to his office although the Crown was during the same period deprived of his services as a member of the police force, and that upon his discharge the officer was paid, and had since been paid and would continue to be paid, a pension. The Attorney-General claimed on behalf of the Crown to be reimbursed in respect of the moneys already paid and which would thereafter be paid to the officer.

HELD: There is a fundamental difference between the domestic relation of servant and master and that of the holder of a public office and the State which he is said to serve. The constable falls within the latter category. His authority is original, not delegated, and is exercised at his own discretion by virtue of his office: he is a ministerial officer exercising statutory rights independently of contract. The essential difference is recognised in the fact that his relationship to the Government is not in ordinary parlance described as that of servant and master.

It would not be in accord with modern notions or with the realities of human relationships today to extend the action to the loss of service of one who, if he can be called a servant at all, is the holder of an office which has for centuries been regarded as a public office.

Metropolitan Police Comr v Lowrey-Nesbitt

[1999] ICR 401, EAT

[5.75] A police officer serving in the Metropolitan Police presented a complaint to the industrial tribunal in respect of an unlawful deduction from wages contrary to the Employment Rights Act 1996, s 13. Section 13(1) stated: 'An employer shall not make a deduction from wages of a worker employed by him...'

HELD: A declaration was made that the applicant was not a worker within the meaning of the Employment Rights Act 1996. 'Service as a member of a constabulary maintained by virtue of an enactment' in the Employment Rights Act 1996, s 200(2)(*a*) included service in one of four statutory police forces not maintained by Home Office grant, whose officers could be regarded as employees, but did not include service in other forces such as the Metropolitan Police. Officers in such other forces were not in an employment relationship. They were office holders, whose terms of service were governed by statute and statutory instrument, not 'workers'.

The comments of McCardie J (see 5.73 above), in *Fisher v Oldham Corporation* represented the high water mark for the proposition that a constable has a contract pursuant to which he is entitled to receive his wages and other benefits. In a most general sense, there are aspects of the conditions of service of a constable which would fit well into a relationship governed by a contract of employment. The relationship between a police constable and the chief officer of police has 'contractual echoes'. However, a police constable's status is governed by statute and he owes allegiance to the community at large, through his oath of office, rather than through private contractual rights and obligations. *Attorney-General for NSW v Perpetual Trustee*, 5.74 above, is high judicial authority, cited with approval by the Court of Appeal in 1989 (*Sheikh v Chief Constable of Greater Manchester Police* [1989] ICR 373, 376), and the case expressed principles of general application.

Whether as a matter of public policy, or because of the nature of his duties as a constable who has taken an oath, or because a police officer is an office holder, there is no room for any further argument, short of the House of Lords, for the proposition that a police officer is in an employment relationship with anyone. The terms on which a constable serves are governed by statute and statutory instrument. The Police Act 1996, s 50(1) empowers the Secretary of State to make 'regulations as to the government, administration and conditions of service of police forces'. Section 50(2) entitles the Secretary of State to make provision in relation to all the terms and conditions of service that might otherwise have been contained in a written contract of employment, including his hours of duty, pay and allowances and disciplinary procedure. The provisions of the Sex Discrimination Act 1975 and Race Relations Act 1976 have subjected police constables to their protection; the Disability Discrimination Act 1995 has not. The general employment protection afforded to civilians working under contracts of employment is not afforded to police officers.

CHAPTER 6
Industrial Disease Claims

Causation and apportionment	[6.1]
Causation in disease claims	[6.1]
Medical evidence	[6.5]
Limits on decision	[6.6]
Apportionment in 'divisible' conditions	[6.7]
Date of knowledge	[6.8]
Apportionment	[6.9]
No duty to dismiss	[6.12]
Pneumoconiosis/Chronic Obstructive Airways Disease	[6.15]
Liability and date of knowledge	[6.16]
Medical evidence, epidemiological evidence and causation	[6.17]
Apportionment	[6.18]
Asbestos: insurance policy	[6.19]
Procedural issues: jurisdiction	[6.20]
Crown immunity	[6.21]
Limitation/accrual of cause of action	[6.25]
Legislation: The Asbestos Industry Regulations 1931	[6.28]
Factories Act 1937, s 47(1)	[6.29]
Factories Act 1961, s 4(1)	[6.30]
Regulations under the Factories Act 1961	
Shipbuilding and Ship-repairing Regulations 1961	[6.31]
Control of Asbestos Regulations 1969	[6.32]
Standards	[6.33]
Application of legislation	[6.34]
Duty of care/date of knowledge	[6.38]
Offset of benefits	[6.45]
Occupational noise-induced hearing loss/deafness claims	[6.46]
Legislation	[6.47]
Vibration White Finger	[6.48]
Date of knowledge	[6.49]
Medical evidence	[6.50]
Vascular	[6.51]
Neurological	[6.52]
Musculo-skeletal	[6.53]
Extent of disability	[6.54]
Effect of cessation of exposure	[6.55]
Diagnosis	[6.56]

Classification [6.57]
apportionment [6.58]
Sensitisation claims: legislation: Control of Substances Hazardous to Health Regulations [6.63]
Asthma [6.64]
Date of knowledge [6.66]
COSHH Regulations [6.67]
Dermatitis [6.68]
Work-related upper limb disorder claims: keyboard claims: Legislation: Health & Safety
(Display Screen Equipment) Regulations 1992 [6.69]
Cases [6.70]
Manual processes: legislation [6.76]
Cases [6.77]
Occupational stress: pre-Hatton [6.83]
Post-Hatton [6.84]
Facts [6.85]
Summary of reasons [6.89]
Cases decided post-Hatton [6.90]
Bullying and harassment [6.92]

CAUSATION AND APPORTIONMENT

Causation in disease claims

Bonnington Castings Ltd v Wardlaw

[1956] AC 613 613, HL (silicosis)

[6.1] The pursuer was employed by the defendants as a steel dresser between 1942 and 1950. The defender produced steel castings, made by pouring molten metal into moulds which consisted of sand with a very high silica content. After the casting was cooled and annealed, any remaining sand had to be removed using grinders, or a hammer or chisel driven by compressed air. Several machines of each type were situated in the dressing shop where the pursuer worked.

The evidence was that each machine would give off dust, part of which was silica from the sand. Originally, the size of the particles was too large to constitute a risk to health through inhalation, but either in the annealing process or through the operation of the machines in the dressing shop, a proportion of the original particles were broken up, with the result that a proportion of the dust produced contained dangerous minute particles of silica.

The evidence was also that in the 1940s there was no known means of preventing the dust from the pneumatic hammers from escaping into the air and no form of mask or respirator had been invented which was effective to protect those exposed to the dust. However, local exhaust appliances had been fitted to the swing grinders but for considerable periods had been choked, causing more dust to escape than would otherwise have been the case. The defender admitted a breach of the relevant regulations in relation to the swing grinders but argued that the pursuer had failed to prove on the balance of probabilities that the dust from the swing grinders (as opposed to the dust from the pneumatic hammer) materially contributed to his disease.

HELD: that any contribution which was not *de minimis* must be material. Even if more dust came from the pneumatic hammer than from the swing grinders, there was enough dust from the grinders to make a substantial contribution towards the pursuer's disease and the pursuer was therefore entitled to succeed.

> Note—See also *Nicholson v Atlas Steel Foundry and Engineering Co Ltd* [1957] 1 All ER 776, HL, for a similar case applying *Bonnington Castings* (silicosis caused by exposure to silica dust in the dressing shop of the defendant's steel foundry).

McGhee v National Coal Board

[1973] 1 WLR 1, HL (dermatitis)

[6.2] The pursuer was employed by the defendant from 1952 to 1967 as a labourer. His normal work was emptying pipe kilns. On Thursday 30 March 1967 he was sent to empty brick kilns, where working conditions were much hotter and dustier. After work, he cycled home with brick dust caked to his skin. The following Sunday, he developed dermatitis.

The medical evidence was that the pursuer's dermatitis was caused by repeated minute abrasions of the outer horny layer of skin, followed by some injury or change to the underlying cells, the precise nature of which had yet to be discovered by medical science. However, profuse sweating for a considerable time causes the outer layer of skin to soften, exposing the tender layer of cells below to the risk of injury or infection. If the skin is not thoroughly washed, the process can continue for some considerable time. By cycling home still caked in dust and sweat, the pursuer was liable to suffer further injury until he could wash himself at home. Washing is the only practicable method of removing the risk of injury. However, the medical experts could not say that the failure to provide showers did any more than increase the risk of that the pursuer would develop dermatitis.

The Lord Ordinary held the employer to be in breach of a duty to provide washing facilities but held that the pursuer had failed to show that this breach materially contributed to the development of his condition.

HELD: The House of Lords overturned the decisions below, finding for the pursuer. Three members of the House (Reid, Simon & Salmon LLJ) held that, in circumstances such as this, the law did not draw a distinction between having materially increased the risk of contracting the disease and having materially contributed to it.

> Note—The decision in *McGhee* should now be read in light of the analysis of the House of Lords in *Fairchild v Glenhaven Funeral Services*, below.

Wilsher v Essex Area Health Authority

[1988] AC 1074, HL

[6.3] The claimant was an infant born nearly three months prematurely. He developed retrolental fibroplasias ('RLF'), causing total blindness in one eye and partial blindness in the other. The evidence was that the defendant health authority failed to take reasonable precautions to prevent one of the possible causative agents (excess oxygen) but that no one could tell whether excess oxygen did or did not cause or contribute to the condition in this case. The claimant's RLF may have been caused by some completely different agent or agents, eg hypercarbia, intraventricular haemorrhage, apnoea or patent ductus arteriosus, all of which have been implicated as possible cause of RLF in addition to excess oxygen. The claimant suffered from each of those conditions at various times in his first two months of life.

HELD: That the principle in *McGhee* should not be extended to these circumstances. In *McGhee*, there was only one candidate (brick dust) which could have caused the dermatitis. Here, there was no satisfactory evidence that excess oxygen was more likely than any of the other four candidates to have caused RLF in this baby.

> *Note*—the decision of the House in *Wilsher* and its analysis of the ratio in *McGhee* should now be read in light of the analysis of the House of Lords in *Fairchild v Glenhaven Funeral Services*, below.

Fairchild v Glenhaven Funeral Services Ltd

[2003] 1 AC 32, HL (mesothelioma)

[6.4] The claimants in three co-joined appeals (*Fairchild v Glenhaven Funeral Services*, *Fox v Spousal (Midland) Ltd*, and *Matthews v Associated Portland Cement Manufacturers (1978) Ltd*) appealed against the Court of Appeal's decision that each claim failed on the burden of proof because the claimants had failed to establish on the balance of probabilities which employer was responsible for the fibre or fibres which caused his condition.

In *Fairchild*, the deceased died from mesothelioma in 1996. The evidence was that he may have been exposed to asbestos whilst working for a sub-contractor to a local authority building packing cases for the transportation of industrial ovens lined with asbestos in the early 1960s. He was also exposed to asbestos whilst working for a builder on a factory owned by the second defendant, cutting asbestos sheets to repair roofs. The second defendant accepted breach of the Factories Act 1961, s 63.

In *Fox*, the deceased died from mesothelioma in 1996. The evidence was that he had been exposed to high levels of asbestos dust between 1953 and 1955 whilst employed by the defendant as a lagger. He was also exposed to asbestos dust whilst working as a docker/holdsman in the Liverpool Docks handling cargoes containing asbestos.

In *Matthews*, the claimant was diagnosed as suffering from mesothelioma in 1999 and had a life expectancy of some months at the date of the appeal hearing. He was exposed to asbestos dust whilst working for the defendant as a boilerman for four years between 1977 and 1981. He was also exposed to asbestos dust whilst working for other employers between 1965 and 1967 and for 5–6 weeks in 1973.

[6.5] The medical evidence was that

> [t]he mechanism by which a normal mesothelial cell is transformed into a mesothelioma cell is not known. It is believed to involve a multi-stage process, in which six or seven genetic changes occur in a normal cell to

render it malignant. Asbestos acts in at least one of those stages and may (but this is uncertain) act in more than one. It is not known what level of exposure to asbestos dust and fibre can be tolerated without significant risk of developing a mesothelioma, but it is known that those living in urban environments (although without occupational exposure) inhale large numbers of asbestos fibres without developing a mesothelioma. It is accepted that the risk of developing a mesothelioma increases in proportion to the quantity of asbestos dust and fibres inhaled: the greater the quantity of dust and fibre inhaled, the greater the risk. But the condition may be caused by a single fibre, or a few fibres, or many fibres: medical opinion holds none of these possibilities to be more probable than any other, and the condition once caused is not aggravated by further exposure…There is no way of identifying, even on a balance of probabilities, the source of the fibre or fibres which initiated the genetic process which culminated in the malignant tumour. It is on this rock of uncertainty, reflecting the point to which medical science has so far advanced, that the three claims were rejected by the Court of Appeal and by two of the three trial judges. (Per Lord Bingham at 310–1.)

HELD: Allowing the claimants' appeals, that the legal test to be applied in each of these cases was whether the defendant's breach had materially increased the risk of injury to the claimant (*McGhee v National Coal Board*).

LIMITS ON DECISION

[6.6] The *McGhee* test requires a less stringent causal connection and represents a departure from the usual 'but for' test (per Nicholls LJ at 337, para 44). Their Lordships indicated that they were not extending the application of the principle beyond the circumstances of the appeals before them.

Per Lord Bingham:

> Where the following conditions are satisfied, C is entitled to recover against both A and B if:
>
> (1) C was employed at different times and for differing periods by both A and B, and
> (2) A and B were both subject to a duty to take reasonable care or to take all practicable measures to prevent C inhaling asbestos dust because of the known risk that asbestos dust (if inhaled) might cause a mesothelioma, and
> (3) both A and B were in breach of that duty in relation to C during the periods of C's employment by each of them with the result that during both periods C inhaled excessive quantities of asbestos dust, and
> (4) C is found to be suffering from a mesothelioma, and
> (5) any cause of C's mesothelioma other than the inhalation of asbestos dust at work can be effectively discounted, but
> (6) C cannot (because of the current limits of human science) prove, on the balance of probabilities, that his mesothelioma was the result

Industrial Diseases Claims

of his inhaling asbestos dust during his employment by A or during his employment by B or by his employment by A and B taken together...

...Where those conditions are satisfied, it seems to me just and in accordance with common sense to treat the conduct of A and B in exposing C to a risk to which he should not have been exposed as making a material contribution to the contracting by C of a condition against which it was the duty of A and B to protect him. It is a conclusion which follows even if either A or B is not before the court. It was not suggested in argument that C's entitlement against either A or B should be for any sum less than the full compensation to which C is entitled, although A and B could of course seek contribution against each other or any other employer liable in respect of the same damage in the ordinary way. No argument on apportionment was addressed to the House. I would in conclusion emphasise that my opinion is directed to cases in which each of the conditions specified in (1)–(6), above, is satisfied and to no other case. It would be unrealistic to suppose that the principle here affirmed will not over time be the subject of incremental and analogical development. Cases seeking to develop the principle must be decided when and as they arise.

Per Lord Nicholls:

I need hardly add that considerable restraint is called for in any relaxation of the threshold 'but for' test of causal connection. The principle applied on these appeals is emphatically not intended to lead to such a relaxation whenever a plaintiff has difficulty, perhaps understandable difficulty, in discharging the burden of proof resting upon him. Unless closely confined in its application this principle could become a source of injustice to defendants. There must be good reason for departing from the normal threshold 'but for' test. The reason must be sufficiently weighty to justify depriving the defendant of the protection this test normally and rightly affords him, and it must be plain and obvious that this is so. Policy questions will loom large when a court has to decide whether the difficulties of proof confronting a plaintiff justify taking this exceptional course. It is impossible to be more specific. [at 337, para 43]

Per Lord Hoffmann:

The question is how narrowly the principle developed in *McGhee's* case and applied in this case should be confined. In my opinion, caution is advisable. *Wilsher's* case shows the dangers of over-generalisation...I would suggest that the rule now laid down by the House should be limited to cases which have the five features I have described.

That does not mean that the principle is not capable of development and application in new situations...But the problems differ quite widely and the fair and just answer will not always be the same... Cases like this are not before the House and should in my view be left for consideration when they arise [at pp 343–5, paras 73–4].

Per Lord Hutton:

I consider that where there is only one causative agent (in this case asbestos dust) the *McGhee* principle can apply notwithstanding that there are a number of tortfeasors...[I]n *Wilsher's* case the House was right to hold that the majority of the Court of Appeal should not have extended the *McGhee* principle to apply where there were five possible candidates which could have caused the claimant's blindness...Subject to this observation on the decision in *Wilsher's* case, I wish to confine my view to the circumstances of these cases. It may be necessary in the future to consider whether the *McGhee* principle should be applied to other cases, but such decisions will have to be taken when such cases arise. (at pp 361–2, paras 115, 118)

Per Lord Rodger:

I would tentatively suggest that certain conditions are necessary, but may not always be sufficient, for applying the principle. All the criteria are satisfied in the present cases.

First, the principle is designed to resolve the difficulty that arises where it is inherently impossible for the claimant to prove exactly how his injury was caused. It applies, therefore, where the claimant has proved all that he possibly can, but the causal link could only ever be established by scientific investigation and the current state of the relevant science leaves it uncertain exactly how the injury was caused and, so, who caused it. *McGhee* and the present cases are examples.

Secondly, part of the underlying rationale of the principle is that the defendant's wrongdoing has materially increased the risk that the claimant will suffer injury. It is therefore essential not just that the defendant's conduct created a material risk of injury to a class of persons but that it actually created a material risk of injury to the claimant himself.

Thirdly, it follows that the defendant's conduct must have been capable of causing the claimant's injury.

Fourthly, the claimant must prove that his injury was caused by the eventuation of the kind of risk created by the defendant's wrongdoing. In McGhee, for instance, the risk created by the defendant's failure was that the pursuer would develop dermatitis due to the brick dust on his skin and he proved that he had developed dermatitis due to brick dust on his skin. By contrast, the principle does not apply where the claimant has merely proved that his injury could have been caused by a number of different events, only one of which is the eventuation of the risk created by the defendant's wrongful act or omission. *Wilsher's* case is an example.

Fifthly, this will usually mean that the claimant must prove that his injury was caused, if not by the same agency as was involved in the defendant's wrongdoing, at least by an agency that operated in substantially the same way. A possible example would be where a workman suffered injury from exposure to dusts coming from two sources, the dusts being particles of different substances each of which, however, could have caused his injury in the same way. Without having heard detailed argument on the point, I incline to the view that the principle was properly applied by the Court of Appeal in *Fitzgerald v Lane* [1987] QB 781.

Sixthly, the principle applies where the other possible source of the claimant's injury is a similar wrongful act or omission of another person, but it can also apply where, as in McGhee, the other possible source of the injury is a similar, but lawful, act or omission of the same defendant. I reserve my opinion as to whether the principle applies where the other possible source of injury is a similar but lawful act or omission of someone else or a natural occurrence.

Apportionment in 'divisible' conditions

Thompson v Smiths Shiprepairers (North Shields) Ltd

[1984] 1 All ER 881 (QBD, Mustill J) (deafness)

[6.7] Claims by nine claimants for noise-induced hearing loss against Swan Hunter Shipbuilders Ltd and Vickers Armstrong Ltd were consolidated. The claimants had been employed as labourers or fitters in the defendants' shipbuilding yards over long periods, stretching from the 1940s or earlier to the 1970s.

DATE OF KNOWLEDGE

[6.8–6.9]

The evidence was that it had been known since 1886, when Thomas Barr published a paper describing the features of noise-induced hearing loss, that persons working in conditions of excessive noise are liable to suffer deafness. Shipyards have been recognised as noisy places since the beginning of the 20th century, if not before. Everybody knew this, but no one did anything about it. Apathy and fatalism prevailed amongst workers, employees, trades unions and legislators alike. Deafness was treated as an inescapable fact of shipyard life. Not until the early 1970s was any effective and systematic provision made for the protection of persons employed in shipbuilding and ship repair yards. (See *Thompson v Smiths Shiprepairers (North Shields) Ltd* [1984] 1 All ER 881, 885 – 888 for a detailed summary of the effect of noise on the human ear and the process for quantifying the degree of hearing loss.)

The legal test is that set out in the judgment of Swanwick J in *Stokes v Guest, Keen and Nettlefold (Bolts and Nuts) Ltd* [1968] 1 WLR 1776, that is, the conduct of the reasonable and prudent employer taking positive thought for the safety of his workers in light of what he knows or ought to know. Where there is a recognised and general practice which has been followed for a substantial period in similar circumstances without mishap, he is entitled to follow it, unless in light of common sense or newer knowledge it is clearly bad. Where there is developing knowledge, he must keep reasonably abreast of it and not be slow to apply it. Where he has greater than average knowledge of the risks, he may be obliged to take more than the average or standard precautions. He must weigh up the risks in terms of the likelihood of injury occurring and the potential consequences if it does, and he must balance against this the probable effectiveness of the precautions that can be taken to meet it and the expense and inconvenience they involve. If he is found to have fallen below the standard to be properly expected of a reasonable and prudent employer in these respects, he is negligent.

In addition to the categories of 'a recognised practice which may be followed without mishap' and one which is 'clearly bad' in light of common sense or increased knowledge, is the type of risk which is regarded at any given time as an inescapable feature of the industry. The employer is not liable for the consequences of such risks, although subsequent changes in social awareness or improvements in knowledge and technology may transfer the risk into the category of those against which the employer can and should take care. An employer is not exonerated by proving that other employers are just as negligent but that the standard of what is negligent is influenced by the practice of industry as a whole. This principle applies not only where the breach of duty is said to consist of a failure to take precautions known to be available as a means of combating a known danger, but also where the omission involves an absence of initiative in seeking out knowledge of facts which are not in themselves obvious. The employer must keep up to date, but the court must be slow to blame him for not ploughing a lone furrow.

In this case, actual knowledge can be proved with effect from 1963 when Smiths Shipbuilders received a copy of the Ministry of Labour publication, 'Noise and the Worker' (Safety, Health & Welfare New Series Booklet no 25). Actual knowledge can be inferred from a much earlier date. After 1963 there was no excuse for ignorance. References in the medical literature to the types of protective devices available became more common in the 1950s and the safety and medical officers of factories and shipyards might have recognised from those sources that ear muffs and protective inserts were on the market and could have set about tracking them down and deciding whether they were worth the considerable effort which would have been required to have put them into use. By 1963, Billesholm wool and reasonably effective ear muffs were available. From 1963, by offering their employees nothing, the defendants were in breach of duty at common law.

The starting point is the principle that the court should so far as possible endeavour to restore the claimant to the position in which he would have found himself but for the defendant's act. The basic principle suggests that employer A should be liable in full, but not more than in full, for the impairment existing when the worker leaves his employment. Ideally, this should be assessed by reference to the damage suffered by the structure of his organs of hearing. But this cannot directly be measured, so it is quantified in terms of the decibel hearing loss. The intermediate step is the ascertainment of the symptoms which are the immediate cause of loss. The symptoms are of two kinds: first, those (if any) the claimant has already suffered and is suffering at the date of trial; and second, those which, because of damage to bodily structure suffered through breach, are definitely going to happen, or may happen, at a future date. In the present case, such symptoms take the shape of (i) the earlier onset of presbyacusis which *will* be suffered by anyone whose 'non-disability' reservoir of hearing impairment has been drawn on by excessive noise, and (ii) the further handicap which *may* be suffered *if* he undergoes further exposure to excessive noise. A proper award of damages against employer A will recognise the existence of both current and potential symptoms.

What of employer B? He has 'taken over' the claimant in a condition where his organs of hearing are already damaged, and where he is already subject to actual and potential symptoms. It would be an injustice to employer B to make him liable for damage already done before he had any connection with the claimant. His liability should be limited to compensation for (a) the perpetuation and amplification of the handicaps already being suffered at the moment when the employment changed hands, and (b) the bringing to fruit in the shape of current hardship those symptoms which had previously been no more than potential.

The result should be that the recoveries against A and B will amount in total to the award which would have been made if the damage had all been caused by the wrongs of a single employer, and, equally, that the assessment of such an award could form at least the starting point of any quantification of the individual liability of employers A and B.

Next, one must consider how this approach can be applied to a case where either (a) there are two successive employers, of whom only the second is at fault, or (b) there is a single employer, who had been guilty of an actionable fault only from a date after the employment began. Logic suggests that the analysis should be the same. Employer B has, once again, 'inherited' a workman whose hearing is already damaged by events with which that employer has had no connection, or at least no connection which makes him liable in law. The fact that, so far as the worker is concerned, the prior events unfortunately give him no cause of action against anyone should not affect the principles on which he recovers from employer B. Justice looks to both parties, not the claimant alone.

This solution presupposes a division of responsibility between A and B, or (in the case of the second example) between non-blameworthy and blameworthy sources of noise. How precise must this division be, before it can found an apportionment in law? …What happens if the apportionment is insufficiently precise? The degree of accuracy demanded should be commensurate with the degree of accuracy possible, in light of existing knowledge, and with the degree of accuracy involved in the remainder of the exercise which leads to the calculation of damages.

Can it be said here that each claimant is suffering from an injury which is one and indivisible? Undoubtedly in one sense it can: for each claimant is hard of hearing, a disability which cannot now be severed into component parts…Nor indeed, if one looks behind the disability and handicap to the measured impairment, is it possible to regard the impairment as indivisible, as if by saying that a hearing loss of 60 dB can be treated as two losses, each of 30 dB. But this is not the end of the story. Even the measured impairment is only a symptom of the deteriorated condition of the organs of hearing. This condition is not the direct product of a group of acts, not necessarily simultaneous, but all converging to bring about one occurrence of damage. Rather, it is the culmination of a progression, the individual stages of which were each brought about by the separate acts of the persons sued, or (as the case may be) the separate non-faulty and faulty acts of the only defendant.

I see no reason why the present impossibility of making a precise apportionment of impairment and disability in terms of time, should in justice lead to the result that the defendants are adjudged liable to pay in full, when it is known that only part of the damage was their fault. What justice does demand is that the court should make the best estimate which it can, in the light of the evidence, making the fullest allowances in favour of the plaintiffs for the uncertainties to be involved in any apportionment. In the end, this has to be regarded as a jury question.

The claimants were people who in 1963 were already going to be hard of hearing in later life, and the breach merely served to accelerate and enhance the process. A monetary value should then be assigned to this additional detriment. An eye should be cast on the general level of damages appropriate where liability is established for the whole of the hearing loss, to make sure that the sums awarded for a part of the impairment are not seriously out of proportion.

Holtby v Brigham & Cowan (Hull) Ltd

[2000] 3 All ER 421, CA (asbestosis)

[6.10] The claimant was employed as a marine fitter from 1942 to 1981. For 12 years, approximately half of this time, he was employed by Brigham & Cowan. For the remainder, he was employed by other employers doing similar work in similar conditions, in some cases for quite long periods (5, 4, 2 and 1½ years) and in other cases for periods measured in months. He subsequently developed pleural disease and asbestosis. The medical evidence was that all exposure to asbestos contributed to the development of his condition and that, had the claimant not been exposed to asbestos whilst working for Brigham & Cowan, he would still have developed the condition but to a lesser extent.

The trial judge found Brigham & Cowan liable for 75% of the claimant's loss.

HELD, on appeal: Trial judge's decision upheld, approving the decision in *Thompson v Smith's Shiprepairers* [1984] QB 405. Asbestosis (that is, pleural or pulmonary fibrosis) is a cumulative or 'indivisible' disease and the progression is linear, depending on the amount of dust inhaled. All dust contributes to the final disability. An employer is liable if its tortious conduct made a material contribution to the claimant's disability but, strictly speaking, the defendant is only liable to the extent of that contribution.

The question of quantification may be difficult and the court has to do the best it can using its common sense. It is not so much a question of apportionment between tortfeasors as one of proof of causation in respect of a quantifiable part of his disability by the claimant against the defendant, and it is not so much a question of discounting the full liability figure, as counting the proportion attributable to the defendant.

It might be said that the judge should have made the defendants liable only to 50%. If the other employers had been before the court, then subject to the exposure which ought to be considered *de minimis*, this is what he would have done. As it is, he erred on the side of generosity to the claimant. This method of dividing responsibility on a time exposure basis is adopted by insurers in such cases as these. In the absence of some unusual feature, such as for example periods of exposure to particularly dangerous blue asbestos during some periods, that seems to be not only the sensible, but the correct approach in law. In practice, many years afterwards, such distinctions are likely to be impossible to prove.

Allen v British Rail Engineering

[2001] EWCA Civ 242, [2001] ICR 942

[6.11] Four lead cases for several hundred claims against British Rail Engineering Ltd were brought by employees who developed vibration white finger (VWF) in the course of their work from the 1950s to the late 1980s. In one of the lead cases, the claimant appealed the apportionment of damages.

In Mr Allen's case, he had started working for BREL in the late 1950s and first developed VWF in 1968. The trial judge found that BREL should have carried out surveys to assess the incidence of VWF in a few of its workshops during the first half of 1973. Had it done so, the surveys would have shown a significant incidence of VWF. BREL could then have widened the surveys to all workshops where vibrating tools were used and devised a programme of prevention for groups of workers found to be at risk. BREL could have taken measures to reduce the rate at which VWF progressed. BREL failed to take those measures. Had it done so, Mr Allen would have been offered a medical examination and advice by mid-1974 and could have been moved to less exposed work within BREL by mid-1975. His work would still have involved some use of vibrating tools. In the event, he left BREL's employment in 1987 for another job which also involved the use of vibrating tools and which did further damage.

The trial judge found that the effects of vibration were cumulative, led to progressive damage to the tissues and that when that damage reaches a certain point, symptoms become apparent. Before symptoms appeared, there would have been tissue changes, but they could not be assessed. Apportioning current symptoms to past vibration exposure was extremely difficult and the whole of the vibration exposure was responsible for the current symptoms.

The judge apportioned liability between 3 periods of life-time exposure, awarding Mr Allen £4,000 of a total damages award of £11,000:
(i) £1,500 for the (non-tortious) exposure period prior to 1976. This amount reflects the fact that about 40% of the claimant's exposure to vibration occurred before the onset of his symptoms in 1968 and a further 10% between 1968 and 1973. The symptoms in 1973 were not severe and were probably at stage 1 on the Taylor-Pelmear scale.
(ii) £1,500 for the period of exposure with his subsequent employer after 1987. 10% of the claimant's exposure to vibration occurred during this period.
(iii) £4,000 for the period between 1976 and 1987. It follows from the above that a further 40% of his exposure occurred during the period of BREL's negligence. The trial judge reduced the damages for this period by half to reflect the fact that Mr Allen was already suffering symptoms by 1973, when BREL should first have discovered the incidence of VWF, and that even if BREL had offered the claimant a medical examination and moved him to other work involving less exposure to vibration by mid-1975, from 1976 he would have been exposed to a degree of vibration in any event. That exposure would have been around $\frac{1}{2}$ to $\frac{2}{3}$ the exposure he actually received. Had BREL taken the action identified, Mr Allen's symptoms would still have progressed to stage 2 (probably nearer to stage 3 than to stage 1) but would not have progressed to stage 3 as they did.

The judge did not apportion damages on a straight line basis because damages should reflect the onset and progress of disability as well as actual damage. She gave greater weight to the exposure after symptoms began than to the early exposure.

HELD, on appeal:The trial judge's approach was upheld. In light of *Bonnington Castings v Wardlaw*, *Thompson v Smiths Shiprepairers* and *Holtby v Brigham & Cowan*, the principles to be applied are as follows:
(i) the employee will establish liability if he can prove that the employer's tortious conduct made a material contribution to the employee's disability.
(ii) There can be cases where the state of evidence is such that it is just to recognise each of two separate tortfeasors as having caused the whole of the damage of which the claimant complains; for instance where a passenger is killed as the

result of a head on collision between two cars each of which was negligently driven and in one of which he was sitting.

(iii) However in principle the amount of the employer's liability will be limited to the extent of the contribution which his tortious conduct made to the employee's disability.

(iv) The court must do the best it can on the evidence to make the apportionment and should not be astute to deny the claimant relief on the basis that he cannot establish with demonstrable accuracy precisely what proportion of his injury is attributable to the defendant's tortious conduct.

(v) The amount of evidence which should be called to enable a judge to make a just apportionment must be proportionate to the amount at stake and the uncertainties which are inherent in making any award of damages for personal injury.

No duty to dismiss

Withers v Perry Chain Co Ltd

[1961] 1 WLR 1314, CA (dermatitis)

[6.12] The claimant developed dermatitis at work. She was off work for a period and, on her return, it was known to both her and her employers that her continuing to work would give rise to a small risk that her dermatitis might recur or be exacerbated.

HELD, on appeal: The finding of liability against the employer was overturned. Per Devlin LJ at 1320:

> [T]here is no legal duty upon an employer to prevent an adult employee from doing work which he or she is willing to do. If there is a slight risk...it is for the employee to weigh it against the desirability, or perhaps the necessity, of employment. The relationship between employer and employee is not that of a schoolmaster and pupil. There is no obligation on an employer to offer alternative safe employment, though no doubt a considerate employer would always try to do so – as the defendants thought they had done here. Nor is there any obligation on an employer to dismiss an employee in the circumstances. It cannot be said that an employer is bound to dismiss an employee rather than allow her to run a small risk. The employee is free to decide for herself what risks she will run.

See also *Kossinski v Chrysler UK Ltd* (1973) 15 KIR 225 (claimant developed epicondylitis of the left elbow as a result of repetitive work removing paint with compressed air. The evidence was that there was no lighter assembly job available. The Court of Appeal held that the defendant was not under an obligation to conduct an investigation as to what, if any, alternative work was available or to warn the claimant that if he wanted to continue with his work, he would do so at his own peril.). Compare Sutherland v Hattsy.

Note—A further example of the application of the *Withers* principle is *Ball v Post Office* [1995] PIQR P5.

Henderson v Wakefield Shirt Co Ltd

[1997] PIQR P413, CA (WRULD)

[6.13] The claimant was employed by the defendant as a final presser at its factory from May 1989 until March 1994. Her job was a factory version of ironing as it is done in almost every home, the difference being that she was doing it all day and under some pressure because there was a bonus system in operation. The evidence was that the claimant would iron approximately 300 shirts per day. The claimant developed a painful stiff neck early in 1991 and was absent from work on sick leave for eight weeks, after which she returned to work. In 1992 her condition deteriorated, with pain and pins and needles in her right arm from the right hand, right elbow, up her arm to her back and a stiff neck. A diagnosis of neck pain and supra-spinatus tendinitis of the right shoulder was made.

At trial, the judge found on the medical evidence that the claimant suffered from pre-existing cervical spondylosis. Because of the nature of her work, this condition manifested itself in the form of neck pain. The critical factor was the flexed position of the head. Most if not all of her other symptoms, in particular her problems with her elbow and supra-spinatus tendinitis of the shoulder, were not related to her work.

HELD, on appeal: That the defendant had no reason to believe previously that their method of work gave rise to a particular risk. The claimant's work was safe for an ordinarily fit person. However, once they had been informed by the claimant of her doctor's opinion that her symptoms were caused by her work following her return to work in August 1991, the defendant became aware of the relationship between her complaints and the job which she was doing. From that point, the defendant came under a duty to reconsider the equipment provided to the claimant and her system of work to see whether either was the likely cause of her symptoms. They did not do so, but if they had, the result would have been that they would have found that the height of the ironing board was entirely acceptable, the weight of the iron was appropriate and there was nothing to criticise in the work pattern undertaken by the claimant. The medical evidence was that job rotation would not have had any beneficial effect unless it extended so far as to the claimant giving up ironing entirely as it was impossible to avoid the flexed position of the head when ironing. The defendant did transfer the claimant to the intermediate pressing area where the weight of the garments was lighter, but it had no effect on her symptoms.

Applying *Withers v Perry Chain Co*, it was held that the defendants were not in breach of duty in permitting the claimant to continue in her work.

Coxall v Goodyear Great Britain Ltd

[2002] EWCA Civ 1010, [2003] 1 WLR 536 (asthma)

[6.14] The claimant was employed by the defendant on the paint and line section from February to May 1996. His duties involved spraying the inside of tyres with a lubricant paint. Shortly after he started working in this capacity, a new lubricant paint was introduced. The claimant and his fellow workers were provided with rubber gloves, goggles and a respirator for use whilst spraying.

Unknown to both the claimant and the defendant, the claimant had a mild constitutional predisposition to asthma. He developed severe headaches and consulted the works nurse and then the works doctor, who advised that he should not work with the new paint. The works doctor wrote a memo to the claimant's line manager which never reached him, with the result that the claimant continued in his work for a further three weeks. The evidence of both the line manager and the health and safety manager was that, had they known of the memo, they would have taken the claimant off the job immediately. In May 1996, the claimant collapsed and was certified unfit to work.

The trial judge held that the defendant was liable for failing to take the claimant off the job.

HELD, on appeal: The trial judge's decision was upheld. Per Simon Brown LJ: The principle in *Withers v Perry Chain Co* remains no less effective today as when it was first adumbrated. However, whether a particular case falls within the principle in *Withers* depends on the actual nature and extent of the known risk. The risk in *Withers* was described as 'some risk', a 'slight risk' and a 'small risk'. In *Kossinski*, the court was concerned only with a tennis elbow. In *Henderson*, the claimant had not even been advised by her own doctor to stop work. There are cases in which, despite the employee's desire to remain at work notwithstanding the risk he runs, the employer will nevertheless be under a duty to dismiss him for his own good so as to protect him against physical danger.

The defendants did not allege contributory negligence on the grounds that the claimant was himself partly to blame, having chosen to continue at work despite knowing of the risk involved and of the works doctor's express advice to his line manager that he should stop working. Had the defendants put forward such a case, it may well have relieved them of part of their liability.

Per Brooke LJ: The trial judge's decision should be upheld on the limited basis that the defendants ought to have discussed with the claimant all the available options once their works doctor had formed the conclusion that the claimant should not continue to work with the new paint. If they had done so and if he then insisted that he wished to go on working, it would have been a different case.

Note—See also *Dugmore v Swansea NHS Trust Trust [2002] EWCA Civ 1689, [2003] 1 All ER 333*

> There is no duty at common law to sack an employee with a particular sensitivity who wants to take the risk of carrying on working in what is for others a reasonably safe environment: see *Withers v Perry Chain Co* [1961] 1 WLR 1314, CA. The judge concluded that the claimant was so anxious to continue her nursing career that even if the problem had been better recognised the probability was that she would still have been working in the ITU in December 1997. The last finding is a finding of primary fact…It is fatal to a finding of

liability in negligence. If no amount of warning would have kept the claimant away until she actually suffered her attack, then the failure to warn cannot have caused it to happen.

But note the Court of Appeal's comment that 'regulations may impose a stricter duty on employers even if the employee is willing to take the risk and may be prejudiced by compliance'.

PNEUMOCONIOSIS/CHRONIC OBSTRUCTIVE AIRWAYS DISEASE

British Coal Respiratory Disease Litigation (sub nom Griffiths v British Coal Corpn)

(1998) LTL, 23 January (QBD, Turner J) (pneumoconiosis)

[6.15] Decision on liability, causation and apportionment in the British Coal Respiratory Disease Litigation group litigation. Eight lead cases were selected from over 100 similar actions and a further 6,000 or so other claims yet to be litigated. The claims involved former miners who developed a range of respiratory conditions as a result of exposure to coal dust whilst working for British Coal between 1 January 1947 (the date on which the liabilities of the formerly private colliery companies vested in British Coal) and the 1970s.

Liability

[6.16] British Coal (formerly known as the 'National Coal Board') was established under the Coal Industry Nationalisation Act 1946. Its primary obligation was to work, get and make supplies of coal available. A secondary obligation was to secure the safety, health and welfare of their employees.

For many years prior to 1947 there had been industry-wide concerns about chronic pulmonary disease, especially in the mines of South Wales. The Medical Research Council was appointed to investigate in 1936 and produced the Bedford & Warner Report in 1943, which found evidence of an association between the incidence of pneumoconiosis (by which was meant all respiratory disease) and the calculated mass concentration of airborne particles, particularly those below 5 microns in size, of coal and other minerals. In 1954, Pneumoconiosis Field Research (now the Institute of Occupational Medicine) was set up to undertake field research into the issue.

In 1949 British Coal introduced the 'Approved Conditions' scheme to enable miners already suffering from pneumoconiosis to continue working in coal mines. Those whose condition was 'seriously incapacitating' were allowed to work on the surface in 'approved dust conditions' (ie reasonably dust free), whilst those whose condition was in its early stages were allowed to continue working below ground, again in 'approved dust conditions'. Under the scheme, atmospheric samples were taken over a short period using a sampling instrument to measure 'periods of maximum dustiness'. In 1956, a new protocol was introduced requiring instead measurement of 'mean shift averages'. British Coal did not take this opportunity to introduce a tighter standard, the reason at the time being it would lead to unnecessary duplication of effort since gravimetric sampling standards were to be introduced in a few years time and that there was not yet a rational or scientific basis on which to set a new standard.

In the event, gravimetric sampling and the new standards were not introduced until 1970. Following the introduction of the new standards, some coal faces that were previously approved failed to meet the new criteria. The evidence demonstrated that, once collieries knew they were not meeting the standards, they set about devising and implementing schemes for reducing dust by making better use of existing technology. These measures included: (a) face infusion; (b) the use of pneumatic picks equipped with water sprays; (c) water designed into coal cutting and getting machines at the pick face; (d) spraying fallen coal and muck with water; (e) reduction of firing, especially on production shifts; (f) attention to chutes, enclosed transfer points and joints on conveyor systems; (g) ventilation in headings and drivages. The measures were largely successful and demonstrated that more could and should have been done before then to minimise exposure of miners to coal dust.

> British Coal appear to have been mesmerised, or corrupted, by the notion that it was only if a face was 'not approved' anything needed to be done to reduce the concentration of dust at such a face. It was not for lack of expertise that such a position was allowed to develop and become institutionalised. British Coal employed a number of talented research and development engineers in the field of dust suppression and measurement. The problem was that they were not given either their heads or the resources to do what was necessary, until statutory regulation, long opposed by British Coal, had become an inevitability....
>
> The conclusion is inescapable: if British Coal had devoted themselves as zealously in the years between 1947 and 1970 as they did, and had to do, after 1970 and especially 1975 to the suppression and control of respirable dust, there is every reason to suppose that the exposure of large numbers of men to avoidable concentrations of such dust would not have taken place.

An obvious measure was to provide respiratory protection. Although respirators existed in 1946, they were crude and uncomfortable to wear. After nationalisation and the introduction of the 'Approved Conditions' scheme, the perception of British Coal was that the widespread introduction and use of respirators would distract attention of officials and workmen from the fundamental task of suppression and control of dust at source and thereafter. However, in 1971, with the advent of statutory regulation not far away, British Coal took a U-turn in its policy, its new position being that respirators should be provided, albeit as a last line of defence in a new system of anti-dust measures.

The generic conclusion is that British Coal failed: (1) to take all reasonable steps to minimise the creation and dispersion of respirable dust by the introduction and use of known and available dust suppression techniques from about 1949 to 1970 and to a lesser extent thereafter; (2) to ensure that suitable instruments for measuring dust were developed and introduced at as early a stage as was practicable; (3) by adhering to the misleading concept of face 'approval' and 'non-approval', to institute an efficient system for ensuring that the obligation to minimise dust was met.

MEDICAL EVIDENCE, EPIDEMIOLOGICAL EVIDENCE AND CAUSATION

[6.17] The proceedings involved claims for the following respiratory conditions:

Coal worker's pneumoconiosis is a condition generally detected radiologically during the claimant's life. 'Simple pneumoconiosis' does not cause respiratory disability and is not usually progressive in that once exposure to mine dust ceases, the condition does not significantly progress. 'Complicated pneumoconiosis' (or 'pulmonary massive fibrosis') is usually progressive, causes respiratory disability in its more advanced forms and may ultimately lead to death. It may develop from simple pneumoconiosis.

Chronic bronchitis as defined by the Medical Research Council is a functional (rather than disease-based) definition. It is defined as 'sputum production on most days for at least three months in the year for at least two consecutive years'. The term is frequently used loosely, particularly in early medical papers, to refer to all diseases and abnormal conditions of the respiratory tract with the exception of tuberculosis. The judge rejected British Coal's contention that chronic bronchitis does not constitute a compensatable injury at law. The judge accepted that the effects of smoking and coal dust are additive. The judge accepted that chronic bronchitis constituted actionable personal injury. Per Turner J:

> [T]he production of excessive quantities of mucus with associated frequent bouts of coughing or expectoration as the result of exposure to dust or other irritant if 'more than trivial' is capable of constituting personal injury sufficient to found a cause of action.

Emphysema is a pathological definition of a condition in the lung characterised by abnormal permanent enlargement of the airspaces distal to the terminal bronchioles with concomitant destruction of the walls of the airspaces, but without fibrosis. The functional result is the destruction of the alveolar walls which are the gas/blood exchange area of the lungs, resulting in a mismatch of exchange of oxygen to, and carbon dioxide from, the blood. Because the lungs have to work harder to try to match the demands of the blood supply for more oxygen, the result will be breathlessness. Three types of emphysema were considered:

(1) Centriacinar (or centrilobular) emphysema, which predominantly affects the central parts of the acinus, that part of the lung tissue proximal to the respiratory bronchiole. The judge found that it can be caused by coal mine dust and by smoking. It may, and usually does, lead to loss of ventilatory capacity.

(2) Panacinar emphysema, which affects the whole of the acinus, but is characteristically more pronounced in the lower lobes of the lung.

(3) Focal dust emphysema, which may or may not be a separate disease entity in itself. It is thought to be caused by the deposit of respirable dust around the respiratory bronchioles where it causes atropy or loss of tone in the smooth

muscle of the bronchial wall. The judge rejected British Coal's contention that focal dust emphysema is the only type of emphysema caused by coal dust or that, where there is no fibrosis, any emphysema cannot have been caused by coal dust.

Small airways disease is a functional description of a condition which results from airway narrowing in the distal bronchioles. It may exist independently of emphysema. It cannot be diagnosed on the basis of clinical assessment alone but a differential diagnosis may be made where there is evidence of reduced flow in the small airways without evidence of emphysema.

Asthma is a condition characterised by variability of symptoms. At times there will be a normal, or near normal, function, while at others there may be severe limitation of air flow. It is diagnostic and a characteristic is that there may be a significant improvement in airflow following inhalation of a bronchodilator drug. Only one claimant in the 8 lead actions was diagnosed as suffering from asthma. The judge held that, on the evidence put before him, not enough is known about the causes of occupationally induced asthma to justify a finding that there is a type which results from exposure to chronic low-dose irritants.

Epidemiological evidence indicates that in the healthy individual, lung function increases with age until it reaches its peak at about 25 years. Thereafter it decreases at the rate of about 30 ml per year, on average. The rate of decline varies between individuals by factors as much as 2 or 3 times. In the same way there will be individual variations in the rate at which lung function declines with age. As between individuals, absolute levels of lung function will be found to vary even after correction for such known variables as height and age: 2.5% of the population will have a lung function which will be 1 litre greater, and 2.5% 1 litre less than, the mean. About 15% of the population will have a 'deficit' when compared to the mean of more than half a litre. Given these known variables, there are obvious theoretical and practical difficulties in determining what was an individual's lung function before it became subject to insult of any kind.

The effect of various epidemiological studies before the court was: (1) the effects of both smoking and exposure to mine dust could cause clinically important respiratory dysfunction and the effects of were additive; (2) the loss of lung function ('forced expiratory volume of air in 1 second', or 'FEV1') increases with previous cumulative dust exposure after allowing for the effects of age, height, smoking and overall colliery differences; (3) miners exposed to excessive amounts of respirable coal dust are at increased risk of premature death, either from PMF, chronic bronchitis or emphysema; (4) the severity of emphysema in coal workers is causally related to coal content in the lung and thus to exposure to coal in life; (5) the effect of dust decreases per unit of exposure as age increases.

APPORTIONMENT

[6.18] Applying *Thompson v Smiths Shiprepairers* ([1984] QB 405, above) and *Knox v Cammell Laird Shipbuilders* (30 July 1990, unreported), the judge held that damages fell to be apportioned, excluding from the award the effects of:

A. tortious but non-actionable exposure prior to 6 June 1954 (excluded by limitation Following *Arnold v Central Electricity Generating Board* [1988] AC 228, HL).
B. non-tortious exposure.
C. smoking.

The evidence was that, at one stage at least, more than 80% of working miners were also tobacco smokers. The medical experts agreed that a person who smokes 20 cigarettes a day for 1 year (defined as '1 pack year') will lose 15 ml of FEV1 per year. The judge accepted the proposition that loss of lung function can be apportioned equally between smoking and dust if a person is an average smoker and has been heavily exposed to dust.

The judge found that apportionment cannot be satisfactorily achieved by reliance on numbers, whether of the exposure to dust day to day, year to year or over the whole period of employment. The solution must be found as an answer to a 'jury question'.

For a summary of the actual awards made in the 8 claims before the court, see the summary table. The claimants received amounts ranging from nil to 36% of the damages they would have received had their condition been entirely due to the defendant's tortious conduct.

ASBESTOS

Insurance policy

Cape plc v Iron Trades Employers Insurance Association Ltd

[1999] PIQR Q212 (QBD, Rix J)

[6.19] Cape plc and its subsidiaries were major manufacturers of asbestos products. In March 1966, Cape took out an employer's liability insurance policy with Iron Trades. The policy continued with the same conditions until 1971. The policy contained an exclusion in respect of 'claims arising from pneumoconiosis or pneumoconiosis accompanied by tuberculosis', which was the agreed wording developed by insurers for the exclusion of pneumoconiosis dating back to its inclusion as a prescribed disease for national insurance purposes in 1948. It was common ground that the medical definition of pneumoconiosis referred to fibrosis of the lung (silicosis or asbestosis, depending on the cause) but mesothelioma (a malignant tumour) was a different disease. The distinction was known by professionals at the time the policy was negotiated but both types of disease were commonly referred to under the general term of 'pneumoconiosis' or 'asbestosis' in the insurance industry.

In anticipation of the introduction of the Employers Liability (Compulsory Insurance) Act 1969, the exclusion clause was removed and thereafter Cape agreed to indemnify Iron Trades in relation to pneumoconiosis and mesothelioma and cancer of the lung associated with pneumoconiosis.

Iron Trades initially accepted and paid some mesothelioma claims in respect of periods under the policy. Having subsequently located underwriting files, they changed their position and denied cover.

HELD: The judge held that the term 'pneumoconiosis' should be construed in light of the medical and statutory definitions, not in the wider and looser understanding of the term common in the insurance industry at the time. The exclusion did not include mesothelioma and Cape were entitled to be indemnified under the policy.

Procedural issues

Jurisdiction

Durham v T & N plc

(1996) LTL, 2 May, CA

[6.20] The claimant was employed by a wholly-owned subsidiary of T&N plc, Atlas Asbestos Co Ltd at its factory in Montreal from September 1955 to August 1956, where he was exposed to asbestos dust. He had been born in England and, following his retirement in 1980, divided his time between England and Florida, finally returning to England to live in 1992. He was diagnosed as suffering from mesothelioma in 1992.

In 1993, the claimant received Can$44,000 compensation for his condition under a statutory compensation scheme. The claimant also issued proceedings in England claiming common law damages.

HELD, on appeal: That the trial judge was correct to strike out the claim on the basis that the English courts had no jurisdiction to deal with it and that the action was statute-barred: (1) The wrongful act complained of (here, the exposure to asbestos dust and the lack of proper precautions to reduce levels of dust in the factory) occurred in Quebec. The fact that England was the seat of the defendant group at the time it exercised its power of control did not alter the position. Nor did the fact that the claimant was resident in England at the time the physical changes to his lungs leading to his death occurred. (2) The wrongful act was done by Atlas as the employer and occupier of the factory. (3) Quebec law was the proper law to be applied (Note that this decision pre-dated the operation of the *Private International Law (Miscellaneous Provisions) Act 1995 Pt III*, although the Court of Appeal doubted that the outcome would have been any different here). (4) The statutory scheme precluded the claimant's common law right of action against Atlas in Quebec. Further, under Quebec law, the claimant had only one year from his date of knowledge within which to bring his claim and these proceedings were issued six months after the expiry of that period. (5) There were no policy reasons to depart from the ordinary double actionability rule.

Note—For an example of the application of the *Spiliada* test to the issue of the correct forum for overseas group litigation, see *Lubbe v Cape plc* [2000] 4 All ER 268, HL.

Crown immunity

[6.21] For a fuller consideration see paragraph 5.65 and following cases

Pearce v Secretary of State for Defence

[1988] AC 755, HL

[6.22] Claim by a soldier for cancer caused by exposure to radiation in atomic tests in 1957–58 barred by the Crown Proceedings Act 1947, s 10; transfer of the Atomic Energy Authority's liability to the Secretary of State did not revive the action.

See paragraph 5.67 above.

Quinn v Ministry of Defence

(1997) LTL, 29 November, CA

[6.23] Claimant exposed to asbestos whilst working as a stoker, stoker mechanic, boiler cleaner and mechanical engineer on board naval vessels; claim barred by the Crown Proceedings Act 1947, s 10.

Matthews v Ministry of Defence

[2003] ULHL 4, [2003] 1 All ER 689

[6.24] Claimant exposed to asbestos whilst working as an electrical mechanic in the Royal Navy between 1955 and 1968; claim barred by the Crown Proceedings Act 1947, s 10; the effect of section 10 is substantive and the issue of a certificate by the Secretary of State under the Act forms part of the substantive law; section 10 is not incompatible with the European Convention on Human Rights, art 6.

Limitation/Accrual of cause of action

[6.25] For cases involving questions of limitation against local authorities, see below.

Arnold v Central Electricity Generating Board

[1988] AC 228, HL

[6.26] Limitation period of 1 year in respect of claims against local authorities under the Limitation Act 1939 preserved by the Limitation Act 1980, Sch 2, para 9(1). The deceased died from mesothelioma in 1982 as a result of exposure to asbestos whilst working for CEGB as a boiler cleaner between 1938 and 1943. The deceased's cause of action accrued in 1943 and was therefore statute barred from 1944 – this date being 12 months after the last date of exposure. Note that the court appears to have accepted that 'damage' for the purposes of the *Limitation Act* is suffered when the fibres are inhaled or on piercing the lung tissue, following *Cartledge v Jopling & Sons Ltd* [1963] AC 758, HL (pneumoconiosis).

Industrial Diseases Claims

Note that it was assumed in this case that the cause of action accrued at the time the asbestos fibres were inhaled. This is consistent with the approach taken under the old Workmen's Compensation Act, eg *Fitzsimons v Ford Motor Co Ltd* [1946] 1 All ER 429, CA (VWF), *Pyrah v Doncaster Corpn* [1949] 1 All ER 883, CA (tuberculosis caused by inhalation of bacterium). See also the more recent case of *Dhak v Insurance Co of North America* [1996] 1 Lloyd's Rep 632, CA – 'The introduction of some foreign matter into the body which causes harmful psychological changes in the structure of the body can...amount to a bodily injury' (per Neill LJ, 637).

Jameson v Central Electricity Generating Board (Babcock Energy, third party)

(31 March 1995, unreported), QBD

[6.27] For an alternative view in the context of mesothelioma, see the first instance decision in *Jameson v Central Electricity Generating Board (Babcock Energy, third party)*, pp 65 – 69; Subsequently appealed to the Court of Appeal [1998] QB 323 and the House of Lords [1999] 1 All ER 193 on a different point, namely whether part settlement of the action against one tortfeasors precluded an action against another tortfeasors for the same damage) in the context of a contractual indemnity in a construction contract. Per Tudor Evans J:

> The question is whether the damage or injury to the deceased occurred before the Works were handed over which it is agreed between Mr McLaren and Mr Woodward was in 1960.
>
> Mr McLaren proffered the construction that the word 'injury does not refer to the type of injury which is necessary to constitute a cause of action. It means the insult to the system when the person inhaled an asbestos fibre or fibres whilst working at the relevant premises which in due time led to the formation of mesothelioma and therefore it does not matter that the insult was not sufficient to cause damage and so ground a cause of action.
>
> ...In my judgment this is not the meaning which should be given to the relevant words. The meaning has to be construed in the context of the language of the whole clause which, in my view, makes it clear that the 'damage or injury' is related to 'all actions, suits, claims...arising in connection therewith', that is actions, and so forth, arising in connection with the damage or injury. The clause is therefore dealing with actionable damage or injury and the question I have to decide is whether actionable damage or injury occurred before the Works were taken over in 1960. This damage or injury has to be more than minimal to be actionable, as the House of Lords held in a case concerned with pneumoconiosis: see *Cartledge v Jopling & Sons Ltd* [1963] AC 758, HL.
>
> ...It is common ground between the doctors that a very large percentage of the general population has asbestos fibres in its lungs without any ill effect whatsoever. According to Dr Rudd, mesothelioma begins with a

malignant transformation of a mesothelium cell: one of the cells lining the pleura escapes from the normal mechanism which controls the growth of the cell. The result is that the cell multiplies and its off-spring multiply until mesothelioma is present. In Dr Rudd's opinion, the tumour begins from about ten years before any symptoms appear but it cannot be known for certain in an individual case when it begins to grow, that is, when microscopic changes occur in the cell. Dr Rudd deduced that this microscopic process begins about ten years before the symptoms. He stated that it is not fully understood how mesothelioma is caused. He referred to two theories: one was the 'lottery ticket' theory whereby one single asbestos fibre was the cause: such a risk is infinitely small. The other theory is that the fibres inhaled are too great a burden for the body to bear.

Professor Jones said one possible mechanism of the cause of mesothelioma is the environment into which the fibres are put. His view is that fibres enter the patient at any time by inhalation and they lie dormant for years and then at some stage the defence mechanism alters and permits the cell to grow. Patients often lead a healthy life during the interval from inhalation which may be a period of anything from 12 to 50 years. The failure of the mechanism may be the result of the presence of fibres or, according to another theory, it may be due to some wholly unrelated factor (for example), another disease such as tuberculosis: it is wrong, said this witness, to attribute the mechanism to asbestos fibres. It may or may not be so.

On this evidence, had damage or injury occurred before the Works were taken over? I find the evidence is far from establishing that any such damage or injury existed at that time. The fibres may have lain dormant causing no trouble not even minimal damage in the cell or cells for many years. If Dr Rudd is right, and his clearly is a tenable theory, the microscopic process of cellular change may have occurred about 10 years before the symptoms appeared. According to Professor Jones, the failure or the mechanism which allows the cell or cells to grow may be due to some unrelated matter.

I find that the evidence does not even establish that minimal microscopic changes occurred before 1960. I find that the damage in this case is the mesothelioma which occurred many years after the deceased finished working. In the result, the claim for an express indemnity must fail.

This approach is to be contrasted with that taken by some US courts when considering when injury occurs for the purposes of determining which insurance policy applies: *Insurance Co of North America v Forty-Eight Insulations Inc* 633 F 2d 1212 (1980) ('each tiny deposit of scar like tissue causes injury to a lung' (the 'exposure theory') Note however that the court in this case held the insurer liable only for its contribution on a time-exposure basis); *Keene Corpn v Insurance Co of North America* 667 F 3d 1034 (1981)('injury' occurs (i) at the time of the initial exposure; (ii) during continued exposure; (iii) on manifestation of symptoms of the disease (the 'triple trigger' theory)).

Legislation

The Asbestos Industry Regulations 1931

[6.28] The regulations applied to occupiers of factories and workshops in which the processes listed in the preamble (breaking, crushing etc of asbestos, manufacture of asbestos cloth, making of asbestos insulation slabs and mattresses, sawing/grinding etc of dry asbestos etc – except where the sawing, grinding etc was carried on occasionally only and no person was employed to do that work for more than 8 hours per week –, and the cleaning of plant used for such processes). They were revoked by the 1969 Regulations. The regulations imposed a duty to provide and maintain exhaust ventilation to prevent the escape of asbestos dust into the work room for the activities listed – ie certain asbestos manufacturing machinery, chambers etc into which loose asbestos is delivered, work benches for the handling of asbestos, places where sacks etc of asbestos are filled, emptied or weighed etc except where the machine or plant is enclosed or does not otherwise give rise to asbestos dust or where the asbestos is wet or otherwise treated to prevent dust (reg 1) and wherever asbestos is mixed or blended by hand (reg 2(a)). Mixing or blending by hand was not to be carried out alongside other work (reg 2(b)). Specific measures were to be taken: when making or repairing asbestos mattresses (reg 3); in relation to storage chambers and bins for loose asbestos (reg 4); in the construction of machinery used in the manufacture of asbestos (reg 5); when cleaning cylinders (reg 6), or in relation to sacks of asbestos (reg 8). Rooms in such factories/workshops were to be kept clean and free of asbestos debris etc (reg 7) and breathing apparatus provided for certain work – ie for any person employed in chambers containing loose asbestos, cleaning dust settling on filtering chambers or apparatus, cleaning cylinders etc using hand strickles & filling, beating etc asbestos mattresses – involving exposure to loose asbestos (reg 10).

Factories Acts 1937 and 1961

FACTORIES ACT 1937, s 47(1)

[6.29]

In every factory in which, in connection with any process carried on, there is given off any dust or fume or other impurity of such a character and to such extent as to be likely to be injurious or offensive to the persons employed, or any substantial quantity of dust of any kind, all practicable measures shall be taken to protect the persons employed against inhalation of the dust or fume or other impurity and to prevent its accumulating in any workroom, and in particular, where the nature of the process makes it practicable, exhaust appliances shall be provided and maintained, as near as possible to the point of origin of the dust or fume or other impurity, so as to prevent it entering the air of any workroom.

Factories Act 1961, s 4(1)

[6.30]

Effective and suitable provision shall be made for securing and maintaining by the circulation of fresh air in each workroom the adequate ventilation of the room, and for rendering harmless, so far as practicable, all fumes, dust and other impurities that may be injurious to health generated in the course of any process or work carried on in the factory.

> Note— a 'workroom' must be a room in the factory, not a compartment within an article (however large) being worked on in the factory (*Ebbs v James Whitson & Co Ltd [1952] 2 QB 877,* [1952] 2 All ER 192).
>
> Note —'Factory' is defined in s 175(1) to mean 'any premises in which, or within the close curtilage or precincts of which, persons are employed in manual labour in any process…by way of trade or for purposes of gain and to or over which the employer of the persons employed therein has the right of access or control'. It also includes shipyards and dry docks in which ships are constructed, repaired, refitted, broken up etc and premises used for the construction, repair etc of locomotives, vehicles and other transport plant (s 175(2)). Section 47 does not appear to apply to work on ships in wet dock (s 126).

Regulations under the Factories Act 1961

Shipbuilding and Ship-repairing Regulations 1961

[6.31] Reg 53(2) imposed a duty to provide and maintain exhaust extraction equipment in similar terms to the Factories Act 1937, s 47(1).

Reg 76 imposed a duty to provide an approved respirator to anyone engaged in certain operations including cutting asbestos materials with a power saw, spraying asbestos, removing asbestos lagging, cleaning asbestos sacks etc.

Control of Asbestos Regulations 1969

[6.32] The 1969 Regulations applied to 'factories' (see Note to para. [6.30] above) and to any process in which asbestos dust can be given off (reg 3). 'Asbestos dust' is defined as 'dust of or containing asbestos to such an extent as is liable to cause danger to the health of employed persons' (reg 2(a)). See *Smith v P & O Bulk Shipping,* below, as support for the contention that the 1969 Regulations do not impose a duty over and above that owed at common law towards employees who suffer only occasional and indirect exposure. The regulations applied to employers, occupiers and building or engineering contractors (reg 5).

The regulations imposed a duty to provide, maintain and inspect exhaust ventilation (reg 7), provide approved respiratory equipment and protective clothing (reg 8), keep work spaces and equipment clean (reg 9) using vacuum cleaning equipment (reg 10). The factory inspector had to be notified of any process involving crocidolite (blue asbestos) (reg 6).

194 *Industrial Diseases Claims*

For legislation after 1969, see the Asbestos (Licensing) Regulations 1983, the Control of Asbestos at Work Regulations 1987 and 2002 and Approved Code of Practice COP 21, the Asbestos (Prohibitions) Regulations 1985, the Asbestos Products (Safety) Regulations 1985, the Control of Asbestos in the Air Regulations 1990, and the Asbestos (Prohibitions) Regulations 1992.

Standards

[6.33] For evidence of the standards applied, see:
HMFI Technical Data Note 35: Control of Asbestos Dust (December 1972),
HMFI Technical Data Note 42: Probable Asbestos Dust Concentrations at Construction Processes (April 1973),
HSE Technical Data Note 52: Health Hazards from Sprayed Asbestos Coatings in Buildings (May 1976),
HSE Guidance Note EH10: Asbestos – Hygiene Standards & Measurements of Airborne Dust Concentrations (May 1976 – revised with new control limits in April 1983 and again in July 1984),
HSE Guidance Note MS13: Asbestos (January 1980),
HSE Guidance Note EH35: Probable Asbestos Dust Concentrations at Construction Processes (October 1984),
HSE Technical Data Note EH37: Work With Asbestos Insulating Board (October 1984),
HSE Guidance Note EH41: Respiratory Protective Equipment for Use Against Asbestos (November 1985),
HSE Guidance Note EH47: The Provision, Use & Maintenance of Hygiene Facilities for Work with Asbestos Insulation and Coatings (September 1986).

Application of legislation

Nurse v Morganite Crucible Ltd

[1989] 1 All ER 113, HL

[6.34] The defendant company was charged with and convicted of a breach of the Factories Act 1961, s 155(2), and reg 8(1) (the duty to provide approved respiratory equipment), reg 9 (the duty to keep plant and equipment free from asbestos waste and dust) and reg 15 (the duty to keep loose asbestos in suitable closed receptacles) of the Asbestos Regulations 1969.

The company was in the business of manufacturing crucibles. It did not use asbestos in the production process. However, in 1984 over the course of 9 days, the company demolished a number of large brick dryers, the roof panels of which contained asbestos insulation.

HELD, on appeal: The conviction was upheld. The use of the word 'process' in the 1969 Regulations and the Factories Act 1961, s 175(1) should not be restricted to a manufacturing process or regular activity carried on as a normal part of the operation of a factory but includes any activity of a more than minimal duration involving the use of asbestos. The single act of knocking a nail into an asbestos panel cannot be considered a 'process'. There has to be some degree of continuity and repetition of a series of acts in order to constitute a process. Here the activity went on over a period of days involving materials containing asbestos and therefore did fall within the Regulations.

Note—See also *Edgson v Vickers plc* [1994] ICR 510 (dry sweeping of asbestos dust constituted a manufacturing process for the purposes of the Factories Act 1961 and regs 15(1)(a) and 2(2) of the Asbestos Regulations 1969 applied).

Jeromson v Shell Tankers (UK) Ltd, Shell Tankers (UK) Ltd v Dawson

[2001] EWCA Civ 100, 101, [2001] ICR 1223

[6.35] The case involved two appeals from defendants in the cases *Dawson v Cherry Tree Machine Co Ltd and Shell Tankers UK Ltd* and *Jeromson v Shell Tankers UK Ltd*. In both, the claimants had been employed and exposed to asbestos dust by Shell Tankers as marine engineers in the 1950s. In *Dawson*, the claimant had also been employed and exposed by Cherry Tree Machine Co as an apprentice fitter in the 1940s.

The *Cherry Tree* appeal

[6.36] Mr Dawson was exposed to asbestos dust whilst working for Cherry Tree. From 1946 to 1948, part of his job consisted of sealing platens of dry cleaner's presses with asbestos to stop steam escaping. He would take a couple of handfuls of asbestos flock, put it in a bucket, mix with water and apply it to the press. He would do this once a week, taking about an hour to seal six machines. The process would generate visible dust which would get into his overalls and remain in the air for two to three minutes, although invisible dust might persist longer.

HELD, on appeal: That the *Asbestos Industry Regulations 1931* applied. The Regulations were passed under the Factory and Workshop Act 1901, ss 79 and 80(1), which empowered the Secretary of State to certify a manufacture, process, description of manual labour etc to be dangerous and to make regulations in respect of all factories and workshops in which the manufacture, process, description of labour etc was used. The Secretary of State certified 'the manipulation of asbestos and the manufacture or repair of articles composed wholly or partly of asbestos and processes incidental thereto' as dangerous in a letter from the Home Office dated 15 September 1931 accompanying the draft regulations. The preamble to the Regulations included the mixing of asbestos in para (i) of the list of processes covered. The court held that the claimant did not fall within the exemption under the preamble in respect of work carried out 'occasionally only' where 'no person is employed therein for more than eight hours per week', upholding the trial judge's interpretation that, for an employee to fall within the exemption, he had first to satisfy both requirements. Here the claimant mixed asbestos on a regular rather than an occasional basis and the exemption therefore did not apply.

196   *Industrial Diseases Claims*

Having found that the 1931 Regulations applied, the Court of Appeal held that the trial judge was right to find Cherry Tree in breach of reg 2 (the duty to provide an exhaust unless not practicable to do so).

The *Shell* appeal

[6.37]   Both Dawson and Jeromson were employed by Shell Tankers as marine engineers on various ships, Mr Dawson between 1951 and 1957 and Mr Jeromson between 1957 and 1961. No specific regulations applied and Shell's duty fell to be assessed at common law. Both men were exposed to asbestos dust when stripping away and replacing asbestos insulation to access leaking joints, when pipes burst and during dry docking. Both parties' occupational health and safety consultants agreed that stripping asbestos lagging by hand, mixing asbestos powder with water and dry sweeping of asbestos debris all gave rise to high concentrations of visible dust. At the time, there was no way of measuring the concentrations and until 1960 there were no published limits. The trial judge held that the marine engineers employed by Shell were likely to be exposed to intense concentrations of asbestos dust, that these exposures would be for minutes rather than hours, but that on occasion the exposures would be for hours and at even higher intensity.

HELD, ON APPEAL: The trial judge's finding that Shell should have foreseen the risk of injury associated with this level of exposure was upheld. The headline message of the Mereweather and Price report of 1930 was that prolonged intense exposure would inevitably lead to asbestosis. It must have been apparent to any careful reader that the effect of much lower levels of exposure was quite unknown. The Asbestos Industry Regulations 1931 only offered a green light to occasional exposure to certain processes. Otherwise, the obligations contained in them were strict and constituted a considerable warning of the dangers involved. Next came the Factories Act 1937, s 47, which prohibited exposure to 'any dust…of such a character and to such an extent as to be likely to be injurious or offensive…or of any substantial quantity of dust of any kind'. The Chief Inspector of Factories' Annual Reports of 1931, 1935 and 1943 contained tabulated data indicating that the shortest occupational exposure to asbestos dust associated with injury had fallen from 4.4 years in 1931 to 0.5 years in 1943. In August 1945, the Chief Inspector of Factories wrote to the shipbuilding and shiprepairing industry of his concerns about asbestos insulation aboard ships, noting that even if the work was temporary, all reasonably practicable steps should nevertheless be taken to reduce the risk to a minimum. The letter suggested various precautions, including provision of a respirator for each workman engaged in the fitting or removal of dry insulating material. The Annual Report of 1949, stressed the dangers of exposure to asbestos dust outside the asbestos industry. The 1956 Annual report referred specifically to the removal of old heat-insulation lagging, commenting that this 'very dry and dusty material presents a serious health hazard, which is all the more serious because the work is often done in confined spaces'. Had Shell made enquiries, there is little doubt as to the advice it would have been given.

Duty of care/date of knowledge

Bryce v Swan Hunter Group plc

[1988] 1 All ER 659 (QBD, Phillips J)

[6.38] The deceased was employed as a painter from 1937 to 1975 in various shipyards. He worked for the three defendant companies for various periods between 1947 and 1970. Throughout the course of his work he was exposed to asbestos dust. He developed mesothelioma and died in 1981.

HELD: The judge held that the defendants should have known of the dangers involved in exposure to asbestos dust throughout the period of his employment with them. In light of the reports of the Factories Inspectorate from 1932 to 1956 and the Chief Inspector of Factories' circular of August 1945 regarding asbestos insulation aboard ships, the duty was not to prevent all exposure to asbestos dust given the state of knowledge at the time, but to take all steps reasonably practicable to reduce the amount of dust. The steps that should have been taken were those identified by Surgeon Commander Harries in his survey on practices in naval dockyards: (1) to improve work methods to reduce the amount of dust; (2) restrict access to areas where asbestos work was taking place to workers whose presence was essential; and (3) to provide those workers necessarily exposed to heavy concentrations of dust with breathing apparatus and protective clothing. There was no reason why the defendants should not have adopted similar precautions. Had they done so, the result would have been to reduce the deceased's exposure to both visible and invisible asbestos fibres that can cause mesothelioma. The evidence of the defendants' own expert witness was that within 15 minutes of completing the mixing of asbestos, the concentration of asbestos fibres in the atmosphere would drop from 264 to 20 fibres per cubic centimetre. Had a system been in place for keeping painters out of dust filled compartments until visible dust had settled, this must sensibly have reduced the quantity of small asbestos fibres inhaled by the deceased.

Whether the defendants' breaches of duty merely added to the number of possible initiators of mesothelioma within the deceased's lungs or whether they also produced a cumulative effect on the reduction of the body's defence mechanisms, they increased the risk of his developing mesothelioma. Applying *McGhee*, the judge held that the claimant had therefore satisfied the legal requirements for causation.

Gunn v Wallsend Slipway and Engineering Co Ltd

(1989) Times, 23 January (QBD, Waterhouse J)

[6.39] The claimant was employed by the defendant. The claimant's wife died from mesothelioma as a result of inhaling asbestos dust from his work clothes.

HELD: The judge held that, prior to the publication of *The Sunday Times* article concerning the dangers of inhalation of asbestos dust on 31 October 1965, no one in the industrialised world directed his mind to the risk of industrial injury from domestic exposure, except in the 'asbestos neighbourhood cases. There was no medical literature, warnings or guidance hinting at the risk from asbestos dust in clothing. A reasonably prudent employer would not have foreseen any risk of injury to the deceased. The defendant therefore did not owe a duty of care to the deceased.

Margereson and Hancock v J W Roberts Ltd

[1996] PIQR P358, CA

[6.40] J W Roberts Ltd were the occupiers of a factory which produced asbestos insulation and related products from the late 19th century until 1958. The factory was in a densely populated area. The two claimants grew up near the factory, Mr Margereson living as a child 200 yards from the factory between 1925 and 1943 and Mrs Hancock living as a child in the neighbourhood from 1938 to 1951. Both claimants were diagnosed as suffering from mesothelioma in 1991 and 1992 respectively.

There was overwhelming evidence that blue asbestos dust escaped from the factory and was deposited outside the perimeter on all sides and into the surrounding atmosphere. Employees would leave the factory covered in asbestos dust. The claimants and other neighbourhood children would play in the loading bays and open yards, jumping up and down on bales of asbestos and using dust to make 'snowballs'.

HELD, on appeal: The trial judge's finding on foreseeability was upheld. The risk of fibrosis of the lung and other respiratory disorders (although not mesothelioma) was known in 1930 following the publication of the Mereweather and Price report, *Effects of Asbestos Dust on the Lungs and Dust Suppression in the Asbestos Industry*, and the *Asbestos Industry Regulations 1931* had come into effect in 1933. The Court of Appeal held that the information which should have operated on the defendants' corporate mind was in existence long before Mr Margereson's birth date (1925). Although the link between mesothelioma and asbestos exposure had yet to be identified in the 1930s, it was foreseeable that the claimants could suffer some injury. The risks should have been foreseen notwithstanding the fact that that the claimants' exposure occurred outside the factory.

O'Toole v Iarnod Eireann (Irish Rail)

[1999] CLY 1535 (QBD, Judge Hayward)

[6.41] The deceased was employed as a fitter by Irish Rail from 1950 to 1955 in the construction of railway carriages in its coach shop at Inichcore in Ireland. He died from mesothelioma in 1987. From 1954, Irish Rail switched from wooden to metal Park Royal carriages insulated with sprayed limpet asbestos, applied by a spray machine supplied and operated by the third defendant, J W Roberts Ltd.

The evidence was that bags of pre-mixed blue asbestos and cement were delivered to the coach shop and loaded by hand by a J W Roberts employee into a mobile spraying machine, not unlike a closed cement mixer. Inside the machine, the mixture was teased, carried up a conveyor belt and sprayed with atomised water and compressed air. The dampened mixture fell to the bottom of the machine and was propelled by compressed air along a hosepipe and out through a nozzle. The hole in the nozzle through which the asbestos and cement mix was ejected was surrounded by water jets. The asbestos/cement mix and atomised water converged approximately 12 inches in front of the nozzle and the resulting mixture was sprayed onto the surface of the carriages. The surface was flattened using a plasterer's float and allowed to dry. During spraying, some of the sprayed asbestos/cement would fall to the floor and would be swept up whilst still damp. The operator would wear a respirator whilst loading the machine, whilst spraying and for 15 to 20 minutes after spraying had stopped.

Spraying would be done by J W Roberts every two to three weeks, with two to three coaches being sprayed each visit. Each coach would take about 4 hours to spray. Once dry, the fitters would start the fitting-out process.

The fitters cut and scraped the dried asbestos to expose holes and channels for the internal fittings. They would sweep up the asbestos that had been cut away.

HELD: The spraying, sweeping of dried limpet asbestos from the carriages, cutting and scraping of dried asbestos and further sweeping of dry asbestos debris all created substantial amounts of dust to which the claimant would have been exposed. Both J W Roberts and Irish Rail were held liable, apportioning liability on a 70:30 basis against J W Roberts.

The judge held that J W Roberts was aware of the risks associated with asbestos before 1954–55. Its liability was wider because of its greater knowledge of the hazard. It knew the nature of the work that was being done in coaches and that Irish Rail employees were working in coaches from time to time in very dusty conditions. It was under a duty to warn Irish Rail of the potential dangers of dust which might escape from the spraying process. It gave no warnings to customers in the 1940s and 1950s for commercial reasons.

J W Roberts was one of a group of companies in the asbestos industry at the forefront of knowledge concerning asbestos. It had been known that asbestos fibres were bad for lungs from the turn of the 20th century. The Mereweather and Price report of 1930 confirmed that heavy exposure to asbestos fibres could lead to asbestosis and led to the introduction of the Asbestos Industry Regulations 1931. In October 1937, the minutes of a J W Roberts board meeting recorded a discussion as to whether their spray workers should be regularly medically examined and that they should wear special respirators. In 1938, one of the companies belonging to J W Roberts' Turner & Newall Group wrote that 'all asbestos fibres dust, whether it arises in a factory or elsewhere, is a danger to lungs, and especially so where the person breathing it has not healthy lungs to start with'. The Factories Inspector's Report of 1938 noted, 'It is not many years ago when the dust of asbestos was regarded as innocuous, but today it is regarded as highly dangerous'. In 1943 Dr Mereweather complained to J W Roberts about the use of juvenile labour in London to do spraying work without use of respirators. The 1945 Factories Inspector's Report advised that approved dust respirators should be provided for men undertaking work with dry asbestos insulating material and asbestos spraying. The 1947 Factories Inspector's Report noted fatal cases (including cancer of the lung) where the asbestos exposure ranged from as little as 6 months to as many as 48 years. The 1949 Factories Inspector's Report referred to the risks associated with the use of portable asbestos spraying plants. In 1954, Dr Knox (Turner & Newall's medical officer) and Dr Doyle completed a report following their study into the causes of death of a Turner & Newall employee, concluding that lung cancer was a specific industrial hazard of asbestos workers and that the risk among men employed for 20 years or more may have been 10 times that experienced by the general population. The report was published in 1955 in Dr Doyle's name only. The judge held that there was evidence that Turner & Newall attempted to stop publication of the report, suggesting that the evidence did not support the doctors' findings. Finally, in 1955 a paper published by Dr McLoughlin reported cases of asbestosis in workers engaged in the lagging of pipes and boilers and that, if asbestos was being sprayed, it was difficult to apply adequate protective measures.

HELD: The judge held that articles and papers in *The Lancet* and the *British Medical Journal* published in the 1930s about the hazards of asbestos dust, largely concerned with risks to employees in the asbestos industries, would have been read by the medical staff at J W Roberts and Turner & Newall.

Smith v P & O Bulk Shipping Ltd

[1998] 2 Lloyd's Rep 81 (QBD, Drake J)

[6.42] The deceased worked as a shore gang worker for New Zealand Shipping Co (later part of the P&O Group) for 17 years from 1954 to 1971 at the Royal Docks in East London. His duties included cleaning and sweeping and helping the chief storeman load cargo. He did not work directly with asbestos lagging. Asbestos sheeting and guttering as well as bags of asbestos were loaded on board near to where the deceased would have worked.

HELD: The judge found that the deceased would have come into contact with asbestos dust from the cargo on an occasional but not rare basis. Over the course of 17 years, such exposure would have exceeded 2 hours, but it was not exposure of the same order as that found in an asbestos factory, for someone living close to an asbestos factory or within an area in which asbestos work was being done. Further, he found that exposure of this magnitude is sufficient to cause mesothelioma.

However, the judge found in favour of the defendant shipowners on the basis that it was not reasonably foreseeable at the time that exposure of this magnitude involved a significant risk of injury. The Asbestos Industry Regulations 1931 did not apply to cases of occasional exposure and were limited to cases where employees were exposed to asbestos dust 8 hours or more per week. A letter sent by the Inspector of Factories in August 1945 to various employers in the shipping industry warning of the health risks associated with exposure to asbestos was not sent to shipowners. Subsequent reports of the Factories Inspectorate in 1949 and 1956, the Wagner medical paper in 1960 and the Shipbuilding and Ship-repairing Regulations 1961 were also concerned with those working directly with asbestos. A letter from the Ministry of Labour of 28 October 1965 recommended only the use of impervious rather than hessian sacks to contain asbestos. *The Sunday Times* article of 31 October 1965 was directed at the dangers of working with or in close proximity to asbestos. The Factories Inspector's Report of 1966 warned of the health risks to persons working in a confined space where asbestos work was going on but the judge did not accept that this was intended to refer to the alleyways or corridors of a ship. A 1967 report following an inquiry in to dockers working with asbestos found no evidence of injury to health as a result of dockers handling asbestos cargo. The Asbestos Regulations 1969 did not apply to workers exposed only occasionally and indirectly to asbestos dust on ships. It was only in 1977, when shipowners, shipbuilders and repairers and master's offices and seamen received the Department of Trade's 'M Notice', that a clear warning of the risk of developing mesothelioma from short exposure to asbestos was received, and a requirement imposed that precautions be taken to protect those who had access to the area where asbestos was being worked.

Babcock International Ltd v National Grid plc

[2000] All ER (D) 810 (QBD, Eady J)

[6.43] The claimant company ('Babcock') was a specialist supplier of boilers and associated pipework. During the 1950s, Babcock undertook construction work at the Barking and Battersea power stations. Most of the installation work was performed as part of the general construction of the power stations themselves. There were a number of contractors and sub-contractors working on these sites at the same time, including lagging firms who were responsible for lagging the boilers and pipework with material containing asbestos. This was standard practice at the time and would have been in accordance with the specifications issued by the Central Electricity Generating Board (the precursor to National Grid plc), the occupier of the power stations.

Mr Hussey was employed by Babcock as a welder. He did not work directly with asbestos himself but would have been exposed to asbestos over the course of his employment. He died from malignant mesothelioma in 1993. Proceedings brought by Mr Hussey's widow were settled by Babcock in April 1997 and Babcock sought contribution from National Grid.

The evidence was that, without extensive use of asbestos lagging materials, it would not have been possible in the 1950s to operate the massive steam boilers required in power stations safely or economically. Both Babcock and CEGB ought to have known that, during the installation of the boilers, laggers would be swarming over the boiler and applying lagging in accordance with the specifications. They would also have known that repair or modification would require removal of the lagging materials and subsequent reinstatement. Everyone with managerial responsibilities on site would have known that there was going to be a great deal of asbestos dust in the atmosphere and would have known in the early mid-1950s of at least the risk of respiratory damage, although the risk of cancer may not have been appreciated until later.

HELD: The claim for contribution failed. CEGB's duty was simply to instruct competent and skilled companies to carry out the necessary steps for the construction of a power station, including the installation of boilers and associated equipment and lagging of pipes in accordance with current standards. Even if CEGB failed in its duty, in this instance the judge would have held Babcock liable to contribute to the extent of 100% on the basis that it had, as employer, a clear non-delegable duty, was aware of the risks of respiratory disorder from exposure to asbestos and did nothing about it. Babcock should have warned its staff and provided them with a suitable type of respirator in use at the time. Moreover, although there was a security presence at the sites on CEGB's behalf, CEGB was not in overall daily control of the work whilst the power stations were under construction.

Milner v Humphreys & Glasgow Ltd

(2002) LTL, 25 July (QBD, Longmore J)

[6.44] The claimant was employed by Humphreys & Glasgow on the construction of two gas-making furnaces for approximately seven months between April and December 1964. He was required to handle, cut and transport insulation slabs containing asbestos and asbestos rope. Clouds of asbestos dust were given off by the activities of other employees on site. The claimant cleaned the site at the end of each working day, sweeping debris and bits of asbestos rope from the cladding slabs. The claimant was also exposed to asbestos with other employers, who were not before the court. His total exposure amounted to 56 months on a time-exposure basis. He subsequently developed pleural plaques, pleural thickening and asbestosis. His symptoms of breathlessness were contributed to by his obesity.

HELD: The risks of asbestosis had been known in the 1960s, in the building and construction industry and generally. The defendant was under a duty to take all steps reasonably practicable to reduce the amount of general dust and asbestos dust in particular. On the defendant's own case, it had not taken any reasonable steps to reduce the amount of dust and it was therefore in breach of its duty.

The judge held that the defendant was responsible for 1/8th of the claimant's total exposure (7 months/56 months); it was not appropriate to make any reduction to take into account the claimant's obesity.

Offset of benefits

Ballantine v Newalls Insulation Co Ltd

[2001] ICR 25, CA

[6.45] The deceased developed mesothelioma and died in 1998. Shortly before his death he applied for and obtained an award of £39,000 under the Pneumoconiosis, etc (Worker's Compensation) Act 1979. The Act entitled a person disabled by pneumoconiosis, byssinosis or diffuse mesothelioma to claim compensation from the state provided 'every relevant employer' has ceased to carry on business and he has not brought a claim for damages in respect of his condition (section 2). The size of the award is determined by the claimant's age and the percentage disablement assessed by the Pneumoconiosis Medical Board.

Proceedings were issued on behalf of the deceased against the defendant for environmental exposure to asbestos. He was not an employee of the defendant at the time of the exposure.

It was agreed that the total amount of the claim was in the order of £144,000, comprised of the deceased's claim for damages under the Law Reform (Miscellaneous Provisions) Act 1934 and the widow's claim for dependency under the Fatal Accidents Act 1976. The Law Reform Act claim totalled approximately £52,100, comprised of £40,000 for pain, suffering and loss of amenity, £5,000 for nursing costs and £7,100 loss of earnings.

HELD: Damages paid under the 1979 Act were deductible from the award.

OCCUPATIONAL NOISE-INDUCED HEARING LOSS/DEAFNESS CLAIMS

[6.46] Prior to 1 January 1990, it is arguable that the relevant standard was that set by the 1972 'Code of Practice for reducing exposure of employed persons to noise', which required that employers take the following steps whenever an employee was exposed to noise exceeding 90 dB(A) over an eight-hour period:
- Identify marked zones where ear protection was to be worn.
- Ensure that employees wore ear protection in those zones.
- Provide 'noise hazard awareness training'.
- Reduce noise levels as far as reasonably practicable.

Legislation

[6.47] Under the *Noise at Work Regulations* (ie from 1 January 1990) the duty was higher. The Regulations enact Directive 86/188/EEC. Note that the new *Physical Agents (Noise) Directive* came into force on 15 February 2003.

Risk assessments had to be carried out whenever employees were likely to be exposed to noise levels averaged over an 8 hour (8 hours per 1 week under the 2003 Directive) day of 85dB(A) or above.

Regular noise assessments had to be conducted and an accurate record kept.

Noise levels had to be reduced to the 'lowest level reasonably practicable' (Under the 2003 Directive, the duty is to eliminate the risk at source or reduce it to a minimum. There is no requirement of reasonable practicability.).

Ear protectors had to be provided at the employee's request where noise levels were between 85dB(A) (and 200 Pa; the threshold limits are 80 dB(A) and 112 Pa under the 2003 Directive) and 90dB(A). Ear protectors were obligatory and the employer was under a duty to ensure employees wore them where noise levels exceeded 90dB(A) (85 dB(A) and 140 Pa under the 2003 Directive).

Ear protection zones had to be clearly marked whenever noise levels exceeded 90dB(A) (85dB(A) and 140 Pa under the 2003 Directive).

Employees have to be provided with information, training and instruction.

As before, noise levels in excess of 90dB(A) had to be reduced 'as far as reasonably practicable'.

Note—See also *Thompson v Smiths Shiprepairers (North Shields) Ltd* [1984] 1 All ER 881, above.

VIBRATION WHITE FINGER

Hall v British Gas plc

(1998) LTL, 1 May (Manchester County Court, Judge Ensor)

[6.48] Six claims were selected as lead claims representing 48 similar claims against British Gas, each involving claims by employees for vibration white finger

204 Industrial Diseases Claims

(VWF) caused by exposure to vibration whilst using hand-held power tools. The evidence was that the claimants were engaged in distribution and excavation and reinstatement work, requiring them to use a variety of tools to lay or access gas pipes.

Around 1966, British Gas introduced power tools on a large scale. Gangs of men in the field were reduced to two or three. They were provided with their own compressors, pneumatic tools and a van. The main types of equipment in use were: (1) the road breaker, the most commonly used implement with either a point attached or a pummel foot, or 'elephant's foot'; (2) the rock drill, similar to a road breaker but with a smaller, long hexagonal shaft with a hardened tip, used to search for gas escapes and for breaking around the edges of concrete surfaces; (3) from the 1980s, the 'wacker', used to consolidate excavations in place of the road breaker; and (4) the wall drill, used for drilling through masonry when fitting new supply to a house. Measurements taken in 1983 indicated that all the breakers and some rock drills and wackers either exceeded acceptable daily exposure limits in the then current standards or reached very high and unacceptable levels. Further, there was no system of maintenance from 1970 until the late 1980s. The tools were in poor condition and in the central Lancashire area were hired in.

DATE OF KNOWLEDGE

[6.49] British Gas was for many years a public utility with the monopoly of the gas industry. By the early 1980s, it employed 18,000 people nationally on manual work. The vast majority of these were employed using vibrating tools. They represented 20–25% of British Gas' workforce nationally. In the 1970s, British Gas employed three full-time medical officers in the North West region and occupational medical officers were employed in all the regions and at Headquarters. The engineering and research station expanded from 250 to 550 persons. British Gas had resources fully capable, if directed, of considering the effect of vibration on this large segment of their workforce.

As early as 1911, it was known that work with pneumatic tools could cause white finger problems. In 1936 and 1937, medical journals in Britain published papers confirming that many vibration tools caused Reynaud's Phenomenon but pneumatic drills were the most frequent offenders. In 1947, a paper pointing out the distinction between the rate of operation of the machine and the characteristics of the vibration transmitted to the hands of the user was published by Agate and Druett in the *British Journal of Industrial Medicine*. The paper included measurements of vibration on a road ripper and a rock drill, distinguishing the vibration frequency from the strike rate. In 1950 the government through the Industrial Injuries Advisory Council (IIAC) delegated a sub-committee to investigate prescription of vibration injuries. In December 1954, they reported that the disease should not be prescribed but found a number of clearly occupational causes of Reynaud's Phenomenon caused by vibrating hand and machine tools. The failure to prescribe the disease was not a decision which would entitle an employer to ignore its implications. British Gas' medical officers would have been aware of the findings of the sub-committee and should have kept a watching brief on the progress of research into VWF.

In 1955 Hunter's Diseases of Occupations was published for the first time. It reviewed the research so far undertaken and gave guidance as to methods of postponing the onset of the disability by the provision of gloves. It concluded that there could be no real solution to the problem short of any entirely new design of portable tools.

In January 1967, the government again instructed IIAC to investigate VWF. British Gas knew of this through its membership of the Confederation of British Industry and their decision to communicate with large employers on the subject. A British Gas memo of June 1967 demonstrates that its medical officers were aware that there was a link between VWF and the use of vibrating tools by men in their employment. They were aware of the government's concern about this problem in other industries. At this stage British Gas was contemplating expanding its supply of vibration tools to distribution workers. By extending the use, they were increasing the risk.

By the late 1960s and early 1970s, reliable accelerometers became available and combined with frequency analysis, vibration spectra were produced. The medical and engineering departments of British Gas could have made themselves aware of these facilities had they so directed themselves.

In 1971, Professor Taylor published a paper in the British Journal of Industrial Medicine on VWF in saw operators. Following the report, the Forestry Commission measured the vibration and required that tools be produced with anti-vibration measures. Given the number of men employed on pneumatic tools and the proportion they represented of the total workforce, British Gas' investigations should have intensified.

In 1972 and 1973, the British Standards Institute circulated drafts of a standard for exposure to vibration, DD43. DD43 was published in February 1975. The Institution of Gas Engineers was one of the many government and industrial bodies under whose auspices it was prepared. Although a draft, it was recommended that it should be applied on a provisional basis in relation to vibration limits. It stated that adherence to those vibration levels would result in a considerable decrease in the incidence of VWF. A further purpose was to categorise the levels of vibration as acceptable/unacceptable, depending on the length of exposure. It recommended that cumulative exposure time to vibration should never exceed 400 minutes and that regular users should not exceed 150 minutes duration. British Gas did not consider DD43 until 1980.

British Gas eventually consulted Professor Taylor in 1980, who advised that road breakers should be regularly examined, that steps should be taken to take stage 2 cases off the job or minimise exposure time, that new entrants and existing employees should be warned of the risk and that gloves should be warm and waterproof. Had this advice been sought in 1975, the judge was satisfied it would have been the same.

HELD: That, by the end of 1975, British Gas should not only have been aware of the injury that vibrating tools were causing their employees but should also have implemented a comprehensive range of measures to minimise the risk. British Gas should have measured the levels of vibration on all tools. Sample tools could have been taken to the engineering and research department or the manufacturers could have been asked to provide the information. Measures identified by British Gas in reports of 1983 and 1994 could have been implemented in 1975, namely: to encourage manufacturers to produce low vibration equipment as a matter of urgency; to measure vibration levels of new equipment before purchase; direct efforts towards reducing vibration levels of existing equipment; to monitor exposure to vibration and establish safe operating limits; review existing operating procedures; introduce a formal system for job rotation and regular medical examinations.

MEDICAL EVIDENCE

[6.50] Vibration can cause injury to the vascular, nervous and musculo-skeletal systems. VWF is the term used to cover all types of injury to the hands and lower arms. The condition forms part of 'Hand-Arm Vibration Syndrome', which includes also vibration-induced carpal tunnel syndrome.

Vascular

[6.51] Vibration can cause damage to the vascular tree leading to attacks of whiteness in the fingers when hands are exposed to cold. Circulation stops in the affected areas which become numb. Attacks often last for 20 to 60 minutes and sometimes longer. When the blood supply returns the hands appear red and this may be accompanied by painful tingling. Warming the hands by artificial means may produce very severe pain. With continued exposure to vibration, attacks may increase in severity and frequency. More digits of the fingers are affected by whiteness. Attacks can occur with small drops in temperature and so occur throughout the year.

Neurological

[6.52] Neurological damage results in tingling and numbness which can become permanent, causing reductions in sensitivity, manual dexterity and grip strength. In severe form, the neurological symptoms can render an individual seriously disabled. Carpal tunnel syndrome can be part of the neurological effects of vibration and has been accepted as part of the prescribed condition since 1992.

Musculo-skeletal

[6.53] The generally accepted effects are reduced grip strength and duration of grip and muscle fatigue.

Extent of disability

[6.54] VWF often restricts outdoor pursuits such as fishing and golf. The victim may be unable to pursue a hobby in cold weather or may have to give up the activity completely. There can be interference with work such that the victim is confined to work in a warm environment and may be unable to manage fine tasks.

Effect of cessation of exposure

[6.55] 1. In respect of vascular symptoms, there can be improvement on cessation of exposure. The likelihood of improvement depends on age, total exposure, length of exposure after development of symptoms and severity of the condition. The worse the condition is, the less improvement there is on cessation of vibration. Some individuals can experience worsening symptoms in the 12 months following cessation of exposure. After 12 months, there is no worsening or improvement.

2. The evidence is less clear in respect of neurological symptoms. There is evidence suggesting symptoms can improve or get worse following cessation of exposure.

Diagnosis

[6.56] Some 4 to 5% of the male population complain of episodes of whiteness of the of the fingers when exposed to cold. By restricting the male population to those in their 30s, 40s or 50s, those developing episodes of whiteness at this age is only about 1% of the population. There is no objective test which can determine whether a person has VWF but it is possible in the vast majority of cases to make a diagnosis. A history of typical symptoms developing after several years of occupational exposure to vibration is very suggestive.

Classification

[6.57] The Taylor Pelmear Scale was developed as a research tool. It has limited usefulness when classifying cases for compensation purposes. It can be misleading in that it underestimates the neurological effects. An individual can have severe neurological changes but not be at stage 1 if they have not developed blanching.

Taylor/Pelmear Scale

Stage	Condition of Digits	Work & Social Interference
0	No blanching of digits	No complaints
0T	Intermittent tingling	No interference with activities
0N	Intermittent numbness	No interference with activities
1	Blanching of one or more fingertips with or without tingling or numbness	No interference with activities
2	Blanching of one or more fingers with numbness. Usually confined to winter.	Slight interference with home and social activities. No interference at work.
3	Extensive blanching. Frequent episodes in summer as well as winter.	Definite interference at work, at home and with social activities. Restriction of hobbies.
4	Extensive blanching. Most fingers; frequent episodes summer and winter.	Occupation changed to avoid further vibration exposures because of severity of signs and symptoms.

The Stockholm Workshop Scale is a more useful scale because it allows for vascular and neurological effects to be assessed separately and to provide separate gradings for each hand and finger.

Stockholm Workshop Scale

Vascular Effects

Stage	Grade	Description
0		No attacks.
1	Mild	Occasional attacks affecting only the tips of one or more fingers.
2	Moderate	Occasional attacks affecting the distal and middle (rarely also proximal) phalanges of one or more fingers.
3	Severe	Frequent attacks affecting all phalanges of most fingers.
4	Very severe	As in Stage 3, with trophic skin changes in the finger tips.

Sensori-neural (or Neurological) Effects

Stage	Symptoms
0SN	Exposed to vibration but no symptoms.
1SN	Intermittent numbness, with or without tingling.
2SN	Intermittent or persistent numbness, reduced sensory perception.
3SN	Intermittent or persistent numbness, reduced tactile discrimination and/or manipulative dexterity.

Sensori-neural staging is carried out for each hand.

APPORTIONMENT

[6.58] The judge held, distinguishing *Thompson v Smiths Shiprepairers* on the grounds that the claimants in that case had hearing which was already damaged to such an extent that they would inevitably have become hard of hearing as part or the normal ageing process, whereas in this case the claimants may not have developed VWF had exposure ceased after 1975, that there should be no apportionment of damages between pre- and post-1975 vibration. Further, there should be no apportionment between tortious and non-tortious vibration after 1975 since the nature of sub-clinical damage places it in the category of *de minimis*.

Armstrong v British Coal Corpn

(1997) 8 Med LR 259, CA

[6.59] Nine claims were selected as lead claims representing 25,000 similar claims against British Coal brought by employees who developed VWF.

The trial judge found that British Coal should have recognised by 1 January 1973 that working with vibratory tools gave rise to a foreseeable risk of

VWF. By 1 January 1975, British coal should have issued warnings and should have introduced a system for surveillance and routine examinations. By 1 January 1976, British Coal should have introduced a system of job rotation.

On the issue of what standard should have been applied to determine the point at which job rotation should have been introduced, the trial judge rejected the standards set out in DD43, a draft document for the development of a British Standard which was the only guidance available in the 1970s, as setting too low a standard. Further guidance was issued in 1986 by the International Organisation for Standards: ISO 5349, *Guidelines for The Measurement and Assessment of Human Exposure to Hand-transmitted Vibration* and in 1987 by the British Standards Institute: BS6842, *Guide to Measurement and Evaluation of Human Exposure to Vibration Transmitted to the Hand* which replaced DD43, in 1989 (ISO 5349) and 1991 (BS 7482).

Before the Court of Appeal, British Coal conceded that the trial judge's decision on this issue should not be set aside. The judge held that the appropriate standard was that set out in the 1994 HSE booklet, 'Hand-Arm Vibration'. In the course of identifying hazardous work and assessing risk, the vibration 'dose' should be measured:

> Vibration 'dose' received by the worker over a typical working day depends on the duration of exposure as well as the vibration magnitude. To allow different patterns to be compared, they are adjusted or 'normalised' to a standard reference period of 8 hours, however long the actual exposure period (para 8).
>
> 'Programmes of preventive measures and health surveillance are recommended where workers' exposure regularly exceeds an A8 of 2.8 m/s2 (para 21) (as per BS 6842:1987).
>
> 'A preventive programme should control the risk of injury if introduced where there is regular prolonged use of tools likely to be hazardous, or where it is known that vibration exposure will exceed the actual level of [2.8 m/s2] (para 22).

HELD, on appeal: The judge's finding of liability was upheld. However, there is no logical reason to impose a duty to reduce all exposure to vibration that is more than *de minimis*. This would have been neither practicable nor reasonable. Although every member of the workforce using vibrating tools was exposed to the risk, only a small proportion would have gone on to develop the condition. In its early manifestations the injury was not very serious and adequate protection would have been provided by a proper warning and surveillance system.

Job rotation should have formed part of a preventive programme where it was or should have been known that vibration levels exceeded A8 2.8 m/s2. If they did so for any significant period, the fact that an individual employee's lifetime average exposure fell below A8 2.8 m/s2 would not provide an unanswerable defence to the a claim in action.

Note the Court of Appeal's comment that

> this conclusion is not intended to lay down guidelines about appropriate levels of exposure in other employments. All it means is that when considering the reasonable safety of those employees exposed to vibrating tools the 1994 booklet provides a standard which it would have been reasonable for the defendants as prudent employers to apply when considering the appropriate level of exposure.

See also *Walker v Wabco*, below in this context.

When considering the warning that should have been given, the terms of the warning must be considered in the context of the practical realities of work in the coal industry. A warning to avoid a problem after it has developed is usually too late. However, in the case of VWF, even after blanching has occurred there is no interference with work or social activities while it remains at stage 1. If caught then, the condition would improve without leaving long term problems. Moreover, in this industry, for many of the men who worked underground in great danger, the prospect of reporting a minor degree of tingling or a small amount of numbness at the end of a tough shift would be demeaning, and the same general approach would be taken by those working away from the immediate dangers underground but engaged in heavy exhausting activity.

To be valuable, warnings must be practical and useful, that is, they should be couched in terms which carry weight with the person or persons to whom they are given. A sensible warning in the context of VWF in the coal industry would have been to the effect, 'If you are working with vibrating tools and you notice that you are getting some whitening or discolouration of any of your fingers then in your own interests you should report this as quickly as possible. If you do nothing you could end up with some very nasty problems in both hands.'

Note—See also *Allen v British Rail Engineering [2001] EWCA Civ 942*, [2001] ICR 942, above.

Heyes v Pilkington Glass Ltd

[1998] PIQR P303, CA

[6.60] The claimant was employed by the defendant as a crane driver in the mid-1960s and from 1967 to 1985. From 1980 he developed VWF as a result of vibration inside the crane cabin. The defendant conceded that from 1976 onwards it knew or ought to have known that excessive exposure to vibration could cause VWF, but contended that this knowledge was confined to hand-operated power tools.

HELD, on appeal: The trial judge's finding of liability was overturned. This was a novel claim. There had never been a previous decision which established that there was a significant risk of injury from vibration for crane drivers. The relevant British Standard confined its recommendations to employers who employed operators of hand-operated power tools. There was virtually no evidence before the judge to suggest that the defendants had fallen below the conduct of a reasonable and prudent employer. Medical knowledge or that disseminated and available to industry generally did not claim or even suggest that the level of vibration from electrically operated cranes was likely to cause any upper limb disorder and still less VWF to the operators. The defendant was entitled to proceed on the basis that it had adopted a recognised and general practice of operating their gantry cranes which had been followed for a substantial period in similar circumstances without mishap. No previous incidents had occurred in their own factory or elsewhere. No complaint was made by any of their operators about any undue vibrations from any of their cranes. Commonsense or newer knowledge did not make the practice bad. The developing knowledge had been confined to hand-held tools. Neither machinery, still less heavy plant, had come under suspicion.

It is significant that the Health & Safety Executive have never considered the possibility, still less issued pamphlets making employers with electrically operated gantry cranes inside a factory aware of any risk or that precautions were called for. There was no evidence that the claimant was particularly susceptible to the risk of vibration.

Walker v Wabco Automotive UK Ltd

(1999) LTL, 11 May, CA

[6.61] The claimant was employed by the defendant as an assembly line worker from 1983 to 1995. In 1991 she moved to work in the compressor department, assembling Perkins and DAF compressors. The work was undertaken in a 4 week cycle, the first 2 weeks spent building the smaller components and the fourth week assembling the larger parts previously assembled. The claimant was required to hold greasy or oiled pieces in one hand and use a vibrating gun in the other on the bolts to assemble the finished product. The claimant would do this work for $7\frac{1}{2}$ hours per day plus a couple of hours overtime, and sometimes on a Saturday or Sunday.

Around the end of June 1991, the claimant developed symptoms of pins and needles in both hands. Her condition was diagnosed as carpal tunnel syndrome. She underwent a decompression operation in her right wrist in April 1993 and a further operation on her left wrist in 1994.

Although HSE advice about the A8 action level for exposure to vibration was not published until 1994, the judge held that there was sufficient information in HSE Guidance Note G60 on work-related upper limb disorders for the defendant to have been aware of problems arising from vibration in 1991.

HELD, on appeal: Applying *Heyes v Pilkington Glass*, the judge's decision on liability was overturned. G60 was too tentative a piece of guidance to justify the imposition of such a heavy a burden on the defendant.

G60 mentioned vibration as a factor to be considered in the context of work-related upper limb disorders but provided no assistance as to the amount or duration of exposure to vibration that was to be avoided. The defendant's evidence was that the claimant was exposed to vibration for 30 minutes per working day, that for that duration of exposure the vibration levels would have had to have been around A8 11 m/s2 in order to have the effect complained of, that the problems relating to carpal tunnel syndrome were not properly presented to employers until the publication of the HSE booklet in 1994 and that carpal tunnel syndrome was not added to the list of prescribed diseases in a context such as this until April 1993. The defendant had been using a well-tried system of work and the level of vibration to which the claimant was exposed was quite limited and did not reach the action level subsequently identified by the HSE in 1994 when they first gave employers detailed guidance about this particular risk. There had been no known instance of injury to any of the defendant's operatives from this method of working until the claimant made her complaint following her second operation in 1994. The claimant herself did not inform the defendant of the association of her condition with her work after her first operation in 1993.

Note—the trial judge had reduced the claimant's damages by one third for contributory negligence on this point.

King v Samsung Heavy Industries

(2002) LTL, 10 April, CA

[6.62] The claimant was employed by Samsung from August 1995 to April 1998, when he was made redundant. He was then employed by Thrall Europe from August to September 1998. In both employments he was exposed to vibration from hand-held power tools. Shortly after he commenced his employment with Thrall, he developed either VWF or carpal tunnel syndrome.

The trial judge held that the claimant's exposure to vibration was limited to approximately 5 minutes per day with Samsung but that he was required to use the tools in a different manner for three 40 minute sessions per day with Thrall. The judge concluded that he could not overlook the coincidence that the claimant had worked for Samsung for over two years but showed signs of carpal tunnel syndrome after working for Thrall for only a few days. The judge found Thrall but not Samsung liable.

HELD, on appeal: The judge's finding of liability was upheld. He was entitled to find that the vibration levels the claimant was exposed to at Thrall were unacceptable. Thrall's breach of duty was not necessarily the main or sole cause of the claimant's condition but it was a material factor contributing to the injury.

SENSITISATION CLAIMS

Legislation

CONTROL OF SUBSTANCES HAZARDOUS TO HEALTH REGULATIONS

[6.63] The 1988 Regulations came into force in 1993 and were replaced by the 1994 Regulations in January 1995. These have since been replaced by the 1999 Regulations and now the 2002 Regulations (in force from 21/11/02).

Generally, the regulations impose a duty to:
conduct and regularly review risk assessments (reg 6)
'prevent' as far as is reasonably practicable or 'adequately control' exposure to any 'substance hazardous to health' (reg 7)

Note—The regulations list the various control measures which must be considered. Whether or not the measures are 'adequate' depends on the substance in question. Certain substances have 'maximum exposure limits' which cannot be exceeded under any circumstances. These are further subdivided into 'short-term exposure limits' ('STEL') and 'long-term exposure limits' ('LTEL'). Others have been assigned an 'occupational exposure standard' which may in some circumstances be exceeded without breaching the regulations provided that prompt action is taken to remedy the situation. Those substances not specifically assigned a MEL or OES are nevertheless covered by the Regulations if they satisfy reg 2(1)(e) – ie, a substance which 'creates a hazard to the health of any person which is comparable with the hazards created' by the listed substances.

regularly maintain, examine and test control measures (such as ventilation systems, respiratory equipment and so on) (regs 8 and 9)

regularly monitor and record exposure levels (reg 10)

conduct pre-employment health screening (reg 11)

instruct and train employees in precautions to be undertaken to avoid exposure (reg 12).

Asthma

Ogden v Airedale Health Authority

(1996) 7 Med LR 153 (QBD, Judge Bentley QC) (X-ray chemicals)

[6.64] The claimant was employed as a radiographer in the X-ray department of the defendant's hospital from 1979 to 1991. In June 1987 (before the COSHH Regulations came into force) he developed sensitisation to X-ray chemicals, with symptoms of dry eyes and a sore throat, with further incidences of symptoms in March 1988 and 1991. Following the 1991 incident, he developed asthma.

HELD: The judge held that the chemicals were capable of having a sensitising effect and that staff were required to carry out duties involving a likelihood of exposure beyond recommended limits. The defendant knew that radiography staff were complaining of health problems and ought to have inquired as to the safety hazards associated with the chemicals and taken steps to control the fumes at source. They took little action until 1988, by which time the claimant had been sensitised.

Dugmore v Swansea NHS Trust

[2002] EWCA Civ 1689, [2003] 1 All ER 333 (latex gloves)

[6.65] The claimant was employed by the first defendant as a nurse at the Singleton Hospital from 1990 to December 1996. At some point between 1993 and 1995, she developed a Type I allergy to latex protein as a result of wearing powdered latex gloves in the course of her work. In June 1996, she suffered a serious reaction and was off work for three days. Following her return, she was supplied with vinyl gloves instead.

In January 1997, she went to work for the second defendant as a nurse in the in the Morriston Hospital, where she was also supplied with vinyl gloves. By this stage, her sensitivity was such that she suffered an anaphylactic attack whilst picking up an empty box which had previously contained powdered latex gloves.

HELD, on appeal: The trial judge's finding of liability against the first defendant was upheld.

Date of knowledge

[6.66] Both defendants ought to have been aware of the risk that latex gloves could sensitise their employees and give rise to skin problems, asthma and even anaphylaxis by 1 January 1997. In April 1996, the Medical Devices Agency had issued a bulletin, *Latex Sensitisation in the Health Care Setting (Use of Latex Gloves)*, which concluded that latex sensitisation had been recognised for many years, that there had been an increase in the number of reported cases and that health care establishments should implement a policy to disseminate information, encourage staff to seek guidance, make adequate occupational health facilities for staff and provide alternatives to latex based devices as necessary. However, the MDA did not issue mandatory advice until 1998. The Royal College of Nursing did not produce a report about it until 1999 and the Health & Safety Executive only circulated a leaflet in 2000. The expert evidence was that employers in the health care industry would be expected to look to the MDA for guidance. Following this guidance, it would take some months to put such a policy into place.

COSHH Regulations

[6.67] HELD, on appeal: The Court of Appeal upheld the claimant's appeal against the first defendant on the grounds that the COSHH Regulations 1988, reg 7 imposed strict liability. Latex is a substance 'which creates a hazard to the health of any person which is comparable with the hazard created' by the substances listed for purposes of the Regulations. Reg 7 imposed a duty to prevent exposure altogether, unless that was not reasonably practicable. Where prevention was not reasonably practicable, the hospital was under a secondary duty adequately to control the exposure and this duty was strict. The defence of reasonable practicability only qualifies the duty of total prevention. 'Adequate' is restrictively defined, the only relevant factors being the nature of the substance and the nature and degree of exposure generally. Reg 7(7) in the 1988 Regulations and Reg 7(11) in the 1994 Regulations: 'In this regulation 'adequate' means adequate having regard only to the nature of the substance and to the nature and degree of exposure to substances hazardous to health and 'adequately' shall be construed accordingly'.

There is no reference to reasonable foreseeability and it does not therefore matter that the hospital could not have foreseen that the claimant would develop such a reaction. Similarly, the duty is not dependent on what a risk assessment under reg 6 would have revealed the risk.

The purpose of the regulations is protective and preventive: they do not rely simply on criminal sanctions or civil liability after the event to induce good practice. They involve positive obligations to seek out the risks and take precautions against them. It is by no means incompatible with their purpose that an employer who fails to discover a risk or rates it so low that he takes no precautions against it should nevertheless be liable to the employee who suffers as a result.

In relation to the second defendant, by the time the claimant arrived, she had already been sensitised. The trial judge found that the hospital could not have done more than carry out blood tests to confirm the diagnosis, issue her with vinyl gloves and advise her to transfer to as latex free an environment as possible. There is no duty at common law to sack an employee with particular sensitivity who wants to take on the risk of carrying on working in what is for others a reasonably safe environment (see *Withers v Perry Chain Co Ltd* [1961] 1 WLR 1314, CA). It is difficult to say that the exposure was adequately controlled in the circumstances, because there were other less latex-laden environments to which she might have been transferred, however unwillingly. The difficulty is that the risk of anaphylactic attack would have remained wherever she had been. In the circumstances, it is difficult to hold that any breach of the regulations was causative of her attack.

Note—See also *Bilton v Fastnet Highlands Ltd* 1998 SLT 1323 (prawn sorter exposed to respirable prawn protein); and *Williams v Farne Salmon and Trout Ltd* 1998 SLT 1329 (exposure to salmonella bacteria in fish).

Per Nimmo Smith LJ, 1998 SLT 1329: The absolute nature of this duty is, in my view, made abundantly clear by the provisions of reg 7(1), which uses the word "ensure" in connection with the employer's duties, subject to a limited defence of reasonable practicability in respect of the duty to prevent the exposure of his employees to substances hazardous to health. The risk assessment provisions of reg 6(1), the monitoring provisions of reg 10(1) and (3), the surveillance provisions of reg 11(1) and the information, instruction and training provisions of reg 12(1) all seem to me to presuppose the actual or potential existence of an objectively verifiable state of affairs, and to place the onus on the employer to discover this, the better to ensure compliance with his absolute duty to protect his employees from exposure to substances hazardous to health.

This analysis was approved by the Court of Appeal in *Dugmore v Swansea NHS Trust*, above.

Note also *Naylor v Volex Group plc* (2003) LTL, 14 February (claimant's asthma caused by exposure to colophony fumes whilst soldering). The Court of Appeal held that the decision in *Dugmore v Swansea NHS Trust* in construing the effect of the COSHH Regulations was of general application and not distinguishable. The fact that the defendant had not received notice from the HSE to the effect that its earlier risk assessment procedure under reg 6 was unreliable was not a defence. In any event, the defendant was on notice of the potential unreliability of the risk assessment, a report from an environmental consultant having raised serious concerns. The defendant should have undertaken a further assessment under reg 6.

Dermatitis

[6.68] For examples of cases involving dermatitis, see
Holmes v Ashford [1950] 2 All ER 76, CA (hair dye – manufacturer);
Pape v Cumbria County Council [1992] 3 All ER 211 (detergents & cleaning solvents); and
Maddox v Rocky Horror London Ltd (1995) LTL, 6 June (ultraviolet grease paint).

WORK-RELATED UPPER LIMB DISORDER CLAIMS (WRULD)

Keyboard claims

Legislation

HEALTH & SAFETY (DISPLAY SCREEN EQUIPMENT) REGULATIONS 1992

[6.69] The Health and Safety (Display Screen Equipment) Regulations 1992 came into effect from 1 January 1993. They are backed by HSE Guidance on Regulations L26.

'Workstation' is given a broad meaning and covers not only computer/keyboard equipment but also the desk/other surface, chair, telephone and immediate work environment (reg 1).

Note that infrequent or occasional users of display screen equipment may not be covered. See the Guidance Note, paras 5 – 18 for guidance on who is a 'user' for the purposes of the Regulations.

Regulation 2   Duty to assess risks and review assessments regularly.
Regulation 3   Workstation to meet certain criteria, including screen specification, keyboard, desk/work surface, chair, leg space etc. (These requirements applied to new workstations from 1 January 1992. Workstations already in use as at 1 January 1993 did not have to comply until 31 December 1996 (reg 3(2)).)
Regulation 4   Duty to plan work routine (ensure regular breaks, varied tasks).
Regulation 6   Duty to provide health and safety training.
Regulation 7   Information to be given to employees in respect of risks arising from the use of the workstation.

For details of the standards against which a workstation will be assessed for the purposes of the Regulations, see the BSI publication *Ergonomics of Design & Use of Visual Display Terminals in Offices* BS 7179.

Cases

Mughal v Reuters

[1993] IRLR 571 (QBD, Judge Prosser QC)

[6.70] The claimant was employed as a journalist by Reuters between 1987 and 1989. Initially he worked as deputy news editor at the financial reporting unit, writing and editing stories and features which would be passed on to the equities desk for processing and then sent to Reuters' customers. He spent more than 50% of his time at his desk, using a computer with two keyboards. The claimant alleged that he received no advice about the safety of the keyboard, of the working posture he should adopt or of the need to take regular breaks from keyboard activity.

On 20 October 1988, the claimant was prescribed Temazepam, an anti-depressant, by his GP, who noted that the claimant was under pressure at work. Seven months later, the claimant was still taking Temazepam and his GP warned of the risks of dependency.

On 31 October 1988, the claimant reluctantly moved to a new position on the equities desk. There he had two screens and two keyboards on his desk, positioned differently to his previous workstation. The keyboards were on the edge of his desk at different heights. The desk was not adjustable although the chair was. The screen was adjustable but he had no footrest. The equities desk was a busy one. The claimant took breaks for tea and the toilet about every hour but irregularly. His typing speed was 60 to 80 words per minute and his key rate 30 to 40 words per minute.

Within a month the move, the claimant began to experience tingling and numbness in his fingers and hand, which then moved up his forearm. The symptoms became worse and on one occasion his left hand seized. His hands became swollen, as if pumped up with air. The nurse in the medical room at Reuters gave him painkillers and told him that his condition was linked to his use of the computer keyboard. The following day he told his union representative. He remained off work until the end of 1988. From that point on, the claimant complained constantly of pain in some part of his body. He was seen by many medical experts of different disciplines. Ultimately, his claim proceeded on the basis that he had developed 'repetitive strain injury' or 'RSI'.

HELD: The judge held that the claimant failed to establish either breach of duty or causation.

The judge reviewed the medical literature and the expert evidence, concluding that 'RSI' had no meaning as a medical term. Certain conditions such as tenosynovitis, peritendonitis crepitans, or epicondylitis have a definite pathology. The symptoms can be seen and the treatment set in motion. Each has attributable causes, some of which can be attributable to the patient's work. The judge was struck in this case by the almost glib use made by treating doctors and others involved in the claimant's treatment of a number of terms such as repetitive strain injury, repetitive strain syndrome, reflex sympathetic dystrophy, and sympathetically maintained pain. These do not denote a disease or diagnosis but are labels used to describe a complex social phenomenon with social, psychological and economic facets, in which claims for compensation for injury at work occur in epidemics which may be localised in one office or involve whole countries, for example, the Australian epidemic in the 1980s. The correct and logical approach is to define the disorder and then consider causation.

The judge further noted that it was difficult to see how any one position for any one individual could be regarded as the correct position for that individual. 'With each operator it has to be a case of trial and error as to comfort of position and, provided that British Standard equipment is provided or available, it is difficult to see what more an employer can do for the comfort and safety of employees'.

Amosu v Financial Times Ltd

(1998) LTL, 31 July (QBD, Kennedy J)

[6.71] Five journalists/sub-editors employed by the *Financial Times* claimed damages as a result of work-related upper limb disorders (tennis elbow, tendonititis, tenovaginitis, carpal tunnel syndrome and golfer's elbow) as a result of repetitive keyboard activity. The evidence was that the amount of keyboard activity increased following the introduction of 'EDWIN', new editing software, in 1998, with periods of particularly intense and continuous keyboard use of up to 3 hours in order to meet publishing deadlines.

Kennedy J held that, although the claimants had suffered transient aches and pains exacerbated by the stress and responsibility of their work and their anxieties over the introduction of the new system, they had failed to establish a compensatable condition. Although the defendant's occupational health physician had reached a diagnosis of RSI, this was based entirely on the claimants' own reported symptoms. There was no objective clinical evidence supporting the diagnosis. Contemporaneous medical records did not substantiate the later diagnoses of work-related upper limb disorders (WRULDs).

HELD: The judge accepted the defendant's medical expert's evidence that there was nothing in the medical literature indicating that VDU use is damaging to health *per se*.

The judge also held that the claimants had failed to show a breach of statutory or common law duty. The fact that claimants were occasionally required to use chairs with broken gas lifts and did not have document holders provided was insufficient for a finding of liability.

Pickford v Imperial Chemical Industries plc

[1998] 1 WLR 1189, HL

[6.72] The claimant was a full-time secretary employed by ICI between 1984 and September 1990. She worked a 7-hour day from 10am to 6pm with a lunch break of 30 minutes. Approximately 50% of her working time was spent typing with the remainder taken up with other secretarial duties (phone calls, filing, photocopying and the like). Between late 1988 and April/May 1989, her typing load increased to the point where it took up around 75% or her working day.

The claimant first complained of pain in her hands in May 1989 and was signed off work. Neither her GP nor the works doctor nor a consultant orthopaedic surgeon could find a physical cause for her symptoms. After returning to work for 3 days in May 1990, she again went off sick and her employment was terminated in September 1990.

The claimant alleged that she had developed prescribed disease A4 ('writer's cramp'). The evidence before the court was that a precise cause of the condition had yet to be established and medical opinion was divided as to whether the condition was 'organic' (ie physical in origin) or 'psychogenic' (ie psychological in origin).

HELD, ON APPEAL: ICI's appeal upheld (Lord Slynn dissenting), restoring the trial judge's decision. The cause of PDA4 might be organic or psychogenic in nature or a combination of both, but in this case the claimant had failed to satisfy him that her symptoms were organic and caused by typing work. The burden of proof was on the claimant to establish the cause of her condition.

The trial judge's finding that it was not reasonably foreseeable that a secretary working to the same work regime as the claimant would be likely to suffer from the condition should not be interfered with. There was no duty to warn the claimant of the risk of developing PDA4 as this was not the practice the in industry at the time and such warnings could be counter productive precipitating the condition it was intended to avoid. Further, there was no duty on ICI to specify rest breaks as the claimant's work was sufficiently varied to allow her to rotate between typing and non typing duties. An employee of the claimant's intelligence and experience would do so without being told.

Alexander v Midland Bank plc

[1999] IRLR 723, CA

[6.73] The five claimants were employed by Midland Bank as part-time data encoders from 1990 to 1992. Their duties were to encode details of cheques and voucher transactions, keying in the relevant information using the right hand keypad. The evidence was that the work required a high degree of both speed and accuracy. Minimum target rates were set, requiring the processing of 1,350 to 1,500 fields per hour depending on the type of work, each field requiring up to 11 keystrokes. There was evidence that local management encouraged encoders to exceed their targets and that fully-trained encoders achieved an average of 2,123 fields per hour (12,700 keystrokes/hr).

The work rate increased in late 1990. Work was brought directly to the operator, a 'no talking' rule introduced and computer chips installed in the encoders to monitor start, finish and breaks from encoding and reduce the need for certain non-keying tasks. In January 1992 the 15 minute tea break was reduced to 10 minutes. An independent ergonomic report commissioned by the bank was critical of the lack of breaks from encoding work.

There was evidence that management encouraged competition between encoders. Each month the 3 most successful encoders' names were put on the 'excellent board'. Encoders were grouped in teams and team performance displayed and set out in a 'league table of achievement' sent out to all centres. Those that failed to meet the minimum standard faced redundancy.

In 1991 the claimants developed pain in their necks, right arms, wrists and hands and were subsequently diagnosed as suffering from 'regional fibro-myalgia', a diffuse condition with no precise pathology. Initially the pain amounted to a transient discomfort but subsequently became sufficiently persistent and intense to amount to a compensatable injury. The trial judge accepted the claimants' medical expert's evidence that it was not possible to identify a precise cause as medical science was unable to explain the precise causes of pain.

HELD, on appeal: The trial judge's decision in favour of the claimants was upheld. The trial judge was entitled to find that the bank was in breach of its duty in failing to ensure the claimants adopted a correct posture and in failing to provide adequate breaks. There was abundant evidence that the bank was aware of the risk of injury but that awareness had not reached those in charge of the claimants' work centre.

On the issue of medical causation, the Court of Appeal held that the judge was entitled to prefer the evidence of the claimants' medical expert that diffuse fibromyalgia is physically based. Even if the condition were shown to be psychogenic, that does not mean that damages are irrecoverable, although it may be impossible for a claimant to establish a causal link between the breach of duty and the injury.

McPherson v LB Camden London Borough

(1999) LTL, 24 May, QBD (Judge Anthony Thornton QC)

[6.74] The claimant was employed in the defendant's housing department from 1980 until her medical retirement on 14 August 1994. She was responsible for arranging accommodation for homeless families and her duties involved liaising with hostels and bed and breakfasts.

In June 1993, the claimant's section was merged with another and the claimant promoted to senior administration and accommodation officer. She was required to use a computer for the first time to prepare procedures and reports and to send and receive email. Keyboard work took up significantly in excess of 50% of her working day from June to December 1993 and approximately 50% in January 1994. Her evidence was that she used her left thumb frequently to depress the left shift key on the keyboard.

In mid-January 1994 the claimant developed intense pain in her left thumb with pain shooting towards her left elbow and neck. She was diagnosed as suffering from De Quervain's tenosynovitis.

HELD: The judge found the local authority to be in breach of the DSE Regulations, reg 2 (see paragraph 6.48 above). No assessment or workplan of any kind was undertaken by the defendant on setting up the workstation. A suitable and sufficient risk assessment would have identified the need for a wrist rest and a flat keyboard, an appropriate posture, a 10 minute break from keyboard activity every hour and avoiding use of the keyboard for more than 50% of the working day. Had the claimant been given the advice, she would have followed it.

The judge accepted the claimant's medical expert's evidence that De Quervain's tenosynovitis can be caused by keyboard work, rejecting the evidence of the defendant's expert based on new Australian studies to the contrary on the grounds it had not been raised before trial.

> *Note*—See also *Conaty v Barclays Bank plc (6 April 2000*, unreported), Central London County Court (Michael Rich QC) for a similar case: claimant bank employee developed DeQuervain's tenosynovitis. Although the defendant's

medical expert produced evidence suggesting keyboard work involved insufficient force to cause the condition, the judge accepted that, in the absence of other identifiable cause to explain the onset of symptoms, it was more probable than not that it was caused by the claimant's work.

Gallagher v Bond Pearce

[2001] CLY 1668 (Judge Tyzack QC, Bournemouth County Court) Leave to appeal was refused by both HH Judge Tyzack QC and the Court of Appeal.

[6.75] The claimant was employed by Bond Pearce as a legal secretary in the firm's commercial department from 1986 to November 1995 when her employment was medically terminated. Her duties involved typing commercial agreements, correspondence and other documents. The evidence was that it was a particularly busy department and that the claimant spent over $5\frac{1}{2}$ hours per day engaged in keyboard work.

In 1992 Bond Pearce carried out a health and safety audit which identified the need for a document holder and footrest, that the claimant's chair needed to be replaced and blinds needed to be fitted to her window. The document holder and footrest were provided around 12 months after the audit. No other changes to the claimant's work were made.

From August 1994, the claimant began to do overtime on Wednesday evenings at a different workstation in addition to her normal work. The evidence was that this consisted of an old wooden desk in a basement, a chair that was too high and no footrest. Around the same time she began to experience aches and pains in her hands and wrists. The claimant informed the personnel manager who told her to see her GP.

By January 1995 she was experiencing stabbing pains in her shoulders whenever she used a keyboard. She was signed off work by her GP for 4 weeks. On her return, she was given a revised timetable incorporating specific breaks and different types of work. She was still required her to do around $5\frac{1}{2}$ hours of typing per day and her symptoms persisted. In June she was moved to the marketing department. On 13 June 1995, her GP diagnosed a repetitive strain injury (RSI) and in November 1995 her employment was terminated.

HELD: The judge found Bond Pearce to be in breach of the Health and Safety (Display Screen Equipment) Regulations 1992. The 1992 audit was inadequate in that the claimant was not given training as required by regulation 6 nor was she informed that it was for the purposes of a workstation assessment. The delay in providing a document holder and footrest constituted a breach of regulation 3 and paragraph 42 of the Guidance Notes to the regulations requiring 'immediate steps to reduce the risk'. Throughout, Bond Pearce failed to ensure the claimant took regular rest breaks, contrary to regulation 4. No assessment was undertaken of the workstation used for overtime work from August 1994 (reg 2).

The judge accepted the claimant's medical expert's diagnosis of a 'diffuse Type 2 work-related upper limb disorder' which was essentially organic characterised by diffuse pain, but with no apparent pathology. He held that the initial trigger was the deficient overtime workstation but that other factors contributing to the development of actual injury in January 1995 included tight deadlines, a heavy workload, poor posture, absence of proper breaks, an absence of changes in working routine and Mrs. Gallagher's own vulnerability.

> *Note*—For a further example of a keyboard case involving factors other than keystroke rate, see *Hadoulis v Trinatours Ltd* ((2002) LTL, 1 October, Recorder Warren QC, Central London CC) (claimant travel agent; alleged combination long working hours without a break, poor posture exacerbated by position of desk leg and failure to warn/provide information about the risk of injury caused her to develop fibro-myalgia; judge accepted breach of regs 2 (duty to assess workstation) and 6 and 7 (duty to provide health and safety information) of the *DSE Regulations* but held that the claimant failed on the evidence to establish that these breaches caused her condition.

Manual processes

Legislation

[6.76] The Manual Handling Operations Regulations 1992 came into effect from 1 January 1993. They are backed by HSE Guidance on Regulations L23.

Note that 'manual handling operation' is defined broadly to mean 'any transporting or supporting of a load (including the lifting, putting down, pushing, pulling, carrying or moving thereof) by hand or bodily force' (but compare the decision in *Gissing v Walkers Smith Snack Foods*, below).

Regulation 4 imposes the following duties:

> 4(1)(a) As far as reasonably practicable, to avoid the need for manual handling operations involving a risk of injury.

> Note—In *Koonjul v Thameslink Healthcare BHS Services* [2000] PIQR P123, CA, Hale LJ stated that for a court to consider what was meant by 'risk' in accordance with reg.4 of the Regulations, it was necessary to reach the conclusion that an injury was really foreseeable and was not just a possibility.

> 4(1)(b)(i) Undertake a suitable and sufficient assessment of manual handling operations.

> 4(1)(b)(ii) Take 'appropriate steps' to reduce the risk of injury to the lowest level reasonably practicable.

> 4(1)(b)(iii) Provide training in correct lifting and manual handling techniques.

> 4(2) Review any assessment if there is reason to suspect it is no longer valid or there is a significant change in the manual handling operation to which it relates.

> Regulation 5 imposes a duty on an employee to 'make full and proper use' of systems introduced in compliance with reg 4(1)(b)(ii).

Cases

[6.77] For an example of a WRULD claim pre-dating the Manual Handling Operations Regulations, see *Burgess v Thorn Consumer Electronics (Newhaven) Ltd* (1983) Times, 16 May, in which the employer was liable for failure to pass on warnings in guidance notes from Department of Employment concerning risk of tenosynovitis in assembly line workers.

Mountenay v Bernard Matthews plc

(1994) 5 Med LR 293 (Judge Mellor, Central London CC)

[6.78] This case involved nine claimants who were employed at two sites owned and operated by Bernard Matthews for the production of turkeys. Their duties involved working on production lines covering killing and evisceration, bagging and boxing and the further cutting and processing of turkeys. The claimants were diagnosed as suffering a range of symptoms – tenosynovitis, trigger thumb, De Quervain's tenosynovitis, carpal tunnel syndrome and 'work-related upper limb disorder' or 'repetitive strain injury'.

The judge considered Bernard Matthews' duty in the context of its knowledge of the risks of developing an upper limb disorder, noting that tenosynovitis had been a prescribed disease (PD 34) for national insurance purposes since 1948, the HSE had issued 'Guidance Note MS10 on Beat Conditions: Tenosynovitis' in 1977 and Bernard Matthews had particular knowledge of the risks as Europe's largest producer of turkey products.

HELD: The judge held that, although Bernard Matthews had issued a notice informing employees of the need to report symptoms as soon as they occurred and of the need for early treatment tenosynovitis in 1983 and had introduced some job rotation, the warning should have gone further and a formal system of job rotation enforced. The warnings should have been sufficient to give workers an opportunity to make an informed choice as to whether to undertake work that involved a risk of RSI as well as requiring them to report symptoms. They should have been given to prospective employees as well as existing employees in the event of a transfer to a job with a known risk of RSI. Further, Bernard Matthews should have ensured new employees were introduced to repetitive work gradually and have been alert to signs of symptoms.

The judge awarded compensation in each case, accepting that pain was 'harm' for the purposes of deciding compensation, regardless of whether its cause was physical or psychological.

Foster v National Power plc

(1997) LTL, 7 May (sorting papers)

[6.79] The claimant was employed by the defendant sorting papers. She developed epicondylitis affecting both elbows. At first instance National Power was found liable on the basis that it should have foreseen the risk. National Power appealed on the grounds that it could not reasonably have been expected to act instantly in response to the publication of the HSE publication relied on by the claimant. The appeal was withdrawn prior to judgment.

Note—See also *Henderson v Wakefield Shirt Co Ltd* [1997] PIQR P413 (WRULD) (pressing shirts), above.

Coley v Securicor

(1998) LTL, 3 February, CA

[6.80] The claimant was employed by Securicor as a part-time cashier from 1978 to March 1995. Her duties involved counting bank notes by hand. The evidence was that she would sit at a table holding a pile of notes in her left hand and use the middle or index finger of her right hand to flick the corners of the notes into her left hand, counting the notes as she did so. She worked 24 hours per week. From August 1990 she volunteered to work additional hours, averaging 42 hours per week until July 1991 when she reverted back to 24 hours per week.

In Christmas 1990, she developed 'trigger finger' affecting her right middle finger, causing it to lock in a flexed position and flick straight when released.

Ergonomic evidence suggested that the work itself would not normally be considered to create a significant risk, although the ergonomists themselves would have issued the claimant with a warning prior to taking on increased hours as a precaution.

HELD, on appeal: The judge's decision that the claim failed on foreseeability was upheld. Nothing in the HSE publications issued prior to 1991 alerted employers to a risk associated with this type of work. Although the ergonomists would themselves have issued a warning to the claimant, the judge was correct to find that this was not the test for determining what standard of care was to be expected of a reasonable employer.

Gissing v Walkers Smith Snack Foods Ltd

[1999] CLY 3983 (Judge Heath, Lincoln County Court)

[6.81] The claimant was employed as a packer. On 14 May 1994 he was tasked to work on a packaging machine producing crisp packets at a rate of 57 bags per minute (3,000 bags per hour) over the course of a 12 hour shift. He had previously worked on the machine without apparent problems for 6 weeks in summer 1993. The evidence was that he would pick up the packets of crisps in one hand, transfer them to the other hand and pack them in boxes of 48.

The medical evidence was that the claimant had developed either tenosynovitis or per-tendinitis crepitans.

HELD: The judge held that the work was rapid and repetitive but did not involve a significant degree of force. The Manual Handling Operations Regulations 1992 did not apply, as they were neither aimed nor directed at this type of work.

Even if the Regulations did apply, Walkers were not in breach. The risk involved was low. It was not reasonably practicable for the work to have been carried out in any other way. The evidence showed that claimant had been fully trained, he had undergone a satisfactory probationary period and had worked on the machine before. The claimant had been warned about the risks and signed a health warning upon commencement of work.

Spencer v Boots the Chemist Ltd

(2002) 146 Sol Jo LB 215, CA

[6.82] The claimant was employed as a pharmacist and store manager from 1970 to April 1997. His duties included dispensing medicines under prescription. The evidence was that he would check the doctor's prescription against the stock bottles, either place the stock bottle in the returns tray or throw it away (if empty), put the medicines in a bag and put the bag out for reception staff to deliver to customers. The counter at which the claimant worked was small (1200mm × 1000mm high × 600mm deep) and he shared this space with a second pharmacist. The returns tray was on a shelf above the counter. The claimant's evidence was that he would complete 250 prescriptions involving on average $2\frac{1}{2}$ items over a $6\frac{1}{2}$ hour shift over the course of an average day. This would equate 90 seconds checking and 37 seconds handling time on average per item.

No manual handling assessment had been carried out.

Following a busy period over Christmas 1996, the claimant developed pericapsulitis affecting his left shoulder.

HELD, on appeal: The trial judge's finding in favour of Boots was upheld. Although the layout of the counter required the claimant to raise his left arm above shoulder height in cramped conditions when replacing stock bottles, the weight of the bottles did not give rise to a foreseeable risk of injury. The judge correctly found that, as far as reasonably practicable, Boots had complied with the Manual Handling Operations Regulations.

OCCUPATIONAL STRESS

Pre-Hatton

Walker v Northumberland CC

[1995] 1 WLR 737 (QBD, Colman J)

[6.83] The claimant was employed as an area social services officer from 1970 to December 1987. He was responsible for managing four teams of social services fieldworkers in an area with a high incidence of child care problems and a growing population. The increasing incidence of child abuse cases was particularly stressful. Despite a growing caseload, the number of available fieldworkers remained static after 1978 and by 1986 the pressure on fieldworkers was considerable.

The claimant suffered a nervous breakdown in November 1986 with symptoms of mental exhaustion, acute anxiety, headaches, sleeplessness, irritability, inability to cope with any form of stress, and a tendency to weep and become upset. He remained off work on his doctor's advice until March 1987. He had no previous history of mental disorder.

Following a meeting with his superior, he agreed to return to work on the basis that he would be provided with assistance in his duties as area officer by a principal fieldwork officer and from other area officers in chairing case conferences in child abuse cases. It was also agreed that his superior would visit him weekly. However, within a month of the claimant's return he was informed that the assistance promised was not available. There were no visits from his superior. Further, the claimant had to deal with a considerable backlog of cases which had built up during his absence. In the meantime, the number of pending cases rose from 148 to 174 between March and July 1987.

The claimant suffered further symptoms of stress. He took two weeks' holiday in August 1987 and shortly after his return ceased work on his doctor's advice. He was dismissed on the grounds of ill-health in February 1988.

HELD: That the local authority was not liable for the first breakdown in November 1986 as it was not reasonably foreseeable that the claimant would suffer psychiatric injury. There was no evidence that the council had previously encountered stress-induced mental illness in its area officers or that others in middle management were particularly vulnerable.

However, the local authority was liable for the second breakdown in September 1997. Following the claimant's return to work, the authority was on notice that the claimant was at risk of mental illness should he be exposed to the same workload. In failing to provide the additional assistance identified, the local authority fell below the standard of care required.

For examples of decisions after *Walker*, see:
Maryniak v Thomas Cook Group Ltd (LTL 1/7/99, Northampton County Court) (claimant manager of a travel agency; alleged harassment from his regional manager; breakdown held to be unforeseeable);
Cowley v Mersey Regional Ambulance NHS Trust (LTL 23/10/01, QBD) (claimant senior manager of regional ambulance service; alleged demanding workload and harassment from chief executive caused two breakdowns; defendant liable for second breakdown having been informed of risk by doctor's letter);
Garret v Camden LBC (LTL 3/4/01) (CA) (claimant council worker; alleged his role systematically undermined, harassment, intimidation etc as a result of his 'whistleblowing'; claim failed on the facts);
Young v The Post Office [2002] EWCA Civ 661, LTL 30/4/02 (CA) (claimant workshop manager; alleged stress and overwork following introduction of new computer system; following first breakdown, flexible working plan agreed but not followed through; second breakdown foreseeable).
Johnson v Unisys 2001 IRLR 279 HC, see paragraph 8.138. Claim for psychiatric damage arising from the manner of dismissal failed. There was no common law remedy for such a dismissal – Parliament had provided for a statutory scheme.

Post-Hatton

Hatton v Sutherland

[2002] 2 All ER 1

[6.84] *Hatton* is a landmark decision in this area. It involved four co-joined appeals. At the time of writing, an appeal from the decision in relation to *Barber* to the House of Lords is awaited.

FACTS

[6.85] Mrs Hatton was employed by the defendant school as a French teacher from 1980 until her retirement on the grounds of ill-health in August 1996. She was signed off in October 1995 for depression after which she never returned to work.

The evidence was that her workload was no greater than that of any other teacher in the school. Although there was some additional preparatory work required by the change to a modular-based course system in 1992, Mrs Hatton did not complain at the time and the effects of the new system were fully absorbed by September 1994. Similarly, any additional workload caused by the use of supply teachers/English teachers ended with the appointment of a new head of department in September 1994, a year before her breakdown.

Mrs Hatton had previous episodes of depression. She had two months off work following the break-up of her marriage. In January 1994 she was off work for one month following an attack in the street. In April 1994 one of her sons was in hospital for a considerable period and she was off work for over a month. She saw a stress counsellor in August 1994 but did not tell the school.

HELD, on appeal: The claim failed.

Barber v Somerset County Council

[6.86] Mr Barber was employed as a maths teacher and Head of Maths from 1984 to November 1996, when he ceased work on his doctor's advice. He accepted early retirement in March 1997.

The evidence was that the school was in a deprived area, its roll had more than halved between the mid-1980s and mid-1990s and resources had fallen accordingly. Under a restructuring plan, Mr Barber, along with the other heads of department, became an 'area of experience co-ordinator' in September 1995. As a result he took sole responsibility for management of the maths department. He also took on the role of project manager in charge of publicity and media relations. He was working long hours but his workload was not so extreme as to put the school on notice that his health was at risk.

Mr Barber developed depressive symptoms during the autumn term 1995 but told no one at the school. In May 1996 he had 3 weeks off work with depression. On his return, he told the headteacher and deputy head that he was finding things difficult, that he could not cope and that the situation was becoming detrimental to his health.

228 *Industrial Diseases Claims*

He did not mention his symptoms of weight loss, lack of sleep and out of body experiences.

At the beginning of the autumn term 1996, the headteacher expressed concern for Mr Barber and asked a colleague to keep an eye on him. The evidence was that there was no indication at this stage that the problems he had identified before the summer holidays were continuing. In October 1996, Mr Barber raised his symptoms with his doctor for the first time. In November 1996 he lost control in the classroom and was advised to stop work immediately.

HELD, on appeal: That it was difficult to identify a point at which the school came under a duty to take positive steps and the claim failed.

Jones v Sandwell Metropolitan Borough Council

[6.87] Mrs Jones was employed as an administrative assistant at a local authority training centre from August 1992 to January 1995 when she went off sick with anxiety and depression. She was made redundant when the centre closed at the end of 1996.

Mrs Jones' position was unique and resulted from a consolidation of training activities on one site. Her duties included submitting monthly claims to the local Training and Enterprise Council. Her tasks were varied and the deadlines tight. The evidence was that she worked far in excess of her contracted 37 hours per week.

Mrs Jones complained of over-work to her immediate manager, who dismissed her complaint and threatened her with loss of her job if she continued to complain. She then complained to head office who promised additional help. The extra help was earmarked for her but diverted by her immediate manager to other tasks. In July 1994, Mrs Jones sent a detailed memo to the personnel officer listing her problems under 'health', 'excessive workload', 'managerial disagreements'. She was again promised extra help but none was provided.

In November 1994, Mrs Jones invoked the grievance procedure but went off sick before the grievance hearing could take place.

HELD, on appeal: The judge's finding in the claimant's favour was confirmed. The combination of the way in which she was treated by her immediate manager, her formal complaints about it and the fact that the need for extra help was identified on two occasions but none was provided made her injury foreseeable.

Bishop v Baker Refractories Ltd

[6.88] Mr Bishop worked in the defendant's factory from 1979 to February 1997, when he had a mental breakdown and attempted suicide. He did not return to work and was dismissed in 1998.

Baker Refractories was taken over by an American company in 1992 and production reorganised. New shift patterns were introduced and employees expected to perform a greater variety of tasks. Mr Bishop's tasks of mixer cleaning and graphite blowing were spread among other employees and Mr Bishop given new duties involving receiving and distributing raw materials.

Mr Bishop had difficulty coping with his new role. He complained to his foreman, who told him there was nothing he could do as his old job did not exist any more. Mr Bishop saw his GP in November 1996 and was advised to change his job. He did not tell anyone at work of this. He was off work from 24 January to 16 February 1997, some of which was due to being off shift and some authorised by his doctor's certificate which stated the reason to be 'neuroasthenia'. On his return, Mr Bishop worked a further two days, was then off shift and returned to work on 24 February. His breakdown took place the following day.

HELD, on appeal: That Mr Bishop's condition was not reasonably foreseeable and the claim failed. There was nothing unusual, excessive or unreasonable about the demands placed on Mr Bishop. He did not tell his employers of his doctor's advice. The sickness certificates were not such clear signs that a reasonable employer would have realised that something had to be done. Even if they had been, there was nothing the employer could have done as the job he wanted was no longer available.

SUMMARY OF REASONS

[6.89] Per Hale LJ:
(1) There are no special control mechanisms applying to claims for psychiatric (or physical) illness or injury arising from the stress of doing the work the employee is required to do. The ordinary principles of employer's liability apply.
(2) The threshold question is whether this kind of harm to this particular employee was reasonably foreseeable: this has two components (a) an injury to health (as distinct from occupational stress) which (b) is attributable to stress at work (as distinct from other factors).
(3) Foreseeability depends upon what the employer knows (or ought reasonably to know) about the individual employee. Because of the nature of mental disorder, it is harder to foresee than physical injury, but may be easier to foresee in a known individual than in the population at large. An employer is usually entitled to assume that the employee can withstand the normal pressures of the job unless he knows of some particular problem or vulnerability.
(4) The test is the same whatever the employment: there are no occupations which should be regarded as intrinsically dangerous to mental health.
(5) Factors likely to be relevant in answering the threshold question include:
   (a) The nature and extent of the work done by the employee. Is the workload much more than is normal for the particular job? Is the work particularly intellectually or emotionally demanding for this employee? Are demands being made of this employee unreasonable when compared with the demands made of others in the same or comparable jobs? Or are there signs that others doing this job are suffering harmful levels of stress? Is there an abnormal level of sickness or absenteeism in the same job or the same department?
   (b) Signs from the employee of impending harm to health. Has he a particular problem or vulnerability? Has he already suffered from illness attributable to stress at work? Have there recently been frequent or prolonged

absences which are uncharacteristic of him? Is there reason to think that these are attributable to stress at work, for example because of complaints or warnings from him or others?

(6) The employer is generally entitled to take what he is told by his employee at face value, unless he has good reason to think to the contrary. He does not generally have to make searching enquiries of the employee or seek permission to make further enquiries of his medical advisers.

(7) To trigger a duty to take steps, the indications of impending harm to health arising from stress at work must be plain enough for any reasonable employer to realise that he should do something about it.

(8) The employer is only in breach of duty if he has failed to take the steps which are reasonable in the circumstances, bearing in mind the magnitude of the risk of harm occurring, the gravity of the harm which may occur, the costs and practicability of preventing it, and the justifications for running the risk.

(9) The size and scope of the employer's operation, its resources and the demands it faces are relevant in deciding what is reasonable; these include the interests of other employees and the need to treat them fairly, for example, in any redistribution of duties.

(10) An employer can only reasonably be expected to take steps which are likely to do some good: the court is likely to need expert evidence on this.

(11) An employer who offers a confidential advice service, with referral to appropriate counselling or treatment services, is unlikely to be found in breach of duty.

(12) If the only reasonable and effective step would have been to dismiss or demote the employee, the employer will not be in breach of duty in allowing a willing employee to continue in the job.

(13) In all cases, therefore, it is necessary to identify the steps which the employer both could and should have taken before finding him in breach of his duty of care.

(14) The claimant must show that that breach of duty has caused or materially contributed to the harm suffered. It is not enough to show that occupational stress has caused the harm.

(15) Where the harm suffered has more than one cause, the employer should only pay for that proportion of the harm suffered which is attributable to his wrongdoing, unless the harm is truly indivisible. It is for the defendant to raise the question of apportionment.

(16) The assessment of damages will take account of any pre-existing disorder or vulnerability and of the chance that the claimant would have succumbed to a stress related disorder in any event.'

Cases decided post-Hatton

Pratley v Surrey County Council

[2002] EWHC 1608, (2002) LTL, 13 August

[6.90] The claimant was employed as a case manager for the elderly in the Surrey County Council's social services department from 1994 to September 1996, when she was diagnosed by her GP as suffering from 'stress' and did not return to work.

The evidence was that the claimant's work involved assessing the needs of elderly clients, formulating a plan and 'purchasing' the appropriate services or equipment. The office in which the claimant worked was under-staffed and under-resourced. Further, money was not available to provide services to the level both social workers and the public would have liked. Elderly clients sometimes remained occupying hospital beds, for which hospital staff blamed the case manager, sometimes in an abusive manner.

The claimant's evidence was that she regularly worked far in excess of her contracted 36 hours per week, taking work home in the evenings and on weekends. She did not tell her manager nor record all the additional time as required for 'time off in lieu'. She first suffered symptoms of stress in March 1996 and took two weeks off work. Her doctor recorded this as 'neuralgia' in the sickness certificate following the claimant's request that he make no reference to stress at work.

In August 1996 an additional 40 cases were to be transferred to the claimant in addition to her existing caseload of 110. She told her manager that she was having difficulty coping but did not say that her health was already suffering or that she had seen her GP. Her manager agreed to ask that a system for 'stacking' be introduced whereby new cases were not allocated immediately, to slow down new work. This had not been introduced by the time the claimant returned from summer holiday in September. The claimant worked for a further $2\frac{1}{2}$ days before going off sick.

HELD: The judge, applying the principles set out in *Hatton* (paragraph 6.84 above), held that the claimant's condition was not reasonably foreseeable. Until the medical certificate of September 1996, there was no clear indication that the claimant's health was at risk. The claimant herself did not go to her GP, the defendant's Occupational Health Department or make use of the counselling services available. The conversation in August 1996 reflected a concern for the future, should the claimant's workload not be reorganised. It was entirely reasonable for the claimant's manager to see how things were on the claimant's return from holiday before taking specific action.

Sparks v HSBC

(2002) LTL, 9 December, CA

[6.91] The claimant was employed by HSBC from 1969 until his retirement on ill-health grounds in June 1998. He first began to suffer from symptoms of depression in 1994 culminating in a breakdown in September 1995. He accepted an offer of a part-time role with fewer responsibilities and was rehabilitated by June 1996. Apart from a couple of instances in which cheques were incorrectly returned in autumn 1996 which led to a disciplinary appraisal, things seemed to be going well. In March 1997 the claimant was promoted to senior lending officer of the branch.

Around the same time, the claimant consulted his GP with chest pains and palpitations, which he associated with stress. He began to exhibit behaviour at work suggestive of stress, such as a short temper, banging the phone down and the like. In June 1997, his manager referred him to Occupational Health, who advised that the claimant would need to be supported at work.

At the beginning of August 1997, the claimant's superior went on holiday and the claimant was 'left to hold the fort' with no replacement provided. The claimant wrongly returned two business cheques that week, resulting in a disciplinary meeting, but the matter was taken no further. At the end of the week, he was signed off work by his GP for two months. A psychiatrist diagnosed him as suffering from moderate reactive depression.

The trial judge found that the claimant's condition was caused by his work but that the claimant had failed to prove that it was due to HSBC's negligence.

HELD, on appeal: The trial judge's decision was upheld. Although HSBC were negligent in failing to provide the support identified by their Occupational Health officer, the claimant's condition had developed some time before that and the claimant had failed to demonstrate an appreciable or measurable exacerbation.

Note—For a further example of a claim applying the principles set out in *Hatton*, see *Barlow v Borough of Broxbourne* [2003] EWHC 50, (2003) LTL, 24 January (claimant a senior operations manager of the defendant local authority's Direct Services Organisation; alleged bullying and harassment from late 1995 by the new Director of Services; claimant failed on the evidence to demonstrate either conduct amounting to 'bullying' or 'harassment' or that the conduct complained of was sufficient to put the defendant on notice of a risk to the claimant's health; the evidence was that the claimant had not appeared to be a vulnerable individual).

BULLYING AND HARASSMENT

Waters v Commissioner of Police of the Metropolis

[2000] 4 All ER 934, HL

[6.92] The claimant was a policewoman who alleged she had been sexually assaulted by a male colleague in police residential accommodation whilst both were off duty. She complained to her reporting Sergeant and other officers and brought proceedings before an industrial tribunal alleging sexual discrimination. She then issued proceedings for a stress-related psychiatric injury caused by the cumulative effects of her treatment by fellow officers, who she alleged had failed to support her, told her to leave the police force, excluded her from duties and the like because she had complained against a fellow officer.

The issue before the House of Lords was whether the claim should have been struck out by the Court of Appeal as disclosing no cause of action.

HELD: The claimant's appeal was upheld. Per Lord Slynn:

> If an employer knows that acts being done by employees during their employment may cause physical or mental harm to a particular fellow employee and he does nothing to supervise or prevent such acts, when it is in his power to do so, it is clearly arguable that he may be in breach of his duty to that employee...he may also be in breach of that duty if he can foresee that such acts may happen and if

they do, that physical or mental harm may be caused to an individual...if this sort of sexual assault is alleged (whether it happened or not) and the officer persists in making complaints about it, it is arguable that it can be foreseen that some retaliatory steps may be taken against the woman and that she may suffer harm as a result. Even if this is not necessarily foreseeable at the beginning it may become foreseeable or indeed obvious to those in charge at various levels who are carrying out the Commissioner's [ie the 'employer's] responsibilities that there is a risk of harm and that some protective steps should be taken.

Ellis v Eagle Place Services

[2002] EWHC 1201

[6.93] The claimant was a junior solicitor who alleged she developed a stress-related psychiatric injury following bullying and harassment by a senior partner. She alleged that he converted compassionate leave to holiday leave against her wishes at a time when he was aware of her grief over her mother's death, humiliated her by telling her she was a '9 to 5' person, would receive a nil pay review and that the review board would laugh at her proposals and accusing her of lying over a failure to return a client's phone call.

HELD: The judge held that the allegations were not supported by the evidence and that the claimant had not been bullied or harassed.

The judge noted that the legal test in claims for bullying/harassment following the Court of Appeal judgment in *Hatton*. In a bullying case the duty falls vicariously on the employer providing there is sufficient connection with the employment. So far as breach is concerned, there are two questions: (1) did the person doing the acts complained of know or ought to have known that there was a risk that what he was doing might cause harm; and (2) could he by exercising reasonable care have avoided it? In considering the allegations, it is necessary to consider the whole picture and the cumulative effect of any conduct upon the claimant paying particular regard to the claimant's condition at the date of any particular complaint. There is a danger that, by concentrating analytically on an individual act in isolation, its impact may become artificially and unfairly trivialised. There is a need to avoid a fragmented approach to the evidence.

Note—The line of authority dealing with claims for injury to feelings arising from a breach of the duty of mutual trust and confidence implied in the contract of employment as an alternative route to claiming damages for conditions falling short of a psychiatric injury: *McCabe v Cornwall County Council* [2002] EWCA Civ 1887, [2003] ICR 501, and *Eastwood v Magnox Electric plc* [2002] EWCA Civ 463, [2002] IRLR 447 (on appeal to HL).

CHAPTER 7

Race, Sex and Disability Discrimination

Direct race discrimination	[7.1]
'Less favourable' treatment	[7.2]
Racial grounds/racial group	[7.6]
Ethnic groups	[7.7]
Identifying an ethnic group in practice	[7.8]
National origins	[7.9]
Racial grounds	[7.10]
Discrimination on the grounds of another person's race	[7.14]
Religions as ethnic groups	[7.16]
Rastafarians	[7.17]
The importance of the discriminatory factor in the decision taken	
An appropriate comparator	[7.21]
Direct sex discrimination	[7.22]
Pregnancy and reasons connected with pregnancy	[7.24]
Failure to carry out a risk assessment	[7.30]
Sexual orientation discrimination	[7.31]
Indirect discrimination	[7.35]
Is full-time work the imposition of a requirement or condition?	[7.40]
'Considerably smaller proportion'	[7.42]
The meaning of 'can comply'	[7.46]
Detriment	[7.47]
Knowledge is not necessary for there to be a detriment	[7.48]
The pool for comparison	[7.49]
Justification	[7.50]
Discrimination on the grounds of gender reassignment	[7.55]
Establishing discriminatory treatment	[7.60]
Discrimination by others	[7.63]
Discrimination by 'qualifying bodies'	[7.66]
Continuing act versus one-off act of discrimination	[7.70]
Work ordinarily outside great britain	[7.74]
Freedom of Movement (EC Treaty, Art 48)	[7.75]
Genuine occupational qualification defence	[7.76]
Victimisation	[7.80]
Is there a need for conscious motivation?	[7.81]
Section 2(1)(b) of the RRA	[7.84]
Victimisation on the grounds of sex	[7.86]

Direct Race Discrimination 235

Instructions to discriminate and pressure to discriminate: Instructions to discriminate	[7.87]
Pressure to discriminate	[7.88]
Vicarious liability or direct liability for acts of employees	[7.90]
Post-employment victimisation	[7.96]
Aiding unlawful acts	[7.100]
Damages for injury to feelings and aggravated damages	[7.103]
Exemplary damages	[7.109]
Disability discrimination	[7.110]
Definition of disability	[7.111]
Physical impairment	[7.112]
Mental impairment	[7.115]
Functional overlay	[7.118]
Substantial and long-term adverse effect	[7.120]
Normal day-to-day activities	[7.123]
Can activities at work constitute normal day-to-day activities?	[7.127]
Progressive conditions	[7.129]
Knowledge of an employee's disability	[7.131]
Scope of the Act for employment purposes	[7.134]
The date at which to assess the question of disability	[7.137]
Small employer exemption	[7.140]
Discrimination against contract workers	[7.142]
Who is an appropriate comparator?	[7.144]
Redundancy selection arrangements	[7.146]
The obligation to make reasonable adjustments	[7.147]
Personal, non-job-related adjustments	[7.150]
Is it relevant that the applicant or advisers can think of no suitable alternatives?	[7.153]
Monetary benefits	[7.154]
Employer's duty when faced with non-co-operation by the employee	[7.155]
Justification	[7.156]
Does an employer need to know of the disability, to rely upon a justification defence?	[7.161]
The role of medical evidence and treatment	[7.162]
Damages	[7.166]
Constructive dismissal and disability discrimination	[7.167]
Post-employment victimisation	[7.168]

DIRECT RACE DISCRIMINATION

[7.1] Under the Race Relations Act 1976 (RRA), s 1:

(1) A person discriminates against another in any circumstances relevant for the provisions of this Act if:
(a) on racial grounds he treats that other less favourably than he treats or would treat other persons.

Under the Sex Discrimination Act 1975 (SDA), s 1:

(1) A person discriminates against another in any circumstances relevant for the provisions of this Act if:
(a) on the grounds of her sex he treats her less favourably than he treats or would treat a man.

'Less favourable' treatment

Birmingham City Council v Equal Opportunities Commission

[1989] AC 1155, HL

[7.2] Birmingham provided 600 places a year to voluntary aided schools. 390 places went to boys and 210 to girls. The EOC brought proceedings against Birmingham City Council alleging breach of SDA s 23(1). The High Court granted a declaration that Birmingham City Council were in breach of section 23(1) and the Court of Appeal dismissed the Council's appeal. Birmingham City Council appealed to the House of Lords.

HELD, on appeal: Dismissing the appeal, motive was not a relevant consideration for liability and that discrimination on the grounds of sex would take place if girls would have received the same treatment as boys but for their sex. It was not necessary to prove that selective education was better than non-selective education, it is sufficient that they were deprived of a choice which is valued by them.

Burrett v West Birmingham Health Authority

[1994] IRLR 7, EAT

[7.3] Ms Burrett was a nurse; both male and female nurses were required to wear a uniform and in some departments female nurses were required to wear cap. A ballot amongst the female nurses was in favour of retaining the cap. Ms Burrett did not like the cap because she thought it stereotypical and refused to wear it. As a result she was disciplined and transferred to another department where caps were not worn. Her transfer meant that she lost the opportunity of being regraded. She complained that she had been discriminated against because female but not male nurses were required to wear the cap. A tribunal rejected her complaint and she appealed to the EAT.

HELD: The tribunal had not erred. Male and female nurses were required to wear a uniform. The fact that the uniform differed and that she objected to wearing one part of it did not amount to less favourable treatment. Less favourable treatment does not require a subjective belief on the part of the applicant, it is an objective decision for the tribunal.

Stewart v Cleveland Guest (Engineering) Ltd

[1994] IRLR 440, EAT

[7.4] Miss Stewart was an inspector and her duties required her to go through the factory where calendars of nude and partially nude women were displayed. She complained to the works manager that the calendars were offensive. Her complaint was treated as trivial and she was told that the company were not going to do anything further. Her union became involved and the pictures were removed although a number of other women in the factory indicated that they did not regard the pictures as offensive. She learnt that the pictures had been removed and did not believe that her employers would protect her from taunts that would be directed at her and she claimed that she had been constructively dismissed and discriminated against on the grounds of sex discrimination. A tribunal found that she genuinely found the pictures offensive and that this was a detriment to her and that when the employers failed to deal with her complaint this was a further detriment to her. However, they held that she had not been discriminated against because the display of the pictures was not aimed at women. She appealed to the EAT.

HELD: The tribunal was correct. The pictures were neutral. They were not aimed at women and a man may equally have found them offensive. If he had complained his complaint would have been treated in a similar manner. There is room for disagreement about what is less favourable treatment. However, a tribunal is best placed to reach such decisions. An appeal should not be allowed simply because the EAT would have reached a different conclusion.

Sidhu v Aerospace Composite Technology Ltd

[2000] IRLR 602, CA

[7.5] On a day out organised by the employers the appellant, a Sikh, and his wife were racially abused by a fellow employee. The appellant was seen to wield a chair aggressively but said he did so in self-defence. An internal disciplinary hearing recommended both should be dismissed. The appellant appealed. Initially, the appeal committee were going to uphold the appeal but following a meeting with the managing director and company solicitor, it decided to confirm the dismissal. A tribunal upheld an unfair dismissal complaint but rejected his claim of racial discrimination because the dismissal decision was based on the company's approach to violent behaviour.

The EAT upheld his appeal. They found that the events had taken place in the course of employment and that the tribunal had been wrong to disregard the fact that the cause of the attack was racial and this amounted to racial conduct. The company appealed to the Court of Appeal

HELD, on appeal: The issue is whether less favourable treatment on racial grounds has been shown by the application of the policy to ignore the provocation and whether a comparator in similar circumstances would be treated less favourably. The company's policy was not directed specifically to racial matters and the tribunal was entitled to find that there had been no racial discrimination. Whilst the company's policy was misguided and unfair it did not amount to racial discrimination.

Racial grounds/racial group

[7.6] Race Relations Act 1976, s 3(1):

Racial grounds means any of the following grounds namely colour, race, nationality, or ethnic or national origins;

Racial group means a group of persons defined by reference to colour, race, nationality or ethnic or national origins and references to a person's racial group refer to any racial group into which he falls.

Ethnic groups

Mandla v Dowell Lee

[1983] IRLR 209, HL

[7.7] This was an appeal to the House of Lords from the decisions of the county court and the Court of Appeal that the Race Relations Act did not apply to Sikhs. The claim arose from the refusal of a private school to allow a Sikh child to wear a turban to school.

HELD, on appeal: The word 'ethnic' is not used in a racial or biological sense, and whilst it retains racial connotations, it extends to include other characteristics. For a group to be an ethnic group it must regard itself and be regarded as a separate group. There are some essential characteristics:
  i. a long shared history of which it is conscious as distinguishing it from other groups and the memory of which it keeps alive; and
  ii. a cultural tradition of its own.

Other non-essential characteristics are:
  iii. a common geographical origin or descent from a small number of ancestors; or
  iv. a common language, but not necessarily peculiar to it;
  v. a common literature;
  vi. a common religion different from those surrounding it; and
  vii. being a group, either a minority or majority within a larger community.

A person may belong to a particular racial group either by birth or adherence.

'Can comply' in section 1(1)(b)(i), means can comply consistently with the customs and cultural traditions of the racial group.

Per Lord Templeman: 'A group of persons defined by ethnic origins must possess some of the characteristics of a race, namely group, descent, a group of geographical origin and a group of history.'

IDENTIFYING AN ETHNIC GROUP IN PRACTICE

Commission for Racial Equality v Dutton

[1989] IRLR 8, CA

[7.8] The respondent was the licensee of a pub. He had in the past had unpleasant experiences with travellers and put out signs saying 'sorry, no travellers'. The signs were brought to the attention of the CRE. The CRE's complaint was that the signs discriminated against gypsies, a racial group. The CRE appealed to the Court of Appeal after the county court found that gypsies were not a racial or ethnic group.

HELD: There was no direct discrimination because the signs applied to travellers in a wider sense than just gypsies. Applying the *Mandla* conditions (see 7.7 above), Nicholls LJ concluded that gypsies were an ethnic group and that despite their long presence in England, there was some evidence that they had not lost their separate identity. A considerably smaller proportion of gypsies could comply with the 'no travellers' requirement than the rest of the population; and gypsies suffered a detriment as a result of the requirement. The ability to comply with a requirement is to be judged at the time it was to be fulfilled.

Per Stocker LJ: the fact that all or most of the *Mandla* conditions might be met does not itself establish that a group is of an ethnic origin.

No finding was made on the question of justification, which was remitted to the county court.

National origins

Northern Joint Police Board v Power

[1997] IRLR 610

[7.9] The appellants advertised the position of Chief Constable, for which the respondent applied. He was unsuccessful and alleged that this was because he was English rather than Scottish. His claim under the RRA, s 3(1) was successful before a tribunal on the basis that the English and Scots are separate racial groups defined by national origins and that England and Scotland are separate nations, but failed on the basis that the two were not distinct ethnic groups.

Lord Johnson in the EAT held: England and Scotland were once separate nations; an individual must show that his origins are embedded in a particular nation and that the criteria to establish this would be self-evident. The *Mandla* conditions (see 7.7 above) are not relevant to the issue of national origin. The Scots, English and Welsh do not fall within separate racial groups based on ethnic origins. The matter was remitted back to the tribunal to establish whether the respondent had English national origins and whether he was discriminated against in that context.

Racial grounds

Tejani v Superintendent Registrar for the District of Peterborough

[1986] IRLR 502, CA

[7.10] The respondent dealt with the registration of marriages. As part of the process he asked those who had been born abroad to produce their birth certificates and passport. There was no requirement for the passport to be produced but it helped ensure that the formalities had been adhered to. The appellant had been born in Uganda but lived in the UK for many years. His fiancée came from India. They were requested to and produced their passports but subsequently learned that there was no requirement to do so. It was accepted by the county court judge that all those born abroad were asked to produce their passports and that there had been no discrimination against the claimant. Mr Tejani appealed.

HELD: There had been no discrimination on racial grounds because everyone who came from abroad was asked to produce their passport. The request was not being made because of racial or national origins. On that basis the appeal was dismissed.

Dhatt v McDonalds Hamburgers Ltd

[1991] IRLR 130, CA

[7.11] The appellant came to the UK from India at the age of six when he was granted indefinite leave to remain. The respondent offered him employment which he commenced, but because he was not a British citizen or from the EC, it wanted him to produce a work permit. It would not accept his passport as sufficient evidence of his right to work and terminated his employment.

An employment tribunal rejected the complaint and the EAT dismissed his appeal. He appealed to the Court of Appeal.

HELD, on appeal: The employer was required to make enquiries about an individual's right to work. The employer had no choice but to make those enquiries. Once British citizens and those from EC countries, who were free to work in the UK, were excluded, all others were treated alike. Nationality was a relevant circumstance because Parliament was seeking to enforce, by reference to nationality, a general division between those who are free to work and those who require permission.

R v Commission for Racial Equality, ex p Westminster City Council

[1985] IRLR 426, CA

[7.12] Westminster's policy until 1979 was to appoint refuse collectors from amongst friends and family of their current employees. All the staff were white. In 1980 under a new procedure a black road sweeper applied for a post as a refuse collector. The union representatives objected to the applicant's appointment because of his poor attendance record and met with the appropriate manager who withdrew the offer. The CRE issued a non-discrimination notice. An application for judicial review was successful and the Council appealed to the Court of Appeal.

HELD: Since the manager believed the union's objection was based on racial grounds, he was obliged to consider the objection with care. The offer of employment was withdrawn because of a racially motivated objection to the transfer. The appeal on this ground and because of an alleged breach of natural justice was dismissed.

Acts may take place on racial grounds even though they are not directed at an individual's race but those of a third party. Nevertheless if the person to whom instructions are given to act in a certain manner on racial grounds brings a complaint that will fall within the meaning of 'acts on racial grounds'.

Din v Carrington Viyella Ltd

[1982] IRLR 281

[7.13] The respondents had a large Asian workforce. It had a policy of allowing employees who wished to return to their native country, but who had used their holiday entitlement, to resign and take extended leave. Upon their return they would be favourably considered for re-employment. The appellant had done this on one occasion. He was due to take another period of extended absence. However, shortly before he left he was asked by the technical foreman to assist another employee with a piece of machinery. He refused and there was an altercation. The appellant's colleagues were unhappy and the appellant was advised not to go back to work. The appellant returned from his trip but was advised that there were no jobs for him. He applied for advertised vacancies but was unsuccessful.

Applying *Seide v Gillette* (see 7.16 below), the tribunal held there had been no discriminatory treatment because the motive for not re-engaging the appellant was the unresolved situation that existed when his employment came to an end. The tribunal found as a fact the foreman had been racially motivated. Mr Din appealed.

HELD: The tribunal had extended *Seide* too far because if an act of racial discrimination gives rise to potential or actual industrial unrest, an employer may discriminate if it removes the unrest by dismissing or not re-employing the person against whom discrimination has been shown. The case was remitted to the employment tribunal.

DISCRIMINATION ON THE GROUNDS OF ANOTHER PERSON'S RACE

Showboat Entertainment Centre Ltd v Owens

[1984] IRLR 7, EAT

[7.14] Mr Owens was the manger of an amusement arcade. He alleged that he was dismissed because he refused to carry out an instruction to exclude young blacks from the centre. The tribunal held that this was unlawful discrimination. The amusement centre appealed.

HELD: The RRA, s 1(1)(a) was wide enough to include discrimination on racial grounds where the racial characteristics were those of a third party.

Weathersfield Ltd (t/a Van and Truck Rentals) v Sargent

[1999] IRLR 94, CA

[7.15] The respondent accepted a job as a receptionist with the appellant. During her induction she was told that if she received a call from any coloureds or Asians she was to advise them that no vehicles were available. On her second day a director asked her if 'the policy' had been explained to her and it was accepted that it had. The respondent subsequently resigned and advised the appellant that it was because of its racist policy. The tribunal found that there had been racial discrimination contrary to the RRA, s 1(1)(a). The EAT agreed and the employer appealed to the Court of Appeal.

HELD, on appeal: The decision in *Showboat Entertainment Centre Ltd v Owens* (see 7.14 above) was correct. The meaning of 'on racial grounds' is wide enough to extend to unfavourable treatment of an employee, if the employee is required to carry out a racially discriminatory trading policy. The finding of constructive dismissal was also upheld.

Religions as ethnic groups

Seide v Gillette Industries Ltd

[1980] IRLR 427, EAT

[7.16] The appellant was Jewish and was subjected to anti-semitic remarks. As a result he was transferred to a different shift. Subsequently, another employee asked to be moved because the appellant was trying to involve this employee in the on-going issues with the first employee. The appellant was moved to day work, which resulted in a loss of salary. His internal grievance was unsuccessful and he commenced proceedings in the tribunal. His claim was rejected and he appealed.

HELD, on appeal: Allowing the appeal, that the tribunal had correctly concluded that being 'Jewish' could refer to a person's religion or to being a member of a race or of a particular ethnic origin. The comments that had been made had been found to be on grounds of race or ethnic origin. However, the fundamental question is whether the activating cause of the employer's actions is less favourable treatment on racial grounds. Here the treatment received was not because of his race or ethnic origin and the appeal failed.

RASTAFARIANS

Dawkins v Department of the Environment

[1993] IRLR 284, [1983] ICR 517, CA

[7.17] The appellant applied for a job with the respondent. He was told that employees were expected to have short hair and that dreadlocks were not acceptable. He was not appointed and commenced proceedings. Applying the *Mandla* principles (see 7.7 above), a tribunal upheld his complaint because 60 years was sufficient for a long shared history, there was a separate cultural tradition, a common language, a common literature of sorts and a sense of being a minority. The EAT allowed an appeal because 60 years was not evidence of a long shared history. Rastafarians were not a separate and distinct community from the general Afro-Caribbean community, nor did they have an organised cultural tradition. The DOE appealed.

HELD, on appeal: Although Rastafarians have identifiable characteristics, they have not established themselves as having a separate identity by reference to their ethnic origins. There was nothing to set them apart from the Afro-Caribbean community in general and they have a short history and a common past to other Afro-Caribbeans when they were taken from Africa to the Caribbean.

Martins v Marks and Spencer plc

[1998] IRLR 326, CA

[7.18] In 1991 the appellant applied for the fourth time for a post as trainee manager. Unknown to her there was a freeze on recruitment for new management posts. Her complaint to a tribunal was settled when the respondent agreed to interview her. The interview was conducted by two people, one of whom was Afro-Caribbean in origin. She performed well at a practical test but was unsuccessful because she could not communicate effectively and lacked decisiveness. She was granted a meeting where her failure was discussed. A tribunal concluded that despite the company's extensive efforts to deal with the public's perception of the respondent as a white middle-class company, it had failed. The tribunal found direct race discrimination and rejected the statutory defence. The EAT allowed the company's appeal and the appellant appealed to the Court of Appeal.

HELD: The correct question to be asked was whether the appellant had been less favourably treated on racial grounds. If the appellant had been treated differently than a person of a different racial group with similar experience and qualifications there would be discriminatory treatment. The tribunal had only looked for bias. The tribunal members had substituted their own views for those of the interviewers; this went beyond drawing on their own experience. The tribunal had also reached a number of contradictory conclusions that made it impossible for a reasonable tribunal to conclude that there had been less favourable treatment on the grounds of race.

Barclays Bank plc v Kapur (No 2)

[1995] IRLR 87, CA

[7.19] The appellants were East African Asians who had been employed by the bank on local contracts in Kenya and Tanzania. They had lost their jobs in those countries but had been offered employment in the UK. UK nationals were also employed in these countries but on UK contracts with pensions maintained in the UK. The consequence of this was that those East African Asians aged under 50 lost the benefit of the pension they would have been entitled to receive. However, the bank implemented a pension compensation package for them. The appellants were offered jobs in the UK but were notified, because they had received pension compensation, that they would not be able to take advantage of the group service rule to take advantage of their employment in Kenya and Tanzania for pension purposes. The comparators, mainly white Europeans, had been allowed to count their service in Kenya/Tanzania, but had not received a compensation payment. A tribunal found that this constituted discrimination on racial grounds. The EAT allowed the bank's appeal and the employees appealed to the Court of Appeal.

HELD: Balcombe LJ distinguished the decisions in *Birmingham City Council v Equal Opportunities Commission* and *James v Eastleigh Borough Council* (see 7.2 above, 7.23 below), because they decided that where a gender-based criterion was applied, it was irrelevant that the motive was benign. The reason to refuse to credit East African service was because the employees had received compensation. The EAT had rejected an overtly racial reason. None of the other possible reasons were based on race and as a result the claim of direct discrimination failed. On the issue of indirect discrimination the Court of Appeal agreed with the EAT that 'an unjustified sense of grievance cannot amount to a detriment or less favourable treatment'. The initial decision to prevent double recovery was justifiable.

The importance of the discriminatory factor in the decision taken

Owen and Briggs v James

[1982] IRLR 502, CA

[7.20] Miss James, a coloured English lady, applied for an advertised position with the appellant. She was unsuccessful. Another advertisement appeared a short time later for which she applied again. She attended the interview and was told that she need not have applied again. A row developed in which she called the interviewer a bigot. Later that afternoon a white English girl was interviewed and appointed. She was told that the employer could not understand why anyone would want to employ coloured girls when 'nice English girls' were available. Miss James was successful in her claim of racial discrimination. The employer unsuccessfully appealed to the EAT and then appealed to the Court of Appeal.

HELD: Dismissing the appeal, that the racial factor does not have to be the sole factor operating. It is only necessary that race is a substantial reason for what has happened. If there are other factors then it is for a tribunal to determine whether discrimination has taken place.

An appropriate comparator

Wakeman v Quick Corpn

[1999] IRLR 424, CA

[7.21] Mr Wakeman and other employees who were British were made redundant. They complained of racial discrimination because secondees to the company, who were all Japanese, were paid substantially more although locally hired Japanese staff were paid at local rates. The company argued that the difference in pay was due to the secondees' status rather than race or nationality because the secondment was treated as part of their Japanese employment structure. The appellants complained of direct racial discrimination. Both the employment tribunal and EAT dismissed the complaint. Mr Wakeman appealed to the Court of Appeal.

HELD: The appeal would be dismissed because the comparators chosen by Mr Wakeman were not appropriate comparators. For a comparison to be fair there must be no material difference in the circumstances relevant to the remuneration of the comparator. It is only if that material difference can be eliminated that it is possible to say the difference in treatment must be attributable to racial grounds. The court found that the use of the word secondee was not synonymous with 'Japanese' and the implications of the secondment that had been identified by the tribunal were all based on the fact that the secondees were employed in another part of the world. None of the factors were race-based or race-determined in the *James v Eastleigh* sense (see 7.23 below). The court noted that in many cases it would be essential to desegregate pay but this was not such a case because the differentials were readily apparent

DIRECT SEX DISCRIMINATION

[7.22] Section 1 of SDA provides:

(1) In any circumstances relevant for the purposes of any provision of this Act, other than a provision to which subsection (2) applies, a person discriminates against a woman if—
(a) on the grounds of her sex he treats her less favourably than he treats or would treat a man....

James v Eastleigh Borough Council

[1990] ICR 554, HL

[7.23] This was an appeal in connection with alleged discriminatory treatment of those using a local authority swimming pool. The appellant and his wife were both 61. Since the appellant had not reached retirement age he was required to pay for admission. However, his wife who had reached statutory retirement age was not. The Court of Appeal found that if there had been discrimination it fell within s 1(1)(b) rather than s 1(1)(a) because the treatment was not on account of the applicant's sex. Mr James appealed to the House of Lords.

HELD, allowing his appeal: This was a case within s 1(1)(a) and that the test to be applied was objective rather than subjective. It was whether the complainant would have received the same treatment but for his or her sex. The House of Lords noted that indirect discrimination arises only where the requirement or condition is applied equally to the complainant and the comparator. Pensionable age was not such a comparator.

Pregnancy and reasons connected with pregnancy

Caisse Nationale d'Assurance Vieillesse des Travailleurs Salariés v Thibault

C-136/95: [1998] IRLR 399, ECJ[query]

[7.24] This was a claim of sex discrimination brought by an employee who was denied a performance review and thereafter a pay review on the grounds that due to her maternity absence she did not have sufficient service in that year to entitle her to such a review. The matter was referred to the European Court of Justice.

HELD: The unfavourable treatment accorded to her arose as a result of her pregnancy and her absence on maternity leave. Such conduct was based directly on the grounds of her sex. The purpose of the Equal Treatment Directive was to ensure substantive equality of treatment for women and that the exercise by them of their rights cannot be the subject of unfavourable treatment. If Ms Thibault had not been pregnant and absent on maternity leave she would have been assessed for the year in question and to deprive her of that right was to discriminate against her as a worker.

Dekker v Stichting Vormingscentrum voor Jong Volwassenen

C-177/88: [1992] ICR 325, ECJ

[7.25] The applicant applied for a post as a training instructor in a youth centre whilst she was pregnant. She was recommended for appointment but the Board rejected her application because the benefits that they would have to pay her whilst pregnant would not be reimbursed by their insurers, because she was already pregnant at the date of appointment. She claimed discrimination against them on the grounds of her sex contrary to the Equal Treatment Directive. The matter was referred to the European Court of Justice.

HELD: An employer acts in breach of the Directive if it refuses to employ an applicant because she is pregnant. If the decision not to appoint is on the grounds of pregnancy this is directly related to the applicant's sex. A refusal to employ based on the adverse financial consequences is deemed also to be based on the fact of pregnancy.

Webb v EMO Air Cargo (UK) Ltd

[1992] 4 All ER 929, HL; refd C-32/93: [1994] QB 718, ECJ; apld [1995] 4 All ER 577, HL

[7.26] The appellant was recruited to act, initially, as maternity cover for one of the respondent's employees. It was anticipated that she would remain in employment when the employee returned to work from maternity leave. Shortly after joining the appellant fell pregnant and informed her employers, who dismissed her. She complained of sexual discrimination. A number of questions were referred by the House of Lords to the European Court of Justice.

HELD: The Equal Treatment Directive precludes the dismissal of an employee who is recruited for an unlimited time who will initially replace another employee on maternity leave because she is pregnant. There was no question of comparing the situation of a pregnant woman with a hypothetical man or a man absent for medical or other reasons.

The matter was returned to the House of Lords who specifically left open the possibility that a person who is recruited for a specific period and is then unable to perform that role through pregnancy, may be lawfully dismissed.

Brown v Rentokil Ltd

C-394/96: [1998] IRLR 445, ECJ

[7.27] This was a claim by a woman who had been dismissed whilst absent from work as a result of a pregnancy-related illness following the end of her maternity leave. Her employers operated a rule that those absent for more than 26 weeks with ill-health could be dismissed.

The House of Lords referred a series of questions to the European Court of Justice.

HELD: Dismissal of a woman during pregnancy because of ill-health absences associated with pregnancy, is direct discrimination on the grounds of sex. The

Equal Treatment Directive protects women from dismissal on account of absences during a period of pregnancy or maternity leave. Where a woman is absent as a result of an illness which is associated with pregnancy or childbirth, then if that illness continues beyond the end of maternity leave any period of absence prior to the end of the maternity leave must be disregarded for the purposes of deciding whether it is fair to dismiss her. However, absence after the end of maternity leave can be taken into account in deciding whether to dismiss an employee.

Caledonia Bureau Investment and Property v Caffrey

[1998] IRLR 110, EAT

[7.28] Following childbirth, an employee suffered post-natal depression and submitted sickness certificates. She was eventually dismissed on the grounds of her ill-health. Her claims of unfair dismissal and sex discrimination succeeded. The dismissal was found to be pregnancy-related and therefore automatically unfair. It was also decided that since the illness was pregnancy-related, the employee had been discriminated against. The company appealed to the EAT.

HELD: A purposive approach should be taken to the legislation. The Employment Rights Act, s 99(1)(a), is not limited to the period of pregnancy/maternity leave but applies after maternity leave has expired provided the contract has been extended. Dismissal on account of illness which is related to having given birth or being pregnant, is discriminatory because the employee is suffering from an illness from which a man could not suffer.

The appeal was dismissed.

GUS Home Shopping Ltd v Green and McLaughlin

[2001] IRLR 75, EAT

[7.29] GUS was to move its marketing department and offered those who worked through to the date of transfer a loyalty bonus. The applicants were pregnant throughout the relevant period and either received no loyalty bonus because they were on maternity leave throughout the entire period, or a reduced bonus. An employment tribunal found that they had not been considered for the loyalty bonus because of their maternity absence and that this was direct sex discrimination. The company appealed.

HELD: The bonus scheme was intimately linked to the contract of employment. To receive a bonus an employee only had to comply with his or her contract. It was not the case of a separate and specific contract or one for a finite duration. The EAT noted that if it had been, then it was possible that there may have been no discrimination. Since the bonus was linked to the contract and the employees could not earn the bonus because of their absence on maternity leave this constituted discrimination on the grounds of their sex. The company's appeal was dismissed.

Failure to carry out a risk assessment

Day v T Pickles Farms Ltd

[1999] IRLR 217, EAT

[7.30] The appellant worked in a sandwich shop and became pregnant. The smell of food made her feel ill and she was certified unfit for work. She was paid SSP only. Eventually she resigned and claimed unfair constructive dismissal and sexual discrimination. Her sex discrimination claim was based on a failure to carry out a risk assessment which would have resulted in suspension on full pay, not being allowed time off for anti-natal care and a failure to pay SSP to which she was due. A tribunal rejected both her complaints, save the pay in respect of anti-natal care and she appealed.

HELD: Her appeal on the risk assessment point would be allowed and the matter referred back to the tribunal to consider whether she was subjected to a detriment as a result of the failure to carry out a risk assessment. There is an obligation on an employer was to carry out a risk assessment at the time women of childbearing age are employed and not at the time that they become pregnant.

Sexual orientation discrimination

Smith v Gardner Merchant Ltd

[1998] IRLR 510, CA

[7.31] Mr Smith was a homosexual and employed as a barman. He was dismissed after a female member of staff complained that he had acted in a threatening and aggressive manner towards her. In return, he alleged that she had made offensive remarks about his sexuality and that she would not have made such remarks to a gay woman. He alleged that his dismissal rather than the woman's amounted to less favourable treatment.

A tribunal and the EAT rejected his complaint because the SDA did not extend to discrimination on the grounds of sexual orientation. He appealed to the Court of Appeal.

HELD: For a homosexual to succeed in a claim of sex discrimination, he must establish that it was because he was a man rather than a woman that caused him to receive the treatment. The correct comparator for a male homosexual was a female homosexual. In sexual harassment cases once the complainant has established that he/she has suffered a detriment, it is still necessary to establish that the detriment constitutes discrimination.

The appeal was dismissed.

Grant v South-West Trains Ltd

C-249/96: [1998] IRLR 206, ECJ

[7.32] The applicant, a woman, was denied concessionary rail-fares for her partner, another woman. Married couples and those in 'common law' heterosexual relationships were entitled to the benefit of concessionary travel. The respondent had adopted an equal opportunities policy that provided individuals would be treated fairly irrespective of, inter alia, sexual preference. Ms Grant commenced proceedings alleging the policy had been incorporated into her contract and was therefore binding.

Her claim was dismissed by the High Court because the contractual conditions specified that they were only available to partners of the opposite sex; the policy was expressed not in contractual but in idealistic terms and had not been incorporated.

Proceedings were also commenced before an employment tribunal. The tribunal referred a number of questions to the European Court of Justice.

HELD: There had been no discrimination directly based on sex even where there was a stable on-going relationship. The requirement to be in a stable relationship with a member of the opposite sex was applied equally to men and women. The ECJ noted that at that time the community did not regard same sex relationships as equivalent to marriage or a stable relationship between two persons of the opposite sex. There had been no discrimination contrary to Article 109 of the Treaty of Rome.

Pearce v Governing Body of Mayfield Secondary School

[2001] EWCA Civ 1347, [2001] IRLR 669

[7.33] The applicant was a lesbian who had taught at the school. She was subject to taunts and abuse by pupils at school in relation to her sexual preference. She brought proceedings against the school alleging sex discrimination. An employment tribunal dismissed her application because only one instance upon which she relied amounted to sex discrimination and the school had dealt with it properly. She appealed and the EAT substituted a finding that none of the pupils' acts amounted to sex discrimination because the SDA did not protect against discrimination on the grounds of sexual orientation. It noted that a male homosexual would have been treated in much the same way. She appealed to the Court of Appeal.

HELD: The appropriate comparator was a male homosexual. There had been no less favourable treatment because a male homosexual would have received the same treatment. The court was bound by the decision in *Smith v Gardiner Merchant* (see 7.31 above).

Secretary of State for Defence v MacDonald

[2002] ICR 174, Court of Session

[7.34] Mr MacDonald was forced to resign from the armed forces because of his admitted homosexuality. He claimed that this constituted sex discrimination. The tribunal rejected his complaint but the EAT found in his favour. The Secretary of State appealed to the Court of Session

HELD: The applicant had been forced to resign because he was sexually attracted to members of his own sex. The appropriate comparator was a woman employed in the armed forces who was sexually attracted to members of her own sex. Since a homosexual woman would have received the same treatment there had been no discrimination on the grounds of his gender. The SDA did not relate to discrimination on the grounds of sexual orientation.

INDIRECT DISCRIMINATION

[7.35] The SDA, s 1 provides

(1) In any circumstances relevant for the purposes of any provision of this Act, other than a provision to which subsection (2) applies, a person discriminates against a woman if—

...

(b) he applies to her a requirement or condition which he applies or would apply equally to a man but—
   (i) which is such that the proportion of women who can comply is substantially smaller than the proportion of men who can comply with it, and
   (ii) which he cannot show is justifiable irrespective of the sex of the person to whom it is applied, and
   (iii) which is to her detriment because she cannot comply with it.

(2) In any circumstances relevant for the purposes of any provision of this Act, other than a provision to which this subsection applies, a person discriminates against a woman if—
(a) on the grounds of her sex he treats her less favourably than he treats or would treat a man, or
(b) he applies to her a provision criterion or practice which he applies or would apply equally to a man but—
   (i) which is such that it would be to the detriment of a considerably larger proportion of women than of men, and
   (ii) which he cannot show to be justifiable irrespective of the sex of the person to whom it is applied, and
   (iii) which is to her detriment.

The RRA, s1(1) provides:

A person discriminates against another in any circumstances relevant for the purposes of this Act if—

...

(b) he applies to that other a requirement or condition which he applies or would apply equally to persons not of the same racial group as that other but—
   (i) which is such that the proportion of persons of the same racial group who can comply with it is considerably smaller than the proportion of persons not of the same racial group who can comply with it; and
   (ii) which he cannot show to be justifiable irrespective of the colour, race, nationality or ethnic origins of the person to whom it is applied; and
   (iii) which is to the detriment of that other because he cannot comply.

Perera v Civil Service Commission (No 2)

[1983] IRLR 166, CA

[7.36] The appellant, a Sri Lankan, brought complaints against the respondent alleging discrimination on the grounds of colour and national origin in relation to applications for employment and to obtaining a bursary. Before the EAT he succeeded in one claim of indirect discrimination because of the imposition of an upper age limit. He appealed to the Court of Appeal.

HELD: His appeal in relation to direct discrimination was rejected. The argument based upon indirect discrimination failed because he complied with the one requirement that was essential. There was no other express requirement or condition. If such a condition could be identified he would have to show it had been applied and that there was a disparate effect upon him. However, since the tribunal had found that he had not been appointed because there were certain personal qualities that he lacked, he had failed to establish indirect discrimination.

Barry v Midland Bank Plc

[1999] IRLR 581, HL

[7.37] The apellant originally worked full-time but following maternity leave returned on a part-time basis under the respondent's key-time scheme. 96% of key-time workers were women. She accepted voluntary severance under the terms of a scheme negotiated by her union based upon her final part-time salary. She argued that this constituted a requirement or condition that was to her detriment because she was treated as if she had been a part-time employee throughout her whole employment. A tribunal rejected her complaint because 92.68% of women in the pool worked full-time. The EAT rejected her appeal because the same rules applied to men and women. The Court of Appeal rejected her appeal and identified the relevant pool as all part-time employees and that the correct comparison was between those who were advantaged and those disadvantaged within that pool. The disadvantaged would be those whose average hours were less at termination than throughout their employment. Her appeal failed because the relevant statistics were not before the tribunal. She appealed to the House of Lords.

HELD: Their Lordships noted the purpose of the scheme was to compensate for future loss not reward past service. The comparison to be made is the proportion of men who are not disadvantaged to those who are and the same proportions for women. The alleged disadvantaged group comprised all employees at the termination date whose average hours exceeded their current hours. The House of Lords also took the view that the scheme could be objectively justified because the objection was to cushion employees against unemployment.

Meer v London Borough of Tower Hamlets

[1988] IRLR 399, CA

[7.38] Mr Meer was of Indian origin and worked in local government. He applied for a position with London Borough of Tower Hamlets. There were 23 applicants, four of whom had worked for London Borough of Tower Hamlets before. Twelve people were selected for interview, including the four who had previous experience with the respondent. Five of them were selected for short-listing, including two of the four who had previous experience with Tower Hamlets.

Mr Meer complained of direct and indirect racial discrimination. Both claims failed and he only pursued the claim of indirect discrimination on appeal.

HELD: The Court of Appeal found that it was bound by the decision in *Perera* (see 7.36 above). Obiter: Balcombe LJ indicated that if he was not bound to follow precedent he thought that the absolute bar construction of 'condition or requirement' may not be consistent with the object of the RDA. Dillon LJ commented that if *Perera* reflected the true state of the law, there were reasons to change it.

Allonby v Accrington and Rossendale College

[2001] EWCA Civ 529, [2001] IRLR 364

[7.39] The applicant was a part-time lecturer. The respondent decided, in the light of impending legislative changes, to employ all part-time staff through a third party as self-employed contractors. The applicant brought various claims against the college and the third party. An employment tribunal found that there was a requirement of full-time work, which was to the applicant's detriment but that this was justified because of the budgetary constraints. Her appeal to the EAT was dismissed and she appealed to the Court of Appeal.

HELD: There had been the imposition of a requirement or condition. It was irrelevant that the employer could show a different and unobjectionable requirement or condition. There was sufficient difference between the proportional impact between men and women to uphold the tribunal's findings. However, it had reached the wrong conclusion on the question of justification because it failed to weigh the justification against its discriminatory effects.

Is full-time work the imposition of a requirement or condition?

Briggs v North Eastern Education and Library Board

[1990] IRLR 181, NICA

[7.40] Mrs Briggs was a teacher who assisted with extra curricular activities including badminton teaching. Following the adoption of her daughter she switched her badminton lesson from after school to lunchtime. She was asked to re-introduce after-school badminton and agreed to do this one day a week. However, she refused to coach these lessons at the leisure centre two-miles away. She was disciplined and her pay reduced. She claimed that this constituted sexual discrimination on the grounds of marital status. A tribunal found that there was a prima facie case of indirect sex discrimination and that the employer had failed to justify its actions. The matter was referred to the Northern Ireland Court of Appeal.

HELD: The fact that an employer requires an individual to do the job he or she was employed to do does not prevent the employer imposing a requirement. A tribunal could take into account its own experience of whether a considerably smaller proportion of women can comply with the requirement and that this means 'can in practice comply'. On the issue of justification the court found the tribunal had misdirected itself because it was required to balance the discriminatory effect of the requirement against the reasonable needs of the employer. Applying that test, coaching at lunchtime was not in the pupils' and the school's interest. The tribunal had reached a decision that no reasonable tribunal could have reached and the employer's actions were justified.

Lord Chancellor v Coker

[2001] EWCA Civ 1756, [2002] IRLR 80

[7.41] This was a complaint by two individuals that they had been discriminated against on the grounds of their sex when the Lord Chancellor decided to appoint a special adviser. He had recommended one person for appointment by the Prime Minister. A tribunal found that a requirement or condition had been applied that the successful candidate must be known to the Lord Chancellor personally. It went on to find that this was to the applicant's detriment and not justifiable. The Lord Chancellor appealed.

The EAT allowed the appeal because there was not a disproportionate impact between men and women and there was no relevant pool because only one person was considered. The two ladies appealed to the Court of Appeal.

HELD: The appeal would be dismissed because a requirement or condition could only have a discriminatory effect if a significant proportion of the pool are able to satisfy the requirement. Making an appointment from within a close circle of friends is unlikely to constitute discrimination. However, conducting a recruitment exercise by word of mouth or personal recommendation may well infringe the discrimination legislation.

'Considerably smaller proportion'

London Underground Ltd v Edwards (No 2)

[1998] IRLR 364, CA

[7.42] The respondent was a single mother who worked for London Underground as a train driver. Following changes to shift patterns she brought a complaint of indirect sex discrimination because she could not comply with the terms of the new roster. A tribunal found that all male drivers could comply with the new roster but only 95.2% of female drivers could. It went on to find that this constituted a considerably smaller proportion of women who could comply with the requirement and rejected arguments on justification.

The EAT dismissed the appellant's appeal because the tribunal was entitled to take account of the absolute numbers of men and women, to consider whether the number of women was so small that it was statistically unreliable and to consider whether there was a generalised assumption that work was 'men's work'. She appealed to the Court of Appeal.

HELD: The only issue was whether a considerably small proportion of female as opposed to male train operators could comply with the requirement or condition. The tribunal was not restricted to considering the selection pool but could take into account its general knowledge and experience of single mothers having child care responsibilities. A tribunal was entitled to take into account the large discrepancy in the numbers of male and female workers in a particular pool. In this case, the small number of women indicated that the job was unattractive to them. The court was not prepared to lay down guidelines for the meaning of 'considerably smaller'.

For Simon Brown LJ the most compelling fact in the case was that despite the large disparity in actual numbers, no men were disadvantaged, whilst of 21 women, one was.

Chief Constable of Avon and Somerset Constabulary v Chew

[2001] All ER (D) 101 (Sep), EAT

[7.43] This was an appeal from the decision of an employment tribunal that a difference of 2.26% was a considerably smaller proportion in the context of a pool of 435 women and 2,581 men.

HELD: It was permissible for a tribunal to have regard to the make up and overall numbers of the workforce, the effect of a change in numbers of men and women, the fact that no man was disadvantaged, the history of the relevant workforce and the likely effect of the condition or requirement.

Whilst the EAT thought that a difference of 2.26% was unlikely to establish a disparate effect, a flexible approach was needed to ensure that a range of factors were taken into account.

Rutherford v Towncircle Ltd (t/a Harvest) (in liquidation) and Secretary of State for Trade and Industry (No 2), Bentley v Secretary of State for Trade and Industry

[2002] IRLR 768, EAT

[7.44] Mr Rutherford was made redundant when he was 67 years old. He sought to bring an unfair dismissal claim and/or a claim for a redundancy payment. The tribunal held the statutory provisions, subject to arguments of justification, did indirectly sexually discriminate. Towncircle appealed.

HELD: The EAT found flaws in the approach taken by the tribunal and allowed the appeal, remitting the case back to the tribunal. The EAT noted:
1. In some cases a disparate impact will be so obvious that simply to look at the numbers alone or the proportions will suffice to show that the members of one sex are considerably disadvantaged.
2. In less obvious cases a tribunal should use more than one form of comparison
3. It will be proper to look not only at proportions but also to numbers and to respective proportions in the disadvantaged groups.
4. Where there is doubt about the obviousness of a case a tribunal should look at several forms of comparison.
5. Over time a better feel for what is a considerable disparity will develop.
6. No distinction is to be drawn between a considerable and a substantial disparity.
7. When it has all the figures for comparison a tribunal should stand back to ascertain whether the criterion or practice in question has a disparate impact that could be described as considerable or substantial

Whiffen v Milham Ford Girls' School

[2001] EWCA Civ 385, [2001] IRLR 468

[7.45] Mrs Whiffen was employed by the school on a series of fixed-term contracts. A redundancy exercise was carried out and in accordance with the local authority's policy those on fixed-term contracts did not have those contracts renewed. Mrs Whiffen claimed that she had been indirectly discriminated against because fewer women could comply with the condition to have full-time contracts. A tribunal found that she had raised a prima facie case of indirect discrimination but that the policy was justified because it was gender neutral. At the time there were eleven teachers at her grade, two were men who were permanent and seven were women of whom five were permanent. The EAT dismissed her appeal. She appealed to the Court of Appeal.

HELD: The policy was not gender neutral. 100% of the male teachers could comply, but only 77% of the female teachers. This was a considerably smaller proportion. The employer had not justified the disparate impact; its argument that it was not inherently discriminatory was flawed.

The meaning of 'can comply'

Raval v Department of Health and Social Security

[1985] IRLR 370, EAT

[7.46] The DHSS required an 'O' level in English GCE for clerical workers on the basis that a knowledge of English was necessary when dealing with the public. The appellant was of Asian origin and educated abroad. She did not have the qualification but was sufficiently fluent to obtain such a qualification.

HELD: In the EAT Waite J identified ten questions to be asked when considering the issue of indirect discrimination. The seventh question considered the proportionate comparison to be made where a job advertisement specifies qualifications that are necessary. He concluded that 'can comply' means an ability to produce proof that the relevant qualification had already been obtained. The court con-sidered that an individual's ability to pass a language exam was affected if the exam was in an examinee's second language. Although there was a finding in the appellant's favour on the issue of whether she could comply, her appeal was dismissed because the tribuna had gone on to find that if there was discrimination, it was justified.

Detriment

Bohon-Mitchell v Common Professional Examination Board and Council of Legal Education

[1978] IRLR 525, IT

[7.47] This was a complaint of discrimination on grounds of national origin or nationality. The applicant applied for, but was refused, a certificate to exempt her from one year of the academic training stage for the Bar exams because she did not have a UK degree. She was a US citizen with a degree in English Literature. She complained to an employment tribunal of indirect discrimination.

HELD: The tribunal found that the applicant's racial group was comprised of those who were not from the United Kingdom or Ireland and that her racial group was defined by nationality and national origins. The fact that she would have to spend an extra academic year constituted a detriment because she would be without income for that year. The appropriate pool for comparison purposes was English-speaking graduates. The proportion of those who had a non-UK or Ireland nationality or origin who could comply with the requirement was considerably smaller than those who had such a nationality or origin. The tribunal went on to consider the issue of justification and found that the requirement or condition could not be justified and found in the applicant's favour.

Knowledge is not necessary for there to be a detriment

Garry v London Borough of Ealing

[2001] EWCA Civ 1282, [2001] IRLR 681

[7.48] Mrs Garry was born in Nigeria and worked as a benefit rent team manager. The manager of the investigation team was told that she had been subject to an investigation in her previous employment. An investigation was conducted but insufficient evidence found. She complained to a tribunal about the manner of the investigation. It was found that, but for the fact that she was Nigerian, the investigation would have been concluded much sooner. A tribunal upheld her complaint of racial discrimination on the grounds of ethnic origin. The EAT allowed an appeal because there had been no detriment suffered by her. She appealed to the Court of Appeal.

HELD: The fact that she was unaware of the ongoing investigation was no defence if there was a detriment to her. The detriment here was the fact that the investigation was known to the council's officers, where attitudes towards her were important with regard to her ongoing employment.

Her appeal was allowed because she had suffered less favourable treatment.

The pool for comparison

Jones v University of Manchester

[1993] IRLR 218, CA

[7.49] The respondent advertised a post for a graduate aged 27 to 35. The respondent wanted someone who was close in age and outlook to its students. The appellant was 46 and was not short-listed for the position. She complained of indirect sex discrimination in respect of women who were mature students. A tribunal upheld her complaint because the age requirement was a complete bar and statistical evidence of mature students showed that a considerably smaller proportion of women than men could comply with the requirement. The EAT allowed an appeal because the correct pool for comparison was all graduates rather than mature graduates.

HELD: The Court of Appeal considered whether a requirement had been applied. Having applied the criteria referred to in *Perera* (see 7.36 above), the Court of Appeal indicated that they were not prepared to interfere with the tribunal's findings. It found that the correct pool for comparison was all those who satisfied the qualification criterion. It did not accept that the relevant ambits were the comparative totals of men and women who could comply but that a comparison of the proportions had to be carried out. It cited with approval the exercise on justification described by Balcombe LJ in *Hampson v DES* (see 7.56 below).

> Note—The following case is very much out of line with other decisions involving claims of indirect discrimination arising from a decision by an employee to work part-time as a result of childbirth.

JUSTIFICATION

[7.50] The provisions for the defence of justification are as follows.

Section 1(1)(b)(ii) of the SDA: 'which he cannot show to be justified irrespective of the sex of the person to whom it is applied'.

Section 1(2)(b)(ii) SDA: 'which he cannot show to be justifiable irrespective of the sex of the person to whom it is applied'.

Section 1(1)(b)(ii) RRA: 'which he cannot show to be justifiable irrespective of the colour, race, nationality or ethnic or national origins of the person to whom it is applied'.

Ojutiku v Manpower Services Commission

[1982] IRLR 418, CA

[7.51] Mr Ojutiku came to Britain from West Africa. He enrolled on a polytechnic course and applied to the MSC for a grant. His application was rejected because he did not have experience in a commercial or managerial position. A tribunal found that he had been discriminated against but that the discrimination was justifiable and dismissed his complaint. The EAT dismissed his appeal and he appealed to the Court of Appeal.

HELD, per Stephenson LJ: The party applying the discriminatory condition must prove that it is justifiable in all the circumstances balancing its discriminatory effect against the discriminator's need for it.

Bilka-Kaufhaus GmbH v Weber von Hartz

170/84: [1986] IRLR 317, ECJ

[7.52] This was an equal pay complaint in connection with a company's policy only to permit staff the benefit of an occupational pension scheme until they had completed 15 years' full-time service . The complainant had 15 years' service but not all was full-time service.

She complained of indirect discrimination. The matter was referred to the European Court of Justice.

HELD: To succeed in a justification defence an employer must show that the means chosen for achieving its objective correspond to a real need on the part of the undertaking, are appropriate with a view to achieving the objective in question and are necessary to that end.

Rainey v Greater Glasgow Health Board

[1987] IRLR 26, HL

[7.53] This was an equal pay claim by Mrs Rainey. It was alleged that the difference in pay between her and her male comparator arose from their different methods of joining the Health Board. A tribunal found this to be the reason and dismissed her claim. Appeals to the EAT and Court of Session were rejected and she appealed to the House of Lords.

HELD: The decision in *Bilka-Kaufhaus* (see 7.52 above) must be accepted as authoritative. The ECJ's decision did not limit the objective grounds that could be taken into account. This meant that objective grounds other those that are economic could be taken into account, such as administrative efficiency. Her appeal was dismissed.

Hampson v Department of Education and Science

[1989] IRLR 69, CA

[7.54] This was a complaint as to whether the refusal of the DES to grant the appellant, a Hong Kong national, qualified teacher status constituted racial discrimination. Her application was refused because her initial training was not comparable to that of UK teachers. A tribunal rejected her complaint because the need for comparable training was a test or yardstick rather than a requirement. The EAT held that there was a requirement but that it was protected pursuant to section 41(1)(b) because it was done in pursuance of an enactment. The EAT found that any discriminatory treatment was justified. The appellant appealed to the Court of Appeal.

HELD: The Court of Appeal upheld the section 41 defence and considered the issue of justification.

Per Balcombe LJ: The defence of justification is an objective test requiring an objective balance between the discriminating effect of the condition and the reasonable needs of the party applying the condition. The court refused to find that *Ojutiku* (7.53 above) had been overruled following *Bilka-Kaufhaus* and the *Rainey* decision (7.52 and 7.53 above). The appeal was dismissed.

DISCRIMINATION ON THE GROUNDS OF GENDER REASSIGNMENT

[7.55] SDA, s 2A provides

(1) A person ('A') discriminates against another person ('B') in any circumstances relevant for the purposes of—

(a) any provision of Part II,
(b) section 35A or 35B, or
(c) any other provision of Part III, so far as it applies to vocational training,

if he treats B less favourably than he treats or would treat other persons, and does so on the ground that B intends to undergo, is undergoing or has undergone gender reassignment.

(2) Subsection (3) applies to arrangements made by any person in relation to another's absence from work or from vocational training.

(3) For the purposes of subsection (1), B is treated less favourably than others under such arrangements if, in the application of the arrangements to any absence due to B undergoing gender reassignment—
(a) he is treated less favourably than he would be if the absence was due to sickness or injury, or
(b) he is treated less favourably than he would be if the absence was due to some other cause and, having regard to the circumstances of the case, it is reasonable for him to be treated no less favourably.

(4) In subsections (2) and (3) 'arrangements' includes terms, conditions or arrangements on which employment, a pupillage or tenancy or vocational training is offered.

(5) For the purposes of subsection (1), a provision mentioned in that subsection framed with reference to discrimination against women shall be treated as applying equally to the treatment of men with such modifications as are requisite.

Section 2A SDA reads:

'gender reassignment' means a process which is undertaken under medical supervision for the purpose of reassigning a person's sex by changing physiological or other characteristics of sex, and includes any part of such a process.

P v S and Cornwall County Council

[1996] IRLR 347

[7.56] P was employed as the general manager of one of the council's education units. He advised his employers that he was to undergo surgery for gender re-assignment and that he would be undergoing a year-long life test which required him to dress as a woman. P took sick leave and the governors were advised of the situation. They gave him three months' notice of dismissal and his employment was terminated. An employment tribunal dismissed his claim of sex discrimination but referred two questions to the European Court of Justice.

HELD: The Equal Treatment Directive expressed a fundamental principle of community law – equality of treatment. The Directive extended to discrimination based primarily on the sex of the person concerned. If discrimination was taking place as a result of gender re-assignment, then a person was being less favourably treated than persons of the sex to which the individual was deemed to belong. Transsexuals were protected.

Chessington World of Adventures Ltd v Reed, ex p News Group Newspapers Ltd

[1997] IRLR 556, [1998] ICR 97, EAT

[7.57] The applicant operated rides at the respondent's theme park. She announced a change of identity from male to female and announced her new name. She was subject to sexual harassment by her colleagues. She made a complaint of sex discrimination which was successful. Her managers knew about the campaign that was being conducted against her and even after she attempted to commit suicide, no action was taken to protect her. Her employers appealed against the decision to the EAT.

HELD: Where the reason for the unfavourable treatment is sex-based, here the intention to undergo a sex change operation, there is no requirement under the Equal Treatment Directive for a male/female comparison to be made. The SDA was interpreted consistently with the decision in *P v S*.

As a result of the decision in *Burton v De Vere* (see 7.94 below) the employer was directly liable for its employee's actions rather than vicariously liable, because the employer knew about the harassment the applicant was suffering from and had done nothing about it.

Ashton v Chief Constable of West Mercia Constabulary

[2001] ICR 67, EAT

[7.58] Ms Ashton was diagnosed as suffering from gender identity dysphoria and wrote to her colleagues explaining her intention to undergo gender reassignment. It was proposed that she should resign from her position as police constable on terms that would be agreed. She agreed to ensure her continued employment. Following the start of her hormone treatment she suffered from depression. Her performance of her new role was not satisfactory and it was recommended that she be dismissed. She was absent from work with depression for five months but recovered and shortly before her gender reassignment operation she was dismissed. She claimed that she had been discriminated against contrary to the SDA and DDA. A tribunal dismissed both claims and she appealed.

HELD: Her medical conditions associated with her gender reassignment were not sex specific and she could not compare herself with a pregnant woman. The comparison that should be made was with a worker who failed to perform satisfactorily during his or her probationary period. As a result her complaint of sex discrimination failed.

A v Chief Constable of West Yorkshire Police

[2002] EWCA Civ 1584, [2003] 1 All ER 255

[7.59] See 7.77 below. Concerns about intimate searches did not justify discriminating against a male to female transsexual.

ESTABLISHING DISCRIMINATORY TREATMENT

King v Great Britain-China Centre

[1992] ICR 516, CA

[7.60] The appellant, who had been born in China of Chinese parents, applied for the post of deputy director. She was not interviewed but was told that the post had been filled from a field of strong candidates. She commenced proceedings for racial discrimination because she did not believe the explanation. A tribunal concluded that there had been racial discrimination because the employer had not satisfied them that racial bias played no part in the appointment process. The EAT allowed an appeal and the appellant appealed.

HELD: Allowing the appeal, Neil LJ distilled from *North West Thames RHA v Noone, Khanna v MOD, Chattopadhyay v Headmaster of Holloway School*, the following principles:

i. The applicant must make out his or her case on the balance of probabilities;
ii. it is unusual to find direct evidence of racial discrimination. In some cases the discrimination will not be ill intentioned;
iii. the outcome will usually depend on what inferences it is proper to draw from the primary facts; this may include equivocal or evasive answers to questionnaires;
iv. a finding of discrimination and a finding of a difference in race will point to racial discrimination. A tribunal will look to the employer for an explanation. If there is no, or an inadequate or unsatisfactory explanation, it will be legitimate for a tribunal to infer that the discrimination was on racial grounds;
v. it is unhelpful to refer to a shifting of the evidential burden. A tribunal should make findings as to the primary facts and draw such inferences as they consider proper. A decision should be reached on the balance of probabilities, bearing in mind the difficulties faced by the complainant and that it is for the complainant to prove his or her case.

Glasgow City Council v Zafar

[1998] ICR 120, HL

[7.61] The appellant was a British citizen of Asian origin who had worked for the respondent for ten years before being dismissed for sexual harassment of clients. He brought proceedings alleging racial discrimination both during employment and in relation to his dismissal and also a claim of unfair dismissal. A tribunal held the dismissal unfair and racially discriminatory. It was unfair because of the manner in which it had been brought about. The respondent was guilty of delay, not issuing warnings and failing to investigate allegations. It found the allegation of racial discrimination established on the basis that the employer's treatment fell below that of a reasonable employer and that the tribunal was bound, in the absence of a non-racial explanation for the conduct, to draw the adverse inference.

The EAT dismissed the respondent's appeal. However, the Court of Session allowed an appeal against the finding of racial discrimination. Mr Zafar appealed.

HELD: The fact that the conduct of a hypothetical reasonable employer would have been different was irrelevant. If an employer acts unreasonably in the context of unfair dismissal it casts no light on whether an employee has been treated less favourably. It cannot be inferred that because an employer acts unreasonably towards one employee it would have acted reasonably towards another. On that basis the tribunal was wrong to conclude that it was bound, in the absence of a non-racial explanation, to infer that the treatment was on grounds of race.

The guidance given by Neil LJ in *King v Great Britain-China Centre Ltd* (see 7.62 above) was quoted with approval.

Anya v University of Oxford

[2001] EWCA Civ 405, [2001] IRLR 377

[7.62] Dr Anya was a black Nigerian permanently resident in the United Kingdom. He applied for a post-doctoral research position but the position was awarded to the other short-listed candidate who was white. One of those interviewing the candidates was Dr Anya's supervisor. The tribunal made a finding of fact that his supervisor formed an adverse view of Dr Anya and passed this on to one of the other interviewers. The University's equal opportunities and recruitment policies for such interviews were not followed. Although there were inconsistencies in the respondent's evidence, a tribunal concluded there had been no discrimination. The EAT dismissed Dr Anya's appeal and he appealed to the Court of Appeal.

HELD: Without findings of primary fact it is impossible to draw inferences. Tribunals must look for indicators from before and after a particular decision which may demonstrate that an ostensibly fair decision was tainted by discrimination. In those circumstances it was necessary to evaluate the totality of the evidence to make findings of fact and to follow them through to reasoned conclusions. Since the candidates had comparable experience and the choice would depend upon how the panel viewed them, if there were any racial factors they would only emerge from the surrounding circumstances and the previous history. The appeal was allowed on the basis that the reasoning of the tribunal was deficient and the matter was referred back to a tribunal.

Discrimination by others

[7.63] Section 7 of RRA makes provision for cases of discrimination by others:

(1) This section applies to any work for a person ('the principal') which is available for doing by individuals ('contract workers') who are employed not by the principal himself but by another person, who supplies their labour under a contract made with the principal.

(2) It is unlawful for the principal, in relation to work to which this section applies to discriminate against a contract worker—
(a) in the terms on which he allows him to do that work; or
(b) by not allowing him to do it or continue to do it; or
(c) in the way he affords him access to any benefits, facilities or services or by refusing or deliberately omitting to afford him access to them; or
(d) by subjecting him to any other detriment.

Similarly section 9 of SDA provides:

(1) This section applies to any work for a person ('the principal') which is available for doing by individuals ('contract workers') who are employed not by the principal himself but by another person, who supplies their labour under a contract made with the principal.

(2) It is unlawful for the principal, in relation to work to which this section applies to discriminate against a woman who is a contract worker—
(a) in the terms on which he allows her to do that work; or
(b) by not allowing her to do it or continue to do it; or
(c) in the way he affords her access to any benefits, facilities or services or by refusing or deliberately omitting to afford her access to them; or
(d) by subjecting her to any other detriment.

Harrods Ltd v Remick

[1997] IRLR 583, CA

[7.64] The respondent worked for a concession working in Harrods. She required Harrods' approval to work in the store. This was withdrawn because of a breach of the dress code. The issue for determination by the Court of Appeal was whether those who worked for concessions within Harrods worked 'for Harrods' within the meaning of section 7 of the SDA.

HELD: In construing section 7 it was necessary to construe the statute in a way that was consistent with the words used but also to achieve the statutory purpose of providing a remedy for victims of discrimination who would not otherwise have one. Whilst the primary obligations of concessionaires was to market goods, there was an obligation to supply labour and in those circumstances Harrods were principals for the purpose of section 7.

Allonby v Accrington and Rossendale College

[2001] EWCA Civ 529, [2001] IRLR 364

[7.65] (For facts, see 7.39 above.) The section is not limited to discrimination between male and female contract workers supplied to a single employer. To do so would be to defeat the purpose of the legislation, which is to remove sex discrimination in the employment field. The section is wide enough to prevent discrimination between a contract worker and an employee employed by the same employer.

The case was remitted to a tribunal to determine inter alia whether the college had discriminated between contract workers and employees.

Discrimination by 'qualifying bodies'

[7.66] Section 12 of the RRA makes unlawful discrimination by 'qualifying bodie':

(1) It is unlawful for an authority or body which can confer an authorisation or qualification which is needed for, facilitates, engagement in a particular

profession or trade to discriminate against a person—
(a) in the terms on which it is prepared to confer on him that authorisation or qualification; or
(b) by refusing, or deliberately omitting to grant his application for it; or
(c) by withdrawing it from him or varying the terms on which he holds it.

Similarly section 13 of the SDA reads:

(1) It is unlawful for an authority or body which can confer an authorisation or qualification which is needed for, engagement in a particular profession or trade to discriminate against a woman
(a) in the terms on which it is prepared to confer on her that authorisation or qualification; or
(b) by refusing, or deliberately omitting to grant her application for it; or
(c) by withdrawing it from him or varying the terms on which she holds it.

Tattari v Private Patients Plan Ltd

[1997] IRLR 586, CA

[7.67] The appellant was a Greek-born British citizen who completed her medical qualifications at Athens University. She had been appointed to the specialist list maintained by the GMC. Her application to register with PPP was rejected because she did not have a relevant qualification. She claimed that she had been discriminated against contrary to RRA, s 12. Both an employment tribunal and the EAT rejected her complaint and she appealed to the Court of Appeal.

HELD: Section 12 has to be read as a whole. The bodies referred to in it are those empowered to grant qualification or recognition for the purposes of practising a profession, calling or trade. It does not apply to a body that stipulates for the purposes of a commercial agreement that a particular qualification is required.

Bohon-Mitchell v Common Professional Examination Board

[7.68] (For facts, see 7.47 above.)

HELD: On the issue of whether the CPE were a qualifying body: the CPE Board were a qualifying Body for the purposes of the Race Relations Act and their decision to refuse Ms Bohon-Mitchell the status of an English national was justifiable by an employment tribunal.

British Judo Association (BJA) v Petty

[1981] IRLR 484, EAT

[7.69] Mrs Petty was a judo instructor and had a certificate to act as a referee from the BJA. She refereed at a men's competition but was then told that a new rule prohibited women refereeing at men's competitions. She brought a complaint under SDA, s 13. A tribunal found in her favour and the BJA appealed

HELD: The tribunal's conclusion was correct. The BJA reached a decision about whether she was qualified to referee at men's competitions. It is irrelevant whether the term was applied when she became a referee or was applied at a later date. The statute requires a complainant to show that the relevant qualification facilitates his or her job prospects and that attached to such qualification is a term which is discriminatory against the sex or race of the complainant. It is not necessary for the complainant to prove that the term had a discriminatory effect upon them.

Continuing act versus one-off act of discrimination

Barclays Bank plc v Kapur

[1991] IRLR 136, HL

[7.70] The complaint arose from the failure of Barclays Bank, having compensated employees for loss of pension rights in East Africa, to treat them in the same way as UK citizens who had been seconded to work in East Africa. The issue before the House of Lords was whether refusing to credit the employees with East African service when they were employed in the UK, was a continuing act of discrimination.

HELD: The failure to provide similar terms was a continuing act throughout the course of employment.

Sougrin v Haringey Health Authority

[1992] IRLR 416, CA

[7.71] The appellant complained about the outcome of a re-grading exercise. The issue before the Court of Appeal was whether the appellant had brought her claim in time and whether there was a continuing act. The appellant's appeal was dismissed because her complaint related to her grading, which was a one-off act. That act had continuing consequences but these were not discriminatory.

HELD, per Lord Donaldson: This case could be distinguished from the position in *Barclays Bank v Kapur* (above) because in *Kapur* there was a policy to pay coloured workers less and it was the policy that was the discriminatory act. In this case all employees on the same grade were paid at the same rate and there was no continuing discriminatory act.

Littlewood Organisation plc v Traynor

[1993] IRLR 154, EAT

[7.72] Mr Traynor brought an internal grievance complaining about racial abuse by his manager. The company undertook steps to deal with his complaint but failed to do so. He resigned and complained of racial discrimination. The issue for determination was whether the complaint was in time, since more than three months had elapsed since the racial abuse. A tribunal found that this constituted a continuing act. The company appealed.

HELD: The EAT rejected the employer's appeal because the decision whether there is a single act or a continuing act must involve a consideration of the particular circumstances. Whilst the remedial measures were not taken, a situation involving racial discrimination continued to exist and that this amounted to a continuing act.

Hendricks v Metropolitan Police Comr

[2002] EWCA Civ 1686, [2003] 1 All ER 654

[7.73] The appellant complained of institutional racism and alleged 99 such acts had taken place in the period 1989 to 1999. These acts were alleged to have been performed by 50 different police officers in five different work places. She also brought separate victimisation proceedings. The issue for determination by the Court of Appeal was what constituted a continuing act.

HELD: The fact that Ms Hendricks was absent from work from March 1999 did not prevent continuing acts of discrimination. The burden was upon the applicant to establish that the alleged incidents of discrimination were linked to one another and that they were evidence of a continuing discriminatory state of affairs.

WORK ORDINARILY OUTSIDE GREAT BRITAIN

[7.74] The provisions for work outside GB are contained in section 10 of the SDA and section 8 of the RRA:

(1) For the purposes of this Part employment is to be regarded as being at an establishment in Great Britain unless the employee does work wholly outside Great Britain

Freedom of Movement (EC Treaty, Art 48)

Bossa v Nordstress Ltd

[1998] IRLR 284, EAT

[7.75] The appellant responded to an advertisement in the UK that advertised jobs for those holding a European Union passport to work in Italy. The apellant was an Italian national living in the UK. He was advised that he could not be interviewed because the company was not permitted by the Italian authorities to take Italian nationals back to Italy. His complaint was dismissed by a tribunal on the grounds that the tribunal had no jurisdiction to determine the complaint because it related to work wholly or mainly outside Great Britain. He appealed.

HELD: Article 48 of the EC Treaty (providing for the free movement of workers) has direct effect (*Van Duyn v Home Office*:41/74 [1975] Ch 358, ECJ applying).

Since Article 48 applied, it was the duty of the tribunal to override any provision of the Act that conflicts with it. The complaint was to be determined by the tribunal despite the fact that the appellant was applying for a job wholly or mainly outside Great Britain.

GENUINE OCCUPATIONAL QUALIFICATION DEFENCE

[7.76] The defence of genuine occupational qualification (GOC) will most generally be available in cases involving direct, as opposed to indirect, discrimination.

It is an exemption from the rigours of the Acts by acknowledging that in certain circumstances it will be necessary to employ an individual with a particular racial or ethnic identity. Section 5 of the RRA provides:

(1) In relation to racial discrimination:
(a) section 4(1)(a) or (c) does not apply to any employment where being of a particular racial group is a genuine occupational qualification for the job, and
(b) section 4(2)(b) does not apply to opportunities for promotion or transfer to or training for, such employment.

(2) Being of a particular racial group is a genuine occupational qualification for a job only where:
(a) the job involves participation in a dramatic performance or other entertainment in a capacity for which a person of that racial group is required for reasons of authenticity, or
(b) the job involves participation as an artist's or photographic model in the production of a work of art, visual image or sequence of visual images for which a person of that racial group if required for reasons of authenticity, or
(c) the job involves working in a place where food or drink is (for payment or not) provided to and consumed by members of the public or a section of the public in a particular setting for which, in that job, a person of that racial group is required for reasons of authenticity, or
(d) the holder of the job provides persons of that racial group with personal services promotion their welfare, and those services can most effectively be provided by a person of that racial group.

(3) Subsection (2) applies where some only of the duties of the job fall within paragraph (a), (b), (c) or (d) as well as where all of them do.

(4) Paragraph (a), (b), (c) or (d) of subsection (2) does not apply in relation to the filling of a vacancy at a time when the employer already has employees of the racial group in question:
(a) who are capable of carrying out the duties falling within that paragraph, and
(b) whom it would be reasonable to employ on this duties, and
(c) whose numbers are sufficient to meet the employer's likely requirements in respect of those duties without undue inconvenience.

Similar provisions are also contained in sections 7A and 7B of the Sex Discrimination Act 1975 relating to gender reassignment.

Tottenham Green Under Fives' Centre v Marshall

[1989] IRLR 147, EAT

[7.77] The centre sought to maintain an ethnic mix amongst both the children and staff. An Afro-Caribbean member of staff left and a decision was taken to replace her with another member of the Afro-Caribbean community. The respondent applied for the position. When it became clear he was white, he was told he would not be suitable. He complained of unlawful racial discrimination. A tribunal upheld his complaint but it could find no special need that was to be fulfilled by the successful candidate. The centre appealed.

HELD: A genuine occupational qualification defence is most likely to succeed in direct discrimination cases. When considering such a defence the following matters need to be considered:
i. the particular racial group will need to be clearly defined because it must be that of the holder of the post and the recipient of the services.;
ii. the holder of the post must be involved in the provision of the services, although not necessarily on a one-to-one basis;
iii. if several personal services are provided, it is only necessary for one service to satisfy section 5(4);
iv. 'promoting their welfare' is a very wide expression; and
v. it is only necessary that the services can most effectively be provided by a person of that racial group.

Considerable weight should be given to a conscious decision by a responsible employer to commit an act of discrimination when deciding whether the defence succeeds.

A similar approach was taken in the following case although on the facts a different result was reached .

Lambeth London Borough Council v Commission for Racial Equality

[1990] IRLR 231, CA

[7.78] Lambeth sought to recruit two Afro-Caribbean housing managers, although they were only going to have limited contact with the public. The CRE sought a declaration that this constituted racial discrimination. A tribunal dismissed the authority's GOQ defence because the racial group of the holder and the recipient of the services was not sufficiently identified. They appealed.

HELD: Based on the tribunal's findings of fact, the appeal was dismissed. Tribunals should take a broad approach to issues of fact. It should not be too difficult to identify genuine defences. The Act requires direct contact in the provision of personal services; here, since there was to be little contact with the public, the defence could not be made out.

A v Chief Constable of West Yorkshire Police

[2002] EWCA Civ 1584, [2003] 1 All ER 255

[7.79] A was a male to female transsexual. She applied to become a police constable and raised as an issue whether there would be any problem with a transsexual carrying out intimate searches. She was told that the police were happy to consider her application further. However, she was subsequently told that the force had decided not to appoint transsexuals. She asserted that she had been discriminated against on the grounds of her sex and the police admitted discrimination but argued that it was lawful. A tribunal found that to give effect to the Chief Constable's concerns in connection with personal searches would be disproportionate to the denial of A's fundamental right to equal treatment and found in her favour. Following this decision the Sex Discrimination Gender Reassignment Regulations came into force. The EAT allowed the appeal but remitted the matter to the tribunal to consider again whether there had been unlawful discrimination. A appealed to the Court of Appeal.

HELD: Following the decision in *Goodwin v UK* (2002) 35 EHRR 447 (see 7.117 below), it was clear that a post-operative male to female transsexual was entitled to be treated for all purposes as a woman. The applicant had to be treated in all respects as a woman. As a result it was not open to the Chief Constable to discriminate against her as a transsexual. A's appeal was allowed.

VICTIMISATION

[7.80] Those who either bring proceedings, give evidence or information in connection with proceedings, do anything by reference to the Act or allege a contravention of either the SDA or RRA are protected by SDA s 4 and RRA, s 2:

> A person ('the discriminator') discriminates against another person ('the person victimised') in any circumstances relevant for the purposes of this Act if he treats the person victimised less favourably than in those circumstances he treats or would treat other persons, and does so by reason that the person victimised has:
>
> (a) brought proceedings against the discriminator or any other person under this Act [or the Equal Pay Act 1970 – SDA];
> (b) given evidence or information in connection with proceedings brought by any person against the discriminator or any other person under this Act [or the Equal Pay Act 1970 – SDA];
> (c) otherwise done anything under or by reference to this Act [or the Equal Pay Act 1970 – SDA] in relation to the discriminator or any other person; or
> (d) alleged that the discriminator or any other person has committed an act which (whether or not the allegation so states) would amount to a contravention of this Act [or the Equal Pay Act 1970 – SDA],
>
> or by reason that the discriminator knows that the person victimised intends to do any of those things or suspects that the person victimised has done, or intends to do, any of them.'

Is there a need for conscious motivation?

[7.81] Whether a conscious motivation is needed has been conclusively determined by the House of Lords.

Nagarajan v London Regional Transport

[1999] IRLR 572, HL

[7.82] The issue before the House of Lords was whether conscious motivation was necessary for victimisation.

HELD: Under section 1(1)(a), the reason a person discriminates against another is irrelevant. This includes sub-conscious motivation. The expression in RRA, s 2(1)(a) 'by reason that' is interchangeable with the words 'on racial grounds' in section 1(1)(a) and the same reasoning applies. Section 4 of the RRA refers to the employer and it is therefore irrelevant that different employees were involved at different stages. Mr Nagarajan's appeal was allowed and the decision of the employment tribunal restored.

The House of Lords commented that *Aziz* (see below) was wrong insofar as it found that 'a motive that is consciously connected with the race relations legislation was needed'.

Aziz v Trinity Street Taxis Ltd

[1988] IRLR 204, CA

[7.83] This was an appeal from dismissal of a complaint of racial discrimination. TST was an incorporated company limited by guarantee for the benefit of its members who were taxi drivers in Coventry. The appellant, who was a member, was required to pay an arbitrary fee to register a third taxi. Believing he might be the subject of racial discrimination he secretly tape-recorded discussions with other members. The tribunal proceedings were unsuccessful but one of those recorded learned of the recordings and decided to take action which resulted in the appellant's expulsion for making the recordings. The issue before the Court of Appeal was whether there had been a breach of the RRA, s 2(1)(c).

HELD: What had formed in the appellant's mind was only the possibility that some form of racial discrimination was taking place. However, this was sufficient for his actions to be 'by reference to the act'. The relevant comparison to be made was to persons who had not done the protected act and that to establish a causal link under section 2(1), the fact that the protected act was done under or by reference to the legislation influenced the alleged discriminator in his unfavourable treatment of the complainant. However, since the fact that the recordings were made by reference to the act did not influence the decision, the causal link had not been established and the appeal failed.

The tests applied in *Kirby* (see below) are not the correct tests.

Section 2(1)(b) of the RRA

Kirby v Manpower Services Commission

[1980] IRLR 229, EAT

[7.84] The appellant was a clerk at a job centre. He spoke to three potential employers who made it clear that they did not want black or coloured applicants. He reported that matter to the British Community Relations Council. When his actions became known he was moved to a less desirable position. He complained that he had been victimised contrary to RRA, s 2. A tribunal dismissed his claim and he appealed.

HELD: For there to be protection under section 2(1)(b) proceedings must be brought, although it is irrelevant whether information is given before or after the proceedings have been commenced. The making of a report to the CRE is done by reference to the Act.

Chief Constable of West Yorkshire Police v Khan

[2001] IRLR 830, HL

[7.85] The respondent was a Detective Sergeant of Indian origin. He had brought proceedings against the appellant on the grounds of racial discrimination but before the hearing he applied for a post with another force. His current employers refused to provide a reference because of his outstanding claim. He added a victimisation claim to the tribunal proceedings. A tribunal found that he had been victimised and appeals to the EAT and the Court of Appeal were rejected. The police authority appealed to the House of Lords.

HELD: Adopting the approach of Slade LJ in *Aziz* (see 7.85 above), the correct comparison was between a person who has done a protected act and others who have not. On that basis the respondent had been treated less favourably. However, the words 'by reason that' require a subjective test to be applied. Here the reference was refused because of the outstanding claim. It was not connected with any racial motive.

Per Lord Scott of Foscote:

> The language of s 2(1) is not the strict language of causation. 'By reason that' suggests it is the real reason, the core reason, causa causans, the motive for the treatment complained of that must be identified.

Victimisation on the grounds of sex

Corneleus v University College of Swansea

[1987] IRLR 141, CA

[7.86] The appellant, who was employed as a secretary, complained that her immediate superior had kissed her and expressed strong feelings for her. She was moved to another post and told that if it did not work out she would be transferred again. She was unhappy and asked for her old post back. Nothing happened. A complaint of sexual discrimination was dismissed and she appealed. Whilst the appeal was outstanding she formally requested that she be transferred back to her old position. The respondent refused until the outcome of her appeal was known. She issued further proceedings and asked that the internal grievance procedure be operated. The college again refused in the light of the outstanding proceedings.

Both the tribunal and EAT dismissed her claims. She appealed to the Court of Appeal.

HELD: For her claim to succeed it would have to be shown that by its actions the college had treated the applicant less favourably than it would have treated others in the same circumstances and that it did so because proceedings had been brought under the Act. Since there was no such evidence her claim failed.

Instructions to discriminate and pressure to discriminate

Instructions to discriminate

[7.87] By SDA, s 39; RRA, s 30:

It is unlawful for a person:
(a) who has authority over another person, or
(b) in accordance with whose wishes that other person is accustomed to act,

to instruct him to do any act which is unlawful by virtue of Part II or III, or procure or attempt to procure the doing by him or any such act.

Pressure to discriminate

[7.88] By RRA, s 31:

(1) It is unlawful to induce, or attempt to induce, a person to do any act which contravenes Part II or III.

(2) An attempted inducement is not prevented from falling within subsection (1) because it is not made directly to the person in question, if it is made in such a way that he is likely to hear of it.

And by SDA, s 40:

(1) it is unlawful to induce, or attempt to induce, a person to do any act which contravenes part II or III by:

providing or offering to provide him with any benefit; or

by subjecting or threatening to subject him to any detriment.

(2) An offer or threat is not prevented from falling within subsection (1) because it is not made directly to the person in question , if it is made in such a way that he is likely to hear of it.

Commission for Racial Equality v Imperial Society of Teachers of Dancing

[1983] IRLR 315, EAT

[7.89] The respondents telephoned a school to ascertain if they had any pupils who would be interested in a job as a filing clerk with general office duties. It was alleged that the respondent advised the school not to send any coloured applicants because they would 'not fit in'. The CRE brought proceedings for breach of the Race Relations Act, ss 30 and 31. A tribunal found that the words had been used and that there was no breach because it was only a request. The CRE appealed.

HELD: The CRE's appeal would be allowed on the ground that 'induce' in s 31 means to 'persuade or prevail upon to bring about'. On that basis induce was wide enough to cover the current situation. In s 30 'procure' and 'attempt to procure' include the use of words that bring about or attempt to bring about a certain result. However, there had been no breach of s 30 because the school was not accustomed to act in accordance with the respondent's wishes.

VICARIOUS LIABILITY OR DIRECT LIABILITY FOR ACTS OF EMPLOYEES

[7.90] Under SDA, s 41 and RRA, s 32:

(1) Anything done by a person in the course of his employment shall be treated for the purposes of this Act (except as regards offences thereunder) as done by his employer as well as by him, whether or not it was done with the employer's knowledge or approval.

(2) Anything done by a person as agent for another person with the authority (whether express or implied, and whether precedent or subsequent) of that other person shall be treated for the purposes of this Act (except as regards offences thereunder) as done by that other person as well as by him.

(3) In proceedings brought under this Act against any person in respect of an act alleged to have been done by an employee of his it shall be a defence for that person to prove that he took such steps as were reasonably practicable to prevent the employee from doing that act, or from doing in the course of his employment acts of that description.'

Jones v Tower Boot Co Ltd

[1997] IRLR 168, CA

[7.91] Mr Jones was coloured. He was assaulted at work by his fellow workers using their work tools. A tribunal found that his employer was vicariously liable for their workers' actions in assaulting Mr Jones. The company's appeal that the assault had not taken place in the course of employment, applying the well-known common law test, was upheld. Mr Jones appealed.

HELD: It was wrong to construe the statutory words in the context of the common law. The purpose of the legislation was to deter discrimination and to extend the range of those responsible for acts of discrimination whilst providing a statutory defence.

Giving the phrase 'in the course of employment' a narrow construction would mean that the more heinous the act the more likely the employer would be to escape. In the current circumstances the employers were liable for their employees' act of assaulting Mr Jones.

Burton and Rhule v De Vere Hotels

[1996] IRLR 596, EAT

[7.92] The appellants were employed as waitresses by the hotel; both were black. The hotel was hosting a function at which Bernard Manning was to speak. During his performance the appellants went into the banqueting hall. Mr Manning was making derogatory remarks about black people and made pointed comments towards them. The two women were upset but continued to work. On the following day they complained to the hotel manager about the treatment to which they had been subjected. The manager unsuccessfully sought to resolve the situation with the appellants. They brought claims for racial discrimination against the hotel.

A tribunal rejected their complaint because although they had suffered a detriment they had not been subjected to it by the hotel. They appealed.

HELD: It is not necessary to show that the discriminator had any intention to discriminate. An employer who knows that racial harassment is taking place or who deliberately closes his eyes to such acts will, if he does not act reasonably to prevent it, have subjected his employees to a detriment. An employer will subject an employee to a detriment if the detriment takes place in circumstances where the employer can control whether it happens or not. Foresight is not necessary, although it might be relevant to whether the employer could control what occurred.

Since the employer could control whether the waitresses went into the banqueting hall while Mr Manning was performing, the hotel had subjected them to a detriment by allowing them to enter during his performance.

Waters v Metropolitan Police Comr

[1997] IRLR 589, CA

[7.93] The appellant lived in police accommodation with other officers. Whilst off duty she was subjected to a serious sexual assault by another off-duty officer. She reported the matter, but despite an internal enquiry no action was taken against the male officer. She alleged that she became the victim of harassment, unfair treatment and bullying. She complained of sex discrimination following the removal of her name from a list of officers trained to conduct important searches. She also commenced a civil action alleging negligence.

The complaint before the tribunal was dismissed because the act had not taken place in the course of employment. An appeal to the EAT was dismissed. She appealed to the Court of Appeal.

HELD: At the time of the assault the attacker and the victim were in no different position than if they had been social acquaintances with no working connection. The argument that the appellant was entitled to protection under SDA, s 4(1)(d) failed because the matters complained of could not have constituted acts of discrimination because the alleged attacker was not acting in the course of his employment at the time of the assault.

Chief Constable of Lincolnshire Police v Stubbs

[1999] IRLR 81, EAT

[7.94] The respondent was seconded from her role with the appellant to another police force. She complained that whilst seconded she was subjected to two incidents of inappropriate behaviour by a member of her force also on secondment. The incident took place in the pub immediately after work. The tribunal upheld her complaint. The issues before the EAT were whether the appellant was responsible for an officer's conduct whilst on secondment and whether the acts had been carried out in the course of employment.

HELD: The respondent remained appointed to her original police force by virtue of the Police Act. Although the incidents took place at social events they were an extension of the workplace because they took place immediately after work or were an organised leaving party. It was a question of fact in each case whether the employer was vicariously liable for its employee's acts but here there was a connection between the event and the workplace and therefore the acts were in the course of employment.

Liversidge v Chief Constable of Bedfordshire Police

[2002] EWCA Civ 894, [2002] IRLR 651

[7.95] This was a complaint by a police constable of racial discrimination by a fellow officer. The Chief Constable was sued on the basis that he was vicariously liable for the acts of officers employed by the authority. The issue was whether, before the Race Relations (Amendment) Act 2000 came into force, a Chief Constable was vicariously liable for acts of racial discrimination committed by a police constable. The matter was appealed to the Court of Appeal.

HELD: Since a police constable was not an employee, the Chief Constable could not be vicariously liable for such acts. Leave to appeal to the House of Lords has been refused.

    Note—This case was distinguished in *Chief Constable of Cumbria v McGlennon* [2002] ICR 1156, EAT.

POST-EMPLOYMENT VICTIMISATION

Adekeye v Post Office (No 2)

[1997] IRLR 105, CA

[7.96] The appellant was dismissed for misconduct and brought an internal appeal. She was unsuccessful and complained of racial discrimination both at the time of dismissal and subsequently on the determination of her appeal. The issue before the Court of Appeal was whether the apellant was 'a person employed at the time of the act complained of' (ie the determination of her appeal).

HELD: RRA, s 4(2) only extends to protect those who are employed at the relevant time. The fact that there was an appeal after the dismissal did not continue the employment. The Equal Treatment Directive did not apply to the RRA and it was not necessary to construe the Act in a manner consistent with the Directive. Gibson and Hirst LJ thought that it was open to argument whether the words of the Directive 'working conditions, including the conditions governing dismissal' are apt to cover an appeal procedure where dismissal has already occurred. Pill LJ thought it was strongly arguable that the words 'conditions governing dismissal' are sufficiently broad to cover a post-dismissal appeal procedure.

A different approach has been taken in sex discrimination cases because there the legislation has to be construed so as to give effect to the Equal Treatment Directive.

Coote v Granada Hospitality Ltd

C-185/97: [1998] IRLR 656, ECJ; apld sub nom Coote v Granada Hospitality (No 2) [1999] IRLR 452, EAT

[7.97] The appellant had been employed by the respondent. She had pursued sex discrimination proceedings against the respondent. Subsequently she had difficulty obtaining employment because the respondent refused to provide a reference for her. She alleged that she was being victimised because of the proceedings previously brought against the respondent. A tribunal rejected her claim, following the reasoning in *Adekeye v Post Office (No 2)* (above). The EAT referred to matter to the European Court of Justice.

HELD: Article 6 requires Member States to introduce measures to enable persons who consider themselves victims of discrimination to pursue their claims by judicial process. The principle of effective judicial control would be deprived of an essential element of its effectiveness if its protection did not extend to a situation where an employer refuses to provide a reference. The matter was then referred to the EAT.

Held by Morrison P: The complaint fell within SDA, s 6 because the language of the section was wide enough to apply to present and former employees and to ensure conformity with the Directive. The decision in *Adekeye* was not so mistaken that it could not be followed, but Morrison P disagreed with it.

Rhys-Harper v Relaxion Group Ltd

[2001] EWCA Civ 634, [2001] IRLR 460

[7.98] The applicant was dismissed on 15 October 1998. She made an allegation of sexual discrimination based upon harassment that occurred during the course of her employment on 9 November 1998. The allegation was investigated and she was advised on 30 November that it had been dismissed. The issue for the Court of Appeal was whether her claim could proceed.

HELD: The appeal would be dismissed. Section 6(2) of the SDA and s 4(2) of the RRA have to be construed in the same way. The EAT was correct to reach the conclusion that a tribunal does not have jurisdiction to determine such a complaint. The decision in *Coote* (above) did not cover the question of whether an employee who was victimised whilst at work could bring a complaint about those acts of victimisation after the employment had ended. *Coote* decided the narrow point that an employee who is victimised after the employment has ended must have the right to have a remedy if victimised in such circumstances.

D'Souza v Lambeth London Borough Council

[2001] EWCA Civ 794

[7.99] Mr D'Souza succeeded in a claim of racial discrimination and obtained a reinstatement order. The respondent argued that it was not practicable to comply with that order and refused to comply. Mr D'Souza complained that this was a further act of discrimination. His claim was rejected by a tribunal and by the EAT. He appealed to the Court of Appeal.

HELD: The appeal was dismissed because *Adekeye v Post Office* (see 7.96 above) was neither wrongly decided nor decided per incurium. Any argument that the applicant's Convention rights were infringed following *Rhys-Harper v Relaxion Group Ltd 2001* (above) could not be sustained.

AIDING UNLAWFUL ACTS

[7.100] Section 42 of the SDA and section 33 of the RRA provide:

(1) A person who knowingly aids another person to do an act made unlawful by this Act shall be treated for the purposes of this Act as himself doing an unlawful act of the like description.

(2) For the purposes of subsection (1) an employee or agent for whose act the employer or principal is liable under section 32 (or would be so liable but for section 32(3)) shall be deemed to aid the doing of the act by the employer or principal.

(3) A person does not under this section knowingly aid another to do an unlawful act if:—
(a) he acts in reliance on a statement made to him by that other person that, by reason of any provision of this Act, the act which he aids would not be unlawful; and
(b) it is reasonable for him to rely on the statement.

A person who knowingly or recklessly makes a statement such as is mentioned in subsection (3)(a) which in a material respect is false or misleading commits an offence, and shall be liable on summary conviction to a fine not exceeding [level 5 on the standard scale].

Anyanwu v South Bank Student Union

[2001] UKHL 14, [2001] IRLR 305

[7.101] Following disciplinary proceedings the appellants had been expelled from the University and subsequently had been dismissed from their positions within the Students Union. They alleged their expulsion was on the grounds of race. The issue in the House of Lords was whether the University had aided the Students Union to do an unlawful act by expelling them as students.

HELD: Allowing the appeals and remitting the matter to an employment tribunal, 'aids' bears its every-day meaning in section 33(1) of the RRA, and that a person aids another if he helps or assists, regardless of whether the help is substantial and productive, provided that it is not so insignificant as to be negligible.

Hallam v Avery

[2001] UKHL 15, [2001] ICR 408, [2001] IRLR 312, HL

[7.102] Proceedings were brought against the police for aiding a local authority to discriminate by passing information to it. The issue in the House of Lords was whether the police had aided the doing of an unlawful act.

HELD: 'Aiding' required a much closer involvement in the act of the principal than encouraging, inducing, causing or procuring. Section 33 of the RRA required more than a general act of helpfulness and co-operation. However, it did not follow that where information was given to another the provider of the information could never be liable under section 33.

DAMAGES FOR INJURY TO FEELINGS AND AGGRAVATED DAMAGES

Vento v Chief Constable of West Yorkshire Police (No 2)

[2002] EWCA Civ 1871, [2003] ICR 318

[7.103] The appellant was employed as a probationary officer. Her marriage broke down and she experienced a change in attitude towards her, with unwarranted interest in her private life; she became the subject of bullying and sexual harassment. A tribunal found in her favour and awarded £50,000 for injury to feelings and £15,000 aggravated damages for the high-handed manner in which the respondents acted. The tribunal noted that over 22 days her private life was subjected to minute scrutiny. The EAT reduced the award to £30,000 for both injury to feelings and aggravated damages. The police appealed to the Court of Appeal.

HELD: The tribunal award was in excess of the JSB guidelines for moderate brain damage involving epilepsy, severe PTSD with permanent effects and total deafness and loss of speech. There are three categories for injury to feelings. In the most serious cases damages should be in the range of £15,000 to £25,000; a moderate band that does not merit an award at a higher end would be in the region of £5,000 to £15,000, and a lower band for less serious cases where there is only an isolated incident would be in the range of £500 to £5,000. Damages of less than £500 were to be avoided. The aggravated damages award was reduced to £5,000 in the light of the totality of the award.

ICTS (UK) Ltd v Tchoula

[2000] IRLR 643, EAT

[7.104] This was an appeal to the EAT from the decision of a tribunal to award a coloured applicant £53,486 compensation, including £22,000 for injury to feeling and £5,000 for aggravated damages, following findings of racial discrimination and five acts of victimisation.

HELD: It was not wrong for a tribunal to take a global approach to assessing damages for injury to feelings and it was not necessary to assign a value to each discriminatory act about which complaint was made. Awards for injury to feelings are compensatory rather than punitive but should not be so low as to diminish respect for the policy of anti-discrimination legislation. Such awards should also have a broad similarity to personal injury awards. The EAT identified two bands of award, an upper and higher band. The cases to which it referred in the lower band were cases where awards of less than £15,000. The court agreed with the approach of Carswell LCJ in *McConnell* (below) that awards for aggravated damages should be included within the personal injury element although sometimes they may be expressed separately.

McConnell v Police Authority for Northern Ireland

[1997] IRLR 625, NICA

[7.105] This was a claim before the Northern Ireland fair employment tribunal on the grounds of religious discrimination where the applicant who was a Catholic and was suitably qualified had failed to succeed in six job applications where the posts had been awarded to Protestants. He was awarded £10,000 damages for injury to feelings and £2,500 aggravated damages.

HELD: The Northern Ireland Court of Appeal (Carswell LCJ) allowed an appeal in part. Aggravated damages should form part of awards for injury to feelings. An honest but misguided attempt to defend an employer's action should not generally be regarded as an aggravating element, nor should the identity or status of the discriminator affect the extent of an award. On that basis the award was reduced to £5,000.

Armitage, Marsden and HM Prison Service v Johnston

[1997] IRLR 162, EAT

[7.106] £20,000 damages for injury to feelings and £7,000 aggravated damages were awarded to a black prison officer who was ostracised by his colleagues and subjected to an eighteen-month campaign, including racist remarks and false accusations. The Prison Service appealed.

HELD: Awards are compensatory and should be just to both parties; they should not be too low because that will diminish respect for legislation; they should be broadly similar to awards in personal injury cases; tribunals should remind themselves of the value of an award in every day life; and regard should be had for the need for public respect for awards. It is a matter for each tribunal whether an award should be made against individuals who are named as respondents. The appeal was dismissed because the award was not grossly out of line with the general range of personal injury awards.

Ministry of Defence v Meredith

[1995] IRLR 539, EAT

[7.107] In dealing with an issue of discoverability of various classes of document, the EAT noted that for aggravated damages to be awarded there must be a causal connection between the exceptional or contumelious conduct or motive in committing the wrong and the loss suffered by the applicant.

Bradford City Metropolitan Council v Arora

[1991] IRLR 165, CA

[7.108] The Court of Appeal noted that aggravated damages can be awarded for the discriminatory conduct and for the manner in which an individual is dealt with thereafter.

Exemplary damages

A B v South West Water Services Ltd

[1993] 1 All ER 609, CA

[7.109] An individual's claim for exemplary damages was dismissed, since the decision in *Rookes v Barnard* ([1964] AC 1129) laid down that such damages were restricted to tort in which such awards had been made at the date of the decision in *Rookes v Barnard* in 1964.

DISABILITY DISCRIMINATION

> Note—The Disability Discrimination Act came into force in 1996. It marked a dramatic change in the legislative landscape by introducing positive rights for those who are disabled and at the same time moved away from some of the concepts familiar in the Sex and Race discrimination legislation that had been introduced in the 1970s.

[7.110] The Disability Discrimination Act 1996 (1995) (DDA) introduced a definition of disability and only those who fall within that definition can claim the protection of the Act. Following the introduction of the Act the courts have had to grapple with a number of difficult concepts such as who is an appropriate comparator, the inter-reaction of tribunals and medical experts and the approach to how one assesses what are normal day-to-day activities and the general approach to be taken in deciding whether these have been affected.

Definition of disability

[7.111] Section 1 of the DDA provides the definition of disability:

> **1.**—(1) Subject to the provisions of Schedule 1, a person has a disability for the purposes of this Act if he has a physical or mental impairment which has a substantial and long-term adverse effect on his ability to carry out normal day-to-day activities.
>
> (2) In this Act 'disabled person' means a person who has a disability.

The definition, whilst capable of being broken down into component parts, has to be read as a whole; satisfying only one part is not sufficient all parts must be satisfied. Helpful guidance on the meaning and interpretation of section 1 is provided in Schedule 1 to the DDA and in the DTI's publication 'Guidance on matters to be taken into account in determining questions relating to the definition of disability'.

Physical impairment

Cruickshank v VAW Motorcast Ltd

[2002] IRLR 24, [2002] ICR 729, EAT

[7.112] The appellant worked in a foundry from 1995 and developed occupational asthma. He was transferred to work away from the fumes causing the asthma. Subsequently his duties were changed so that he worked nearer the area creating fumes causing his asthma. His asthma was triggered again and he had a significant period of sickness absence. This resulted in his dismissal because there were no other vacancies available. His claim of disability discrimination was dismissed by an employment tribunal on the basis that he was not disabled because there was no effect upon his ability to carry out normal day-to-day activities outside work. The dismissal was found to be fair.

HELD: His appeal was allowed by the EAT because the time at which the condition must be examined is at the time of the alleged discriminatory act. In the EAT's opinion no distinction is drawn between whether an impairment is caused at work or outside work. Where there is a varying effect, then the effect upon normal day-to-day activities is to be considered both at work and away from work. This can take into account what the individual can and cannot do at work and also outside work. The tribunal must assess the impact of an impairment taking all circumstances into account. The case was remitted to a new tribunal.

College of Ripon and York St John v Hobbs

[2002] IRLR 185, EAT

[7.113] The respondent suffered, she alleged, from progressive muscle weakening, and wasting and twitching muscles. She was absent from work for a substantial period of time and eventually brought a claim alleging disability discrimination on the grounds that the college had failed to make reasonable adjustments. A preliminary hearing was held to determine the issue of disability. The tribunal had before it a medical report that indicated there was nothing 'organically' wrong with the respondent. The tribunal concluded that she was disabled by interpreting 'physical impairment' to mean that there was something wrong with the body and that her symptoms were physical manifestations of those symptoms.

HELD: On appeal the EAT refused to interfere with the tribunal's findings, based on the evidence before it, because the physical symptoms were sufficient to permit a finding of physical impairment. The medical report did not suggest that there was no physical impairment and this was not a case where the tribunal had reached a conclusion contrary to the expert evidence.

Howden v Capital Copiers

(ET No.S/400005/97), (1997) IRLIB 586

[7.114] The applicant suffered gripping pains which resulted in him being admitted to hospital on a number of occasions. No cause could be identified for the pains suffered by the applicant. An employment tribunal accepted that there was a physical impairment even though no cause could be identified for the pain. The pain caused lack of mobility, manual dexterity, and problems with physical co-ordination.

Note—Cf *McNicol v Balfour Beatty Rail Maintenance* (see 7.118 below).

Mental impairment

[7.115] The definition in section 1 is supplemented by Schedule 1 of the DDA, which provides that:

1 (1) Mental impairment' includes an impairment resulting from or consisting of a mental illness only if the illness is a clinically well-recognised illness.

Goodwin v Patent Office

[1999] IRLR 4, [1999] ICR 302, EAT

[7.116] The appellant was employed as a patent examiner and suffered from paranoid schizophrenia which manifested itself in auditory hallucinations and thought-broadcasting. This meant that he was unable to concentrate for prolonged periods of time. An employment tribunal found no substantial adverse effect on the appellant's normal day-to-day activities because he could carry out his domestic activities.

HELD: On appeal to the EAT, Morrison P. considered the proper approach for tribunals to take. He noted that it would be good practice to make standard directions or arrange a directions hearing; that tribunals should adopt a purposive approach to the legislation; in cases involving mental illness regard should be had to the World Health Organisation International Classification of Diseases; that tribunals should focus on what an individual cannot do, and tribunals should note that disabilities may have a cumulative effect. Tribunals should be slow to rely upon an individual's capabilities at a hearing and should take into account the deduced effects.

By focusing on what the applicant could do at home rather than what he could not do, the tribunal had reached the wrong conclusion. It was apparent from the evidence that his capacity to concentrate and communicate were adversely affected. The tribunal should have had regard to the effect of medication upon Mr Goodwin and then considered the deduced effects, ie the condition he would have been in without the medication. If either the actual or deduced effects are more than trivial the individual is a disabled person.

The EAT commented that this type of legislation should be given a purposive interpretation in a way that gives effect to Parliament's intention.

The case was remitted to a new tribunal to consider the issue of justification.

Subsequently the EAT have indicated the potential routes for establishing a mental impairment. See paragraph 7.118 below.

Staffordshire University v Morgan

[2002] IRLR 190, [2002] ICR 475, EAT

[7.117] The appellant was assaulted at work by her supervisor. On her return to work she was offered alternative roles but there was no guarantee she would avoid contact with the supervisor who had assaulted her. She resigned and claimed constructive dismissal. Later a formal disability claim was pleaded relying on the anxiety and stress she had suffered. A tribunal rejected her complaint because it was unable to satisfy itself that she had a mental impairment within the meaning of the DDA.

HELD: Her appeal failed because references to stress, anxiety and depression were not sufficient by themselves to establish a claim. The EAT commented on the possible routes to establish a successful claim based on mental impairment. These were proof of:

i.   a mental illness referred to by the World Health Organisation International Classification of Diseases;
ii. a mental illness referred to by another publication of equal standing;
iii. a mental illness recognised by a respected body of medical opinion; and
iv   proof of a state that is a mental impairment but which is not caused by a mental illness.

FUNCTIONAL OVERLAY

McNicol v Balfour Beatty Rail Maintenance Ltd

[2001] IRLR 644, [2002] ICR 381, EAT

[7.118] Mr McNicol's appeal related to functional or psychological overlay, a condition where the applicant alleges physical injury but medical opinion suggests that the illness is a result of the applicant's psychological state.

Mr McNicol worked on the railways from 1992 but suffered an injury in 1995 caused by a jolt whilst going over a pot-hole. He was absent from work until he presented a complaint in 1998. He had been in discussions with his employers for some time but could not agree on the basis for his return to work. A consultant spinal surgeon prepared a report indicating that organically he could find no injury and suggested a referral to a psychiatrist or clinical psychologist.

An employment tribunal dismissed the claim on the basis that the cause of Mr McNicol's problems were psychological rather than physical. The tribunal accepted that pain may be a consequence of a mental condition without any physical cause, but rejected the suggestion that because it caused pain it became a physical impairment. The tribunal noted that there was no evidence that psychological overlay was a well-recognised mental illness and rejected the complaint.

The EAT upheld the tribunal's decision, holding that the distinction between a physical and a mental impairment depends on whether the cause of the impairment is physical or mental, and not the effects of the impairment. Mr McNicol appealed to the Court of Appeal.

HELD: In dismissing his appeal, it held that there had been no evidence of a physical cause of his impairment and there was no evidence of a clinically well-recognised mental illness. The Court of Appeal noted that an impairment within Schedule 1 may result from an illness or it may consist of an illness.

Power v Panasonic UK Ltd

[2003] IRLR 151, EAT

[7.119] The applicant alleged that she suffered from phobic anxiety and that she had become clinically depressed which caused her to drink heavily. Before the tribunal expert evidence was given to determine whether the applicant became depressed because she was drinking heavily or drank heavily because she was depressed. The tribunal concluded on the basis of the evidence that she was not a person with a disability. It also found that her phobic anxiety was not a disability. She appealed.

HELD: The tribunal's decision with regard to phobic anxiety could not be said to be perverse. However, the tribunal had misdirected itself on the issue of alcoholism and depression. Tribunals are not required to consider how the impairment from which a person was suffering was caused, but whether the impairment from which the person suffers at the material time is a disability within the meaning of the DDA or whether it is an impairment that is excluded from being a disability. By focusing upon whether the depression caused the alcoholism or was caused by it the tribunal had asked itself the wrong question. The case was remitted back to the tribunal to determine whether she suffered from a disability at the time of dismissal.

Substantial and long-term adverse effect

[7.120] Schedule 1 of DDA provides:

2.—(1) The effect of an impairment is a long-term effect if—

(a) it has lasted at least 12 months;

(b) the period for which it lasts is likely to be at least 12 months; or

(c) it is likely to last for the rest of the life of the person affected.

(2) Where an impairment ceases to have a substantial adverse effect on a person's ability to carry out normal day-to-day activities, it is to be treated as continuing to have that effect if that effect is likely to recur.

Vicary v British Telecommunications plc

[1999] IRLR 680, EAT

[7.121] This was an appeal to the EAT from a tribunal decision that the applicant, who had an upper arm condition which meant that she could not cut up meat, roast potatoes, do DIY, file nails, knit and cut with scissors, was not disabled because there was not a substantial adverse effect upon the appellant's ability to carry out normal day-to-day activities.

HELD: Morrisons P in the EAT, held that the statutory definition of 'substantial' is something which is more than a minor or trivial effect and that the list of day-to-day activities in the Code is illustrative and not exhaustive. Tribunals must use their own judgment to determine what are normal day-to-day activities and whether adverse effects are substantial. If an individual is able to mitigate the effects of a disability, this does not mean that they are not disabled.

Kirton v Tetrosil Ltd

[2002] IRLR 840, EAT

[7.122] Mr Kirton developed prostate cancer. Following an operation to remove the tumour he had urinary incontinence and he gave evidence that carrying heavy loads caused him a problem and that he used the toilet more frequently. A tribunal concluded, based upon expert medical opinion which noted that he wore incontinence pads and did not wet his clothes, and also using its members' own personal experience, that this did not have a substantial adverse effect upon his ability to carry out normal day-to-day activities. He appealed.

HELD: The EAT dismissed his appeal and held that the tribunal members were entitled to take into account their own experience. It also found that he did not have a progressive condition. His symptoms were as a result of the treatment he underwent and not as a result of his condition; as a result he was not protected by paragraph 8 of Schedule 1.

Normal day-to-day activities

[7.123] This area is most likely to cause difficulty in practice and a substantial body of case law has begun to develop in this area.

'Normal day-to-day activities' are exhaustively defined by paragraph 4 of Schedule 1 to the DDA.

> 4.—(1) An impairment is to be taken to affect the ability of the person concerned to carry out normal day-to-day activities only if it affects one of the following—
> (a) mobility;
> (b) manual dexterity;
> (c) physical co-ordination;
> (d) continence;
> (e) ability to lift, carry or otherwise move everyday objects;
> (f) speech, hearing or eyesight;
> (g) memory or ability to concentrate, learn or understand; or
> (h) perception of the risk of physical danger.

Further assistance on these issues is given by the Guidance.

Leonard v Southern Derbyshire Chamber of Commerce

[2001] IRLR 19, EAT

[7.124] The applicant was employed by the respondent from 1993 and was dismissed on grounds of capability in October 1998, having been absent from work with clinical depression since March 1998. A tribunal concluded that she was not a disabled person because there was no substantial adverse effect on normal day-to-day activities. In the reasoning of the tribunal it appears to have read the Guidance as a gauge and balanced out what the appellant could and could not do.

HELD: Nelson J in the EAT held that the tribunal should have focused on those things the appellant could not do or could only do with difficulty, rather than conducting a balancing exercise of what she could and could not do.

Abadeh v British Telecommunications plc

[2001] ICR 156, [2001] IRLR 23, EAT

[7.125] Mr Abadeh was a telephone operator. He received a burst of high pitched noise through his headset which resulted in permanent hearing loss in his left ear, tinnitus and post-traumatic stress disorder. He claimed the BT had discriminated against him following the incident. The appellant's DDA claim was dismissed on the preliminary point that the adverse effects were not substantial and he was therefore not disabled. The tribunal found that since he did not live in London, travel by underground was not a day-to-day activity and neither was flying. Mr Abadeh appealed.

HELD: Normal day-to-day activities must be considered without regard to whether it is normal for the particular individual concerned. When considering the ability to travel by public transport it is not necessary to consider each form of transport in isolation, but by looking at transport as a whole. The tribunal should have found that both travel by underground and aeroplane were normal day-to-day activities and then whether on the facts of this case his inability to use these forms of transport amounted to an impairment that had a substantial and long-term adverse effect. Whether an inability to use one or more forms of transport has a substantial adverse effect will depend upon the facts of each individual case.

Ekpe v Metropolitan Police Comr

[2001] ICR 1084, [2001] IRLR 605, EAT

[7.126] The appellant suffered from a wasting of the muscles in her right hand. She was required to move to a new job involving the use of a keyboard. She complained of discrimination and a preliminary hearing was held on the issue of disability. Her evidence was that she could not carry heavy shopping, scrub pans, peel, grate or sew. She also gave evidence that she sometimes used her left hand to feed herself and apply make-up. A tribunal concluded that she was not disabled because it was only the heavier shopping she could not carry and she was able to make adjustments. They did not think that applying make-up and using hair-rollers were normal day-to-day activities because these were normally done by women as opposed to the population at large.

HELD: Allowing the appellant's appeal, the EAT held that the tribunal had focused on specific problems highlighted by the appellant rather than considering the issue of whether her manual dexterity or ability to move every-day objects was impaired. It noted that if an ability within paragraph 4(1) of Schedule 1 is affected, it is almost inevitable that there will be an impact on normal day-to-day activities. At that point a tribunal must consider whether the impact has a substantial adverse affect on normal day-to-day activities. In this context normal means not abnormal or unusual. A tribunal can take account of the appellant's actions before it. However, if a tribunal is to do that, it should raise that issue at the hearing. A finding that the applicant was disabled was substituted for the tribunal's original decision.

CAN ACTIVITIES AT WORK CONSTITUTE NORMAL DAY-TO-DAY ACTIVITIES?

Law Hospital NHS Trust v Rush

[2001] IRLR 611, Ct of Sess

[7.127] The respondent was employed as a nurse. In 1984 she injured her back at work and was absent on sick leave for 14 months. Her disability was assessed at 7% and when she returned to work she was employed on light duties. She suffered a further injury to her back in 1997 and remained off work until dismissed in 1999. The respondent denied that she was disabled. Evidence was given that she could perform her nursing duties but the tribunal rejected evidence of what she could do at work on the grounds that this was not a matter for them to consider. The tribunal preferred her evidence that her mobility was affected, that she could not lift with her right hand, that she needed help dressing and took pain-killers daily.

The EAT dismissed the employer's appeal and they appealed to the Court of Session.

HELD: Although their appeal was rejected on the basis that they had not led direct evidence of what the applicant could do at work, the Court of Session noted that the particular duties at work could not be equated with normal day-to-day activities but that an individual's work may include some normal day-to-day activities and that evidence of what an individual can do at work may have a bearing on a witness' credibility.

Quinlan v B & Q plc

[1999] Disc LR 76, EAT

[7.128] Mr Quinlan worked for B&Q. He underwent open heart surgery which meant that when he returned to work as an assistant in the garden department he was unable to undertake heavy lifting. He was able to carry everyday shopping and move everyday items.

HELD: He was not disabled because his ability to carry out normal day-to-day activities had not been affected.

Progressive conditions

[7.129] Specific protection is given to those suffering from a condition that is progressive such a cancer, multiple sclerosis and HIV/AIDS, by paragraph 8 of Schedule 1 to DDA:

8.—(1) Where—
(a) a person has a progressive condition (such as cancer, multiple sclerosis or muscular dystrophy or infection by the human immunodeficiency virus),
(b) as a result of that condition, he has an impairment which has (or had) an effect on his ability to carry out normal day-to-day activities, but
(c) that effect is not (or was not) a substantial adverse effect,

he shall be taken to have an impairment which has such a substantial adverse effect if the condition is likely to result in his having such an impairment.

(2) Regulations may make provision, for the purposes of this paragraph—
(a) for conditions of a prescribed description to be treated as being progressive;
(b) for conditions of a prescribed description to be treated as not being progressive.

However, it is clear that simply being diagnosed as suffering from such a condition will not ensure protection under the Act.

Mowat-Brown v University of Surrey

[2002] IRLR 235, EAT

[7.130] The appellant complained of discrimination following a reduction in his teaching hours. He alleged that he was disabled following a diagnosis of multiple sclerosis. A tribunal rejected his complaint on the basis that he had few symptoms and it did not consider his condition, based upon the medical evidence, to be progressive. Mr Mowat-Brown appealed.

HELD: The EAT rejected his appeal because on the evidence the tribunal had made a permissible finding. It noted that in determining whether a condition is progressive an applicant must establish that on the balance of probabilities his condition will have a substantial adverse effect on his ability to perform normal day-to-day activities at some stage in the future. The appellant had failed to cross this threshold and his appeal failed.

KNOWLEDGE OF AN EMPLOYEE'S DISABILITY

H J Heinz & Co Ltd v Kenrick

[2000] IRLR 144, [2000] ICR 491, EAT

[7.131] Mr Kenrick worked for Heinz from 1979 until he became ill in May 1996 with an unidentified illness but which he told the company he thought was chronic fatigue syndrome (CFS). He was absent from work from May 1996. In February 1997 he was warned that his continued absence could result in his dismissal unless he could indicate when he was due to return. He was dismissed in April 1997 when the company's doctor advised that he did not know when the respondent was likely to return. Mr Kenrick asked that the decision be delayed until he had seen an immunologist. The company refused. Subsequently a diagnosis of CFS was confirmed.

A tribunal found that the company knew the details of the respondent's condition even though they did not know exactly what he was suffering from and concluded that he had been discriminated against. The company appealed to the EAT.

HELD: Heinz had sufficient knowledge of the manifestations of Mr Kenrick's illness at the time of his dismissal for them to have treated him less favourably by reason of his disability. The DDA does not require a subjective approach to be taken to a company's treatment of an individual, the company's treatment should be judged objectively and the question was whether there was a relationship between the disability and the treatment rather than whether the employer knew of the disability.

O'Neill v Symm & Co Ltd

[1998] IRLR 233, [1998] ICR 481, [1999] Disc LR 59

[7.132] At her interview Mrs O'Neill told the respondent that she suffered from viral pneumonia for which she had taken time off work that year. She was appointed and her employment commenced in September 1996. She was off work in October with a viral illness. She was signed off work again at the end of November and remained absent from work until her dismissal on 3 December 1996. During the course of her employment Miss O'Neill had a number of hospital appointments in an endeavour to identify the cause of her problems.

Prior to her dismissal the applicant had been diagnosed as suffering from ME/CFS. She alleged that on the day before her dismissal the respondent should have received a sickness certificate which would have confirmed this diagnosis. The respondent denied this.

A tribunal dismissed her complaint because the respondent was not aware that she had a disability.

HELD: The EAT dismised her complaint. Knowledge of the disability or the material features of it are relevant to the reason whether the employer's actions relate to the employee's disability. Without such knowledge the employer could not be liable for disability discrimination.

The decision in O'Neill has been subjected to criticism and the decision in *Heinz* is to be preferred.

Ridout v TC Group

[1998] IRLR 628, [1999] Disc LR 8, EAT

[7.133] Ms Ridout applied for a job and in her application form she noted that she suffered from photosensitive epilepsy. She was not contacted prior to her interview about any arrangements she might need for the interview. She arrived for her interview wearing sunglasses around her neck. The interview was conducted in a room with strip-lighting and she commented that she might be disadvantaged. The employers thought this was a reference to her sunglasses.

A tribunal found that there was no discrimination because there was no onus on the employer to make every possible enquiry about her condition. She appealed to the EAT.

HELD: Morison P, dismissing her appeal, held that as a matter of evidence the appellant had not put the respondent on notice that the environment in which the interview was conducted was placing her at a substantial disadvantage. There was no duty to make reasonable adjustments because no reasonable employer could be expected to know that the arrangements made could disadvantage the appellant. The employer's duty had to be judged in the light of section 6(6)(b) of the DDA which provided that there was no duty to make an adjustment if the employer does not know and could not be reasonably be expected to know that the individual has a disability. It is not desirable that employers should be required to ask detailed questions about a person's disability.

Scope of the Act for employment purposes

[7.134] Section 5 of the DDA provides that the within the employment provisions of the Act 'discrimination' means

(1) For the purposes of this Part, an employer discriminates against a disabled person if—
(a) for a reason which relates to the disabled person's disability, he treats him less favourably than he treats or would treat others to whom that reason does not or would not apply; and
(b) he cannot show that the treatment in question is justified.

(2) For the purposes of this Part, an employer also discriminates against a disabled person if—
(a) he fails to comply with a section 6 duty imposed on him in relation to the disabled person; and
(b) he cannot show that his failure to comply with that duty is justified.

Kent County Council v Mingo

[2000] IRLR 90, EAT

[7.135] Mr Mingo worked as an assistant cook until he hurt his back. Following sick leave he returned to work as a helper and was advised by his doctor that he could not undertake work that involved lifting or heavy work. It was recommended that he be re-deployed. The council categorised him as a Category B re-deployee. Category A re-deployees were those staff who were at risk of redundancy. Mr Mingo expressed interest in a number of jobs but was told that they were reserved for Category A staff. He was also turned down for a position which he was told he would have been appointed to if he had been a Category A re-deployee. Eventually his supernumerary role as a helper came to an end and he was dismissed.

A tribunal found he had been discriminated against contrary to section 5(1) and (2). The council appealed to the EAT

HELD: A scheme that gives precedence to those being made redundant did not adequately give effect to the council's obligations under the DDA. Had the council permitted Mr Mingo to be treated as a Category A re-deployee he would not have been dismissed; as a result he had been subjected to less favourable treatment because the re-deployment policy placed him at a disadvantage compared to other employees.

Hammersmith and Fulham London Borough v Farnsworth

[2000] IRLR 691, EAT

[7.136] Ms Farnsworth was offered employment subject to medical clearance by the Borough's occupational health physician (OHP). This revealed that she had a history of mental illness. The OHP's report indicated that if the illness recurred her attendance and performance would be affected. This resulted in the withdrawal of the offer. Ms Farnsworth complained to a tribunal of disability discrimination.

A tribunal found in her favour because the OHP was acting as the council's agent and the council were on notice of the illness and should have made further enquiries about it. It also concluded that the discrimination was not justified. The council appealed to the EAT.

HELD: Charles J held that the OHP was acting as the council's agent and on the facts of this case no distinction could be made between the council and the OHP. By denying itself knowledge of Ms Farnsworth's medical history, the council caused the OHP to become a relevant decision-maker. Knowledge of disability at the section 5(1)(a) stage is irrelevant. However, knowledge is necessary when considering the duty to make adjustments in section 6. Equally knowledge, or the lack of knowledge, is not a necessary ingredient for the purposes of section 5(1)(b). The appeal was dismissed.

The date at which to assess the question of disability

Goodwin v Patent Office

[1999] ICR 302, EAT

[7.137] (For facts, see 7.116 above.) In *Goodwin* the EAT regarded the appropriate time at which to decide whether the employee was a person with a disability was the date of the discriminatory act.

Greenwood v British Airways plc

[1999] IRLR 600, [1999] ICR 969, EAT

[7.138] Mr Greenwood had worked for the respondent for a number of years and suffered from nervous tension. He saw the company's physician who diagnosed a chronic underlying medical problem which included flashbacks which could prevent him from working. He was absent from work for a period of time and eventually returned. He was intermittently on medication from 1994 to September 1997. Mr Greenwood eventually applied for promotion but was unsuccessful because he was regarded as unreliable due to his sickness record. He brought a claim under the DDA.

A tribunal concluded that he was not disabled and he appealed.

HELD: Tribunals should look at the total period of illness both before and after the alleged discriminatory act up to the date of the tribunal hearing to conclude whether an individual is or is not a person suffering from a disability. Taking into account his illness since the date of the discriminatory act, he was a person with a disability. The EAT also concluded that he was a person who had been suffering from a disability and that the adverse effect had recurred.

Cruickshank v VAW Motorcast Ltd

[2002] IRLR 24, EAT

[7.139] Mr Cruickshank worked in a foundry. As a result of his job he developed occupational asthma. The company's doctor advised that he should not work where he would be exposed to fumes. His role was changed, however, as a reorganisation resulted in him being exposed to fumes again and this resulted in periods of absence due to sickness. It was recommended that he should work outside the foundry either in the yard or the office. Despite this, his condition worsened and his employment was terminated. Once away from the foundry his condition improved. He claimed both unfair dismissal and that he had been discriminated against on the grounds of his disability.

A tribunal considered his condition at the time of the hearing and dismissed his claim under the DDA because he had not shown that his asthma had a substantial adverse effect upon his ability to carry out normal day-to-day activities. His unfair dismissal claim was also dismissed and he appealed to the EAT.

HELD: The tribunal was wrong to consider his condition at the time of the hearing; the material time was at the time of the discriminatory act. Where a person's condition fluctuates a tribunal should consider whether a person's ability to carry out normal day-to-day activities is affected both at work and outside work. Symptoms that occur at work which have a substantial adverse effect should not be disregarded provided that the employee's ability to undertake day-to-day tasks can be measured. Where an employee is dismissed because of the effect of an impairment upon his abilities at work it is that effect that should be measured.

In the circumstances Mr Cruickshank was a person suffering from a disability.

Small employer exemption

[7.140] When originally introduced, the DDA applied only to those employers who had 20 or more employees. This was reduced to 15 from 1 December 1998 as a result of the Disability Discrimination (Exemption for Small Employers) Order 1998.

Hardie v C D Northern Ltd

[2000] IRLR 87

[7.141] Lindsay P heard an appeal from a tribunal decision that in considering whether an employer fell within the small employer exemption, reference was only to be made to the particular employer rather than any associated or subsidiary companies. In upholding the tribunal's decision, Lindsay P noted that the provisions of section 68 of the DDA (the definitions section) are clear. There was no justification for extending the ambit of the Act to associated employers. The question in each case was whether the particular employer fell within the small employer exemption.

Discrimination against contract workers

[7.142] Disabled workers who provide services under a contract are protected by virtue of DDA, s 12:

> 12.—(1) It is unlawful for a principal, in relation to contract work, to discriminate against a disabled person—
> (a) in the terms on which he allows him to do that work;
> (b) by not allowing him to do it or continue to do it;
> (c) in the way he affords him access to any benefits or by refusing or deliberately omitting to afford him access to them; or
> (d) by subjecting him to any other detriment.
> .....
>
> (6) In this section—
> 'principal' means a person ('A') who makes work available for doing by individuals who are employed by another person who supplies them under a contract made with A;
> 'contract work' means work so made available; and
> 'contract worker' means any individual who is supplied to the principal under such a contract.

The extent of the protection was seen in *Abbey Life v Tansell*.

Abbey Life Assurance Co Ltd v Tansell

[2000] IRLR 387 , CA

[7.143] Mr Tansell was the sole shareholder and one of four directors in a company called Intelligents Ltd. Intelligents registered with MHC, an employment agency. MHC entered into an agreement with Abbey Life for the provision of Mr Tansell's services. Mr Tansell was disabled and Abbey Life rejected his services. Mr Tansell claimed that both MHC and Abbey Life had discriminated against him and were liable under DDA, s 12.

In the EAT, Morrison P held that where there was a chain of inter-linked contracts, the principle for the purposes of section 12(6) is the end-user. As a result, Abbey Life were the appropriate target rather than MHC, who were merely a link in the chain. Abbey Life appealed to the Court of Appeal.

HELD: Mummery LJ. upheld the EAT's decision, noting that it is not necessary for there to be a direct contractual link between the principle and the worker; all that it necessary is the supply of an individual under a contract.

WHO IS AN APPROPRIATE COMPARATOR?

[7.144] There was initially much debate over the question of how potentially discriminatory treatment was to be judged using the familiar concept of a comparator from sex and race discrimination. That question appears to have been conclusively answered.

Clark v TDG Ltd (t/a Novacold)

[1999] 2 All ER 977, [1999] ICR 951, [1999] IRLR 318, CA

[7.145] Mr Clark was a process operator in a manual and physically demanding job. He suffered a back injury at work and was absent from September 1996. The company obtained a medical report in December 1996 from his GP, indicating that it was difficult to anticipate his return to work in the near future. At the end of December his orthopaedic surgeon suggested that the injury should improve over 12 months from the date of the injury. No exact date was given for his return and, as a result, he was dismissed in January 1997.

An employment tribunal concluded that although he had been dismissed for a section 5(1) reason, there had been no discrimination under section 5(2) because he was treated in a similar manner to those who had been off work for a comparable period of time, but for a non-disablement reason. The EAT upheld his appeal on the section 5(2) ground because they said it was not contingent on a claim under section 5(1). In addition, the tribunal were wrong to find that a section 6 duty does not arise on dismissal. The EAT remitted the case to a tribunal to determine whether there had been discrimination under section 5(2). Mr Clark appealed to the Court of Appeal against the finding that he had not been discriminated against contrary to section 5(1) and that there had not been a failure to make reasonable adjustments.

HELD: Treatment is less favourable if the reason for it does not apply to others. The comparison to be made was with others who had no difficulty performing their role rather than others who had difficulty for a non-disability reason. Dismissal falls within section 5(1) rather than section 5(2) of the DDA. Where an employee has been dismissed there is no duty to make reasonable adjustments under the Act. A claim under section 5(2) is independent of a claim under section 5(1). An employee who has been dismissed may bring a claim under section 5(2) for acts of discrimination arising prior to the dismissal. Where there is a section 5(2) claim, section 6 and the duty to make reasonable adjustments is relevant. There had been less favourable treatment under section 5(1)(a) and the question of justification was remitted to a tribunal.

REDUNDANCY SELECTION ARRANGEMENTS

British Sugar plc v Kirker

[1998] IRLR 624, EAT

[7.146] This was an appeal from the decision of a tribunal that Mr Kirker, a severely visually impaired employee who was eligible for full blind registration, had been discriminated against in a redundancy selection process. There was evidence before the tribunal of acts by the company that showed they were ill-disposed to him because of his poor eye sight which, he had been told, prevented his promotion on previous occasions. The company chose well-known redundancy selection criteria which were: flexibility, team work, self-motivation, initiative, skills, customer and business focus, qualifications, performance and competence, potential, current disciplinary record and attendance. Mr Kirker scored very poorly in some of these categories and was selected for redundancy. The tribunal found that if reasonable adjustments had been made he would have scored close to the top of the selection pool. It therefore found that discrimination had taken place. The company appealed.

HELD: Judge Peter Clark in the EAT held that the tribunal was entitled to take into account the company's conduct in the period pre-dating the DDA to determine whether or not old perceptions of the applicant's value as an employee were carried through into the assessment process. It is not necessary for a tribunal to identify an appropriate comparator because a like-for-like comparison was not required. It was also noted that if disability discrimination was found in a dismissal case, it would be highly exceptional not to find that the dismissal was also unfair.

The obligation to make reasonable adjustments

[7.147] DDA, s 6 provides:

> 6.—(1) Where—
> (a) any arrangements made by or on behalf of an employer, or
> (b) any physical feature of premises occupied by the employer,
>
> place the disabled person concerned at a substantial disadvantage in comparison with persons who are not disabled, it is the duty of the employer to take such steps as it is reasonable, in all the circumstances of the case, for him to have to take in order to prevent the arrangements or feature having that effect.
>
> (2) Subsection (1)(a) applies only in relation to—
> (a) arrangements for determining to whom employment should be offered;
> (b) any term, condition or arrangements on which employment, promotion, a transfer, training or any other benefit is offered or afforded.
>
> (3) The following are examples of steps which an employer may have to take in relation to a disabled person in order to comply with subsection (1)—
> (a) making adjustments to premises;
> (b) allocating some of the disabled person's duties to another person;
> (c) transferring him to fill an existing vacancy;
> (d) altering his working hours;
> (e) assigning him to a different place of work;
> (f) allowing him to be absent during working hours for rehabilitation, assessment or treatment;
> (g) giving him, or arranging for him to be given, training;
> (h) acquiring or modifying equipment;

(i) modifying instructions or reference manuals;
(j) modifying procedures for testing or assessment;
(k) providing a reader or interpreter;
(l) providing supervision.

(4) In determining whether it is reasonable for an employer to have to take a particular step in order to comply with subsection (1), regard shall be had, in particular, to—
(a) the extent to which taking the step would prevent the effect in question;
(b) the extent to which it is practicable for the employer to take the step;
(c) the financial and other costs which would be incurred by the employer in taking the step and the extent to which taking it would disrupt any of his activities;
(d) the extent of the employer's financial and other resources;
(e) the availability to the employer of financial or other assistance with respect to taking the step.

This subsection is subject to any provision of regulations made under subsection (8).

Morse v Wiltshire County Council

[1998] ICR 1023, [1998] IRLR 352, EAT

[7.148] This was an appeal against a finding that the Mr Morse's disability was so severe that dismissal was justified because no reasonable adjustments could have been made to working conditions. Mr Morse was a road worker. He suffered from a lack of grip in his right hand, stiffness in his right leg and susceptibility to blackouts, as a result of which he refused to undertake driving duties. Duties assigned to him consisted of assisting others and labouring if power tools were needed. A financial problem forced the council to consider a reduction in employees. A major consideration was the need to provide a winter road service, which included driving duties. Redundancy selection was performed and a key criterion was the ability to drive. On that basis the Mr Morse was selected for dismissal.

HELD in the EAT, per Bell J: That the tribunal had failed to adopt the correct approach in deciding that there had not been a breach of section 5(2) and that section 6(1) does not apply to dismissals. Tribunals are required to follow a number of sequential steps:
1. Do s 6(1) and s 6(2) impose a s 6(1) duty?
2. If yes, has the employer taken such steps as are reasonable for it to take to prevent the disabled person being placed at a substantial disadvantage?
3. Could the employer have taken any other steps set out in s 6(3)?
4. Tribunals must have regard to the factors in s 6(4) when carrying out step (3); and only after following these steps and having found a breach of section 6(1) does the issue of justification arise.

Since the tribunal had not adopted the correct approach and had not considered whether there were any steps that could be taken in accordance with section 6(3) which might have enabled Mr Morse to be kept on, the matter was remitted back to the tribunal.

Fu v London Borough of Camden

[2001] IRLR 186, EAT

[7.149] Ms Fu was a housing officer who suffered two accidents at work in 1993, resulting in a year's absence; after the accidents she needed to use a walking-stick. She suffered another accident in 1997 which caused further absence. Ms Fu asked for changes to be made to the working arrangements but a report from the Borough's occupational health unit indicated that it did not know whether the Ms Fu would be able to return to work. She was given the option of ill-health retirement or dismissal. She chose ill-health retirement.

A disability discrimination claim was brought before a tribunal which dismissed it, indicating that the Borough's decision to dismiss when it was unclear whether she would ever return to work was reasonable. She appealed to the EAT.

HELD: The tribunal had failed to consider whether the Borough had met its pre-dismissal obligations by considering whether the adjustments requested by her would have overcome her symptoms, which would have allowed her to return to work. Section 6 required consideration not only of the proposed adjustments, but also whether there were reasonable adjustments to make and whether the Borough were justified in not making them. A tribunal is under a duty to consider the extent to which the employee's proposals might have overcome the symptoms that had prevented a return to work.

The matter was remitted back to the tribunal.

Personal, non-job-related adjustments

[7.150] The extent to which an employer is required to make adjustments for a disabled employee is central to the issue of reasonable adjustments. It is not all of a disabled person's needs that have to be catered for under the duty of reasonable adjustment.

Kenny v Hampshire Constabulary

[1999] IRLR 76, [1999] ICR 27, EAT

[7.151] Mr Kenny was physically disabled, suffering from cerebral palsy. He needed assistance to go to the toilet and open food packets at lunch. He was offered employment by the Hampshire Constabulary subject to suitable arrangements being made for his personal needs. None of those working at the office were willing to volunteer to assist him. He suggested a computer link to his house, but this was not practicable because he would be handling material of a sensitive nature. Mr Kenny considered whether his mother could attend the office to help him but the idea was rejected and an application was made for a support worker. However, Social Services could not confirm when a decision would be taken on that issue and the offer was eventually withdrawn.

A tribunal found that the appellant had been discriminated against but that it had been justified. Both the appellant and the respondent appealed.

HELD, per Morrison P, allowing the respondent's cross-appeal: That an employer's duty to make reasonable adjustments extended to the job and the premises; it did not extend to non-job-related matters such as the provision of an assistant to cope with an individual's personal needs. The claim under section 5(2) failed, but the claim under section 5(1) was remitted to another tribunal to determine the issue of whether the respondent was justified in not waiting for the support worker application to be determined.

British Gas Services Ltd v McCaull

[2001] IRLR 60, EAT

[7.152] Mr McCaull was a driver. He suffered an epileptic fit at work and wrote off his van. The occupational health adviser advised him that he could return to work subject to working under supervision, not driving and not working with electrical equipment. He was offered clerical work or termination. He was not given information that would normally be provided in these circumstances and rejected the offer that was made to him which was for a 30% reduction in salary. Mr McCaull was dismissed.

A tribunal upheld his complaint on the grounds of less favourable treatment and failure to make reasonable adjustments. His unfair dismissal complaint was upheld because the employers had acted unreasonably in treating the rejection of the offer as a sufficient reason to dismiss. The employer appealed to the EAT.

HELD: The application had been made in time because the relevant date in cases of less favourable treatment involving dismissal was the date of dismissal. When considering the duty to make reasonable adjustments in DDA, s 6, an employer can fulfil that obligation without consciously considering the section 6 duties. The test in section 6 is an objective one and the focus should be on what an employer did and did not do, rather than what it considered. The finding of unfair dismissal was held to be perverse because Mr McCaull had been offered the only available job.

Is it relevant that the applicant or advisers can think of no suitable alternatives?

Cosgrove v Caesar and Howie

[2001] IRLR 653, EAT

[7.153] This was an appeal from the decision of a tribunal dismissing the appellants complaint of disability discrimination where she had been dismissed after being absent from work for a year with depression. The tribunal held that the employer was justified in taking such action where there was no date for her return and others who had been absent for a similar period would have been dismissed. In addition, neither the applicant nor her solicitor could make any suggestions for adjustments.

HELD: Following the decision in *Clark v TDG Ltd (t/a Novacold)* (see 7.145 above), the tribunal had applied an incorrect test. The applicant had been dismissed for her absence and someone who had not been absent would not have been dismissed. The employers were in breach of their section 6 duty (to make reasonable adjustments) because they had given no thought to them. The fact that the applicant and her advisers could not think of any adjustments did not remove the duty from the employer. The appeal was allowed and the case remitted to the tribuna.

Monetary benefits

London Clubs Management Ltd v Hood

[2001] IRLR 719

[7.154] This was an appeal from the decision of a tribunal that an employee who was disabled by reason of cluster headaches suffered less favourable treatment when the employer decided to exercise its discretion generally not to pay sick pay to employees absent through illness.

HELD: The tribunal had erred in law because it should have considered whether the applicant failed to receive sick pay for a reason related to his disability. For a section 6 duty to arise, the employer's arrangements must place the disabled person at a substantial disadvantage. The tribunal failed to indicate whether it had reached this conclusion. If the tribunal had expressly considered the issue of whether he was placed at a substantial disadvantage by non-payment of sick pay it might have reached a different conclusion. Section 6 applies to monetary benefits and reasonable adjustments can include the payment of sick pay.

Employer's duty when faced with non-co-operation by the employee

[7.155] See *Callagan v Glasgow City Council* (7.160 below).

Justification

[7.156] Unlike the other discrimination legislation, an employer may seek to justify its act of direct and indirect disability discrimination (DDA, s 5):

(3) Subject to subsection (5), for the purposes of subsection (1) treatment is justified if, but only if, the reason for it is both material to the circumstances of the particular case and substantial.

(4) For the purposes of subsection (2), failure to comply with a section 6 duty is justified if, but only if, the reason for the failure is both material to the circumstances of the particular case and substantial.

(5) If, in a case falling within subsection (1), the employer is under a section 6 duty in relation to the disabled person but fails without justification to comply with that duty, his treatment of that person cannot be justified under subsection (3) unless it would have been justified even if he had complied with the section 6 duty.

Jones v Post Office

[2001] EWCA Civ 558, [2001] IRLR 384

[7.157] Mr Jones had been a van driver since 1977. Two years later he was diagnosed as having non-insulin dependent diabetes. He suffered a heart attack in 1997 and was subsequently treated with insulin. His driving duties were removed because the respondent's medical fitness standards did not permit drivers to take insulin. After presenting a disability complaint, the respondent agreed to review its decision. As a result the appellant was permitted to return to limited driving duties but driving was limited to two hours driving duty in any 24-hour period. This job offer was rejected and proceedings commenced. The respondent conceded that discrimination had taken place before the offer. The tribunal found the offer of two hours driving duty was not justified because the medical evidence relied upon was incorrect and in their opinion this meant that the justification could not be either material or substantial.

The EAT allowed the employer's appeal and remitted the case to an employment tribunal. Mr Jones appealed to the Court of Appeal.

HELD: For an employer to rely on DDA, s 5(3), it has to establish that the reason given satisfies the statutory criteria. The respondent's medical experts were suitably qualified and the opinions expressed by them provided a reason that was both material and substantial. A tribunal is not permitted, when dealing with competent experts, to form its own opinion of whether or not the assessment was correct. The role of the tribunal is not very different from that which it performs in unfair dismissal cases; the tribunal members might have come to a different conclusion, but their function was to assess the materiality and substantiality of the employer's reasons.

The appeal was dismissed

Surrey Police v Marshall

[2002] IRLR 843, EAT

[7.158] Despite suffering from manic depression Ms Marshall was offered a position as a finger print officer, subject to medical approval. The appellant's medical officer decided that she did not meet the medical standards and was concerned about the respondent's and other's safety, particularly since she had stopped taking her medication. A tribunal held that the appellant had failed to show that their treatment was justified because they had not obtained a suitable medical opinion and at the time of making the decision no medical evidence had been obtained. They disregarded medical evidence obtained after the decision had been reached. The police appealed.

HELD: In allowing their appeal, that there was evidence before the police's medical officer at the time she reached her decision that could support the decision she made and it was a decision open to a reasonable person to make based upon the material available. Tribunals were warned that they should not set too high a requirement for medical advice when considering the issue of justification. The tribunal was able to consider medical evidence obtained after her rejection because that went to the issue of whether the decision could have been taken at the time and to its reasonableness.

Baynton v Saurus General Engineers Ltd

[1999] IRLR 604, [2000] ICR 375, EAT

[7.159] Appeal from a tribunal decision that the apellant failed to establish that he had been less favourably treated. Mr Baynton suffered an injury at work which resulted in a 15% disability to his left hand. He was off work from February 1997 to 30 January 1998 when his employment was terminated due to his sickness absence. Following the decision in *Clark v TDG Ltd t/a Novacold* (see 7.146 above), it was accepted that there had been less favourable treatment and the issue on appeal was justification.

HELD: When considering the issue of justification, tribunals must conduct a balancing exercise taking into account the interests of the employer and the employee and reviewing all the circumstances. Since the tribunal had failed to do that, the appeal would be upheld and the case remitted to the tribunal to consider the issue of justification.

Callaghan v Glasgow City Council

[2001] IRLR 724, EAT

[7.160] This was an appeal by Mr Callaghan from the decision of a tribunal that he had not been discriminated against despite a finding that he was disabled. Mr Callaghan had increasing periods of sickness absence and failed to follow notification procedures. He received a warning and subsequent meetings were arranged, but he failed to attend. The tribunal found his dismissal was justified, given his long period of absence and that there had been no breach of a section 6 duty by failing to offer part-time work. Mr Callaghan appealed.

HELD, per Lord Johnston, dismissing the appeal: That following *Jones v Post Office* (see 7.157 above), there had to be a causal connection between the discriminatory act and the justifying circumstances. Disagreeing with the decision of the EAT in *Quinn v Schwarzkopf* (below), he held that the knowledge of the disability is not essential to establishing justification. At the time of dismissal the appellant was not fit and it was not known when he would be fit. The justification defence was made out. In the particular circumstances of this case, including the employee's non-co-operation, there was no duty to consider part-time work.

Does an employer need to know of the disability, to rely upon a justification defence?

Quinn v Schwarzkopf

[2002] IRLR 602, Ct of Sess

[7.161] Mr Quinn became ill and was diagnosed as suffering a form of rheumatoid arthritis and was eventually dismissed. The employment tribunal found that the employers did not know at the time of dismissal that he was disabled and they thought he was on sick leave. As a result the tribunal found that the appellant was disabled but that his dismissal was justified. In the EAT it was held that the burden is on the employer objectively to justify its actions. That burden cannot be satisfied if the employer does not know of the condition from which the employee is suffering. The EAT considered that without knowledge of the disability at the time of the act such a defence could not be raised after the relevant events. Mr Quinn appealed to the Court of Session. It was conceded on the appeal that the EAT had misdirected itself on the issue of justification and knowledge of the disability.

HELD: The tribunal had not misdirected itself on the issue of justification by holding that an employer does not discharge its duty under DDA, s 5 if, during the course of employment, it did not consider what should be done because it did not know of the disability. The tribunal was not wrong to find that the employer was justified in its act of dismissing Mr Quinn. It was not necessary for the tribunal to consider and mention every kind of adjustment that could have been made. In the circumstances of this case the company were justified in terminating Mr Quinn's employment. The tribunal's decision was restored.

The role of medical evidence and treatment

Woodrup v London Borough of Southwark

[2002] EWCA Civ 1716, [2003] IRLR 111

[7.162] Miss Woodrup appealed from the determination of a preliminary question of whether she was a person suffering from a disability. She attended the tribunal hearing without a medical report but armed with four 'medical' documents relating to her medical condition; a letter from 1992 confirming that she had been a patient at a psychiatric clinic being treated for a general anxiety disorder, a sick note from 1993, a GP's letter dated November 1999 indicating that she suffered from an anxiety neurosis and had been receiving medical treatment for five years and a letter from her consultant which confirmed that her treatment was continuing and that it was too soon for her to stop attending counselling sessions. At the hearing she argued that if she ceased to attend the counselling sessions her condition would return. The tribunal concluded that there was insufficient medical evidence for her to substantiate her claim and it was dismissed. She appealed to the EAT where the issue was whether the tribunal had considered the deduced effects of the impairment. The EAT concluded that she had failed to establish that if her treatment had been discontinued there would have been a substantial adverse effect and dismissed her appeal. She appealed to the Court of Appeal.

HELD: Since Miss Woodrup had not called any medical evidence to support her argument that the tribunal should have disregarded the effects of her medical treatment, she had failed to establish that if her therapy had been discontinued there would have been a substantial adverse effect upon her ability to carry out normal day-to-day activities. In a case involving deduced effects the claimant is required to prove his or her case with some particularity. The documents produced by the applicant together with her evidence were insufficient to prove her case.

Where a tribunal is dealing with an unrepresented applicant it is not required to adopt a more interventionist or inquisitorial approach than it would otherwise do, on the grounds that the DDA requires all service providers to make reasonable adjustments approach. The court was not convinced that a tribunal is a service provider.

Kapadia v London Borough of Lambeth

[2000] IRLR 699, CA

[7.163] In 1995 Mr Kapadia was diagnosed as suffering from reactive depression. He received counselling over the next two years. In 1996 he was promoted but took time off work due to the pressure of work and was subsequently declared permanently unfit in 1997 and medically retired.

Medical evidence was presented to the tribunal by doctors on behalf of Mr Kapadia. However, the tribunal found that although suffering from a clinically well recognised illness, it had only a trivial effect on his normal day-to-day activities. The EAT upheld the his appeal and made a declaration that he was disabled, because the tribunal had substituted its view of Mr Kapadia for that of his medical experts. His evidence was uncontested. The EAT also found that the tribunal had failed to take account of the deduced effects of the impairment in the light of evidence that the condition would have been more severe without the counselling sessions. The employer appealed to the Court of Appeal.

HELD: The tribunal was not entitled to disregard uncontested medical evidence where it was clear that the tribunal had not rejected the basis upon which the opinion had been formed or where there was no evidence that the doctors had misunderstood their instructions. The tribunal, in the light of the uncontested medical evidence, was bound to find that Mr Kapadia had proved his case and the EAT were entitled to make a declaration to that effect.

The appeal was dismissed.

Abadeh v British Telecommunications plc

[2001] IRLR 23, [2001] ICR 156, EAT

[7.164] (See paragraph 7.126 above.) Mr Abadeh was a telephone operator. He received a burst of high pitched noise through his headset which resulted in permanent hearing loss in his left ear, tinnitus and post-traumatic stress disorder. He claimed the BT had discriminated against him following the incident. The appellant's DDA claim was dismissed on the preliminary point that the adverse effects were not substantial and he was therefore not disabled. The tribunal relied heavily on the finding of the BT's Regional Medical Officer who gave oral evidence that she could find nothing to suggest that his impairments were sufficiently severe to have a substantial adverse effect, although there were two written medical reports submitted on behalf of Mr Abadeh.

HELD: The tribunal had relied too heavily on the respondent's medical evidence, making that opinion their own. The tribunal misdirected itself in law in the way it dealt with the expert evidence. Where medical treatment is continuing, the effect of that medical treatment must be ignored unless there has been a permanent improvement, when that improvement must be taken into account. Where treatment has ceased, the effects of the treatment must also be taken into account. In this case it was not clear whether there had been a permanent improvement. Since the tribunal had substituted the RMO's opinion for its own and because it was unclear whether there had been a permanent improvement, on that basis the matter was to be referred back to a new tribunal.

Edwards v Mid-Suffolk District Council

[2001] IRLR 190, [2001] ICR 616, EAT

[7.165] Mr Edwards, who was Head of Corporate Development, was diagnosed with post-viral fatigue syndrome in 1989 and subsequently developed an anxiety state for which he received treatment. He was required to work with a re-deployed assistant, which exacerbated his anxiety state. His GP prepared a report that indicated he was medically fit but that inter-personal difficulties were the problem rather than illness. In December 1997 he was dismissed because of an irretrievable breakdown of the relationship of trust and confidence.

A tribunal rejected his complaints of unfair dismissal because he refused to manage the re-deployee and because they considered that the internal appeal panel were entitled to believe the fault was his. His disability complaint was dismissed because he did not establish a link between his illness and his behaviour. The tribunal thought he was using his mental illness as a device to attack his employer.

HELD, the EAT allowing his appeal: That the tribunal had erred in law because it had not made a finding with regard to the impact of his disability on his behaviour and his ability to work. It is not permissible for a tribunal to find no connection between an applicant's behaviour and disability without explaining its reason for the finding. Tribunals must make findings as to the nature and extent of a disability and consider its impact on an applicant's ability to work. A tribunal is required to take into account medical evidence and if it disagrees with it, explain why. The case was remitted to another tribunal.

Damages

Buxton v Equinox Design Ltd

[1999] IRLR 158, EAT

[7.166] This was an appeal from the decision of the employment tribunal to award the apellant, who suffered from multiple sclerosis, £7,627.50 (including £500 for injury to feelings) following an accident at work. A report had been prepared by the respondent's employment medical advisory service which suggested that the apellant should consider re-training because a decision about his future would need to be taken within a year. When the apellant refused, he was dismissed by the respondent. He appealed against the imposition of a one year limit and an award of £500 for injury to feelings.

HELD: Defining a future loss limited to one year could not be sustained on the evidence because it involved a finding in relation to a risk assessment that had not been completed and a disease that had variable effects. The award of £500 for injury to feeling could not be interfered with and the issue of future loss was to be remitted back to the tribunal.

Constructive dismissal and disability discrimination

Metropolitan Police Comr v Harley

[2001] IRLR 263, EAT

[7.167] Ms Harley suffered from bulimia nervosa. She signed a document at work that resulted in disciplinary proceedings and demotion on 12 February 1999. She appealed against the findings on 5 March on the grounds that it was not deliberate and occurred when she was ill because of her disability. The appeal was held on 2 June 1999 and she subsequently advised the apellant on 20 June that if her appeal failed, she would consider her employment terminated. A month later she treated her employment as terminated and the appeal decision, rejecting her appeal, was received a day later. She lodged her IT1 on 17 September claiming disability discrimination.

The tribunal held, on a preliminary point, that the proceedings had been commenced within time because her constructive dismissal fell within section 4(2)(d). The EAT allowed the employer's appeal on the grounds that section 4(2)(d) was not wide enough to include a constructive dismissal. The statutory language required an act by the employer rather than an election by the employee. The EAT noted that even if they were wrong on that point, the three-month time-limit for bringing a complaint ran from the date of the alleged repudiatory breach rather than the acceptance. In reaching that decision they preferred the decision in *Cast v Croydon College* [1998] IRLR 318, CA, rather than *Reed v Stedman* [1999] IRLR 299, EAT.

Post-employment victimisation

[7.168] Section 4 of the DDA provides:

(1) It is unlawful for an employer to discriminate against a disabled person—
(a) in the arrangements which he makes for the purpose of determining to whom he should offer employment;
(b) in the terms on which he offers that person employment; or
(c) by refusing to offer, or deliberately not offering, him employment.

(2) It is unlawful for an employer to discriminate against a disabled person whom he employs—
(a) in the terms of employment which he affords him;
(b) in the opportunities which he affords him for promotion, a transfer, training or receiving any other benefit;
(c) by refusing to afford him, or deliberately not affording him, any such opportunity; or
(d) by dismissing him, or subjecting him to any other detriment.

Jones v 3M Healthcare Ltd, Kirker v British Sugar plc, Angel v New Possibilities NHS Trust, Bond v Hackney Citizens' Advice Bureau

[2002] EWCA Civ 304, 70 BMLR 1

[7.169] Four appeals were heard together from decisions of the EAT. Each raised the issue of whether a tribunal had jurisdiction to hear complaints of disability discrimination or victimisation where the events complained of occurred after the date of termination.

HELD: There is no binding decision on s 4(2) which is differently constructed to the other discrimination acts. The meaning of the section is plain. An employee's right to protection under s 4(2) is terminated with the cessation of their employment along with their other employment rights. If that were not the case dismissed employees would be in a position to continue to bring claims under s 4(2) for many years after the termination of their employment in respect of post termination acts which may be committed many years later, such as the non provision of a reference

CHAPTER 8

Unfair Dismissal

The law of unfair dismissal – background	[8.1]
General	[8.2]
Eligibility to make an unfair dismissal claim	[8.5]
Normal retiring age: Retirement age	[8.7]
Excluded classes of employees	[8.12]
Was there a dismissal?	[8.14]
Termination by agreement	[8.20]
Ambiguous language	[8.21]
Frustration and fixed-term contracts	[8.24]
Date of dismissal and 'effective date of termination'	[8.27]
Dismissal with notice	[8.30]
Section 97(2) of ERA]	[8.35]
Time at which the dismissal takes effect	[8.36]
Reason for dismissal	[8.37]
Correctly identifying the reason for dismissal	[8.40]
Burden of proof	[8.41]
Establishing the reason	[8.44]
When is the reason to be determined?	[8.46]
Capability	[8.48]
Lack of capability due to ill-health	[8.50]
Conduct	[8.55]
Criminal acts	[8.60]
Breach of a statutory enactment	[8.62]
Redundancy: *Redundancy procedure*	[8.65]
Some other substantial reason	[8.67]
Protection of interest of business	[8.70]
Imprisonment	[8.72]
Dismissal following a transfer of an undertaking	[8.74]
Dismissal for economic, technical or organisational reasons	[8.75]
Dismissals connected with the transfer	[8.76]
Cases on dismissal for economic, technical or organisational reasons	[8.77]
Dismissals 'connected with the transfer'	[8.79]
Automatically unfair reasons: *Leave for family reasons*	[8.80]
Health and safety reason	[8.83]
Refusal to work on a Sunday	[8.87]
Occupational pension scheme trustee	[8.88]
Employee representative	[8.89]

Unfair Dismissal

Trade union reasons	[8.90]
Selection for redundancy	[8.92]
Public interest disclosure	[8.94]
Assertion of a statutory right	[8.96]
The national minimum wage	[8.97]
Tax credit	[8.98]
Procedure	[8.99]
A fair procedure?	[8.100]
The band of reasonable responses	[8.104]
Constructive dismissal	[8.111]
Duty promptly to redress grievances	[8.123]
Remedies: Re-employment	[8.124]
Order for reinstatement	[8.125]
Order for re-engagement	[8.126]
Choice of order and its terms	[8.127]
Compensation: General considerations	[8.136]
The duty to mitigate	[8.141]
Deductions for contributory fault	[8.144]
Just and equitable	[8.148]
Loss of wages	[8.152]

THE LAW OF UNFAIR DISMISSAL – BACKGROUND

[8.1] There follows a short summary of the law of unfair dismissal designed to offer the reader an introduction to the law in this area.

An employee's rights to claim unfair dismissal are found predominantly in the Employment Rights Act 1996 (ERA). This is a consolidating Act. Although the law has been developed and minor changes made over time, it has remained largely unaltered for over 25 years.

For a claim to be accepted as valid by an employment tribunal, it must have been presented within three months of the effective date of termination of employment, or within such later period as the tribunal may allow in appropriate cases.

To claim, certain qualifying criteria must be met and these are found in ERA, ss 108, 109. These in the main, require an employee to have been continuously employed for one year, and to be under the age of sixty-five (or such lower age which may apply as the usual retiring age in the employee's undertaking or business).

ERA sets out a general test of fairness in section 98, which applies to all claims. It is for an employer to show that the reason, or if more than one, the principal reason for dismissal falls within the list of the fair reasons set out in the Act. These are: *capability* of the employee to perform the work, *conduct* of the employee, that the employee was *redundant,* that his continued work would contravene a restriction imposed by any other enactment, or that there was *some other substantial reason* of a kind justifying dismissal of the employee holding the position which he held.

If the employer can point to one or more of these reasons, it must then be able to show that it acted reasonably in all the circumstances in treating it as a sufficient reason for dismissing the employee. This latter requirement is often referred to as being able to show procedural fairness when implementing the dismissal. Unless the employer can establish it had one or more of the fair reasons, the fact that it acted fairly when dismissing may still lead to a finding of unfair dismissal by an employment tribunal.

Remedies for unfair dismissal range from re-engagement (meaning re-employing the employee in a different position), re-instatement (meaning re-employing the employee in the same position) or compensation.

Compensation is made up of two elements – a basic award and a compensatory award. Both are capped at levels, which are indexed-linked annually. The basic award broadly aims to compensate for length of service. The compensatory award sets out to compensate principally for loss of earnings over the period of loss claimed by the employee.

If an employee can be said to have contributed to his own dismissal, then there is a power to reduce compensation by such proportion as the employment tribunal considers just and equitable.

Other incidental rights overlay these rights and will often affect the outcome to a claim.

General

Addison v Babcock FATA Ltd

[1987] IRLR 173, CA

[8.2] Mr Addison was dismissed by reason of redundancy and received his redundancy pay, payment in lieu of notice and an ex gratia payment.

The decision of the tribunal to deduct the value of the payment in lieu and the ex gratia payment from the compensatory award was reversed by the EAT who held that a payment in lieu does not fall to be deducted from the compensatory award.

HELD, on appeal: Babcock's appeal was allowed and the compensatory award reduced by the value of the payment made in lieu of notice. Where an award for lost wages is taken from the date of dismissal, any payment in lieu of notice should be deducted, as an employee should not be able to essentially recover twice for the same period.

Igbo v Johnson Matthey Chemicals Ltd

[1986] IRLR 215, [1986] ICR 505, CA

[8.3] Mrs Igbo wanted extended holiday leave. Her employer granted her the leave provided that she signed a document entitled 'contractual letter for provision of extended holiday absence'. This stated: 'you are required to work your normal shift … (if you fail to return) immediately after the end of your holiday … on 28.9.83 … your contract of employment will automatically terminate on that date'. Upon return to England Mrs Igbo was unwell and sent a medical certificate to her employers explaining her absence. However, her employment was terminated on the basis of the signed letter.

Mrs Igbo claimed unfair dismissal. Following *British Leyland v Ashraf* (1978) the tribunal held the employment had been terminated by a consensual agreement and consequently there was no dismissal. Mrs Igbo appealed.

HELD: Her appeal would be allowed. *British Leyland v Ashraf* was wrongly decided and would be overruled. The provisions in the 'contractual letter' converted the right not to be unfairly dismissed into a conditional right. A term that provides if an employee is, for example, late for work for any reason their contract will automatically terminate, will limit the operation of the statutory terms. Such a provision is void.

Logan Salton v Durham County Council

[1989] IRLR 99, EAT

[8.4] Mr Logan Salton was informed of a disciplinary decision to dismiss him summarily. He then negotiated terms with his employers (via a union representative). This resulted in preparation of a written agreement stipulating that his employment would end by mutual agreement on 31 March 1987, and detailing the financial terms agreed. Mr Salton then claimed unfair dismissal.

He appealed from the tribunal's decision that he had been fairly dismissed and that his employment had been terminated by mutual agreement.

HELD: The agreement was effective, and was not void under ERA, s 203. The 'contract' was separate from, and not a variation of, his contract of employment. He entered into this contract willingly, without duress, after proper advice and for good consideration. Neither did termination depend upon the happening of a, definite or possible, future event. In these circumstances such an agreement should be effective. Whether an agreement is effective is an issue of fact for the tribunal.

ELIGIBILITY TO MAKE AN UNFAIR DISMISSAL CLAIM

[8.5] In order to bring a claim for unfair dismissal employees generally need to have one year's continuous service ERA, s 108(1):

> Section 94 does not apply to the dismissal of an employee unless he has been continuously employed for a period of not less than two years ending with the effective date of termination.

The right only applies to 'employees'.

Ironmonger v Movefield Ltd (t/a Deering Appointments)

[1988] IRLR 461, EAT

[8.6] Mr Ironmonger was employed as a contractor by an employment agency (Deerings) who provided his services to his previous employers. Upon commencement of his first contract Deerings had written to Mr Ironmonger stating that he was 'employed by Unilever', but that they would be responsible for tax and national insurance deductions. After his contract with Unilever came to an end he was employed on a similar basis by another company. Eventually this contract was terminated and Deerings offered him other positions that he turned down. His engagement came to an end and he sued Deerings for unfair dismissal. His claim was rejected by a tribunal because although it found there was an employment contract, it was for a specific purpose which had come to an end.

HELD, on appeal: There was no contract of service between the Mr Ironmonger and Deerings. The applicant had been 'self-employed'. The EAT upheld the tribunal's decision that there was no dismissal, as the project for which the applicant was engaged was merely completed.

Normal retiring age

Retirement age

[8.7] ERA, s 109 provides:

(1) Section 94 does not apply to the dismissal of an employee if on or before the effective date of termination he has attained—
(a) in a case where—
   (i) in the undertaking in which the employee was employed there was a normal retiring age for an employee holding the position held by the employee, and
   (ii) the age was the same whether the employee holding that position was a man or a woman,
that normal retiring age, and
(b) in any other case, the age of sixty-five.

ERA, s156 provides:

(1) An employee does not have any right to a redundancy payment if before the relevant date he has attained—
(a) in a case where—
   (i) in the business for the purposes of which the employee was employed there was a normal retiring age of less than sixty-five for an employee holding the position held by the employee, and
   (ii) the age was the same whether the employee holding that position was a man or woman,
that normal retiring age, and
(b) in any other case, the age of sixty-five.

Brooks v British Telecommunications plc

[1991] IRLR 4, [1991] ICR 286, EAT

[8.8] Claims of unfair dismissal were brought by 23 former employees of BT. When their employment was terminated they were all between the ages of 60 and 64. BT challenged the jurisdiction of the tribunal to hear the claims, given each claimant had reached the company's normal retiring age of 60. The tribunal dismissed their claims on the ground that it had no jurisdiction to hear the claims because the claimants were all over the normal retiring age for that organisation.

HELD, on appeal: To determine whether an applicant was over normal retiring age at the effective date of termination, the tribunal had to (i) identify the undertaking in which they were employed, (ii) identify who in that undertaking held the same position, and (iii) establish what was the normal retiring age for an employee holding that position. Following application of the facts to these qualifications, the tribunal held in each case the normal retiring age was 60. The tribunal was correct to conclude that it had no jurisdiction to hear the claims of unfair dismissal, or for redundancy payments.

Waite v Government Communications Headquarters

[1983] IRLR 341, [1983] 2 AC 714, [1983] ICR 653, [1983] 3 WLR 389, [1983] 2 All ER 1013, HL

[8.9] Mr Waite had been employed as a civil servant. When he was $60\frac{1}{2}$ years old his employment was terminated and he was re-employed in a less senior position. He claimed that he had been unfairly dismissal. The tribunal, EAT and the Court of Appeal all dismissed his claim, given that at the effective date of termination he had reached the normal retiring age for his position. Mr Waite appealed to the House of Lords.

HELD: The test for ascertaining normal retiring age is what would be the reasonable expectation or understanding of employees holding that position at the relevant time.

Rutherford v Towncircle Ltd (t/a Harvest) (in liquidation) and Secretary of State for Trade and Industry (No 2), Bentley v Secretary of State for Trade and Industry

[2002] IRLR 768, EAT

[8.10–8.11] Mr Rutherford was made redundant when he was 67 years old. He sought to bring an unfair dismissal claim and/or a claim for a redundancy payment. The tribunal held the statutory provisions, subject to arguments of justification, did indirectly sexually discriminate. Towncircle appealed. The EAT found flaws in the approach taken by the tribunal and allowed the appeal, remitting the case back to the tribunal.

HELD: At the rehearing, the tribunal found ERA, ss 109 and 156 indirectly discriminated against men, and the Secretary of State had not objectively justified the limitation on claiming unfair dismissal, and redundancy payments, to those under 65. Therefore, Mr Rutherford was entitled to bring a claim for unfair dismissal, despite being 67 at the date of termination of employment.

Note—Towncircle has been appealed. The appeal was listed for May 2003.

Excluded classes of employees

[8.12] ERA, s 111 provides:

(1) A complaint may be presented to an industrial tribunal against an employer by any person that he was unfairly dismissed by the employer.

(2) Subject to subsection (3), an industrial tribunal shall not consider a complaint under this section unless it is presented to the tribunal—
(a) before the end of the period of three months beginning with the effective date of termination, or
(b) within such further period as the tribunal considers reasonable in a case where it is satisfied that it was not reasonably practicable for the complaint to be presented before the end of that period of three months.

(3) Where a dismissal is with notice, an industrial tribunal shall consider a complaint under this section if it is presented after the notice is given but before the effective date of termination.

(4) In relation to a complaint which is presented as mentioned in subsection (3), the provisions of this Act, so far as they relate to unfair dismissal, have effect as if—
(a) references to a complaint by a person that he was unfairly dismissed by his employer included references to a complaint by a person that his employer has given him notice in such circumstances that he will be unfairly dismissed when the notice expires,
(b) references to reinstatement included references to the withdrawal of the notice by the employer,
(c) references to the effective date of termination included references to the date which would be the effective date of termination on the expiry of the notice, and
(d) references to an employee ceasing to be employed included references to an employee having been given notice of dismissal.

Patel v Nagesan

[1995] IRLR 370, [1995] ICR 989, CA

[8.13] Mr Patel took over the nursing home where Mrs Nagesan was employed as matron. Mr Patel gave notice that he was going to change the terms of all contracts of employment. The new contract specified a retirement age of 60. Mrs Nagesan objected to this as she would soon turn 60, and refused to accept the changes. Nevertheless, Mrs Nagesan was given notice of termination of her employment, expiring on 19 December. On 19 November Mrs Nagesan lodged a complaint of unfair dismissal at the tribunal. On 20 November Mr Patel summarily dismissed Mrs Nagesan. The tribunal and EAT both held that the tribunal had jurisdiction to hear her unfair dismissal complaint notwithstanding that it was presented before her summary dismissal. Mr Patel appealed to the Court of Appeal and argued that since Mrs Nagesan was summarily dismissed without notice after her claim had been lodged, she should have made a separate application in respect of the summary dismissal.

HELD: The tribunal did have jurisdiction to hear the complaint of unfair dismissal. On 19 and 20 November as Mrs Nagesan was under notice of dismissal (ERA, s 111 applied). The application of section 111(3) was unaffected by a subsequent summary dismissal and an employer could not invalidate a complaint by proceeding at a later date to dismiss summarily.

WAS THERE A DISMISSAL?

Alcan Extrusions v Yates

[1996] IRLR 327, EAT

[8.14] Mr Yates had worked a 37-hour week on shifts and was paid overtime for weekends and bank holidays. Alcan proposed introducing a continuous shift pattern including weekends and bank holidays. No overtime would be paid for these extra days, and the times at which holiday could be taken was more restricted. The union failed to negotiate an agreement, but Alcan decided to impose the changes regardless. Mr Yates claimed unfair dismissal. The tribunal concluded that Mr Yates had been directly dismissed, as his employment contract had been removed and replaced by a more demanding and uncontemplated regime. The company appealed.

HELD: Departure from the terms of an existing contract may be so substantial as to pass beyond repudiatory variation and actually amount to withdrawal of the whole contract. Whether this has occurred is a question of fact for the tribunal, provided it asks itself the correct question – 'was the old contract being withdrawn or removed from the employee?'

Sheffield v Oxford Controls Co Ltd

[1979] IRLR 133, EAT

[8.15] Mr Sheffield was employed as a director. There was a disagreement between his wife and the controlling shareholders of the company and she was told that she would have to leave the company. He informed the company that if his wife left he would leave also. He was asked how much he wanted to be paid to leave. He was subsequently told that if he did not leave he would be dismissed. An agreement setting out the terms of his departure was agreed and initialled. Mr Sheffield subsequently claimed that he had been unfairly dismissed. A tribunal dismissed his claim and he appealed to the EAT.

HELD: On the facts of this case the tribunal was entitled to find that Mr Sheffield had resigned once an agreement acceptable to him had been reached. This was not a case where he was told that he had the choice of resigning or being dismissed. It was a matter of causation. His employment had terminated because he had reached an agreement that was acceptable to him. His appeal was dismissed.

Martin v MBS Fastenings (Glynwed) Distribution Ltd

[1983] IRLR 198, [1983] ICR 511, CA

[8.16] Mr Martin was permitted to keep a company minibus at his home. One evening he drove the minibus after consuming 6 or 7 pints of beer and had an accident. After explaining what had happened to MBS, Mr Martin was advised that a disciplinary hearing would probably result in dismissal and that it would be better to resign rather than face such an inquiry. He subsequently resigned, and then claimed unfair dismissal. The tribunal found upon the facts before it that there had not been a dismissal and that he had resigned. He appealed to the EAT who upheld his appeal and the company appealed to the Court of Appeal.

HELD: Mr Martin had voluntarily resigned and had not been dismissed. The question in such cases is always the same, 'who really terminated the contract of employment?'

Morris v London Iron and Steel Co Ltd

[1987] IRLR 182, CA

[8.17] A tribunal was unable to reach a decision on the preliminary issue of whether Mr Morris had been dismissed or resigned, and consequently held Mr Morris had failed to satisfy it that he had been dismissed in law. The tribunal commented on its inability to make a finding of fact as to which evidence it preferred. Mr Morris appealed and the EAT remitted the hearing back to the tribunal, holding that it had left the case undecided by failing to come to a conclusion on the issues of fact. The London Iron and Steel Company then appealed to the Court of Appeal.

HELD: The tribunal was not obliged to make a finding of fact if, on all the evidence, it could not. In such circumstances the tribunal was entitled to fall back on the burden of proof, which lays the onus on the employee to prove that he has been dismissed. Since the tribunal had not been satisfied that he had discharged the burden of proof the tribunal had reached the correct conclusion.

Ready Case Ltd v Jackson

[1981] IRLR 312, EAT

[8.18] Mr Jackson had indicated to his employer that he was considering resigning and if he did he would leave in March or April. However, he changed his mind, but Ready Case wrote to him saying he must leave by 30 April at the latest. Mr Jackson found alternative employment in March and asked if he could leave early. He was told that he must complete what he was currently working on. On 22 March the MD told Mr Jackson 'so far as I am concerned you can piss off'. Mr Jackson did not go back into work and the company wrote to him saying that he was in breach of his contract. He claimed that he had been unfairly dismissed.

HELD: The tribunal with the EAT in agreement, found that he had been unfairly dismissed as a result of the company's letter. The tribunal was entitled to find the words used by the MD amounted to an agreement that Mr Jackson could leave early and notice of dismissal would be shortened.

Alternatively, when Mr Jackson notified the MD of his intention to leave early, this could be construed as giving notice to terminate within the employer's notice period. Mr Jackson could then rely on section (ERA, s 95(2)) to say that he was dismissed at the end of the notice period, notwithstanding his notice was shorter than any contractual or statutory minimum period he was required to give.

Martin v Yeoman Aggregates Ltd

[1983] IRLR 49, EAT

[8.19] Following an argument with a director Mr Martin was dismissed. Realising that he had failed to follow standard disciplinary procedure, the director informed Mr Martin, within 5 minutes of the original argument, that he was only suspended. Mr Martin claimed unfair dismissal. A tribunal found that he had not been dismissed and he appealed.

HELD: Despite the use of unambiguous words of dismissal, the words used during the argument were withdrawn almost immediately. It is a matter of plain common sense that an employer or employee should have the opportunity of recanting from words spoken in the heat of the moment. It is a question of degree whether the change of mind comes too late.

Termination by agreement

Birch and Humber v University of Liverpool

[1985] IRLR 165, CA

[8.20] The University notified its staff that due to a reduction in funding expenditure would need to be cut. The University hoped this could be achieved by 'natural wastage' through retirements and resignations, but did not rule out the possibility of making redundancies. Six months later eligible staff were informed of a premature retirement compensation scheme. The applicants both applied for, and were granted, premature retirement. They then claimed redundancy payments.

A tribunal held that any request for premature retirement had to be approved by the University and that the University had terminated their employment. The EAT allowed the University's appeal, stating that the termination was by mutual agreement and not by dismissal. The applicants appealed to the Court of Appeal.

HELD: Application of the facts to section (ERA, s 136) is a matter of law and the EAT correctly held, within the meaning of this section, that the contracts had been terminated by mutual agreement. As defined, dismissal is not consistent with a situation where termination has been by the freely given mutual consent of the employer and employee. Here the termination would not have taken place but for the University's acceptance of the application for premature retirement.

Ambiguous language

Futty v D & D Brekkes Ltd

[1974] IRLR 130

[8.21] Mr Futty was a fish filleter, and was told by the respondent's foreman 'If you do not like the job, fuck off'. Mr Futty believed this amounted to a dismissal and subsequently claimed unfair dismissal.

HELD: The tribunal held Mr Futty had not been dismissed. The meaning of the words used must be assessed in the light of the custom of the trade in which they are used, in this case against the background of the fish dock. These words had previously been used to mean get on with your job or, if you do not like what you are doing, clock off until you feel more disposed to work.

Sovereign House Security Services Ltd v Savage

[1989] IRLR 115, CA

[8.22] Mr Savage, a security officer, was suspended pending police investigations into a missing sum of money belonging to the employer. When he was informed Mr Savage stated 'I am not having any of that, you can stuff it. I am not taking the rap for that'. Shortly after this, Mr Savage agreed with his superior that he was 'jacking the job in'.

HELD: Both the EAT and the Court of Appeal upheld the tribunal's decision that Mr Savage had been unfairly dismissed. Where unambiguous words of resignation are used by an employee and are so understood by the employer, the proper conclusion of fact is that the employee has resigned. However, in some cases there may be something in the context of the 'resignation' or the circumstances of the employee that despite first appearances there is no resignation. In this instance there was evidence that the words used by Mr Savage were used 'in the heat of the moment' and should not have been accepted at full face value by his employers.

Sothern v Franks Charlesly & Co

[1981] IRLR 278, CA

[8.23] Franks Charlesly & Co appealed against the decision of a tribunal and the EAT to the Court of Appeal that Mrs Sothern's statement, 'I am resigning', during a partners' meeting was ambiguous and not a statement of resignation.

HELD, on appeal: The words used by Mrs Sothern indicated a present intention of resigning. Where words of resignation are unambiguous, and so understood by the employers, the question of what a reasonable employer might have understood does not arise.

Frustration and fixed-term contracts

Notcutt v Universal Equipment Co (London) Ltd

[1986] IRLR 218, CA

[8.24] Mr Notcutt was absent from work following a heart attack. Following provision of a medical report stating Mr Notcutt would not be able to work again, the employers terminated his employment. In defending Mr Notcutt's claim for sick pay, the employers contended the employment contract had been frustrated and in these circumstances they were not liable to make such payments. The county court held that his contract had been frustrated before the notice to terminate had been served. Mr Notcutt appealed.

HELD: The county court were correct that the contract had been frustrated by Mr Notcutt's illness. There is no reason why a periodic contract should not in appropriate circumstances be held to have been terminated without notice by frustration. In this case, the heart attack left Mr Notcutt unable to work again. This was an unexpected occurrence that made performance of his contractual obligations impossible.

Dixon v BBC

[1979] IRLR 114, CA

[8.25] Mr Dixon claimed unfair dismissal after his fixed-term contract expired and was not renewed. The BBC asserted that as his contract included a term that it could be determined by one week's notice, it was not for a fixed term. This was an appeal by the BBC against the finding of the EAT that both Mr Dixon and Mr Constanti had been unfairly dismissed. A tribunal found that there had not been a dismissal. The EAT upheld their appeal and found that they had been dismissed. The BBC appealed.

HELD: A contract is for a fixed term even though it is determinable by notice within that term. To have held otherwise would result in the absurd position of an employer being able to evade claims for unfair dismissal by inserting notice provisions into all contracts for a fixed period.

Wiltshire County Council v National Association of Teachers in Further and Higher Education and Guy

[1980] IRLR 198, CA

[8.26] Mrs Guy was a part-time teacher. Each academic year she was employed on a new contract, which set out the days and hours she would teach. Whenever the courses she taught finished, or the Principal decided there were not enough students for her course, she ceased working. Eventually her contract was not renewed and she claimed unfair dismissal.

Both a tribunal and the EAT found that she had been employed under a fixed-term contract which had expired without being renewed and that she had therefore been dismissed. The local authority appealed to the Court of Appeal.

HELD: Her contract was a contract for a fixed term. Although her contract could come to an end during the course of an academic year it was not a contract which was discharged by performance. The fact that the contract could be brought to an end by the Principal did not prevent it being a contract for a fixed term; when her contract was not renewed she was dismissed. The local authority's appeal was dismissed.

The Court of Appeal noted that if someone is contracted to carry out a particular task or for a particular purpose, when the task or purpose comes to an end the contract is discharged by performance. There is no contract for a fixed term, and no dismissal when the contract ends.

DATE OF DISMISSAL AND 'EFFECTIVE DATE OF TERMINATION'

[8.27] Section 97 of ERA sets out how an employee's effective date of termination is ascertained. This date is important because a complaint of unfair dismissal must be brought within three months' of the effective date of dismissal.

> (1) Subject to the following provisions of this section, in this Part 'the effective date of termination'—

(a) in relation to an employee whose contract of employment is terminated by notice, whether given by his employer or by the employee, means the date on which the notice expires,
(b) in relation to an employee whose contract of employment is terminated without notice, means the date on which the termination takes effect, and
(c) in relation to an employee who is employed under a contract for a fixed term which expires without being renewed under the same contract, means the date on which the term expires.

(2) Where—
(a) the contract of employment is terminated by the employer, and
(b) the notice required by section 86 to be given by an employer would, if duly given on the material date, expire on a date later than the effective date of termination (as defined by subsection (1)),

for the purposes of sections 108(1), 119(1) and 227(3) the later date is the effective date of termination.

(3) In subsection (2)(b) 'the material date' means—
(a) the date when notice of termination was given by the employer, or
(b) where no notice was given, the date when the contract of employment was terminated by the employer.

(4) Where—
(a) the contract of employment is terminated by the employee,
(b) the material date does not fall during a period of notice given by the employer to terminate that contract, and
(c) had the contract been terminated not by the employee but by notice given on the material date by the employer, that notice would have been required by section 86 to expire on a date later than the effective date of termination (as defined by subsection (1)),

for the purposes of sections 108(1), 119(1) and 227(3) the later date is the effective date of termination.

(5) In subsection (4) 'the material date' means—
(a) the date when notice of termination was given by the employee, or
(b) where no notice was given, the date when the contract of employment was terminated by the employee.

(6) Where an employee is taken to be dismissed for the purposes of this Part by virtue of section 96, references in this Part to the effective date of termination are to the notified date of return.

McMaster v Manchester Airport plc

[1998] IRLR 112, EAT

[8.28] Mr McMaster was notified of his summary dismissal by post, but was absent from his home on the date the letter of dismissal arrived. A tribunal concluded that the effective date of termination was the date the letter arrived, regardless of whether or not he was at home to receive the letter. This meant that he had presented his IT1 one day too late and his claim was therefore dismissed. He appealed to the EAT.

HELD: The doctrine of constructive or presumed knowledge, that may be used in relation to the service of formal documents, has no place in relation to parties private employment rights. As such, the date of termination could not be earlier than the date on which he received notification of his dismissal. The effective date of termination was accordingly one day later than alleged by Manchester airport and the IT1 had been presented in time.

Lambert v Croydon College

[1999] IRLR 346, EAT

[8.29] Mr Lambert had been away from work on sick leave. Croydon College wrote to him at the beginning of 1996 indicating that he could draw pension benefits from 1 January 1996 and therefore proposed to terminate his employment on 31 December 1995. He eventually reached an agreement with the College as to the terms of his dismissal and a compromise agreement was drawn up, dated 7 March 1996. However, the date of termination was recorded as being 31 December 1995. After signing the compromise agreement Mr Lambert attempted to bring unfair dismissal proceedings against the College in June 1996. He submitted that the effective date of termination was 7 March 1996, and his IT1 was consequently in time. A tribunal held that his effective date of termination was, as agreed between the parties, 31 December 1995 and dismissed his claim because it had been lodged too late. He appealed

HELD: There was no reason why the effective date of termination should not be a date agreed between the parties. In this case, Lambert reached agreement with Croydon College and the effective date of termination was as recorded in the agreement, namely the 31 December 1995.

Dismissal with notice

Adams v GKN Sankey Ltd

[1980] IRLR 416, EAT

[8.30] Mrs Adams received a letter giving her 12 weeks' notice of dismissal, commencing on 5 November, but informing her that she would be paid in lieu of notice. She brought a claim of unfair dismissal, which was dismissed as time-barred by the tribunal as it held her employment had terminated on 5 November. She appealed.

HELD: Where an employee is given notice, but then paid in lieu of that notice, the effective date of termination is the date the notice expires, not the date it is given. This should be distinguished from the situation where an employee's employment is terminated with immediate effect, but monies are then paid in lieu of that notice period as damages. In that situation the effective date of termination is the date notice of termination is given.

Marshall (Cambridge) Ltd v Hamblin

[1994] IRLR 260, EAT

[8.31] Mr Hamblin had resigned giving notice, but Marshall wanted him to leave immediately and attempted to agree a sum that should be paid to him in compensation. These discussions were not successful. Marshall refused to allow him to continue working and Mr Hamblin resigned and claimed that he had been unfairly dismissed. A tribunal found that Mr Hamblin had been unfairly dismissed. Marshall appealed.

HELD: Mr Hamblin had resigned, and had not been dismissed. Where an employee gives notice, until that notice expires, the contract of employment continues and an employer can take advantage of terms in that contract to bring the contract to an end at an earlier date. Therefore, when an employer wants to cut short the period of notice given by an employee, if they make a payment in lieu of notice in accordance with the terms of the contract, they will not be in breach of contract.

Newham London Borough v Ward

[1985] IRLR 509, CA

[8.32] Mr Ward was summarily dismissed in February 1983 and pursued the internal appeal process. This was concluded in June 1983. His P45 was not sent to him until June 1983. He issued proceedings for unfair dismissal in June 1983. A tribunal concluded that the effective date of dismissal was on the date of his dismissal in February 1983 and that the claim was out of time. His appeal to the EAT was allowed because his employment was found to have continued until such time as he received his P45 in June. The company appealed.

HELD: The effective date of termination of Mr Ward's employment was the date on which he was summarily dismissed. The fact he only received his P45 some 4 months after he was dismissed had nothing to do with the date on which his employment terminated.

Stapp v Shaftesbury Society

[1982] IRLR 326, CA

[8.33] Mr Stapp was given one month's notice of dismissal. If the full month was taken into account, he would have become eligible to make a claim of unfair dismissal. Before the end of the period of notice, he submitted a claim to the tribunal and also initiated the Society's grievance procedure in respect of the dismissal. As soon as the employer became aware of this he was summarily dismissed. The Society enclosed a cheque to cover the remainder of the notice period. A tribunal dismissed his claim because he lacked the requisite service. His appeal to the EAT was dismissed and he appealed to the Court of Appeal.

HELD: By summarily dismissing him, the Society had brought forward the date of termination of employment. In this situation, the Society had reason to dismiss him summarily and this was not done in order to defeat his right to complain of unfair dismissal. The tribunal and the EAT had correctly found that he lacked the necessary service to bring a claim against the Society

J Sainsbury Ltd v Savage

[1980] IRLR 109, CA

[8.34] Mr Savage was summarily dismissed. He appealed against the decision, the company's policies provided that where an appeal was lodged employment would continue until the appeal was determined but that the employee would receive no pay. By the time the appeal was determined he would have had sufficient service to qualify for the right not to be unfairly dismissed. A tribunal determined that his employment had not ceased until the appeal was determined and that he qualified for the right not to be unfairly dismissed. The EAT allowed the company's appeal. Mr Savage appealed.

HELD: The EAT correctly held that the effective date of termination, following summary dismissal, is the date on which termination of the contract of employment takes effect.

If an employee appeals against the decision to dismiss summarily, as in this case, the effective date of termination is not extended until the date of the appeal. The effect of the company's policy was that the employee would be reinstated if his appeal was successful but if his appeal was unsuccessful the employment would take effect on the original date.

Section 97(2) of ERA

Fox Maintenance Ltd v Jackson

[1977] IRLR 306

[8.35] Mr Jackson's contract provided that he was entitled to receive one month's notice. He was dismissed with one month's pay in lieu of notice, although he worked one week of his notice period. He was three weeks short of achieving the necessary qualifying service. A tribunal construed the relevant statutory provision as extending his notice to the date when his contractual notice would have expired. The company appealed.

HELD: The tribunal was wrong. The only statutory requirement was to take account of the statutory minimum notice period. If the statutory minimum period of notice was taken into account he still lacked the necessary qualifying service.

Time at which the dismissal takes effect

Octavius Atkinson & Sons Ltd v Morris

[1989] IRLR 158, CA

[8.36] Mr Morris was made redundant and summarily dismissed at lunchtime and then sent home. When he arrived home, Octavius received an urgent call for work and offered this to two others who had also been made redundant at the same time as Mr Morris. The company's redundancy policy made it clear that Mr Morris should have been offered the work first. A tribunal held that as Morris remained in employment for the entirety of the day on which he was dismissed, the failure to offer him the extra work rendered his dismissal unfair. The company appealed unsuccessfully to the EAT and then to the Court of Appeal.

HELD: Where an employee is summarily dismissed without notice, the contract of employment and the status of the employee must end at the moment dismissal is communicated. Summary dismissal constitutes either an immediate termination of the contract or an immediate repudiation of the contract which is accepted by the employee.

REASON FOR DISMISSAL

[8.37] Section 98 of ERA provides:

(1) In determining for the purposes of this Part whether the dismissal of an employee is fair or unfair, it is for the employer to show—
(a) the reason (or, if more than one, the principal reason) for the dismissal, and
(b) that it is either a reason falling within subsection (2) or some other substantial reason of a kind such as to justify the dismissal of an employee holding the position which the employee held.

(2) A reason falls within this subsection if it—
(a) relates to the capability or qualifications of the employee for performing work of the kind which he was employed by the employer to do,
(b) relates to the conduct of the employee,
(c) is that the employee was redundant, or
(d) is that the employee could not continue to work in the position which he held without contravention (either on his part or on that of his employer) of a duty or restriction imposed by or under an enactment.

(3) In subsection (2)(a)—
(a) 'capability', in relation to an employee, means his capability assessed by reference to skill, aptitude, health or any other physical or mental quality, and
(b) 'qualifications', in relation to an employee, means any degree, diploma or other academic, technical or professional qualification relevant to the position which he held.

Murphy v Epsom College

[1983] IRLR 395, EAT; affd [1984] IRLR 271, CA

[8.38] Mr Murphy was employed as a resident plumber. He was selected for redundancy after the College decided to appoint a resident heating engineer who could deal with work that Mr Murphy had refused to carry out. The College argued that reason for dismissal was redundancy. Mr Murphy claimed unfair dismissal. The tribunal dismissed his complaint, holding that he had been dismissed by reason of redundancy, or for some other substantial reason – although this latter reason was not specifically pleaded nor argued before them. He appealed.

HELD, on appeal: Mr Murphy had been properly dismissed on the grounds of redundancy. However, the EAT held redundancy was the only reason for dismissal on which the College could rely. If 'some other substantial reason' for dismissal is relied upon, the matter should be expressly raised before the tribunal. The rules of natural justice require a party not to have a case decided against them without having the opportunity to be heard. This decision was upheld by the Court of Appeal.

Wilson v Post Office

[2000] IRLR 834, CA

[8.39] Mr Wilson had a history of absence from work, for various medical reasons. As a result of his unsatisfactory attendance record and failure to improve his attendance record, he was dismissed. The Post Office recorded their reason for dismissal in their IT3 as being 'incapability by reason of unsatisfactory attendance record'.

The tribunal interpreted the word 'incapability' as a reference to ERA, s 98(2)(a), that the reason for dismissal related to capability. This resulted in confusion, as the Post Office did not actually rely on capability as defined, but rather the unsatisfactory attendance record. Nevertheless, the tribunal found the actual reason for dismissal was capability, but given he was certified as fit to work, the Post Office had acted unreasonably in using this reason for dismissal. The Post Office appealed.

The EAT found the tribunal had mistakenly identified the appropriate reason for dismissal as capability. The reason for his dismissal was due to his poor attendance record and this amounted to some other substantial reason. The EAT found on the basis of the facts found by the tribunal that the dismissal was fair. Mr Wilson appealed.

HELD: By failing to correctly identify the reason for dismissal the tribunal had made an error of law. The correct characterisation of the reason for dismissal was the attendance record which constituted dismissal for some other substantial reason.

However, the EAT, as an appellate body, should have then remitted the case to the tribunal for a decision on whether dismissal for this reason was unfair.

Correctly identifying the reason for dismissal

Abernethy v Mott, Hay and Anderson

[1974] IRLR 213, CA

[8.40] Mr Abernethy had been employed for several years working at the respondent's head office, although originally he had worked on site. However, the project upon which he was engaged was coming to an end and, as there was no more work available for him at head office, he was offered a job working on site. He refused this and was dismissed.

A tribunal and the NIRC found that although he had not been dismissed for redundancy (the reason given by the employers at the time of dismissal), he had been fairly dismissed by reason of capability. He appealed to the Court of Appeal.

HELD: An incorrect label given by an employer at the time of dismissal does not preclude the employer from relying on another reason for dismissal before the tribunal. Per Lord Denning: an employer can only rely on the actual reason for dismissal, if the facts are sufficiently known or made known to the individual. The fact that the wrong label was attached to the reasons is not relevant.

Burden of proof

Post Office (Counters) Ltd v Heavey

[1989] IRLR 513, EAT

[8.41] Mr Heavey was dismissed as a counter clerk for allegedly obtaining money fraudulently in a promotional scheme run by the Post Office. It was alleged that he had obtained the money by using false names and addresses and the crucial evidence against him was that the money had been paid out against promotional cards bearing his counter stamp. A tribunal found his dismissal unfair as it was not satisfied that an appropriate investigation had been conducted and that therefore the employers had not established that he had been dismissed for a reason relating to his conduct. The Post Office appealed.

HELD: The tribunal was wrong not to find that the reason for the dismissal was misconduct. The adequacy of employer's investigations did not affect the reason for the dismissal. The burden of showing the reason for dismissal falls upon the employer. In this case, no one had suggested that the reason for dismissal was anything other than misconduct.

Only when the reason has been established, should consideration be given to whether the employer acted reasonably in treating that reason as sufficient to dismiss the employee. However, in this respect there is no burden of proof. It is not for the employer to 'show', nor the tribunal to be 'satisfied', as these are terms that indicate the existence of a burden of proof.

Maund v Penwith District Council

[1984] IRLR 24, CA

[8.42] Mr Maund was made redundant by the council who decided that they did not require his services but would instead use contractors. He argued that he had been dismissed because of his union activities and that his dismissal was unfair. A tribunal dismissed his claim finding that he was redundant and his dismissal was fair. He appealed successfully to the EAT and the council appealed to the Court of Appeal.

HELD: If there is a dispute between an employee and an employer as to the real reason for dismissal the legal burden of proving the reason, or principal reason if more than one exists, for dismissal rests on the employer. If the employer fails to convince the tribunal as to the reason, the dismissal will be unfair.

If the employer discharges this burden, the employee is then under an evidential burden to show there is a real issue as to whether this was the real reason for dismissal. However, this burden is lighter than that on the employer, and the employee need only provide evidence sufficient to raise doubt about the supposed reason.

In this case the tribunal had wrongly placed the burden on Mr Maund to show that his dismissal was not for redundancy and was because of his trade union activities.

The case was remitted back to the tribunal by the Court of Appeal.

Ely v YKK Fasteners (UK) Ltd

[1993] IRLR 500, CA

[8.43] Mr Ely received a job offer from an associated company of the respondent, based in Australia. He informed YKK that he intended to accept this job and would be resigning in due course. Since he did not give a date for his departure, YKK made it clear to him that if no date was provided, his last day of employment would be 21 December. On 21 December Mr Ely announced he no longer wished to leave, but YKK maintained he had resigned, bringing his employment to an end. Mr Ely claimed unfair dismissal.

Despite YKK's assertion that Mr Ely had resigned, the tribunal held that he had been dismissed. However, the tribunal went on to hold that his dismissal was for some other substantial reason and was reasonable and justified in the circumstances. Mr Ely appealed to the EAT and the Court of Appeal.

HELD: The Court of Appeal upheld the tribunal's decision, relying on the principles in *Abernethy v Mott, Hay and Anderson* (see 8.40 above). The principle in *Abernethy* could validly be extended. Such an extension could allow for substitution of the reason upon which the employer had relied, but was in fact invalid or misdescribed, with a valid reason based on a state of facts known to and relied on by the employer at the time. The employee would then be supplied with a reason for dismissal which he was only prevented from treating as such at the time as a consequence of his misapprehension, of the true nature of the circumstances. The company had been wrong to argue that he had resigned but given the facts known to the company, the company's dismissal was for some other substantial reason. The issue of fairness was not raised as a ground of appeal and it was not necessary for the court to make a finding on that point.

Establishing the reason

Amor v Galliard Homes Ltd

(2001) EAT/47/01, EAT

[8.44] Mr Amor was made redundant from his job as a fork lift truck driver and was then given a job as a labourer on the same pay. However, due to his disruptive behaviour, Galliard claimed they then had to go ahead and 'implement the redundancy'.

The tribunal held that he had been unfairly dismissed and that the reason for his dismissal was his disruptive behaviour. His dismissal was unfair because there had been a lack of consultation prior to the redundancy. Mr Amor appealed against the value of the award made, on the basis that if the reasoning of the tribunal had been different the actual sum awarded would have been greater.

HELD: There was no finding of fact that could justify the conclusion that Mr Amor's job as a labourer had become redundant. The findings of fact appeared to show Mr Amor was dismissed because of his disruptive behaviour. Consequently the tribunal's conclusion could not be justified. Given this finding, and as the only reason advanced before the tribunal for dismissal was redundancy, Galliard had failed to establish that the reason for dismissal was within section 98 of ERA. The dismissal was therefore unfair.

The matter was remitted back to the tribunal to determine the question of compensation.

Maintenance Co Ltd v Dormer

[1982] IRLR 491, EAT

[8.45] Mr Dormer was managing director of The Maintenance Company. He was suspected of dishonesty as he arranged for company vehicles to be sold to a member of his own family, who was making a profit on the transactions. Mr Dormer was confronted by the company's chief executive. As a result, his employment was terminated. He claimed that he had been unfairly dismissed, and the tribunal agreed. The tribunal found that the employer's stated reason for dismissal, dishonesty, was not founded on reasonable grounds and Mr Dormer was dismissed before a reasonable investigation had taken place. The company appealed.

HELD: From the tribunal's findings of facts it was clear the chief executive of the company genuinely believed Mr Dormer was dishonest. In reaching its decision the tribunal had stated dishonesty could not be the reason for dismissal because it was not founded on reasonable grounds and dismissal took place before reasonable investigations had been carried out. In this respect the tribunal had misdirected itself as the only relevant question was 'what was the employer's actual reason?'. In failing properly to identify the reason for dismissal, the rest of the decision was vitiated. The tribunal was required to identify the reason for the dismissal and then go on to consider the reasonableness of the decision.

Given that Mr Dormer occupied a position of trust, had been given an adequate opportunity to explain his actions but had failed to provide an explanation for them. The EAT substituted a finding that the dismissal was fair.

When is the reason to be determined?

W Devis & Sons Ltd v Atkins

[1977] IRLR 314, HL

[8.46] Mr Atkins was the manager of an abattoir. He was told that he was being dismissed because of the company's dissatisfaction with his purchasing methods. His dismissal took place and the company then discovered facts that would have entitled them to have dismissed summarily. Mr Atkins claimed that he had been unfairly dismissed. A tribunal found that his dismissal was unfair. The company's appeal eventually reached the House of Lords.

HELD: The tribunal's decision that he had been unfairly dismissed was correct. The evidence of his misconduct that came to light after his dismissal was irrelevant to the question of whether his dismissal was fair. An employer cannot establish that a dismissal is fair by relying upon matters which he ought to have known but did not. The fairness of a dismissal is to be judged by what the employer knew at the time of the dismissal.

>Note—Facts coming to light after a dismissal can be taken into account when the question of deciding what compensation it would be just and equitable to award the employee.

Parkinson v March Consulting Ltd

[1997] IRLR 308, CA

[8.47] Mr Parkinson was told that he was to be dismissed by reason of redundancy because the company intended to reorganise the company's financial management. However, approximately one month later Mr Parkinson was informed that the extent of the reorganisation had not yet been determined, but one option was to make his role redundant. Nine days later his dismissal was confirmed. He claimed that he had been unfairly dismissed. A tribunal held the reason for dismissal fell within 'some other substantial reason', but due to the failure to properly consult, he was unfairly dismissed. However, had he been consulted he would still have been dismissed and was not therefore entitled to a compensatory award. The EAT dismissed his appeal and he appealed to the Court of Appeal.

HELD: Where employment to terminate is given in accordance with the terms of an employee's contract the employer's reasons for dismissal have to be judged not only by reference to the reason at the time of dismissal but also by reference to the reason at the time that notice to dismiss is given. Since the decision to reorganise had not been taken at the time Mr Parkinson was given notice of termination, the tribunal erred in finding the reason for dismissal was for the purposes of reorganisation. Nevertheless, this error was merely technical, since a valid six month notice could have been served, this gave rise to no more than nominal compensation. As a result his appeal was dismissed.

CAPABILITY

Abernethy v Mott, Hay and Anderson

[1974] IRLR 213, CA

[8.48] Mr Abernethy had been employed for several years working in head office although originally he had worked on site. However, the project upon which he was engaged was coming to an end and there was no more work available for him in head office and he was offered a job working on site. He refused it and was dismissed.

A tribunal and the NIRC found that although he had not been dismissed for redundancy, the reason given by the employers at the time of dismissal, he had been fairly dismissed by reason of capability. He appealed to the Court of Appeal.

HELD: That the actual reason for dismissal of Abernethy was capability. In this case, Abernethy's inflexibility and lack of adaptability falls within an individual's aptitude and mental capabilities, which fell within the statutory definition of 'capability'.

Per Lord Denning: dismissal of an individual may not be justified if the sole reason for dismissal is that they have reached the limit of their ability and are not fit to be promoted.

(See also 8.40 above.)

Sutton & Gates (Luton) Ltd v Boxall

[1978] IRLR 486, EAT

[8.49] Mr Boxall was an electrician. Following various complaints about his work, and the refusal of certain contractors to have him work on their sites, he was dismissed. A tribunal found his dismissal unfair because he was not afforded an opportunity to have his point of view heard. The company appealed.

HELD: The tribunal's decision that Mr Boxall had been unfairly dismissed would not be set aside. If an employee is falling down at work for a reason over which the employee has control, then the employee should be warned about his performance and given the opportunity to improve. If the employee is unable to reach their former standard due to illness or disability the employer is entitled to dismiss provided they handle the situation sensibly and give the employee a final opportunity to improve. In this situation the decision of the tribunal that Boxall should have been given a last chance could not be set aside.

Obiter dicta: In giving their judgment the EAT also commented on the differences between cases of capability and conduct. Where a person has not come up to standard through their own carelessness or negligence it may be better dealt with as a case of conduct/misconduct rather than capability. The tribunal must identify incapability due to an inherent incapacity to function, as opposed to failure to exercise to the full such talent as the employee possesses. The EAT in *Kraft Foods Ltd v Fox* ([1977] IRLR 431) did not hold that where there is a capability dismissal there can never be a deduction for contributory fault by the employee

Lack of capability due to ill-health

British Gas Services Ltd v McCaull

[2001] IRLR 60, EAT

[8.50] Following the onset of epilepsy, Mr McCaull, whose work included driving a van, was informed by the company's occupational health adviser that he could not continue in his current position as a service engineer. He was then offered an alternative role carrying out clerical work. This new role involved a pay cut of approximately 25–30%. Mr McCaull rejected this offer and as there were no other suitable alternative positions available he was dismissed. A tribunal upheld his unfair dismissal complaint because the job offered to him was not reasonable. The company appealed.

HELD: The company had offered him alternative work of a kind that was within his capacity, and he was offered this work at the prevailing rate of pay for such work. This was the only alternative employment available that he was capable of carrying out. The employer's dismissal following his rejection of the clerical position was within the range of reasonable responses and the appeal was allowed.

London Fire and Civil Defence Authority v Betty

[1994] IRLR 384, EAT

[8.51] Mr Betty was retired on health grounds following a nervous breakdown. The breakdown had been preceded by groundless accusations by fellow employees of racial discrimination and harassment. The tribunal upheld Mr Betty's claim that his dismissal was unfair on the basis that his illness was due to the treatment he received from by his employers. The Authority appealed.

HELD: Mr Betty was dismissed by reason of capability, by reference to ill-health. In these circumstances, the question of whether the dismissal was fair should be unaffected by considerations of whether the illness was caused or was contributed to by the employer. Whether the dismissal was fair depended upon the employee's medical condition and the employer's enquiries and procedures used before taking the decision to dismiss. If the employer has breached its duty to the employee by causing him injury, the employee can claim appropriate compensation in the county court.

Edwards v Governors of Hanson School

[2001] IRLR 733, EAT

[8.52] Mr Edwards was a teacher and had been away from work since September 1996 suffering from stress. He alleged that this was due to the treatment he had received at the hands of the headmaster. He had a poor attendance record and when he returned to school in March 1997 a disciplinary hearing was arranged to consider his poor attendance record. Mr Edwards was immediately away sick and an occupational health adviser informed the school it was unlikely he would return to teaching in the foreseeable future. He was dismissed. His internal appeal was unsuccessful. He claimed that he had been unfairly dismissed because of the inadequate consultation with him. The tribunal considered it was not necessary to decide why he had been ill. At a remedies hearing the tribunal again decided that his allegation about his treatment by the headmaster were irrelevant to determining what sum to award him on the just and equitable ground, this decision was reached in the light of the decision in *London Fire and Civil Defence v Betty* (see 8.51 above). Mr Edwards appealed. The EAT dismissed his appeal; he appealed to the Court of Appeal who referred the matter back to the EAT because it was arguable that it was not just and equitable to deny an applicant an award where the employer had caused the illness for which he was dismissed.

HELD in the EAT: The tribunal was wrong to conclude that the cause of Mr Edward's illness was irrelevant to the issue of what compensation it was just and equitable to award him. Bringing in questions of responsibility for illness at the stage of assessing whether it is just and equitable to make a compensatory award will not lead to endless disputes with which a tribunal is ill equipped to deal. By failing to take into account the allegation made by Mr Edwards a decision had been reached which resulted in an award that was arguably not just and equitable.

HJ Heinz Co Ltd v Kenrick

[2000] IRLR 144, EAT

[8.53] Mr Kenrick was off work sick for approximately one year before he was dismissed, as he was not fit to return to work. At the time of his dismissal his condition had not been identified; after his dismissal he was diagnosed as suffering from chronic fatigue syndrome (CFS). He claimed disability discrimination and unfair dismissal. The tribunal found that he had been discriminated against and in the light of that finding found the dismissal unfair. The company appealed.

HELD: The tribunal had identified that dismissal was on the grounds of capability. However, the tribunal had relied on its findings in relation to the disability discrimination claim to satisfy itself that the dismissal was also unfair. Since it appeared that the tribunal might have been proceeding upon the basis that a dismissal which is in breach of the Disability Discrimination Act and not justified was automatically unfair, the appeal would be allowed. The nature of the statutory language allows there to be a disability related dismissal which is fair. The tribunal must give separate consideration to the fairness of a dismissal under the ERA. The finding of unfair dismissal was set aside.

International Sports Co Ltd v Thomson

[1980] IRLR 340, EAT

[8.54] Mrs Thomson was absent, on average, for 25% of the time by reason of a variety of unconnected illnesses; she was not suffering any long-term chronic illness. She received four warnings about her level of absenteeism, the first was oral and the subsequent three were written. The company consulted the general practitioner employed by them who advised, after considering her medical records that there was no point in examining her because the illnesses she had suffered could not be verified by examination. She was eventually dismissed and a tribunal found the dismissal unfair. The company appealed.

HELD: The tribunal was wrong in law to find the dismissal unfair. The reason for the applicant's dismissal was conduct rather than capability. The EAT distinguished this case from cases concerning incapability relating to ill-health. In this case dismissal was not purported to be on the ground of incapability and there was no allegation of deliberate malingering. This case was concerned with the impact of an unacceptable level of intermittent absences due to unconnected minor ailments.

It would be to place too heavy a burden on an employer to carry out a formal medical investigation. In a case such as this, the employer must fairly review the attendance record and the reasons for it, give the employee the chance to make representations, and then give appropriate warnings if necessary. If the attendance record does not improve, in many cases the employer will be justified in treating the persistent absences as sufficient reason for dismissing the employee. In this case the company sought medical advice and there was no ground to criticise the quality of that advice.

CONDUCT

British Home Stores Ltd v Burchell

[1978] IRLR 379, EAT

[8.55] Mrs Burchell was dismissed with other employees who were alleged to be involved with acts of dishonesty. A tribunal found her dismissal unfair and the company appealed.

HELD: The tribunal had applied too strict a standard. In each case concerning dismissal for alleged misconduct, the tribunal must decide whether the employer entertained a reasonable suspicion amounting to a belief in the guilt of the employee of that misconduct at that time:

> First of all, there must be established by the employer the fact of that belief; that the employer did believe it. Secondly, that the employer had in his mind reasonable grounds upon which to sustain that belief. And thirdly, that the employer at the stage at which he formed that belief on those grounds, at any rate at the final stage at which he formed that belief on those grounds, had carried out as much investigation into the matter as was reasonable in all the circumstances of the case.

Since the employers had a genuine belief in the employee's guilt based upon reasonable grounds following a reasonable investigation, the appeal was allowed. The test is reasonableness and the EAT commented that a conclusion on the balance of probabilities will in any surmisable circumstance be a reasonable conclusion.

Boys and Girls Welfare Society v McDonald

[1996] IRLR 129, EAT

[8.56] Mr McDonald was a residential social worker. He was dismissed after a disciplinary hearing had been called after he allegedly spat at and hit a child in his care. He admitted at the hearing that he spat at one of the children and that he may have caught the child in the face while trying to push him away.

A tribunal held this was an unfair dismissal. While the employers had a genuine belief in his guilt, the tribunal found the employers did not have reasonable grounds for this belief and that they had failed to conduct a reasonable investigation into the matter. The employers appealed.

HELD: A simplistic application of the test set out in *BHS v Burchell* (see 8.55 above) in every conduct case raised the danger of falling into error. Since *Burchell* had been decided, the burden of proof on the employer to satisfy the tribunal that they acted reasonably had been removed. Secondly, application of the *Burchell* test is appropriate where there is a conflict of facts. If there is no debate as to whether the dishonest conduct occurred, there is little scope for the investigation referred to in *Burchell*. A tribunal must remember to consider whether the dismissal of the employee falls within the range of reasonable responses open to a reasonable employer.

Neary and Neary v Dean of Westminster

[1999] IRLR 288, Visitor (Westminster)

[8.57] Mr and Mrs Neary were summarily dismissed for gross misconduct for taking fixed fees in relation to Westminster Abbey events and retaining surpluses accruing from such events, but there was no allegation of dishonesty. Dr Neary was master of choristers and Mrs Neary was the concert secretary. The Nearys claimed their scheme, and the payments received, had been approved. Lord Jauncey of Tullichettle was appointed as a special commissioner to resolve the dispute.

HELD, per Lord Jauncey: Summary dismissal was justified. It was accepted that a spirit of openness was required, and in failing to inform the Abbey of their scheme and making a secret profit, the Nearys fatally undermined the relationship of trust and confidence which should have existed between them, the Abbey and the Dean and Chapter.

Where gross misconduct is alleged, it must so undermine the trust and confidence inherent in that particular contract that the employer should no longer be required to retain the employee. Whether misconduct justifies summary dismissal is a question of fact. In determining the extent of the breach, the nature of the institution, the role played by the employee and the degree of trust required in that relationship must all be considered. Dishonesty is not a necessary element for a breach that goes to the whole contract.

Adamson v B & L Cleaning Services Ltd

[1995] IRLR 193, EAT

[8.58] Mr Adamson was employed as a foreman on a contract. He told his employers that he intended to tender for the work when the time came for it to be retendered and that he had asked for his name to be put on the tender. He was suspended, he refused to confirm either that he would not tender for the work or that he would resign before he tendered for the work. He was dismissed. A tribunal found the dismissal fair on the grounds that tendering would be a breach of his duty of fidelity and that termination would be on the grounds of conduct. He appealed.

HELD: Tendering for future business of an employer's customers in competition with the employer is as much a breach of an employee's obligation to give faithful service as is soliciting an employer's customers to transfer their custom. It is different from indicating an intention to set up in competition, it is competing whilst still employed. On the facts of this case Mr Adamson's dismissal was fair.

John Lewis plc v Coyne

[2001] IRLR 139, EAT

[8.59] Mrs Coyne had been employed by John Lewis for 14 years. The company took a serious view of employees who used company telephones for personal purposes and this was made clear in an employee guide. Mrs Coyne suffered a miscarriage and although she had returned to work she was still upset and would occasionally telephone her husband. She was also in the habit of calling a member of staff who covered her work at weekends. The company investigated telephone calls to certain numbers including her work colleague, her mobile telephone and another telephone. Her departmental manager did not mention the problems that Mrs Coyne was having. She was summoned to a disciplinary meeting and suspended. She did not mention the fact of her miscarriage and that the calls she made were to her husband. A recommendation was made that she should be dismissed. Prior to her dismissal she offered to pay for the personal calls but the company thought the offer came too late and she was dismissed. At the tribunal hearing the company relied on their disciplinary policy and strict rule prohibiting use of departmental phones for personal calls to justify their summary dismissal of Mrs Coyne for making such calls. The tribunal found the dismissal unfair and the company appealed.

HELD: While the rules in place allowed John Lewis to dismiss Mrs Coyne, this was not an inevitable consequence. John Lewis remained under a duty to act reasonably. In failing to investigate the seriousness of the offence, ie the number and purpose of the calls, whether such conduct was persistent and whether it resulted from a personal crisis, they had failed in this duty.

The test for dishonesty is not objective. The best working test is that propounded in *R v Ghosh*: to determine whether there has been dishonesty it must be determined (i) whether according to the standards of reasonable and honest people what was done was dishonest, and, if so (ii) whether the person concerned must have realised that what they were doing was by those standards dishonest.

In this case it was not obvious that the use of the telephone for personal purposes was dishonest. The company did not investigate the question of dishonesty but assumed it from the making of personal calls, putting it into the same category as stealing money. Her dishonesty did not necessarily mean that she should have been dismissed. The appeal was dismissed.

Criminal acts

Harris and Shepherd v Courage (Eastern) Ltd

[1982] IRLR 509, CA

[8.60] The employees should have taken their lorry to a garage for repair, but were seen at one of the company's depots. The supervisor attempted to close the depot gates but the employees forced the lorry through the gates. They were later arrested and charged with theft. They were suspended and the company pursued a disciplinary procedure. The employees' union objected to disciplinary proceedings on behalf of the employees on the grounds the employees could not take part for fear of jeopardising their bail conditions. The employees were advised not to attend a disciplinary hearing because of the pending criminal trial. They were dismissed and a tribunal found the dismissal fair. They appealed to the EAT and then to the Court of Appeal.

HELD: Where an employee has been charged by the police the employer does not have to wait for the outcome of the criminal trial before dealing with, and in this case dismissing, the employee. It is essential that the employee should be given the opportunity to explain, and that the employee is aware dismissal is being contemplated. However, if the employee chooses not to make a statement at this stage, a reasonable employer can consider the evidence they have, and if this is sufficiently indicative of guilt then they may be entitled to dismiss. The appeal was dismissed.

Read v Phoenix Preservation Ltd

[1985] IRLR 93, EAT

[8.61] Mr Read was alleged to have struck his supervisor and was called to a meeting to discuss the matter. Two policemen were also present at the meeting. Mr Read was cautioned, and he claimed the policemen led the interview. He was dismissed and complained that this was unfair. A tribunal found that his dismissal was fair because he had been given every opportunity to state his case and there had been a fair investigation. No findings were made by the tribunal about his knowledge of whether the police would be present at the disciplinary hearing. He appealed.

HELD: The tribunal had made inadequate findings of fact so that it was unsafe to allow the decision to stand. If the police officers were present without Mr Read's consent and foreknowledge, that was a wholly improper course to take. Given the tribunal's lack of findings it was impossible to say whether the dismissal was fair or unfair. The matter was remitted back to the tribunal.

BREACH OF A STATUTORY ENACTMENT

Appleyard v F M Smith (Hull) Ltd

[1972] IRLR 19, IT

[8.62] The applicant was employed as a driver. He lost his licence for 12 months and was dismissed as a result. He attempted to argue he was only a temporary driver and that most of his work was spent undertaking maintenance. The respondent argued that it required all of its employees to drive and that it arranged for those who could not drive to be taught to drive. If Mr Appleyard drove it would be a breach of a statutory enactment.

HELD: It was inherent in this particular employment that the employee was required to drive and he was dismissed because to continue driving would breach a statutory enactment. In the circumstances in which this employer operated it was a requirement that employees should be able to drive. Mr Appleyard's termination was in the circumstances fair.

Obiter: In a large firm it might be possible keep an employee in a workshop The tribunal accepted the employer's argument and ruled the dismissal fair by reason of the statutory qualification provision.

Bouchaala v Trusthouse Forte Hotels Ltd

[1980] IRLR 382, EAT

[8.63] Trust House Forte was given information from the Home Office that it would be unlawful to continue to employ Mr Bouchaala, who was a Tunisian national, because he was no longer working as a student in accordance with the terms of his visa. Upon receiving this information, he was dismissed. The Home Office corrected its advice, but by the time the letter was received by the employer, the dismissal had taken place. Mr Bouchaala argued he had been unfairly dismissed. The tribunal accepted the employer's argument that the employee could not have continued work without breaching a convention, rule or obligation. Notwithstanding that the employer had been given incorrect information, and the employee could have remained in employment lawfully, the tribunal held that at the time the employer dismissed, the employer genuinely believed the employment relationship could not continue.

The tribunal also held that if it were wrong, then the dismissal would fall within the head of 'some other substantial reason' of a kind to have justified the dismissal. The substantial reason was the employer's genuine belief. Mr Bouchaala appealed.

HELD: Since he could have continued working without contravening any enactment, the reason for his dismissal could not fall within the statutory qualification rule. However, a genuine belief held by an employer that it is impossible to continue to employ an employee due to a statutory prohibition can constitute some other substantial reason justifying a dismissal. His appeal was dismissed.

Sandhu v Department of Education and Science and London Borough of Hillingdon

[1978] IRLR 208, EAT

[8.64] Mr Sandhu was dismissed from his job as a trainee science teacher after failing to complete his probationary period satisfactorily. The school and local education authority argued that the decision to dismiss fell within the Schools Regulations and was therefore justifiable. Mr Sandhu argued that the dismissal was because of his race and that he had never be given the chance to prove himself during his probationary period. An employment tribunal held that the dismissal was fair and held that once the Department of Education and Science (DES) had determined that he was unsuitable, the school and Local Authority had to follow the provisions of the Schools Regulations. Mr Sandhu appealed.

HELD: It is not automatically fair to dismiss an employee where it is unlawful to continue to employ him. The tribunal was required to investigate whether any of

Mr Sandhu's allegations were true and to consider whether the local authority had acted reasonably in deciding to dismiss him. Once the DES had deemed the employee unsuitable, the employee had the right to have his allegations that he had not been supported or given a chance to improve, tested.

REDUNDANCY

Redundancy procedure

Williams v Compair Maxam Ltd

[1982] IRLR 83, EAT

[8.65] The respondent sought to make redundancies from its business. When not enough people volunteered for redundancy, the managers concerned drew up lists of the employees they considered it would be best for the business to retain. Those employees not on the lists were dismissed as redundant. They brought unfair dismissal claims against the business.

HELD, on appeal: In a redundancy situation it was not enough for the tribunal to be satisfied that it was reasonable for an employee to be dismissed for redundancy. The fairness of the selection of that particular employee for redundancy had to be considered. The EAT set out the following principles that should generally be followed by employers in redundancy situations, unless there was some good reason to justify departure from the principles:

1. As much warning as possible of the redundancies should be given to the employees and any trade union recognised by the employer in respect of the employees.
2. Consultation should take place with any recognised union about the criteria to be applied in selecting the employees to be made redundant.
3. Whether or not there is an agreement with a trade union about the selection criteria, as far as possible the selection criteria should not depend solely on the opinion of the person making the selection, but should be capable of being objectively verified. Examples of criteria that could be objectively verified were given as attendance record, efficiency at the job, experience and length of service.
4. The selection should be made fairly in accordance with the criteria. The employer should consider any representations that may be made by a recognised trade union in respect of the selection.
5. The employer should investigate whether the employee could be offered alternative employment instead of being dismissed.

These principles are not principles of law but standards of behaviour. They will not stay immutable for all time.

Elkouil v Coney Island Ltd

[2002] IRLR 174, EAT

[8.66] The employee worked as a credit controller for the company's night-clubs. Between May 1998 and July 1999, new systems and procedures were introduced, which resulted in the bulk of the employee's work being transferred to the company's head office and individual managers. Following this, the employee was dismissed as redundant without any warning in July 1999.

The employment tribunal found that the reason for dismissal was redundancy, and that the lack of consultation made the dismissal unfair. However, it only awarded the employee two week's wages as compensation, on the basis that he would still have been made redundant even if there was proper consultation, and proper consultation would only have taken another two weeks to carry out. The applicant appealed.

HELD: The EAT substituted an award of ten weeks wages. They found that it must have been apparent to the employers by May 1999 at the latest that the employee was going to be made redundant. They should have started consultation with him at that stage. If they had, he could have begun to start looking for work some ten weeks earlier than he actually did start looking for work. If he had done this, he would have got another job substantially earlier than he actually did. The tribunal is obliged to consider under section 127(1) what is a just and equitable award in all the circumstances.

SOME OTHER SUBSTANTIAL REASON

Dobie v Burns International Security Services (UK) Ltd

[1984] IRLR 329, CA

[8.67] Mr Dobie was employed as a security officer by Burns at Liverpool airport, which was controlled by the local authority who reserved the right to refuse to permit anyone to work there. Mr Dobie fell out with his immediate superior who was a council employee and his employer was told to remove him from site. He was offered alternative employment at a reduced rate. He claimed that he had been unfairly dismissed. A tribunal found that he had been dismissed for some other substantial reason and that the dismissal was fair. He appealed to the EAT who dismissed his appeal. He appealed to the Court of Appeal.

HELD: Both the tribunal and the EAT had misdirected themselves in law.

Mr Dobie had been dismissed for 'some other substantial reason'. The tribunal was required to consider whether the reason found for dismissal could justify the dismissal of an employee and not the particular employee in question, holding the position that the particular employee holds. Consequently, different justifiable reasons for dismissal could be used for different members of staff. Different types of reason *could* justify dismissal of an office boy from those that *could* justify dismissal of a managing director. The tribunal was entitled to find that pressure from the local authority could justify dismissal.

The tribunal, when considering the reasonableness of the employer's actions should have considered the injustice to the employee. This will include a consideration of an employee's length of service, whether it has been satisfactory, and the difficulty he may have in securing alternative employment.

Kent County Council v Gilham

[1985] IRLR 18, CA

[8.68] Mrs Gilham and her colleagues were dinner ladies who were employed by the council at the council's schools. The council decided that in order to continue providing the service it was necessary to change the dinner ladies terms and conditions. The majority accepted the new terms, but Mrs Gilham and her colleagues refused them and claimed that they had been unfairly dismissed. The council argued that the dismissals were for some other substantial reason which was the need to achieve economies. The tribunal found that this was not a substantial reason and that even if it was, a reasonable employer would not have acted in the manner the employer did. The EAT found that the tribunal was wrong not to find that dismissal was for some other substantial reason but did not disturb the finding that the dismissal was unfair. The council appealed to the Court of Appeal.

HELD: The tribunal was entitled, as a matter of fact, to find that the council had not acted reasonably in dismissing the dinner ladies. The tribunal's decision could not be criticised because it did not recite all of the facts which were not in dispute; it did not mean that they had been overlooked. The tribunal had not misdirected itself in law.

Obiter dicta, the [s 98(1)] 'hurdle' of placing the onus on the employer to show a substantial reason for dismissal is designed to deter dismissal for trivial and unworthy reasons. If on the face of it the reason could justify dismissal, the enquiry moves to s [98(4)] and the question of reasonableness.

In this case the decision of the tribunal that dinner ladies had been unfairly dismissed, following imposition of new holiday pay terms that breached a national agreement, was upheld.

Murphy v Epsom College

[1983] IRLR 395, EAT; affd [1984] IRLR 271, CA

Hollister v National Farmers' Union

[1979] IRLR 238, CA

[8.69] The NFU decided to reorganise their operations. This resulted in a transfer of insurance business to a different organisation, which in turn resulted in a change in the terms and conditions enjoyed by employees. Mr Hollister could not be persuaded to accept these new terms and was dismissed. His claim was dismissed by a tribunal. The EAT allowed his appeal on the grounds that there had been insufficient consultation. The NFU appealed.

HELD: The EAT had put a gloss on the statute. There was no requirement that there should be negotiation and consultation in the statute. They were factors that had to be taken into account in determining the fairness of an employer's decision to dismiss. In this case it was absolutely essential for new contracts to be agreed and the only way to do this was to terminate current agreements and offer new ones. This was a substantial reason of a kind sufficient to justify dismissal.

(See 8.38 above.)

Protection of interest of business

R S Components Ltd v Irwin

[1973] IRLR 239, NIRC

[8.70] RS Components was losing business due to the competitive activities of former employees. As a result it sought to place its sales force under a reasonable restrictive covenant. Mr Irwin refused to sign the new agreement and was dismissed. A tribunal found his dismissal to be unfair and construed the words 'some other substantial reason' ejusdem generis with the other potentially fair reasons for dismissal. The company appealed.

HELD: The NIRC upheld the employer's appeal against the decision that they had unfairly dismissed Irwin. The words 'some other substantial reason' do not have to be construed ejusdem generis with the other potentially fair reasons for dismissal. The tribunal had made unanimous findings of fact that the proposed restrictive covenant was fair, the company was entitled to defend itself, and the effect on the company of Mr Irwin's refusal to sign the new agreement was substantial enough to justify dismissal. Had the tribunal construed the meaning of 'other substantial reason' correctly it would have found the dismissal had been fair.

North Yorkshire County Council v Fay

[1985] IRLR 247, CA

[8.71] Mrs Fay was employed under four fixed, short-term successive contracts. Each engagement was to fill a temporary gap. When the final contract was not renewed she complained that she had been made redundant, and had been unfairly dismissed. A tribunal found that she had been dismissed on the grounds of some other substantial reason. The EAT allowed her appeal because it thought that she had been dismissed to facilitate a reduction in staff. She appealed to the Court of Appeal.

HELD: Mrs Fay had been dismissed for some other substantial reason, and this was reasonable in all the circumstances. There was no suggestion there had been a redundancy situation. Mrs Fay was employed on the ordinary kind of short-term fixed contract. The contracts were for a genuine purpose, to cover for temporary absence of a teacher. She knew this and was also aware that when this purpose came to an end and someone else filled the post her short-term contract would not be renewed. These facts are capable of constituting dismissal for some other substantial reason.

Imprisonment

Kingston v British Railways Board

[1984] IRLR 146, CA

[8.72] Mr Kingston was convicted of assaulting a police officer in the execution of his duty and sentenced to three months' imprisonment (the conviction was later quashed). During his incarceration the British Railways Board informed him that his employment had been frustrated and he would consequently be summarily dismissed. A tribunal held that he had been fairly dismissed, not because his contract had been frustrated, but because of the length of his sentence and the nature of the offence. He appealed to the EAT and then to the Court of Appeal.

HELD, on appeal: A three-month prison sentence was capable of being 'another substantial reason'. In this case, it was not necessary for disciplinary procedures to be followed, as the employee was in prison. In addition, the tribunal had been right to also look at the nature of the offence.

Grootcon (UK) Ltd v Keld

[1984] IRLR 302, EAT

[8.73] Three days before the end of his tour of duty on a rig, Mr Keld sustained a knee injury and was sent home. His GP confirmed that he would be fit to return to work after his usual period of leave. However, he was dismissed. The tribunal found the actual reason for dismissal was capability, but that his dismissal was unfair. The company appealed.

HELD: The company had failed to establish the reason for dismissal. There was no medical evidence about his condition, and Mr Keld was initially told that he was being dismissed by reason of redundancy. Claims by the company that they had been instructed by BP not to employ Mr Keld further, which could amount to a substantial reason to justify dismissal, were also not established. The company had failed to provide sufficient evidence to discharge the onus upon them to show the reason for dismissal.

DISMISSAL FOLLOWING A TRANSFER OF AN UNDERTAKING

[8.74] Regulation 8 of the Transfer of Undertakings (Protection of Employment) Regulations 1981 (TUPE) provides:

(1) Where either before or after a relevant transfer, any employee of the transferor or transferee is dismissed, that employee shall be treated for the purposes of Part V of the 1978 Act and Articles 20 to 41 of the 1976 Order (unfair dismissal) as unfairly dismissed if the transfer or a reason connected with it is the reason or principal reason for his dismissal.

(2) Where an economic, technical or organisational reason entailing a change in the workforce of either the transferor or transferee before or after a relevant transfer is the reason or principal reason for dismissing an employee;
(a) paragraph (1) shall not apply.....

Dismissal for economic, technical or organisational reasons

Kerry Foods Ltd v Creber

[2000] IRLR 10, EAT

[8.75] The employees worked in a sausage-making factory. The factory got into financial difficulties, and receivers were appointed on Friday 24 January. On

Monday 27 January, all staff regarded as non-essential were dismissed with immediate effect. The receivers sought to sell the business as a going concern, but eventually only the brand name and goodwill were sold to Kerry Foods, which produced the sausages from a different factory.

Issues arose concerning whether there was a transfer of an undertaking and, if so, whether the employees were employed immediately prior to the transfer, whether the dismissals were for a reason connected with the transfer and/or an economic, technical or organisational reason entailing changes in the workforce ('an ETO reason').

HELD, on appeal: There was a transfer of an undertaking. Although Kerry Foods did not continue to make sausages in the factory or employ any of the employees, they had acquired the goodwill of the business, and were selling the same sausages (albeit manufactured elsewhere) to the same customers. On the facts, the dismissals were for a reason connected with the transfer, and liability for the dismissals transferred to Kerry Foods. Liability for failure to consult over the transfer also transferred to Kerry Foods.

Per Morison J:

> (1) Every dismissal is effective to terminate the employment relationship.
>
> (2) A dismissal by the transferor by reason of the impending transfer will be automatically unfair.
>
> (3) The employees concerned will enforce their remedies in relation to that dismissal against the transferee, in accordance with the *Litster* principle.
>
> (4) If the main reason for the dismissal by the transferor is an ETO reason, neither reg 8(1) nor the *Litster* principle will apply.
>
> (5) If the reason for the dismissal is an ETO reason but the dismissal is nonetheless unfair, then the principle in the previous point (4) remains true … It is only when reg 8(1) applies that the *Litster* principle operates.
>
> (6) If the dismissal is effected by the transferee then the employee's remedy lies against the transferee. A transferee may dismiss by reason of the transfer or for an ETO reason.'

Dismissals connected with the transfer

Litster v Forth Dry Dock and Engineering Co Ltd

[1989] IRLR 161, HL

[8.76] TUPE are intended to implement the Acquired Rights Directive (a European Directive) into UK law.

The stated objective of the Directive was 'to provide for the protection of employees in the event of a change of employer'.

Regulation 5(1) of TUPE provides that:

> A relevant transfer shall not operate so as to terminate the contract of employment of any person employed by the transferor in the undertaking or part transferred but any such contract which would otherwise have been terminated by the transfer shall have effect after the transfer as if originally made between the person so employed and the transferee.

Regulation 5(3) states that 'Any reference ... to a person employed in an undertaking or part of one transferred by a relevant transfer is a reference to a person so employed immediately before the transfer ...'

Regulation 8(1) goes on to say that any dismissal of an employee, either before or after a relevant transfer, will be unfair if the transfer or a reason connected with it is the reason or principal reason for the dismissal. However, regulation 8(2) says that regulation 8(1) will not apply where the reason or principal reason for the dismissal is an economic, technical or organisational reason entailing changes in the workforce.

Forth Dry Dock dismissed the twelve appellants in this case one hour before selling its business assets to another business, Forth Estuary.

The appellants brought unfair dismissal cases against Forth Dry Dock (which was in receivership) and Forth Estuary. Their rights depended on the question of whether they could be said to have been 'employed immediately before the transfer' under regulation 5(3), even though they had been dismissed one hour before the transfer.

HELD, on appeal: The UK courts must as far as possible adopt a purposive approach to the interpretation of UK regulations implementing European directives, even if this requires a departure from the strict and literal application of the wording of the regulations.

Because of this, and following the European Court of Justice case of *P Bork International A/S v Foreningen af Arbejdsledere i Danmark*:101/87 [1989] IRLR 41, ECJ, the reference to 'a person ... employed immediately before the transfer' must be read as if it were immediately followed by the words 'or would have been so employed if he had not been unfairly dismissed in the circumstances described in regulation 8(1)'.

On the facts of the case, the reason for the dismissal had been the imminent transfer of the business, so the appellants were entitled to be treated as if they had been employed immediately before the transfer.

Cases on dismissal for economic, technical or organisational reasons

Delabole Slate Ltd v Berriman

[1985] IRLR 305, CA

[8.77] Berriman (B) was employed as a quarryman. The business in which he worked was transferred to Delabole (D). This transfer amounted to a transfer of an undertaking. After the transfer, D wrote to B seeking to change his pay rates so as to make them comply with their current collective agreement with their trade union. B objected to the new rates, which would involve a reduction in his guaranteed salary. He resigned, claiming to have been constructively dismissed, and brought a claim alleging unfair dismissal.

By the time the case reached the Court of Appeal, it was not disputed that B was constructively dismissed by the attempt to impose a lower guaranteed wage. The question for the Court of Appeal was whether the dismissal was for an 'economic, technical or organisational reason entailing changes in the workforce'. If so, TUPE, reg 8(2) provided that the dismissal was potentially fair as being for 'some other substantial reason' under what is now ERA, s 98.

HELD: Per Brown-Wilkinson LJ:

> ...the phrase 'economic, technical or organisational reason entailing changes in the workforce' in our judgment requires that the change in the workforce is part of the economic, technical or organisational reason. The employer's plan must be to achieve changes in the workforce. It must be an objective of the plan, not just a possible consequence of it...

> ... we do not think that the dismissal of one employee followed by the engagement of another in his place constitutes a change in the 'workforce'. To our minds, the word 'workforce' connotes the whole body of employees as an entity: it corresponds to the 'strength' or the 'establishment'. Changes in the identity of the individuals who make up the workforce do not constitute changes in the workforce itself so long as the overall numbers and functions of the employees looked at as a whole remain unchanged.

It followed that B's dismissal was not for an economic, technical or organisational reason entailing changes in the workforce.

Whitehouse v Charles A Blatchford & Sons Ltd

[1999] IRLR 492, CA

[8.78] W was employed as a technician by S, whose main business was in the supply of prosthetic appliances to the Northern General Hospital. When the contract for supply of prosthetic appliances was put out to tender, B won the contract. The change in supplier from S to B was a transfer of an undertaking, and B took on S's employees. However, one condition of the contract being awarded by the hospital to B was a reduction in costs, including a reduction of the number of technicians from 13 to 12. After a redundancy selection exercise, B dismissed W as redundant. He complained that he had been unfairly dismissed, and that his dismissal was automatically unfair under the TUPE, reg 8(1). B contended that the dismissal was fair, and that it was for an economic, technical or organisational reason within reg 8(2).

HELD, on appeal: The dismissal was for an economic, technical or organisational reason entailing changes in the workforce. The reduction in the numbers of staff was directly connected with the provision of the services to the hospital, and the conduct of any business which provided them. This was not analogous to a case in which a vendor of a business dismissed employees for the purpose solely of achieving the best price for his business.

Dismissals 'connected with the transfer'

Rossiter v Pendragon plc, Crosby-Clarke v Air Foyle Ltd

[2002] EWCA Civ 745, [2002] ICR 1063

[8.79] Regulation 5(1) of TUPE provides for the automatic transfer of an employee's contract of employment from transferor to transferee.

Regulation 5(4A) provides that an employee will not be automatically transferred if they notify the transferor or transferee that they object to the transfer. Regulation 5(4B) goes on to say that where the employee notifies the transferor that he objects, his employment with the transferor will end, but he is not to be treated, for any purpose, as having been dismissed by the transferor.

Regulation 5(5) provides that 'paragraphs (1) and (4A) above are without prejudice to any right of an employee arising apart from these Regulations to terminate his contract of employment without notice if a substantial change is made in his working conditions to his detriment …'

In normal circumstances, an employee will be entitled to terminate their contract of employment without notice where his or her employer commits a fundamental breach of their contract of employment. In these cases, the Court of Appeal considered the question of whether regulation 5(5) extended the normal rule so that an employee could, on a transfer of an undertaking, claim to have been constructively dismissed by reason of a substantial change in their working conditions where that change in their working conditions did not amount to a breach of their employment contract.

In *Rossiter*, a car salesman's commission scheme was revised when he was transferred to a new employer. In *Crosby-Clarke*, the maximum number of days an airline pilot could work without a break were extended on the transfer of his employment from an airline regulated under UK law to one regulated under Belgian law. Neither of these changes amounted to a breach of contract.

HELD, on appeal: Regulation 5(5) did not extend the normal test for constructive dismissal. Even in the context of a transfer of an undertaking, it was necessary for an employee to show a breach of their contract before there could be a constructive dismissal.

AUTOMATICALLY UNFAIR REASONS

Leave for family reasons

[8.80] Section 99 of ERA provides:

(1) An employee who is dismissed shall be regarded for the purposes of this Part as unfairly dismissed if—
(a) the reason or principal reason for the dismissal is of a prescribed kind, or
(b) the dismissal takes place in prescribed circumstances.

(2) In this section 'prescribed' means prescribed by regulations made by the Secretary of State.

(3) A reason or set of circumstances prescribed under this section must relate to—
(a) pregnancy, childbirth or maternity,
(b) ordinary, compulsory or additional maternity leave,
(c) parental leave, or
(d) time off under section 57A;

and it may also relate to redundancy or other factors.

(4) A reason or set of circumstances prescribed under subsection (1) satisfies subsection (3)(c) or (d) if it relates to action which an employee—
(a) takes,
(b) agrees to take, or
(c) refuses to take,

under or in respect of a collective or workforce agreement which deals with parental leave.

(5) Regulations under this section may—
(a) make different provision for different cases or circumstances;
(b) apply any enactment, in such circumstances as may be specified and subject to any conditions specified, in relation to persons regarded as unfairly dismissed by reason of this section.

Del Monte Foods Ltd v Mundon

[1980] IRLR 224, EAT

[8.81] The applicant had a poor absence record and was off for long periods of time for a variety of reasons. Eventually, her employer wrote to her to express its concerns over her sickness record and gave her two months in which to improve her attendance. After this the applicant again went off sick. After the two-month period, the respondent decided to terminate her employment. However, before steps could be taken to dismiss, she informed her employer that she was pregnant. Despite this, the employer went ahead and dismissed her. A tribunal held that this was an automatically unfair dismissal under (what is now) ERA, s 99. The employer appealed.

HELD: The tribunal had been wrong to decide that the employee had been automatically unfairly dismissed. When the employer made the decision to dismiss, it did not know that she was pregnant. The decision to dismiss was because of her continued sickness absence. The fact that the employer subsequently discovered that the employee was pregnant, but still dismissed, was not enough to show they had dismissed by reason of the pregnancy. Nor was there evidence that her absence was because she was pregnant.

Under ERA, s 99, a dismissal will be unfair if either the reason or principal reason for the dismissal was that the employee was pregnant or was for a reason connected with pregnancy. The employer must have known or believed that the woman was pregnant or that they were dismissing her for some pregnancy-related reason if the employee was to succeed. If the only matter that can be found is knowledge of the pregnancy without a change in the decision to dismiss, that will not justify upholding the complaint.

Caledonia Bureau Investment and Property v Caffrey

[1998] IRLR 110, EAT

[8.82] Following childbirth, an employee suffered post-natal depression and submitted sickness certificates. She was eventually dismissed on the grounds of her ill-health. Her claims of unfair dismissal and sex discrimination succeeded. The dismissal was found to be pregnancy-related and therefore automatically unfair. It was also decided that since the illness was pregnancy-related, the employee had been discriminated against. The company appealed to the EAT.

HELD: A purposive approach should be taken to the legislation. Section 99(1)(a) of ERA is not limited to the period of pregnancy/maternity leave but applies after maternity leave has expired provided the contract has been extended.

Dismissal on account of illness which is related to having given birth or being pregnant, is discriminatory because the employee is suffering from an illness from which a man could not suffer. The appeal was dismissed.

Health and safety reason

[8.83] Section 100 of ERA provides:

(1) An employee who is dismissed shall be regarded for the purposes of this Part as unfairly dismissed if the reason (or, if more than one, the principal reason) for the dismissal is that—
(a) having been designated by the employer to carry out activities in connection with preventing or reducing risks to health and safety at work, the employee carried out (or proposed to carry out) any such activities,
(b) being a representative of workers on matters of health and safety at work or member of a safety committee—
  (i) in accordance with arrangements established under or by virtue of any enactment, or
  (ii) by reason of being acknowledged as such by the employer,
the employee performed (or proposed to perform) any functions as such a representative or a member of such a committee,

348   *Unfair Dismissal*

    (c) being an employee at a place where—
        (i) there was no such representative or safety committee, or
        (ii) there was such a representative or safety committee but it was not reasonably practicable for the employee to raise the matter by those means,
    he brought to his employer's attention, by reasonable means, circumstances connected with his work which he reasonably believed were harmful or potentially harmful to health or safety,
    (d) in circumstances of danger which the employee reasonably believed to be serious and imminent and which he could not reasonably have been expected to avert, he left (or proposed to leave) or (while the danger persisted) refused to return to his place of work or any dangerous part of his place of work, or
    (e) in circumstances of danger which the employee reasonably believed to be serious and imminent, he took (or proposed to take) appropriate steps to protect himself or other persons from the danger.

(2) For the purposes of subsection (1)(e) whether steps which an employee took (or proposed to take) were appropriate is to be judged by reference to all the circumstances including, in particular, his knowledge and the facilities and advice available to him at the time.

Goodwin v Cabletel UK Ltd

[1997] IRLR 665, EAT

[8.84] Mr Goodwin was employed as a construction manager. Part of his responsibilities were to ensure that sub-contractors complied with health and safety requirements and procedures. Mr Goodwin was concerned about the health and safety record of one of the sub-contractors. Mr Goodwin's employers did not share his view of taking further action against the sub-contractors, but wanted to take a more conciliatory approach.

Relations between Mr Goodwin and the sub-contractors did not improve and his employers decided to remove Mr Goodwin from any dealings with them by changing his job to that of Assistant Construction Manager. Mr Goodwin resigned and claimed that he had been constructively dismissed and that the dismissal was automatically unfair as he was raising a concern over health and safety and should be protected under the Employment Protection (Consolidation) Act 1975, s 57A as a 'designated employee' (now ERA, s 100).

A tribunal concluded that the dismissal was not unfair since ERA, s 100 only applied where the dismissal was because of the way a 'designated employee' was carrying out health and safety duties. Since Mr Goodwin was never prevented or limited in performing his health and safety duties, his claim failed. He appealed to the EAT.

HELD: Appeal allowed. Mr Goodwin was dismissed because he was carrying out his health and safety duties. The Act protected health and safety employees from dismissal when they were carrying out their duties. The tribunal should have considered if the way the employer had approached his concerns was within the scope of his health and safety activities or whether he had behaved in such a manner that he was no longer entitled to the protection afforded to him by the Act.

The matter was remitted back to the tribunal.

Harvest Press Ltd v McCaffrey

[1999] IRLR 778, EAT

[8.85] Mr McCaffrey was dismissed after he walked out of a factory and left a machine unattended during the nightshift. Mr McCaffrey argued that the reason why he left the factory and went home was because his co-worker had been abusive to him and he had feared for his health and safety. He said that he would not return to work unless he had assurances about his safety. The employer preferred the co-worker's version of events and told Mr McCaffrey that he had resigned from his job by walking out and going home. Mr McCaffrey argued that he had been constructively dismissed and that his dismissal fell within ERA, s 100(1)(d) in that he had left employment 'in circumstances of danger which the employee reasonably believed to be serious and imminent…'. The tribunal accepted this argument and held the dismissal unfair. The employer appealed.

HELD: The behaviour of fellow employees in the workplace could give rise to a 'serious and imminent' danger falling within ERA, s 100(1)(d), and therefore it could be automatically unfair to dismiss. 'Danger' was intended to cover any danger, without limitation, therefore the employer's appeal failed.

Masiak v City Restaurants (UK) Ltd

[1999] IRLR 780, EAT

[8.86] Mr Masiak walked out of his job as a chef after less than a month after claiming that he considered the restaurant a potential hazard to public health. He then issued proceedings for breach of contract and automatic unfair dismissal under ERA, s 100(1)(e), on the basis that he reasonably believed there to be a serious and imminent danger, and he took 'appropriate steps to protect himself or other persons from the danger'. The employment tribunal dismissed his claim as it believed that 'other persons' within s 100(1)(e) did not include members of the public but only other employees. He appealed to the EAT.

HELD: 'Other persons' in s 100(1)(e) extends to include members of the public as well as fellow workers.

Refusal to work on a Sunday

[8.87] Section 101 of ERA provides:

(1) Where an employee who is—
(a) a protected shop worker or an opted-out shop worker, or
(b) a protected betting worker or an opted-out betting worker,

is dismissed, he shall be regarded for the purposes of this Part as unfairly dismissed if the reason (or, if more than one, the principal reason) for the dismissal is that he refused (or proposed to refuse) to do shop work, or betting work, on Sunday or on a particular Sunday.

Occupational pension scheme trustee

[8.88] Section 102 of ERA provides:

(1) An employee who is dismissed shall be regarded for the purposes of this Part as unfairly dismissed if the reason (or, if more than one, the principal reason) for the dismissal is that, being a trustee of a relevant occupational pension scheme which relates to his employment, the employee performed (or proposed to perform) any functions as such a trustee.

Employee representative

[8.89] Section 103 of ERA provides:

An employee who is dismissed shall be regarded for the purposes of this Part as unfairly dismissed if the reason (or, if more than one, the principal reason) for the dismissal is that the employee, being—
(a) an employee representative for the purposes of Chapter II of Part IV of the Trade Union and Labour Relations (Consolidation) Act 1992 (redundancies) or Regulations 10 and 11 of the Transfer of Undertakings (Protection of Employment) Regulations 1981, or
(b) a candidate in an election in which any person elected will, on being elected, be such an employee representative,

Trade union reasons

(Trade Union and Labour Relations Consolidation Act 1992, s 152.)

Speciality Care plc v Pachela
[1996] IRLR 248, EAT

[8.90] The employer sought to change the employee's shift from a double day shift of 8 am to 4 pm and 1 pm to 9.30 pm to a single day shift from 8 am to 8 pm.

The employees objected to the change. They joined a trade union to help them resist the proposed changes. The employer imposed the changes, and when the employees refused to work to the new shift patterns they were dismissed. They brought an unfair dismissal claim under the Trade Union and Labour Relations (Consolidation) Act 1992, s 152(1) alleging that they had been dismissed on account of their trade union membership or activities.

HELD, per Clark J:

> ... where a complaint of dismissal by reason of union membership is made, as in this case, it will be for the tribunal to find as a fact

whether or not the reason or principal reason for dismissal related to the applicant's trade union membership not only by reference to whether he or she had simply joined a union, but also by reference to whether the introduction of union representation into the employment relationship had led the employer to dismiss the employee. Tribunals should answer that question robustly, based on their findings as to what really caused the dismissal in the mind of the employer.

Fitzpatrick v British Railways Board

[1991] IRLR 376, CA

[8.91] The employee took part in trade union activities at British Rail. She was dismissed when her disruptive trade union activities at previous employers became apparent. The employment tribunal found that the reason for her dismissal was because of the disruptive reputation she had acquired on account of her trade union activities while at previous employers. The employment tribunal held that this was not automatically unfair under what is now the Trade Union and Labour Relations (Consolidation) Act 1992, s 152. It considered that to fall within s 152(1)(b) there must be some identifiable act in her present employment for which the employee had been dismissed, and it was not enough for the dismissal to be on account of possible trouble in the future.

HELD, per Leggatt LJ:

> The sole question in this appeal is whether the principal reason why the appellant was dismissed by the respondents was that she proposed to take part in trade union activities within the meaning of [s 152(1)(b)]. It is common ground that she did propose to take part in trade union activities and it was only because she proposed to do so that her reputation as a trouble-maker, mainly, if not wholly, acquired by reference to her previous trade union activities, can reasonably be regarded as having been relevant. She was dismissed because on account of that reputation the respondents apprehended that the way in which she participated in trade union activities would or might be objectionable. In short, the principal reason for her dismissal was that she, a reputed trouble-maker, proposed to take part in trade union activities.'

Her appeal was allowed because the only rational reason for the dismissal was her proposed trade union activities.

Selection for redundancy

Dundon v GPT Ltd

[1995] IRLR 403, EAT

[8.92] The applicant was a long-standing employee who had, over the years, become more and more involved in trade union activities, ultimately becoming a senior representative. The employers agreed to an arrangement whereby he would spend 50% of his time on his trade union responsibilities and 50% of his time actually carrying out his normal work. In practice, however, he spent less than 20% of his time on his normal work, and his employers had tacitly consented to this.

When the employer came to make redundancies, six criteria were agreed. The applicant was marked as 'very poor' against one of the criteria, which was 'quantity of work'. This marking was said to be due to 'time spent on unofficial union duties ... and his regular appalling time-keeping'. This marking was confirmed on an appeal, when the markers were told to make allowance for his union activities on the basis that he should have been dividing his time equally between union activities and work.

The employment tribunal found that the redundancy was genuine, and that the employer was not motivated by malice in selecting the applicant for redundancy. It went on to hold that his selection for redundancy was not on account of his trade union activities.

Section 152(1)(b) protects an individual from dismissal on account of union activities taking place at 'an appropriate time'. 'An appropriate time' is defined in sub-section (2)(b) as including 'a time within his working hours at which, in accordance with arrangements agreed with or consent given by his employer, it is permissible for him to take part in the activities of a trade union'.

HELD, on appeal: It was not a requirement of the Trade Union and Labour Relations (Consolidation) Act 1992, s 152 or s 153 that the employer must have maliciously or deliberately selected an employee for redundancy or dismissal on account of trade union activities. Selection for redundancy was unfair if the reason for selection was that he was spending too much time on trade union duties at 'an appropriate time'. The employers had, albeit tacitly and reluctantly, consented to him spending 80% of his time on union duties. The tribunal should have concluded that the selection was automatically unfair as the applicant had been selected for redundancy because he had taken part in trade union activities at an appropriate time. However, the EAT considered that the employee had contributed to his dismissal by 33%.

O'Dea v ISC Chemicals Ltd

[1995] IRLR 599, CA

[8.93] Section 153 of the Trade Union and Labour Relations (Consolidation) Act 1992 provides that a dismissal is unfair where the principal reason for a dismissal is redundancy, but:
  (a) the circumstances constituting the redundancy applied equally to one or more employees in the same undertaking who held positions similar to that held by him and who have not been dismissed by the employer, and
  (b) ... the reason .. why he was selected for dismissal was one of those specified in s152(1) [including taking part in trade union activities]...

The applicant was employed as a technical services operator, but did not actually do that job. Instead, he spent at least 50% of his time on trade union activities and the remainder of his time as a packaging operator.

The packaging department was shut down. The applicant was dismissed as redundant, although neither of the other two technical services operators were dismissed. The tribunal dismissed his claim and he appealed to the EAT.

HELD: In considering whether there were other employees who held positions similar to those held by the applicant for the purposes of s 153(a) it was necessary to ignore the time that the applicant spent on trade union activities. The tribunal should limit its consideration to his status as a skilled manual worker, the nature of his work and the terms and conditions of his employment. It was not appropriate to compare the applicant to the other technical services operators since although that was his job title it was not the role he actually undertook. This was the case even though the reason he had moved from being a technical services operator to being a packaging operator was to allow him time to carry out his trade union activities. In this case there were no comparators as the applicant was the only person employed as a packaging operator but on the (more favourable) technical services operator terms and conditions. The tribunal had been right to conclude that the trade union activities were not the principal reason for the redundancy selection.

Public interest disclosure

[8.94] The Public Interest Disclosure Act 1998 has been incorporated into the Employment Rights Act 1996 in Part IVA, as follows (section 103A of ERA):

> An employee who is dismissed shall be regarded for the purposes of this Part as unfairly dismissed if the reason (or, if more than one, the principal reason) for the dismissal is that the employee made a protected disclosure.

Miklaszewicz v Stolt Offshore Ltd

[2002] IRLR 344, Ct of Sess

[8.95] In 1993 the applicant was dismissed because he reported his employer to the Inland Revenue. The applicant continued to work within the oil industry, however, following a number of transfers he found himself again employed by Stolt Offshore Limited in 1999. The applicant was dismissed again by the respondent in 1999, the reason given was redundancy. However, the applicant argued that the real reason was the disclosure he had made in 1993 and claimed that this was a protected disclosure and therefore his dismissal was automatically unfair under ERA, s 103A.

The primary issue was whether Mr Miklaszewicz could argue the disclosure in 1993 was protected since it happened before the enactment of the Public Interest Disclosure Act. The tribunal found that the disclosure was not protected because it predated the enactment of the Act and therefore the tribunal did not have jurisdiction to hear his complaint. The EAT overturned this decision and the employers appealed to the Court of Session.

HELD: Notwithstanding that the disclosure had taken place more than six years earlier and prior to the coming into force of the PIDA, the applicant was entitled to protection. The important point in time is when the employer chooses to dismiss. Only at this point are the statutory remedies triggered. Such an interpretation of the legislation poses no unfairness to employers. Since the employer dismissed after the PIDA and ERA were enacted, the employee was entitled to protection. This interpretation was consistent with the main purpose of the PIDA.

Assertion of a statutory right

[8.96] Section 104 of ERA provides:

(1) An employee who is dismissed shall be regarded for the purposes of this Part as unfairly dismissed if the reason (or, if more than one, the principal reason) for the dismissal is that the employee—
(a) brought proceedings against the employer to enforce a right of his which is a relevant statutory right, or
(b) alleged that the employer had infringed a right of his which is a relevant statutory right.

The national minimum wage

[8.97] Section 104A(1) of ERA:

An employee who is dismissed shall be regarded for the purposes of this Part as unfairly dismissed if the reason (or, if more than one, the principal reason) for the dismissal is that—
(a) any action was taken, or was proposed to be taken, by or on behalf of the employee with a view to enforcing, or otherwise securing the benefit of, a right of the employee's to which this section applies; or
(b) the employer was prosecuted for an offence under section 31 of the National Minimum Wage Act 1998 as a result of action taken by or on behalf of the employee for the purpose of enforcing, or otherwise securing the benefit of, a right of the employee's to which this section applies; or
(c) the employee qualifies, or will or might qualify, for the national minimum wage or for a particular rate of national minimum wage.

Tax credit

[8.98] Section 104B(1) of ERA:

An employee who is dismissed shall be regarded for the purposes of this Part as unfairly dismissed if the reason (or, if more than one, the principal reason) for the dismissal is that—
(a) any action was taken, or was proposed to be taken, by or on behalf of the employee with a view to enforcing, or otherwise securing the benefit of, a right conferred on the employee by regulations under section 6(2)(a) or (c) of the Tax Credits Act 1999;
(b) a penalty was imposed on the employer, or proceedings for a penalty were brought against him, under section 9 of that Act, as a result of action

taken by or on behalf of the employee for the purpose of enforcing, or otherwise securing the benefit of, such a right; or
(c) the employee is entitled, or will or may be entitled, to working families' tax credit or disabled person's tax credit

PROCEDURE

[8.99] Section 98(4) of ERA provides that once an employer has shown a potentially fair reason for dismissal the tribunal must then decide whether the employer has acted fairly in deciding to dismiss.

> (4) Where the employer has fulfilled the requirements of subsection (1), the determination of the question whether the dismissal is fair or unfair (having regard to the reason shown by the employer)—
> (a) depends on whether in the circumstances (including the size and administrative resources of the employer's undertaking) the employer acted reasonably or unreasonably in treating it as a sufficient reason for dismissing the employee, and
> (b) shall be determined in accordance with equity and the substantial merits of the case.

A fair procedure?

Polkey v A E Dauton (or Dayton) Services Ltd (Formerly Edmund Walker Holdings Ltd)

[1987] IRLR 503, HL

[8.100] The applicant was one of three van drivers made redundant by the employer. The applicant was not given any prior warning of the redundancy situation, and no consultation procedure was followed. Mr Polkey brought unfair dismissal proceedings against his former employer.

The employment tribunal dismissed Mr Polkey's claim and the EAT and Court of Appeal upheld this decision on appeal. The Court of Appeal agreed that the tribunal was bound by the decision in *British Labour Pump Co Ltd v Byrne* [1979] IRLR 94, EAT. Under this principle, the tribunal had no choice but to accept that even if the employer had consulted with Mr Polkey or given him prior warning, it would have made no difference to the outcome and therefore, the dismissal was fair. The employee appealed to the House of Lords.

HELD: When determining whether a dismissal is fair or unfair the decision will depend on what the employer actually did and not what he might have done. It is not for the tribunal to consider if the employer had acted differently, whether the employee would have been dismissed fairly as this is relying on matters not known to the employer before the dismissal. The *British Labour Pump* decision was out of line with the spirit of unfair dismissal protection and would lead to injustice for the employee. What must be considered is what a 'reasonable employer' would have had in mind at the time he decided to dismiss. The statutory tests require that consideration is given not only to the reason for dismissal but also to the manner of dismissal.

If the employer could reasonably have concluded at the time of dismissal that consultation or warning would be 'utterly useless' the employer might well have a defence for failing to follow fair procedure. However, such an argument must be judged on the circumstances known by the employer at the time of the dismissal. This is particularly relevant when assessing compensation.

Slater v Leicestershire Health Authority

[1989] IRLR 16, CA

[8.101] Allegations were made against Mr Slater, who was a staff nurse, that he had hit an elderly patient in his care. He was suspended from his duties pending an investigation. The hospital's director of nursing investigated the complaint and saw that the patient had red marks on his body. Mr Slater was called to a disciplinary hearing conducted by the director of nursing who concluded that Mr Slater had slapped the patient in a temper. The director of nursing also took the decision to dismiss Mr Slater for gross misconduct. The tribunal found that the dismissal was fair despite the fact that the nursing director had conducted the investigation and the disciplinary hearing. Mr Later appealed, unsuccessfully, to the EAT and then to the Court of Appeal.

HELD: Mr Slater's argument that he was unfairly dismissed because the director was investigator, judge and jury had considerable force. Although there were issues as to whether the disciplinary hearing had been conducted fairly, the tribunal concluded that it had been.

It was ill advised for the nursing director to conduct the investigation, but in this case the existence of marks on the patient were not in issue. The principal issue in the disciplinary meeting was the credibility of Mr Slater. Since the tribunal had not misdirected itself the Court of Appeal dismissed Mr Slater's appeal.

Whitbread plc v Hall

[2001] EWCA Civ 268, [2001] IRLR 275

[8.102] Mr Hall was a manager of a hotel. During his employment there had been stock control problems and he received a warning. Further problems occurred and were investigated by the area manager, he was suspended during the investigation. At a disciplinary meeting conducted by the area manager he admitted the offences and was dismissed for gross misconduct. He appealed and the appeal was heard by the operations manager.

He complained of unfair dismissal because the area manager had conducted the investigation and conducted the disciplinary hearing. A tribunal upheld his claim on the grounds of procedural unfairness, finding that the defects had not been cured by the appeal. The EAT dismissed the employer's appeal because the area manager's role offended the principle that justice should not only be done but be seen to be done. The employers appealed to the Court of Appeal.

HELD: Even in circumstances where misconduct is admitted an employer is not free from any requirement to act in a reasonable fashion. Section 98(4) requires tribunals to decide whether an employer has acted reasonably in treating the reason as a reason to dismiss. In this case the offence was not so heinous as to require necessarily that dismissal was the only sanction. Too heavy a procedural burden should not be placed upon employers. There are some cases which are so heinous that a large employer well versed in employment practices might decide to dismiss regardless of the explanation.

Thomas v St Johnstone Football Club Ltd

(EAT/48/02)

[8.103] The appellant, Mr Thomas, was dismissed for gross misconduct following allegations that he had taken drugs in a public place. He appealed against the football club's decision to the Scottish Premier League. Under the terms of that appeal an independent commission was convened. At this hearing, chaired by a Queen's Counsel, the Commission decided to reduce the penalty to serious misconduct and quash the dismissal. The football club in turn appealed to the Scottish Football Association's (SFA) Appeals Committee. Mr Thomas was not allowed to make submissions to this appeal committee. The SFA's Appeal Committee upheld the football club's original decision to dismiss, although no reasons were given for that decision.

Mr Thomas brought a claim for unfair dismissal which was dismissed by an employment tribunal. He appealed.

HELD, on appeal: Procedural defects in a decision-making process leading to dismissal can be cured by a full appeal hearing. The tribunal's decision was quashed and a finding of unfair dismissal held.

THE BAND OF REASONABLE RESPONSES (SECTION 98(4) OF ERA)

Iceland Frozen Foods Ltd v Jones

[1982] IRLR 439, EAT

[8.104] Mr Jones was employed as a night shift foreman. Allegations were raised, which included an allegation that he had not secured an office in the warehouse contrary to his responsibilities and that he had not re-activated the security alarm. The employer drew an inference of misconduct and dismissed Mr Jones summarily. A tribunal held that the dismissal was unfair and that it was not reasonable to dismiss Mr Jones in the circumstances, nor had the employer followed a fair procedure. The tribunal noted that he had not been allowed to be accompanied by a union representative and that the discussions with his employer were too short to allow him to state his case. The company appealed to the EAT.

HELD: The tribunal had failed to consider whether the decision fell within the band of reasonable responses. The EAT also held that there were five points the tribunal had to take into consideration, these are (per Mr Justice Browne-Wilkinson at para 24):

(1) the starting point should always be [ERA, s 98(4)] themselves];

(2) in applying the section an employment tribunal must consider the reasonableness of the employer's conduct, not simply whether they (the members of the employment tribunal) consider the dismissal to be fair;

(3) in judging the reasonableness of the employer's conduct an employment tribunal must not substitute its decision as to what was the right course to adopt for that of the employer;

(4) in many (though not all) cases there is a band of reasonable responses to the employee's conduct within which one employer might reasonably take one view, another quite reasonably take another;

(5) the function of the employment tribunal, as an industrial jury, is to determine whether in particular circumstances of each case the decision to dismiss the employee fell within the band of reasonable responses which a reasonable employer might have adopted. If the dismissal falls within the band the dismissal is fair: if the dismissal falls outside the band it is unfair.'

The tribunal's decision on procedural unfairness could not be supported. The tribunal had not been correct to deal with the reasonableness of the substantive decision and the reasonableness of the procedure separately.

The appeal was allowed and the matter remitted to a new tribunal.

Hereford and Worcester County Council v Neale

[1986] IRLR 168, CA

[8.105] Mr Neale was dismissed from his role as head of music following an incident which occurred whilst he was invigilating an 'A' level music exam, where he wrote on an examination paper to assist one of his pupils. The decision to dismiss him was taken by a specially convened meeting of the council's sub-committee. Mr Neale complained of unfair dismissal.

Although the tribunal was critical of the sub-committee, it held that the decision to dismiss was within the band of reasonable responses. The EAT disagreed with the tribunal's decision. It felt the employer had acted with too much haste and there was too much stubbornness and secrecy surrounding the decision-making of the committee. As a result it concluded that the council acted unfairly. The council appealed to the Court of Appeal.

HELD: Although there were some procedural deficiencies in the council's procedure, the decision to dismiss fell within the band of reasonable responses. The EAT had substituted its own views for that of the tribunal's decision. It is for the tribunal to find the facts, apply the relevant law and to reach its conclusion. If the tribunal has acted in this way, it is rare that its decision should be interfered with unless it can be said to be perverse. The tribunal in the present case had not misdirected itself, nor had acted perversely. The dismissal was therefore fair.

Foley v Post Office; HSBC Bank (formerly Midland Bank plc) v Madden

[2000] IRLR 827, CA

[8.106] These cases were heard together as in both cases the employees had been dismissed for alleged acts of misconduct. Mr Foley was allowed time off for what he said was to deal with a family issue. However, he was spotted in a nearby pub by an off duty manager shortly after leaving work. Mr Foley said that he had gone to the pub to phone for a taxi and could not have been seen by the manager at the time the manager said he saw him. Following an internal hearing and appeal, the employer dismissed Mr Foley. Mr Foley then brought a claim for unfair dismissal which was dismissed by the tribunal, but was allowed on appeal. The EAT allowed the appeal on the basis that the tribunal had not given any consideration to the range of reasonable responses.

Mr Madden was dismissed after it was found he had been involved in misappropriating and fraudulently using customers' debit cards. He complained to the tribunal and it, and the EAT, held the dismissal was unfair. The EAT held that in a disputed misconduct case, the tribunal was free to substitute its own view for that of the employer. Both employers appealed to the Court of Appeal.

HELD: The 'band of reasonable responses' test was still good law. If a tribunal misinterprets the test then an appellate court could interfere with its decision. The court appreciated that in some cases there would not be a band or range to consider, as sometimes there can be only one response. However, where there would be disagreement between reasonable employers over the sanction to impose, then the tribunal should consider the 'range of reasonable responses'.

The court made clear (as stated in *Iceland Frozen Foods v Jones* [1982] IRLR 439), that it is not for the tribunal to substitute its own views. Instead the role of the tribunal is to determine whether what the employer did and the decision it made was within the band of reasonable responses 'which a reasonable employer might have adopted'. The 'reasonable employer' is an objective and hypothetical employer and is not someone whom the tribunal substitutes with reference to their own subjective views. The court also held that the test laid down in *British Home Stores Ltd v Burchell* [1978] IRLR 379, was binding.

Both appeals were allowed and the complaints of unfair dismissal dismissed.

    Note—See *British Home Stores Ltd v Burchell* [1978] IRLR 379 (see 8.55 above).

Fuller v Lloyds Bank plc

[1991] IRLR 336, EAT

[8.107] It was alleged that Mr Fuller had smashed a glass into the face of a work colleague at a pub on Christmas Eve. Mr Fuller stated that the injury was a result of an accident and was not malicious. The employer questioned a number of witnesses during its investigations and statements were prepared. These statements were never revealed to the applicant or his union representative, despite requests. On the basis of these statements, the bank decided that the injury to the employee was a deliberate act and not an accident as Mr Fuller maintained. As a result he was dismissed.

A tribunal dismissed Mr Fuller's complaint of unfair dismissal as it held that a failure to disclose the witness statements did not mean the decision to dismiss fell outside the range of reasonable responses. The tribunal accepted that the allegation against Mr Fuller was clear and there was no need to explain it further. Mr Fuller appealed to the EAT.

HELD: It is generally desirable that witness statements and other evidence that forms the basis of an employer's decision should be revealed to the employee prior to the disciplinary hearing. Failing to provide such evidence will not inevitably make a dismissal unfair.

If there is a defect in a disciplinary procedure, this must be considered in the light of what occurred. A tribunal should consider whether the defect makes the procedure unfair or whether the results of the defect looked at overall makes it unfair. If a defect is serious so as to render the procedure unfair then a dismissal will be held to be unfair. In this case the tribunal had correctly assessed that the defect was not sufficiently serious to render the procedure unfair and that the overall process was fair.

Sainsbury's Supermarkets Ltd v Hitt

[2002] EWCA Civ 1588, [2003] IRLR 23, CA

[8.108] Mr Hitt had eight years' service with Sainsbury's until he was dismissed for gross misconduct. Razor blades went missing from the store and following a locker search, they were found in Mr Hitt's locker. Mr Hitt maintained that someone else had put them there and named members of staff who had keys to his locker. Sainsbury's investigated the matter and also the comments that other key holders could have stolen the goods and stored them in his locker. The store concluded that the other key holders could not have taken the goods and subsequently Mr Hitt was dismissed for gross misconduct.

The tribunal and the EAT held that Sainsbury's had unfairly dismissed Mr Hitt in that it had not acted fairly in investigating the alleged theft. Sainsbury's appealed to the Court of Appeal.

HELD: Tribunals should apply the objective standards of the reasonable employer, the 'band of reasonable responses' test, in determining every aspect of whether the employee had been fairly or unfairly dismissed, including the initial investigation. Whether Sainsbury's had conducted a fair investigation should be judged in the light of what a reasonable employer would have done. It was not necessary for them to follow every possible line of enquiry.

The purpose of an investigation process is not to determine as a court of law would, the guilt of an employee, but to establish whether there was a reasonable belief that the employee had committed an act of misconduct to which a reasonable response would be dismissal. To ask more of the employer, as the tribunal had done in this case, amounted to the tribunal substituting its own standards of what constituted a reasonable investigation, this was not permissible.

O'Flynn v Airlinks the Airport Coach Co Ltd

(EAT/0269/01)

[8.109] The applicant was dismissed after failing to comply with the respondent's drink and drugs policy. The respondent had introduced a drink and drugs policy in 1999 which promoted zero tolerance of drugs and also introduced random screening of 10% of its workforce each year. The applicant had not complained about this policy at the time it was introduced. She was selected for a random drugs test. Prior to the test she admitted that she had taken cocaine and had smoked cannabis, although only cannabis was found in her system. She was dismissed.

She argued that the decision to dismiss her was not within the band of reasonable responses and a lesser sanction was more appropriate. The tribunal held that she was well aware of the policy and made no objections to it when it was introduced, therefore it formed part of her contract of employment. The tribunal also commented that as part of the her duties she could be required to assist drivers in manoeuvring coaches and also to serve hot drinks to passengers on moving coaches, therefore the policy was necessary from a health and safety perspective. Finally she argued that the policy and the testing had been a breach of her human rights. The tribunal did not consider there was a human rights issue and found the decision to dismiss was neither unfair or wrongful. The applicant appealed.

HELD: The policy formed part of her contract of employment and was necessary on the grounds of health and safety because it protected the employer's customers. As a result the decision to dismiss fell within the range of reasonable responses. The EAT agreed with the tribunal that there was no human rights issue.

Nkengfack v London Borough of Southwark

[2001] EWCA Civ 711, CA

[8.110] The applicant was employed as a teacher. Her employer was concerned about the amount of time she was taking off due to sickness. They believed that she was taking time off to work in a hair salon which she owned. During one of these periods of sickness, the head teacher at the applicant's school and another teacher went to the applicant's salon and found her working there. The applicant denied that she had been working but that she had been in bed with back pains. However during the disciplinary hearing, the evidence of the head and another teacher was preferred and the applicant was dismissed. The applicant complained of unfair dismissal and also sex and race discrimination. The respondent submitted that the offence was so serious, and involved dishonesty, that dismissal was the only option. The tribunal dismissed all of her complaints and accepted that the employer had acted reasonably in dismissing the employee for gross misconduct. She appealed to the EAT arguing that insufficient consideration had been given by the disciplinary panel to a sanction other than dismissal. Her appeal was unsuccessful and she appealed to the Court of Appeal.

HELD: It is for the tribunal to consider what an employer did in the circumstances and whether the employer acted reasonably or unreasonably in treating that reason as a 'sufficient reason' to dismiss. What is considered is not some other action which the employer might have but did not take. As was held in *Iceland Frozen Foods Ltd v Jones* [1982] IRLR 439, EAT at para 24 per Browne-Wilkinson J: 'If the dismissal falls within the band it is fair: if the dismissal falls outside the band it is unfair'.

If the dismissal fell within the band of reasonable responses to the employee's conduct which a reasonable employer might had adopted, then the court held, that is the end of the tribunal's enquiry.

In this instance the tribunal found that the respondent carried out a proper investigation, that the disciplinary panels acted fairly when they accepted evidence that she was working and reached the conclusion that they acted fairly in dismissing her. Dismissal for gross misconduct fell within the range of reasonable responses. The appeal was dismissed.

CONSTRUCTIVE DISMISSAL

[8.111] Section 95 of ERA provides that where an employee is entitled to treat himself as dismissed by reason of his employer's conduct that can constitute an unfair dismissal:

(1) For the purposes of this Part an employee is dismissed by his employer if (and, subject to subsection (2) and section 96, only if)—
  (a) the contract under which he is employed is terminated by the employer (whether with or without notice),
  (b) he is employed under a contract for a fixed term and that term expires without being renewed under the same contract, or
  (c) the employee terminates the contract under which he is employed (with or without notice) in circumstances in which he is entitled to terminate it without notice by reason of the employer's conduct.

(2) An employee shall be taken to be dismissed by his employer for the purposes of this Part if—
  (a) the employer gives notice to the employee to terminate his contract of employment, and
  (b) at a time within the period of that notice the employee gives notice to the employer to terminate the contract of employment on a date earlier than the date on which the employer's notice is due to expire;

and the reason for the dismissal is to be taken to be the reason for which the employer's notice is given.

Western Excavating (ECC) Ltd v Sharp

[1978] IRLR 27, CA

[8.112] Mr Sharp requested time off work but was refused. However, he took the time off and was dismissed with two weeks' notice. He pursued an internal appeal and the decision was changed to five days' suspension without pay. He asked his employers for an advance on his accrued holiday pay but they refused unless the holiday was taken. He then asked them for a loan but this was also refused. Eventually he resigned to obtain his accrued holiday pay and then claimed that he had been unfairly dismissed.

A tribunal found that he had been unfairly dismissed and the EAT dismissed the employer's appeal. The employer appealed to the Court of Appeal.

HELD: In determining whether an employee has been constructively dismissed, the contract test is to be applied. This provides that where an employer is guilty of conduct that is a significant breach going to the root of the contract, or where the employer shows that he no longer intends to be bound by one or more of the essential terms of the contract, the employee is required to make up his mind soon after the conduct about which he complains. If he continues for any length of time, the employee will be regarded as having affirmed the contract. Since the employers were not in breach of the employment contract, their appeal was upheld.

Per Lawton L J:

> It is not necessary or advisable to express an opinion as to what principles of law operate to bring a contract of employment to an end by reason of an employer's conduct. Sensible persons have no difficulty recognising such conduct when they hear about it.

W E Cox Toner (International) Ltd v Crook

[1981] IRLR 443, EAT

[8.113] The respondent was a director and employee of the appellant. Relations between him and the other directors were poor. In July 1979 he decided that he had to travel urgently to Holland on business. Upon his return he took the rest of the week off. He received a letter of censure from the other directors warning him about his conduct on 31 July. He sought a withdrawal of the allegations contained in the letter and after further correspondence between solicitors when it became clear that the allegations were not to be withdrawn, he gave one month's notice and resigned on 3 March 1980 on the grounds that the refusal to withdraw the allegations set out in the July letter constituted a repudiation of the contract.

A tribunal upheld his complaint because the delay did not indicate an affirmation of the contract. The tribunal also believed that a one month delay following confirmation that the allegations would not be withdrawn was not unreasonable. The company appealed.

HELD: The tribunal had misdirected itself. Employees faced with a repudiatory breach of contract are in a difficult position because by going to work they are affirming the contract, and accepting wages increases the risk of affirmatory conduct. However, delay by itself will not be fatal but what is important is what happens during the period of delay. Provided an employee makes clear his objection to what is being done, he will not, for a limited period, be taken to have confirmed the contract by continuing to work and draw pay.

Since the respondent had continued to work without saying that he was doing so on a without-prejudice basis for a period of six months, when his final ultimatum was rejected there was no justification in his continuing to delay acceptance of the repudiatory breach any longer. In those circumstances the court determined that by virtue of his delay he had affirmed the contract. The company's appeal was allowed.

London Transport Executive v Clarke

[1981] IRLR 166, CA

[8.114] LTE operated a policy that staff who wished to take extended leave to travel overseas could do so once every three years. Mr Clarke took such leave in 1977 and applied for extended leave again in 1979. His application was refused. However, Mr Clarke had bought a ticket and was told that if he went in any event 'his name would be removed from the books'. He took the holiday and LTE sought an explanation for his absence, requiring a response within 14 days. His wife, who remained in the country, asked the company to treat him with leniency. Upon his return he complained that he had been unfairly dismissed. A tribunal found in his favour and the EAT dismissed LTE's appeal. LTE appealed to the Court of Appeal.

HELD: Where there is a repudiatory breach of contract the contract is only determined when there is acceptance by the innocent party. Where the employer accepts the breach it must show that it acted reasonably in treating the repudiatory conduct as sufficient to determine the contract. In this instance LTE had established that they had acted reasonably, having regard to equity and the substantial merits of the case, and their appeal was allowed.

Hilton International Hotels (UK) Ltd v Protopapa

[1990] IRLR 316, EAT

[8.115] The respondent resigned after she had been given an officious and insensitive reprimand by her immediate superior which humiliated, intimidated and degraded her in front of others when she had made a dental appointment during work hours. She resigned and claimed that she had been constructively dismissed because of her employer's breach of the term of mutual trust and confidence.

A tribunal found that the appellant's conduct was a breach of the implied term of mutual trust and confidence and held that she had been unfairly dismissed. The company appealed.

HELD: The fact that the respondent pursued three other grounds of complaint which did not constitute a repudiatory breach did not affect the tribunal's ability to find that the conduct on the day in question was repudiatory. The general law of vicarious liability applies to this area of law and an employer will be liable for the conduct of a supervisory employee where they are carrying out their duties, if the manner in which they carry out those duties constitutes a repudiatory breach. It is not necessary for such an employee to have the power of dismissal. The company's appeal was dismissed.

Greenaway Harrison Ltd v Wiles

[1994] IRLR 380, EAT

[8.116] The respondent was one of three telephonists who worked shifts. She and another worked the day shift and the third an evening shift. The employee working the evening shift was dismissed and the remaining employees were told they would have to cover her shift. They were given four weeks' notice of the change and told that if they did not agree, they would be dismissed. The respondent resigned.

A tribunal upheld her complaint of constructive dismissal. In the EAT it was argued that the employers had endeavoured to negotiate a new contract and had only threatened to give lawful notice.

HELD: It is implicit in the principle of constructive dismissal that the contract of employment is deemed to continue. The Court of Appeal in *Western Excavating v Sharp* did not have in mind the giving of lawful notice which would give rise to an unfair dismissal claim. In this instance the employers had committed a significant anticipatory breach of contract by threatening to give notice to terminate the employment contract. The appeal was dismissed.

Lewis v Motorworld Garages Ltd

[1985] IRLR 465, CA

[8.117] Mr Lewis was employed as an after-sales manager. Following a reshuffle in 1981 he was demoted, which resulted in him receiving a smaller car for business and a reduced salary. During 1982 he was subjected to criticism and resigned in August. He complained that he had been unfairly dismissed.

An employment tribunal rejected his complaint because although the demotion was a repudiatory breach of contract, he had delayed too long before he resigned. It found that the employer's criticism was unjustified but the criticisms were not of great substance. He appealed to the EAT and then to the Court of Appeal.

HELD: Where an employer commits a repudiatory breach of contract, even if that breach is not accepted, if there is then a series of actions by the employer that might, together, constitute a breach, the employee can rely upon the employer's original and subsequent acts. A tribunal must consider the cumulative effect of the employer's actions. The employer's intention when carrying out those acts is irrelevant. The test is whether the conduct is repudiatory viewed objectively. It is not necessary for the last action which leads to the employee leaving to be a breach of contract. In the circumstances the company's conduct amounted to a repudiatory breach which Mr Lewis was entitled to accept. His appeal was allowed.

Brown v J B D Engineering Ltd

[1993] IRLR 568, EAT

[8.118] Mr Brown was a director and shareholder of JBD. Following an incident at a board meeting, Mr Brown had no further contact with the company and negotiations were conducted to buy his shares. He remained away from the business save for one occasion and was certified sick. JBD appointed another person to carry out his job and customers were told that Mr Brown was no longer employed by the company. When this came to his attention he resigned and claimed that he had been constructively dismissed. JBD defended the claim on the basis that they believed that agreement had been reached on the terms of his departure. The tribunal upheld JBD's defence and dismissed the claim. Mr Brown appealed.

HELD: The fact that a party acted on a genuine but mistaken belief is not sufficient to prevent its conduct being repudiatory. Such a belief is only a factor to be taken into account in determining whether there has been repudiatory conduct. Mr Brown's appeal was allowed.

Savoia v Chiltern Herb Farms Ltd

[1981] IRLR 65, EAT; affd [1982] IRLR 166, CA

[8.119] The appellant was a supervisor for the respondent. He was away from work ill. During this time the employers found his replacement more co-operative. The appellant subsequently returned from sick leave and a short time later the production manager died. The appellant was offered the position of production manager, which was a promotion. However, he refused to accept it, claiming that he would suffer conjunctivitis as a result of the heat and smoke in the production department. He refused to be examined by a doctor to determine the truth of this statement. The company told him that he was not permitted to return to his original post and that he would receive a termination letter. This did not arrive and eventually he resigned and claimed that he had been constructively dismissed.

A tribunal found that he had been constructively dismissed but that this was fair because the employers had provided him with an opportunity to prove their doubts about his reasons for refusing the promotion unfounded. However, it found that there was a substantial reason for his dismissal and it was found to be fair. An appeal to the EAT was dismissed. Mr Savoia appealed to the Court of Appeal.

HELD: In certain limited circumstances a constructive dismissal may be fair, although it is more likely than not to be an unfair dismissal.

Malik and Mahmud v Bank of Credit and Commerce International SA

[1997] IRLR 462, HL

[8.120] Mr Malik and Mr Mahmud had been senior employees of the bank before they were made redundant. Following their redundancy they were unable to obtain other jobs because their reputations had been tainted by the bank's fraudulent practices. They sued the bank for damages arising from a breach of the implied term of mutual confidence and trust.

The Liquidator, High Court and Court of Appeal rejected their claims and they appealed to the House of Lords.

HELD: The court recognised the implied term that an employer shall not without reasonable and proper cause, conduct itself in a manner calculated and likely to destroy or seriously damage the relationship of confidence and trust between employer and employee.

The bank had conducted its business in a dishonest and corrupt manner, this was a breach of the implied term of mutual trust and confidence. It was not necessary for the trust destroying conduct to be directed at the employee and the employer's motives are not relevant in assessing a claim for damages. It is not essential that there should be a subjective loss of confidence in the employer

The House of Lords went on to make findings in respect of an employee's ability to recover damages for loss of reputation.

Gogay v Hertfordshire County Council

[2000] IRLR 703, CA

[8.121] Ms Gogay was a care worker in a home run by the county council. One of the children for whom she cared became obsessed with her and behaved in a sexually provocative manner. Guidelines were drawn up which made it clear that no adult should be left alone with the child. The child subsequently made allegations against Ms Gogay and she was suspended pending the conclusion of the investigation. It decided that there was no case to answer. Ms Gogay was unable to return to work because of clinical depression that had been brought about by her suspension. Ms Gogay sued the county council and relied upon a breach of her contract of employment.

In the county court it was held that the employers were in breach of the term of mutual trust and confidence and damages were awarded in her favour. The council appealed.

HELD: The council's actions in suspending her by letter were calculated to seriously damage the relationship of trust and confidence between employer and employee. The council had not considered whether the duties it owed to the child could be met by transferring Ms Gogay to another position during the investigation. The council's actions in this instance amounted to a breach of its implied obligation not without reasonable and proper cause to act in a way which seriously damages the relationship of confidence and trust. The appeal was dismissed.

Hilton v Shiner Ltd – Builders Mercants

[2001] IRLR 727, EAT

[8.122] Mr Hilton worked for a builder and served customers dealing with cash transactions. His employers found out that on three occasions customers had left the yard without paying. Mr Hilton could not explain why this had happened. His employers suspected him of theft but because of his long service they decided not to dismiss him but to transfer him to a non-cash handling position. He believed that he had been constructively dismissed and brought proceedings in the tribunal. The tribunal dismissed his complaint because there was no repudiatory breach of contract because the employers had made a genuine offer. He appealed to the EAT.

HELD: The employer's actions in changing Mr Hilton's job could not be imposed upon him without his consent. To do so would potentially be a repudiatory breach; it has to be viewed objectively by reference to its impact upon the employee. There had been a significant change to the employee's job; if the change was sufficiently material the reason for the change is irrelevant; an allegation of dishonesty is irrelevant.

The implied term recognised in *Malik v BCCI* is qualified by the requirement that the conduct must not be indulged in without reasonable and proper cause.

Since the tribunal had failed to give sufficient reasons for concluding that there had been no material change to Mr Hilton's terms and conditions the matter was remitted to another tribunal. The EAT thought that the real issue would be whether the employer had acted reasonably or unreasonably in seeking to change his job.

Duty promptly to redress grievances

WA Goold (Pearmak) Ltd v McConnell

[1995] IRLR 516, EAT

[8.123] A re-organisation at the respondents' place of work resulted in their receiving lower take-home pay. They complained and asked for the matter to be looked into. The company dismissed the matter and their solicitors wrote threatening to bring claims for constructive dismissal unless acceptable proposals were forthcoming. The company had a number of meetings with the employees, none of which resolved their concerns about pay. They eventually resigned and claimed constructive dismissal.

A tribunal concluded that the company's failure to introduce a system to deal with the employees' complaints was conduct that entitled them to resign and claim constructive dismissal. The company appealed to the EAT.

HELD: That the tribunal had been correct. There is an implied term in the contract of employment that employers will reasonably and promptly afford a reasonable opportunity to their employees to obtain redress of any grievance they may have.

REMEDIES

RE-EMPLOYMENT

[8.124] The remedies for an unfair dismissal are set out in ERA, ss 112 to 117. The main remedy is for compensation, but a tribunal can also order reinstatement and re-engagement

Order for reinstatement

[8.125] Section 114 provides:

(1) An order for reinstatement is an order that the employer shall treat the complainant in all respects as if he had not been dismissed.

Remedies 369

(2) On making an order for reinstatement the tribunal shall specify—
(a) any amount payable by the employer in respect of any benefit which the complainant might reasonably be expected to have had but for the dismissal (including arrears of pay) for the period between the date of termination of employment and the date of reinstatement,
(b) any rights and privileges (including seniority and pension rights) which must be restored to the employee, and
(c) the date by which the order must be complied with.

Order for re-engagement

[8.126] Section 115 provides:

(1) An order for re-engagement is an order, on such terms as the tribunal may decide, that the complainant be engaged by the employer, or by a successor of the employer or by an associated employer, in employment comparable to that from which he was dismissed or other suitable employment.(2) On making an order for re-engagement the tribunal shall specify the terms on which re-engagement is to take place, including—
(a) the identity of the employer,
(b) the nature of the employment,
(c) the remuneration for the employment,
(d) any amount payable by the employer in respect of any benefit which the complainant might reasonably be expected to have had but for the dismissal (including arrears of pay) for the period between the date of termination of employment and the date of re-engagement,
(e) any rights and privileges (including seniority and pension rights) which must be restored to the employee, and
(f) the date by which the order must be complied with.

Choice of order and its terms

[8.127] Section 116 of ERA is as follows:

(1) In exercising its discretion under section 113 the tribunal shall first consider whether to make an order for reinstatement and in so doing shall take into account—
(a) whether the complainant wishes to be reinstated,
(b) whether it is practicable for the employer to comply with an order for reinstatement, and
(c) where the complainant caused or contributed to some extent to the dismissal, whether it would be just to order his reinstatement.

(2) If the tribunal decides not to make an order for reinstatement it shall then consider whether to make an order for re-engagement and, if so, on what terms.(3) In so doing the tribunal shall take into account—
(a) any wish expressed by the complainant as to the nature of the order to be made,

(b) whether it is practicable for the employer (or a successor or an associated employer) to comply with an order for re-engagement, and

(c) where the complainant caused or contributed to some extent to the dismissal, whether it would be just to order his re-engagement and (if so) on what terms

Cowley v Manson Timber Ltd

[1995] IRLR 153, CA

[8.128] Mr Cowley succeeded in an unfair dismissal claim following dismissal for redundancy. The tribunal held that if a fair procedure had been followed his employment would have been extended by 14 days. He appealed. The basis of his appeal was that the available remedies to him other than compensation were not explained to him. The EAT dismissed his appeal and he appealed to the Court of Appeal.

HELD: Dismissing his appeal that if a tribunal fails to explain the available remedies to a claimant, that will not make the tribunal's decision a nullity.

Port of London Authority v Payne

[1994] IRLR 9, CA

[8.129] Mr Payne and the other appellants were dock workers and shop stewards with the TGWU. Following a restructuring they were made redundant with a number of others. A tribunal concluded that they had been selected because of their union membership and that their dismissal was unfair and an order for re-engagement was made. PLA failed to re-engage them and argued it was not practical because there were no vacancies. The tribunal found that PLA should have enquired about whether any of its employees wished to accept voluntary severance. The EAT allowed PLA's appeal because the tribunal had substituted its own commercial judgment and failed to make a final determination on the issue of practicability. Mr Payne appealed to the Court of Appeal.

HELD: Before making a re-engagement order a tribunal must make a preliminary determination of whether it is practicable for an employee to be re-engaged. A final determination on this issue is only made when the employer ascertains whether he can comply with the order. When applying this part of the test the standard should not be set too high and regard should be had to the commercial judgment of the management, provided that their evidence is accepted.

If the tribunal had directed itself correctly, it would have been bound to find that it was not practical to re-engage the employees, and Mr Payne's appeal was dismissed.

Wood Group Heavy Industrial Turbines Ltd v Crossan

[1998] IRLR 680, EAT

[8.130] Mr Crosson had been employed for 16 years. He was dismissed following allegations of drug-taking, drug dealing and time-keeping and clocking offences. The employer carried out some investigations and formed a genuine belief that he was guilty of the allegations. A tribunal concluded that the dismissal was unfair because the employer had not conducted a reasonable investigation and ordered Mr Crosson's re-engagement. The company appealed to the EAT.

HELD: The tribunal had failed to consider the practicality of re-engagement. Where there is a genuine belief by an employer in an employee's guilt, the essential bond of trust and confidence will have been broken. In circumstances where there is a breakdown in trust and confidence, re-engagement will only rarely be a relevant consideration.

Artisan Press Ltd v Srawley and Parker

[1986] IRLR 126, EAT

[8.131] A tribunal originally found that Mr Srawley and Mr Parker had been unfairly dismissed and ordered that they be reinstated to their security jobs. The company purported to comply with the order by giving them cleaning jobs with minor security roles. They complained to a tribunal which found in their favour. The company appealed.

HELD: An order for reinstatement requires that it be in all respects as if the employee had not been dismissed. The employees had not been reinstated and it was an abuse of the English language to say that the order had been fully complied with. The company's appeal was dismissed.

O'Laoire v Jackel International Ltd (No 2)

[1991] IRLR 170, CA

[8.132] Mr O'Laoire was employed on the understanding that he would be promoted to managing director in two years. This did not happen and eventually he was dismissed. He sued for wrongful and unfair dismissal. An employment tribunal made a reinstatement order and found that the intention was that he would become the managing director, which had become a contractual term. The company failed to comply with the order. Mr O'Laoire sought to enforce the order.

HELD, on appeal: A reinstatement order is not enforceable save under the relevant legislation. To do that the claimant had to apply to a tribunal and compensation would be subject to the statutory maximum. In addition, a reinstatement order should specify amounts payable by reference to rates of pay or other formulae to enable calculations to be made when the date of reinstatement is known.

Rank Xerox (UK) Ltd v Stryczek

[1995] IRLR 568, EAT

[8.133] Mr Stryczek was dismissed and his employers accepted that his dismissal was unfair. When issuing his claim he had indicated that he wanted compensation but subsequently that he wanted reinstatement. At the hearing he indicated, at the chairman's instigation, that he wished to be re-engaged. The tribunal ordered re-engagement in a specific post at a higher salary. The company appealed.

HELD: The general principle is that an order for re-engagement should be realistic. In this instance the order would have led to a promotion and the tribunal is not permitted to order re-engagement in employment significantly more favourable. In addition, it is undesirable to order re-engagement in a specific position.

Mabirizi v National Hospital for Nervous Diseases

[1990] IRLR 133, EAT

[8.134] Mrs Mabirizi was dismissed because the hospital believed she was moonlighting. However, a tribunal found that the dismissal had been unfair. Reinstatement was ordered, together with compensation of £15,400. At the hearing it was argued that there had been a breakdown of trust and confidence, but no evidence of impracticality was presented. Mrs Mabirizi was not reinstated and a third hearing took place at which she was awarded £8,000. She appealed this decision.

HELD, on appeal: There can only be one order for compensation following an unfair dismissal. Mrs Mabirizi had failed to mitigate her losses and this was a relevant factor to be taken into account when assessing the value of the additional award. Another relevant factor is the employer's conduct, including the reason for their failure to comply with the order. An additional award is not intended to be precisely calculated.

Selfridges Ltd v Malik

[1997] IRLR 577, EAT

[8.135] Mr Malik was unfairly dismissed and a reinstatement order was made. This included an award of £25,000 for lost wages. The employers refused to comply with the order and the tribunal made an award of £43,647, which included a basic award, a compensatory award (£11,000), an additional award (£5,000), and the £25,000 originally awarded. Selfridges appealed because the award exceeded the sum permitted by ERA, s 124(4).

HELD: Section 124(4) of ERA ensures that the employer is not in a better position by refusing to reinstate an employee than by complying with the Order. Where an employer reinstates, an employee is entitled to compensation awarded under ERA, s 114. This award is not free-standing and is only payable under a reinstatement Order that is complied with. If the employee is not reinstated, the employee is entitled to a compensatory award under ERA, s 117(3). The gross compensatory award will include the section 114 award and future losses. The award is limited; however: section 124(4) provides that where an award is made under section 117(3)(a), section 124(1)(a) can be exceeded to the extent of the section 114 loss less the additional award. Selfridges' appeal was allowed and an award of £26,887.89 was substituted.

COMPENSATION

General considerations

[8.136] Section 123 of ERA sets out the matters that a tribunal must consider when determining an applicant's loss for the purposes of the compensatory award:

> (1) Subject to the provisions of this section and sections 124 and 126, the amount of the compensatory award shall be such amount as the tribunal considers just and equitable in all the circumstances having regard to the loss

sustained by the complainant in consequence of the dismissal in so far as that loss is attributable to action taken by the employer.

(2) The loss referred to in subsection (1) shall be taken to include—
(a) any expenses reasonably incurred by the complainant in consequence of the dismissal, and
(b) subject to subsection (3), loss of any benefit which he might reasonably be expected to have had but for the dismissal.

(3) The loss referred to in subsection (1) shall be taken to include in respect of any loss of—
(a) any entitlement or potential entitlement to a payment on account of dismissal by reason of redundancy (whether in pursuance of Part XI or otherwise), or
(b) any expectation of such a payment,

only the loss referable to the amount (if any) by which the amount of that payment would have exceeded the amount of a basic award (apart from any reduction under section 122) in respect of the same dismissal.

(4) In ascertaining the loss referred to in subsection (1) the tribunal shall apply the same rule concerning the duty of a person to mitigate his loss as applies to damages recoverable under the common law of England and Wales or (as the case may be) Scotland.

(5) In determining, for the purposes of subsection (1), how far any loss sustained by the complainant was attributable to action taken by the employer, no account shall be taken of any pressure which by—
(a) calling, organising, procuring or financing a strike or other industrial action, or
(b) threatening to do so,

was exercised on the employer to dismiss the employee; and that question shall be determined as if no such pressure had been exercised.

(6) Where the tribunal finds that the dismissal was to any extent caused or contributed to by any action of the complainant, it shall reduce the amount of the compensatory award by such proportion as it considers just and equitable having regard to that finding.

(7) If the amount of any payment made by the employer to the employee on the ground that the dismissal was by reason of redundancy (whether in pursuance of Part XI or otherwise) exceeds the amount of the basic award which would be payable but for section 122(4), that excess goes to reduce the amount of the compensatory award.

Norton Tool Co Ltd v Tewson

[1972] IRLR 86, NIRC

[8.137] Mr Tewson was found to have been unfairly dismissed by his former employer and was awarded £250 in compensation by the employment tribunal. The employer appealed against this level of award.

HELD: There are two general principles to consider when assessing compensation for unfair dismissal:

—That the applicant should be compensated fully; and

—That the sum awarded in compensation must be 'just and equitable' in all the circumstances having regard to the losses sustained by the employee. Loss does not include an injury to the employee's pride or feelings.

The burden of proving loss rests with the applicant and it is not for the tribunal to take into account anything other than what the applicant has lost.

The categories of compensation a tribunal may award are:

the applicant's immediate loss of earnings in situations where he/she was dismissed without notice or a payment in lieu of notice;

the manner of dismissal, if the manner of dismissal could give rise to a risk of financial loss at a later stage, for example if it made the applicant less attractive to future employers;

any future loss of earnings;

loss of the statutory protection not to be unfairly dismissed.

Johnson v Unisys Ltd

[2001] UKHL 13, [2001] IRLR 279

[8.138] Mr Johnson commenced work with Unisys in 1971. In 1985 he suffered a psychological illness brought on by work-related stress but he remained employed by the company. In 1987, Mr Johnson was made redundant but was re-employed by the company. However, in 1994 he was dismissed summarily for alleged irregularities. An employment tribunal held that he was unfairly dismissed and awarded him the maximum tribunal award at that time, which was reduced by 25% for contributory fault, giving a total award of £11,700.

Two years later, Mr Johnson brought a claim against Unisys in the county court alleging that his dismissal had been in breach of, amongst other things, the implied term of mutual trust and confidence as he was dismissed without a fair hearing and also that dismissal was in breach of company procedures. Mr Johnson argued that the manner of his dismissal had caused him to suffer a mental breakdown which affected his family life and made it impossible to find alternative employment. He also brought a tortious action on the grounds that it was reasonably foreseeable that dismissing him as the company did was likely to cause psychiatric damage. Mr Johnson's claims were originally struck out on the ground there was no cause of action at common law. He was given leave to appeal to the House of Lords

HELD: It is not for the courts to develop at common law a remedy for the manner of dismissal. Such a common law right would not sit with the statutory right not to be unfairly dismissed. Similarly, their Lordships were not prepared to develop a duty of care argument.

On the issue of compensation for unfair dismissal, their Lordships commented that the statutory framework already gives a wide discretion to tribunals in awarding compensation for unfair dismissal.

In contrast to the ruling in *Norton Tool Co Ltd* (see 8.137 above), Lord Hoffman commented that the definition of 'loss' as equating to financial loss only is too restrictive a construction. Lord Hoffman's opinion was that if compensation is to be awarded on what is fair and equitable, there was no reason why this could not include compensation for distress, humiliation, damage to reputation in the community or to family life. The Employment Appeal Tribunal has held that such awards should not be made: see *Dunnachie v Kingston upon Hull* [2003] IRLR 384.

Simrad Ltd v Scott
[1997] IRLR 147, EAT

[8.139] Ms Scott was made redundant from her job as an electronic technician. She had difficulty in finding a similar position and decided instead to take a lower paying job which had no prospects. Eventually she decided to retrain as a nurse and started a three-year course for which she received an annual grant.

Ms Scott was found to have been unfairly dismissed by her employer. When the tribunal came to assess her compensation, it included a sum for future loss of earnings over a 15-month period by comparing her previous salary to the grant she was receiving. The tribunal felt that the decision to retrain as a nurse was a reasonable one. Her employer appealed on the basis that it was not for the tribunal to consider if the applicant had acted 'reasonably' in pursuing a career in nursing, but whether her losses were attributable to the dismissal.

HELD: The EAT held that section 123(1) of ERA required a three stage assessment: the tribunal must assess what actual losses have arisen from the dismissal; it must then consider whether each of those losses is directly attributable to the dismissal; and it must then consider the overall award and whether it is just and equitable to make the proposed award.

In assessing future loss, the EAT held that there must be a direct and natural link between the dismissal and the losses sustained. Unless this can be shown, the losses will be too remote. In Ms Scott's case, although her decision to retrain was a reasonable one it was too remote in time to be linked to the employer's decision to dismiss. The tribunal had been wrong to regard a loan which the employers had agreed need not be repaid as an ex gratia payment and therefore to be deducted from the compensatory award.

Paggetti v Cobb
[2002] IRLR 861, EAT

[8.140] Mr Paggetti was adjudged to have been unfairly dismissed. He was awarded £900 basic award and £598 compensatory award. He was said to have contributed 30% to his dismissal and the compensatory award was reduced accordingly. The applicant appealed against the tribunal's method of calculation.

The issue arose in the EAT as to the correct wage rate which should be applied to the calculations. The applicant took home on average £111 per week, for a

63.5 hour week. This equated to £1.88 per hour. The tribunal had calculated his compensatory award on the basis of his actual weekly net wage. However, the applicant sought to argue that the minimum wage rate should have been used, although he had not brought a national minimum wage claim at the original hearing.

HELD: The starting place for calculating the compensatory award was the net weekly wage the applicant was entitled to receive under his contract of employment. The tribunal accepted in this case that this would be a sum not less than the national minimum wage and accordingly calculated a weekly wage based on it, less notional tax and national insurance. The award was subject to the 30% reduction for his contributory conduct.

THE DUTY TO MITIGATE

Wilding v British Telecommunications plc

[2002] EWCA Civ 349, [2002] IRLR 524

[8.141] Mr Wilding was employed by BT for 29 years and was well regarded. He was involved in a road accident and injured his back. His condition deteriorated and despite a number of adjustments it became no longer possible for him to work and he was dismissed in March 1998.

A tribunal concluded that his dismissal was both discriminatory and unfair because insufficient enquiries had been made into his condition and no thought had been given to whether he could work on a part-time basis. Before the remedies hearing his solicitors asked for a re-engagement order and BT offered him re-engagement on part-time work; they also appealed against the tribunal's decision. BT's offer was rejected by Mr Wilding who thought it a sham and listed a number of reasons for refusing it. A tribunal concluded that he had not acted reasonably in refusing the order and had not mitigated his loss. The EAT dismissed his appeal. He appealed to the Court of Appeal and argued that the tribunal had incorrectly applied a subjective rather than objective test.

HELD: A claimant is bound to take reasonable steps to mitigate his loss. The principles that are to be applied are (i) Mr Wilding must act to mitigate his loss without the expectation of an award by the tribunal, (ii) the onus is upon the wrongdoer to show Mr Wilding acted unreasonably, (iii) the test of unreasonableness is an objective one base on all the evidence, (iv) in applying the test all the circumstances will be taken into account, (v) the tribunal should not be too stringent in its expectations of the injured party.

If an offer is made that is reasonable and which is refused it will be necessary to consider the claimant's subjective reasons, which may critically affect the reasonableness of the decision. Since Mr Wilding had always said he wanted to go back to BT on a part-time basis the tribunal was entitled to enquire what had caused him to change his mind following the liability hearing. There was no burden of proof on BT to prove that the offer had been made in good faith.

Bessenden Properties Ltd v Corness

[1974] IRLR 338, CA

[8.142] Mrs Corness was unfairly selected for redundancy and was awarded £50.50 redundancy pay and £438 compensation for unfair dismissal. The company appealed to the NIRC and then to the Court of Appeal.

The issue before the Court of Appeal was whether the tribunal had been correct to award compensation of £438 because it was alleged that she had failed to mitigate her loss by accepting other employment.

HELD, on appeal: Questions of mitigation are questions of fact. If a party seeks to allege that the other has failed to take steps to mitigate their loss it is for the party making the allegation to prove it.

Fyffe v Scientific Furnishings Ltd

[1989] IRLR 331, EAT

[8.143] Mr Fyffe's employment was terminated on the grounds of redundancy. The dismissal was held to be unfair. On the evening of his dismissal he had been offered a generous early retirement package which he refused. The tribunal found that he had failed to mitigate his loss and made a nil award. Mr Fyffe appealed.

HELD: The common law rules on mitigation apply: the issue may be raised by either the tribunal or the respondent. The onus of proof does not shift from the respondent to the plaintiff. When dealing with the question of reasonableness the surrounding circumstances need to be considered, including any offer that have been made, the way that the employee has been treated. Since the tribunal ignored the surrounding factors, it could not be said that had the tribunal considered all the factors it would have reached the same conclusion. For that reason the appeal was allowed.

Deductions for contributory fault

Nelson v BBC (No 2)

[1980] ICR 110, [1979] IRLR 346, CA

[8.144] Mr Nelson worked for the BBC on the Caribbean service. His position became redundant and he was offered another position but would have to serve a probationary period. He did not accept the offer and was eventually dismissed. Both the tribunal and EAT held that the dismissal was fair but his appeal was allowed by the Court of Appeal who remitted his case to the tribunal for a remedies hearing.

The tribunal refused his request for re-engagement and awarded him compensation having made a reduction of 60% for contributory fault. The EAT permitted the decision of the original tribunal to be placed before it and affirmed the tribunal's decision in connection with contributory fault and non-re-engagement but varied the award in respect of three elements of the calculation. He appealed to the Court of Appeal.

HELD: In order to make reductions for contributory conduct, there must be conduct relating to the complaint and it must be just and equitable to make a reduction. The conduct on the part of the claimant in relation to the dismissal must be culpable or blameworthy. Such conduct includes conduct which amounts to a breach of contract or tort and other conduct which is perverse, foolish or bloody-minded.

It is desirable for tribunals to make express findings on the issue of blameworthiness and culpability. The tribunal erred in law in deciding that it was entitled to reduce the award by 60% because it did not take into account the earlier Court of Appeal decision that he had been unfairly dismissed. The tribunal had to take into account the legal position between the two parties, although this was not determinative of the issue.

Since the tribunal had misdirected itself, Mr Nelson's appeal was allowed.

Friend v Civil Aviation Authority

[2001] EWCA Civ 1204, [2001] IRLR 819

[8.145] Captain Friend was a flight operations inspector. He objected to inspecting helicopters because the team did not contain a helicopter pilot. This caused tension with others in the team and resulted in adverse reports being filed about him. He was subjected to a disciplinary hearing that exonerated him and made recommendations that were not adhered to and he was dismissed.

A tribunal found his dismissal unfair but made a reduction of 100%. He appealed to the EAT and then the Court of Appeal unsuccessfully. Captain Friend then began proceedings in the High Court where the proceedings were struck out and he appealed again to the Court of Appeal.

HELD: Chadwick LJ commented obiter that a tribunal is not required to consider the issue of contribution unless it is satisfied that some part of the loss is attributable to the employer's action. If no part of the loss can be attributed to the employer's actions then section 123 is not relevant. As a result a 100% reduction under section 123(6) will be exceptional.

Polentarutti v Autokraft Ltd

[1991] IRLR 457, EAT

[8.146] Mr Polentarutti was responsible for machining parts for hand-built cars. 23 out of a batch of 24 parts were defective and his employers had to pay an outside contractor to correct the defect. They refused to pay him for some overtime he had worked. He resigned and claimed constructive dismissal.

A tribunal upheld his complaint and reduced his award by 66% because of his contributory conduct. Mr Polentarutti appealed.

HELD: It did not follow that because the employers had failed to show a reason for the dismissal there could not be a reduction in the compensation awarded to Mr Polentarutti. It is not necessary when dealing with a constructively dismissed employee that there should be exceptional circumstances for making a reduction in the award. Although there had been a repudiatory breach of contract the employer's conduct was causally linked to Mr Polentarutti's actions. A causal link is sufficient for there to be a reduction for contributory fault.

Hollier v Plysu Ltd

[1983] IRLR 260, CA

[8.147] Mrs Hollier had bought goods from a lorry driver from whom she and other employees had been warned not to buy goods. Following a police investigation in which stolen goods that she had bought from the lorry driver were found at her home, she was dismissed.

A tribunal found the dismissal unfair but reduced her award by 75% because of her contributory conduct: the factors taken into account by the tribunal were her evasive responses to the police; she should have been suspicious because of the low prices, and the warning given by her employers. She appealed and the EAT substituted a reduction of 25%. The company appealed.

HELD: The EAT should not have interfered with the tribunal's finding unless the tribunal had erred in law or its decision was perverse. A tribunal's function is to take a broad common sense view on an appeal. The finding that she had been evasive with the police was a finding of fact that could be taken into account in determining a reduction for contributory conduct.

The tribunal's original award was substituted for that of the EAT.

JUST AND EQUITABLE

O'Donoghue v Redcar and Cleveland Borough Council

[2001] EWCA Civ 701, [2001] IRLR 615

[8.148] The applicant, Ms O'Donoghue, brought a sex discrimination case against her employer for failing to appoint her to a position which was eventually offered to a man. Following the conclusion of those proceedings but before the decision was received she was suspended. Her employer commenced disciplinary proceedings against her which resulted in her dismissal. She brought proceedings against the employer for victimisation and unfair dismissal.

A tribunal agreed that the dismissal was unfair but held that she would have been dismissed in any event within six months because of her attitude and behaviour towards her other colleagues and reduced her compensation accordingly. She appealed to the EAT.

HELD: The tribunal had been correct in assessing that the applicant would have left the company within six months in any event and were right to give a cut off for compensation at this point. It is for the tribunal to award compensation on the basis of what is just and equitable. If a tribunal concludes that although dismissed unfairly, the applicant would have been bound soon after to have been dismissed fairly because of her conduct or attitude, then it is just and equitable that compensation for unfair dismissal should be awarded on this basis.

King v Eaton Ltd (No 2)

[1998] IRLR 686, Ct of Sess

[8.149] The appellant employees were dismissed for reason of redundancy. They brought claims for unfair dismissal which the tribunal upheld. At the remedies hearing, the employers sought to argue under the principle laid down in *Polkey v A E Dayton Services* (see 8.100 above), on the basis that the employees would still have been selected for dismissal even if a fair procedure had been followed and therefore compensation should be reduced. Part of the tribunal's conclusion was that it could not assess, based upon the evidence, what would have happened if there had been adequate consultation. The EAT allowed the employers' appeal, because although there had been no individual consultation there had been consultation with the employees' union. The employees appealed to the Court of Session.

HELD: It is not always possible for the employer to put forward evidence that compensation should be reduced because the employee would have been dismissed in any event. In assessing what would have happened, the EAT held there was a distinction between a merely procedural lapse and a more genuinely substantive lapse from proper procedures. If there was merely a procedural lapse or omission, a tribunal may be able to consider what would have happened if the procedures had been correct. However, if what went wrong was more fundamental, it may be difficult to assess what would have happened. In this case the tribunal was correct not to allow the employer to present evidence as to whether consultation would have made any difference.

Rao v Civil Aviation Authority

[1994] IRLR 240, CA

[8.150] Mr Rao was dismissed for gross misconduct on 18 February 1998. Mr Rao was successful in arguing that he had been unfairly dismissed. When considering compensation, the tribunal made three important findings: that Mr Rao's employment would have ended on 8 March 1998 in any event, that there was only a 20% chance that his employment would have continued after this date, and that he had contributed to his dismissal. Mr Rao appealed on the basis that to reduce compensation on the basis that his employment would only have continued for another month and on the basis of his contributory fault was unfair and imposed a double penalty. The EAT dismissed the appeal. He appealed to the Court of Appeal.

HELD: The tribunal had not erred in reducing the award on the basis of contributory fault and on the basis there was an 80% chance he would have been dismissed if the employers had followed a fair procedure.

A tribunal should first assess the total loss including the possibility that employment could have carried on had the employee not been unfairly dismissed. The tribunal should determine the extent to which the employee contributed to his dismissal and the amount by which it is just and equitable to reduce the award on the grounds of his contributory conduct. In this case the tribunal had concluded that there was only a 20% chance of the job continuing after 8 March, in the light of that finding the tribunal was required to consider whether it was just and equitable to reduce the award further.

Edwards v Governors of Hanson School

[2001] IRLR 733, EAT

[8.151] See facts at 8.52 above. It was necessary to determine what had caused Mr Edward's illness in order to determine what award was just and equitable.

Loss of wages

Dench v Flynn & Partners

[1998] IRLR 653, CA

[8.152] The applicant was made redundant from her role as a solicitor. She accepted a position with a new firm of solicitors. Her employment was terminated shortly after joining because of disagreements with her new boss. She brought a claim for unfair against her former firm. The tribunal held her dismissal was unfair but held that her compensatory award was to be assessed over a period between the date her employment terminated and the date she took up the new employment. The tribunal's view was that the job at the new firm was a permanent position with the expectation of unlimited duration. The fact that she lost her job as a result of a conflict with her new employer was unfortunate, but was not the responsibility of her former employer. She appealed to the EAT who dismissed her appeal and she appealed to the Court of Appeal.

HELD: The acceptance of new employment does not prevent losses arising thereafter from being related to the original unfair dismissal. The principle to be applied in deciding whether there is a connection between an unfair dismissal and its consequences is a question of law. The tribunal misdirected itself. The tribunal should have considered for what period of time after her dismissal from her new employer the consequences of her losses flowed from her original dismissal.

The matter was remitted back to the tribunal to determine for what period of time the losses claimed by the applicant should be awarded.

The court disagreed with the judgement in *Whelan (t/a Cheers Off Licence) v Richardson* [1998] IRLR 114 (EAT) (see 8.153 below) which concluded that the chain of causation was always broken as soon as the applicant obtains permanent employment.

Whelan (t/a Cheers Off Licence) v Richardson

[1998] IRLR 114, EAT

[8.153] Mrs Richardson argued successfully before a tribunal that she had been unfairly dismissed. Following dismissal, Mrs Richardson had been out of work for two weeks. She was then employed for 18 weeks at a rate of £51.60 per week. Following this, she took a new job that paid her £95.82 per week. She was still in that job at the remedies hearing. Her original job with the respondent paid her £72 per week. The tribunal had to decide over what period compensation should be calculated – up to the date when she found higher paying employment (less monies earned from the first job) or up until the date of the remedies hearing giving credit for all sums earned from dismissal? The tribunal preferred the first approach and the employer's appealed.

HELD: The tribunal had adopted the correct approach. As soon as the applicant obtains higher paid alternative employment the chain of causation is broken. The loss cannot be revived if that employment is lost, for example, if the applicant losses the job either through his own or through the new employer's actions.

If an applicant takes up temporary employment following dismissal he is not prevented from claiming losses either up to the remedies hearing or until permanent employment is found (whichever is the soonest date). However, credit must be given for all earnings from that short-term work.

Morganite Electrical Carbon Ltd v Donne

[1987] IRLR 363, EAT

[8.154] Following a successful unfair dismissal claim, the tribunal ordered that the applicant be re-engaged into his previous position or into a similar role. The tribunal had to calculate the applicant's loss of earnings from the period of dismissal to re-engagement. The employer appealed against the tribunal's award on the grounds that the total period over which loss of earnings was assessed was excessive, that compensation should be reduced on the ground of contributory fault, and that an additional award of 26 weeks' pay was too high.

HELD: The tribunal had erred in awarding the maximum additional award for failing to comply with a re-engagement order. Whilst there was a wide discretion, the tribunal had to carry out a proper assessment to determine what the award should be. The tribunal had failed to address the issue of the applicant's duty to mitigate his loss when making any assessment of compensation. This applies both to losses to the date of the remedies hearing and any future losses that might be awarded. The tribunal also failed to take into account the applicant's own contributory fault.

Fougère v Phoenix Motor Co Ltd

[1976] IRLR 259, EAT

[8.155] The applicant was awarded £298.46 in compensation for unfair dismissal. He was a man of 58 years of age and in poor health. He appealed against this award as the tribunal did not take these two factors into account when assessing his compensation.

HELD: A tribunal is able to take into account the personal characteristics of the applicant provided they existed at the date of the dismissal. The tribunal had erred in not taking these issues into account when assessing compensation. The tribunal should consider how long a particular applicant is likely to remain out of work and not consider the issue on the basis of a notional applicant.

Tribunals are obliged only to consider compensation quickly and fairly. Tribunals operate in a rough and ready way to give a broad brush approach. If tribunals were required to calculate losses to the nearest penny it would be impractical and would not serve either applicants or respondents. The tribunal procedure is intended to be quick, open and simple. If there was a serious error in the calculation then the EAT would interfere, but the EAT is not there to quibble over trifling amounts or errors.

William Muir (Bond 9) Ltd v Lamb

[1985] IRLR 95, EAT

[8.156] Mr Lamb was found to have been unfairly dismissed. The tribunal made a full award to him and his employer appealed to the EAT on the ground that because he had not used an internal appeal procedure his damages should be reduced by 50%.

HELD: By failing to follow the internal appeal procedure Mr Lamb had not failed to mitigate his loss. There is no obligation upon an employee to follow an internal appeal procedure. It is purely speculative to attempt to determine what would have happened if the internal appeal procedure had been followed. It would be quite wrong to penalise an employee for not following such a procedure.

Lock v Connell Estate Agents

[1994] IRLR 444, EAT

[8.157] Mr Lock was given notice of dismissal for failing to achieve performance targets but was not required to work his notice. He did not pursue an internal appeal procedure but alleged that he had been unfairly dismissed. A tribunal found his dismissal unfair but reduced his basic and compensatory awards by 50% because he had not used the company's appeal procedures. He appealed to the EAT.

HELD: A failure to operate an internal appeals procedure can never result in a reduction of the basic award. Furthermore such a failure does not, as a matter of law, represent a failure to mitigate loss. In the present circumstances it was inappropriate to reduce the compensatory award. The decision of the EAT in *William Muir (Bond 9) Ltd v Lamb* [1985] IRLR 95 (see 8.156 above) was followed.

McCarthy v British Insulated Callenders Cables plc

[1985] IRLR 94, EAT

[8.158] Mr McCarthy was dismissed and paid an ex gratia sum of £1,274. He succeeded in his claim of unfair dismissal and was awarded £15,820 before the imposition of the statutory cap. His ex gratia payment was then deducted from the award. This meant that he received less than the statutory maximum award and he appealed.

HELD: Mr McCarthy's ex gratia payment was to be taken into account before the statutory cap was applied to reduce the value of the award. The statutory cap was to be applied at that point.

Gilham v Kent County Council (No 3)

[1986] ICR 52, EAT

[8.159] The appellant was a dinner lady. She and her colleagues were dismissed and offered new contracts on less advantageous terms. They refused the new contracts and succeeded in their claims of unfair dismissal (see 8.68 above). A remedies hearing was held two years later. It was argued that if the new terms had not been imposed the dinner service would have ceased to operate within 12 months and contractors would have been appointed. A tribunal accepted that argument and limited the loss to 12 months despite the fact that the dinner service was still in operation. The appellants appealed.

HELD: At the date of the remedies hearing the school meals service continued. As a result it was not necessary or appropriate to ascertain what might have happened to the dinner service following the date of dismissal. Regard had to be had to what had occurred in reality.

Clancy v Cannock Chase Technical College

[2001] IRLR 331, EAT

[8.160] Mr Clancy was found to have been unfairly selected for redundancy. At the remedies hearing the tribunal refused to order re-engagement and assessed the value of his lost pension by reference to the employer's financial contribution, taking into account the tribunal's own guidelines. Mr Clancy appealed.

HELD: The tribunal had been correct not to order re-engagement given the worsening redundancy situation at the College and the decline in popularity of Mr Clancy's subject. However, pension guidelines which had been published in 1991, did not provide any yardstick for assessing loss in a case where income benefits and a lump sum were derived. The matter was therefore remitted to the same tribunal to calculate his pension loss.

Tele-Trading Ltd v Jenkins

[1990] IRLR 430, CA

[8.161] Mr Jenkins was dismissed after it was discovered that his salary cheque had been altered to increase it by £30 and his employers believed that he had made the alteration himself. A tribunal found the dismissal unfair because they had not conducted a reasonable investigation and could not have a genuine belief in his guilt. The EAT dismissed the company's appeal.

At the remedies hearing evidence about the police investigation was admitted. The tribunal refused to reduce the award and the EAT dismissed the company's appeal. The company appealed and argued that the tribunal should have considered both whether there had been contributory fault and whether there should be a reduction on the just and equitable ground.

HELD: At the time of dismissal the company did not have reasonable grounds for belief in Mr Jenkins' guilt and the tribunal was not wrong in those circumstances to refuse to reduce the award. The compensatory award can be reduced either on the grounds of contributory conduct or on the just and equitable ground. Reductions for contributory fault occur when the employer knows of the misconduct at the time of dismissal. Reductions on the just and equitable ground occur when the company becomes aware of matters after the date of dismissal.

Since no evidence had been adduced here to show that the employers had reasonable grounds for their belief, either at the time of the dismissal or subsequently, the appeal would be dismissed.

CHAPTER 9

Practice and Procedure

A   HIGH COURT AND COUNTY COURT

Introduction	[9.1]
Procedural steps: *Default judgment*	[9.2]
Summary judgment	[9.4]
Interim applications	[9.7]
Expert evidence	[9.10]
Commencing proceedings: *Pre-action protocol*	[9.13]
Vexatious litigants	[9.14]
Parties to the action	[9.16]
Issuing proceedings	[9.17]
Serving proceedings	[9.20]
Pleading requirements	[9.34]
Amendments	[9.35]
Resiling from admission of liability	[9.36]
Group litigation	[9.37]
Costs	[9.38]
Limitation	[9.41]
Running of time	[9.51]
Date of knowledge	[9.53]
Limitation defence	[9.65]
Extending the time-limits – (section 33)	[9.69]
New claims in pending action – (section 35)	[9.76]
Commencing second action out of time	[9.78]
Striking out (CPR)	[9.80]
Claim or defence itself alleged to be objectionable	[9.81]
Manner in which claim pursued	[9.84]
Trial: *allocation*	[9.92]
Adjournments	[9.93]
Submission of no case to answer	[9.96]
Costs (CPR)	[9.97]
Summary assessment	[9.98]
In the court's discretion	[9.100]
Effect of Part 36	[9.110]
Indemnity basis	[9.113]
Conditional fee agreements	[9.118]
Costs orders against non-parties	[9124]
Wasted costs orders	[9.125]

B EMPLOYMENT TRIBUNAL PRACTICE AND PROCEDURE

Introduction	[9.128]
Chairman sitting alone or sitting with one lay member	[9.129]
Jurisdiction	[9.132]
Calculating time: *Unfair dismissal – 'reasonably practical'*	[9.132]
Just and equitable to extend the time-limit	[9.138]
'Reasonably practicable' – effect of criminal proceedings	[9.140]
Effect of tribunal being closed on the last day to lodge IT1	[9.142]
Lodging claim forms by post	[9.144]
Limitation period where none specified by statute	[9.145]
Amending the grounds of claim after they have been lodged with the tribunal	[9.146]
The jurisdiction to hear breach of contract claims	[9.148]
Preliminary issues	[9.149]
The need to sit in public	[9.151]
Adjournments	[9.152]
Procedure at the hearing	[9.153]
Tribunals must exercise their discretion judicially	[9.154]
The need to investigate pleaded claims	[9.155]
The power of a tribunal to limit cross examination	[9.156]
The status of a tribunal chairman's notes of evidence	[9.157]
The use of written submissions	[9.158]
Further particulars	[9.160]
Directions	[9.161]
Disclosure of documents	[9.162]
Witness orders	[9.166]
Striking out (Employment Tribunal Regs)	[9.168]
The tribunal's decision	[9.170]
The need to make findings of fact	[9.171]
The tribunal's power to grant a remedy for unpleaded cause of action	[9.172]
The power to review decisions	[9.173]
Costs (Employment Tribunal Regs)	[9.175]
Unreasonable conduct by a trade union representative	[9.176]
The applicant's ability to pay	[9.177]

A HIGH COURT AND COUNTY COURT

INTRODUCTION

[9.1] The Civil Procedure Rules 1998, SI 1998/3132, came into force in April 1999. The former distinction between the rules that governed High Court and County Court actions was abolished and in its place is one unified set of rules. All civil cases, whatever their size or subject matter, are now governed by the 'overriding objective' that cases should be dealt with 'justly'. This objective is to be achieved primarily through reference to the factors highlighted in Part 1, and reference should be made to the commentary in the White Book.

The intention is two-fold: the court should use active case management and the parties should co-operate with each other at all stages of the pre-action and litigation process. Co-operation takes many forms but includes complying fully with any relevant pre-action protocol (such as the protocol for personal injury actions), attempting to narrow the areas of dispute, making admissions where appropriate, contesting only those issues that are genuinely likely to succeed at trial; agreeing a timetable, and making early payments in or offers to settle. Whether this has been practitioners' experience is open to question!

A further change is requiring the court in almost every case to allocate the claim to one of three tracks:
i. the small claims track (CPR Pt 27), covering cases where the financial value of the claim is less than £5,000 *and*, where relevant, any claim for general damages in a personal injury action is less than £1,000.
ii. The fast track (CPR Pt 28), covering cases where the value of the claim as a whole is not expected to exceed £15,000 *and* the trial is not likely to last more than a day.
iii. The multi track (CPR Pt 29), covering all other cases, and especially suitable for large value or more complicated actions.

As a result of the sea change in the way in which practice and procedure is now to be considered by the courts, pre-CPR cases are of less and less relevance and must be treated with caution. Instead a new body of case law has sprung up in which the new principles have generally been expressly applied. Unless the older case sets down a rule which has not been brought into question by the CPR or which is otherwise unambiguous, this section deals primarily with the newer authorities.

PROCEDURAL STEPS

Default judgment

[9.2] The situations in which a claimant can obtain judgment in default are set out in Part 12 of the CPR.

In addition to certain situations in which the court must set aside judgment in default (CPR 13.2), the court has a discretion to set it aside if (CPR 13.3):
i. the defendant has a real prospect of successfully defending the claim; or
ii. it appears to the court that there is some other good reason why the judgment should be set aside or varied or the defendant should be allowed to defend the action

Alpine Bulk Transport Co Inc v Saudi Eagle Shipping Co Inc

[1986] 2 Lloyd's Rep 221, CA

[9.3] In providing that the defendant had to show a real prospect of success, the Court of Appeal referred to an arguable defence that carried some degree of conviction.

Summary judgment

[9.4] The court may give summary judgment against a claimant or a defendant on the whole of a claim or on a particular issue if it considers that (CPR 24.2):

i. the claimant has no real prospect of succeeding on the claim or issue; or
ii. the defendant has no real prospect of successfully defending the claim or issue; and
iii. that there is no other compelling reason why the case or issue should be disposed of at trial.

Swain v Hillman

[2001] 1 All ER 91, CA

[9.5] 'Real' in the context of CPR 24.2 (and, it would appear, an application under CPR 13.3 to set aside judgment in default) meant 'realistic, as opposed to a fanciful prospect of success'. A court hearing an application for summary judgment is not required to undertake a 'mini trial'.

Interim applications

[9.6] The court has discretion under CPR 25 to grant a wide range of interim remedies and reference should be made to CPR 25.1

Interim payments

[9.7] CPR 25.6 and 25.7 set out the procedure whereby claimants can apply for interim payments. The court may order an interim payment of not more than a reasonable proportion of the likely amount of the final judgment (CPR 25.7(4)) to be made where (CPR 27.2(5)):
i. the defendant has admitted liability to pay damages or some other sum of money to the claimant;
ii. the claimant has obtained judgment for damages to be assessed or for a sum of money other than costs to be assessed;
iii. it is satisfied that if the claim went to trial the claimant would obtain judgment for a substantial sum of money against the defendant (taking into account contributory negligence and any relevant set-off or counterclaim.

In addition, in a claim for personal injuries the court may only make an order for an interim payment where:
i. the defendant is insured in respect of the claim;
ii. the defendant's liability will be met by an insurer under section 151 of the Road Traffic Act 1998 or by an insurer acting under the Motor Insurers Bureau Agreement or by the Motor Insurers Bureau; or
iii. the defendant is a public body

If there are two or more defendants to a personal injuries action the court may make the order against any of the defendants, even though there has been no determination as to which is liable, as long as it is satisfied that the claimant would obtain judgment for substantial damages against at least one of them and CPR 25.7(2) at paragraph 9.7 above is satisfied in relation to each defendant.

Note—the provisions of the Social Security (Recovery of Benefits) Act 1997 mean that a person making an interim payment is obliged to repay to the Secretary of State an amount equal to the total certified recoverable benefits (s 6(1)). Accordingly parties must ensure that any order sets out the amount by which the payment is to be reduced and the net amount that will be payable to the claimant.

Stringman v McArdle

[1994] 1 WLR 1653, CA

[9.8] The claimant does not have to demonstrate that a certain sum is required to cover any particular need over and above the general need that a claimant has to be paid his damages as soon as can reasonably be done.

Campbell v Mylchreest

[1998] PIQR P20, QBD

[9.9] The court is not concerned with what the claimant proposes to do with the money received although it can in its discretion consider what practical effect an interim payment would have on the conduct of the litigation.

Expert evidence

Daniels v Walker

[2000] 1 WLR 1382, CA

[9.10] The defendant was permitted to obtain evidence from a singly instructed expert even though the parties had previously agreed to and had obtained evidence from a joint expert. The value of the claim in respect of which additional evidence was sought was high and was a vital part of the quantum claim. Further, the defendant's concerns about the joint expert's report were not fanciful.

Cosgrove v Pattison

[2001] 2 CPLR 177

[9.11] The factors to be taken into account in considering whether a party was to be permitted to adduce evidence from an expert where a joint expert's report had already been obtained included the nature of the dispute, the number of disputes on which the expert evidence was relevant, the reasons for needing another expert report, the amount of money at stake, the effect of allowing a further expert witness on the conduct of the trial, the delay that calling a further expert would cause, any other special features and the overall justice to the parties in the context of the litigation.

Peet v Mid-Kent Healthcare Trust

[2001] EWCA Civ 1703, [2002] 1 WLR 210

[9.12] Parties were not entitled to have any contact with a single joint expert that was not transparent. It was not appropriate for an expert to attend a conference with counsel for one side in the absence of the other side. The Court of Appeal said, obiter, that usually there would not be a need to amplify or test the report of a single joint expert at trial by cross-examination.

COMMENCING PROCEEDINGS

Pre-action protocol

[9.13] The objectives of the pre-action protocol are:
i. to encourage the exchange of early and full information about the prospective legal claim;
ii. to enable parties to avoid litigation by agreeing a settlement of the claim before the commencement of proceedings;
iii. to support the efficient management of proceedings where litigation cannot be avoided.

The court has great discretion to penalise parties who are considered to have failed to comply with the substance of an approved protocol. Such penalties might involve:
i. a order that the party at fault pay the costs of the proceedings of the other party (if for example litigation would have been avoided by full compliance);
ii. an order that the party at fault pay such costs on an indemnity basis;
iii. an order depriving the party who is at fault but who eventually succeeds of part of the interest that would otherwise have been payable;
iv. an order that the party at fault who is eventually ordered to make payment of damages do in addition pay interest at a higher rate.

If a party has entered into a funding agreement within the meaning of CPR 43.2(1)(k) but fails to notify the other side, he is unable to recover any additional liability to which he might otherwise be entitled for the period during which he failed to provide the necessary funding information to the other side.

In employer's liability claims involving personal injuries the claimant will send a letter of claim to the employer. A request for early disclosure will generally be included. The protocol provides that standard disclosure in workplace claims will generally include the documents set out at CPR C2–019 to C2–020 and it is not necessary to reproduce the entire list here.

Vexatious litigants

Grepe v Loam

(1887) 37 Ch D 168, CA

[9.14] Applicants who persist in making frivolous applications to the court in the context of specific actions can be restrained from making any further applications in that action without the court's permission. If notice of any such application is given without such leave being obtained, the respondents to the application are not required to appear upon such application, and the application will be dismissed without being heard.

This can assist weary respondents to persistent applications in existing proceedings where there is no real prospect that the applicant will be held to be vexatious under the Supreme Court Act 1981, s 42.

Ebert v Venvil

[2000] Ch 484, CA

[9.15] The court had inherent jurisdiction to make extended '*Grepe v Loam*' orders to prevent the initiation of fresh proceedings which were likely to amount to an abuse of process without leave of the court. Such an order could in appropriate circumstances apply to county court as well as High Court proceedings. The order needed to be sufficiently certain so as to enable the person at whom it was directed to know what he was, and was not, entitled to do.

Parties to the action

Re Harvest Lane Motor Bodies Ltd

[1969] 1 Ch 457

[9.16] The claimant was the widow of a man killed in a road accident as a result, so she alleged, of the negligence of the limited company. She commenced proceedings but whilst the action was proceeding the company's name was struck off the register under the Companies Act 1948, s 353 (now the Companies Act 1985, s 653). She brought a petition to restore the company's name to the register.

HELD: That, on the true construction of section 353(6) of the Act of 1948, 'creditor' should be construed widely to include a creditor whose debt was contingen or prospective, and that, accordingly, the court would order that the name of the company be restored to the register.

Issuing proceedings

[9.17] The claim form must contain a statement of value identifying whether the claim is likely to exceed £5,000 or £15,000 (where appropriate) as well as identifying whether a claim for personal injuries is likely to exceed £1,000.

The claim form and any statement of case must include a signed statement of truth verifying its contents (CPR Part 22). Electronic signatures are permitted.

Clarke v Marlborough Fine Art (London) Ltd

[2002] 1 WLR 1731

[9.18] If the claimant pleads two alternative sets of facts and makes the alternative case clear that it is pleaded as such, the claimant is not necessarily stating that he believes both sets of facts are true. Unless it can be said that one of the alternatives is unsupported by any evidence and is therefore pure speculation or invention on the claimant's part then it is still permissible for the claimant to sign the statement of truth. Here, alternative pleas of actual and presumed undue influence were not on the facts mutually inconsistent.

Alex Lawrie Factors Ltd v Morgan

(1999) Times 18 August, CA

[9.19] The defendant swore an affidavit drafted by lawyers which included a sophisticated legal argument to which she herself would not be readily able to speak if cross-examined on her affidavits. Affidavits were there for witnesses to say in their own words what the relevant evidence was and they were not to be used as a vehicle for complex legal argument. Those considerations applied just as much to statements of truth under the CPR as they did to affidavits.

Serving proceedings

[9.20] The claim form must be served on the defendant (CPR 7.5):
i. within 4 months after the date of issue
ii. within 6 months after the date of issue where the claim form is to be served out of the jurisdiction

Molins plc v GD SpA

[2000] 1 WLR 1741, CA

[9.21] The pre-condition for service of process by fax is that the party to be served must have given prior written consent. That is not satisfied merely by including a fax number on the company's standard letterhead.

Zoan v Rouamba

[2000] 1 WLR 1509, CA

[9.22] HELD: In the context of interpreting a hire agreement, the usual meaning of the word 'after' in the context of reckoning time was that the day 'after' which a period of time was to be reckoned was not included in the period. That was so in order to avoid disputes as to fractions of a day and to give the party who had to comply maximum time for that compliance.

Nanglegan v Royal Free Hampstead NHS Trust

[2001] EWCA Civ 127, [2002] 1 WLR 1043

[9.23] Where the putative defendant in an action had nominated solicitors to accept service of a claim form, rule 6.5(4) of the CPR applied and the claimant was required to serve the claim form on the nominated solicitors. Posting the claim form to the defendant was not valid service, particularly where it had been sent to an incorrect postcode. Further, CPR 6.8, which dealt with service by an alternative method, was quite clearly directed to the notion of substituted service and did not apply to rectify errors of service retrospectively.

Smith v Probyn

(2000) Times 29 March, QBD

[9.24] Service of a claim form on solicitors in the mistaken belief that they were authorised to accept service would not justify an extension of time for service under CPR 7.6(3)(b) where no prior written notification had been obtained from the solicitors as required for such service by CPR 6.4(2). There was nothing to prevent personal service on the defendant and it could not be said that the claimant had taken all reasonable steps to serve the claim form but had been unable to do so.

Vinos v Marks & Spencer plc

[2001] 3 All ER 784, CA

[9.25] The claimant served a claim form seeking damages for an accident at work nine days after the expiry of the four months period for doing so. No explanation was given except that it was an oversight.

HELD: The meaning of CPR 7.6(3) was plain. The court had power to extend time for serving the claim form after the period for its service had run out 'only if' the stipulated conditions were fulfilled. That meant that the court did not have power to do so otherwise.

Kaur v CTP Coil Ltd

(2000) LTL, 10 July

[9.26] The claimants sought damages for injuries sustained as a result of their employment. The claim form was issued shortly before limitation expired. The claimants' solicitor had difficulties drafting the schedule of loss and delayed service of the claim form until four days after the expiry of the four month period. The judge granted an extension of time for service under CPR 7.6(3) on the basis that the claimants had taken all reasonable steps but were unable to serve the claim form because of difficulties drafting the schedule.

HELD, allowing the appeal: The judge had erred in holding that the claimants had satisfied the provisions of CPR 7.6(3)(b). The word 'serve' in CPR 7.6(3)(b) meant what it said, the clause being concerned with the actual process of service and as to whether it had been reasonably attempted. Difficulties preparing schedules were not matters that could be taken into account, and delaying preparing schedules until the last minute would not in any event count as reasonable.

Elmes v Hygrade Food Products plc

[2001] EWCA Civ 121, [2001] CP Rep 71

[9.27] The claimant served a claim form in respect of an accident at work on the defendant's insurers rather than on the defendant. The claimant sought to rely on CPR 3.9 and 3.10 to remedy a procedural error and on CPR 6.8 permitting service by an alternative method.

HELD: CPR 6.8 could not be applied retrospectively to permit an error. Service on the wrong party was not a procedural error and there was no power to correct the consequences.

Infantino v MacLean

[2001] 3 All ER 802, CA

[9.28] The claimant's solicitors inadvertently sent particulars of claim to the wrong DX number. When the error was discovered the documents were sent again but were a day late. There was no dispute that the claimant could not bring herself within CPR 7.6. The defendant contended that, following *Vinos v Marks & Spencer plc* and *Kaur v CTP Coil Ltd* (9.25 and 9.26 above) the claim must be struck out.

HELD: An order for dispensing with service would be made under CPR 6.9, which had to be read and applied together with the rules as to the overriding objective of enabling the court to deal with cases justly. On the facts of this extremely complicated case, the claimant's solicitors had gone well beyond the requirements of the clinical negligence pre-action protocol, had provided the fullest detail of the claim and had twice extended the time for the defendant's response in order to assist him and his experts. It would not enable the court to do justice if the claim were struck out.

Note— May LJ disapproved of this decision in *Godwin v Swindon Borough Council* (below)

Godwin v Swindon Borough Council

[2001] EWCA Civ 1478, [2002] 1 WLR 997

[9.29] The claimant issued a claim for damages for personal injuries sustained at work shortly before the expiry of the limitation period. The time for service of the claim form was 8 September 2000. His solicitors posted the claim form on 7 September 2000. Under CPR 6.7(1) service was deemed to be effected out of time on 9 September. In fact it was received within time on 8 September.

HELD: The date specified as the deemed date of service had to be treated as the date of service irrespective of proof of the date of actual service. A claimant who is as a matter of fact having to seek an extension of time to extricate him from the consequences of late service is only entitled to one when he can bring himself within CPR 7.6(3).

Rimer J considered that a defendant could prove that service was in fact effected later than the deemed date; overruled in *Anderton v Clwyd County Council* (below).

Anderton v Clwyd County Council

[2002] EWCA Civ 933, [2002] 1 WLR 3174

[9.30] These were five appeals concerning the construction and interpretation of CPR 6 and CPR 7.

HELD: Saturday and Sunday are not excluded from calculation of the day of deemed service. There was power in exceptional circumstances to dispense with service of the claim form retrospectively as well as prospectively. Such power was not available to be prayed in aid by claimants who had not attempted to serve within time. It could however avail a claimant who had made an ineffective attempt to serve in time where the defendant did receive the claim form before the end of the period for service.

Wilkey v BBC

[2002] EWCA Civ 1561, [2003] 1 WLR 1

[9.31] This case considered the second category of cases in *Anderton v Clwyd County Council* (above).

HELD: In cases which remained to be determined in which the deemed late service was prior to the decision of the Court of Appeal in *Anderton*, the discretion should ordinarily be exercised in the claimant's favour unless the defendant could prove prejudice or there was some other good reason not to exercise that discretion. In cases in which there was deemed late service after the decision in *Anderton* no such presumption should apply and the court should ordinarily adopt a strict approach to the exercise of its discretion.

Per Carnworth LJ: the matter had now been exhaustively reviewed in three judgments of the Court of Appeal and the transition period regarding the construction of the CPR on rules of service was now to be taken to have come to an end.

> *Note*— It would appear that, however detailed the letter of claim and however co-operative the claimant had tried to be, *Infantino v Maclean* (9.28 above) would now be decided differently

Particulars of claim must (CPR 7.4):
i. be contained in or served with the claim form; or
ii. be served within 14 days after service of the claim form; and
iii. in any case, not later than the last time for service of the claim form.

Totty v Snowden

[2001] EWCA Civ 1415, [2002] 1 WLR 1384

[9.32] The court had a discretion to grant an extension of time to a claimant who had served a claim form within the time prescribed by the CPR but who either had not served particulars of claim, or had failed to serve particulars complying with the requirements of CPR 16 within the period prescribed by CPR 7.5. A distinction could be drawn between failure to serve a claim form in time (as in *Vinos v Marks & Spencer plc, see* 9.25 above) and a failure to serve particulars. There was no justification for concluding, in the absence of express words to that effect, that the particulars of claim came within the provisions of rule 7.6 by implication.

Charles v NTL Group Ltd

(2002) LTL, 13 December

[9.33] The rules for formal service of documents contained in CPR Part 6 did not apply to the making of a CPR Part 36 offer. It was sufficient that the offer was communicated in writing to the offeree and that the offeree received it.

Pleading requirements

[9.34] The requirements as to the contents of the particulars of claim and defence are set out at Part 16. In particular note:

i. The claimant must set out specifically a claim for interest, aggravated damages, exemplary damages and provisional damages (CPR 16.4);
ii. In personal injury actions the particulars of claim must include the claimant's date of birth and brief details of the personal injuries suffered (PD 16 para 4.1);
iii. The claimant must attach a schedule of details of past and future expenses and losses to the particulars of claim (PD 16 para 4.2);
iv. Where the claimant is relying on the evidence of a medical practitioner a report from the same must be attached to the particulars of claim (CPR 16.4.3);
v. Where the claimant makes a claim for provisional damages he must state that whether he makes the claim under the Supreme Court Act 1981, s 32A or the County Courts Act 1984, s 51; that there is a chance that at some future time the claimant will develop a serious disease or suffer some serious deterioration in his physical or mental condition; and specify the disease or type of deterioration in respect of which an application may be made (CPR 16.4.4).

Amendments

Hay v London Brick Co Ltd

[1989] 2 Lloyd's Rep 7, CA

[9.35] The claimant was involved in an accident at work in which he injured his back falling from a stack of bricks. He commenced proceedings contending that the accident occurred on 18 November 1974. Subsequent disclosure of documents showed that the accident in fact occurred on 3 December 1975. The claimant applied to amend the pleadings. The judge at first instance refused the application on the basis that it introduced a new cause of action.

HELD: The amendment did not introduce a new cause of action. The cause of action was the allegation of negligence and breach of statutory duty in poorly stacking bricks on which the claimant had to stand. On those facts, the date was not a material part of the cause of action.

Resiling from admission of liability

Gale v Superdrug Stores plc

[1996] 3 All ER 468, CA

[9.36] The claimant was injured in the course of her employment with the defendant when she was struck by the door of a delivery van while unloading it. The defendant's insurers indicated that they did not intend to dispute liability. An interim payment was made on account of damages. Proceedings were then issued and a defence served denying liability. The defence was struck out as an abuse of process.

HELD, allowing the appeal: There was no distinction to be drawn from an application to resile from an admission by amendment to a pleaded case. The test is whether in all the circumstances it is just to relieve the defendant of his admission having regard to the interests of both sides and to the extent to which either side may be injured. The party resisting the retraction of an admission must produce clear and cogent evidence of prejudice, rather than mere disappointment, before the court will restrain the defendant from exercising his right to change his mind.

GROUP LITIGATION

[9.37] The procedures involved in group actions are contained in Part 19 of the CPR. In particular individuals can seek a Group Litigation Order (GLO) if there are likely to be a number of claims giving rise to the GLO issues.

If the court makes a GLO it must:
  i. give directions about the establishment of a 'group register' on which all claims managed under the GLO will be entered;
  ii. specify the GLO issues;
  iii. specify the court which will manage the claims.

If the court makes an order or gives a judgment in a claim governed by a GLO:
  i. the order or judgment will be binding on all parties entered on the group register at the time the order is made unless the court otherwise orders (CPR 19.12(1)(a));
  ii. the court may give directions as to the extent to which the judgment or order binds parties who are subsequently entered on the group register (CPR 19.12.(1)(b));
  iii. no party to a claim entered on the group register may apply for the judgment or order to be set aside, varied or stayed or may appeal the judgment or order. Such parties can however apply for an order that the judgment or order is not binding on him (CPR 19.12(3));
  iv. disclosure to one party to a claim on the group register is disclosure to all parties to claims on the group register including those subsequently entered on the register unless the court orders otherwise.
  Note—practitioners must notify both the Law Society and the Senior Master of the Queen's Bench Division of any GLO made (CPR PD 19B para.29).

COSTS

Ochwat v Watson Burton (a firm)

(10 December 1999, unreported), CA

[9.38] In proceedings where two out of five lead cases went to trial and were dismissed, the Court of Appeal ordered that all claimants should contribute to 75% of the defendant's costs. It was impossible to say that the claimants and their advisors did not intend that the costs of the lead actions be borne proportionately by all of them.

Allen v BREL Ltd

[2000] CLY 454

[9.39] In vibration white finger litigation four claimants succeeded on liability. One failed to beat the defendant's payment in. The court held that all parties had effectively treated the cases as test cases, primarily for the benefit of the defendant seeking an authoritative judgment. The defendant was ordered to pay 90% of the claimants' costs on the common issues from the date of the payment in and the unsuccessful claimant was ordered to pay 10% of the defendant's costs from the same date.

Sayers v Merck SmithKline Beecham plc

[2001] EWCA Civ 2017, [2002] 1 WLR 2274

[9.40] In making a costs-sharing order in a multi-party action, it was not appropriate to order that a claimant who discontinued his action would be liable for individual costs together with his several share of the costs, but rather to order that liability for common costs and disbursements would be determined following the trial of common issues with permission to apply if such a trial did not take place.

LIMITATION

BACKGROUND

[9.41] A general rule for limitation of actions in tort and simple contract requiring such actions to be commenced within six years from the cause of action arising was established by the Statute of Limitation of 1623, which remained in force (with some accretion of exceptions and amendments) until supplanted by the Limitation Act 1939. The six year period was maintained by s 2 of that Act. A proviso was added to that section by the Law Reform (Limitation of Actions) Act 1954 reducing the limitation period to three years in actions of negligence, nuisance and breach of duty for damages in respect of personal injuries. That Act also helpfully abolished or amended to three years a variety of special periods of limitation contained in particular statutes. The Limitation Act 1963 gave the court power to disapply the limitation period of three years so as to enable a plaintiff to pursue an action for damages for personal injury when material facts 'of a decisive character' were proved to have been outside his knowledge, in effect, when the cause of action arose. The Act also by s 4m prescribed a time limit of two years for contribution proceedings. The Limitation Act 1975 simplified the elaborate provisions of the 1963 Act for disapplying or extending the three-year period and, by ss 2A, 2B and 2C added to the 1939 Act, made rules for determining the date from which time began to run in personal injury and fatal accident cases. A further section inserted as 2D in the 1939 Act provided a new and more liberal rule by which to disapply the three-year period in certain cases. The Limitation Act 1980 (in force from 1 May 1981) repealed and re-enacted with some amendments and additions the surviving provisions of the earlier acts so far as they related to the subject matter of this book.

Practice and Procedure

[9.42] The Latent Damage Act 1986 (amending the Limitation Act by inserting sections 14A and 14B) added an alternative limitation period in situations where damage could not be discovered until after the ordinary limitation period had expired. These provisions are discussed in more detail below.

As some cases in this Chapter refer to provisions of the Limitation Acts before 1980 the following destination table may be useful:

Limitation Act 1963	Limitation Act 1980
s 4	s 10

Limitation Act 1939	Limitation Act 1980
s 2	s 2 Tort, s 5 Contract
s 2A	s 11, 14
s 2B	s 2, 14
s 2C	s 13
s 2D	s 33

A few cases dealing with the provisions of s 35 of the Limitation Act 1980 have been reported. What guidance has been provided by the courts can be found at paras [20.2]–[20.9]. Useful general points are as follows:

1. Defendant wishing to rely on the statute of limitation must plead it (CPR PD 16 para 1).
2. 'Damage only' claims have a six-year limitation period (s 2).
3. The day on which the cause of action arose is excluded from the computation of the limitation period.
4. In the case of plaintiffs under age, times does not begin to run until after their 18th birthday.
5. The limitation period for trespass to persons is six years.

The Limitation Act 1980

2 Time limit for actions founded on tort

[9.43]

An action founded on tort shall not be brought after the expiration of six years from the date on which the cause of action accrued.

5 Time limit for actions founded on simple contract

[9.44]

An action founded on simple contract shall not be brought after the expiration of six years from the date on which the cause of action accrued.

ACTIONS IN RESPECT OF WRONGS CAUSING PERSONAL INJURIES OR DEATH

[9.45]

11 Special time limit for actions in respect of personal injuries

(1) This section applies to any action for damages for negligence, nuisance or breach of duty (whether the duty exists by virtue of a contract of provision made by or under a statute or independently of any contract or any such provision) where the damages claimed by the plaintiff for the negligence, nuisance or breach of duty consist of or include damages in respect of personal injuries to the plaintiff or any other person.

(2) None of the time limits given in the preceding provisions of this Act shall apply to an action to which this section applies.

(3) An action to which this section applies shall not be brought after the expiration of the period applicable in accordance with subsection (4) or (5) below.

(4) Except where sub-s (5) below applies, the period applicable is three years from—
(a) the date on which the cause of action accrued, or
(b) the date of knowledge (if later) of the person injured.

(5) If the person injured dies before the expiration of the period mentioned in sub-s (4) above, the period applicable as respects the cause of action surviving for the benefit of his estate by virtue of s 1 of the Law Reform (Miscellaneous Provisions) Act 1934 shall be three years from—
(a) the date of death; or
(b) the date of the personal representative's knowledge;

whichever is the later.

(6) For the purposes of this section 'personal representative' includes any person who is or has been a personal representative of the deceased, including an executor who has not proved the will (whether or not he has renounced probate) but not anyone appointed only as a special personal representative in relation to settled land; and regard shall be had to any knowledge acquired by any such person while personal representative or previously.

(7) If there is more than one personal representative, and their dates of knowledge are different, sub-s (5)(b) above shall be read as referring to the earliest of those dates.

12 Special time limit for actions under Fatal Accidents legislation

[9.46]

(1) An action under the Fatal Accidents Act 1976 shall not be brought if the death occurred when the person injured could no longer maintain an action

and recover damages in respect of the injury (whether because of a time limit in this Act or in any other Act, or for any other reason).

Where any such action by the injured person would have been barred by the time limit in s 11 of this Act, no account shall be taken of the possibility of that time limit being overridden under s 33 of this Act.

(2) None of the time limits given in the preceding provisions of this Act shall apply to an action under the Fatal Accidents Act 1976, but no such action shall be brought after the expiration of three years from—
(a) the date of death; or
(b) the date of knowledge of the person for whose benefit the action is brought;

whichever is the later.

(3) An action under the Fatal Accidents Act 1976 shall be one to which ss 28, 33 and 35 of this Act apply, and the application to any such action of the time limit under sub-s (2) above shall be subject to s 39; but otherwise Parts II and III of this Act shall not apply to any such action.

13 Operation of time limit under s 12 in relation to different dependants

[9.47]

(1) Where there is more than one person for whose benefit an action under the Fatal Accidents Act 1976 is brought, s 12(2)(b) of this Act shall be applied separately to each of them.

(2) Subject to sub-s (3) below, if by virtue of sub-s (1) above the action would be outside the time limit given by sub-s 12(2) as regards one or more, but not all, of the persons for whose benefit is brought, the court shall direct that any person as regards whom the action would be outside that time limit shall be excluded from those for whom the action is brought.

(3) The court shall not give such a direction if it is shown that if the action were brought exclusively for the benefit of the person in question it would not be defeated by a defence of limitation (whether in consequence of s 28 of this Act or an agreement between the parties not to raise the defence, or otherwise).

14 Definition of date of knowledge for purposes of ss 11 and 12

[9.48]

(1) In s 11 of this Act references to a person's date of knowledge are references to the date on which he first had knowledge of the following facts—
(a) that the injury in question was significant; and

(b) that the injury was attributable in whole or in part to the act or omission which is alleged to constitute negligence, nuisance or breach of duty; and
(c) the identity of the defendant; and
(d) if it is alleged that the act or omission was that of a person other than the defendant, the identity of that person and the additional facts supporting the fringing of an action against the defendant;

and knowledge that any acts or omissions did or did not, as a matter of law, involve negligence, nuisance or breach of duty is irrelevant.

(2) For the purposes of this section an injury is significant if the person whose date of knowledge is in question would reasonably have considered it sufficiently serious to justify his instituting proceedings for damages against a defendant who did not dispute liability and was able to satisfy a judgement.

(3) For the purposes of this section a person's knowledge includes knowledge which he might reasonably have been expected to acquire—
(a) from facts observable or ascertainable by him; or
(b) from facts ascertainable by him with the help of medical or other appropriate expert advice which it is reasonable for him to seek;

but a person shall not be fixed under this subsection with knowledge of a fact ascertainable only with the help of expert advice so long as he has taken all reasonable steps to obtain (and, where appropriate, to act on) that advice.

14A Special time limit for negligence actions where facts relevant to cause of action are not known at date of accrual

[9.49]

(1) This section applies to any action for damages for negligence, other than one to which section 11 of this Act applies, where the starting date for reckoning the period of limitation under subsection (4)(b) below falls after the date on which the cause of action accrued.

(2) Section 2 of this Act shall not apply to an action to which this section applies.

(3) An action to which this section applies shall not be brought after the expiration of the period applicable in accordance with subsection (4) below.

(4) That period is either—
(a) six years from the date on which the cause of action accrued; or
(b) three years from the starting date as defined by subsection (5) below, if that period expires later than the period mentioned in paragraph (a) above.

(5) For the purposes of this section, the starting date for reckoning the period of limitation under subsection (4)(b) above is the earliest date on which the plaintiff or any person in whom the cause of action was vested before him first had both the knowledge required for bringing an action for damages in respect of the relevant damage and a right to bring such an action.

(6) In subsection (5) above 'the knowledge required for bringing an action for damages in respect of the relevant damage' means knowledge both—
(a) of the material facts about the damage in respect of which damages are claimed; and
(b) of the other facts relevant to the current action mentioned in subsection (8) below.

(7) For the purpose of subsection (6)(a) above, the material facts about the damage are such as would lead a reasonable person who had suffered such damage to consider it sufficiently serious to justify his instituting proceedings for damages against a defendant who did not dispute liability and was able to satisfy a judgement.

(8) The other facts referred to in subsection (6)(b) above are—
(a) that the damage was attributable in whole or in part to the act or omission which is alleged to constitute negligence; and
(b) the identity of the defendant; and
(c) if it is alleged that the act or omission was that of a person other than the defendant, the identity of that person and the additional facts supporting the bringing of an action against the defendant.

(9) Knowledge that any acts or omissions did or did not, as a matter of law, involve negligence is irrelevant for the purposes of subsection (5) above.

(10) For the purposes of this section a person's knowledge includes knowledge which he might reasonable have been expected to acquire—
(a) from facts observable or ascertainable by him; or
(b) from facts ascertainable by him with the help of appropriate expert advice which it is reasonable for him to seek;

but a person shall not be taken by virtue of this subsection to have knowledge of a fact ascertainable only with the help of expert advice so long as he has taken all reasonable step s to obtain (and, where appropriate, to act on) that advice.

14B Overriding time limit for negligence actions not involving personal injuries

[9.50]

(1) An action for damages for negligence, other than one to which section 11 of this Act applies, shall not be brought after the expiration of fifteen years from the date(or, if more than one, from the last of the dates) in which there occurred any act or omission—

(a) which is alleged to constitute negligence; and
(b) to which the damage in respect of which damages are claimed is alleged to be attributable (in whole or part).

(2) This section bars the right of action in a case to which subsection (1) above applies not withstanding that—
(a) the cause of action has not yet accrued; or
(b) where section 14A of this Act applies to the action, the date which is for the purposes of that section the starting date for reckoning the period mentioned in subsection (4)(b) of that section has not yet occurred;

before the end of the period of limitation prescribed by this section.

Running of time

Marren v Dawson Bentley & Co Ltd

[1961] 2 QB 135, [1961] 2 All ER 270

[9.51] The claim occurred at 1.30pm on 8 November 1954. The writ was issued on 8 November 1957. The defendant contended that he was out of time.

HELD: The day on which the cause of action arose is excluded from the computation of the three year period. The claim was in time.

Smith v White Knight Laundry Ltd

[2001] EWCA Civ 660, [2001] 3 All ER 862, [2002] 1 WLR 616

[9.52] The claimant's husband worked for the defendant from 1950 to 1956. His work brought him into contact with asbestos. The defendant was dissolved in 1963. The claimant's husband died of mesothelioma on 5 February 1995. In December 1997 the claimant applied to the Companies Court for an order under the Companies Act 1985, s 651 declaring the dissolution to have been void and restoring the defendant's name to the register. The order was made on 23 January 1998 and included an order that the period between dissolution and restoration should not count for limitation purposes. The action was commenced by writ on 14 April 1999. The defendant pleaded a limitation defence. The claimant contended that the defence was bound to fail in the light of the order made. The order was subsequently varied and the claimant appealed.

HELD, dismissing the appeal: Since the effect on an order under section 651 rendered the company's dissolution void ab initio, any cause of action against the defendant accrued on the date on which it would otherwise have accrued but for the dissolution. Accordingly the claimant's claim was statute-barred and she would have to make a Limitation Act 1980, s 33 application in the usual way. As a general rule a section 651 direction should not normally be made unless (a) notice of the application has been given to all those who might oppose it, including insurers, (b) the court is satisfied that it has before it all the evidence which the parties would wish to adduce on a section 33 application and that this application would be bound to succeed.

Date of knowledge

Driscoll-Varley v Parkside Health Authority

[1991] 2 Med LR 346

[9.53] The claimant was assaulted by her husband and suffered serious injuries including fractures to her right leg on 18 April 1984. She was in traction for 12 days. Thereafter she received a long course of medical treatment from the defendant which she claimed had made her condition worse. In mid-1985 she was told that there was some dead bone in the leg causing problems but even when this had been removed she continued to have difficulties and union of the fracture failed to take place. The claimant consulted solicitors in late 1986 but was reluctant to issue because she feared that her consultant would cease treating her. Expert evidence was obtained in June 1988 stating the cause of the problems was the premature stopping of traction. The claimant argued that she had only realised at a late stage of the treatment that certain aspects of the treatment were aggravating her condition and alleged that she only had the requisite knowledge from that point.

HELD: 'Knowledge' is a high standard and mere suspicion is not enough. The claimant needed to be more or less sure that her injuries were attributable to the defendants' negligence. The injury was not 'significant' until September 1985 when the dead bone was discovered but the claimant did not have 'knowledge' until June 1988. Claim allowed to proceed.

O'Driscoll v Dudley Health Authority

[1998] Lloyd's Rep Med 210, CA

[9.54] The claimant had cerebral palsy and although not a patient, left management of her affairs to her parents. Her parents had the requisite knowledge some years before she did that her condition was probably due to negligence during her birth.

HELD: The court must have regard simply to what the claimant herself knew as opposed to what her parents knew. Her parents were not to be treated as agents for the purposes of the Limitation Act 1980. However the claimant herself had actual knowledge more than three years prior to the date of issuing proceedings and, on the specific facts, she was out of time.

Halford v Brookes

[1991] 3 All ER 559, [1991] 1 WLR 428, CA

[9.55] The claimant was the mother of a girl murdered on 3 April 1978. The second defendant confessed to inflicting injuries on the girl at the instigation of the first defendant. He was subsequently tried and acquitted of murder. After the trial further evidence came to light implicating the first defendant but despite the family's best efforts the authorities refused to prosecute him. In July 1985 the claimant consulted solicitors and counsel advised that a civil action claiming damages on behalf of the daughter's estate was feasible. A writ was issued on 1 April 1987. The defendants pleaded that the action was statute-barred.

HELD: The claimant had the requisite knowledge at the conclusion of the second defendant's trial in 1978. She did not need expert knowledge. The claim was statute-barred (although the Court of Appeal overturned the lower court's refusal to exercise its section 33 discretion).

Harding v People's Dispensary for Sick Animals

[1994] PIQR P270 , CA

[9.56] The claimant worked for the defendant. She suffered an injury at work. She had previously suffered a similar injury which had cleared up and concluded that it was not worth suing. In fact her symptoms did not resolve. She issued proceedings more than three years after the accident. The defendant pleaded that the claim was out of time.

HELD: The claimant did not know that the injury was 'significant' within the meaning of the Limitation Act 1980, s 14(2) until it became clear that the second injury was more serious than the first and would not clear up. Claim allowed to proceed.

Spargo v North Essex District Health Authority

[1997] PIQR 235, CA

[9.57] The claimant was wrongly diagnosed as suffering from organic brain damage in 1975 and as a result was detained in a psychiatric hospital for six years. This had a catastrophic effect on her life. In January 1986 the diagnosing doctor's secretary informed her that the doctor accepted that he had made a mistake. In October 1986 she consulted solicitors. She stated that she was clear in her own mind at this time that her suffering stemmed from the mistaken diagnosis. A negative expert opinion was obtained in 1989 and a positive opinion was not obtained until 1991. The writ was issued in December 1993. The defendant pleaded that the action was out of time.

HELD, per Lord Justice Brooke: various principles could be deduced from the authorities: (1) the knowledge required to satisfy section 14(1)(b) of the Limitation Act 1980 is a broad knowledge of the essence of the causally relevant act or omission to which the injury is attributable; (2) 'attributable' means 'capable of being attributed to' in the sense of being a real possibility; (3) the claimant has the requisite knowledge when she knows enough to make it reasonable for her to begin to investigate whether she has a case. Having a sufficiently firm belief to go to a solicitor to seek advice would indicate sufficient knowledge; (4) if the claimant thinks she knows what to investigate but is 'barking up the wrong tree' or her knowledge is vague or general or she needs to check first with an expert, that would not constitute knowledge. The claimant had the requisite knowledge in October 1986 and the claim was out of time.

Corbin v Penfold Metalising Co Ltd

[2000] Lloyd's Rep Med 247, CA

[9.58] The claimant was employed by the defendant between 1979 and 1992 as a metal sprayer. In 1992 he suffered a chest complaint and underwent a lung biopsy in August 1992. He was told that he had deposits of iron in the lung which did not necessarily indicate an industrial injury. Following further tests medical opinion changed and in February 1993 he was told by a leading consultant that everyone was now convinced that he had an inhaled disease. Further investigations followed. The claimant consulted solicitors in September 1993. In March 1995 an expert confirmed that the dusts in the claimant's lungs were identifiable with those in the factory. Proceedings were issued on 19 August 1996 and served on 16 June 1998. The defendant pleaded a limitation defence.

HELD: Following *Spargo* (9.57 above) the claimant had the requisite knowledge to make it reasonable for him to begin to investigate whether he had a claim against the defendant when he was told by a leading consultant that he was suffering from an inhaled disease. There could have been no source other than his employment with the defendant. The claimant did not need to have detailed knowledge or certainty as to whether there was a causal connection.

Simpson v Norwest Holst Southern Ltd

[1980] 1 WLR 968, CA

[9.59] The claimant was employed as a carpenter on a building site. The company's statement of terms provided to him as well as his wage slips gave his employer's name as 'Norwest Holst Group', which was not a legal entity. He was injured at work on 4 August 1976. Despite making several enquiries neither he nor his solicitors were informed of the correct identity of the defendant until 4 July 1979. The summons was issued on 17 August 1979. The court at first instance refused the defendant's application to dismiss the claim for being out of time.

HELD: The appeal was dismissed. The identity of the claimant's employer and the correct defendant was not known until 4 July 1979. The claimant was entitled to assume that 'Norwest Holst Group' was his employer and time did not begin to run until he could reasonably have discovered that he was employed by another company in the same group.

Farmer v National Coal Board

(1985) Times, 27 April, CA

[9.60] Reliance on expert advice is limited to questions of fact. The claimant cannot rely on incorrect legal advice he has received as a ground for postponing the date of knowledge.

Central Asbestos Co Ltd v Dodd

[1973] AC 518, HL

[9.61] The claimants were claiming damages for asbestos-related diseases from the defendant employer. Some of them had been told by the defendant's works manager that, as a matter of law, they could not claim both a disability pension from the defendant and sue for damages.

HELD: The appeal was dismissed. The claimants' misapprehension on this point amounted to ignorance of a material fact.

Note—See *Harper v National Coal Board* [1974] QB 614, where a two-man Court of Appeal declined to follow the ratio decidendi on the basis that there was none. See also *McGee* on Limitation (4th edition) at 8.020; case could not be decided this way under the 1980 Act but should apply still on the basis that the defendant should be estopped from pleading limitation by reason of the conduct of its works manager.

Henderson v Temple Pier Co Ltd

[1998] 3 All ER 324, [1998] 1 WLR 1540, CA

[9.62] The claimant suffered an injury on the defendant's moored ship on 28 January 1993. She instructed solicitors on 22 February 1993 but they did not identify the defendant as owners of the ship until July 1994. Proceedings were issued on 30 April 1997. The defendant applied to strike out the claim as being statute-barred.

HELD: The claimant could have acquired knowledge as to the identity of the defendant from the facts attainable or ascertainable by her. She did not require expert advice. The claimant was fixed with the constructive knowledge that her solicitors ought to have acquired at an earlier stage. Claim struck out.

Sniezek v Bundy (Letchworth) Ltd

[2000] PIQR P213, CA

[9.63] It was necessary to distinguish between a claimant who has a firm belief that he has a significant injury attributable to his working conditions and a claimant who believes that he may have, or even probably has, a significant injury which is attributable to his working conditions but is not sure and feels it necessary to have expert advice on those questions. It was possible to have the requisite knowledge but not yet be in a position to initiate proceedings because the necessary evidence is not yet available.

Walkin v South Manchester Health Authority

[1995] 1 WLR 1543, CA

[9.64] By writ dated 10 October 1991 the claimant sought damages for negligent sterilisation treatment causing economic loss of bringing up a child born in September 1987 following a sterilisation operation. No claim was made for personal injuries but the defence pleaded that it was in fact for personal injuries and so out of time.

HELD: The court had to look at the substance of the claim rather than the way in which it was pleaded. The unwanted conception was a personal injury and all of the claim arose out of the same cause of action. The claim was time-barred.

Limitation defence

Wright v John Bagnall & Sons Ltd

[1900] 2 QB 240, CA

Rendall v Hill's Dry Docks & Engineering Co

[1900] 2 QB 245, CA

[9.65] In both claims the claimant was suing his employer for damages as a result of an accident at work. In both cases liability was admitted. In both cases the writ was issued outside the applicable time-limit and the defendant argued that the claim was out of time.

HELD: An unambiguous admission of liability precluded the defendant from relying on the statute.

The judgments do not make clear whether the admission was to be viewed as an agreement not to rely on the statute or on more equitable grounds.

>   *Note*—See also *Cotterell v Leeds Day (a firm)* (2000) LTL, 3 January (9.67 below) – judge doubting proposition that admission could preclude reliance on expiry of statutory limitation period.

Lubovsky v Snelling

[1944] KB 44, CA

[9.66] The claimant's husband was killed in a road accident as a result of the defendant's negligence. The defendant's solicitors agreed not to contest liability but reserved the question of quantum. A defective writ was issued in time but by the time this had been corrected time had expired. The defendant sought to rely on the statutory limitation.

HELD: The defendant had agreed not to contest liability so the date of the writ was immaterial. They would not be permitted to attempt to dispute liability in its entirety.

Cotterell (Reece's Executrix) v Leeds Day (a firm)

(2000) LTL, 3 January

[9.67] The claimant sought damages for professional negligence from her former solicitors. The defendant admitted liability. The defendant further assured the claimant that she would not suffer loss financially because the defendant was insured. The writ was issued out of time. The defendant pleaded a limitation defence.

HELD: A bare admission, however unequivocal, did not itself prevent time from running or otherwise entitle a claimant to avoid the 1980 Act. It was clear that at the time of the meeting and the letter both parties had in mind only the possibility of some future liability to inheritance tax, and not the Act. In those circumstances, it was impossible to find any contract, whether express or implied, to the effect that the defendant would not take the limitation point if the claimant forbore to sue. Similar considerations also meant that no estoppel arose.

Bridgeman v McAlpine Brown

(19 January 2000, unreported), CA

[9.68] The claimant's car was struck from behind on 29 February 1996. She spoke to the defendant, a man in the car behind who gave his details. His insurers admitted liability. The claimant issued proceedings on 19 February 1999. A defence was filed claiming that the defendant's wife had been the driver. The defendant applied to strike the claim out.

HELD: The case was remitted for a trial on the issue of liability. The defendant was ordered to pay the costs on an indemnity basis, the court deploring the fact that the defendant had taken a wholly unmeritorious technical point in the hope of preventing the court from deciding the case on its true merits.

Extending the time-limits (section)

Hinks v Channel 4 Television Corp

(3 March 2000, unreported) (Morland J)

[9.69] This case involved a claim for libel. There is a similar discretion to extend time limits in claims for libel. The claimants wished to sue the defendant for libel arising out of a Channel 4 programme broadcast on 26 May 1998 in which they both appeared and which they said defamed them by portraying them as fences of stolen goods. They instructed solicitors in June 1998. The solicitor negligently consulted an out of date textbook which gave the limitation period as three years instead of the one year period it by then was. Proceedings were issued out of time.

HELD: It was not 'equitable' within the meaning of section 32A of the 1980 Act to disapply the one year limitation period. The claimants had an apparently unanswerable claim against their solicitors. There was real risk that documents crucial to the defendant's intended plea of justification would have been lost after four years and recollections blurred. The balance of prejudice favoured the defendant.

Corbin v Penfold

(Facts as in 9.58 above.)

[9.70] The claimant sought relief under s 33 of the 1980 Act. The defendant pointed to long periods of delay attributable to the claimant's solicitors.

HELD: There is no law requiring a court to visit the faults of the lawyers upon the claimant. Where the claimant is merely a passive observer this cannot be said in any realistic way to contribute to any delay.

Mold v Hayton

(17 April 2000, unreported), CA

[9.71] The claimant went to her general practitioner in 1979 to early 1980 with symptoms which were eventually diagnosed in September 1980 as cervical cancer. She contended that she should have been examined vaginally and referred to hospital at an earlier stage and that, had they done so, she would have required lower doses of radiation and would have spared a number of unpleasant side effects. She issued proceedings on 13 October 1998. The defendant pleaded a limitation defence. The judge at first instance allowed the claim to continue pursuant to section 33 of the 1980 Act.

HELD: If a judge is minded to give as long an extension of time as 15 years, he is under a duty to explain his reasons with meticulous care. Here the defendants had done nothing to add to the delay and the first warning of the allegedly negligent omission was some 18 years after the event. It was not equitable to allow the action to continue.

Thompson v Brown Construction (Ebbw Vale) Ltd

[1981] 1 WLR 744, HL

[9.72] The claimant was employed by the defendant. He was injured on 4 March 1976 when scaffolding on which he was working collapsed. His solicitors notified his claim to the defendant on 27 April 1976. On 17 March 1977 the defendant's insurers wrote saying they were prepared to make an offer in settlement. The claimant's solicitors mislaid the file at some date after August 1977 and it was not found until spring 1979. A writ was issued on 10 April 1979, 37 days after limitation expired. The defendant pleaded that the action was out of time. The judge at first instance considered that the claimant had a cast iron claim against his solicitors so he would not be prejudiced if the statutory limitation was held to apply.

HELD: A judge determining an application to exercise discretion to extend time had to consider all the circumstances of the case and particularly the six matters singled out for mention in the 1980 Act. The delay referred to in what is now section 33(3)(a) referred to the delay after the primary limitation period expired and the effect on the cogency of the evidence likely to be adduced was the effect attributable to this period of delay. The judge had fettered his discretion and the matter was remitted to him for further consideration.

Donovan v Gwentoys Ltd

[1990] 1 WLR 472, HL

[9.73] The claimant was employed by the defendant. She suffered an accident at work in December 1979 when aged 16. She turned 18 on 25 April 1981. She consulted solicitors on 6 April 1984, 19 days before limitation expired. They did not issue until 10 October 1984, five and a half months out of time. The defendant argued that they should not be faced with a stale claim of which they had not been notified until around five years after the accident. The trial judge and Court of Appeal considered that they were bound to consider only the prejudice caused by the five and a half month delay and this was minimal.

HELD: Section 33 of the Limitation Act 1980 provides an unfettered discretion to a judge to allow a claim to continue if it is just and equitable in all the circumstances. The court is entitled to take account of delay overall. The balance of prejudice came down heavily in the defendant's favour and the claimant could be left to her remedy against her solicitors.

Dale v British Coal Corpn

[1993] 1 All ER 317, CA

[9.74] The test as to whether the claimant acted reasonably in bringing the case late was an objective one. A trade union member could usually be said to act reasonably if he took and followed union advice.

Thomas v Plaistow

[1997] PIQR P540, CA

[9.75] 'Disability' within the meaning of section 33(3)(d) of the 1980 Act meant only mental disorder within the meaning of the Mental Health Act 1983. It did not include a wider range of symptoms such as forgetfulness, depression and an inability to concentrate. However such symptoms might be relevant as part of 'all of the circumstances of the case' under section 33(3)(a).

New claims in pending action – (section 35)

Leicester Wholesale Fruit Market Ltd v Grundy

[1990] 1 WLR 107, CA

[9.76] If the claimant is trying by amendment to include a defendant after the time at which the limitation period against that defendant had expired, the court should decline if, had the claimant commenced fresh proceedings against that defendant, the defendant could successfully have applied to strike out the action as being out of time.

Welsh Development Agency v Redpath Dorman Long Ltd

[1994] 1 WLR 1409, CA

[9.77] A new claim under the Limitation Act 1980, s 35(3) is not made until the date on which the statement of case is actually amended, which cannot be earlier than the date on which permission to amend is given. Unless the case falls within one of the exceptions such permission cannot be given even though time might not have expired at the time the application to amend was made.

Commencing second action out of time

Walkley v Precision Forgings Ltd

[1979] 2 All ER 548, [1979] 1 WLR 606, HL

[9.78] The claimant was employed by the defendant between 1966 and 1971. He contracted an industrial disease in his hands. He was fixed with knowledge from 1969. A writ was issued on 7 October 1971 but never served, the claimant having been told by his solicitors that he did not have a good claim. The claimant went to other solicitors in 1973. The defendant indicated that it would make an application to have the claim dismissed for want of prosecution if the claim was resurrected. The claimant went to a third firm of solicitors who issued a fresh writ on 6 December 1976 asserting the same cause of action. The defendant applied for an order that the second writ be struck out and the claim dismissed. The master made the order but the action was restored on appeal.

HELD: Once a claimant had started an action within the primary limitation period it was only in the most exceptional circumstances that he would be able to bring himself within the discretionary ambit of section 2D of the 1939 Act (now section 33 of the 1980 Act) since it was not the provisions of any statutory limitation period that caused him prejudice but rather dilatoriness. The only exceptional circumstance envisaged might be where the claimant had been induced to discontinue the first action by a misrepresentation or other improper conduct by the defendant.

Shapland v Palmer

[1999] 1 WLR 2068, CA

[9.79] The 'Walkley' principle (above) served to exclude only those cases from the ambit of section 33 of the 1980 Act where precisely the same claimant and defendant were involved in both actions and the same cause of action was pleaded. Here, where the first action was against the defendant's employers rather than the defendant personally, it did not apply and the court was not prevented from considering exercising its discretion under section 33.

STRIKING OUT (CPR)

[9.80] The CPR, Part 3 states:

> 3.4 (2) The court may strike out a statement of case if it appears to the court—
> (a) that the statement of case discloses no reasonable grounds for bringing or defending the claim;
> (b) that the statement of case is an abuse of the court's process or is otherwise likely to obstruct the just disposal of the proceedings; or
> (c) that there has been a failure to comply with a rule, practice direction or court order.
>
> ...
>
> (5) Paragraph 2 does not limit any other power of the court to strike out a statement of case.

The court's powers to strike out a statement of case are generally exercised in two broad sets of circumstances: (1) where there is something objectionable about the claim (or defence) itself; and (2) where, although the claim itself is not objectionable, it has been pursued in such a manner as to justify striking it out. An example of the former might be where the particulars of claim, even if they are factually accurate, do not disclose a cause of action in law, or disclose a cause of action which is statute-barred. An example of the latter might be where the claimant has thoroughly disregarded court orders, or has so delayed that a fair trial is no longer possible.

CLAIM OR DEFENCE ITSELF ALLEGED TO BE OBJECTIONABLE

[9.81] The court's jurisdiction to strike out the whole or part of a statement of case under rule 3.4 [?] paragraph 2(a) is to be contrasted with the power to give summary judgment (for either party) under Part 24 (see 9.4 above). On a summary judgment application, the court, if able to do so, resolves issues of fact. By contrast an application under CPR rule 3(2)(a) requires the court to assume that the facts in the statements of case are accurate and consider whether, if so, there are reasonable grounds for bringing or defending the claim.

Bridgeman v McAlpine Brown

(19 January 2000, unreported), CA

[9.82] (See paragraph 9.68 above.) The claimant was in her car when another car drove into the back of it. There was no dispute that the driver of the other car was liable. Just before the expiry of the limitation period, the claimant issued proceedings. She was met with the defence that the driver had been the defendant's wife. The defendant applied to strike out the claim and the judge did so. The claimant appealed.

HELD: There was a live issue as to the identity of the driver and the judge was wrong to have sought to determine this issue on an application to strike out. The correct course was to arrange for a hearing, with oral evidence, of the factual dispute.

Farah v British Airways plc

(2000) Times, 26 January, CA

[9.83] The claimants were refused entry to BA's flight to London because the Home Office had advised BA that the claimants' travel documents were invalid. The claimants contended that their documents were valid and that they had suffered loss. They sought damages from BA and the Home Office. The Home Office sought to strike the action out as disclosing no reasonable grounds, since they denied owing the claimants a duty of care. It was accepted by both parties to the application that there was no decided authority on the point.

HELD, per Chadwick LJ: This case raised legal issues which could fairly be regarded as developing as the boundaries in this area became settled by decided cases. The development of the law should be on the basis of decided rather than assumed facts. The court needed a full understanding of the facts and should therefore allow the claim to go to trial.

Manner in which claim pursued

[9.84] Under the RSC and CCR there were numerous authorities as to the circumstances in which a claim should be struck out for want of prosecution or disobedience to court direction. The party seeking to strike out his opponent needed to show either: (i) inordinate and inexcusable delay such as gave rise to a substantial risk that a fair trial was not possible or otherwise prejudiced the party seeking the strike-out; or (ii) intentional or contumelious disregard of the court's orders, or conduct amounting to an abuse of the process of the court (see *Birkett v James* [1978] AC 297, HL). In broad terms this remains the case. However, the CPR have modified the position in certain ways. The court's approach is much broader, having regard to overall principles of justice rather than the detail of pre-CPR authorities. The court now has a range of sanctions short of striking-out and need not necessarily strike out a party's case where it would be more appropriate to apply one of these sanctions instead. On the other hand the court is likely to be less forgiving of delay in progressing actions, particularly delay which took place after the advent of the CPR (and thus could in an appropriate case strike out a claim even if the strict *Birkett v James* criteria were not met). In cases in which the court finds that delay has resulted in a real risk of an unfair trial, however, the position is unchanged – the court will not allow an unfair trail to go ahead. The authorities set out below, where they predate the CPR, have been endorsed in cases decided since the enactment of the CPR.

Arbuthnot Latham Bank Ltd v Trafalgar Holdings Ltd

[1998] 1 WLR 1426, CA

[9.85] (1) In assessing delay and whether it has caused prejudice, the court should under the CPR consider not only prejudice to the parties, but also to other litigants waiting to have their cases heard and to the due administration of civil justice. (2) The practice of 'warehousing' claims, i.e. commencing several actions and only proceeding with some of them, must cease.

Grovit v Doctor

[1997] 1 WLR 640, HL

[9.86] It is an abuse of process to continue litigation with no intention of bringing it to an end.

Biguzzi v Rank Leisure plc

[1999] 1 WLR 1926, CA

[9.87] The claimant was injured at work in November 1993. He served his claim in October 1995. A trial was set for August 1996 but was vacated at the claimant's request. The parties 'ambled' towards trial, but little happened until, in early 1999, the defendant applied to strike out the claim on the grounds of delay. The county court judge declined to do so, holding that a fair trial was still possible and should take place at the earliest opportunity. Old authorities on delay, he held, should not be taken as binding or probably even persuasive; references to old decisions and old rules were a distraction. The defendant appealed.

HELD, per Lord Woolf MR: (1) The judge's approach to pre-CPR authorities was commendable. (2) Under the CPR the keeping of time-limits is more important than formerly. (3) However, the CPR are more flexible than the old rules and authorities: thus the court could in an appropriate case order a party at fault to pay the costs or part of the costs, if necessary on an indemnity basis, or to pay money into court. (4) In this case the judge had been correct to find on the facts that a fair trial was still possible and to make directions to enable this to take place quickly.

Habib Bank Ltd v Jaffer

[2000] CPLR 438, CA

[9.88] In January 1992 the claimant bank sued the defendants on unsatisfied guarantees. After an application for summary judgment and an appeal therefrom the defendants were given leave to defend. They filed defences in September 1993. The defence was that the guarantees were never intended to be enforced. A direction required discovery to take place by the end of January 1994. The bank served a request for further and better particulars of the defence in January 1994. No discovery took place and the request went unanswered. In January 1996 the bank issued a summons for directions but the hearing of the summons was adjourned by consent. Nothing further was done to progress the claim apart from a notice of change of the bank's solicitors in November 1997. The limitation period expired in January 1998 and the defendants immediately applied to strike the claim out. There was evidence that during the period of complete inactivity from January 1994 and November 1997 the bank had repeatedly been advised by its solicitors of the obligation to give full discovery, but had chosen to ignore this advice. The master struck the claim out but his decision was reversed by the judge. The defendants appealed to the Court of Appeal.

HELD, striking the claim out: (1) (Following *Choraria v Sethia* [1998] CLC 625, CA) delay which involves complete, total or wholesale disregard of the rules of court with full awareness of the consequences is capable of amounting to such an abuse that, if it is fair to do so, the claim will be struck out; (2) here the bank had acted in wholesale disregard of the norms of conducting serious litigation; moreover it did so in full awareness of the consequences; (3) the CPR gave the court a welcome flexibility in dealing with applications to strike out (as stated in *Biguzzi v Rank Leisure plc,* see 9.87 above), but an abuse of process remained an abuse of process; although there might be cases of abuse which did not justify striking out, this was not one of them.

Securum Finance Ltd v Ashton

[2001] Ch 291, CA

[9.89] The defendants gave a guarantee of a company's obligations to the bank. They also gave a legal charge to secure their obligations under the guarantee. In August 1989 the claimant bank commenced proceedings on the guarantee. Little happened in those proceedings and they were struck out in December 1997 (see *Arbuthnot Latham Bank Ltd v Trafalgar Holdings Ltd*, 9.85 above). In September 1998 the bank commenced an action to enforce its rights on the charge (the limitation period of 12 years not having yet expired); the bank sought payment under the covenant in the charge and possession of the property charged. The defendants sought to strike out the new proceedings as an abuse of process. The bank relied on the principle (see *Birkett v James*, in 8.85 above) that it was entitled to bring an action at any time within the limitation period and could not be penalised for delay in the earlier proceedings which had taken place before the issue of later proceedings.

HELD: The position under the CPR was different. Because of the need to consider the appropriate allocation of the court's resources (see CPR 1.1(2)(e)), it was no longer the case that a party whose action had been struck out within the limitation period could commence a fresh action with impunity. Rather, where a party had already had one action struck out, there needed to be some special reason before he would be permitted to have a 'second bite of the cherry'. Here, had the second action been for payment alone it would have been struck out since it was in substance the same action as the earlier one which had been struck out and there was no reason to permit a second action. However, since it also included a claim for possession it was not truly a second action and would be permitted to continue.

Collins v CPS Fuels Ltd

[2001] EWCA Civ 1597, [2001] All ER (D) 124 (Oct)

[9.90] HELD per Judge LJ: The words 'some special reason' (see 9.89 above) are not statutory and should not be treated as if they are. They are an attractive form of forensic shorthand for the broad approach to the decision-making process to be made when one action has been struck out and the court is considering whether to permit a second action. Semantic analysis of this or that factor to see whether it is sufficiently 'special' is unhelpful.

Hamblin v Field

[2000] BPIR 621, CA

[9.91] It is of little assistance to the court in considering questions of delay and striking out to have cited to it decisions on the application of the overriding objective to particular circumstances. Excessive citation of authorities bedevilled this area in pre-CPR days and must not be allowed to do so again.

TRIAL

Allocation

Maguire v Molin

[2002] EWCA Civ 1083, [2002] 4 All ER 325

[9.92] A claim originally allocated to the fast track does not automatically have to be re-allocated to the multi track simply because an amendment is made which increases the damages claimed to in excess of £15,000. So long as a claim remains on the fast track a district judge has jurisdiction to hear it.

Adjournments

Fox v Graham Group Ltd

(2001) Times, 3 August

[9.93] The court should be slow to refuse an application to adjourn a trial made by a litigant in person on the grounds of ill-health, provided that it is his first application and his case has some prospect of success.

Rollinson v Kimberley Clark

(1999) Times, 22 June, CA

[9.94] It is not acceptable to instruct an expert shortly before trial without checking availability for the trial date. Application to vacate trial date dismissed.

Matthews v Tarmac Bricks and Tiles Ltd

(1999) 54 BMLR 139, CA

[9.95] This was an application to appeal a decision listing trial date on a day when one medical expert could not attend, but no reasons had been provided to the court as to the reasons for his unavailability. Appeal dismissed. It was essential, if parties wanted cases to be fixed for hearing in accordance with the dates which met their convenience, that those dates should be fixed as early as possible. Doctors who held themselves out as practising in the medico-legal field had to be prepared to arrange their affairs to meet the commitments of the courts where that was practical. If there was no agreement as to the dates which were acceptable to the court, the lawyers for the parties had to be in a position to give the reasons why certain dates were not convenient to the doctors.

SUBMISSION OF NO CASE TO ANSWER

Mullan v Birmingham City Council

(1999) Times, 29 July, QBD

[9.96] The trial judge is entitled to entertain a submission of no case to answer at the close of the claimant's case without requiring the defendant to elect not to call evidence in the event that his submission fails.

Note—Relied on and upheld in *Worsley v Tambrands Ltd* (1999) LTL, 3 December

COSTS (CPR)

[9.97] The best guidance on the area of costs is still to be found in the White Book, CPR 43 to 48. This chapter is not intended to do more than highlight those cases which practitioners may find helpful. For full particulars and detailed analysis the reader is referred to the commentaries in the White Book.

The introduction of the Civil Procedure Rules brought about many changes in this field. The main areas could be summarised:

i. Fast track trial costs recoverable from the paying party limited in all but the most exceptional cases. Claims with a value of up to £3,000 warrant a brief fee for counsel of not more than £350; claims up to £10,000 limit a fee to £500 and claims between £10,000 and £15,000 provide an upper limit of £750 (CPR 46).

ii. In addition, the cost of a solicitor attending a fast track trial is limited to £250.

iii. Following hearings which last for less than a day the general rule is that the judge will conduct a summary assessment of the costs which he has ordered to be paid by one party to another (CPR PD 44 para 13).
iv. The general rule is that the unsuccessful party will pay the successful party's costs but the court has discretion to make a different order (CPR 44.3(2)).
v. The court is expressly directed to consider a number of factors in making a costs order including the parties' conduct, the extent to which either side has succeeded, any attempts at settlement etc (CPR 44.3)

Summary assessment

Macdonald v Taree Holdings Ltd

(2000) Times, 28 December

[9.98] Notwithstanding the requirement that parties serve schedules of costs on each other no less than 24 hours before the hearing, the court should not deprive a successful party of his costs where the only factor against awarding costs was merely a failure to serve a schedule without aggravating factors. The court should take the matter into account but its reaction should be proportionate. The question the court should ask itself was what if any prejudice had there been to the paying party and how should that prejudice be dealt with.

1–800 Flowers Inc v Phonenames Ltd

[2001] EWCA Civ 721, [2001] 2 Costs LR 286

[9.99] In summary assessments the court must focus on the detailed breakdown of costs actually incurred by the party in question as shown in its statement of costs and carry out the assessment by reference to the items appearing in that statement. The court could then go on to consider whether the sum overall fell within the bounds of what was reasonable and proportionate. The jurisdiction to assess costs summarily was not to be used as a vehicle for the introduction of a scale of judicial tariffs for different categories of case.

In the court's discretion

AEI Rediffusion Music Ltd v Phonographic Performance Ltd (No 2)

[1999] 1 WLR 1507, CA

[9.100] Dealing with an appeal from the Copyright Tribunal but referring to the changes brought about by the CPR, Lord Woolf commented that the most significant change of emphasis of the CPR was to require courts to be more ready to make separate orders which reflect the outcome of different issues.

Customs and Excise Com rs v Anchor Foods Ltd

[1999] 3 All ER 268, ChD

[9.101] Notwithstanding rule 44.3 of the Civil Procedure Rules which allowed the court a wide discretion as to costs, once a costs order was made it was not generally open to the court to re-visit it as an appellate court in respect of its own order. Only in the most exceptional circumstances such as those involving fraud or the slip rule, could the court re-visit an order for costs.

Daniels v Walker

[2000] 1 WLR 1382, CA

[9.102] The Court of Appeal allowed an appeal so as to entitle the defendant to adduce its own expert care evidence following receipt of an unfavourable joint expert's report, but it ordered the defendant to pay the costs of the appeal in any event because of the way the defendant's lawyers had conducted themselves in the court below.

Antonelli v Allen

[2000] NLJR 1825

[9.103] Costs factors to be taken into account where a party has succeeded on part of his case include: the reasonableness of the successful party taking the point on which he was unsuccessful; the manner in which the successful party took the point and conducted his case generally; whether it was reasonable for the successful party to have taken the point in the circumstances; the extra costs in terms of preparing for the trial and preparing witness statements, documents and so on; the extra time taken up in court over the particular issue; the extent to which the unsuccessful point was inter-related, in terms of evidence and argument, with the points on which the successful party succeeded; the extent to which it was just in all the circumstances to deprive the successful party of all or any of its costs.

Dunnett v Railtrack plc (in administration)

[2002] EWCA Civ 303, [2002] 1 WLR 2434

[9.104] The claimant, who was for a while representing herself, made attempts to persuade the defendant to agree to alternative dispute resolution. The court also advised ADR. The defendant refused, although it did make small offers of financial compensation which the claimant rejected. At trial the defendant succeeded.

HELD: In making no order as to costs, the parties to litigation are obliged by CPR 1.3 to further the overriding objective. Since the court in exercising its discretion as to costs under CPR Pt 44 is bound to take into account all the circumstances of the case, including the conduct of the parties, any settlement offers made by the successful party may be disregarded in the assessment of costs where it refused to contemplate alternative dispute resolution before the costs started to flow.

Hurst v Leeming

[2002] EWHC 1051 (Ch), [2003] 1 Lloyd's Rep 379

[9.105] On the facts, the defendant barrister who had declined to mediate the claimant's claim against him for professional negligence was not to be deprived of his costs since mediation had no realistic prospect of success.

English v Emery Reimbold & Strick Ltd

[2002] EWCA Civ 605, [2002] 3 All ER 385, [2002] 1 WLR 2409

[9.106] These were three appeals concerning the adequacy of reasons given by judges for their judgments, including those on costs.

HELD: The judge had a duty to give reasons, but a party should not seek to upset a judgment on this ground alone unless he was unable to understand why the judge had reached that decision. If permission was sought on this basis the judge should consider whether his judgment was defective and consider whether to remedy the defect by provision of additional reasons. When permission was sought from the appellate court, it should consider inviting further reasons or explanations from the judge. Where permission was granted, the appellate court should review the judgment in the light of the evidence and submissions in order to determine whether it was apparent why the judge reached his decision.

In particular on costs: a 'percentage' order whereby the judge assesses the percentage of costs to be paid will often produce a fairer result than an 'issues based' order under CPR 44.3(6)(f) which requires the costs judge to assess the extent to which different issues have increased the overall costs incurred.

Lownds v Home Office

[2002] EWCA Civ 365, [2002] 4 All ER 775, [2002] 1 WLR 2450

[9.107] In giving guidelines for the way 'proportionality' should be approached under the CPR when assessing costs, the Court of Appeal stated that this should be decided having regard to what it was reasonable for the party in question to believe might be recovered. Therefore the proportionality of costs recovered by the claimant should be determined having regard to the sum that it was reasonable for him to believe that he might recover at the time he made his claim and the proportionality of the costs incurred by the defendant should be determined having regard to the sum that it was reasonable for him to believe that the claimant might recover, should his claim succeed.

Hall v Rover Financial Services (GB) Ltd

[2002] EWCA Civ 1514, [2002] 45 LS Gaz R 34

[9.108] If the court is to deprive a successful litigant of all of the costs of the proceedings on the basis of misconduct, this misconduct must be in the context of the proceedings and not in ordinary life.

Devine v Franklin

[2002] EWCA Civ 1846

[9.109] Where the claimant exaggerated the extent of injuries he had sustained, with the result that at trial he was awarded less than £1,000, it would generally be reasonable to restrict his claim for costs to that which he would have been awarded had the claim proceeded on the correct track for small claims, namely the fixed costs allowed under CPR 27.14. The court did in any event have discretion to increase any award if the paying party had behaved unreasonably.

Effect of Part 36

Petrotrade Inc v Texaco Ltd

[2002] 1 WLR 947, CA

[9.110] The provisions of Part 36 apply only where judgment has been given at trial (CPR 36.20 and 36.21). Accordingly they do not apply where one party has succeeded in obtaining summary judgment. The court nonetheless has a wide discretion on both interest and costs.

Huck v Robson

[2002] EWCA Civ 398, [2002] 3 All ER 263

[9.111] A Part 36 offer on liability in the ratio 95 to 5 was a genuine offer and there was nothing unjust in permitting the normal rule to have effect. The claimant was therefore awarded costs on the indemnity basis.

McPhilemy v Times Newspapers Ltd (No 2)

[2001] EWCA Civ 933, [2001] 4 All ER 861, [2002] 1 WLR 934

[9.112] The making of an order for costs on the indemnity basis where the claimant has beaten his own Part 36 offer does not carry any implied disapproval of the defendant's conduct, nor any stigma. The making of such an order in a case to which CPR 36.21 applies indicates only that the court, when addressing the task which it is set by that rule, has not considered it unjust to make the order for indemnity costs for which the rule provides.

Indemnity basis

Reid Minty (a firm) v Taylor

[2001] EWCA Civ 1723, [2002] 2 All ER 150, [2002] 1 WLR 2800

[9.113] Where Part 36 did not apply and an application for indemnity costs was made, the court did not have to restrict itself to cases where it wished to indicate its disapproval of the paying party. Indemnity costs could be awarded against a party whose conduct had been unreasonable even though it could not be regarded as lacking moral probity or deserving moral condemnation.

Kiam v MGN Ltd (No 2)

[2002] EWCA Civ 66, [2002] 2 All ER 242, [2002] 1 WLR 2810

[9.114] The simple refusal of a settlement offer would rarely amount to conduct so unreasonable as to warrant an award of costs on the indemnity basis.

Clark v Associated Newspapers Ltd

[1998] 1 WLR 1558, ChD

[9.115] An uncalled for and excessive personal attack on the claimant during cross-examination merited an order of indemnity costs for that portion of the trial.

Baron v Lovell

[2000] PIQR P20, CA

[9.116] If a litigant, or in appropriate cases his insurer, acted unreasonably by not attending or sending a representative with appropriate authority to attend a pre-trial review in breach of a direction of the court, the court could make an order for indemnity costs against him or exercise its power to award interest on damages at a much higher rate than usual.

Brawley v Marczynski

[2002] EWCA Civ 1453, CA

[9.117] The fact that a party was in receipt of public funding and so would not benefit directly was no impediment to the court ordering that the costs payable to that party should be on the indemnity basis.

Conditional fee agreements

[9.118] Any agreement entered into before April 1999 is champertous and no uplift will be awarded.

The language of the Conditional Fee Agreements Regulations 2000 (SI 2000/692) relating to the provision of information in a CFA is mandatory and failure to comply with the relevant client care provisions renders the CFA unenforceable, with the result that the losing party does not have to pay any portion of the successful party's costs. In particular the CFA must state:

i. the particular proceedings or parts of them to which the CFA relates;
ii. the circumstances in which the legal representative's fees are payable;
iii. what payment is due eg on termination of the CFA for any reason;
iv. that the requirements of regulation 4 have been complied with.

Callery v Gray

[2001] EWCA Civ 117, [2001] 3 All ER 833

[9.119] In considering the recoverability of success fees and insurance premiums, the Court of Appeal held (and was subsequently upheld by the House of Lords [2002] UKHL 28, [2002] 1 WLR 2000, which additionally confirmed that such areas were better left to the Court of Appeal) that: (1) It is permissible for a claimant to enter into a CFA and to take out ATE insurance when he first consults his solicitor; (2) In relation to modest and straightforward road traffic claims, the maximum permissible uplift should be 20%; (3) ATE premiums are in principle recoverable as a part of the claimant's costs even though his claim may be resolved quickly and without need for proceedings; (4) Two stage uplift agreements were permissible.

Callery v Gray (No 2)

[2001] EWCA Civ 1246, [2001] 4 All ER 1

[9.120] On a proper construction of the Access to Justice Act 1999, s 29, the words 'insurance against the risk of incurring a [costs] liability' meant 'insurance against the risk of incurring a costs liability that could not be passed on to the opposing party' and, therefore, the cost to a claimant of insuring against the risk of having to pay his own disbursements could be recovered as part of his costs. Accordingly the whole of the ATE insurance premium paid by the claimant could be recovered from the other side as part of the claimant's costs. The court considered that whether a premium was reasonable depended on the relationship between the premium and the risk but that on the facts a premium of £350 was proportionate and reasonable.

Re Claims Direct Test Cases

(19 July 2002, unreported)

[9.121] These were test cases to deal with the situation in which claimants paid money to Claims Direct plc by way of insurance cover in claims they wished to pursue for injuries sustained in a number of ways (road accidents, accidents at work, slipping accidents and so on). They contended that the money spent amounted to premiums which were recoverable in full under the Access to Justice Act 1999, s 29. The defendants contended that the recoverable premium was only that part which related to the risk bearing element.

HELD, by the Senior Costs Judge: The claimants were entitled to recover the reasonable cost of the insurance element but that, properly analysed, the claimants received more for their agreements than insurance alone and the total premium recoverable was around half of that paid by the claimants.

Sarwar v Alam

[2001] EWCA Civ 1401, [2002] 1 WLR 125

[9.122] The claimant sought and obtained ATE insurance to cover a claim against the defendant for injuries sustained in a road accident. No steps were taken to ascertain whether the claimant had the benefit of any BTE insurance cover. The Court of Appeal considered that solicitors needed to take basic steps such as asking the client to bring to a first interview relevant motor policy documentation, household insurance policies and so on, but that if no such cover was available it would be reasonable thereafter to enter into a CFA with ATE cover in accordance with *Callery v Gray* (9.120 above). It would not normally be reasonable to expect a claimant to take advantage of cover provided by the defendant (eg as a passenger in the defendant driver's car covered by the defendant's motor policy) where this would give the defendant's insurers full conduct and control of the claimant's case against the defendant.

Arkin v Borchard Lines Ltd (No 2)

[2001] CP Rep 108

Ashworth v Peterborough United Football Club

(10 June 2002, unreported)

[9.123] The claimant purchased an ATE insurance policy with a premium of some £45,000. The parties eventually settled the claim in the sum of £66,000 plus costs on the standard basis, the defendant having at no stage been informed of the size of the premium the claimant would seek to recover.

HELD, by the costs judge: That the claimant would probably not have found an alternative insurer charging a lower premium, that no collateral benefits were provided for which a charge was made by the insurers and so the entirety of the sum charged was an insurance premium, that there was no obligation on parties to notify the other side of the precise amount of the premium. The premium was allowed in full.

COSTS ORDERS AGAINST NON-PARTIES

[9.124] The following cases illustrate the principles for costs orders against non-parties:
  i. *Symphony Group plc v Hodgson* [1993] 4 All ER 143, CA
  ii. *Secretary of State for Trade and Industry v Backhouse* (2001) 145 Sol Jo LB 53, CA
  iii. *Murphy v Young & Co's Brewery plc* [1997] 1 WLR 1591, CA
  iv. *Pendennis Shipyard Ltd v Ma grathea (Pendennis) Ltd (In liquidation)* [1998] 1 Lloyd's Rep 315
  v. *TGA Chapman Ltd v Christopher* [1998] 1 WLR 12, CA
  vi. *Cormack v Excess Insurance Co Ltd* (2000) Times, 30 March, CA.

WASTED COSTS ORDERS

Ridehalgh v Horsefield

[1994] Ch 205, CA

[9.125] On a true construction of s 51(7) of the Supreme Court Act 1981 the words 'improper, unreasonable or negligent' bore their established meaning; that 'improper' applied to conduct which amounted to any significant breach of a substantial duty imposed by a relevant code of professional conduct and included conduct so regarded by the consensus of professional opinion; that 'unreasonable' described conduct which did not permit of a reasonable explanation; that 'negligent' was to be understood in an untechnical way to denote a failure to act with the competence reasonably to be expected of ordinary members of the profession; that in any event orders should only be made under section 51(6) where and to the extent that the conduct so characterised had been established as directly causative of wasted costs.

Kilroy v Kilroy

[1997] PNLR 66, CA

[9.126] The judge should identify the conduct of the legal representative relating to delay in the conduct of proceedings which is improper, unreasonable or negligent and then make an assessment of the costs actually wasted as a result.

Re Stathams (Wasted Costs Order)

[1997] PIQR P464, CA

[9.127] Where a party is legally aided the solicitor is under a duty under the Civil Legal Aid (General) Regulations 1989 to serve notice of revocation or discharge of legal aid on all other parties, counsel and the court. Failure to do so could in appropriate circumstances amount to unreasonable behaviour and the costs suffered by the other parties as a result should not be borne by the Legal Aid Board.

B EMPLOYMENT TRIBUNAL PRACTICE AND PROCEDURE

INTRODUCTION

[9.128] Employment tribunals are a creature of statute. Their rights and obligations are defined by the Employment Tribunals Act 1996. This Act gives the Secretary of State power by regulation to make such provisions as appear to him to be necessary or expedient with respect to proceedings before them. The current regulations are the Employment Tribunals (Constitution and Rules of Procedure) Regulations 2001.

CHAIRMAN SITTING ALONE OR SITTING WITH ONE LAY MEMBER

Morgan v Brith Gof Cyf

[2001] ICR 978

[9.129] Mr Morgan claimed the respondent had breached his oral contract of employment. The tribunal dismissed his claim. Mr Morgan appealed. One of the grounds of appeal was that the chairman of the tribunal had wrongly decided to hear the case sitting alone in circumstances where a full panel should have heard the claim, as it involved disputes of fact.

HELD: The chairman was entitled to sit alone as the claim was for breach of contract. Numerous claims involve disputes of fact and in such cases there is no requirement for the chairman to convene a panel, especially where this is not requested.

Tsangacos v Amalgamated Chemicals Ltd

[1997] IRLR 4, EAT

[9.130] Mr Tsangacos made a claim for unfair dismissal and discrimination. A month after he made his claim the company went into liquidation and the business was sold to an associated company. Mr Tsangacos attempted to amend his IT1 to include the acquiring company and another respondent.

A tribunal chairman sitting alone heard his application. He concluded that the dismissal was not related to the transfer and therefore not caught by the TUPE regulations. Mr Tsangacos appealed to the EAT on two grounds: did a chairman sitting alone have jurisdiction to determine such matters by himself, and the correctness of the decision.

HELD: A chairman sitting alone is entitled, subject to the exceptions in rule 13(8), to make decisions of every kind. Rule 6 expressly permits a chairman sitting alone to determine jurisdictional points and all other matters in connection with an originating application. The decision in *Mobbs v Nuclear Electric plc* [1996] IRLR 536 was wrong.

His appeal on the substantive point of law was also dismissed.

Sogbetun v London Borough of Hackney

[1998] IRLR 676, EAT

[9.131] Ms Sogbetun was dismissed because of the level of her sickness absence. When she had met her employers, prior to her dismissal, to discuss her absences she explained that her problems had been overcome following a surgical procedure and she wanted to show her employers a letter from her consultant. Her employers refused to allow the letter to be produced and relied upon the evidence of the occupational health adviser.

After the IT1 and IT3 had been lodged the parties were advised that the tribunal had decided to hear the complaint with a tribunal chairman sitting alone. Both parties indicated, in writing, that this was acceptable. No objection was raised during the hearing which included evidence from five witnesses. Ms Sogbetun was unsuccessful and appealed to the EAT. A major part of the appeal related to the chairman's jurisdiction to hear the matter sitting alone.

HELD: The Employment Tribunals Act 1996, s 4, provides the power for a chairman to sit alone. Before a chairman sits alone section 4(5) requires a two stage process: (i) the proceedings must be identified as qualifying proceedings, (ii) a chairman must have exercised his discretion and decided not to hear the case with a full tribunal. No reasonable chairman could have concluded otherwise than that it was desirable for this case to be determined by a full tribunal. If lay members are dispensed with in unfair dismissal cases that is a radical departure from Parliament's intention. Even if it was correct to hear the proceedings by a chairman alone, the proceedings were not qualifying proceedings at the time that the discretion was exercised because the parties had not applied to have the matter heard by a chairman sitting alone. It is not possible to confer authority upon a statutory tribunal either by consent or estoppel.

Ms Sogbetun's appeal was allowed and the matter was referred back to another tribunal.

JURISDICTION: CALCULATING TIME

Unfair dismissal – 'reasonably practical'

[9.132] The Employment Rights Act 1996, s 111 provides:

(1) A complaint may be presented to an industrial tribunal against an employer by any person that he was unfairly dismissed by the employer.

(2) Subject to subsection (3), an industrial tribunal shall not consider a complaint under this section unless it is presented to the tribunal—

(a) before the end of the period of three months beginning with the effective date of termination, or
(b) within such further period as the tribunal considers reasonable in a case where it is satisfied that it was not reasonably practicable for the complaint to be presented before the end of that period of three months.

(3) Where a dismissal is with notice, an industrial tribunal shall consider a complaint under this section if it is presented after the notice is given but before the effective date of termination.

Porter v Bandridge Ltd

[1978] IRLR 271, CA

[9.133] Mr Porter was dismissed May 1976 after being charged with theft from his employer. The criminal trial was heard in March 1977 but no prosecution evidence was offered. In April 1977 Mr Porter submitted his claim of unfair dismissal. A tribunal held that it was not satisfied that it was not reasonably practicable to lodge the claim in time. The EAT dismissed her appeal and she appealed to the Court of Appeal.

HELD: The onus of proving that it was not reasonably practicable to present the complaint within three months was upon the applicant. The applicant has to satisfy the tribunal that he did not know his rights during the whole period of delay and that there was no reason why he should make enquiries or should know of his rights during that period.

London International College v Sen

[1993] IRLR 333, CA

[9.134] Mr Sen was dismissed on 9 July and was aware he had to present a claim for unfair dismissal within three months. However, he did not know when the three month period expired. Mr Sen contacted a solicitor, and was incorrectly informed that he should submit his application by 9 October at the latest. Staff at the tribunal office later confirmed this advice. Consequently, Mr Sen lodged his application at the tribunal on 9 October, one day too late.

In deciding whether it had jurisdiction to hear the claim, the tribunal found that given the erroneous advice Mr Sen received from the tribunal office, it was not reasonably practicable for him to have made his complaint in time. The one day delay was reasonable, and it therefore had jurisdiction. The college appealed to the EAT and then to the Court of Appeal.

HELD: Whether it was reasonably practicable to submit an IT1 within time is a question of fact. A prospective complainant does not lose for all time his right to rely on the 'not reasonably practicable' defence after they consult a solicitor if they then distrust that advice and seek further advice from an organisation such as the tribunal.

It is also a question of fact which advice the applicant relies on, in this case the tribunal was entitled to find Mr Sen relied on the advice from the tribunal officer.

Sir Thomas Bingham also stated, obiter, that if it is the state of mind of the applicant that matters – as it appears to be – it would be strange that an applicant misled by incorrect advice into misapprehending his rights is unable to rely on the escape clause in section 67(2) of the Employment Protection (Consolidation) Act 1978. If the rationale for that is that it would be the adviser and not the employer who should then be liable to compensate the applicant, there would be a distinction between solicitors, who are prima facie liable, and other sources of advice, such as the tribunal, whose liability is far from clear.

However, Sir Thomas Bingham also commented that, but for authority on the point, the submission that it was reasonably practicable for Mr Sen to present his application in time, before he sought any advice, would have been accepted. It was clear the only issue Mr Sen sought advice upon was the date when the three month period expired. Mr Sen was aware he could bring a complaint, that this had a time-limit, and the time-limit was three months. Therefore, it would be difficult to see how inaccurate advice as to the expiry date rendered it not reasonably practicable to present the claim in time.

Machine Tool Industry Research Association v Simpson

[1988] IRLR 212, CA

[9.135] Ms Simpson's claim to the tribunal was three days out of time. She had been made redundant, and only perceived there to have been any unfairness to her dismissal after she heard another employee was re-engaged.

The tribunal held it had not been reasonably practicable for Ms Simpson to present her claim in time, and that it was presented within a reasonable time thereafter. The EAT and the Court of Appeal dismissed the employer's appeal against this decision.

HELD: The Court of Appeal gave guidance on the factual knowledge of an applicant. The tribunal had been entitled to find that during the three month limitation period there were crucial/important facts unknown, or reasonably unknown, to the applicant which then became known and led her to hold a genuine belief that she had a claim.

In determining whether it was reasonably practicable for the employee to present his claim in time, the subjective state of mind of the employee when she decides that there is a claim to be brought must be examined. To be allowed to present a claim out of time, it is not necessary for the employee to establish the veracity of the fact that led her to make the claim.

The expression 'reasonably practicable' imports three stages, the burden of proof of which rests upon the applicant. Firstly, it was reasonable for applicant not to be aware of the factual basis upon which she could bring an application to the tribunal during the three month period. Secondly, the applicant must establish the knowledge she has was reasonably gained and is either crucial, fundamental or important to her change in belief: 'an objective qualification of reasonableness, in the circumstances, to a subjective test of the applicant's state of mind'. Finally, acquisition of this knowledge must be crucial to the decision to bring a claim in any event.

Hammond v Haigh Castle & Co Ltd

[1973] 2 All ER 289, NIRC

[9.136] Mr Hammond claimed he had been unfairly dismissed. He was informed by his trade association that a claim for unfair dismissal must be posted the tribunal 'to arrive before the end of August'. However, this would have meant his claim was received out of time. He followed the advice and his claim was received late. A tribunal ruled that it did not have jurisdiction to hear his complaint.

HELD: The time period had expired, and it was reasonably practicable for Mr Hammond to have submitted his application in time. A claim is only presented to the tribunal when it is received by the tribunal, whether or not it is immediately dealt with upon receipt. A claim delivered by post on a Saturday is presented that day, even if it is not registered as received until the Monday. However, a claim is not presented by the act of posting it addressed to the tribunal.

Biggs v Somerset County Council

[1996] IRLR 203, CA

[9.137] Mrs Biggs was a part-time teacher who worked 14 hours a week, and under the legislation at the time lacked the relevant qualifying service because she did not work sufficient hours each week. She was dismissed in 1976 but did not bring her claim for unfair dismissal until 1994 when the House of Lords held that the need to work more than a certain number of hours discriminated against women. Her claim was brought within three months of that decision. Her claim was dismissed by a tribunal as was her appeal and she appealed to the Court of Appeal.

HELD: It was reasonably practicable for the claim to be lodged in time. Mrs Biggs was mistaken as to her rights, this was a mistake of law as opposed to fact. The House of Lords decision was declaratory of what the law had always been. The words reasonably practical are directed to difficulties faced by an individual applicant such as illness or some other temporary impediment.

Just and equitable to extend the time-limit

Hutchinson v Westward Television Ltd

[1977] IRLR 69, EAT

[9.138] In this case Mrs Hutchinson decided not to bring a claim of sex discrimination after she formed a belief she would not succeed. It was only on reading a newspaper article about another case that she thought she might succeed. Therefore, Mrs Hutchinson submitted her application to the tribunal approximately 10 days late.

Both the tribunal and the EAT held it was not just and equitable to allow Hutchinson's claim, submitted out of time, to go forward.

HELD, in the EAT: The tribunal has a very wide discretion to do what it considers just and equitable in the circumstances with regard to extension of the time-limit for submitting a claim. Because this discretion is so wide appealing against a negative decision of the tribunal is a heavy task. In this case, the applicant was intelligent, well educated and a trade union member. She did not consult the union's legal advisers, and essentially she made a conscious decision not to pursue a claim.

British Coal Corpcxn v Keeble

[1997] IRLR 336, EAT

[9.139] Mrs Keeble was made redundant in 1989. The corporation's voluntary redundancy scheme was based upon a retirement age of 65 for men and 60 for women. Abatement provisions applied to women under 55 and men under 60.

Her application was made to a tribunal in July 1991, 22 months after her dismissal, following the decision of the ECJ in *Barber* in 1990. The claim was brought under the Sex Discrimination Act 1975. A tribunal decided that it was just and equitable to extend the time for lodging the complaint. British Coal appealed. The EAT referred the matter back to the tribunal. The tribunal took into account the decision of the Court of Appeal in *Biggs v Somerset County Council* (see 9.137 above), which had held, on the issue of whether it was reasonably practicable for a part-time worker to bring an unfair dismissal complaint within three months of dismissal, that part-time workers could not pursue such claims out of time. because it had been reasonably practicable to do so. The tribunal distinguished *Biggs* and considered that the issue was, whether in the light of the Limitation Act 1980, s 33 it was 'just and equitable' to hear the complaint out of time, and ruled that it was. British Coal appealed.

HELD: The decision in *Biggs* was not intended to apply to all limitation periods. The discretion tribunals have to permit a discrimination claim lodged out of time is much wider than the discretion to permit unfair dismissal claims to proceed. If *Biggs* was right, it would not be possible to take all the circumstances of the case into account. The decision in *Biggs* applied only to unfair dismissal cases.

Since the tribunal had not misdirected itself the appeal was dismissed.

'Reasonably practicable' – effect of criminal proceedings

Palmer and Saunders v Southend-on-Sea Borough Council

[1984] IRLR 119, CA

[9.140] Mr Saunders and Mr Palmer had been employed by the council for 25 years when they were charged with theft. The council suspended them on half pay, informing them that if they were convicted they would be dismissed but that if they were acquitted they would be reimbursed their lost pay. They were told that their employment had been terminated forthwith and of their right to appeal. They appealed unsuccessfully against the decision to dismiss. They were told that if they appealed the Crown Court's decision the council would reconsider the matter. The Court of Appeal quashed their convictions in December 1982 and in March 1983 they sought reinstatement. This was refused and they lodged claims for unfair dismissal in April 1982.

A tribunal dismissed their claims on the ground that they had been presented out of time. In the tribunal's view since they were sure of their innocence they should have presented the tribunal claims much earlier, within three months of dismissal. The EAT dismissed their appeals and they appealed to the Court of Appeal.

HELD: The claims had been presented out of time. To construe the words reasonably practicable as equivalent to reasonable is to adopt a view too favourable to the employee. Reasonably practicable means more than what is reasonably capable of being done. Each decision depends largely on its own facts. It might be relevant for a tribunal to enquire what an individual knew about his rights, whether the individual was being advised at the time and whether there has been any substantial fault on the part of the employee and his adviser. The tribunal had not misdirected itself and the appeal was dismissed.

Dedman v British Building and Engineering Appliances Ltd

[1973] IRLR 379, CA

[9.141] Mr Dedman was dismissed without notice and paid in lieu of notice to the end of the month. He consulted solicitors who did not advise him of the time-limit within which to lodge a complaint for unfair dismissal. A tribunal found that his complaint was within time because he had been paid to the end of the month and taking that extra period into account his claim was in time. The company appealed and it was held that his complaint was out of time. Mr Dedman appealed to the Court of Appeal.

HELD: Despite the fact that he had received a cheque paying him to the end of the month, the effective date of termination was the date upon which he received his letter of dismissal. His complaint had been presented out of time. Ignorance of his rights does not mean that it was not practicable to lodge the claim. Unless a specific and acceptable explanation can be shown for not acting within time the claim will be time-barred.

Effect of tribunal being closed on the last day to lodge IT1

Swainston v Hetton Victory Club Ltd

[1983] 1 All ER 1179, [1983] IRLR 164, CA

[9.142] Mr Swainston was dismissed. The last day to lodge his claim was Sunday 6 December. The tribunal office was closed at weekends but there was a letterbox. The complaint was not presented until the Monday. It was argued at the tribunal that the claim was out of time. The tribunal held that since the limitation period expired at the weekend it was extended to the following day. The employer appealed. The EAT held that the claim was presented out of time. Mr Swainston appealed to the Court of Appeal.

HELD: Since it was possible to lodge the claim in time, by posting it through the tribunal office's letterbox at the weekend the claim was out of time.

Ford v Stakis Hotels and Inns Ltd

[1988] IRLR 46, EAT

[9.143] Mr Ford was dismissed. His last day to lodge a complaint of unfair dismissal was 27 May 1985, a bank holiday. The tribunal's office had no post box, but his solicitor was in the habit of slipping documents under the door, although on this occasion had not done so and the claim was delivered the day after the bank holiday. Given the solicitor's evidence the tribunal found that it had been possible to deliver the document in time and dismissed the complaint. Mr Ford appealed to the EAT.

HELD: The tribunal had been wrong to dismiss the complaint. Even if the solicitor had been in the habit of delivering documents by pushing them under the door there was no evidence that the tribunal approved of such a practice. As a result there was no proper means for delivering documents when the tribunal office was closed. This meant that the time for lodging the claim was extended to the first day that the tribunal was open.

Lodging claim forms by post

Consignia plc v Sealy

[2002] EWCA Civ 878, [2002] IRLR 624

[9.144] Mr Sealy was a postman. He was summarily dismissed on 9 July 2000. The last day to lodge his claim was 8 October 2000. He posted his application to the tribunal on 6 October and it was received on 10 October, two days late. A tribunal found, in its summary reasons it was not reasonably practicable to lodge the claim in time because if it had arrived in the ordinary course of the post it would have arrived either on the Saturday, in time or on the Monday, which was the first day after the period had expired. In their extended reasons they held he had a reasonable expectation that the claim would arrive on the Saturday. Not to permit the claim to be heard would be to allow a procedural reason to deny the hearing of a substantive claim.

The EAT dismissed the employer's appeal and they appealed to the Court of Appeal.

HELD: The tribunal, in its summary reasons, had found that the claim would have arrived either on the Saturday or the Monday. There was no evidence to support the alleged expectation that it would have arrived on the Saturday. The time-limit expired on the Sunday. When lodging a compliant it is permissible to rely upon the ordinary course of post.

Complaints are presented to tribunals when they are received by them. If it is not possible to deliver documents at weekends because the tribunal's offices are locked it will be possible to argue that it was not reasonably practicable to present the complaint in time. If a complaint is sent by post it will be assumed to have been effected at the time when it would have arrived in the ordinary course of post. If sent by first class post this will mean the second day after it was posted. If a form is date stamped Monday and the limitation period expired over the weekend it will be possible for a tribunal to find that it was posted on the Thursday and that it arrived on the Saturday, or to extend the limitation period.

Limitation period where none specified by statute

Greenwich Health Authority v Skinner and Ward

[1989] IRLR 238, EAT

[9.145] Mrs Skinner and Mrs Ward were employed under the Whitley Council Agreement. As employees of the health authority they were excluded from the right to receive statutory redundancy payments but were entitled to equivalent payments under the Whitley Council Agreement. Claims for such a payment were to be made within six months. Mrs Skinner and Mrs Ward complained to a tribunal after six months seeking an 'equivalent payment'. There is no time within which such complaints must be presented set out in the statute. However, Greenwich argued that the time-limit should be six months in accordance with the time-limits for redundancy payments. The tribunal dismissed this argument and found in favour of Mrs Skinner and Mrs Ward. Greenwich appealed.

HELD: Since there was no time-limit specified in the Act for bringing complaints about a contractual redundancy payment before a tribunal the normal, six year, limitation period would be applied.

Amending the grounds of claim after they have been lodged with the tribunal

Selkent Bus Co Ltd (t/a Stagecoach Selkent) v Moore

[1996] IRLR 661, EAT

[9.146] In his originating application Mr Moore claimed unfair dismissal but did not mention that dismissal may have been for a reason connected with his trade union membership. Mr Moore then sought to amend the application to state dismissal was by reason of his involvement in trade union activities. Leave was given to Mr Moore to amend the application, against which Selkent appealed.

HELD: The EAT allowed Selkent's appeal. In giving judgment the EAT outlined what the tribunal should consider when deciding whether to grant leave to amend.

The tribunal should take into account all the circumstances and balance the injustice and hardship of allowing the amendment against the injustice and hardship of refusing it. Relevant circumstances include:
  (i) the nature of the amendment, ie whether it merely adds factual details to existing allegations, or on the other hand makes entirely new factual allegations which change the basis of the existing claim;

(ii) the applicability of statutory time-limits. If a new complaint or cause of action is proposed by the amendment, the tribunal should consider whether that complaint is out of time; and

(iii) the timing and manner of the application. An application should not be refused solely because of a delay in making it. There are no time-limits laid down for the making of amendments. However, it is relevant to consider why the application was not made earlier and why it is now being made.

In this case, the requested amendment pleaded facts not previously pleaded, in support of a new case. Fresh primary facts would need to be established. No explanation was given as to why these were not included in the original application. Finally, refusal of leave to amend would cause no hardship, as Moore could still claim unfair dismissal. Indeed, because of the nature of the new allegation, if the amendment was made further costs were likely to have been incurred.

Housing Corpn v Bryant

[1999] ICR 123, CA

[9.147] Mrs Bryant pleaded her grounds of complaint as unfair dismissal, sex discrimination and unlawful deductions from wages. A preliminary hearing was held to determine whether the complaint of sex discrimination, presented outside the three month time-limit, should go forward.

The tribunal held it was not just and equitable to extend the time-limit. Following this, Mrs Bryant's representative wrote to the tribunal requesting amendment to the original application to include a claim of victimisation, allegedly arising by way of the same facts already pleaded. The tribunal dismissed this application because the case as pleaded revealed no grounds for such a claim and it would not be just or equitable to extend the time-limit. Mrs Bryant appealed successfully to the EAT and the company appealed.

HELD: If there had been a claim of victimisation set out in the IT1, there would have been no need for amendment. It is not enough to say the document reveals some grounds for a claim of victimisation, or indicates there is a question as to the linkage between the alleged discrimination and the dismissal. Such a linkage must be demonstrated in the document itself.

The jurisdiction to hear breach of contract claims

Capek v Lincolnshire County Council

[2000] IRLR 590, CA

[9.148] Mr Clark was subjected to disciplinary proceedings in October 1994 and dismissed on 2 January 1995. He appealed and although his dismissal was upheld the effective date was changed to 7 July 1995, the date of the appeal decision. Mr Capek had presented a complaint to the tribunal in November 1994 alleging breach of contract, including a failure to pay salary during his period of suspension and arrears of pay due to a failure to conduct a proper review exercise.

A tribunal found that it did not have jurisdiction to determine the breach of contract complaint because it was brought before the effective date of termination. He appealed to the EAT who allowed his appeal because the causes of action were outstanding at the date of termination. Both parties appealed to the Court of Appeal. The council sought to restore the tribunal's decision and Mr Clark appealed on the ground that the tribunal had not considered his claim as a one for unauthorised deductions from wages.

HELD: The tribunal's jurisdiction to hear claims in respect of breach of contract are determined by the (Employment) Tribunals Extension of Jurisdiction (England and Wales) Order 1994. The tribunal's jurisdiction to hear matters in relation to breach of contract only arises upon the effective date of termination, such claims must be brought within three months of that date. His appeal on the breach of contract point failed. However, the Court of Appeal referred the matter back to a tribunal to determine whether there had been unauthorised deductions.

PRELIMINARY ISSUES

(Employment Tribunals (Constitution and Rules of Procedure) Regulations 2001)

Wellcome Foundation v Darby

[1996] IRLR 538, EAT

[9.149] Mrs Darby brought claims for equal pay and sex discrimination. However, she asked for the case to be adjourned until judgment was delivered by the ECJ in a different but relevant case. After the decision of the ECJ was made, a chairman ordered a preliminary hearing on whether on the basis of this case her claim of sex discrimination was without foundation. At the preliminary hearing the tribunal decided the complaint of sex discrimination should proceed to a full merits hearing. The Wellcome Foundation appealed against the tribunal's failure to dismiss her claim since in the light of the ECJ's judgment it was bound to fail.

HELD: Whether or not the effect of a decision in another case is that the complaint fails, is a substantive issue which can only be decided after hearing all the evidence. It is not a matter for a preliminary hearing. The question for the tribunal in deciding whether to hold a preliminary hearing or not must always be, 'is this a self-contained issue and is its resolution capable of being determinative of the whole case'?

Obiter, when parties request a preliminary hearing with the intention of shortening proceedings, parties and the tribunal should first consider whether the issue is one that should be taken in advance of a full hearing, and whether its resolution in one party's favour will dispose of the whole case.

Smith v Gardner Merchant Ltd

[1998] IRLR 510, CA

[9.150] Mr Smith brought a claim of sex discrimination against Gardner Merchant. The tribunal identified as a preliminary point of law the issue of whether or not a claim of discrimination on grounds of sexual orientation was within the tribunal's jurisdiction under the Sex Discrimination Act and held a preliminary hearing at which it dismissed the claim. The EAT dismissed Mr Smith's appeal. He appealed.

HELD: The appeal would be allowed. Per Ward LJ: he would discourage tribunals from trying to identify preliminary points of law in cases in which the facts are in dispute, and when it is far from clear what facts will ultimately be found by the tribunal and what facts should be assumed to be necessary to form the basis of the proposed point of law.

The need to sit in public

Storer v British Gas plc

[2000] IRLR 495, CA

[9.151] Mr Storer accepted an offer of voluntary redundancy, and then lodged a complaint that he had been constructively and unfairly dismissed. The complaint was submitted outside the three month limitation period, and a preliminary hearing was arranged to decide whether time should be extended. As no tribunal room was available this hearing was held in the regional chairman's office. This office was behind a locked door, in what was described as a 'secure area' protected by a push button coded lock and was also marked 'private'. The chairman found it was reasonably practicable for Mr Storer to have submitted his claim in time.

Mr Storer appealed, raising the point that his case had not been heard in public, per rule 8(2) of the Employment Tribunal Rules of Procedure. The EAT dismissed his appeal. Mr Storer appealed to the Court of Appeal.

HELD: Whether a court is sitting in public may be, in any individual case, a question of fact and degree for the judge, a matter of discretion. However, it would be a wrong exercise of that discretion not to take proper account of the need for that rule. In this case, the locked door was a physical barrier to prevent all access to the public. There was no chance of a member of the public dropping in to see how the tribunal was conducted. The fact that no one attempted to sit in on the hearing does not show that this tribunal was conducting the hearing in public. In this case the tribunal was sitting in private, but did not have the jurisdiction to sit in private. Accordingly, the decision of the tribunal was quashed and the matter remitted for rehearing.

Adjournments

Bastick v James Lane (Turf Accountants) Ltd

[1979] ICR 778, EAT

[9.152] Mr Bastick was employed as a manager, and claimed unfair dismissal after he was dismissed for allegedly defrauding the company. The tribunal refused Mr Bastick's application for the tribunal hearing to be adjourned until after his criminal trial because he did not want to give evidence that might be prejudicial to that trial. Mr Bastick appealed.

HELD: The chairman had considered all relevant matters, there was no matter that had been improperly taken into consideration and the decision of the chairman could not be said to be perverse. In such circumstances there was no ground to interfere with the chairman's decision.

PROCEDURE AT THE HEARING

[9.153] Rule 11 of Schedule 1 of the Employment Tribunals (Constitution Rules of Procedure) Regs 2001 provides:

> The tribunal shall, so far as it appears to it appropriate, seek to avoid formality in its proceedings and shall not be bound by any enactment or rule of law relating to the admissibility of evidence in proceedings before the courts of law. The tribunal shall make such enquiries of persons appearing before it and witnesses as it considers appropriate and shall otherwise conduct the hearing in such manner as it considers most appropriate for the clarification of the issues before it and generally to the just handling of the proceedings.
>
> (2) Subject to paragraph (1), at the hearing of the originating application a party shall be entitled to give evidence, to call witnesses, to question any witnesses and to address the tribunal.
>
> (3) If a party fails to attend or to be represented at the time and place fixed for the hearing, the tribunal may, if that party is an applicant, dismiss or, in any case, dispose of the application in the absence of that party or may adjourn the hearing to a later date; provided that before dismissing or disposing of any application in the absence of a party the tribunal shall consider his originating application or notice of appearance, any representations in writing presented by him in pursuance of rule 10(5) and any written answer furnished to the tribunal pursuant to rule 4(3).
>
> (4) A tribunal may require any witness to give evidence on oath or affirmation and for that purpose there may be administered an oath or affirmation in due form.

Tribunals must exercise their discretion judicially

Aberdeen Steak Houses Group plc v Ibrahim

[1988] IRLR 420, EAT

[9.154] The employer appealed against a decision of a tribunal that it had dismissed the employee unfairly. During the tribunal hearing, the applicant's counsel had been allowed to recall the applicant after giving his evidence. This was part of the applicant's strategy in the case. However, the employer's counsel was not permitted to recall one of its witnesses to re-examine them on the same point. The employers argued that such treatment was prejudicial to their case.

HELD: The tribunal should not have allowed the applicant's counsel to re-call the applicant as a witness. The applicant's counsel chose, as a matter of tactics, to leave a question of evidence until the applicant was recalled which could have been dealt with in cross-examination of the respondent's witnesses.

Although the tribunal has ultimate case management discretion during a hearing, that discretion must be used judicially. Whilst tribunals are informal, that informality must not go too far and the tribunal must be aware of tactics used to present evidence.

The need to investigate pleaded claims

Mensah v East Hertfordshire NHS Trust

[1998] IRLR 531, CA

[9.155] Mrs Mensah brought a complaint of race discrimination again the NHS Trust for failing to consider her applications for positions in the maternity and the neonatal units at one of the its hospitals. The tribunal dismissed her claim. In its extended reasons the tribunal dealt solely with the issue of discrimination with regard to vacancies within the maternity unit. Mrs Mensah appealed on the basis that the tribunal had failed to consider allegations of discrimination with regard to the vacancies in the neonatal ward.

The EAT allowed the appeal and the respondent appealed.

HELD: The tribunal had not erred in failing to consider the allegations of racial discrimination with regard to the neonatal unit vacancies. Although the allegation was raised in her application, the applicant did not pursue it as part of her case in the tribunal. The tribunal is not under a duty to ensure that every issue referred to in the IT1 is dealt with and the EAT had erred in holding there to be a duty.

Whilst it is good practice for the tribunal to clarify with the applicants (especially if they are unrepresented) the precise matters in the IT1 they are pursuing, it is for the tribunal to decide if, in the circumstances, it should investigate any pleaded complaint which it is for the applicant to prove but which she is not setting out to prove.

The applicant in this case had been given every opportunity to pursue her allegations but chose not to do so, therefore it could not be said she was not given the opportunity to plead her case.

The power of a tribunal to limit cross examination

Zurich Insurance Co v Gulson

[1998] IRLR 118, EAT

[9.156] During the applicant's maternity leave, the respondents changed its working patterns. The applicant informed the respondent that she could not meet these new requirements when she returned to work. Following her return she was told she would have to comply with the new working arrangements and after unsuccessful negotiations she was dismissed. She argued that she had been discriminated against, both directly and indirectly. The employer argued that she could comply because she and her husband could afford a full time nanny.

The applicant and her husband gave evidence about their income and monthly expenditure and argued that they could not afford a nanny. The applicant was elaborately cross-examined by the respondent's counsel, however, the tribunal ruled that the applicant had been questioned about this enough and it was not necessary for the tribunal to consider financial evidence in a manner similar to a divorce court.

The employer's appealed against the decision to limit cross-examination.

HELD: The tribunal has discretion over the conduct of the proceedings and has a duty to keep enquiry within its proper bounds. A party does not have an absolute right to cross-examine and there is no sense in allowing a lengthy and detailed cross-examination which will not assist the tribunal. In the present case, the tribunal had identified the issue and there was no need to allow the examination further. The tribunal had not wrongly exercised its discretion.

The status of a tribunal chairman's notes of evidence

Houston v Lightwater Farms Ltd; Walker v Lakhdari (t/a Mayfair Newsagency)

[1990] IRLR 469, EAT

[9.157] In both cases the tribunal chairmen involved were requested by the registrar of the EAT to disclose their notes of evidence. Both chairmen refused. The tribunal chairmen argued that their notes were produced as an aide-memoire and were not intended to be an accurate note of the proceedings. Both employees appealed.

HELD: The chairmen had erred in refusing to comply with the registrar's request for the notes of evidence. In a tribunal, the chairman acts in a judicial capacity and the notes produced are not merely an aide-memoire but are tools to assist the appeal courts. In requesting the notes of evidence the EAT has to balanced the burden of the chairman in providing the notes and the reason put forward by the parties for needing the notes. An order was made to disclose the notes.

The use of written submissions

Barking and Dagenham London Borough v Oguoko

[2000] IRLR 179, EAT

[9.158] Mr Oguoko brought claims for racial discrimination and victimisation against the respondents. During the tribunal it was agreed that both parties would submit written submissions. The parties duly did but the tribunal did not copy the submissions to the other party. The tribunal met in chambers and upheld the claim of race discrimination but dismissed the victimisation claim.

The employers appealed on the basis that the decision had been reached without it being able to see the other side's submissions. The tribunal wrote to both parties and asked if the extended reasons would have been changed if either party had had a chance to see each other's submissions. After considering these issues, the tribunal decided that its decision would not have been changed, therefore the application for review was refused.

The employers appealed against the decision of the tribunal and also, that the failure to serve copies of the submissions and give them an opportunity to comment before the tribunal met to consider its decision, amounted to a breach of the rules of natural justice.

HELD: The EAT dismissed the appeal. The EAT gave some guidance on asking for written submissions as follows:

Whilst written submissions may be requested by the tribunal it has to be with the consent of the parties and once the consent is given it is the responsibility of the chairman to ensure that the procedure is implemented in accordance with the rules of natural justice.

This means that the tribunal should cross-serve the submissions on both parties and ask for any comments they have to be forwarded within 14 days.

The parties should be warned that if they do not give their comments that the tribunal would proceed and reach its finding.

The failure of the tribunal to serve the submissions on the other party was a breach of the rules of natural justice. However, any breach of the rules of natural justice were remedied when the tribunal sought comments from both parties. The tribunal had conducted their procedures overall in a fair way and the appeal would be dismissed.

Masiak v City Restaurants (UK) Ltd

[1999] IRLR 780, EAT

[9.159] Mr Masiak was employed as a chef. He walked out after a month because he refused to cook food that he regarded as a potential hazard to public health and then lodged complaints with a tribunal alleging breach of contract and unfair dismissal. A tribunal dismissed his claim because s 100(1)(e) of the Employment Rights Act 1996 relates to other employees and not to members of the public at large. It rejected his claim for breach of contract because his length of service was insufficient to qualify for statutory minimum notice. He appealed to the EAT.

HELD: The tribunal had misdirected itself on the contract claim. Every employee at common law is entitled to a reasonable period of notice. A tribunal has jurisdiction to determine claims for breach of contract by virtue of the Employment Tribunals Act 1996, s 3(2).

The EAT also concluded that section 100(1)(e) was wide enough to include members of the public and did not just relate to other employees.

The appeal was allowed and the matter remitted to a new tribunal.

Further particulars

Byrne v Financial Times Ltd

[1991] IRLR 417, EAT

[9.160] The applicants brought an equal pay claim, claiming to have been employed on like work or work of equal value to various different comparators. The employer argued that there were a number of different material factors accounting for the differences in pay, and gave voluntary disclosure of the salary history of the comparators.

The applicants sought as further particulars a detailed breakdown of the difference in salary and an allocation of a specific sum or a specific fraction of that difference to a particular fact in the work record or history of each comparator. The application was refused by a tribunal chairman and the applicants appealed.

HELD: Where there was an obvious relationship between a factor and an amount, for example, a merit award, this could be pleaded. However, in realistic industrial situations it was impossible to attribute a particular weight to a particular factor when fixing a wage. The situation would quite often occur where it is impossible to attribute a particular percentage or amount to a specific part of the variation. The employment tribunal chairman's decision not to order the further particulars would be upheld.

Per Wood J:

> General principles affecting the ordering of further and better particulars include that parties should not be taken by surprise at the last minute; that particulars should only be ordered when necessary in order to do justice in the case or to prevent adjournment; that the order should not be oppressive; that particulars are for the purposes of identifying the issues, not for the production of the evidence; and that complicated pleadings battles should not be encouraged.

The appeal was dismissed.

Directions

Martins v Marks & Spencer plc

[1998] IRLR 326, CA

[9.161] Ms Martins brought proceedings for racial discrimination against Marks & Spencer after she had applied four times for a post as a trainee manager. Her complaint was upheld by a tribunal but the company appealed successfully to the EAT and Ms Martins appealed to the Court of Appeal.

HELD: Her appeal was unsuccessful. The Court of Appeal commented on good tribunal practice when dealing with race discrimination claims. Obiter:

> Good case management is 'critical to a fair, orderly just and efficient hearing'. 'In most cases of race discrimination, it would be good practice to hold a meeting for preliminary directions, so as to ensure, as far as possible, that the

parties and the tribunal identify the issues before the hearing of the case begins. The chairman can consider making directions, such as agreement on the issues falling for determination at the hearing and, if appropriate, the exchange of witness statements in advance of the hearing. It would also be important to obtain from the parties at that stage a reliable estimate of the likely length of the hearing. The parties should be asked to justify that estimate by reference to the number of documents which the tribunal is likely to be asked to examine and the number of witnesses likely to be called to give evidence on relevant issues.

Disclosure of documents

Knight v Department of Social Security

[2002] IRLR 249, EAT

[9.162] The applicant brought a disability discrimination claim, claiming to have been discriminated against in his application for a particular position. To support his case, the applicant sought disclosure of test papers which he and others had completed as part of the process of applying for the job. He also sought disclosure of the model answers to the test.

The respondent agreed to disclose the model answers to the applicant's solicitors, on condition that (1) no copies of the model answers were made and (2) that the model answers were not shown to anyone other than the applicant, and then only in the presence of a member of the applicant's solicitors' firm. They contended that if the test questions and answers were to enter the public domain, a new test would have to be set at a cost of between £150,000 to £200,000.

HELD: Confidentiality was not in itself a basis for refusing disclosure of otherwise relevant information. The requested documents were relevant to the case, and disclosure would be ordered. However, the disclosure order would be based on that contained in rule 31.22 of the CPR restricting or prohibiting the use of a document which has been disclosed in legal proceedings.

Science Research Council v Nassé; Leyland Cars v Vyas

[1980] AC 1028, [1979] IRLR 465, HL

[9.163] Applicants in a sex discrimination claim and a race discrimination claim requested disclosure of confidential employment records relating to their comparators. Disclosure was ordered by the Court of Appeal and the employers appealed to the House of Lords.

HELD: There is no presumption against disclosure of confidential documents. The ultimate test is whether disclosure is necessary for disposing fairly of the proceedings. If it is, then disclosure must be ordered notwithstanding confidentiality.

Where there is a need to preserve confidentiality in a particular case, then the tribuna should consider whether the necessary information can be obtained by other means, not involving a breach of confidence.

In order to reach a conclusion on whether disclosure is necessary notwithstanding confidentiality, the tribunal should inspect the documents, and should also consider whether justice can be done by special measures such as 'covering up', substituting anonymous references for specific names, or, in rare cases, a hearing in private.

Asda Stores Ltd v Thompson

[2002] IRLR 245, EAT

[9.164] The applicants were dismissed following a formal investigation into allegations that they had been involved in the use and supply of drugs at a work party and a training event.

In the course of their unfair dismissal claim, the applicants asked for disclosure of witness statements which had been relied upon by the employer in its disciplinary proceedings against them.

The employer refused to disclose the witness statements, arguing that (1) the witness statements had been taken from the witnesses under a promise that they would be kept confidential, (2) the reason for the promise of confidentiality was a fear of reprisals against the makers of the statements, and (3) the disclosure of the statements, and in particular of the identities of the makers of the statements, was not necessary for a fair hearing of the case.

HELD: It was not necessary for the fair and proper conduct of the proceedings for the applicants to know the identities of those who made the allegations against them. The tribunal should direct disclosure of documents in an anonymised or edited form, so that the makers of the statements could not be identified. If this meant that some of the statements had to be entirely excluded because it was not possible to conceal the identity of the makers of the statement, then that is what would have to occur, and the case would have to be judged on that basis.

West Midlands Passenger Transport Executive v Singh

[1988] IRLR 186, CA

[9.165] The applicant alleged that his failure to obtain promotion was caused by race discrimination. In support of his claim, he sought disclosure from his employer of the details of the ethnic origins of applicants and appointees to positions broadly comparable to the one for which he had unsuccessfully applied.

HELD: The details he required were relevant to his case, and disclosure would be ordered.

Witness orders

Clapson v British Airways plc

[2001] IRLR 184, EAT

[9.166] Rule 4(5)(a) of the Employment Tribunals Rules of Procedure provides that:

A tribunal may, on the application of a party or of its own motion, require the attendance of any person in Great Britain, including a party, either to give evidence or to produce documents or both and may appoint the time and place at which the person is to attend, and, if so required, to produce any document ...

During the course of an employment tribunal hearing, the applicant's counsel, having previously indicated that she intended to call the applicant as a witness, and having questioned the respondent's witnesses on this basis, then announced that she did not intend to call the applicant as a witness. The respondent invited the tribunal (of its own motion) to order the applicant to attend and give evidence. The tribunal made the order requested. The respondent did not want to apply for a formal witness order itself, since it feared that if it were to be treated as calling the applicant as a witness it would not be allowed to cross-examine him.

HELD: The tribunal had an unrestricted power to call a witness of its own motion. Tribunals should be cautious before exercising that power. Although the EAT had reservations about the order which the tribunal had made, it could not say that the tribunal's decision to make the order was so wrong that it should be overturned on appeal.

Dada v Metal Box Co Ltd

[1974] IRLR 251, NIRC

[9.167] The applicant requested five witness orders. The tribunal refused to grant the orders, on the basis that, amongst other things, the applicant had not shown that the witnesses were unwilling to attend voluntarily.

HELD: The tribunal was wrong to reject the application for witness orders on the basis that applicant had not shown that the witnesses were unwilling to attend voluntarily.

The only two matters of which the tribunal should be satisfied before making witness orders were: whether the witness could give relevant evidence, and that it was necessary to issue a witness order.

In making an application for a witness order, a party should indicate the subject matter of the evidence that the witness could give, and the relevance of it. A party should invite a witness to attend before making an application for a witness order. If the witness agrees to attend, and the party is satisfied that the witness will attend, then it is not necessary to issue an order. An order may be considered necessary if a witness refuses to attend, equivocates, or agrees to attend but says that a witness order would make it easier for them to attend, as may be the case if an employer is unwilling to release a witness to attend a tribunal hearing.

STRIKING OUT (EMPLOYMENT TRIBUNAL REGS)

[9.168] Rule 15 of Schedule 1 of the Employment Tribunals (Constitution and Rules of Procedure) Regs 2001 provide:

(1) Subject to the provisions of these rules, a tribunal may regulate its own procedure.

(2) A tribunal may—
(a) if the applicant at any time gives notice of the withdrawal of his originating application, dismiss the proceedings;
(b) if both or all the parties agree in writing upon the terms of a decision to be made by the tribunal, decide accordingly;
(c) subject to paragraph (3), at any stage of the proceedings, order to be struck out or amended any originating application or notice of appearance, or anything in such application or notice of appearance, on the grounds that it is scandalous, misconceived or vexatious;
(d) subject to paragraph (3), at any stage of the proceedings, order to be struck out any originating application or notice of appearance on the grounds that the manner in which the proceedings have been conducted by or on behalf of the applicant or, as the case may be, respondent has been scandalous, unreasonable or vexatious; and
(e) subject to paragraph (3), on the application of the respondent, or of its own motion, order an originating application to be struck out for want of prosecution. (3) Before making an order under sub-paragraph (c), (d) or (e) of paragraph (2) the tribunal shall send notice to the party against whom it is proposed that the order should be made giving him an opportunity to show cause why the order should not be made; but this paragraph shall not be taken to require the tribunal to send such notice to that party if the party has been given an opportunity to show cause orally why the order should not be made.

Bennett v London Borough of Southwark

[2002] EWCA Civ 223, [2002] IRLR 407

[9.169] Following her dismissal from employment, Mrs Bennett brought sex and race discrimination and victimisation proceedings against her employer. The case was listed for a ten-day hearing, however this was not enough to dispose of the case fully and the case was adjourned. On the reconvened date Mrs Bennett could not attend and her representative sought an adjournment. The application was opposed and the tribunal refused the postponement application. The applicant's representative reapplied for an adjournment. The representative said to the tribunal 'if I were a white barrister I would not be treated in this way' and also that 'if I were an Oxford-educated white barrister with a plummy voice I would not be put in this position'. The tribunal decided it could not go on to hear the case and discharged itself.

A freshly convened tribunal concluded that the representative's actions had been 'scandalous' and therefore the applicant's claims should be struck out under Rule 13 of the Employment Tribunals (Constitution and Rules of Procedure) Regulations 1993. The applicant appealed.

The EAT held that the first tribunal had been wrong to discharge itself so readily. As a result the second tribunal did not have authority to strike out her claims. However, the EAT used its powers under the Employment Tribunals Act, s 35(1)(a) to substitute its own view for that of the tribunal and struck out the proceedings. The applicant appealed to the Court of Appeal.

HELD: The EAT had been correct in finding that the first tribunal had been too quick to discharge itself. Where a representative behaves appallingly the hearing should not be aborted until the situation has been given a chance to calm down. Although a tribunal cannot ignore claims of being racist, it should give the representative a chance to reconsider and take back what he or she has said. If he does there is no reason why the tribunal cannot continue. If he does not withdraw the remarks, the tribunal may still decide to go ahead with the hearing after considering the time and expense of reconvening to a different panel. The tribunal could always invite the Attorney General to consider whether the representative is in contempt of court.

The second tribunal and the EAT had been incorrect in striking out the applicant's claim because of her representative's actions. The power of the court to strike out claims under Rule 13(2)(e) is not simply that the representative's conduct is scandalous but it refers to the manner in which he has conducted the proceedings on the applicant's behalf. This requires consideration of three issues:

The manner in which a party's proceedings are conducted is not the same as, though it may be demonstrated by, the applicant's representative's behaviour.

What is done in a party's name is presumptively, but not without question, on his or her behalf;

When considering the word 'scandalous' this does not mean 'shocking'.

The behaviour in question must be proportionate with striking out. In the present case, the representative had acted improperly but not 'scandalously'. Therefore the applicant's appeal was allowed.

The EAT had also erred in using its powers under Employment Tribunals Act, s 35(1), in substituting its own view for the tribunal. The EAT may only use this power where it is clear that a properly directed tribunal would have reached the same conclusion. In this case, striking out was not a foregone conclusion and therefore it was not open for the EAT to substitute its own decision for that of the tribunal.

THE TRIBUNAL'S DECISION

[9.170] Rule 12 of the Employment Tribunals (Constitution and Rules of Procedure) Regs 2001 provides:

(1) Where a tribunal is composed of three members its decision may be taken by a majority; and if a tribunal is composed of two members only, the chairman shall have a second or casting vote.

(2) The decision of a tribunal, which may be given orally at the end of a hearing or reserved, shall be recorded in a document signed by the chairman.

(3) The tribunal shall give reasons for its decision in a document signed by the chairman. That document shall contain a statement as to whether the reasonsare given in summary or extended form and where the tribunal—

(a) makes an award of compensation, or
(b) comes to any other determination by virtue of which one party is required to pay a sum to another (excluding an award of costs or allowances),

the document shall also contain a statement of the amount of compensation awarded, or of the sum required to be paid, followed either by a table showing how the amount or sum has been calculated or by a description of the manner in which it has been calculated.

The need to make findings of fact

Morris v London Iron and Steel Co Ltd

[1987] IRLR 182, CA

[9.171] Mr Morris brought unfair dismissal proceedings against his former employer. The tribunal heard conflicting evidence from both parties as to whether Mr Morris had been dismissed in law. The tribunal was unable to reach a decision as to whether Mr Morris resigned or was dismissed and held that Mr Morris complaint be dismissed. The employee appealed. The EAT upheld the appeal and remitted the case back to a fresh tribunal. The employer appealed.

HELD: The employment tribunal is not under an absolute obligation to reach a finding of fact in every case. In exceptional cases, a tribunal may not be able to decide what the decision should be, and the tribunal should not be obligated to embark on a detailed analysis as to its reasons and the way in which it reached its ultimate decision. When all the evidence is presented it is for the tribunal to consider this evidence in its totality, draw whatever inferences are necessary and consider this evidence on the balance of probabilities.

The tribunal's power to grant a remedy for unpleaded cause of action

Chapman v Simon

[1994] IRLR 124, CA

[9.172] Ms Simon brought a claim for race discrimination against the head teacher of the school where she worked and also against the local education authority (LEA). Her claim was upheld by the employment tribunal who accepted that there was an element of 'prejudgement' by the head teacher on the basis of Ms Simon's race following a complaint that had been made by her about another member of staff and also that Ms Simon's had been treated less favourably in other respects. Ms Chapman and the LEA appealed.

The EAT upheld the appeal against the decision that there was any 'prejudgement' but dismissed the appeal that there was no discrimination in any other respects. The head teacher and LEA again appealed and the applicant cross-appealed asking that the tribunal's original decision be restored.

HELD: The Court of Appeal dismissed the cross-appeal but upheld the appellant's appeal. The tribunal had decided incorrectly that the head teacher had discriminated against Ms Simon by unfairly prejudging a complaint she had made as this was not the subject of complaint in the original IT1. The tribunal may only consider complaints which have been made to it. If the tribunal finds that acts complained of are not proved, it is not open to it to give a remedy in respect of another unpleaded act. The tribunal may consider other issues but only where the IT1 is amended.

There were, in any event, no primary facts to enable the tribunal to draw inferences that there was a subconscious or unconscious racial prejudice on the part of the head teacher.

The power to review decisions

[9.173] Rule 13 of the Employment Tribunals (Constitution and Rules of Procedure) Regs 2001 provides:

(1) Subject to the provisions of this rule, a tribunal shall have power, on the application of a party or of its own motion, to review any decision on the grounds that—
  (a) the decision was wrongly made as a result of an error on the part of the tribunal staff;
  (b) a party did not receive notice of the proceedings leading to the decision;
  (c) the decision was made in the absence of a party;
  (d) new evidence has become available since the conclusion of the hearing to which the decision relates, provided that its existence could not have been reasonably known of or foreseen at the time of the hearing; or
  (e) the interests of justice require such a review.

Aparau v Iceland Frozen Foods plc

[2000] IRLR 196, CA

[9.174] The applicant originally worked for the Bejam Group. In her terms and conditions there was no reference to either a place of work or any mobility provisions. In 1989, Bejam was taken over by Iceland. Iceland issued new terms and conditions which included the clause 'you will normally be located at ... but you may be required to move to a different location at any time'. The applicant did not sign the new contract but continued to work for the respondent.

The applicant was asked to transfer to another branch following a dispute with her manager. The applicant refused and resigned claiming constructive unfair dismissal. The tribunal dismissed her claim on the grounds there was an express mobility clause in her contract of employment which the applicant had made no objection to. The EAT held that the tribunal had misdirected itself and the case was remitted to a fresh tribunal to consider the issue over whether the mobility clause had been incorporated into her contract of employment.

Prior to the re-hearing the respondent's solicitors wrote to the tribunal conceding that the applicant had been constructively unfairly dismissed. However, they asked that the tribunal grant permission for them to amend their IT3 to include a defence that the applicant was dismissed for some other substantial reason and that the dismissal was fair. The tribunal allowed the amendment. The applicant did not object. The tribunal held that the dismissal was for some other substantial reason and was fair. The applicant appealed. The EAT refused the appeal. The applicant appealed to the Court of Appeal.

HELD: On appeal, the applicant sought leave to amend her notice of appeal to argue that the tribunal had acted outside its jurisdiction. The Court of Appeal granted leave to amend the notice of appeal.

The EAT had remitted the case to a fresh tribunal to consider whether the mobility clause had been incorporated into the applicant's contract of employment. The tribunal had considered whether the applicant was dismissed for refusing to obey a lawful instruction. It acted outside its jurisdiction.

Although the tribunal has a limited power to review its decision, its jurisdiction is exhausted once that final judgment is given. It is not for the tribunal to re-open proceedings or to consider different issues from that which have been remitted to it. The tribunal does not have the power to entitle a party to amend its case prior to remission to raise issues which were not previously before it. It is also not for the parties to consent to extending the tribunal's jurisdiction. The tribunal's jurisdiction is to be exercised in accordance with statutory rules of procedure which cannot be changed by consent of the parties.

COSTS (EMPLOYMENT TRIBUNAL REGS)

[9.175] Rule 14 of the Employment Tribunals (Constitution and Rules of Procedure) Regs 2001 provides:

(1) Where, in the opinion of the tribunal, a party has in bringing the proceedings, or a party or a party's representative has in conducting the proceedings, acted vexatiously, abusively, disruptively or otherwise unreasonably, or the bringing or conducting of the proceedings by a party has been misconceived, the tribunal shall consider making, and if it so decides, may make—
(a) an order containing an award against that party in respect of the costs incurred by another party;
(b) an order that that party shall pay to the Secretary of State the whole, or any part, of any allowances (other than allowances paid to members of tribunals) paid by the Secretary of State under section 5(2) or (3) of the 1996 Act to any person for the purposes of, or in connection with, his attendance at the tribunal.

(2) Paragraph (1) applies to a respondent who has not entered an appearance in relation to the conduct of any part in the proceedings which he has taken.

Unreasonable conduct by a trade union representative

Beynon v Scadden

[1999] IRLR 700, EAT

[9.176] The applicant and 12 other colleagues complained that there had been a transfer of the business in which they worked and the employers had failed to comply with their obligations under the Transfer of Undertakings (Protection of Employment) Regulations 1981. The applicant's union (Unison) supported their claims. The tribunal held there had been no transfer as there had been a share sale. The claims were dismissed.

The tribunal made an order for costs against the applicant on the basis that 'such costs to be taxed, if not agreed, on an indemnity basis on the higher county court scale'. The order also stated that: 'This award has been made having taken into account both the involvement of and the means of the applicants' union, Unison'. The tribunal held that the union should and could have been aware there was no reasonable prospect of success in this case but continued to proceed for their own sake, which included forcing the employers to recognise the union.

Costs were awarded under rule 12(1) of the Employment Tribunals (Constitution and Rules of Procedure) Regulations 1993 [now Rule 14 of the Employment Tribunals (Constitution and Rules of Procedure) Regulations 2001, schedule 1].

The applicants appealed against the order for costs on the following grounds:
that there was no case to award costs;
that the order for costs had failed to take into account the applicants' means;
the order had wrongly taken into account the role of Unison;
if the order for costs was appropriate, the tribunal had exceeded its jurisdiction in specifying that costs should be assessed on an indemnity basis, as there was not a good ground to order costs indemnity basis.

HELD: The tribunal was right to order costs where the union had acted unreasonably in pursuing a claim which it knew, or ought to have known, had no reasonable prospects of success. The union also pursued this claim for its own benefit. The tribunal has discretion to order costs where a party has acted 'frivolously, vexatiously, abusively, disruptively or otherwise unreasonably' in bringing or conducting proceedings. This applies whether it is the fault of the party of their representative. The tribunal was right to take into account the means of the union when making an order for costs. The tribunal had not exceeded its jurisdiction in specifying that the costs should be taxed on the indemnity basis rather than on a standard basis.

The applicant's ability to pay

Kovacs v Queen Mary and Westfield College

[2002] EWCA Civ 352, [2002] IRLR 414

[9.177] The applicant brought claims for unfair dismissal and unlawful race and sex discrimination against the first respondent and unlawful sex and race discrimination against The Royal Hospitals NHS Trust. A tribunal dismissed her claims against the second respondent and ordered her to pay its taxed costs under Rule 12(1) of the Employment Tribunals (Constitution and Rules of Procedure) 1993.

Although the tribunal recognised the applicant had limited finances, in the circumstances, it considered it reasonable to order her to pay all of the second respondent's costs. Costs were eventually assessed by the county court to be £62,000.

The applicant appealed against the decision. The EAT dismissed the appeal. The applicant appealed to the Court of Appeal.

HELD: The tribunal did not have to take into account the applicant's ability to pay when ordering costs against her. A party's ability to pay is not a factor in deciding whether to make an order for costs. Once the tribunal has considered a party has acted 'frivolously, vexatiously, abusively, disruptively or otherwise unreasonably', there is no reason why the party in question should not be required to compensate his opponent for costs which he plainly should not have had to incur.

CHAPTER 10

Health and Safety Prosecutions

Health and Safety at Work etc Act 1974: *Introduction* [10.1]
The test of *'reasonably practicability'* and *'conducting an undertaking'* [10.9]
Personal liability of corporate officers [10.16]
Limits of practicability (HSWA, s 40) [10.19]
Sentencing and level of fines [10.20]
Corporate manslaughter [10.26]

HEALTH AND SAFETY AT WORK ETC ACT 1974

Introduction

[10.1] The Health and Safety at Work etc Act 1974 (HSWA) remains the principal source of criminal liability in this area. A number of general duties are imposed upon the employer under sections 2–9 of the Act, failure to comply with which is made a specific offence and may lead to prosecution pursuant to sub-sections 33(1)(a)–(b).

Perhaps the most important of these duties can found in sections 2 and 3 of HSWA which require the employer to ensure, so far as is reasonably practicable, the health, safety and welfare at work of all of his employees and any person affected by the conduct of his undertaking.

That HSWA is the basis for almost all health and safety prosecutions stems from the combination of these two sections, the importance of which ought not to be underestimated. In addition section 15 of the Act (see 10.12 below) is the source of the large number of Regulations that compose the bulk of health and safety law, *any* breach of which is criminalised and may lead to prosecution pursuant to sub-section 33(c). As a result of the foregoing, employers face criminal sanction for any breach of a wide variety of obligations.

It is beyond the remit of this chapter to consider the provisions of the relevant Regulations but specific attention is drawn to the Management of Health and Safety at Work Regulations 1992 and the obligations imposed by the Reporting of Injuries, Diseases and Dangerous Occurrences Regulations 1995.

Provisions of HSWA

[10.2]

2 General duties of employers to their employees

(1) It shall be the duty of every employee to ensure, so far as is reasonably practicable, the health, safety and welfare at work of all his employees.

(2) Without prejudice to the generality of an employer's duty under the preceding subsection, the matters to which that duty extends include in particular—
  (a) the provision and maintenance of plant and systems of work that are, so far as is reasonably practicable, safe and without risks to health;
  (b) arrangements for ensuring, so far as is reasonably practicable, safety and absence of risks to health in connection with the use, handling, storage and transport of articles and substances;
  (c) the provision of such information, instruction, training and supervision as is necessary to ensure, so far as is reasonable practicable, the health and safety at work of his employees;
  (d) so far as is reasonably practicable as regards any place of work under the employer's control, the maintenance of it in a condition that is safe and without risks to health and the provision and maintenance of means and access to and egress from it that are safe and without such risks;
  (e) the provision and maintenance of a safe working environment for his employees that is, so far as is reasonably practicable, safe, without risks to health, and adequate as regards facilities and arrangements for their welfare at work.

(3) Except in such cases as may be prescribed, it shall be the duty of every employer to prepare and as often may be appropriate revise a written statement of his general policy with respect to the health and safety at work of his employees and the organisation and arrangements for the time being in force for carrying out that policy, and to bring the statement and any revision of it to the notice of all of his employees.

(4) Regulations made by the Secretary of State may provide for the appointment in prescribed cases by recognised trade unions (within the meaning of the regulations) of safety representatives from amongst the employees, and those representatives shall represent the employees in consultation with the employers under subsection (6) below and shall have such other functions as may be prescribed.

(5) …

(6) It shall be the duty of every employer to consult any such representatives with a view to the making and maintenance of arrangements which will enable him and his employees to co-operate effectively in promoting and developing measures to ensure the health and safety at work of the employees, and in checking the effectiveness of such measures.

(7) In such cases as may be prescribed it shall be the duty of every employer, if requested to do so by the safety representatives mentioned in subsection 4 above, to establish, in accordance with regulations made by the Secretary of State, a safety committee having the function of keeping under review the measures taken to ensure the health and safety at work of his employees and such other functions as may be prescribed.

[10.3]

3 General duties of employers and self-employed to persons other than their employees

(1) It shall by the duty of every employer to conduct his undertaking in such a way as to ensure, so far as is reasonably practicable, that persons not in his employment who may be affected thereby are not thereby exposed to risks to their health or safety.

(2) It shall be the duty of every self-employed person to conduct his undertaking in such a way as to ensure, so far as is reasonably practicable, that he and other persons (not being his employees) who may be affected thereby are not thereby exposed to risks to their health or safety.

(3) In such cases as may be prescribed, it shall be the duty of every employer and every self-employed person, in the prescribed circumstances and in the prescribed manner, to give to persons (not being his employees) who may be affected by the way in which he conducts his undertaking the prescribed information about such aspects of the way in which he conducts his undertaking as might affect their health or safety.

[10.4]

4 General duties of persons concerned with premises to persons other than their employees

(1) This section has effect for imposing on persons duties in relation to those who—
(a) are not their employees: but
(b) use non-domestic premises made available to them as a place of work or as a place where they may use plant or substances provided for their use there,

and applies to premises so made available and other non-domestic premises used in connection with them.

(2) It shall be the duty of each person who has, to any extent, control of premises to which this section applies or of the means of access thereto or egress therefrom or of any plant or substance in such premises to take such measures as it is reasonable for a person in his position to take to ensure, so far as is reasonably practicable, that the premises, all means of access thereto or egress therefrom available for use by persons using the premises or, as the case may be, provided for use there, is or are safe with out risks to health.

(3) Where a person has, by virtue of any contract or tenancy, an obligation of any extent in relation to—
(a) the maintenance or repair of any premises to which this section applies or any means of access thereto or egress therefrom; or
(b) the safety or the absence or health to risks arising from plant or substances in any such premises;

that person shall be treated for the purposes of subsection (2) above, as being as a person who has control of the matters to which his obligation extends.

(4) Any reference in this section to a person having control of any premises or matter is a reference to a person having control of the premises or matter in connection with the carrying on by him of a trade, business or other undertaking (whether for profit or not).

...

[10.5]

6 General duties of manufacturers etc as regards articles and substances for use at work

(1) It shall be the duty of every person who designs, manufactures, imports or supplies any article for use at work or any article or fairground equipment—
(a) to ensure, so far as is reasonably practicable, that the article is so designed and constructed that it will be safe and without risks to health at all times when it is being set, used, cleaned or maintained by a person at work;
(b) to carry out or arrange for the carrying out of such testing and examination as may be necessary for the performance of the duty imposed by him by the preceding paragraph;
(c) to take such steps as are necessary to secure that persons supplied by the person with that article are provided with adequate information about the use for which the article is designed or has been tested and about any conditions necessary to ensure that it will be safe and without risks to health at all such times as are mentioned in paragraph (a) above and when it is being dismantled or disposed of; and
(d) to take such steps as are necessary to secure, so far as is reasonably practicable, that persons so supplied are provided with all such revisions of information provided to them by virtue of the preceding paragraph as are necessary by reason of its becoming known that anything gives rise to a serious risk to health or safety.

(1A) It shall be the duty of any person who designs, manufactures, imports or supplies any article of fairground equipment—
(a) to ensure, so far as is reasonably practicable, that the article is so designed and constructed that it will be safe and without risks to health at all times when it is being used for or in connection with the entertainment of members of the public;

(b) to carry out or arrange for the carrying out of such testing and examination as may be necessary for the performance of the duty imposed upon him by the preceding paragraph;
(c) to take such steps as are necessary to secure that persons supplied by that person with the article are provided with adequate information about the use for which the article is designed or has been tested and about any conditions necessary to ensure that it will be safe and without risks to health and safety at all times when it is being for or in connection with the entertainment of member so of the public; and
(d) to take such steps as are necessary to secure, so far as is reasonably practicable, that persons so supplied are provided with all such revisions of information provided to them by virtue of the preceding paragraph as are necessary by reason of its becoming known that anything gives rise to a serious risk to health or safety.

(2) It shall be the duty of any person who undertakes the design or manufacture of any article for use at work or of any article of fairground equipment to carry out or arrange for the carrying out of any necessary research with a view to the discovery and, so far as is reasonably practicable, the elimination or minimisation of any risks to health and safety to which the design or article give rise.

(3) It shall be the duty of any person who erects or installs any article for use at work in any premises where that article is to be used by persons at work or who erects or installs any article of fairground equipment to ensure, so far as is reasonably practicable, that nothing about the way in which the article is erected or installed makes it unsafe or a risk to health at any such time as is mentioned in paragraph (a) of subsection (1) or, as the case may be, in paragraph (a) of subsections (1) or (1A) above.

(4) It shall be the duty of any person who manufactures, imports or supplies any substance—
(a) to ensure, so far as is reasonably practicable, that the substance will be safe and without risks to health at all times when it is being used, handled, processed, stored or transported by a person at work or in premises to which section 4 above applies;
(b) to carry out or arrange for the carrying out of such testing and examination as may be necessary for the performance of the duty imposed upon him by the preceding paragraph;
(c) to take such steps as are necessary to secure that persons supplied by that person with the substance are provided with adequate information about risks to health or safety to which the inherent properties to the substance may give rise, about the results of any tests which have been carried out on or in connection with the substance and about any conditions necessary to ensure that the substance will be safe and without risks to health at all such times as are mentioned in paragraph (a) above and when the substance is being disposed of; and
(d) to take such steps as are necessary to secure, so far as is reasonably practicable, that persons so supplied are provided with all such revisions

of information provided to them by virtue of the preceding paragraph as are necessary by reason of its becoming known that anything gives rise to a serious risk to health or safety.

(5) It shall be the duty of any person who undertakes the manufacture of any substance to carry out or arrange for the carrying out of any necessary research with a view to the discovery and, so far as is reasonably practicable, the elimination or minimisation of any risks to health or safety to which the substance may give rise at all such times as are mentioned in paragraph (a) of the subsection (4) above.

(6) Nothing in the preceding provisions of this section shall be taken to require a person to repeat any testing, examination or research which has been carried out otherwise than by him or at his instance, in so far as it is reasonable for him to rely on the results thereof for the purposes of those provisions.

(7) Any duty imposed upon any person by any of the preceding provisions of this section shall extend only to things done in the course of trade, business or other undertaking carried on by him (whether for profit or not) and to matters within his control.

(8) Where a person designs, manufactures, imports or supplies an article for use at work or on an article of fairground equipment and does so for or to another on the basis of a written undertaking by that other to take specified steps sufficient to ensure, so far as is reasonably practicable, that the article will be safe and without risks to health at all such times as are mentioned in paragraph (a) of subsection (1) or, as the case may be, in paragraph (a) of subsection (1) or (1A) above, the undertaking shall have the effect of relieving the first-mentioned person of the duty imposed by virtue of that paragraph to such extent as is reasonable having regard to the terms of the undertaking.

(8A) Nothing in subsection (7) or (8) above shall relieve any person who imports any article or substance from any duty in respect of anything which—
(a) in the case of an article designed outside the United Kingdom, was done by and in the course of any trade, profession or other undertaking carried on by, or was within the control of, the person who designed the article; or
(b) in the case of an article or substance manufactured outside the United Kingdom, was done by and in the course of any trade, profession or other undertaking carried on by, or was within the control of, the person who manufactured the article or substance.

(9) Where a person ('the ostensible supplier') supplies any article or substance to another ('the customer') under a hire-purchase agreement, conditional sale agreement or credit-sale agreement, and the ostensible supplier—
(a) carries on the business of financing the acquisition of goods by others by means of such agreements; and

(b) in the course of that business acquired his interest in the article or substance supplied to the customer as a means of financing its acquisition by the customer from a third person ('the effective supplier'),

the effective supplier and not the ostensible supplier shall be treated for the purposes of this section as supplying the article or substance to the customer, and any duty imposed by the preceding provisions of this section on suppliers shall accordingly fall on the effective supplier and not on the ostensible supplier.

(10) For the purposes of this section an absence of safety or a risk to health shall be disregarded in so far as the case in or in relation to which it would arise is shown to be the one occurrence of which could not reasonably be foreseen; and in determining whether any duty imposed by virtue of paragraph (a) of subsection (1), (1A) or (4) above has been performed regard shall be had to any relevant information or advice which has been provided to any person by the person by whom the article has been designed, manufactured , imported or supplied or, as the case may be, by the person by whom the substance has been manufactured, imported or supplied.

[10.6]

7 General duties of employees at work

It shall be the general duty of every employee while at work—
(a) to take reasonable care for the health and safety of himself and of other persons who may be affected by his acts or omissions at work; and
(b) as regards any duty or requirement imposed on his employer or any other person by or under any of the relevant statutory provisions, to cooperate with him so far as is necessary to enable that duty or requirement to be performed or complied with.

[10.7]

8 Duty not to interfere with or misuse things provided pursuant to certain provisions

No person shall intentionally or recklessly interfere with or misuse anything provided in the interests of health, safety or welfare in pursuance of any of the relevant statutory provisions.

[10.8]

9 Duty not to charge employees for things done or provided pursuant to certain specific requirements

No employer shall levy or permit to be levied on any employee of his any charge in respect of anything done or provided in pursuance of any specific requirement of the statutory provisions.

The test of 'reasonably practicability' and 'conducting an undertaking'

R v Gateway Foodmarkets Ltd

[1997] 3 All ER 78, CA

[10.9] The appellant company employed a firm of lift contractors to carry out maintenance and repair works in each of its stores. Unknown to the company's head office, in contravention of policy, management at one of the stores developed a practice of manually rectifying a recurring problem with a lift without recourse to the specialist contractors. The duty manager at the store was killed in pursuance of this practice, falling down a lift shaft whilst attempting to rectify a problem with the lift. The company was prosecuted under HSWA, s 2(1), for failing to ensure, so far as was reasonably practicable, the health, safety and welfare at work of all their employees. On a preliminary point, the judge ruled that the offence was one of strict liability, whereupon the appellant pleaded guilty and were fined £10,000. Appeal against conviction.

HELD: The appeal would be dismissed. In considering the correct interpretation of section 2(1) of the Act, Evans LJ recited with approval the approach taken by Lord Hoffmann in *R v Associated Octel Co Ltd* [1996] 4 All ER 846 when considering the ambit section 3(1) of the same Act. Subject to reasonable practicability, section 2(1) imposes strict liability on an employer whenever there is a failure to ensure an employees health, safety and welfare at work. In the instant case, there had been a clear failure at store management level which was attributable to the employer. The appellant company could not rely upon the adequacy of the measures put in place at head office level to avoid liability. Appeal dismissed.

> *Note*— Evans LJ left open the question of whether or not an employer would be liable for an error or failure at a more junior or individual level, page 84f–g.

R v Associated Octel Co Ltd

[1996] 4 All ER 846, HL

[10.10] The appellant operated a large chemical plant, which the Health and Safety Executive had designated a 'major hazard site'. For a number of years it retained a small firm of specialist contractors to carry out certain repairs and maintenance. In accordance with the appellant company's standard policy, the smaller firm operated under a 'permit to work' system whereby it was required to complete a form in respect of every job that it was to carry out, stating what was to be done and seeking authorisation from the appellant's engineers.

During the course of the annual maintenance programme, an employee of the independent contractors was inside a tank, cleaning the lining by the light of an electric bulb. The light broke, causing a bucket of highly inflammable acetone used in the cleaning process to ignite, leaving the workman with severe burns. The appellant was charged with a breach of HSWA, s 3(1), which imposed a duty upon the appellant to conduct its undertaking in such a way as to ensure, so far as reasonably practicable, that persons not in his employment who might be affected thereby would not thereby be exposed to risk to health and safety.

At trial, the appellant argued that it had no case to answer because the injury to the workman had not occurred as a result of the manner in which it conducted its undertaking within the meaning of section 3(1). Rather, as an employee of the independent contractors, he had been injured as a result of the manner in which that company had conducted its undertaking, consisting of carrying out the repair and maintenance works and, in particular, cleaning the tank. The appellant contended that it had no right to control the way in which the smaller firm carried out its work.

The appellant company was convicted and fined £25,000. It appealed to the Court of Appeal, which held that the phrase 'conduct his undertaking' was wide enough to encompass the activities of independent contractors carrying out cleaning, repair and maintenance work which was necessary for the conduct of the employer's business of enterprise and, accordingly, dismissed the appeal. The appellant appealed to the House of Lords.

HELD: It was important not to confuse two quite different concepts, namely: an employer's vicarious liability for the tortious act of another and a duty imposed upon the employer himself. The former depended upon the nature of the contractual relationship between the employer and tortfeasor, in general terms the question being whether or not the tortfeasor was acting within the scope of his duties under the contract of employment at the time. In contrast, the statutory duty under section 3 is defined by reference to a certain kind of activity, namely the conduct by the employer of his undertaking. This duty arises irrespective of any contractual relationship by which the employer chooses to carry out the task. If the employer engaged an independent contractor to carry out work forming part of his undertaking, he was required by section 3(1) to stipulate whatever conditions were reasonably practicable to avoid employees of the independent contractor being exposed to risks to their health and safety. The key issue of whether or not the activity in question could be described as part of the employer's undertaking was a question of fact to be decided in each case. On the facts of this case, repairs and maintenance work carried out in the tank was almost certainly part of the appellant's undertaking. In particular, the court noted that the work formed part of the appellant's structured maintenance programme and that the workmen involved, although employed by an independent contractor, were almost permanently integrated into the appellant's system of work. Appeal dismissed.

R v Nelson Group Services (Maintenance) Ltd

[1998] 4 All ER 331, CA

[10.11] The appellant company installed, serviced and maintained gas fires nationally. In separate trails arising out of different facts, it was charged with failing to discharge its duty under HSWA, s 3(1), to 'conduct its undertaking in such a way as to ensure, so far as reasonably practicable' that persons not in its employment who might be affected thereby were not exposed to risks to their health and safety. In the third case, one of the appellant's fitters had removed a dangerous and defective gas fire in a private house but failed thereafter to cap the gas supply. The judge directed the jury that if it found that the fitter had made such an error, it could not find that the appellants had done all that was reasonably practicable to ensure that the occupier was not exposed to a risk to her health and safety. The appellants were convicted and appealed.

HELD: There could be no doubt that the activities of individual fitters formed part of the conduct of the appellant's undertaking within the meaning of the Act, and that their acts or omissions had exposed householders to risks to their health and safety. However, of itself that did not prevent the appellant from establishing the statutory defence of reasonable practicability. The court derived great assistance from the reasoning of Evans LJ in *R v Gateway Foodmarkets Ltd* [1997] 3 All ER 78 (see 10.9 above). In the instant case, the negligence or failure to take reasonable precautions had taken place at fitting, rather than at any management level. Having regard to the distinction drawn in the regulations between the duties of employers and the duties of those performing the works, it was not necessary for the adequate protection of the public that the employer be held criminally liable under the Act for an employee's negligent act, since that person was himself potentially liable to criminal sanction. Once the exposure to risk had been established, it was for the employer to prove on the balance of probability that all that was reasonably practicable had been done to ensure that such risks would not arise. Accordingly, the judge had misdirected the jury and the appeal would be allowed on this point.

[10.12]

15 Health and safety regulations

(1) Subject to the provisions of section 50, the Secretary of State ... shall have power to make regulations under this section for any of the general purposes of this Part (and regulations so made are in this Part referred to as 'health and safety regulations').

(2) Without prejudice to the generality of the preceding subsection, health and safety regulations may for any of the general purposes of this Part make provision for any of the purposes mentioned in Schedule 3.

(3) Health and safety regulations—
(a) may repeal or modify any of the existing statutory provisions;
(b) may exclude or modify in relation to any specified class of case any of the provisions of sections 2 to 9 or any of the existing statutory provisions;
(c) may make a specified authority or class of authorities responsible, to such extent as may be specified, for the enforcement of any of the relevant statutory provisions.

(4) Health and safety regulations—
(a) may impose requirements by reference to the approval of the Commission or any other specified body or person;
(b) may provide for references in the regulations to any specified document to operate as references to that document as revised or re-issued from time to time.

(5) Health and safety regulations—
(a) may provide (either unconditionally or subject to conditions, and with or without limit of time) for exemptions for any requirement or prohibition imposed by or under any of the relevant statutory provisions.
(b) may enable exemptions from any requirement or prohibition imposed by or under any of the relevant statutory provisions to be granted (either unconditionally or subject to conditions, and with or without limit of time) by any specified person or by any person authorised in that behalf by a specified authority.

(6) Health and safety regulations—
(a) may specify the person or classes of persons who, in the event of a contravention of a requirement or prohibition imposed by or under the regulations, are to be guilty of an offence, whether in addition to or to the exclusion of other persons or classes of persons;
(b) may provide for any specified defence to be available in proceedings for any offence under the relevant statutory provisions either generally or in specified circumstances;
(c) may exclude proceedings on indictment in relation to offences consisting of a contravention of a requirement or prohibition imposed by or under any of the existing statutory provisions, sections 2 to 9 or health and safety regulations;
(d) may restrict the punishments (other than the maximum fine on conviction on indictment) which can be imposed in respect of any such offence as is mentioned in paragraph (c) above;
(e) in the case of regulations made for any purpose mentioned in section 1 (1) of the Offshore Safety Act 1992, may provide that any offence consisting of a contravention of the regulations, or of any requirement or prohibition imposed by or under them, shall be punishable on conviction on indictment by imprisonment for a term not exceeding two years, or a fine, or both.

(7) Without prejudice to section 35, health and safety regulations may make provision for enabling offences under any of the relevant statutory provisions to be treated as having been committed at any specified place for the purpose of bringing any such offence within the field of responsibility of any enforcing authority or conferring jurisdiction on any court to entertain proceedings for any such offence.

(8) Health and safety regulations may take the form of regulations applying to particular circumstances only or to a particular case only (for example, regulations applying to particular premises only).

(9) If an Order in Council is made under section 84(3) providing that this section shall apply to or in relation to persons, premises or work outside Great Britain then, notwithstanding the Order, health and safety regulations shall not apply to or in relation to aircraft in flight, vessels, hovercraft or offshore installations outside Great Britain or persons at work outside Great Britain in connection with submarine cables or submarine pipelines except insofar as the regulations so provide.

[10.13]

33 Offences

(1) It is an offence for a person—
(a) to fail to discharge a duty to which he is subject by virtue of sections 2 to 7;
(b) to contravene sections 8 or 9;
(c) to contravene any health and safety regulations ... or any requirement or prohibition imposed under any such regulations (including any requirement or prohibition to which he is subject by virtue of the terms of or any condition or restriction attached to any licence, approval, exemption or other authority issued, given or granted under the regulations);
(d) to contravene any requirement imposed by or under regulations under section 14 or intentionally to obstruct any person in the exercise of his powers under that section;
(e) to contravene any requirement imposed by an inspector under section 20 or 25;
(f) to prevent or attempt to prevent any other person from appearing before an inspector or from answering any question to which an inspector may by virtue of section 20(2) require an answer;
(g) to contravene any requirement or prohibition imposed by an improvement notice or a prohibition notice (including any such notice as modified on appeal);
(h) intentionally to obstruct an inspector in the exercise or performance of his powers or duties [or to obstruct a customs officer in the exercise of his powers under section 25A];
(i) to contravene any requirement imposed by a notice under section 27(1);
(j) to use or disclose any information imposed by a notice under section 27(4) or 28;
(k) to make a statement which he knows to be false or recklessly to make a statement which is false where the statement is made—
   (i) in purported compliance with a requirement to furnish any information imposed by or under any or the relevant statutory provisions; or
   (ii) for the purpose of obtaining the issue of a document under any or the relevant statutory provisions to himself or another person;
(l) intentionally to make a false entry in any register, book, notice or other document required by or under any of the relevant statutory provisions to be kept, served or given or, with intent to deceive, to made use of any such entry which he knows to be false;
(m) with intent to deceive, to ... use a document issued or authorised to be issued under any of the relevant statutory provisions or required for any purpose thereunder or to make or have in his possession a document so closely resembling any such document as to be calculated to deceive;
(n) falsely pretend to be an inspector;
(o) to fail to comply with an order made by the court under section 42.

(1A) Subject to any provision made by virtue of section 15(6)(d), a person guilty of an offence under subsection (1)(a) above consisting of failing to discharge a duty to which he is subject by virtue of sections 2 to 6 shall be liable—
(a) on summary conviction, to imprisonment for a term not exceeding six months, or a fine not exceeding £20,000, or both;
(b) on conviction on indictment, to imprisonment for a term not exceeding two years, or a fine, or both.

(2) A person guilty of an offence under paragraph (d), (f), (h) or (n) of subsection (1) above, or of an offence under paragraph (e) of that subsection consisting of contravening a requirement imposed by an inspector under section 20, shall be liable on summary conviction to a fine not exceeding [level five of the standard scale].

(2A) A person guilty of an offence under subsection (1)(g) or (o) shall be liable—
(a) on summary conviction, to imprisonment for a term not exceeding six months, or a fine not exceeding £20,000, or both;
(b) on conviction on indictment, to imprisonment for a term not exceeding two years, or a fine or both.

(3) Subject to any provision made by virtue of section 15(6)(d) [or (e)] or by virtue of paragraph (2)(2) of Schedule 3, a person guilty of [an offence under subsection 1 above not falling within [1A], (2) or (2A) above], or of an offence under any of the existing statutory provisions, being an offence for which no other penalty is specified, shall be liable—
(a) on summary conviction, to a fine not exceeding [the prescribed sum];
(b) on conviction in indictment—
   (i) if the offence is one to which this sub-paragraph applies, to imprisonment for a term not exceeding two years, or a fine, or both;
   (ii) if the offence is not one to which the preceding sub-paragraph applies, to a fine.

(4) Subsection (3)(b)(i) above applies to the following offences—
(a) an offence consisting of contravening any of the relevant statutory provisions be doing otherwise than under the authority of licence issued by the Executive ... something for the doing of which such a licence is necessary under the relevant statutory provisions;
(b) an offence consisting of contravening a term of or a condition or restriction attached to any such licence as is mentioned in the preceding paragraph;
(c) an offence consisting of acquiring or attempting to acquire, possessing or using an explosive article or substance (within the meaning of any of the relevant statutory provisions) in contravention of any of the relevant statutory provisions;
(d) ...
(e) an offence under subsection (1)(j) above.

(5), (6) ...

[10.14]

36 Offences due to the fault of other person

(1) Where the commission by any person of an offence under any or the relevant statutory provisions is due the act or default of some other person, that other person shall be guilty of the offence by virtue of this subsection, and a person may be charged with and convicted of the offence by virtue of the this subsections whether or not proceedings are taken against the first-mentioned person.

(2) Where there would be or have been the commission of an offence under section 33 by the Crown but for the circumstance that that section does not bind the Crown, and that fact is due to the act or default of a person other than the Crown, that person shall be guilty of an offence which, but for that circumstance, the Crown would be committing or would have committed, and may be charged with and convicted of that offence accordingly.

(3) The preceding provisions of this section are subject to any provisions made by virtue of section 15(6).

[10.15]

37 Offences by bodies corporate

(1) Where an offence under any of the relevant statutory provisions committed by a body corporate is proved to have been committed with the consent or connivance of, or to have been attributable to any neglect on the part of, any director, manager, secretary or other similar officer of the body corporate or a person who was purporting to act in any such capacity, he as well as the body corporate shall be liable to be proceeded against and punished accordingly.

(2) Where the affairs of a body corporate are managed by its members, the preceding subsection shall apply in relation to the acts and defaults of a member in connection with his functions of management as if he were a director of the body corporate.

Personal liability of corporate officers

Huckerby v Elliott

[1970] 1 All ER 189

[10.16] The appellant was a director of a company charged with being a provider of premises used for the purpose of gaming without the appropriate licence, as required by the Finance Act 1966, s 13(1). The company and the company secretary, 'L' (a fellow director), pleaded guilty to charges brought under s 305(3) of the Act. It was clear from the evidence at trial that the appellant knew little of the conduct of the business, which had been left in the hands of L. She was aware that a licence was required and knew that money had been set aside to obtain the same, but had no knowledge whether or not such a licence had actually been obtained. Appeal against conviction by way of case stated.

HELD: The appeal would be allowed and the conviction quashed. The prosecution had failed to prove that the principal offence was 'attributable to any neglect' on the part of the appellant. She was entitled to leave certain matters to be dealt with by another director or other competent official on behalf of the company. Business can only operate on principles of trust and the appellant had left the issue of licences to be dealt with by L. She had no reason to distrust him and could not be said to have neglected her duty simply by failing to enquire how such money had in fact been spent.

Armour v Skeen

[1977] IRLR 310

[10.17] The appellant, who was director for roads for the local council, was prosecuted under the HSWA, s 37(1). He was found guilty of five charges arising from the accidental death of one the council's employees who sustained a fatal fall in the course of repainting a bridge spanning the river Clyde. The sheriff court found that there had been neglect on the appellant's part due to his failure to fulfil various responsibilities for health and safety placed upon those in his position by the council. The appellant appealed; arguing first that he was under no personal duty to provide a safe system of work and that, as such, the accident could not be said to be attributable to any neglect of duty. Secondly, he argued that he did not fall within the meaning of section 37(1).

HELD: The appeal would be dismissed on both grounds. As to the first issue, section 37(1) referred to *any* neglect of duty, however that duty may be constituted. Having regard to the council's own 'Statement of Safety Policy' and the terms of a follow up memo sent to the directors of various departments, including that of the appellant, the court was satisfied that he had been under a duty to prepare a general safety policy in relation to the work of his own department (which he had failed to do). In relation to the second ground of appeal, whilst it was accepted that there could no question of equating the appellant's status as director of roads with the term 'director' in section 37(1), he nonetheless came within the ambit of the broader class of persons referred to. The court had particular regard to the actual part played by the appellant in the organisation of the council, emphasising the duty imposed upon him as set out above.

R v Boal

[1992] 3 All ER 177, CA

[10.18] The appellant worked in a bookshop and had recently been promoted to the position of assistant general manager. There was no evidence to suggest that he had received formal managerial training, nor any instruction in respect of heath and safety or fire precautions. Whilst he was in charge of the bookshop (the general manager was on a week's holiday) the premises were inspected by the local fire authority who found serious breaches of the fire certificate.

The appellant was charged (along with the company who owned the premises) with 11 offences under the Fire Precautions Act 1971 on the basis that he was a manager within the meaning of section 23(1) thereof, which provided that, 'Where an offence under the Act committed by a body corporate is proved ... to be attributable to any neglect on the part of, any director, manager, secretary or other similar office ... he as well as the body corporate shall be guilty of that offence'. At trial, the appellant pleaded guilty to three counts as a result of legal advice to the effect that he would be unable to effectively challenge his status as manager within the meaning of section 23(1). The appellant was also convicted on seven further counts. He appealed against conviction.

HELD: The appeal would be allowed. The intended scope of section 23 of the Act was to fix with criminal liability those in a position of real authority, with the power and responsibility to decide corporate policy and strategy. It was intended to catch those responsible for putting proper procedures in place but was not meant to strike at the underlings. Had a defence to the effect that the appellant was not a manager within the meaning of the act been run, it would in all likelihood have succeeded.

Limits of practicability (HSWA, s 40)

[10.19]

40 Onus of proving limits of what is practicable etc

In any proceedings for an offence under any of the relevant statutory provisions consisting of a failure to comply with a duty or requirement to do something so far as is practicable or so far as is reasonably practicable, or to use the best means to do something, it shall be for the accused to prove (as the case may be) that it was not practicable or not reasonably practicable to do more than was in fact done to satisfy the duty or requirement, or that there was no better practicable means that was in fact used to satisfy the duty or requirement.

Sentencing and level of fines

[10.20] The statutory basis of the sentencing powers exercised by the courts in health and safety prosecutions are to be found in HSWA, s 33, above.

In *R v F Howe & Son (Engineers) Ltd* [1999] 2 All ER 249 (see 10.21 below), the Court of Appeal expressly recognised public disquiet that the level of fines imposed in health and safety prosecutions had been too low. In a series of decisions, the courts have emphasised that the underlying purpose of carrying out such prosecutions is to promote the objective of safe workplaces for employees and members of the public alike. Fines should therefore be large enough to bring that message home to managers and shareholders, but should not generally be such as to put a company at risk of bankruptcy.

The judgment in Howe summarises the principal aggravating and mitigating factors to be taken into account when determining the level of fine to be imposed. Whilst a defendant's impecuniosity is no mitigation, the fine should reflect its means. Any company seeking to make submissions in this respect should provide the necessary financial information to the prosecution and the court in advance of the hearing. Failure to do so may have adverse consequences.

Practitioners should also be aware of procedural guidance offered by the Court of Appeal in *R v Friskies Petcare (UK) Ltd* [2000] 2 Cr App Rep (S) 401. Where a prosecution is to be brought the Health and Safety Executive should provide a statement outlining those facts as identified in *Howe* which it says aggravates the offence. If the matter proceeds to a sentencing hearing, the defence should serve a statement in response detailing the relevant mitigating factors upon which it intends to rely.

R v F Howe & Son (Engineers) Ltd

[1999] 2 All ER 249, CA

[10.21] The appellant company pleaded guilty to five offences under HSWA. The prosecution arose from a fatal accident involving one of its employees, a 20 year old cleaner, who was electrocuted in the course of his employment. Following submissions from the prosecution, the magistrates declined jurisdiction and the matter came before the Crown Court for sentencing. The appellant, who was ordered to pay a fine of £48,000 as well as £7,500 costs, appealed against sentence.

HELD: Disquiet had been expressed in various quarters that the level of fines imposed for health and safety offences was too low, which concern the court shared. Whilst it was impossible to lay down any tariff or to say that a fine should bear any specific relationship to turnover or net profit, the factors considered below were relevant.

In assessing the gravity of an offence it is important to have regard to how far short of the appropriate standard the defendant fell. Where death is a consequence of the breach, it will generally be regarded as an aggravating factor and the fine should reflect public disquiet at such an unnecessary loss of life. It is important to note that the standard of care imposed remains the same irrespective of the size of the company. As a result, a defendant company could not rely upon its own relative impecuniosity in mitigation.

Particular aggravating factors will include: (1) a failure to heed warnings; and (2) where a defendant has deliberately profited financially from a failure to take the necessary health and safety steps or specifically run a risk to save money.

Particular mitigating factors will include: (1) prompt admissions of responsibility and a timely plea of guilty; (2) steps to remedy deficiencies after they are drawn to the defendant's attention; and (3) a good safety record.

Any fine imposed should reflect not only the gravity of the offence but also the means of the offender. If the defendant company wishes to make submissions as to its ability to pay a fine it should supply copies of its accounts, and any other financial information upon which it intends to rely, to both the prosecution and the court prior to the hearing. Where such information is deliberately not supplied, the court will be entitled to infer that the defendant can meet any fine imposed.

To meet the legislative objective, fines in health and safety prosecutions need to be large enough to bring home a message to the company, including its shareholders. In the instant case, whilst the various breaches had been of a serious nature and had resulted in a fatality, the defendant was a small company with limited resources. In all the circumstances, the fine would be reduced to £15,000, the costs order would remain the same.

R v Balfour Beatty Civil Engineering Ltd and Geoconsult GES

(1999) LTL, 22 March

[10.22] Balfour Beatty Civil Engineering Ltd (BB), was the main contractor in the construction of a railway tunnel under the Piccadilly Line which also ran beneath the central terminal at Heathrow Airport. Geoconsult GES (G), was the specialist tunnel advisor to BB. On 20 October 1994, in one of the worst civil engineering disasters in Britain for many years, the tunnel collapsed. The expert evidence was that the principal cause of the collapse was the condition of an unrepaired lateral support within the tunnel, and that there had been indications of faults in the lining of the same from at least August 1994. BB pleaded guilty to two counts under HSWA, G was found guilty of two similar counts after trial. The Health and Safety Executive applied for costs against the two defendants.

HELD: The appropriate sentencing guidelines in this type of case were to be found in *R v F Howe & Son (Engineers) Ltd* [1999] 2 All ER 249, CA (see 10.21 above).

BB had fallen seriously short of the appropriate standard in failing to meet the 'reasonably practicable' test. It had been a matter of chance whether death or serious injury resulted from the serious breaches identified and the company had put its concerns as to scheduling above taking proper action to protect its employees and the public at large. The failure to heed warnings was a particular aggravating factor. Mitigating factors were the prompt guilty plea and the exemplary conduct of BB post-accident.

G had also fallen seriously short of the appropriate standard and as with its co-defendant it had been a matter of chance whether or not death or serious injury resulted. However, the court took the view that G bore the lesser responsibility in relation to the collapse and accepted its previously clean health and safety record and the steps taken post-accident as mitigating factors.

The objective for prosecuting health and safety offences in the work place was to achieve a safe environment for employees and members of the public who might be affected thereby. When the defendant was a company the fine had to be large enough to bring the message home to managers and shareholders alike. The fine payable by G would be reduced having regard to its resources and the effect that any fine would have on the business.

BB fined £1.2 million and £100,000 costs, payable in 14 days. G ordered to pay £500,000 and £100,000 costs, the fine to be paid at the rate of £50,000 per quarter and the costs within 12 months.

R v Great Western Trains Co Ltd (1999)

(1999) LTL, 13 August

[10.23] (See paragraphs 10.28, 10.29.) Following the Southall rail crash in September 1997, where one of the defendant company's trains passed through a red light and was involved in a high speed collision killing seven passengers and injuring 150 more, prosecutions were brought alleging seven counts of manslaughter and one count under HSWA. The defendant company pleaded guilty to contravening HSWA, leaving the quantum of fine to be imposed as the remaining issue. The prosecution submitted that the defendant's liability for the accident arose not only as a result of its drivers failure to stop but also due to its management failure in allowing the train to run without the Automatic Warning System (AWS) being isolated. The defence argued that the reasons it had not reversed the train to fit an effective AWS system at the front were fourfold. First, it had not been required by the rules to do so. Secondly, neither Railtrack nor the Railways Inspectorate had suggested such a course of action. Thirdly, it was not the practice of any train operating company to do so and finally, AWS isolation was a category B rather than a category A failure which permitted the train to continue on its journey.

HELD: Passengers were entitled to expect the highest standards of care from train operators. The defendant had failed to meet such a standard by more than it was prepared to admit. Notwithstanding the fact that the primary cause of the collision had been its driver's failure to stop, the AWS isolation was a substantial contributing factor. This accident would not have happened had the train in question been fitted with Automatic Train Protection which British Rail undertook to introduce as standard within five years of the Clapham rail disaster in 1988

The defendant was fined £1.5 million, which reflected the risk created by the degree of its failure to reach the highest standard of care; the extent of the disaster in terms of the number of fatalities and injured passengers and the need to remind those in charge of large public transport undertakings of the need for eternal vigilance to prevent accidents of this type from occurring. The sentence took into account the early guilty plea; the prompt remedial action taken by the defendant after the accident; its previous clean safety record as well as the fact that the defendant had not been in breach of any safety requirements imposed by either Railtrack or the Railways Inspectorate.

R v Friskies Petcare (UK) Ltd

[2000] 2 Cr App Rep (S) 401, CA

[10.24] The appellant company, which operated a large manufacturing concern producing and packaging pet food, pleaded guilty to failing to discharge its duty under HSWA, s 2(1) and contravening the Management of Health and Safety at Work Regulations 1992, reg 3.

The appellant's factory contained 11 stainless steel silos, used to mix meat produce. From time to time the mixing process would halt to allow two technicians to get into the silo and effect repairs and maintenance. Whilst carrying out such works, one of the technicians apparently suffered an electric shock. The other got out of the silo and went to turn off the power supply, which involved climbing a ladder, moving along a gantry and passing through a locked gate before reaching the off switch. The first technician died from electrocution. A subsequent inspection revealed that the underlying cause of death was that welding with a potentially lethal voltage was taking place in a confined, conductive and damp environment.

No proper risk assessment had been carried out nor had any adequate steps been taken to warn the employees of the dangers involved. When sentencing, the trial judge recited what he perceived to be the aggravating and mitigating factors of the case, noting that this was a very serious matter. In particular, he stated that he considered this to be an instance where profit had been put before safety. The appellant, who was ordered to pay a fine of £600,000 in addition to prosecution costs, appealed against sentence.

HELD: The prosecution had not put forward its case on the basis that profit had been put before safety. As such, the Crown Court had been wrong to find that aggravating factor proven.

Applying the principles stated in *R v F Howe & Son (Engineers) Ltd* [1999] 2 All ER 249, CA:

> the aggravating features of the case were: the death of the technician; the inaccessibility of the on/off switch; the fact that the breaches had been going on for some time; the failure to alert employees to the contents of the relevant Health and Safety pamphlets and the failure on the appellant's part to conduct any or any adequate risk assessment in relation to the task being carried out. The mitigating factors were the appellant's prompt admission and guilty plea as well as their good safety record. Taking into account the financial position of the appellant company, whose business generated pre-tax profits of £40 million, the appropriate fine was £250,000.

By way of general guidance, the court recommended that whenever the Health and Safety Executive commenced proceedings, it should list in writing not only the facts of the case but also what it perceived to be the aggravating factors as set out in *Howe*. This document should be served on both the court and defence. If the defendant pleaded guilty it should submit a similar document outlining the mitigating factors to be taken into account. Where the plea was put on an agreed basis, that should be put into writing so that there was no doubt such as had arisen in the instant matter as to the basis upon which the court was to pass sentence.

R v Colthrop Board Mills Ltd

(2002) LTL, 18 March, CA

[10.25] The appellant company specialised in the manufacture of carton board which it produced on an extremely large machine measuring up to one hundred and fifty metres in length. There were approximately 200 access points into the machinery known as running nips. In October 1999, a Health and Safety Inspector issued an Improvement Notice requiring the appellant to carry out a programme of risk assessment by 30January 2000. In a letter accompanying the Improvement Notice express reference was made to the need to provide safe means of access to the machine for the purposes of cleaning and maintenance. It was emphasised that where significant risks were found they should be remedied immediately.

A risk assessment was carried out in respect of the running nip which would become the subject of this prosecution by no later than 12January 2000. The likelihood of an accident involving the same was recorded as 'moderate' whilst the risk of death or serious injury to an employee was said to 'substantial'. On 20 February 2000, one of the claimant's employees sustained a serious crush injury to his right arm when it passed or was pulled through the nip. Whilst the employee was unable to remember precisely what had happened, the evidence was that he had been leaning through the handrails of a cross-machine platform attempting to clean a nip-roll or to deflate an air bubble between the layers of cardboard.

The appellant company was prosecuted and convicted of two offences in relation to this one incident pursuant to HSWA, s 2(1), and under the Provision and Use of Work Equipment Regulations 1998, reg 11. The trial judge, having been informed that a sale of the company had realised £17 million, imposed a total fine of £350,000. In its appeal, the company relied upon three primary submissions, namely that: (1) the conviction depended upon a flawed finding that the employee had been cleaning the machine at the time of the accident; (2) the court below had been provided with misleading information as to its true value; and (3) that the fines imposed were too high.

HELD: In his judgment, the trial judge had listed the aggravating and mitigating factors of the case and had been correct to hold that the company had fallen very short of what could reasonably and practically have been expected of it following the issue of the Improvement Notice. It was noted that the appellant company had two previous convictions arsing from similar accidents in December 1994 and March 1995 (albeit in respect of different machines).

The appellant's first submission failed because the fact remained that the company had, by its neglect, permitted access to dangerous parts of the machinery for cleaning purposes at the very least.

The second and third submissions could be dealt with together. In considering the proper scale of any financial penalty two decisions were of particular assistance: *R v F Howe & Son (Engineers) Ltd* [1999] 2 All ER 249 (see 10.21 above) and *R v Friskies Petcare (UK) Ltd* [2000] 2 Cr App Rep (S) 401, CA (see 10.24 above). These authorities suggested that fines of up to or around £500,000 are appropriate for cases which result in the death or perhaps the serious injury of a single employee. This upper limit ought not to be regarded as set in stone and might be revisited in time and with the increase of safety issue awareness. In this case, the trial judge had not been given accurate financial information and the fines imposed were excessive. The company was in fact of relatively modest size and it had to be acknowledged that there had been a serious injury rather than a fatality. The total fine would be varied to £200,000, to be split evenly between each offence.

Corporate manslaughter

[10.26] The offence of involuntary manslaughter is committed upon proof of unlawful killing without intent to kill or cause grievous bodily harm. The law relating to manslaughter by gross negligence has been clarified and may principally be found in the decision of the House of Lords in *R v Adomako* [1995] 1 AC 171, below.

R v Adomako

[1995] 1 AC 171, HL

[10.27] The defendant, an anaesthetist, was acting as such during the course of an eye operation which involved paralysing the patient, when a tube became disconnected from a ventilator. The patient suffered a cardiac arrest and subsequently died. The defendant was convicted of manslaughter by reason of his breach of duty.

The Court of Appeal dismissed the appeal against conviction. The defendant appealed to the House of Lords on the issue of the true legal nature of involuntary manslaughter.

HELD: The appeal would be dismissed. The ordinary principles of the law of negligence apply to ascertain whether or not the defendant has been in breach of a duty of care towards the victim who has died. If it can be established that the breach of duty caused the death, the jury must go on to consider whether that breach should be characterised as gross negligence and therefore criminal. The question of how far from accepted standards conduct must depart before it will be considered criminal will, necessarily, be a matter of degree in each case. The issue to be determined by the jury is whether, having regard to the risk of death involved, the conduct of the defendant was so bad in all the circumstances as to amount to a criminal act or omission.

R v Great Western Trains Co Ltd

(1999) LTL, 8 November

[10.28] (See paragraph 10.23 above.) On 19 September 1997, a passenger train operated by Great Western Trains (GWT), ran through a red signal and collided with a freight train travelling in the opposite direction. Seven people were killed in the accident which occurred at Southall, a short distance from Paddington station. Both the company and its driver faced seven charges of manslaughter under HSWA.

Prior to the trial of the company, the Crown sought clarification by way of preliminary ruling as to how to put its case and as to the law regarding manslaughter by a corporation generally. Three alternatives were suggested, namely: (1) that there had been a serious breach of personal duty owed by GWT to each of the deceased; (2) that there could be an identification of a sufficiently senior employee in the company who was guilty of the offence himself (in this case, the managing director); (3) whether it could be inferred that there was the existence of a sufficiently senior employee in the company who was guilty of manslaughter.

The Crown argued that the decision of the House of Lords in *R v Adomako* [1995] 1 AC 171 which held that the test for involuntary manslaughter based on gross negligence was a purely objective one not requiring the establishment of mens rea, required a reconsideration of the law as enunciated in *R v P & O European Ferries (Dover) Ltd* (1990) 93 Cr App Rep.

HELD: The allegation against GWT was that its system had failed, there being no suggestion that it bore criminal responsibility for the act of its driver. The prosecution in the *P & O European Ferries* case had been terminated when the jury was directed that there was no proper basis upon which it could convict. In order for such a prosecution to succeed, it had to be shown that there was an identifiable individual in the company guilty of the same offence. In the context of a large corporate body, the only way in which liability could be established was under the directing mind principle. It was acknowledged that this rendered a successful prosecution virtually impossible, particularly where the allegation was one of system failure.

Whilst gross negligence manslaughter might not be a crime involving mens rea in the strict sense, the court did not accept that it was an entirely objective matter. (*Note*—the learned judge erred on this point, see AG's Reference No 2 of 1999, below.). It was still necessary to look for a directing mind in the company and identify whose gross negligence it was that fixed the company with criminal responsibility. The judgment in *Adomako* did not touch upon the circumstances in which a corporation could be held liable for manslaughter, or indeed any other offence.

The ingredients of the offence of manslaughter would have to be established against an individual of a company before that company could be convicted. The only basis on which the Crown could advance a case against GWT was by identifying some person within that company whose negligence was that of the company itself.

A-G's Reference (No 2 of 1999)

[2000] 3 All ER 182, CA

[10.29] The Attorney-General referred to questions two questions for the opinion of the court, namely: (1) Can a defendant be properly convicted of manslaughter by gross negligence in the absence of evidence as to that defendant's state of mind? (2) Can a non-human defendant be convicted of the crime of manslaughter by gross negligence in the absence of evidence establishing the guilt of an identified human individual for the same crime?

HELD: (1) The answer to the first question was 'Yes'. Whilst there might be cases where the defendant's state of mind was relevant to the grossness and criminality of his conduct, such evidence was not a prerequisite to a conviction for manslaughter by gross negligence. As such, the judges ruling on that issue had been wrong. The test set out in *Adomako* is objective, but a defendant who is reckless as defined in *R v Stone* [1977] QB 354, CA, may well be the more readily found to be grossly negligent to a criminal degree.

(2) The answer to the second question was 'No'. The trial judge was correct in his finding that a corporation's liability for manslaughter was based solely on the principle of identification, which was just as relevant to the actus reus as to the mens rea of the offence. Unless an identified individual's conduct, characterisable as gross criminal negligence, can be attributed to the company, that company is not liable for manslaughter. The ordinary rules of civil negligence as, for example, set out in *Wilsons & Clyde Coal Co Ltd v English* [1938] AC 57, HL, were not apt to confer criminal liability upon a corporation.

CHAPTER 11

EU LAW

Introduction	[11.1]
Direct effect of Treaty provisions	[11.2]
Direct effect of Regulations and decisions	[11.3]
Direct effect of Directives	[11.5]
The concept of an emanation of the State	[11.9]
'Indirect effect' of Directives – The obligation to construe National law in conformity with Directives	[11.10]
'Incidental' horizontal effects	[11.12]
Supremacy of community law	[11.13]
Effectiveness of EC law remedies	[11.14]
State liability for breach of EC law	[11.17]
The approach to EC law taken by the UK courts: *European Communities Act 1972*	[11.19]
Substantive EU law	[11.24]

[11.1] The aim of this chapter is merely to provide an initial reference point for those confronted with a case involving European Union law.

European directives dealing with employers and employees can have direct effect. They can alter the construction of statutes and statutory instruments. For this reason some of the most important principles and cases are summarised below.

DIRECT EFFECT OF TREATY PROVISIONS

Case 26/62: NV Algemene Transporten Expeditie Onderneming van Gend en Loos v Nederlandse Administratie Der Belastingen

[1963] ECR 1, ECJ

[11.2] A company was charged with an import duty allegedly increased since the entry into force of the EEC Treaty, which they claimed was contrary to Article 12 (now 25) of that Treaty. In Dutch legal proceedings a question was raised as to whether nationals of a Member State can claim individual rights, on the basis of the Article in question, which the courts must protect.

HELD: According to the spirit, the general scheme and the wording of the EEC Treaty, Article 12 must be interpreted as producing direct effects and creating individual rights which national courts must protect. The European Community constitutes a new legal order of international law for the benefit of which the states have limited their sovereign rights, albeit within limited fields, and the subjects of which comprise not only Member States but also their nationals. Community law not only imposes obligations on individuals but is also intended to confer upon them rights which become part of their legal heritage. These rights arise not only where they are expressly granted by the Treaty, but also by reason of obligations which the Treaty imposes in a clearly defined way upon individuals as well as upon the Member States and upon the institutions of the Community. The Treaty Article in question has 'direct effect' because it is clear and unconditional, negative, contains no reservation on the part of the Member State and is not dependent on any national implementing measure.

DIRECT EFFECT OF REGULATIONS AND DECISIONS

[11.3] Article 249 (ex 189) of the Treaty states that a *regulation* (made by the EU, and not to be confused with UK-made regulations) 'shall be binding in its entirety and directly applicable in all Member States'.

Case 50/76: Amsterdam Bulb BV v Produktschap voor Siergewassen

[1977] ECR 137, ECJ

[11.4] HELD: As the Court has previously confirmed, the direct application of a Community Regulation means that its entry into force and its application in favour of or against those subject to it are independent of any measure of reception into national law. Member States are under a duty not to obstruct the direct effect inherent in regulations and other rules of Community law. Strict compliance with this obligation is an indispensable condition of simultaneous and uniform application of Community regulations throughout the Community. Therefore, the Member States may neither adopt nor allow national organizations having legislative power to adopt any measure which would conceal the Community nature and effects of any legal provision from the person to whom it applies.

> *Note*—Article 249 (ex 189) of the Treaty states that a *decision* is 'binding in its entirety upon those to whom it is addressed'. If a decision is sufficiently unconditional, clear and precise, it will be directly effective (Case 9/70, *Grad v Finanzamt Traunstein* [1970] ECR 825).

DIRECT EFFECT OF DIRECTIVES

[11.5] Article 249 (ex 189) of the Treaty states that a directive 'is binding as to the result to be achieved...but shall leave to the national authorities the choice of form and methods'

Case 41/74: Van Duyn v Home Office

[1974] ECR 1337, ECJ

[11.6] Van Duyn was refused leave to enter the UK on grounds of her association with the Church of Scientology, which the Government asserted was harmful to society. In the course of proceedings in the High Court, a question was referred to the ECJ: whether the provisions of Directive 64/221 were capable of direct effect. The Directive enabled Member States to restrict movement of non-nationals on grounds such as public policy, but did not indicate what would be a legitimate public policy issue.

HELD: It is necessary to examine, in every case, whether the nature, general scheme and wording of a provision are capable of having direct effects on the relations between Member States and individuals. The obligation imposed by the provision of the Directive was clear, precise and legally complete.

Case 152/84: Marshall v Southampton and South West Hampshire Area Health Authority (Teaching)

[1986] QB 401, [1986] ECR 723, ECJ

[11.7] On the basis that she had passed the normal retiring age for women (60), Marshall was dismissed by the respondent, a public authority employer. Men were required by the Authority as a matter of policy to retire at 65. The Sex Discrimination Act 1975 did not on its face encompass retirement issues. Marshall sought to argue that Directive 76/207/EEC (the Equal Treatment Directive) was infringed by her dismissal. The Court of Appeal requested a preliminary ruling.

HELD: The practice of compulsory retirement for women and men at different ages was discriminatory and unlawful, being contrary to the Equal Treatment Directive, Art 5(1). Marshall was entitled to rely upon Article 5(1) of the Directive against a state in its capacity as an employer. As to the argument that a directive may not be relied upon against an individual (referred to by Advocate General Slynn as 'horizontal effect'): a directive may not of itself impose obligations on an individual and a provision of a directive may not be relied upon as such against such a person.

Case C-91/92: Dori v Recreb Srl

[1995] All ER (EC) 1, [1994] ECR I-3325, ECJ

[11.8] The parties had entered into a contract for an English course after one approached the other at Milan Railway Station. The consumer wished to cancel the contract shortly afterwards. She sought to rely upon Directive 85/577/EEC, which concerned the protection of a consumer in a contract negotiated away from business premises. Italy had however failed to implement the Directive. The Italian court made a reference on the issue of whether she could rely on the Directive and her purported cancellation on the basis of the Directive.

HELD: Given that the Member State had not taken measures transposing Directive 85/577/EEC into Italian state law within the prescribed time limit, it was not possible for consumers to derive from the Directive itself a right of cancellation as against private contracting parties. Likewise it was not possible to enforce such a right in a national court against a private trader. However when applying provisions of national law, whether adopted before or after the Directive, the court had to interpret them as far as possible in the light of the wording and purpose of the Directive.

>   *Note*—The latter comment refers to 'indirect effect' dealt with below. *Dori v Recreb* confirmed that directives may not have horizontal direct effect. Thus it is only against an emanation of the State that a directive may have direct effect (vertical direct effect).

THE CONCEPT OF AN EMANATION OF THE STATE

Case C-188/89: Foster v British Gas plc

[1990] ECR I-3313, ECJ

[11.9] A number of female employees of British Gas claimed that they were discriminated against on grounds of sex, in that it was the policy of British Gas to require women to retire at 60 and men at 65. At the relevant time, British Gas was a nationalised industry, with responsibility for and a monopoly of the UK gas supply. The Court of Appeal held that the female employees had not been discriminated against on grounds of sex by being obliged to retire at 60. The House of Lords referred a question to the ECJ: if the Equal Treatment Directive (76/207/EEC), Art 5(1) could be invoked by the female employees against a body such as British Gas.

HELD: Unconditional and sufficiently precise provisions of a directive could be relied on against organizations or bodies subject to the authority or control of the State or which had special powers beyond those which result from the normal rules applicable between individuals. The Court has previously held that provisions of a directive could be relied on against tax authorities, local or regional authorities, constitutionally independent authorities responsible for the maintenance of public order and safety, and public authorities providing public health services. It follows that a body, whatever its legal form, which has been made responsible, pursuant to a measure adopted by the State, for providing a public service under the control of the State and has for that purpose special powers beyond those which resulted from the normal rules applicable in relations between individuals, is included in any event among the bodies against which the provisions of a directive capable of having direct effect may be relied upon. In *Marshall v Southampton and South West Area Health Authority*: Case 152/84 [1986] QB 401 it was shown that Article 5(1) was unconditional and sufficiently precise to be relied on by an individual and to be applied by the national courts although it had not been formally adopted by the member state.

>   *Note*—The House of Lords subsequently ruled that British Gas was indeed a body against which Article 5(1) of the Directive could be enforced, having regard to the ECJ's criteria. Although the criteria for determining whether a body is an emanation of the state are somewhat loosely defined, *Foster* continues to be the primary source of guidance on this issue.

'INDIRECT EFFECT' OF DIRECTIVES – THE OBLIGATION TO CONSTRUE NATIONAL LAW IN CONFORMITY WITH DIRECTIVES

Case 14/83: Von Colson and Kamann v Land Nordrhein-Westfalen, Case 79/83: Harz v Deutsche Tradax GmbH

[1984] ECR 1891, 1921, [1986] 2 CMLR 430, ECJ

[11.10] A private individual sought to rely, as against a public authority employer, upon the provisions of a directive which had been defectively implemented.

HELD: Member States have an obligation arising from a directive to achieve the result envisaged by the directive, and a duty under Article 5 (now Article 10) of the Treaty, to take all appropriate measures, whether general or particular, to ensure the fulfilment of that obligation. The obligation and duty are binding on all the authorities of the Member States, including, for matters within their jurisdiction, the courts. Thus, in applying the national law, and in particular the provisions of a national law specifically introduced to implement Directive 76/207, national courts are obliged to interpret their national law in the light of the wording and purpose of the Directive in order to achieve the result referred to in the third paragraph of Article 189 (now 249). The national courts must interpret the national legislation adopted for the purpose of implementing the directive in conformity with the requirements of Community law, insofar as it is given discretion to do so under national law.

Case C-106/89: Marleasing SA v La Comercial Internacional de Alimentación SA

[1990] ECR I-4135, ECJ

[11.11] In proceedings between two companies, the Spanish court referred a question to the ECJ, asking whether a particular Directive was capable of having direct effect between individuals so as to preclude a declaration of nullity of a company on grounds other than those set out in the Directive.

HELD: The ECJ reframed the question: whether a national court hearing a case which falls within Directive 68/151 is required to interpret its national law in the light of the wording and purpose of that Directive in order to preclude a declaration of nullity of a public limited company on a ground other than those listed in Article 11 of the Directive. It follows from what was stated in *Von Colson* that, in applying national law, whether the provisions in question were adopted before or after a directive, the national court called upon to interpret it is required to do so, as far as possible, in the light of the wording and the purpose of the directive in order to achieve the result pursued by the latter and thereby comply with the third paragraph of Article 189 (now 249) of the Treaty.

'Incidental' horizontal effects

Case C-443/98: Unilever Italia SpA v Central Food SpA

[2000] ECR I-7535, ECJ

[11.12] The case concerned a contractual dispute between two companies. The labelling of olive oil delivered by the plaintiff under a contract for delivery of the oil complied with EC law, but not with the disputed Italian law affecting labelling. The Italian law had been adopted in breach of a standstill clause under Directive 83/189. It was argued that the terms of the Directive could be relied upon to have the Italian law disapplied. The effect would be to impose a contractual obligation on the defendant on the basis of a Directive in private litigation, which would not be imposed if the Italian law applied.

HELD: A national court is required, in civil proceedings between individuals concerning contractual rights and obligations, to refuse to apply a national technical regulation which was adopted during a period of postponement of adoption prescribed by Article 9 of Directive 83/189. Application of the Italian law adopted in breach of Directive 83/189, Art 9, is liable to hinder the plaintiff in marketing the oil which it offers for sale. In *CIA Security International SA v Signalson and Securitel*: C-194/94 [1996] ECR I-2201, ECJ, the finding of inapplicability as a legal consequence of breach of the obligation of notification was made in response to a request for a preliminary ruling arising from proceedings between competing undertakings based on national provisions prohibiting unfair trading. It follows from the Court's case-law that the inapplicability of a technical regulation which has not been notified in accordance with Directive 83/189, Art 8, can be invoked in proceedings between individuals. The same applies to non-compliance with Article 9's obligations, and there is no reason, in that connection, to distinguish disputes between individuals relating to unfair competition from disputes between individuals concerning contractual rights and obligations, as here. Whilst it is correct to state that a directive cannot of itself impose obligations on an individual and cannot therefore be relied on as such against an individual (see *Dori v Recreb)*, that case-law does not apply where non-compliance with Directive 83/189, Arts 8 or 9, which constitutes a substantial procedural defect, renders a technical regulation adopted in breach of either of those Articles inapplicable. Unlike the case of non-transposition of directives, Directive 83/189 does not in any way define the substantive scope of the legal rule on the basis of which the national court must decide the case before it. It creates neither rights nor obligations for individuals.

> Note—Cases such as *Unilever Italia* and *CIA Security* undermine the bright line distinction of no horizontal direct effect set out in *Marshall* (see 11.7 above) and *Dori v Recreb* (see 11.8 above). The extent to which the rule is undermined is far from certain. Increasing use is made of directives in private litigation in various different ways, and practitioners must proceed with caution. Even where a directive has yet to be implemented, or where a national law conflicts with a directive, directives are having effect in different ways in litigation between private parties.

Supremacy of Community law

Case 106/77: Amminstrazione delle Finanze dello Stato v Simmenthal SpA

[1978] ECR 629, ECJ

[11.13] Italian tax authorities argued that a national court could not simply refuse to apply a national law which conflicted with EC law. It claimed that the Italian Constitutional Court would need to decide such a matter and declare it unconstitutional.

HELD: It is not necessary for the national court to request or await the prior setting aside, by legislative or other constitutional means, of a provision of national legislation conflicting with Community law. Every national court, in a case within its jurisdiction, must apply Community law in its entirety and is under a duty to give full effect to Community law provisions, if necessary refusing of its own motion to apply any conflicting provision of national legislation, whether adopted prior or subsequent to the Community rule in question.

Effectiveness of EC law remedies

Case 33/76: Rewe-Zentralfinanz GmbH v Landwirtschaftskammer für Saarland

[1976] ECR 1989, ECJ

[11.14] A claim for a refund of charges was made by the applicants when the charges were found to have been made in breach of Community law.

HELD: The national courts are entrusted with securing the legal protection which citizens derive from directly effective Community law. Accordingly, in the absence of Community rules on this subject, the domestic legal systems must determine the procedural conditions governing actions at law intended to ensure the protection of the rights which citizens have from the direct effect of Community law. Such conditions cannot be less favourable than those relating to similar actions of a domestic nature. In the absence of harmonisation measures, the right conferred by Community law must be exercised before the national courts in accordance with the conditions laid down by national rules, unless the conditions and time-limits made it impossible in practice to exercise the rights which the national courts are obliged to protect. Limitation periods which are reasonable do not infringe this principle.

Case C-213/89: R v Secretary of State for Transport, ex p Factortame Ltd (No 2)

[1991] 1 AC 603, [1990] ECR I-2433, ECJ

[11.15] The Merchant Shipping Act 1988 required fresh registration of all British fishing vessels. The Act included new conditions, such as requiring that there be a 75% nationality requirement for directors and shareholders. Factortame was a company with mainly Spanish directors and shareholders. It had been registered as a British vessel under the previous legislation, but was unable to be registered under the 1988 Act because it could not comply with the new conditions. It argued that the new conditions breached Community law and sought interim relief. The House of Lords ruled that interim relief could not be granted in this case, because of a common law rule that no interim injunction could be granted against the Crown, and because of a presumption that an Act of Parliament is in conformity with EC law absent a decision on its compatibility with EC law. The House of Lords made a reference to the ECJ.

HELD: A national court, in a Community law case, which finds that the sole obstacle precluding it from granting interim relief is a rule of national law, must disapply that national law. The full effectiveness of Community law would be impaired if a rule of national law could prevent a court, in a case governed by Community law, from granting interim relief in order to ensure the full effectiveness of the judgment to be given on the existence of the rights claimed under Community law. Therefore, a court which in those circumstances would grant interim relief, but for the rule of national law, is obliged to set aside that rule.

Case C-271/91: Marshall v Southampton and South West Hampshire Area Health Authority (No 2)

[1994] QB 126, [1993] ECR I-4367, ECJ

[11.16] UK laws imposed a statutory cap on Marshall's damages for her discriminatory dismissal, and there was uncertainty as to whether the industrial tribunal had power to award interest in the circumstances of the case. The House of Lords made a request to the ECJ, asking whether she was entitled to full compensation for her loss and whether Directive 76/207, Art 6 could be relied upon to challenge the national rules limiting compensation.

HELD: Compensation for dismissal on grounds of sex could not be limited by the national law, and interest was an essential component of such compensation for the purpose of restoring equality of treatment. Directive 76/207, Art 6 places Member States under a duty to take the necessary measures to enable all persons who consider themselves wronged by discrimination to pursue their claims by judicial process. Article 6 does not prescribe a specific measure, but the objective is to arrive at real equality of opportunity. The measures taken by the Member State must be such as to guarantee real and effective judicial protection and have a real deterrent effect on the employer. Where financial compensation is the chosen remedy, it must be adequate, in the sense that it must enable the loss and damage actually sustained as a result of the discriminatory dismissal to be made in full in accordance with the national rules. The fixing of an upper limit of the kind in question cannot, by definition, constitute proper implementation of Article 6. Interest is an essential component of full compensation for the purpose of restoring real equality of treatment because factors affecting full compensation, such as the effluxion of time, cannot be left out of account.

Note—Cases such as *Marshall (No 2)* represent something of a high water mark for the ECJ's robust approach to effective remedies. Cases such as

Steenhorst-Neerings v Bestuur van de Bedrijfsvereniging voor Detailhandel:C-338/91 [1993] ECR I-5475, ECJ and *R v Secretary of State for Social Security, ex p Sutton*: C-66/95 [1997] ECR I-2163, ECJ, suggested a retreat. In the latter case, for example, interest was held not be an essential component of the right to payments by way of social security benefit, on the facts, distinguishing *Marshall (No 2)*. The recent approach tends towards balancing the scope and purpose of the particular national rule, against the significance of the particular Community right. For example, in *Hoechst AG v IRC and A-G*: C-397, 410/98 [2001] ECR I-1727, ECJ, the Court overcame an objection that the law of England and Wales did not make restitutionary remedies available in the circumstances; and also distinguished *Sutton* in holding that an award of interest would be essential to repair damage caused by a breach of Article 52 of the Treaty.

STATE LIABILITY FOR BREACH OF EC LAW

Joined Cases C-6/90 and C-9/90: Francovich and Bonifaci v Italy

[1991] ECR I-5357, [1995] ICR 722, ECJ

[11.17] The applicant employees were owed wages by their employers. The Italian Government had failed to implement Directive 80/987, which aimed to protect employees of undertakings which had become insolvent by providing employees with a minimum level of protection. The applicants claimed that the State was liable to pay them the sums outstanding.

HELD: The full effectiveness of Community rules would be impaired if individuals were unable to obtain compensation when their rights are infringed by a breach of Community law for which a Member State can be held responsible. A Member State was required to make good damage to individuals arising from the non-implementation of the Directive. State liability for harm caused to individuals by breaches of Community law for which the State can be held responsible is inherent in the Treaty, but the conditions for state liability giving rise to a right to compensation depend on the nature of the breach. In the case of non-implementation of a directive, the conditions for liability were threefold.

Firstly, the result prescribed by the directive should entail the grant of rights to individuals.

Secondly, it should be possible to identify the content of those rights on the basis of the directive's provisions.

Thirdly, there must be a causal link between the breach of the State's obligation and the harm suffered by the injured parties.

In the absence of Community legislation, it is for the national courts of each system to lay down the detailed procedural rules for legal proceedings to safeguard the rights which individuals derive from Community law. Those national substantive and procedural conditions on compensation for harm may not be less favourable than those relating to similar internal claims, and may not be framed as to make it virtually impossible or excessively difficult to obtain compensation.

Joined Cases C-46/93 & C-48/93: Brasserie du Pecheur SA v Germany R v Secretary of State for Transport, ex p Factortame Ltd

[1996] QB 404, [1996] ECR I-1029, ECJ

[11.18] References for preliminary rulings as to state liability where a Member State retained laws which were incompatible with EC law were made in separate German and British proceedings.

In the German case, a French brewery had suffered loss when it had been obliged to discontinue exporting beer to Germany because the French beer did not conform to German beer purity laws. (These purity laws had been held to be incompatible with Article 30 of the Treaty (now Article 28) in Case 178/84: *EC Commission v Germany* [1987] ECR 1227.) The French brewery claimed damages from the German State.

The British proceedings arose out of the same set of facts described above in the first *Factortame* case. In the second *Factortame* case C-221/89: [1991] ECR I-3905, the ECJ had ruled that the provisions of the Merchant Shipping Act 1988 concerning the registration of Spanish fishing vessels in the UK were incompatible with Article 52 (now 43) of Treaty on freedom of establishment. In these proceedings, the Spanish fishermen claimed damages from the United Kingdom.

HELD: Breaches of Articles 28 (ex Article 30) and Articles 43 (ex Article 52) could give rise to a right to compensation. Member States were obliged to make good damage caused to individuals by breaches of Community law attributable to the State where the national legislature was responsible for the breach in question. The conditions of state liability for breach of Community law must be based on the principles developed by the Court for non-contractual liability of the Community institutions for breach of Community law. These rules take into account, inter alia, the complexity of situations to be regulated, difficulties in the application or interpretation of the texts and the margin of discretion available to the author of the act in question. The reparation for the loss or damage which Member States had caused must be commensurate with the loss or damage sustained. Three conditions had to be met: the rule of law infringed must be intended to confer rights on individuals; the breach must be sufficiently serious; and there must be a direct causal link between the breach of the obligation resting on the state and the damage sustained by the injured parties. Those conditions correspond in substance to the principles of liability of the Community for damage caused to individuals by unlawful legislative measures adopted by its institutions. As to the second condition, the decisive test for finding that a breach of Community law is sufficiently serious is whether the Member State or Community institution manifestly and gravely disregarded the limits on its discretion. The factors which the national court may consider include: the clarity and provision of the rule breaches, the measure of discretion left by the rule to the national or Community authority, whether the infringement and the damage caused was intentional or involuntary, whether any error of law was excusable, the fact that the position taken by a Community institution may have contributed towards the omission, and the adoption or retention of national measures or practices contrary to Community law. On any view, a breach will clearly be sufficiently serious if it has persisted despite a judgment finding the infringement to be established, or a preliminary ruling or settled ECJ case-law from which it is clear that the conduct in question constituted an infringement.

Subsequently, the Divisional Court in the *Factortame* litigation ([1998] 1 All ER 736n) determined that the breaches of Community law were sufficiently serious to give rise to liability for any damage that may subsequently be shown to have been caused to the applicants.

> *Note*—in Cases C-178–190/94: *Dillenkofer v Germany* [1997] QB 259, [1996] ECR I-4845, ECJ, it was held that *Francovich* had established that the failure to take any measure to transpose a directive in order to achieve the result it prescribed within the period laid down was in itself a sufficiently serious breach of Community law.
>
> See also Case C-453/99: *Courage Ltd v Crehan* [2001] ECR I-6297, ECJ. In that case, the principle of liability for breach of Community law was extended to a situation where a private party had committed the breach. The judgment requires that national courts must make available an action in damages against a private party for loss caused by a contract or conduct liable to restrict or distort competition. Whether or not this will extend to breaches of directly effective Community rules outside the competition law field remains to be seen.

THE APPROACH TO EC LAW TAKEN BY THE UK COURTS

European Communities Act 1972

[11.19] Section 2(1) provides:

All such rights, powers, liabilities, obligations and restrictions from time to time created or arising by or under the Treaties, and all such remedies and procedures from time to time provided for by or under the Treaties, as in accordance with the Treaties are without further enactment to be given legal effect or used in the United Kingdom shall be recognised and available in law, and be enforced, allowed and followed accordingly; and the expression 'enforceable Community right' and similar expressions shall be read as referring to one to which this subsection applies.

> *Note*—Section 2(2) provides that Community obligations may be implemented by means of Order in Council or statutory instrument, not just primary legislation.

Section 2(4) provides:

The provision that may be made under subsection 2(4) above includes, subject to Schedule 2 to this Act, any such provision (of any such extent) as might be made by Act of Parliament, and any enactment passed or to be passed, other than one contained in this Part of this Act, shall be construed and have effect subject to the foregoing provisions of this section …

> *Note*—The Schedule referred to by section 2(4) contains a number of powers, like legislating retroactively, which cannot be exercised by Order in Council or delegated legislation.

Section 3 provides:

> For the purposes of all legal proceedings any question as to the meaning or effect of any of the Treaties, or as to the validity, meaning or effect of any Community instrument, shall be treated as a question of law (and, if not referred to the European Court, be for determination as such in accordance with the principles laid down by and any relevant decision of the European Court or any court attached thereto).

Litster v Forth Dry Dock and Engineering Co Ltd (in receivership)

[1990] 1 AC 546, [1989] 1 All ER 1134, HL

[11.20] Employees were dismissed at 3.30 pm by the receiver of the employer. Just one hour later, the receiver sold the assets of the company to the transferee. The transferee of the business had obtained a new lease of the work premises. A question arose concerning the construction of the TUPE Regulations 1981 and whether the transferee of the business was liable to pay compensation for unfair dismissal of the employees.

HELD: The courts are under a duty to give a purposive construction to EC Directives and Regulations, in line with ECJ guidance. Having regard to EC Directive 77/187 and ECJ case-law, TUPE 1981, regulation 5(3) should not be limited to 'workers employed immediately before the transfer in point of time' but must be read so as to cover 'workers employed immediately before the transfer or who would have been so employed if they had not been unfairly dismissed before the transfer for a reason connected with the transfer'.

Webb v EMO Air Cargo (UK) Ltd

[1992] ICR 445, CA; on appeal [1993] 1 WLR 49, HL; refd C-32/93: [1994] QB 718, ECJ; apld [1995] 1 WLR 1454, HL

[11.21] The applicant had been recruited with a view to her replacing an employee who had become pregnant. She then discovered that she had become pregnant shortly after her appointment. The employer dismissed her once it had discovered this fact. Her claim that her dismissal was contrary to the Sex Discrimination Act 1975, s 1 was dismissed by the industrial tribunal. Her appeals to the EAT and Court of Appeal were dismissed.

The Court of Appeal ([1992] ICR 445) considered that a man who had been recruited to take over a pregnant worker's job and who had said he would be absent for a like period, would have been dismissed in similar circumstances, and thus there was no sex discrimination. It plainly stated that the construction of the Sex Discrimination Act contended for by the applicant's counsel would distort the meaning of the Act. It stated that *Von Colson* and *Marleasing* did not require the national courts to give a distorted meaning to a domestic statute in order to achieve the aim of a directive.

The House of Lords, on appeal ([1993] 1 WLR 49), agreed that *Marleasing* did not require the distortion of a domestic statute, but made a reference to the ECJ.

The ECJ (C-32/93: [1994] QB 718) held that the dismissal on grounds of pregnancy amounted to direct sex discrimination. The national courts were wrong in their selection of a comparator, as a woman finding herself to be incapable of performing the task for which she was recruited because of pregnancy could not be compared to a man incapable of such tasks because of a medical or other condition. Article 2(1) read with Article 5(1) of Directive 76/207 precludes dismissal of an employee who is recruited for an unlimited term with a view, initially, to replacing another employee during the latter's maternity leave and who cannot do so because, shortly after recruitment, she is herself found to be pregnant.

When the case returned to the House of Lords ((*Lords Keith, Griffiths, Browne-Wilkinson, Mustill and Slynn*) [1995] 1 WLR 1454), the House had to construe section 1 (1)(a) and section 5(3) of the Sex Discrimination Act 1975 so as to accord if at all possible with Directive 76/207 and the ECJ's ruling. The House noted the problem of how to fit the terms of the precise statutory test of unlawful discrimination of the 1975 Act into the ECJ's ruling, which was based on an interpretation of the broad principles of Articles 2(1) and 5(1) of Directive 76/207. Lord Keith, giving the only full judgment, stated:

> ... The only way of doing so is to hold that, in a case where a woman is engaged for an indefinite period, the fact that the reason why she will be temporarily unavailable for work at a time when to her knowledge her services will be particularly required is pregnancy is a circumstance relevant to her case, being a circumstance which could not be present in the case of the hypothetical man. It does not necessarily follow that pregnancy would be a relevant circumstance in the situation where the woman is denied employment for a fixed period in the future during the whole of which her pregnancy would make her unavailable for work, nor in the situation where after engagement for such a period the discovery of her pregnancy leads to cancellation of the engagement.

Note—Lord Keith did not refer to the House's previous view (and certainly that of the Court of Appeal) that such strained interpretations would distort the meaning of the statute, and that *Marleasing* did not require a distorted meaning to be given. This therefore demonstrates the extent to which the powerful obligation to construe UK law in conformity with EC law has been accepted by the UK courts, and throws doubt on the 'as far as possible' limit stated in *Marleasing*.

R v Secretary of State for Employment, ex p Equal Opportunities Commission

[1995] 1 AC 1, [1994] 1 All ER 910, HL (Lords Keith, Jauncey, Lowry, Browne-Wilkinson and Slynn)

[11.22] The EOC considered that certain provisions of the Employment Protection (Consolidation) Act 1978 concerning part-time workers were discriminatory against women, as they were less likely to comply with the threshold conditions for claiming unfair dismissal and redundancy. The Employment Secretary in a letter to the EOC refused to accept that the UK was in breach of EC law in this regard, and the EOC commenced judicial review of the Minister's decision. The applicant, D, was joined as a party. She had not qualified for a redundancy payment because of the threshold conditions, as she had worked 11 hours a week for less than five years. The Minister contended that the national court had no jurisdiction to make a declaration that the UK or Minister were in breach of an EC law obligation.

HELD: The appropriate forum for D's claim was the industrial tribunal.

As to the EOC's claim, the threshold conditions for entitlement to unfair dismissal and redundancy claims in the Employment Protection (Consolidation) Act 1978 were incompatible with Article 119 of the EEC Treaty and Directives 75/117/EEC and 207/EEC/EEC. Declarations should be made that those parts of the 1978 Act were incompatible with the EC law provisions. (per Lord Keith, Lord Lowry, Lord Browne-Wilkinson and Lord Slynn). The Divisional Court had jurisdiction to determine the substantive issues and to declare that primary legislation was incompatible with Community law. The *Factortame* litigation set a precedent in this regard. (per Lord Keith, Lord Browne-Wilkinson and Lord Slynn).

Stark v Post Office

[2000] ICR 1013, [2000] PIQR P105, CA (Waller LJ, Robert Walker LJ)

[11.23] Stark was a postman, to whom the Post Office had provided a bicycle with which to make his deliveries. He suffered personal injury in the course of his employment, when a part of the front brake broke. The trial judge found as a fact that the cause of the failure of the brake part was would not have been revealed on inspection. The Provision and Use of Work Equipment Regulations 1992, reg 6(1) stated: 'Every employer shall ensure that work equipment is maintained in an efficient state, in efficient working order and in good repair'. The Post Office relied upon Council Directive 89/655/EEC, (the Work Equipment Directive) and Council Directive 89/391/EEC, (the Framework Directive) which the Regulations had been intended to implement, to argue that something less than an absolute duty had been the purpose of the Directives. Stark, on the other hand, said that regulation 6 created an absolute obligation.

HELD: The Directives set forth minimum standards. Nothing precluded a Member State from imposing stricter requirements than the Directives required. Moreover, other health and safety regulations contained the same form of words, which had been held to impose an absolute obligation, considering *Galashiels Gas Co Ltd v O'Donnell (or Millar)* [1949] AC 275, HL, and *Hamilton v National Coal Board* [1960] AC 633, HL. The Regulations imposed an absolute obligation in relation to the provision and use of work equipment, including the bicycle which had caused the accident, notwithstanding the trial judge's finding of fact.

SUBSTANTIVE EU LAW

[11.24] It is not proposed in a work of this kind to cover the many substantive areas of EU law which bear upon employers' liability. Attempt has been made to refer to these substantive areas in other chapters of this book as appropriate. Instead reference is made here to a source of substantive EU law which forms a useful reference point. The European Union's Charter of Fundamental Rights was 'solemnly proclaimed' at Nice on 7 December 2000. It does not yet have formally binding legal status, although it looks set to become the bedrock of the future European constitution presently being considered by the Convention working on the Future of the Union. Moreover, it has already produced legal effects. For an article dealing with the legal effects, actual and potential, of the Charter, set in the UK context, see Ian Rogers, 'From the Human Rights Act to the Charter: Not another Human Rights Instrument to Consider?' [2002] 3 European Human Rights Law Review 343.

Advocate General Tizzano in *R (on the applicaion of BECTU) v Secretary of State for Trade and Industry*: Case C-173/99 [2001] All ER (EC) 647 described it as a 'substantive point of reference' for all those involved in the Community context, and stated:

> In proceedings concerned with the nature and scope of a fundamental right, the relevant statements of the Charter cannot be ignored.

The European Court of First Instance has already relied expressly on Charter provisions in its rulings (*Max.mobil Telekommunikation Service v EC Commission*: Case T-54/99 [2002] 4 CMLR 1356, CFI; *Jego-Quere v EC Commission*: Case T 177/01 [2002] All ER (EC) 932, CFI).

[11.25] Some of the Charter provisions relevant to employers' liability are set out below.

CHAPTER IV

SOLIDARITY

Article 27

Workers' right to information and consultation within the undertaking

Workers or their representatives must, at the appropriate levels, be guaranteed information and consultation in good time in the cases and under the conditions provided for by Community law and national laws and practices.

Article 28

Right of collective bargaining and action

Workers and employers, or their respective organisations, have, in accordance with Community law and national laws and practices, the right to negotiate and conclude collective agreements at the appropriate levels and, in cases of conflicts of interest, to take collective action to defend their interests, including strike action.

Article 29

Right of access to placement services

Everyone has the right of access to a free placement service.

Article 30

Protection in the event of unjustified dismissal

Every worker has the right to protection against unjustified dismissal, in accordance with Community law and national laws and practices.

Article 31

Fair and just working conditions

1. Every worker has the right to working conditions which respect his or her health, safety and dignity.

2. Every worker has the right to limitation of maximum working hours, to daily and weekly rest periods and to an annual period of paid leave.

Article 32

Prohibition of child labour and protection of young people at work

The employment of children is prohibited. The minimum age of admission to employment may not be lower than the minimum school-leaving age, without prejudice to such rules as may be more favourable to young people and except for limited derogations.

Young people admitted to work must have working conditions appropriate to their age and be protected against economic exploitation and any work likely to harm their safety, health or physical, mental, moral or social development or to interfere with their education.

Article 33

Family and professional life

1. The family shall enjoy legal, economic and social protection.

2. To reconcile family and professional life, everyone shall have the right to protection from dismissal for a reason connected with maternity and the right to paid maternity leave and to parental leave following the birth or adoption of a child.

Article 34

Social security and social assistance

1. The Union recognises and respects the entitlement to social security benefits and social services providing protection in cases such as maternity, illness, industrial accidents, dependency or old age, and in the case of loss of employment, in accordance with the rules laid down by Community law and national laws and practices.

2. Everyone residing and moving legally within the European Union is entitled to social security benefits and social advantages in accordance with Community law and national laws and practices.

3. In order to combat social exclusion and poverty, the Union recognises and respects the right to social and housing assistance so as to ensure a decent

existence for all those who lack sufficient resources, in accordance with the rules laid down by Community law and national laws and practices.

Note—The Charter is accompanied by an invaluable Explanatory Text, which sets out the sources of the rights and occasionally points to areas in which the rights in the Charter may be wider than the rights as originally expressed. The Explanatory Text to Article 31 of the Charter is set out here by way of example. The Explanatory Text, CHARTE 4473/00, 21.10.2000 can be found at *http://www.europarl.eu.int/charter/convent49_en.htm*.

Explanation

1. This Article is based on Directive 89/391/EEC on the introduction of measures to encourage improvements in the safety and health of workers at work. It also draws on Article 3 of the Social Charter and point 19 of the Community Charter on the rights of workers, and, as regards dignity at work, on Article 26 of the revised Social Charter. The expression "working conditions" must be understood in the sense of Article 140 of the EC Treaty.

2. Paragraph 2 is based on Directive 93/104/EC concerning certain aspects of the organisation of working time, Article 2 of the European Social Charter and point 8 of the Community Charter on the rights of workers.

CHAPTER 12

Insurance

Compulsory insurance	[12.1]
Employers' Liability (Compulsory Insurance) Act 1969	[12.2]
Nature of liability under 1969 Act	[12.9]
Insolvency	[12.10]
Employer's liability insurance and motor insurance	[12.13]
Personal insurance	[12.14]

COMPULSORY INSURANCE

[12.1] There is a requirement pursuant to the Employers' Liability (Compulsory Insurance) Act 1969 to insure against the liability for injuries sustained by an employee whilst acting in the course of his employment.

Any failure to effect a policy amounts to a criminal offence by virtue of section 5 (see 12.6 below) and can result in a prosecution.

Employers' Liability (Compulsory Insurance) Act 1969

[12.2]

1 Insurance against liability for employees

(1) Except as otherwise provided by this Act, every employer carrying on any business in Great Britain shall insure, and maintain insurance, under one of more approved policies with an authorised insurer or insurers against liability for bodily injury or disease sustained by his employees, and arising out of and in the course of their employment in Great Britain in that business, but except in so far as regulations otherwise provide not including injury or disease suffered or contracted outside Great Britain.

(2) Regulations may provide that the amount for which an employer is required by this Act to insure and maintain insurance shall, either generally or in such cases or classes of case as may be prescribed by the regulations, be limited in such manner as may be so prescribed.

(3) For the purposes of this Act—
(a) 'approved policy' means a policy of insurance not subject to any conditions or exceptions prohibited for those purposes by regulations;
(b) 'authorised insurer' means a person or body of persons lawfully carrying on in [the United Kingdom insurance business of a class specified in Schedule 1 or 2 to the Insurance Companies Act [1982]][, or, being an insurance company the head office of which is in a member state, lawfully carrying on in a member State other than the United Kingdom insurance business of a corresponding class,] and issuing the policy or policies in the course thereof;
(c) 'business' includes a trade or profession, and includes any activity carried on by a body of persons, whether corporate or unincorporate;
(d) except as otherwise provided by regulations, an employer not having a place of business in Great Britain shall be deemed not to carry on business there.

[12.3]

2 Employees to be covered

(1) For the purposes of this Act the term 'employee' means an individual who has entered into or works under a contract of service or apprenticeship with an employer whether by way of manual labour, clerical work or otherwise, whether such contract is expressed or implied, oral or in writing.

(2) This Act shall not require an employer to insure—
(a) in respect of an employee of whom the employer is the husband, wife, father, mother, grandfather, grandmother, step-father, step-mother, son, daughter, grandson, granddaughter, stepson, stepdaughter, brother, sister, half-brother or half-sister; or
(b) except as otherwise provided by regulations, in respect of employees not ordinarily resident in Great Britain.

[12.4]

3 Employers exempted from insurance

(1) This Act shall not require any insurance to be effected by—
(a) any such authority as is mentioned in subsection (2) below; or
(b) any body corporate established by or under any enactment for the carrying on of any industry or part of an industry, or of any undertaking, under national ownership or control; or
(c) in relation to any such cases as may be specified in the regulations, any employer exempted by regulations.

(2) The authorities referred to in subsection (1)(a) above
[(a) a health service body, as defined in section 60(7) of the National Health Service and Community Care Act 1990, ... a National Health Service trust established under Part I of that Act or the National Health Service (Scotland) Act 1978 [and a Primary Care Trust established under section 16A of the National Health Service Act 1977]; and

(b)] are the Common Council of the City of London, ... , the council of a London borough, the council of a county, ... or county district in England [the council of a county or county borough in Wales], [the Broads Authority,] [a National Park authority] [a council constituted under section 2 of the Local Government etc (Scotland) Act 1994 in] Scotland, any joint board or joint committee in England and Wales or joint committee in Scotland which is so constituted as to include among its members representatives of any such council [the Strathclyde Passenger Transport Authority], [... a joint authority established by Part IV of the Local Government Act 1985], [, any police authority, the Service Authority for the National Criminal Intelligence Service and the Service Authority for the National Crime Squad].

[12.5]

4 Certificates of insurance

(1) Provision may be made by regulations for securing that certificates of insurance in such form and containing such particulars as may be prescribed by the regulations, are issued by insurers to employers entering into contracts of insurance in accordance with the requirements of this Act and for the surrender in such circumstances as may be so prescribed of certificates so issued.

(2) Where a certificate of insurance is required to be issued to an employer in accordance with regulations under subsection (1) above, the employer (subject to any provision made by the regulations as to the surrender of the certificate) shall during the currency of the insurance and such further period (if any) as may be provided by regulations—
(a) comply with any regulations requiring him to display copies of the certificate of insurance for the information of his employees;
(b) produce the certificate of insurance or a copy thereof on demand to any inspector duly authorised by the Secretary of State for the purposes of this Act and produce or send the certificate or a copy thereof to such other persons, at such place and in such circumstances as may be prescribed by regulations;
(c) permit the policy of insurance or a copy thereof to be inspected by such persons and in such circumstances as may be so prescribed.

(3) A person who fails to comply with a requirement imposed by or under this section shall be liable on summary conviction to a fine not exceeding [level 3 on the standard scale].

[12.6]

5 Penalty for failure to insure

An employer who on any day is not insured in accordance with this Act when required to be so shall be guilty of an offence and shall be liable on summary conviction to a fine not exceeding [level 4 on the standard scale]; and where an offence under this section committed by a corporation has been committed with the consent or connivance of, or facilitated by any neglect on the part of, any director, manager, secretary or other officer of the corporation, he, as well as the corporation shall be deemed to be guilty of that offence and shall be liable to be proceeded against and punished accordingly.

[12.7]

6 Regulations

(1) The Secretary of State may by statutory instrument make regulations for any purpose for which regulations are authorised to be made by this Act, but any such statutory instrument shall be subject to annulment in pursuance of a resolution of either House of Parliament.

(2) Any regulations under this Act may make different provision for different cases or classes of case, and may contain such incidental and supplementary provisions as appear to the Secretary of State to be necessary or expedient for the purposes of the regulations.

[12.8]

7 Short title, extent and commencement

(1) This Act may be cited as the Employers' Liability (Compulsory Insurance) Act 1969.

(2) This Act shall not extend to Northern Ireland.

(3) This Act shall come into force for any purpose on such date as the Secretary of State may by order contained in a statutory instrument appoint, and the purposes for which this Act is to come into force at any time may be defined by reference to the nature of an employer's business, or to that of an employee's work, or in any other way.

Nature of liability under 1969 Act

Regulations made under the Act have defined what risks need to be covered.

Richardson v Pitt-Stanley

[1995] 1 All ER 460, CA

[12.9] The plaintiff's employer Bridge Metals (Basildon) Ltd failed to take out compulsory insurance under the Employers' Liability (Compulsory Insurance) Act 1969. The plaintiff brought proceedings on the basis that he had suffered 'loss in an amount equal to the sum which he would have recovered inclusive of damages, interest and costs against the said company had it been properly insured'. The claim was struck out as disclosing no reasonable cause of action but reinstated on appeal. The matter came before the Court of Appeal.

HELD: The 1969 Act created a criminal liability and not a civil liability. Any civil action for damages should be brought for breach of the common law duty of care or breach of a statutory duty under relevant legislation. The defendants did not have a civil liability to pay damages as a result of their failure to insure and the appeal was dismissed.

INSOLVENCY

[12.10] In the event of the insolvency of the insured employer the employee will still have rights under the Third Party (Rights Against Insurers) Act 1930. The insurer may rely on certain defences under the policy, but their rights have been limited by the Employers' Liability (Compulsory Insurance) Regulations 1998. These regulations prevent the insurers from relying on a failure to comply with reporting conditions; record keeping requirements and requirements to take reasonable care to protect employees.

Further the employee is not required to pay arrears of premiums.

Murray v Legal & General Assurance Society

[1970] 2 QB 495 Cumming Bruce J.

[12.11] The Claimant made a claim for personal injuries against his employers. The claim was passed to the insurers. They indicated that they proposed to set off against the claim the amount owing by way of premium. The employers went into voluntary liquidation. In 1966 judgment was entered against the employers and the insurers were notified that the Claimant intended to pursue a claim under the 1930 Act. Damages were assessed at £1,750 and costs at £186. The outstanding premiums were £1708. In proceedings brought under the 1930 Act the insurers contended that the sum of £1708 should be set off.

HELD: There should be no set off. The liabilities of the insolvent insured to the insurer were not transferred to the third party Claimant under the 1930 Act. Any defences to a claim under the policy had to arise 'in respect of the liability' to the third party Claimant. The premiums did not arise in respect of such liability.

However any such rights under the 1930 Act had to be established before the insolvent insured company is dissolved.

Bradley v Eagle Star Insurance Co

[1989] AC 957 House of Lords

[12.12] Mrs Bradley was employed by Dart Mill Limited. At the time Dart Mill Limited was insured by Eagle Star. Mrs Bradley suffered from byssinosis (a respiratory disease caused by the inhalation of cotton dust). In 1976 Dart Mill Limited was dissolved. In 1984 Mrs Bradley sought pre-action discovery of the insurer's policy of insurance. The insurers resisted on the basis that no liability had been established against Dart Mill Limited. The District Judge made the order. It was set aside on appeal by the Judge, whose decision was affirmed by the Court of Appeal. On appeal to the House of Lords:

HELD: The insured person could not sue for an indemnity from the insurers unless and until the existence and amount of his liability to a third party had been established by a judgment of a Court or by agreement. The dissolution of Dart Mill Limited made this impossible.

It should be noted that an application can be made pursuant to section 651 of the Companies Act 1985 to treat the dissolution as void.

EMPLOYER'S LIABILITY INSURANCE AND MOTOR INSURANCE

[12.13] There have often been disputes between motor insurers and employer's liability insurers when an employee has an accident in a motor vehicle. Compulsory insurance is required for both employees and vehicles and the dispute usually centred around whether or not the employee was acting in the course of his employment at the time the accident occurred.

The matter is now governed by the provisions of the Third Council Directive 90/232/EEC dated 14 May 1990. "Domestic effect" has been given to the Directive in the amendments to the Employer's Liability (Compulsory Insurance) Regulations and the Motor Vehicles (Compulsory Insurance) Regulations 2000.

The Regulations now provide that there is no requirement for a policy of employers' liability insurance to provide cover for bodily injury sustained by an employee when the employee is 'carried in or upon a vehicle or entering into or getting on to, or alighting from, a vehicle … and where that bodily injury is caused by, or arises out of, the use by the employer of a vehicle on a road or other public place'. The relevant insurance must be provided by the policy of motor insurance.

As a result of these claims made by persons suffering lifting accidents in a motor vehicle are now covered by policies of motor insurance. Although this has avoided many of the disputes between motor insurers and employers' liability insurers there are still possibilities (depending on the wording of the employers' liability policy – and experience has shown that not all policies have been reworded to take account of the statutory changes) for both motor insurers and employers' liability insurers to have liabilities in respect of the accident.

For a case involving conflicts between employer's liability and public liability insurers, see paragraph 3.22 above.

PERSONAL INSURANCE

[12.14] There is no duty to obtain personal accident insurance for an employee working overseas or to advise such an employee to affect such insurance.

Reid v Rush & Tompkins Group plc

[1989] 3 All ER 228, CA

[12.15] The claimant was injured in a road traffic accident in Ethiopia. He was at the time of the accident in the course of his employment with the defendant as a quarry foreman on a project in Ethiopia. The accident was the fault of the driver of a vehicle which collided with the vehicle in which the claimant was travelling. However this individual was never identified and there was no scheme to cover uninsured third parties in Ethiopia. The claimant therefore claimed against the defendant alleging that its failure either to insure the claimant or to advise him to obtain such cover for himself amounted to a breach of its duty of care owed to him in negligence. On an application for strike out for failure to disclose a cause of action, the claimant appealed to the Court of Appeal.

HELD, dismissing the appeal: It was conceded on the part of the claimant that his claim amounted to a claim for pure economic loss and that hitherto the duty of a master to his servant had not been extended to the taking of reasonable care to protect the servant from economic loss. There are several scenarios at English law where an individual might suffer injury as a result of the fault of another yet be unable to recover the money compensation to which the law entitles him. There was no basis for implying a term into the contract of employment which imposed a duty on the defendant to provide advice. Such a term would have to be express. On the basis of the facts alleged in the pleadings there could be no finding of a voluntary assumption of responsibility on the part of the defendant to advise the claimant to take out personal insurance, nor did such a duty fall within the scope of the defendant's general duty as employer which is limited to protection of the employee from physical harm.

Index

A

Agency workers 1.20–1.24
  contract of employment 1.23
  control 1.24
  mutuality of obligations 1.24
  temporary staff 1.22
Armed forces 5.64–5.72
  Crown Proceedings Act 1947, section10 5.64–5.68
  Crown Proceedings (Armed Forces) Act 1987, 5.65
  human rights, and 5.72
  soldier in war zone 5.69
  supervision 5.70, 5.71
Asbestos. *see* Industrial disease claims
Asthma. *see* Industrial disease claims

B

Breach of statutory duty 4.1–4.99
  absolute duty 4.4, 4.10
  causation 4.3
  civil liability under health and safety legislation 4.52–4.99
    by whom duties are owed 4.53
    sources of law 4.52
    to whom duties are owed 4.53
    UK Regulations 4.57–4.99
    work equipment 4.55, 4.56
  common law duty, and 4.11
  construction of penal provisions 4.26–4.40
    'being of good construction' 4.29
    'dangerous' 4.31
    effective and suitable provision for ventilation 4.34
    failure to use guard 4.33
    'in motion' 4.37

Breach of statutory duty – *contd*
  construction of penal provisions – *contd*
    lenient approach 4.27
    manual handling 4.40
    plain, lateral and grammatical meaning of words 4.32
    plain meaning 4.26
    'plant' 4.39
    'process' 4.35, 4.36
    risk assessments 4.40
    'securely fenced' 4.38
    shot-firer, duty of 4.30
    'so far as is reasonably practicable' 4.28
  Control of Substances Hazardous to Health Regulations 2002, 4.86- 4.97
    application 4.89
    definitions 4.87
    duties 4.88
    health surveillance 4.96
    information 4.97
    instruction 4.97
    maintenance, examination and testing of control measures 4.94
    monitoring exposure at workplace 4.95
    prevention or control of exposure 4.91, 4.92
    risk assessment 4.90
    training 4.97
    use of control measures 4.93
  duties of employers 4.80
    evaluation of tasks 4.83
    risk assessment 4.84
  Employers Liability (Defective Equipment) Act 1969, 4.98, 4.99
  fencing of machinery 4.20
  foreseeable or unforeseeable risk 4.5
  Framework Directive 89/391/EEC 4.54
  guard rail 4.21
  ineffective protection 4.7

Breach of statutory duty – *contd*
  liability of employer 4.2
  Manual Handling Operations Regulations 1992, 4.79–4.85
    definitions 4.79
    duties of employees 4.81
  nature of action 4.2–4.15
  objectives of European legislation 4.54–4.56
  occupier of shipbuilding yard 4.17
  'wreck' 4.16
  Pedestrian Crossing Places (Traffic) Regulations 1941, 4.6
  person to whom duty owed 4.41–4.51
    'a person' 4.50–4.51
    customer 4.44
    employee of independent contactor 4.48
    employee or sub-contractor 4.45
    independent contractor 4.42
    labour-only contractor 4.46
    off-duty employee 4.49
    'office premises' 4.47
    seller or hirer 4.43
  proper maintenance of apparatus 4.22–4.25
  protection of class of public 4.14
  Provision and Use of Work Equipment Regulations 1998, 4.69–4.78
    application 4.70
    definitions 4.69
    information 4.76
    instruction 4.76
    maintenance 4.73–4.75
    suitability of work equipment 4.71, 4.72
    training 4.77, 4.78
  reasonable forseeability 4.13
  reasonableness 4.8
  'reasonably practicable' 4.12
  specific working place 4.41
  suitable goggles, provision of 4.10
  temporary use 4.18
  unfenced machinery 4.9
  work equipment 4.15
  Workplace (Health, Safety and Welfare) Regulations 1992, 4.57–4.68
    building 4.60
    condition of floors and traffic routes 4.64–4.66
    control over premises 4.59
    definitions 4.57
    falls or falling objects 4.67–4.68
    maintenance 4.61
    requirements 4.58
    seating 4.62
    workstations 4.62, 4.63

Bullying 6.92, 6.93

C

Causation. *see* Common law duties
Common law duties
  accident in course of employment 2.27
  acts normally and reasonably incidental to work 2.19
  advice as to insurance 2.28
  assessment of damages 2.80
  causation 2.38–2.87
    absence of hand-rail 2.64
    act of third party, and 2.72
    acts of trespass committed by third parties 2.85
    balance of probabilities 2.86
    breach of duty materially contributing to injury 2.55
    breach of safety regulations 2.43
    breach of statutory duty 2.66
    'but for' principle 2.71
    claimant sole author of misfortune 2.62
    conditions likely to cause disease 2.65
    disability 2.82
    employee acting unreasonably 2.77
    equal apportionment 2.46
    failure of employees to use safety belts 2.65, 2.70
    failure to provide look-out 2.50
    joint defendants 2.49
    ladder, absence of 2.73
    material contribution 2.55, 2.56, 2.57, 2.58
    meaning 2.51
    medical evidence 2.83
    medical negligence, and 2.75
    negligence of employee, and 2.48
    public policy 2.79
    reasonable conduct in emergency situation 2.42
    repetitive strain injury 2.87
    standard of proof 2.53
    sufficient causal nexus 2.58
    suicide 2.54, 2.76
    two competing causes 2.84
    two or more factors 2.81
    warlike operation 2.41
  common employment, doctrine of 2.18
  contract, claim pleaded in 2.32–2.33
  contributory negligence 2.38–2.87
    common sense principles 2.47
    degree of care 2.40

Common law duties – *contd*
  contributory negligence – *contd*
    employee deliberately incurring risk 2.78
    protective equipment 2.61
    rescuer 2.63
    respondent declining to be escorted 2.60
    secure fencing 2.52
  dangerous animal 2.25–2.26
  duty of employee to perform duties with proper care 2.30
  employee doing permitted action in prohibited way 2.26
  employee with learning difficulty 2.74
  employee waiting for transport 2.24
  estoppel, and 2.42
  ex turpi causa non oritur actio 2.23
  excessive working hours 2.34
  failure of employee to obey training officer 2.22
  failure to mitigate damage 2.83
  failure to protect employee's goods against theft 2.20
  fault of fellow employee 2.21
  forseeability 2.44
    established test 2.66
  limits 2.18–2.37
  novus actus interveniens 2.39, 2.45
  obligation to inform employee as to pension entitlement 2.29
  provision of fit and proper machinery 2.36
  references, provision of 2.88–2.90
  remoteness 2.38–2.87
    public policy 2.79
  safe system of work 2.59
  'thin skull' rule 2.69
  volenti non fit injuria 2.39
Common law liability 2.1–2.87
Constructive dismissal 8.111–8.123
  breach of implied term of mutual trust and confidence 8.115, 8.120, 8.121
  change on terms of contract 8.122
  disability discrimination, and 7.167
  duty promptly to redress grievances 8.123
  fair 8.119
  repudiatory breach of contract 8.113, 8.114, 8.115–8.118
  significant breach of contract 8.112
Contract of employment
  Crown, and 5.62, 5.63
Contract of service 1.1–1.16. *see also* Employee
  conditions 1.4, 1.5

Contract of service – *contd*
  control 1.16, 1.2, 1.3
  irreducible minimum obligation 1.9
  label given to relationship, and 1.6, 1.7
  lack of mutuality of obligation 1.13, 1.15
  obligation to provide services personally 1.14
  tests for 1.4, 1.5
  training contract, and 1.8
  trawlermen 1.10
Contributory negligence. *see* Common law duties
Corporate manslaughter 10.26–10.29
  gross negligence 10.29
  mens rea 10.28
  negligence, principles of 10.27
Crown employees 5.58–5.75
  contracts of employment, and 5.62, 5.63
  Crown Proceedings Act 1947, 5.58
  Defective Premises Act 1972, section5 5.60
  Occupiers' liability Act 1957, section6 5.59
  Occupiers' Liability Act 1984, section3 5.61
  statutory liability of Crown 5.58–5.61

D

Disability discrimination 7.11–7.169
  appropriate comparator 7.145, 7.146
  constructive dismissal, and 7.167
  contract workers 7.143, 7.144
  damages 7.166
  date at which to assess disability 7.138–7.140
    time of discriminatory act 7.140
  disability, meaning 7.112
  justification 7.156–7.161
    balancing exercise 7.159
    causal connection with discriminatory act 7.160
    knowledge, and 7.161
    medical evidence 7.158
    statutory criteria 7.157
  knowledge of disability 7.132–7.134
    absence of 7.133
    duty of employer to enquire 7.134
    objective test 7.132
  medical evidence and treatment, role of 7.162–7.165
  mutual impairment 7.116
    functional overlay 7.119
    phobic anxiety 7.120

Disability discrimination – *contd*
  normal day-to-day activities 7.124–7.129
    activities at work 7.128
    manual dexterity 7.127
    travel by public transport 7.126
    physical impairment 7.113–7.115
    post-employment victimisation 7.168, 7.169
    progressive conditions 7.130–7.131
    re-employment policy, and 7.136
  reasonable adjustments 7.148–7.155
    monetary benefits 7.154
    no suitable alternative 7.153
    non-co-operation by employee 7.155
    non-job-related 7.151, 7.152
    personal 7.151, 7.152
    relevant date 7.153
    request by employee 7.150
    sequential steps 7.149
  redundancy selection arrangements 7.147
  scope, for employment purposes 7.135–7.137
  small employer exemption 7.141, 7.142
  substantial and long-term adverse effect 7.121–7.123

E

Employee 1.1–1.16
  agency workers, 1.20–1.24. *see also* Agency workers
  contract of service, 1.1–1.16. *see also* Contract of service
  independent contractor, and 1.11, 1.12
  label given to relationship with employer, and 1.6, 1.7
Employer 1.17–1.19
  control by 1.18, 1.19
  who is 1.17–1.19
Employer's duty of care 2.1–2.17
  advice of competent advisor 2.15
  delegation 2.2
  enquiring as to safety hazards 2.17
  fencing of machinery 2.6
  good practice, and 2.5
  guard rail 2.14
  lack of self-control of employee 2.16
  magnitude of risk, and 2.3
  maintenance of floor 2.7
  masks, need for 2.12
  parts of machine 'in motion or use' 2.9
  practice of ignoring obvious danger 2.8
  protective clothing 2.11
  provision of suitable medical care 2.13
  supply of reasonably safe tool 2.10

Employment
  definition 1.1–1.45
  scope 1.1–1.45
Employment tribunal practice and procedure 9.128–9.177
  amending grounds of claim after lodged with tribunal 9.146, 9.147
  calculating time 9.132–9.137
    effect of tribunal being closed on last day to lodge IT! 9.142, 9.143
    limitation period where none specified by statute 9.145
    lodging claim forms by post 9.144
    'reasonably practicable' – effect of criminal proceedings 9.140–9.141
  chairman sitting alone or with one lay member 9.129–9.131
  costs 9.175–9.177
  decision 9.170–9.174
  directions 9.161
  disclosure of documents 9.162
  findings of fact 9.171
  further particulars 9.160
  jurisdiction to hear breach of contract claims 9.148
  just and equitable to extend time-limit 9.138–9.139
  need to investigate pleaded claims 9.155
  power to review decisions 9.173, 9.174
  power of tribunal to limit cross examination 9.156
  preliminary issues 9.149–9.152
  procedure at hearing 9.153–9.167
  tribunals must exercise discretion judicially 9.154
  remedy for unpleaded cause of action 9.172
  status of tribunal chairman's notes of evidence 9.157
  striking out 9.168, 9.169
  use of written submissions 9.158, 9.159
  witness orders 9.166
EU Charter of Fundamental Rights 11.24, 11.25
European Union law 11.1–11.25
  approach to EC law taken by UK courts 11.19–11.24
  Charter of Fundamental Rights 11.24, 11.25
  direct effect of Directives 11.5–11.8
  direct effect of Regulations and Decisions 11.3, 11.4
  direct effect of Treaty provisions 11.2
  effectiveness of EC law remedies 11.14–11.16
  emanation of the state, concept of 11.9

European Union law – *contd*
  European Communities Act 1972, s.2(1) 11.19
  'incidental' horizontal effects 11.12
  'indirect effect' of Directives 11.10–11.16
  obligation to construe national law in conformity with Directives 11.10–11.16
  sex discrimination 11.21, 11.22
  state liability for breach of EC law 11.17, 11.18
  substantive 11.24, 11.25
  supremacy of community law 11.13
  transfer of undertakings 11.20
  work equipment 11.23

H

Harassment 6.92, 6.93
Health and Safety at Work, etc., Act 1974, 10.1–10.29
  'conducting an undertaking' 10.9–10.11
  corporate manslaughter, 10.26–10.29. *see also* Corporate manslaughter
  duty not to charge employees for things done or provided 10.8
  duty not to interfere with or misuse things 10.7
  fines, level of 10.20–10.25
  general duties of employees at work 10.6
  general duties of employers to employees 10.2
  general duties of manufacturers 10.5
  general duties of persons concerned with premises 10.4
  general duties to persons other than employees 10.3
  health and safety regulations 10.12
  limits of practicability 10.19
  offences 10.13
  offences by bodies corporate 10.15–10.18
  offences due to fault of another person 10.14
  'reasonable practicability' 10.9–10.11
  sentencing 10.20–10.25
    aggravating factors 10.21, 10.24, 10.25
    guidelines 10.22
    mitigating factors 10.21, 10.25
    train operators 10.23

Health and safety prosecutions 10.1–10.29
Human rights 5.1–5.75
  analysis of 1998 Act 5.22–5.31
    'austerity of tabulated legalism' 5.26
    principles 5.22–5.31
  armed forces, and 5.72
  cases affecting employers' liability 5.44–5.57
    Article4 5.45
    Article6 5.46
    Article8 5.47–5.51
    Article9 5.52–5.55
    Article10 5.56
    Article14 5.57
  Convention rights 5.1
    interpretation 5.2
    interpretation of legislation 5.3
    safeguards for existing rights 5.10
  declarations of incompatibility 5.4, 5.36–5.40
  discretionary area of judgment 5.32–5.35
  effect of Act of 1998 on employers' liability 5.41–5.75
    amendment of primary legislation, and 5.43
    statutory interpretation, and 5.42
  fair trial, right to 5.16
  freedom of assembly and association 5.20
  freedom of expression 5.11, 5.19
  freedom of thought, conscience and religion 5.12, 5.18
  general comments on when to raise human rights point 5.26, 5.27
  horizontal effect of Act of 1998, 5.30, 5.31
  Human Rights Act 1998, 5.1–5.12
  judicial acts 5.9
  judicial remedies 5.8
  prohibition of discrimination 5.21
  prohibition of slavery and forced labour 5.15
  prohibition of torture 5.14
  proportionality 5.32–5.35
  public authorities 5.6–5.8
    acts of 5.6
    proceedings 5.7
  public authority
    definition 5.28, 5.29
  right of Crown to intervene 5.5
  right to life 5.13
  right to respect for private and family life 5.17
  statutory interpretation under section 3, Act of 1998, 5.36–5.40

I

Independent contractor 3.2–3.13
  business on own account 1.11, 1.12
  'casual negligence' 3.7–3.11
  'collateral negligence' 3.7–3.11
  competence of 3.6
  delegation, and 3.2, 3.4, 3.6
  duty of care of employer, and 3.5
  liability for acts of 3.2–3.13
  practical joke 3.3
  ultra-hazardous activities 3.12, 3.13
Industrial disease claims 6.1–6.93
  apportionment of liability 6.7–6.11
    date of knowledge 6.8–6.9
    material contribution to disease, and 6.1
    vibration white finger 6.11
  asbestos 6.19–6.45
    accrual of cause of action 6.25–6.27
    application of legislation 6.34–6.37
    Asbestos Industry Regulations 1931, 6.28
    awareness of risk 6.41, 6.43, 6.44
    Control of Asbestos Regulations 1969, 6.32
    Crown immunity 6.21–6.24
    date of knowledge 6.38–6.44
    duty of care 6.38–6.44
    Factories Act 1937, s.47(1) 6.29
    Factories Act 1961, s.4(1) 6.30
    foreseeability 6.39, 6.40–6.42
    increased risk 6.38
    insurance policy 6.19
    jurisdiction 6.20
    legislation 6.28–6.32
    limitation 6.25–6.27
    offset of benefits 6.45
    procedural issues 6.20–6.27
    Shipbuilding and Ship-Repairing Regulations 1961, 6.31
    standards 6.33
  asthma 6.64–6.67
    COSHH Regulations 6.67
    date of knowledge 6.66
  bullying 6.92, 6.93
  causation 6.1–6.18
    apportionment in 'divisible' conditions 6.7–6.11
    increase in risk 6.2, 6.3
    material 6.1
    medical evidence 6.5, 6.6
    more than one employer 6.4
    no duty to dismiss 6.12–6.14
  dermatitis 6.68
  harassment 6.92, 6.93

Industrial disease claims – *contd*
  occupational noise-induced hearing loss 6.46, 6.47
  occupational stress, 6.83–6.91. *see also* Occupational stress
  pneumoconiosis 6.15–6.18
    apportionment 6.18
    causation 6.17
    date of knowledge 6.16
    epidemiological evidence 6.17
    medical evidence 6.17
  sensitisation claims 6.63–6.68
    Control of Substances Hazardous to Health Regulations 6.63
    legislation 6.63
  vibration white finger, 6.48–6.62. *see also* Vibration white finger
  work-related upper limb disorder, 6.69–6.82. *see also* Work-related upper limb disorder
Insolvency 12.10
Insurance 12.1–12.15
  compulsory 12.1–12.9
  employer's liability 12.13
  Employer's Liability (Compulsory Insurance) Act1969 12.1–12.8
    certificates of insurance 12.5
    criminal liability 12.9
    employees to be covered 12.3
    exempted employees 12.4
    insurance against liability for employees 12.2
    nature of liability under 12.9
    penalty for failure to insure 12.6
    Regulations 12.7
  interaction between employer's liability insurance and motor insurance 12.13
    authorised act in unauthorised way 12.11
    course of employment, and 12.10–12.15
    employment abroad 12.15
    "frolic of the servant" 12.12
    personal 12.14

N

National minimum wage
  unfair dismissal, and 8.97
Negligence
  vicarious liability, and 1.43–1.45
Non-employees, liability for 3.1–3.37
  Australian approach 3.35–3.37
  extra-hazardous work 3.37

Non-employees, liability for – *contd*
  independent contractor. *see* Independent contractor
  non-delegable duty 3.36
  workers subject to another's control, 3.14–3.34. *see also* Workers subject to another's control

O

Occupational stress 6.83–6.91
  cases decided post-Hatton 6.90, 6.91
  duty of employer to take positive steps 6.86
  foreseeability 6.87, 6.88
  post-Hatton 6.84–6.88
  pre-Hatton 6.83
  summary of reasons in Hatton 6.89

P

Police 5.73–5.75
  employment relationships 5.73, 5.74, 5.75
Practical jokes
  vicarious liability, and 1.43–1.45
Practice and procedure 9.1–9.177
  commencing proceedings 9.13–9.36
  costs 9.97–9.127
    conditional fee agreements 9.118–9.123
    discretion of court 9.100–9.109
    indemnity basis 9.113–9.117
    orders against non-parties 9.124
    Part 36, effect of 9.110–9.112
    summary assessment 9.98, 9.99
    wasted costs orders 9.125–9.127
  county court 9.1–9.127
  default judgment 9.2
  employment tribunal. *see* Employment tribunal practice and procedure
  expert evidence 9.10–9.12
  group litigation 9.37–9.40
    costs 9.38–9.40
  High Court 9.1–9.127
  interim applications 9.6
  interim payments 9.7–9.9
  issuing proceedings 9.17
  limitation 9.41–9.79
    Act of 1980 9.43–9.50
      actions founded on simple contract 9.44
      actions founded on tort 9.43

Practice and procedure – *contd*
  limitation – *contd*
    date of knowledge 9.48
    facts not known at date of accrual of cause of action 9.49
    Fatal Accidents legislation 9.46, 9.47
    legislation 9.42
    overriding time limit for negligence cases not involving personal injuries 9.50
    personal injuries actions 9.45
    commencing second action out of time 9.78, 9.79
    date of knowledge 9.53–9.64
    defence 9.65–9.68
    extending time-limits 9.69–9.75
    new claims in pending action 9.76, 9.77
    running out of time 9.51, 9.52
  parties to action 9.16
  pleading requirements 9.34
    amendments 9.35, 9.36
    resiling from admission of liability 9.36
  pre-action protocol 9.13
  procedural steps 9.2–9.12
  serving proceedings 9.20–9.33
  striking out 9.80–9.91
    claim or defence alleged to be objectionable 9.81–9.83
    manner in which claim pursued 9.84–9.91
  submission of no case to answer 9.96
  summary judgment 9.4, 9.5
  trial 9.92–9.95
    adjournments 9.93–9.95
    allocation 9.92
  vexatious litigation 9.14, 9.15
Pregnancy
  unfair dismissal, and 8.81–8.82
Pregnancy. *see also* Sex discrimination
Public interest disclosure
  unfair dismissal, and 8.94, 8.95

R

Race discrimination 7.1–7.169
  aggravated damages 7.104, 7.107, 7.109
  aiding unlawful acts 7.102–7.104
  appropriate comparator 7.21
  continuing act 7.72, 7.74, 7.75
  direct 7.1–7.21
  discrimination by others 7.65

Race discrimination – *contd*
  discrimination on grounds of another
      person's race 7.14–7.15
  dismissal for violence
      racial attack, and 7.5
  establishing discriminatory treatment
      7.62
  ethnic groups 7.7
      gypsies 7.8
      identifying 7.8
      national origins 7.9
  genuine occupational qualifications
      7.78–7.81
  importance of discriminatory factor in
      decision taken 7.20
  inference of 7.63, 7.64
  injury to feelings 7.105, 7.107
  justification 7.53, 7.55
  less favourable treatment 7.5, 7.18
  pressure to discriminate 7.90, 7.91
  qualifying bodies, by 7.68, 7.69, 7.70
  racial grounds 7.10–7.13
      motive 7.13
      production of passport 7.10
      racially motivated objection to transfer
          7.12
      work permit, requirement for 7.11
  racial grounds/ racial group 7.6
  Rastafarians 7.17
  religions as ethnic groups 7.16–7.19
  unjustified sense of grievance 7.19
  vicarious liability 7.92–7.97
  victimisation 7.82–7.89
      conscious motivation 7.83, 7.84
      less favourable treatment 7.88
      motive 7.87
      report to CRE 7.86
      secret tape-recordings 7.85
  work ordinarily outside Great Britain
      7.76, 7.77
Redundancy
  unfair dismissal, and 8.65, 8.66
Religious discrimination
  aggravated damages 7.106

S

Sex discrimination 7.1–7.169
  aggravated damages 7.104
  aiding unlawful acts 7.102–7.104
  concessionaires, obligations of 7.66
  continuing act 7.73
  contract workers 7.67
  direct 7.1, 7.22–7.34
      display of offensive pictures 7.4
      nurse required to wear cap 7.3
  discrimination by others 7.65

Sex discrimination – *contd*
  gender reassignment 7.57–7.61
      equality of treatment 7.58
      medical conditions 7.60
      sexual harassment 7.59
  genuine occupational qualification
      7.78–7.81
  indirect 7.35–7.51
      'can comply', meaning 7.46
      'condition or requirement' 7.38, 7.39
      'considerably smaller proportion'
          7.42–7.45
      detriment 7.49
      disproportionate impact between men
          and women 7.41
      full-time work, whether imposition of
          requirement or condition 7.40
      knowledge not necessary for detriment
          7.50
      pool for comparison 7.51
      proportion of disadvantaged employees
          7.37
      requirement 7.36
  injury to feelings 7.104
  instructions to discriminate 7.89
  justification 7.54, 7.55
  less favourable treatment 7.2
  objective test 7.23
  pregnancy 7.24–7.29
      failure to carry out risk assessment 7.30
  qualifying bodies, by 7.68, 7.71
  sexual orientation discrimination
      7.31–7.34
  vicarious liability 7.92–7.97
  victimisation 7.82–7.89
      post-employment 7.99, 7.100, 7.101
  work ordinarily outside Great Britain
      7.76, 7.77
Sub-contractor. *see* Independent contractor

T

Trade union
  unfair dismissal, and 8.90–8.93
Transfer of undertaking
  unfair dismissal, and. *see* Unfair dismissal
Travel
  vicarious liability, and 1.38–1.42

U

Unfair dismissal 8.1–8.160
  assertion of statutory right 8.96

Unfair dismissal – *contd*
  automatically unfair reasons 8.80–8.99
  band of reasonable responses
      8.104–8.110
    health and safety, and 8.109
    'sufficient reason' 8.110
    test for 8.106–8.109
  breach of statutory enactment 8.62–8.64
  capability 8.48–8.54
    ill-health 8.50–8.54
  compensation 8.136–8.160
    deductions for contributory fault
        8.144–8.147
    duty to mitigate 8.141–8.143
    heads of damage 8.137
    just and equitable 8.148–8.151
    loss of wages 8.152–8.160
    manner of dismissal 8.138
    nature of tribunal jurisdiction 8.155
    net weekly wage 8.140
    pension loss 8.159
    reductions on just and equitable ground
        8.160
    three-stage assessment 8.139
  compensatory award 8.2
  conduct 8.55–8.61
    breach of duty of fidelity 8.58
    criminal acts 8.60, 8.61
    gross misconduct 8.57
    range of reasonable responses 8.56
    reasonable belief in guilt 8.55
    test for dishonesty 8.59
  constructive dismissal, 8.111–8.123. *see
      also* Constructive dismissal
  date of dismissal 8.27–8.34
  dismissal, whether 8.14–8.26
    ambiguous language 8.21–8.23
    burden of proof 8.17
    change of mind 8.19
    fixed-term contract 8.25, 8.26
    frustration, and 8.24
    notice, and 8.18
    resignation, and 8.16
    variation of terms of contract 8.14
  effective date of termination 8.27–8.34
    agreed between parties 8.29
    appeal against summary dismissal, and
        8.34
    constructive knowledge 8.28
    notice, and 8.30–8.35
  eligibility to make claim 8.5, 8.6
  employee representative 8.89
  employees 8.5, 8.6
  excluded classes of employees 8.12, 8.13
  health and safety reason 8.83–8.86
  later summary dismissal, and 8.13

Unfair dismissal – *contd*
  leave for family reasons 8.80
  national minimum wage 8.97
  occupational pension scheme trustee 8.88
  pregnancy 8.81–8.82
  procedure 8.99–8.103
    appeal 8.103
    investigation 8.101, 8.102
    unfair, effect of 8.100
  public interest disclosure 8.94, 8.95
  re-employment 8.124–8.135
    choice of order 8.127–8.135
    terms of order 8.127–8.135
  re-engagement 8.126–8.135
  reason for dismissal 8.37–8.73
    actual reason 8.45
    burden of proof 8.41, 8.42
    correct characterisation 8.39, 8.40
    establishing 8.44, 8.45
    fairness, and 8.43
    redundancy 8.38
    when to be determined 8.46, 8.47
  redundancy 8.65, 8.66
  refusal to work on Sunday 8.87
  reinstatement 8.125–8.135
  remedies 8.124–8.160
  retirement age 8.7–8.11
  some other substantial reason 8.67–8.73
    agreement for new contract, and 8.69
    burden of proof 8.73
    imprisonment 8.72
    protection of interest of business 8.70
    reasonableness, and 8.67, 8.68
    short-term contract, and 8.71
  summary of law 8.1
  tax credit 8.98
  termination of employment by consensual
      agreement, and 8.3, 8.4, 8.15, 8.20
  time at which dismissal takes effect 8.36
  trade union reasons 8.90–8.93
  transfer of undertaking, and 8.74–8.79
    economic, technical or organisational
        reasons 8.77, 8.78
    reason connected with 8.75, 8.76, 8.79

V

Vibration white finger 6.48–6.62
  apportionment 6.58
  breach of duty, and 6.62
  classification 6.57
  date of knowledge 6.49
  diagnosis 6.56
  effect of cessation of exposure 6.55

Vibration white finger – *contd*
  extent of disability 6.54
  knowledge of employer 6.60, 6.61
  medical evidence 6.50
  musculo-skeletal damage 6.53
  neurological damage 6.52
  Stockholm Workshop Scale 6.57
  Taylor Pelmear Scale 6.57
  vascular damage 6.51
Vicarious liability 1.25–1.45
  authorised work in wrongful manner 1.26–1.29
  course of employment 1.26–1.29
  express prohibition 1.30–1.33
  international acts of employee 1.34–1.37
  negligence 1.43–1.45
  practical jokes 1.43–1.45
  race discrimination 7.92–7.97
  sex discrimination 7.92–7.97
  travel 1.38–1.42
  unsafe method of work 1.32

W

Work-related upper limb disorder 6.69–6.82
  keyboard claims 6.69–6.75
    breach of duty 6.73
    causation 6.73
    Health and Safety (Display Screen Equipment) Regulations 1992 6.69

Work-related upper limb disorder – *contd*
  keyboard claims – *contd*
    legislation 6.69
    medical evidence 6.71, 6.74, 6.75
    terminology 6.70
    warnings 6.72
  manual processes 6.76–6.82
    forseeability of risk 6.79, 6.80, 6.82
    legislation 6.76
    pain 6.78
    warnings 6.81
Workers subject to another's control 3.14–3.34
  architects 3.23, 3.24
  demolition contractor 3.24
  drover 3.18
  educational authorities 3.15
  employee of contractor 3.31
  employee loaned to another enterprise 3.19–3.22
  employer's undertaking 3.28
  employment abroad 3.33
  inappropriate equipment 3.32
  main contractor 3.27
  occupier, and 3.30
  police duties owed to prisoners 3.17
  principal contractor 3.26
  respondent superior, doctrine of 3.25
  superintendence 3.29
  third party injured by employee 3.34
  youth centres 3.16